THE NEVER-ENDING CYCLE OF DEVELOPMENT PROGRESSION, AND FUN.

CW00386046

THE TRESPASS MISSION IS ACCESS FOR ALL!
WE CATER FOR ALL LEVELS. FIND YOURS WITHOUT
COMPROMISING ON PERFORMANCE.
GO TRESPASS . . . GO FURTHER.

TRESPASS®
WWW.TRESPASS.CO.UK GO FURTHER
TIME TO GET SERIOUS
RIDER: LUKE PAULL | SHOOTER: JAMES BRYANT | LOCATION: AVORIAZ FRANCE
DANGER
AIM SERIES
SNOWBOARD & SKI

Compiled, written & edited by Steve Dowle & Pete Coombs

Front cover: pic: Natalie Mayer, boarder: Chris Goulder taken in Tignes, Jan 04
Back cover, next page and additional photos: Zoë Webber, zoermwebber@hotmail.com

Book design by Steve Dowle,
Icons by Jim, www.DoctorPuss.com

Original Idea by Tony Brown

Contributions: Tony Finding, James Woodward, Jon Mitchell, Richard Schnider, Jen Schlemk, Dan Collins, Tim Wilkinson, Lauris, Martins, Paul Slack , Anna Dimitrova, ,Rigmor Anita Hauger, Sonic, Marcelo

Big thanks to: Tony Brown, Bob Dowle, the 215 crew, Woody, Tonys mum, Martin, Jim P, the advertisers, resorts , the photographers and anyone else we've missed

WORLD SNOWBOARD GUIDE 2005
ISBN 0-9548014-0-7
9th edition – September 2004
First published 1996

Published by:
World Snowboard Guide Ltd
Medius House, 2 Sheraton Street
London W1F 8BH
England

Telephone: +44 (0)207 748 6136
Fax: +44 (0)207 748 6137
Email: info@worldsnowboardguide.com
Web: www.worldsnowboardguide.com

Distributed by:
Vine House Distribution Ltd
Telephone: +44 (0)1825 723 398

Printed in England by:
Antony Rowe Ltd
Telephone: +44 (0)1249 659705

WORLD SNOWBOARD GUIDE 2005

From Canada to Kazakhstan, the 9th edition of the legendary World Snowboard Guide takes you to over 40 countries visiting 800 of the best resorts. Written for boarders by boarders, you'll find the best places to ride, stay and party. Completely revised and updated ready for the new season.

WORLD SNOWBOARD GUIDE 2005

CONTENTS

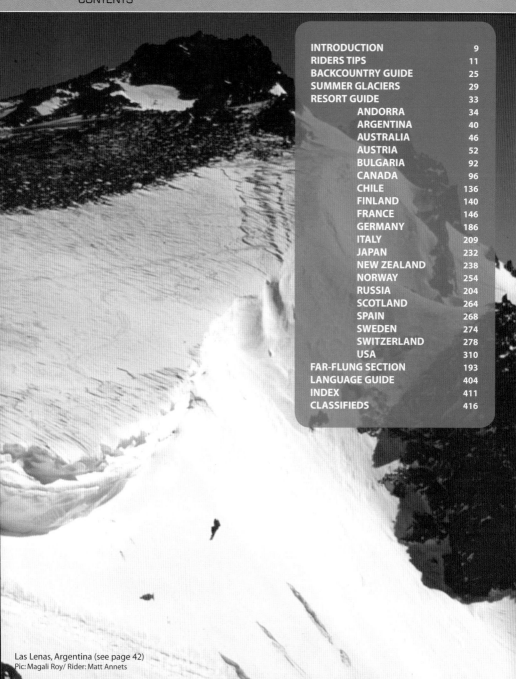

Las Lenas, Argentina (see page 42)
Pic: Magali Roy/ Rider: Matt Annets

INTRODUCTION

This is the 9th edition of the World Snowboard Guide, its fully updated and revised for the 2004/5 season. There are **800** resorts listed in this guide, 300 of which are detailed. Where available we've listed prices for the new season, but expect a small fluctuation. There's information on resorts, major improvements for the new season, and every resort has been checked and updated.

We will inform you of every aspect of the resort from a snowboarders perspective, from piste to pub, from hidden spots to kicking night clubs, from Canada to Kazakhstan. When you pick up this guide, you inherit the inside knowledge from our worldwide team of snowboarders. The pistes have been boarded and the bars have been drunk in. This is categorically the best snowboard guide you can buy, written by boarders for boarders.

Let us know of your travels and adventures, we've fifty copies of the next edition to bribe you into telling us the best secret spots and bars. At the back of the book you'll find details on our website, enter the code shown and get free access to the members only area.

There is also information on **summer riding** on Europe's glaciers. Early starts and boarding in t-shirts in the sunshine, we've details and piste maps of the glaciers in Austria, France, Switzerland and Canada.

In the middle of the book, you'll find our guide on boarding in some **far flung** places. Not all are extreme and remote, and there's sure to be places that surprise you.

Towards the back of the book is a handy snow related **language guide** in French, German, Italian, Japanese, Norwegian and Spanish.

A big **thanks** to everyone who has contributed to this book, past and present. Special thanks to the advertisers for their continued support, please mention WSG when responding to any advertisements.

Read on for the **riders tips** and **backcountry guide**.

Enjoy.

Sunset at Furtschellas, St.Mortiz (see page 300)
pic: Christof Sonderegger/St.Mortiz Tourism

CHOOSING A RESORT

Before you book that holiday or jump in your car, ask yourself what is it you want from a resort. Do you need instruction? Are you there for the boarding or the night life? Freeride or Freestyle? Do you need a hotel to pamper you or do you want the freedom of your own apartment? And the big one, how much cash do you have?

In the Northern Hemisphere most resorts open fully in mid December but some open late November. If you get early snow you could find yourself alone on the slopes. Resorts generally close in late April with some high altitude resorts having summer boarding on glaciers. Christmas, New Year, February half term and Easter are steer clear times, the resorts are always packed and accommodations at a premium. If you have to go at these times pick a resort with an extensive lift system or you'll find you're queuing more than boarding. The choice of holiday options has never been better. If you want to spend big you can with some European resorts offering 5 star hotels on the piste. If cash is short you can often find a bunk house. You can also get great last minute deals with tour operators offering hassle free half board chalet based weeks.

ALTITUDE
Altitude is vital. Some of the lower resort's struggle for snow and often rely on artificial snowmaking. Higher normally means better snow fall and coverage although some high resorts suffer from strong winds which damages the off piste conditions as well as the piste. Altitude of the resorts town as well as it slopes is important, the higher the better or you may find yourself picking your way through rocks and grass if you want to board back to your accommodation. The higher resorts mostly come with a higher price. If money is no problem head high, it could mean the difference between a great trip and a good one.

SMALL MAY BE BETTER
Often small resorts which may be cheaper will join up with huge interlinked areas, such as Le Trois Vallees in France or the Port du Soleil which links 14 resorts in France and Switzerland. Before rushing to a huge area and paying that hard earned cash for a expensive lift pass think about your standard. Beginners will only use a few pistes and most riders tend to find favourite spots and stick to those, some just hit the fun parks and don't even need a lift pass. In most resorts you can buy a daily upgrade on your pass which allows you to board other valleys. This could save you money if the weather turns bad and the top lifts are shut all week, and gives you the freedom to decide on the day.

Alpes D'Huez, France (see page 148)
© nuts.fr/JP NOISILLIER/OT ALPE D'HUEZ

GETTING THERE

Please give that man a beer. Who was it that came up with the idea of budget airfares? If you're lucky enough to live near an airport serviced by a budget airline, and you want to go to the Alps, get a map out, take your driving licence, and you may find yourself a short drive from the slopes for less money than you'll spend on the first round of beers. The cheapest way is to book as far in advance as possible, but of course that means you won't know what the snow conditions will be. If you can fly early morning and mid week it's far cheaper than on a weekend. A lot of the arrival airports are in the middle of a cow field, so if you can't rent a car do some research into public transport before you arrive or you maybe turning up in the resort on the back of a bull. A down side to budget airlines is if it goes wrong there's little back up. If your flight is cancelled you're normally met with a long queue and only the offer of a flight in a few days time or your money back.

ROLLING YOUR OWN
If you're taking your own kit with you, make sure you check to see if they charge you for the privilege. Most of the tour operators do, and for the budget airlines it's a given, expect to be charged around £20. It looks like Ryan Air won't even allow you to take your kit with you, so check the situation out before you turn up to the airport.

FLY DRIVE
Fly drive is always a winner in North America, it also gives you the freedom to roam resorts at will and follow the snow. If you're boarding in one of the more remote parts of the world then you should defiantly go it alone, and try to hang with the locals, not just steamroller through their country in the back of a motor.

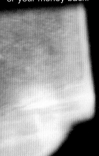
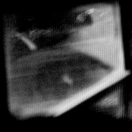

GOING IT ALONE
The main benefit of going alone is the freedom, as you can visit many resorts in a week. Look on the web find the best snow and head straight to it, but be careful if you're trying to do it on the cheap side as you could find yourself stuck in a full resort and stumping up for an expensive room. When looking for accommodation in a resort try the Tourist Info Office first, they can normally help you with finding and sometimes booking accommodation, and they'll usually speak good English.

TOUR OPERATORS
If time is short tour operators can be great. They will sort out your flights and arrange a transfer to and from resort. If you've booked half-board you'll get breakfast, afternoon tea, and with dinner often free wine. You may have to hold your nose to get it down but it's free. They can also arrange hotels and self-catering apartments. Be careful to find out exactly where your accommodation is located or you could have a long bus ride or walk to the lifts each morning. The two main draw backs to organized holidays is if there's no snow your scuppered, and the holiday reps will try to bleed you dry by wanting to sell you stupid après ski fondue nights.

TRAINS
Many resorts are close to major train links. It sure beats bus services for speed, but make sure that you plan ahead and don't turn up to the airport knowing the next step. From London you can hop on the snow train on a Thursday night and hop out at Bourg St.Maurice at 7am ready for the lifts to open in Les Arcs.

COACHES
20 hours in a coach doesn't sound like fun, and make no mistake, its not. But then again, if you're small and want a cheap getaway then perfect. There's many companies offering very cheap boarding weekends and holidays by coach, that leave from various parts of the UK to various places in France. You'll travel overnight and possibly get there in time for a few hours on the slope, or at worst first at the bar

13

Bus Reflections, Zoë Webber

whitelines
snowboard magazine

This season in White Lines snowboarding magazine

Learn and progress with technical tips and advice

Find out about the destinations you want to visit, whatever your budget

See aspirational stunts and lines

Find the equipment that's suited to you, and how you should look after it

Keep up-to-date with the pro's, comp's and the British scene

Improve your boarding knowledge, no matter what your standard

Will Hughes, Tignes. Photo: James McPhail

SPECIAL SUBSCRIPTION OFFER

When you subscribe to White Lines, every issue will be delivered to your door for less than you would pay in the shops, and you'll get loads of free stuff!

For only £24.95 you'll get:

| 6 issues of White Lines delivered to your door | 3 FREE DVDS with the first three issues of the season | FREE White Lines t-shirt | FREE Xscape Saver Card 2 hours for the price of 1 at Xscape real snow slope |

Call Now: 01235 536229 (PLEASE QUOTE W012)   www.whitelines.com

RIDING

FREERIDE OR FREESTYLE?

Our reviews are broken down into two main snowboarding genres: freeride and freestyle.

Freeriding is exactly what it suggests, riding freely around the mountain, be it on the piste, through the trees or best of all descending virgin snow at mach 20 leaving a cloud of snow in your wake. If that's your thing this guide will tell you if a resort has trees, if there's easy access to off piste, what the lift systems like and most importantly what part of the resort to head for. Be warned never take on anything above your ability and if you do go off piste always wear a transceiver, carry a shovel

and follow the resorts advice on avalanche risk.

Freestylers are the big air merchants. They love fun parks and half pipes. It's all about the moves - there's no point in going big if there's no style involved; a huge floating grabbed 360 looks far better than a rushed 540. If methods and misty flips are your tip then let WSG inform you of a resorts fun park and pipes. Many resorts claim to have fun parks but when you turn up its a few bumps on an icy piste. A resort with any snowboarding credibility will have got a pro rider or at least the local riders to help with the design and building of the park. Good

parks will have a fulltime employee designated to the upkeep of the hits and pipe. If not you could ask for a shovel at the lift hut and do some pipe-shaping yourself, but only wield a shovel with permission and knowledge. If you don't know what you're doing and destroy a pipe wall, or spoil a hit's take-off you'll be liable to get a slap.

Carvers love wide well maintained piste so they can crank it over in their turns. Carvers mostly wear hard boots and use an asymmetric board. WSG will tell you of piste style and a resort's track record on slope maintenance.

LEARNING

Beginners should always look closely at the level of instruction a resort can offer. Look for a specialized snowboard school. Being taught to board by an Austrian with little English who normally teaches skiing just won't do. Don't think you won't need lessons. A good posture and stance leads to good balance which is everything in snowboarding. You may get away with leaning back and swinging your arms around on the nursery slopes but once you reach an intermediate level your progress will be hindered by your early bad habits; how can you ever expect to land a jump if you're unbalanced on the approach? Don't try to teach your spouse becuase its bound to end in a fight and there's nothing more annoying than wasting your holiday standing on a green run wishing you were somewhere else. Let someone who knows what they're doing deal with it. Intermediates will benefit from an advanced lesson and some schools offer freestyle and off piste classes. There are also great opportunities for summer freestyle camps where you're taught by professional riders.

Rider: Victoria Jealouse
Photo: Jeff Curtes
Burton Snowboards

IT'S FUN.
IT'S EDGY.
IT'S ADDICTIVE.

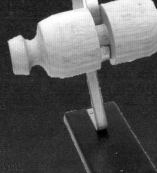

LIFTS

Lifts will vary around the world, the most basic are **Drag lifts** which normally entail sticking something uncomfortable between your legs and letting it pull you up the hill. Beginners will often find themselves being dragged up the mountain with their face in the snow. Beginners are advised to travel on drag lifts with their rear foot released from its binding, as it allows for a quick getaway should you fall off, and just try and relax your body and look forward.

Chair lifts make for a more comfortable journey and should also be used with your rear foot out of its binding, just remember to keep the board flat and pointing straight when getting on and off.

Bubble/Gondola and **Cable Cars** are enclosed shells, normally with seats which are suspended from a cable and usually the fastest way to the top of the mountain. Some resorts have Funiculars which are underground trains that are incredibly efficient. Some resorts won't let you on the lifts without a leash on your board so stick one in your pocket in case you meet a fussy lift operator.

LIFT PASSES

Most resorts offer a range of lift passes which can usually be bought on a daily or multiple-day basis. **Weekly tickets** will normally require an attached picture, so take a passport-sized photo with you. Riders staying for a few months can buy season passes, and although expensive, you will make a massive saving in the long run. You may have the choice of one resort or an interlinked area, sometimes you may even get a free day in a nearby affiliated resort. Ask at the office when you buy your pass. Discounted passes are available for kids, old age pensioners, locals and sometimes students. You'll also find prices changes during the season; at low season you can pay around 25% less. Resorts have their own polices on reimbursement if lifts are shut.

Many resorts offer **beginner packages** that offer good value for money. You get a lesson, full equipment hire and a lift pass that gives you access to the beginners slopes. Its also possible to get terrain park only lift passes at some resorts, and a few even have a few free beginner lifts, so make sure you check before shelling out on a full pass if you're not going to use it.

Lift Chairs, Zoë Webber

WHAT TO WEAR

Don't dress just to look fly! Make sure you're wearing the right kit. Outer layers should be water and wind proof and if possible breathable. The best way to stay warm is to wear layers rather than one huge jumper, so that the air is trapped between the layers and warmed from your body heat. You can buy technical tops to wear next to your skin which are designed to be fast drying and whip the sweat away. if you sweat in cotton it stays wet.

Hiring Kit

If you plan to rent snowboard equipment, it may be better to hire in-resort. You only pay for the days you use the equipment, and it gives you the freedom to change the board and boots if they are not right. Another plus side is if you like the set up you may be able to buy it less the rental price at the end of the hire. Don't settle for substandard kit. Things are much better than they used to be and most resorts will have a snowboard specialist. Gone are the days when you had to choose between a few old boards in the back of a ski hire shop. A positive side to hiring before you leave is there maybe a wider choice and if you wanted a specific brand or size you should be able to reserve it also many shops will offer a standard package or you can pay more to hire top of the range kit.

The main things to check are that the base and edges are in good condition and that the bindings are set up for you not just screwed in any old way. For a beginner the bindings should be set centrally on the board, the front at 10/15 degrees and the back 5/10 degrees both forward, they should be about shoulder width apart and there should be no excessive boot overhang. The board should come up to your chin. A short board is good to learn on but once you start picking up speed a longer board will be more stable. Always check on screws and other parts of your kit; if bits do come loose on the mountain, then look for maintenance tools located at most lift stations. It's a good idea to buy, and carry, a mini-binding tool when on the slopes.

Kids

As more kids take up snowboarding the rental equipment for them has improved. A good store should have genuine children's kit. It's a good idea to hire a safety helmet and wrist-guards as you don't want to spend your time down the valley with little Billy while he gets put back together.

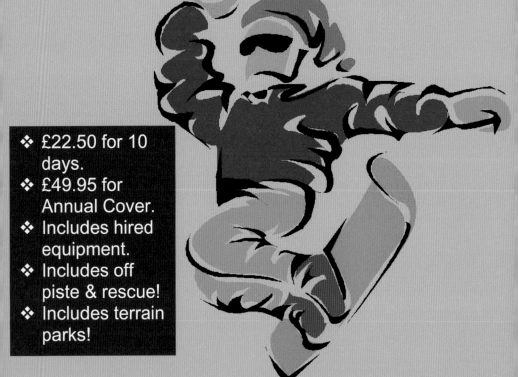

INSURANCE

Shine a torch into the ear of a boarder without insurance and sure enough there'll be light coming out the other side. Only a fool would hit the slopes without good insurance. The main things to check in the small print of your policy is that it states:

- Snowboarding
- Off Piste (you don't want to be crawling back to the piste with a busted leg)
- Personal Injury including repatriation.
- Personal Belongings including your board
- Curtailments, cancellation of flights etc

If hiring kit make sure it's insured on your policy or covered by the hire shop. It's possible to get insurance with your lift pass in some countries but this will normally only cover getting you off the slopes and to the hospital.

EUROPEAN HEALTH INSURANCE CARD

All EU nationals (inc UK) can get the free European Health Insurance Card which has replaced the old E111, pick up the form from the post office. This is no replacement for insurance but makes sure you're covered for medical care and not charged, and is valid across all member states.

THEFT

At least once when you go boarding you'll hear the story that a van turned up at the resort and nicked a load of boards from outside a bar. Make sure you look after your board and that your insurance policy covers the full value of it. Its worth spending a tenner and buying a board lock. It may not look cool, but it'll save you when you stumble back to the bar you started drinking in 8 hours ago trying to find it.

If you do get anything stolen then contact the police, you probably won't get it back, but it will help with your claim.

Lake Tahoe sunset, USA
pic WSG

OFF THE SLOPES

HEALTH ON THE HILL

To get the most out of any snowboard trip you should have a reasonable level of fitness. You need not be an Olympic athlete but to avoid feeling like you've been hit by a truck do some exercise before reaching the slopes. In resort the best things to do each day to prevent injury is do a warm up before that first run, even if it's just a few stretches warm mussels won't tear as easily as when cold.

Just because a resort has hotels and chair lifts don't let it fool you, it's still a mountain and should be treated with respect. There's less oxygen at altitude and you'll find yourself puffing even on a short up hill walk. Add that to the 15 pints of beer you drank last night and the cold air, and suddenly dehydration is a real issue so drink plenty of water. The sun is really strong in the mountains and reflects off the snow, making your face redder than pie eating football fan's beer belly in Benidorm. Get 100%UV approved goggles and sunglasses, wear high factor sun screen and remember to reapply.

OFF THE SLOPE

There is often loads to do in resorts other than boarding. Some resorts offer ice-climbing, snowmobiling, paragliding and even tandem freefall parachute jumps. Lots of resorts have indoor sports facilities like swimming pools, ice rinks, bowling alleys and gyms. Most importantly all have pubs, bars, night clubs and restaurants. It shouldn't take long to find the best places to hang out, just ask a local to point you in the right direction. Try to stay away from the humourless hat wearing skier bars that play euro pop and sell cocktails with stupid names. Restaurants on the mountain are always more expensive than those in the town, some criminally so. Most places will have a wide range of eateries from street food to fine dining.

Snowboarding is there for you to enjoy. Party Hard but Ride Harder.

Steamboat Colorado, USA (see page 350)
Larry Pierce/Steamboat Resort

the
british snowboard
association

bsa

www.thebsa.org

Back in those dark days before snowboarding, when people were thinking of new ways to descend a slope it wasn't the green run to the café or a 540 they had in mind. It was havin-it down a wide open powder field at full speed sending a plume of light fluffy snow skyward in their wake. That's what Snowboards were made for and anyone who's had the joy of doing it will tell you there's nothing else like it. Those first turns in virgin snow will have you screaming with joy and boring your mates rotten in the bar for days.

Like any extreme sport there's a cost and in Back Country/ Off piste Boarding it can be high. People die every year in avalanches boarding Back Country, 90% of people who are caught in an avalanche either set it off themselves or someone in their party did.

Prior Preparation Prevents Piss Pore Performance. Before you think of heading Back Country there is knowledge and equipment you must have. Read any information on avalanches and back country travel you can get your hands on, watch videos, look at the web and don't skimp on equipment if you have a transceiver and no shovel all you can do is find where you should be digging. Over 90% of people buried in an avalanche survive if dug out within 15 minuets, try digging in avalanche debris with the end of your board, it doesn't work. Pack your back pack for all eventualities. Remember the weather in the mountains can change fast, because you started the day in sunshine doesn't mean that you won't end it stuck Back Country in a white out. Always be prepared to stay over night.

There is advice out there, so seek it out and take note of it. Avalanche Risk Warnings are posted in resorts, often there's an advice line you can call for information on the weather and snow conditions. The resort mountain staff will know the mountain well, local inside knowledge is invaluable. Check if there's any Back country tours available, take a local registered guide, if you can't afford one at least ask their advice. Many resorts will have Heli-boarding or a snowcat service which is a fantastic and easy way to access the back country, most commercially run trips will include a local guide in the price.

Rider: Jussi Oksannen
Photo: Dean Blotto Gray
Burton Snowboards

Canadian Rockies

INSURANCE

Never go back county alone or without adequate Insurance, check the small print make sure it states back country or off piste. If you brake a leg and need airlifting out you're going to be paying for it for a long time if your insurance won't cover it.

If you are going on a pre-organised trip with a specialist snowboard or ski organisation, check their insurance cover. Find out if their instructors and guides are properly qualified with a recognised certificate and have public liability insurance.

BACKCOUNTRY LAW

In Europe, you are warned not to ride outside restricted areas. However, you are seldom stopped and in many cases it is not actually illegal, although some areas are National Parks and therefore protected, get caught in these and you could get a fine. In France if you set off an avalanche which ends up killing someone on the piste below you'll be charged with manslaughter.

In the US and Canada, riding in marked-off areas is simply not tolerated. The patrols are extremely strict about riding 'out-of-bounds' and apart from getting yourself kicked off the slopes, you could also face police charges.

RIDE BACKCOUNTRY PACK
Unfolds to hold board, includes hard-shell pockets for shades

ACCESS

Back Country Terrain can sometimes be accessed straight off a lift or you may have to hike to it. Both should be treated with the same respect just because you hopped off a piste doesn't make it safe. Choosing the size of and who's in your party is very important. When hiking four is a good size for a group it's easy to monitor each other and if someone has an accident one can stay with the casualty and the other two can go for help. All members of the party must be competent riders, be trusted to keep cool and help if it all goes belly up and most importantly have the correct equipment and know how to use it. It's also important to have an experienced party leader, decisions on route finding and if you should turn back or change the objective should fall to one person. Never split the party unless you need to send for help.

ROUTE FINDING

Route Finding is vital to safe travel in the back country. Always listen and watch the mountain for activity and try to avoid narrow valleys or gullies as they can channel avalanches. Note the profile of the slopes, are they straight, convex or concave? How

SNOWSHOE
Makes lighter work of hiking, by MSR contact www.msrcorp.com for more details

steep is the area and what features exist? Gullies, bowls or ridges? Do you know what landscape lies under the snow? Grass, bushes, rocks or trees?

Avoid travelling along routes after heavy snowfalls where you can see previous avalanche activity, such as damaged trees, snow cookies or dirty snow slopes. If possible, always travel high and stay above large stashes of snow. If walking along a corniced ridge stay to the windward side as the cornices edge may well be unstable and could fracture with your extra weight.

Descending or crossing a face should be done one at a time so as not to overload the slope. You should always try to enter a slope or snow stash at its top, if you enter its middle and it slides all the snow from above could come down on you. When choosing your line down try to keep it narrow, don't cut across the whole slope if there is a trigger point you're much more likely to find it by traversing across the whole thing. Once you've got to the bottom move to a safe place to watch you friends descend, if they set off a slide and your standing in its path your in trouble. Never ever cut across a slope if someone is on it below you, if you do then you deserve the smack in the mouth your likely to get. Once your friend has descended safely take a line next to theirs. Avoid jumping on a suspect slope as the extra weight from the landing could trigger a slide.

AVALANCHES

AVALANCHE VIDEO
Distributed by Black Diamond Films

Avalanches are the biggest killer of back country boarders. If you don't know about the power of avalanches then you shouldn't even start to think about going off piste. The 12 people who died in their chalets on 9th February 1999 in the Montroc Avalanche Chamonix France probably felt safe, until 300,000 cubic meters of snow travelling at 60miles/hr destroyed 14 buildings. If a building can be flattened think what it could do to you.

As a guide slopes less than 30 degrees aren't steep enough to slide and slopes over 60 degrees normally can't hold enough snow to slide. 38 is the magic number, slopes of 38 degrees are the most likely to slide, can you tell the difference between a safe slope of 30 and a potentially dangerous one at 38? No so get a slope inclinometer a handy little piece of kit for measuring slope angles. Snow pits are the best way to

assess a slopes stability learn how to dig one and how to read the snow pack. Look for indicator slopes a slope of similar angle and position to the sun as the one your thinking of descending. If it has avalanche debris on it then it's highly likely yours will slide to. Rain on fresh snow leads to a high avalanche risk as does high wind and severe temperature change. Get as much information as you can, piece it all together and make a decision.

RESCUE
If you get caught in an avalanche try to board out of its side. Try to grab at a grounded object such as a tree. If you get knocked over swim with the slide trying to stay near its surface, if you feel the slide slowing try to clear an air pocket around your mouth and reach for the surface.

Transceivers save lives. They are a small device which sends out a signal and can be switched to receive if one of your party gets buried. You and all the people in your party must wear them and know how to use them.

Survival after an avalanche is all down to the response time of your party 92% after 15mins falls to 25% after 45mins so knowledge of your kit is vital, every minute counts. If one of your party gets caught then watch their path if you lose sight of them under

pic: Les Deux Alpes Tourism

GENERAL ITEMS

Over-boots & Gaiters
Clothing layers
Spare torch batteries
Mobile 'phone & batteries
Collapsible poles
Snowprobe poles
Board tune-up kit
Spare binding screws
Spare binding parts
10m of avalanche cord

FOR ICE & GLACIERS

Crampons & Ice axe
Safety helmet
Carabiners, Rope/Harness

NIGHTWISE

Tent & Sleeping bag
Stove & Cooking utensils

TENT, PROBE & BOOT
Compact mountaineering tent by Black Diamond, avalanche probe & Ride boots (UK size 10) www.ridesnowboards.com

the snow follow the snows path where they were until it stops.

All new transceivers use the same frequency world wide, read and follow the manufactures guide lines carefully. If you carry a mobile phone, also check that the phone doesn't interfere with transceiver. Always wear them under your jacket, never put them in a pocket or in your back pack. Practice finding them and always check them before you leave home.

Recco produce a small reflector which when worn can be detected by rescue services in most major mountain resorts, the main problem here is response time. However you can purchase a pair for around £25, and they never need batteries. Contact www.Recco.com for more info.

One person should take charge of a rescue search, all transceivers should be turned to receive, someone should be posted to look out for secondary avalanches and you should always make sure you have an escape route you're not going to be of any help if you get buried as well.

Between 1985-2003 2694 people died in avalanches in alpine resorts world wide, around 100 a year die in the alps don't be one of them.

FIRST AID

Mountain first aid is a skill that needs to be learnt and practised. Nothing could be worse than seeing a close friend in pain, when all you can do is stand there looking dumb without a clue of what to do. Buy a book on mountain first aid procedures and learn the basics before you go away. Even better, enrol on a professional first aid course.

The following is a very basic guide for immediate first aid, to help relieve pain and to stop further injury until

FIRST AID ESSENTIALS

Waterproof plasters,
Bandages and safety pins
A sling
Antiseptic cream
Gauze pads
First Aid tape
Asprin or other pain relief
Splint

help is at hand. General rules when helping a casualty: clear the airways and check the patient frequently. Arrest bleeding, apply dressings and immobilise broken limbs. Finally treat for shock, relieve pain and then evacuate the casualty A.S.A.P. If in doubt, do as little as possible to avoid worsening the situation
Never go backcountry riding without a well equipped first-aid kit.

WEATHER INJURIES
Hypothermia (exposure) is caused by body heat loss to below 37C. To prevent, eat properly and wear technical, waterproof, warm clothing. To treat, get the casualty under shelter and out of wet clothing, while doing all you can to increase body heat.

Frostbite/Frostnip is full or partial freezing of the skin and its tissues, causing numbness and no reaction to pain. To prevent, avoid exposure of bare skin, and wear correct clothing. To treat, warm the affected areas but never apply direct heat.

Snowblindness is temporary, partial, or total blindness, caused by direct and indirect ultra-violet light, even on dull days when the sun can't be seen. To prevent, wear suitable eyewear that has a 100% UVA & UVB rating. To treat, cover eyes and apply wet cloth to the forehead. Keep out of bright areas.

Dehydration occurs because of depleted fluids. Dizziness and nausea are early warning signs of dehydration. To prevent, drink regular amounts of fluid, such as water or healthy sport drinks. To treat, take a rest and drink as much fluid needed to re-hydrate your system.

WATER CARRIER
Fits inside most backcountry packs

SUMMER GLACIER GUIDE

INTRODUCTION

Spring is here and if you're not up with the lifty then by the time you hit the slopes it's more like wakeboarding than snowboarding. You can't sit down without getting a soaking wet arse and the board is headed for the cupboard under the stairs for the next 7 months. It needn't be like that, there's a whole range of choices out there for the die hard boarder.

Summer camps are a great way to learn or improve freestyle skills. Camps are arranged for all abilities, you don't have to be a pro to ride a pipe. In the winter the top of a pipe can be a scary spot to sit, the locals fly past you enter the pipe and pull some smooth aerial before re-entering the pipe as if they'd never left the ground, a touch intimidating. So how are you ever going to learn a pipe and feel at ease? You could get a group of beginners and start a turf war with the locals, or a little less confrontational go on a summer camp and get expert tuition. Then next winter you'll be the one styling out the pipe.

If you've got time on your hands or loads of cash for the flight you could always head south for the winter to **New Zealand, Australia** or **South America**. A bit far for a weekend or even a week, so why not head for the Alps or north to Norway the land of the midnight sun, for one of the many camps on offer. You may even get to see the Northern Lights while boarding how cool is that?

Another option if the god of wealth is smiling down on you, is **Heliboarding** in the **Himalayan massif** Kyrgyzstan and Kazakhstan both great places to travel through as well as board and really cheep outside of the Helicopter. One thing to keep an eye on is the stability of some countries. Kashmir in India good late spring, is a great place to Heliboard but until last year was a war zone and could well be again by the time you plan a visit. The Caucasus mountains in Russia are great for summer boarding as long as you don't mind getting shot by the Chechen rebels or robbed by the Russian army who haven't been paid in months, having said that successful camps are run on MounElbrus. The best thing to do is check out www.fco.gov.uk for the latest travel advice.

Many of the **Glacial resorts** in Europe have restricted or stopped their summer programs, due to climate change and the erosion cased by boards and skis, many resorts combat this by opening early morning and closing at lunch, which leaves you free to chill out skate or if possible wake board in the afternoon. The mountains are our playground not our right lets treat them with respect, if you cause damage by boarding don't board.

HELI-BOARDING

Oh Mr Pilot could you drop me at the top of that one please. What could be cooler than having your own helicopter to drop you where ever you want? Nothing !!

Heliboarding is the chance to ride virgin powder all day without seeing another soul, there nothings in it league. You may think it's just for the rich and famous it's not, you don't have to be famous. Heliboarding's cost will vary amazingly depending on where in the world you are, how many drops you want , how high you want to go and of course how many of you there are. If you can fill the chopper with your mates and strike a deal for a few drops telling them to drop the overpriced lunch etc then it might just be the best £100 or so pounds you'll ever spend.

In **Europe** you have a few options in **France** you can fly over the border into Italy for a couple of runs. Heliboarding is band in France, as most undeveloped areas are National Park. You can get a helicopter from Chamonix and Tignes. Most of the Heliboarding in **Italy** takes place in the Val Grisenche and Monte Rosa areas.

Switzerland has a healthy policy to heliboarding. Most of the larger resorts allowing you access to the back country without you having to braking into a sweat, other than when you hand over the cash that is. You can also Heliboard in **Spain, Georgia, Turkey** pretty much anywhere there's a mountain with snow on it if you've got the cash you can board it.

The **US** and **Canada** have some amazing possibilities Fernie, Red Mountain and Whistler in Canada, Colorado and the big boy Alaska in the U.S. and that's just to name a few.

INDIA

Has commercial Heliboarding operations in late April. The Himalayan region of Hanuman Tibba, Deo Tibba, Rohtang Pass and Chandrakhani Pass all close to Manali which is a wild valley where loads of marijuana is grown. Also Gulmarg in Kashkir offer heliboarding. Only experienced travellers and boarders should try these places firstly as people disappear in Manali and secondly if you have an accident on your board it's a long way for any help. www.himachal.com run heli boarding trips in early spring.

KAZAKHSTAN + KYRGYZSTAN

In July and August its possible to Heliboard in the Tien Shan Mountains this is real high from 4500m up to 5800m using an Russian Helicopter you can fly from Karkara base camp up to the Northen Tien Shan. In a weeks program its possible for 7/8 dissents of 700/800meters a day. After a few days acclimatising to the altitude you will board from 5500 meters down to 4000meters up to 4 times in one day. On the last day if you're lucky you can board from Semeyonov Peak 5816m down to 4000m.

AUSTRIA

Austria has one of the largest options for summer snowboarding as well as some of the best glaciers. Burton Snowboards holds most of its training camps on Austria's glaciers and many national teams train here during summer. Resorts offer good local services and slopes are crowd free although glaciers like Stubai and others within easy reach of Innsbruck, do tend to get a lot of one day two plankers on special tourist trips. Summer riding in Austria is cheaper than in winter but note some village services close during parts of May and June.

KAPRUN
Kaprun is a favourite summer destination where snowboard teams spend a lot of time training. The ride area is located

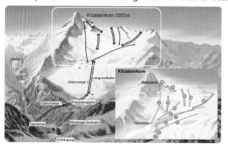

on one of Austria's best glaciers, the Kitzsteinhorn Glacier, which reaches an altitude of 3,203 metres, making it a perfect place to ride. Being a glacier resort, you can ride here all year and no matter what month you visit, riders of all levels will find something to shred. There is a terrain park & pipe located off the Magnetkopfellifte t-bar. Lift tickets are €27 per day. More info on www.kitzsteinhorn.at

SOLDEN
Summer sees both of Solden's glaciers open with carparks at the foot of the **Tiefenbach** and **Rettenbach** glaciers. There's buses from town to the glacier (45mins), or to

drive, follow the main town road as if driving to Oberghurgal then take a right as you leave town at the sign for the glacier. At the foot of the Rettenbach glacier, you'll find a restaurant, the excellent Salomon bar and a couple of shops. The 2 summer terrain parks are also located here and includes rails (straight, kinked, rainbow, etc), wallride, and various size kickers.

The Tiefenbach glacier is a further drive through the tunnel, theres a restaurant at the base and plenty of parking. To board between the 2 glaciers take the new Gondola from the Rettenbach base to the top and board through the skitunnel, to return take the chair at the bottom of the Tiefenbach.

Summer 2004 Burton, Salomon, Volkl & Deeluxe and Scott held team weeks. A week at a BASE camp costs 520€ for Lift ticket, Half Board and coaching.

SUMMER PERIODS:Opens end of June to begining of August
LIFT PASSES: 1 day pass 30 euros
LIFTS OPEN: :2 Gondolas, 1 Chair, 5 t-bars
ELEVATION:2796m to 3309m
TERRAIN PARKS:2

STUBAI GLACIER

45 minutes drive from the centre of Innsbruck is the Stubai Glacier. Stubai claims to be Austria's largest glacier ski resort although in the summer the ski area shrinks to only 4 t-bars, and a couple of runs. The lifts are open from 8am to 4:15pm daily

CANADA

The **Blackcomb mountain** and glacier are the only areas which offer all year round snowboarding in the country. Nearly all of Canada's other resorts close at the end of April with a few closing in mid May.

Blackcomb, which neighbours **Whistler**, is located on the west coast just north of **Vancouver**. Loads of snowboard camps are held here annually on the Horstman glacier. You don't have to be on a camp to ride here during the main summer months, but you may not be allowed in the pipe or park if you are not.

There's 112 acres of terrain open in the summer on the **Horstman Glacier** serviced by 2 t-bars and open from June

7th to August from 12pm to 3pm. It takes 45 minutes from the base of blackcomb to get to the glacier, involving 3 chairs and a bus. Once there you'll find the terrain park has between 4-6 rails/jibs, 2 spine jumps and a halfpipe. Tickets $45CDN per day. In addition to the facilities offered by the resort, there are a number of specialist summer camps with access to their own private terrain parks & pipes. Prices start from $600CDN a week including tuition.

SUMMER GLACIER GUIDE

FRANCE

It's surprising that in a country with so many good winter resorts, has so little to offer for summer snowboarding. 99% of French resorts switch off their lift systems at the end of April regardless of how much snow is still on the slopes. The few resorts that do operate in summer provide a lot of high altitude services with snowboarding only a small part of the mountain activities on offer, with climbing and mountain biking the main attractions.

LA PLAGNE

Ski pass €24.50 a day. Up on the **Glacier de la Chiaupe** with its peak of 3250 meters there are some easy runs. Some of the board schools should be open, but theres no camps of such and no park or pipe, just 3 or 4 easy short pistes. Open from 26/6 to 28/08 a great spot for beginners.

LES DEUX ALPS

A great time to vist this place is summer, as the glacier allows for some fine summer riding in T-shirts. A lot of camps are held here in June and July, with camp programmes mainly aimed at freestylers.Theres 2 half-pipes
Open from 19th June to 28th August from 7:30am to 1:30pm, theres 8 runs open and 11 lifts to get you around. Tickets 29 euros per day.

In summer 2004 Northwave/Drake, Rossignol,Protest,Atomic & SIMS ran summer camps, with prices for 2/3 days 382/576 euros all inclusive

TIGNES

Tignes is one of the major snowboard resorts in France, and has long been hosting national and international events. Tignes lies at 2,100m, and is with out doubt the best summer snowboard destination in France and a match for any of the top glacier resorts of Austria and Switzerland. Access to the glacier area is first done by taking the underground funicular train located at Val Claret. The glacier in the summer is

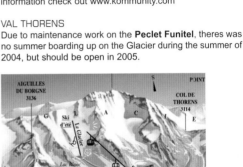

home to 20km of pistes with 750m of vertical, a days lift pass will set you back 30 euros. The snowpark has a range of table tops and rails to suit all levels, and there's a beginners and super pipe.

Kommunity run freestyle summer camps in the last 2 weeks of July. Prices are £500 per week and include tuition, lift pass and half-board accommodation. For more information check out www.kommunity.com

VAL THORENS

Due to maintenance work on the **Peclet Funitel**, theres was no summer boarding up on the Glacier during the summer of 2004, but should be open in 2005.

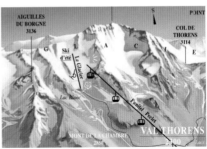

ITALY

Italy offers some of the cheapest summer snowboarding opportunities in the whole of Europe. Although don't expect a great deal in terms of the size and ability of the terrain available. Italy's summer snow cover on its glaciers is okay but, not as good as Austrian or the Swiss glaciers. You won't find many summer halfpipes or parks to ride, but there are snowboard camps with hits to get air from. One place that holds camps is **Passo Stelvio Glacier.** Its the highest glacier resort in Europe and not far from Bormio. Here you get the chance to ride a good park and pipe through out May and June.

CERVINIA

Summer boarding at Cevinia is up at the **Plateau Rosà glacier** and is open from the end of June to early September. The park known as **Indian Park** has a number kickers, rails and a superpipe. Big A run summer camps from mid July to mid August with all-in prices from €350 for the week.

SUMMER GLACIER GUIDE

NORWAY

STRYN

Stryn is located at the base of the **Jostedalsbreen glacier** and is Norway's most famous summer resort (in fact the only one of note really). The glacier gets so much snow during the winter (five metres plus) that the lifts are usually totally buried so they couldn't run them even if they wanted to.

The glacier opens at the end of May to late july. There are some beginners runs, but head to the park. It's got the

usual arrangement of various kickers and rails but no pipe. Lift passes are 280 KR.

Snowboard Norge run summer camps during the last 2 weeks of June, prices are roughly £230 for a weeks instruction and lift pass. For more info check out www.snowboard.no

SWITZERLAND

Switzerland ranks equal with Austria as being the best country in Europe offering summer snowboarding facilities. The Swiss boast a number of great destinations which all provide halfpipes or funparks and like everything else in Switzerland, they are of a very high standard. One of the main places to check out is Saas Fee which boasts to having Europe's only all year round halfpipe and terrain park where loads of pro-rider's hold camps. Swiss local services are good and in most cases lodging is available at the base area of the slopes or close by.

LES DIABLERETS

The glacier is open from mid June 19th to the end of July.Theres 4 easy pistes open. The cable car runs from 8.20am til 4.50pm. One slope is open and the snowpark and the halfpipe. There are a number of summer boarding camps Euroboardtours (www.demonium-mc.com) and Choriqueso Camps (www.choriqueso-camps.ch). Visit www.glacier3000.ch for more information

SAAS-FEE

Saas-Fee has been a resort well known to snowboarders for many years. With its high altitude glacier, Saas-Fee also provides a mountain where you can ride fast and hard in the summer months,

indeed for some, this is the only time worth visiting. The glacier opens in early July until September with access to 20km off pistes and a terrain park with kickers, ¼ pipe, tabletops, rails and a half-pipe. A lift pass will set you back 60CHF a day. Team Nitro are run freestyle camps during July check out www.nitro-snowboards.ch for more info

ZERMATT

Zermatt has the largest summer boarding area in Switzerland high up on the **Klein Matterhorn**. The glacier opens in June until September and theres a number of easy/intermediate

runs all serviced by t-bars and a terrain park.The Gravity Park has a series of kickers and rails and a super-pipe alongside the lift. A lift pass will cost you 60CHF, but the area is only open from 7:30 to 1:30pm so you need to get up early before it starts getting slushy. In the afternoon you can take a look at the worlds highest ice pavilion at 3810m if you're that way inclined.

Stoked run 2 weeks of summer camps in July. A 6 night package including tuition, accommodation, lift pass etc will set you back 630 euros, for more info take a look at www.stoked.ch

RUSSIA

In the heart of the **Caucasus mountains** is **Mt Elbrus** at 5633meters it's the highest mountain in Europe and home for the last 4 years to a summer camp run by SPC. Run in June and July it could be a great laugh if you want good snow and a lot of vodka. The parks built at 4400 meters so be sure to take it easy until you've acclimatised. Once you're there its cheep a pints about 50p and dinners not much more. The camps 850 euros for 9 days excluding international flight.

ICELAND

Iceland Park Project is now in its 4 year, accommodations in a sea side hostel with only a 20 min minibus ride to the park which is on the Snaefelles Glacier. It's a fantastic setting 300km north west of Reykjavik a short drive from Keflavik Airport. It's 500euros for 1 weeks half board and transfer to the park.

We've split the resort information into sections covering mountain, snow, facilities/prices. terrain, and location and contact.

LINKED AREAS
Where a mountain is part of a linked area, we try and specify in the review the size of the linked area, but give details of the local mountain for the resort.

MOUNTAIN STATS
The total ride area is either given in KM's as the length of the combined pistes, or in acres/hectares as the whole boardable area.

The % OF BEGINNER TO EXPERT RUNS are indicated in percentage bars. The lightest shade of grey indicates the beginner easy slopes of green and blue, then intermediate (red) slopes in the middle, finally the black indicates the advanced black and double black slopes.

PRICES
All prices unless stated are for an adult, and for peak season. Lift passes, you can expect to pay up to 25% less for other parts of the season, lessons and hire generally stay the same throughout the season

TERRAIN
We've split the mountain into freeride, freestyle and carving, to indicate the proportion of mountain for your style.
Freeriders as the name suggests like to roam utilising the full area of the resort, so we indicate trees and available area.
Freestylers need their hits, so the higher the percentage the better man-made and natural things there are to fling yourself off of.
Carvers prefer to keep to the pistes, and need nice smooth fast slopes to do so.

COUNTRIES
There's some pretty self-explanatory information on each of the country pages. We've included some very rough currency conversion information, it was correct at the time of going to press, but will change.

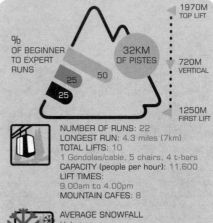

%
OF BEGINNER
TO EXPERT
RUNS

32KM
OF PISTES

25   50
25

1970M
TOP LIFT

720M
VERTICAL

1250M
FIRST LIFT

NUMBER OF RUNS: 22
LONGEST RUN: 4.3 miles (7km)
TOTAL LIFTS: 10
1 Gondolas/cable, 5 chairs, 4 t-bars
CAPACITY (people per hour): 11,600
LIFT TIMES:
9.00am to 4.00pm
MOUNTAIN CAFES: 8

AVERAGE SNOWFALL
Unknown
SNOWMAKING
none

WINTER PERIODS
none
SUMMER PERIODS
July to Sept
Lift Passes
1 Day pass - 49-86 pesos
6 Day pass - 278-484 pesos
Heli Boarding
No
Hire/Board Schools
Yes/Yes

FREERIDE 50%
Some trees and off-piste
FREESTYLE 30%
1Terrain park
CARVING 20%

FLY
to Buenos Aires and then inland to Bariloche and then take a bus or taxi to Chapelco
TRAIN
to Bariloche with a two hour transfer time to the resort with onward travel by bus or taxi to Chapelco.
CAR
Via Bariloche, head north to San Martin de Los Andes on highway 234 and then take the bumpy dirt road Hwy 19 to reach the resort.

Tourist office Chapelco
Cumbres de Chapelco
233 Suipacha LOC 20.
Tel: ++54 (0) 1 350 021
Web: www.cerrochapelco.com
Email:chapelco@fibertel.com.ar

33

Pic - Andorra Tourism

Andorra is a self-governing principality under the joint sovereignty of France and Spain, and has become known as the cheap snow-package tour centre of Europe - a reputation richly deserved. Over the years its also been steadily climbing the leaderboad and now is the 4th most popular destination for British snow hounds, behind France, Austria and Italy. Nestled high in the Pyrenees, Andorra is a very friendly, laid back place which is constantly improving the on-slope facilities, how ever this place has not always had a great snow record.

Andorra has a number of very small resorts, that are ideal for total beginners, and just okay for intermediates on a three day visit. In general, though, there's no challenging terrain for expert riders, or at least nothing that won't take more than a few hours to tackle. A week here will bore the tits off any rider who likes to ride steep, fast and challenging terrain.

All the areas are located within a short distance of each other and can be reached via France or Spain. The nearest international airport is in **Barcelona**, but transfer is not easy if you don't have a car. The resorts offer basic local services, with lots of apartments available.

Andorra is well known for its very boozy nightlife, helping to make it a party-style hangout. Overall this isn't a bad country to visit so as long as it's for no more than a week.

Capital City: Andorra La Vella
Population: 69,865
Highest Peak: Coma Pedrosa 2946m
Language: Catalan-Spanish-French
Legal Drink Age: 18
Drug Laws: Cannabis is illegal and frowned upon
Age of consent: 16
Electricity: 240 Volts AC 2-pin
International Dialing Code: +376

Currency: euro
Exchange Rate:
UK£1 = 1.5 euro
US$1 = 0.8 euro

Driving Guide
All vehicles drive on the right hand side of the road
Speed limits:
In towns 40kph
In rural areas 70kph
Emergency
Police/Ambulance Service - 17
Fire Service - 18
Tolls
None
Documentation
Driving license, insurance and vehicle registration, along with your passport.

Time Zone
UTC/GMT +1 hr
Daylight saving time: +1 hour

Office de Tourisme de la Principauté d'Andorre
Director: Sr. Enric Riba
26, avenue de l'Opéra - 75001 Paris
Tel.: (01) 42 61 50 55
Fax: (01) 42 61 41 91
Minitel: 3615 Andorra
E-mail: OT_ANDORRA@wanadoo.fr
Web: www.tourisme-andorre.net

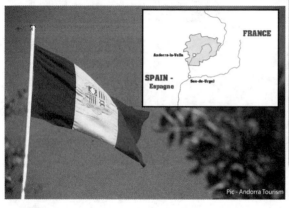

FRANCE
Andorra-la-Vella
SPAIN - Espagne
Seo-de-Urgel

Pic - Andorra Tourism

ARCALIS - ORDINO

5 OUT OF 10

Ok for a few easy days

Arcalis is the least known, least visited, and most remote of all Andorra's resorts. An undeveloped area, **Arcalis** doesn't come with the immediate resort facilities demanded by tour operators and skiers. The 18 miles of snow-sure terrain is perched much above the tree

Pic - Ordino Tourism

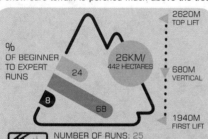

2620M
TOP LIFT

%
OF BEGINNER
TO EXPERT
RUNS

24

26KM/
442 HECTARES

8

68

680M
VERTICAL

1940M
FIRST LIFT

NUMBER OF RUNS: 25
TOTAL LIFTS: 13
5 chairs, 8 drags
CAPACITY (people per hour): 16,510
MOUNTAIN CAFES: 3

AVERAGE SNOWFALL:
Unkown
SNOWMAKING:
30%

WINTER PERIODS:
Dec to April
Lift Passes
1 day 27.50, 5 days 103,season 475
Board School
Group lessons 3 hours 17,25 euros
Nightboarding
No

FREERIDE 40%
Trees and some off-piste
FREESTYLE 20%
No park or pipe
CARVING 40%

Tourist Information
Tel. +376 836 963
Web:www.vallordino.com
Email: ito@andorra.ad

Fly
Barcelona 220km, Tolouse 210km
Bus
9 services daily from Andorra la Vella to Ordino. 0.90 euros. Various daily coach services from Barcelona (ALSINA GRAELLS) and Toulouse (AUTOCARS NADAL) to Andorra la Vella
Train
L'Hospitalet près l'Andorre in France is 8km away. Puigcerdà in Spain is 60km away.
Car
From Andorra la Vella drive to Ordino via La Massana or Canillo.

line, and offers some of the best terrain in the whole principality, with a small number of modest but quite difficult trails. All styles will find that a day or two here is not a waste of money. There are some nice spots for intermediate freeriders to check out, but hardcore freestylers forget it. There's nothing in the way of big jumps, although you will always find plenty of small kickers to trip off. One thing the slopes do offer, is excellent areas for beginners, with easy to reach trails, that make up some 55% of the snowboard area.

THE TOWN
Local facilities can be found in down Ordino which is about 10 miles or 16 km away What you get is very dull.

Pic - Ordino Tourism

5
OUT OF 10

Okay for beginners

Pic - Pal-Arinsal Tourism

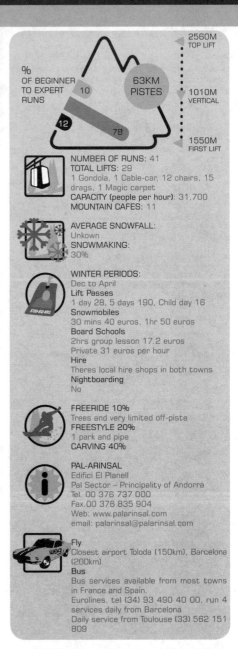

% OF BEGINNER TO EXPERT RUNS

10
12
78

63KM PISTES

2560M TOP LIFT

1010M VERTICAL

1550M FIRST LIFT

NUMBER OF RUNS: 41
TOTAL LIFTS: 29
1 Gondola, 1 Cable-car, 12 chairs, 15 drags, 1 Magic carpet
CAPACITY (people per hour): 31,700
MOUNTAIN CAFES: 11

AVERAGE SNOWFALL:
Unkown
SNOWMAKING:
30%

WINTER PERIODS:
Dec to April
Lift Passes
1 day 28, 5 days 190, Child day 16
Snowmobiles
30 mins 40 euros, 1hr 50 euros
Board Schools
2hrs group lesson 17.2 euros
Private 31 euros per hour
Hire
Theres local hire shops in both towns
Nightboarding
No

FREERIDE 10%
Trees and very limited off-piste
FREESTYLE 20%
1 park and pipe
CARVING 40%

PAL-ARINSAL
Edifici El Planell
Pal Sector – Principality of Andorra
Tel. 00 376 737 000
Fax. 00 376 835 904
Web: www.palarinsal.com
email: palarinsal@palarinsal.com

Fly
Closest airport Toloda (150km), Barcelona (200km)
Bus
Bus services available from most towns in France and Spain.
Eurolines, tel (34) 93 490 40 00, run 4 services daily from Barcelona
Daily service from Toulouse (33) 562 151 809

PAL

Pal is a slightly bigger and better resort than that of its near neighbour Arinsal, with which it shares a lift pass. It also has more interesting terrain than Arinsal and is not quite as rowdy both on and off the slopes. The area is, however, a place for total novices and slow learning intermediates with 95% of the terrain graded blue and red. There's absolutely nothing of note for advanced riders, no matter your style of riding. Only 5% of marked-out trails are black, and even some of these are over-rated, especially if you can ride at a competent level. Most riders will have the whole joint licked in the time it takes to smoke a good joint. Easy-going freeriders will find some wooded areas that on a good day allow for some off-piste through the trees; beginners have nearly the whole place to roam around with a degree of total ease. Freestylers may find the odd log to grind, but that's about all.

THE TOWN: Pal has very basic local services a few miles away.

ARINSAL

Arinsal is a rather a boring resort with miserable features and dull terrain. However, Arinsal is linked directly by cable car to the resort of **Pal** enabling you to escape the place with ease. In Arinsal's defence, a group of beginners on their first snowboard holiday

Pal-Arinsal Mountain Park

Pic - Pal-Arinsal Tourism

SECTOR SETÚRIA

SECTOR ARINSAL

SECTOR PAL

will find the place absolutely perfect and well worth the money - just don't expect any progression once you pass the novice rating. Intermediate carvers may also find a few trails to while away an hour or two but for advanced freestylers forget it.

THE TOWN:Cheap lodging is available in the village of Arinsal which is a few minutes from the slopes and has the reputation of having very lively night-life. Local services are basic but cheap. Information tel: ++376 737 000

Pic - Pal-Arinsal Tourism

PAS DE LA CASA

4 OUT OF 10

Great for beginners, but others will get bored quickly

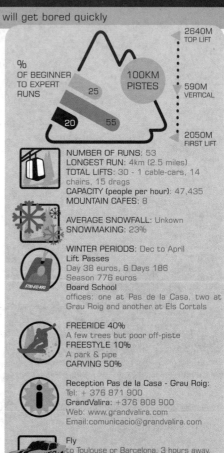

**%
OF BEGINNER
TO EXPERT
RUNS**

25

20 55

**100KM
PISTES**

2640M TOP LIFT

590M VERTICAL

2050M FIRST LIFT

NUMBER OF RUNS: 53
LONGEST RUN: 4km (2.5 miles)
TOTAL LIFTS: 30 - 1 cable-cars, 14 chairs, 15 drags
CAPACITY (people per hour): 47,435
MOUNTAIN CAFES: 8

AVERAGE SNOWFALL: Unkown
SNOWMAKING: 23%

WINTER PERIODS: Dec to April
Lift Passes
Day 38 euros, 6 Days 186
Season 776 euros
Board School
offices: one at Pas de la Casa, two at Grau Roig and another at Els Cortals

FREERIDE 40%
A few trees but poor off-piste
FREESTYLE 10%
A park & pipe
CARVING 50%

Reception Pas de la Casa - Grau Roig:
Tel: + 376 871 900
GrandValira: +376 808 900
Web: www.grandvalira.com
Email:comunicacio@grandvalira.com

Fly
to Toulouse or Barcelona, 3 hours away.
Bus
from airports take 4 hours. Regular daily ski bus to surrounding villages
Car
Drive from Barcelona, head north on the A17 and N152 roads.

NEW
New for 04/05 season
new 8-seat chair to link El Tarter (1710m) with Pla de Riba Escorxada. new 6-seat detachable chair lift in Grau Roig to replace the Coma I ski lift. Terrain park at Pas de la Casa undergoing improvements.

P as de La Casa is the second largest snowboard resort in Andorra, lying in the eastern section of the country along Route N2, close to the **French border.** It now forms part of the linked area **Grand Valira,** currently linking to **Soldeu** and accessing 192km of pistes, but with talk of linking it to Porte Puymorens in France. Each year, the resort attracts more and more riders in groups of lively revellers at novice stage, looking for an easy resort to sample a few beginner bruises. Pas de La Casa shares its slopes with an area known as **Grau Roig** (pronounced 'grau rosh'). Both are lift-linked, offering a collective area of easy-to-master intermediate terrain, with an excellent walk to beginner slopes and a few advanced black runs which can be ridden over a day or two. Three days or more will bore adventurous riders, but a week for beginners is ideal. The mountain is well serviced by some 30 lifts, although quite a few are drag lifts and not beginner friendly.

FREERIDERS should be advised that this is not a freeriding metropolis. However, the area can offer some good powder stashes after a recent dump. The best riding is on the **Grau Roig**, up on the main slope and down the other side. Once in the Grau Roig, you can take a chair up the mountain to gain access to a whole new area, and if you take the main run down the hill and across the top of the black run, you will find some okay powder fields.

FREESTYLERS will find a number of natural hits on the Grau Roig area. However, you will need to plan your route using the piste map if you want to avoid a long walk back to the lift station. Overall, this is not a hot freestyle resort even though there is a well looked after fun-park and pipe off the Coma 111 trail, which is reached by taking the Number 1 chair.

CARVERS have a respectable 25 mile trail which can be done at speed. Avoid trail 37 or Isards, which are pure crap.

BEGINNERS can take most advantage here, with good novice areas reached by foot from the village. The flats are perfect for novices and it won't be too long before you can tackle the rest.

THE TOWN
Local services at the foot of the slopes are cheap and

cheerful, offering a host of duty-free shops, supermarkets, restaurants and bars that stay open very late, and see a fair share of hardcore partying. Shops and **night-life** are within walking distance, doing away with the need for a car or public transport in the evenings. Cool hangouts are *Pub Milwaukee* for happy hour with a very lively atmosphere and *Billboard* for a late night dance, beer and holiday talent.

6 OUT OF 10

Cheap, tacky and the best terrain in Andorra

Soldeu - El Tarter makes up the biggest rideable area in Andorra, with some 92km of linked terrain. Its also linked to **Pas** creating the **Grand Valira** area totalling 192km of pistes. This the country's most popular resort which makes the place hellishly busy, with clogged up lifts and slopes. Budget-conscious skiers have been flocking here for years, and it is now also becoming a popular snowboard destination. Cheap and tacky maybe, but it is still okay for your first snowboard

Pic - Andorra Tourism

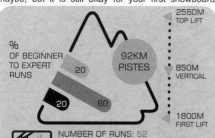

2560M TOP LIFT

% OF BEGINNER TO EXPERT RUNS

92KM PISTES

20

20   60

850M VERTICAL

1800M FIRST LIFT

NUMBER OF RUNS: 52
LONGEST RUN: 8km (5 miles)
TOTAL LIFTS: 32 - 2 cable-cars, 13 chairs, 12 drags, 5 Magic Carpets
CAPACITY (people per hour): 38,100
MOUNTAIN CAFES: 5

AVERAGE SNOWFALL: Unkown
SNOWMAKING: 36%

WINTER PERIODS: Dec to April
Lift Passes
Day 38 euros, 6 Days 186
Season 776 euros
Nightboarding
No

FREERIDE 40%
A few trees and a bit of off-piste
FREESTYLE 20%
A park & pipe
CARVING 40%

Soldeau/ El Tarter
Tel - +376 890 500
Web: www.soldeu.ad
Email:info@soldeu.ad

Fly
to Toulouse or Barcelona, both 3 hrs away.
Bus
Bus services from airports take 4 hours.
Car
Drive from Barcelona, head north on the A17 and N152 roads.

NEW

New for 04/05 season
new 8-seat chair to link El Tarter (1710m) with Pla de Riba Escorxada.
new 6-seat detachable chair lift in Grau Roig to replace the Coma I ski lift
Terrain park at Pas de la Casa undergoing improvements.

holiday. Although this is the largest area in Andorra, there is still not much to brag about. The terrain is not adventurous and basically poor for riders with ability. There are only a couple of black runs to choose from. However, Soldeu has a good snowboard scene and plays host to a number of locally organised snowboard events, which include boardercross competitions that attract the odd pro.

FREERIDERS will find that Soldeau has the best terrain in Andorra, especially for off-piste. The unpisted runs graded black and red, running down from the summit area of **Pic D'enc Ampadana**, are good freeriding areas. The trail starts off in a fast open section before dropping through a thick tree-lined area. For something to suit a novice rider, the red run that descends from the main summit, through the open expanse of the **Riba Escorxada**, is cool.

FREESTYLERS are offered a park and 120m halfpipe. The "**Free SET**" has a quarter pipe, ridges, various jumps, rails and boxes. However its not always well maintained. There are also plenty of cool natural hits to catch air, but nothing is really big so there's no need to call air traffic control. Look out for locals spotting hits to know where to ride

CARVERS have plenty of flats, with the option to ride hard and fast down a number of blacks, or the more sedate, pisted red and blue trails off the Tosa Espiolets chair.

BEGINNERS have a great little mountain to explore with lots of easy, green nursery slopes to learn on, even if they do get clogged. Unfortunately, the easy runs are serviced by T-bars. Novices can ride down a series of open green trails, which will take you through trees and back to Soldeu.

THE TOWN

An overload of apartments are available at the base of the slopes, with some very cheap lodging options. Like the rest of Andorra, local facilities are basic, somewhat dull, but perfectly adequate for a week's stay. **Night-life** is fast, raunchy, with booze, booze and more booze - the streets are pebble-dashed with diced carrots on a nightly basis. Lively bars to check out are the *Piccadilly*, *Pub Iceberg* or *Fat Alberts*.

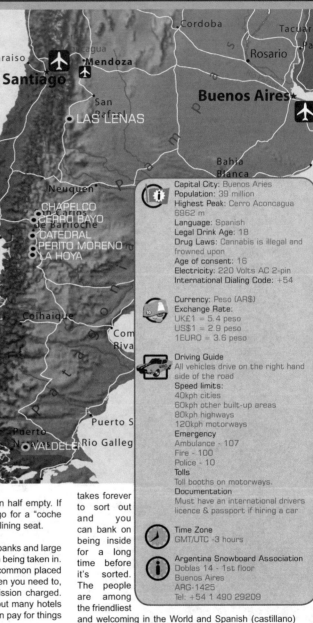

Argentina is a country that is split by the awesome **Andes Mountain range** which is home to a vast array of ski resorts, from large 'internationally acclaimed' chic areas to small and humble 'local hills'. Take your pick: they're relatively easy to get to and can be pretty cheap when you're there.

Argentinean resorts are mainly located in two regions along the Andes; the High Andes between Santiago (Chile) and **Mendoza** (Argentina), and the Lake District/ **Patagonia** further south. The regions differ in many aspects; the High Andes region contains a bunch of resorts in the area around South America's highest peak, Aconcagua, close to areas such as Los Penitentes and Las Lenas. The resorts are high, much above the tree line, and receive good light snow due to their high altitude. They are also considered to be 'top notch' resorts and this is reflected in their prices of accommodation and other resort services.

Flights from London to either Buenos Aries cost from £600 return, and take about 14 hours. The airport is well out of town so a taxi back into the city centre costs around £20, but try bargaining as it works. Car hire is expensive; from AR$120 a day plus mileage. Argentina has an exhaustive network of long distance buses which aren't your stereotype 'latin America' affair. Distances are long but the buses are comfy, and due to the heavy competition are often half empty. If you can spare the extra few dollars go for a "coche cama" which means 'bed coach' or reclining seat.

Traveller's cheques may be cashed at banks and large hotels but with dire rates of commission being taken in. It's better to bring plastic and use the common placed cash machines to withdraw money when you need to, you get a better rate and less commission charged. The peso is more stable these days, but many hotels still quote in US$, and you can still often pay for things in US$.

Night clubs in Argentina usually do not start until midnight. All common drugs (dope etc) are illegal with heavy penalties if caught. Paperwork, if you are rumbled,

takes forever to sort out and you can bank on being inside for a long time before it's sorted. The people are among the friendliest and welcoming in the World and Spanish (castillano) is the main language. It's worth having a few phrases of Spanish up your sleeve, though many people in the tourism industry and local boarders can often speak some English.

Capital City: Buenos Aries
Population: 39 million
Highest Peak: Cerro Aconcagua 6962 m
Language: Spanish
Legal Drink Age: 18
Drug Laws: Cannabis is illegal and frowned upon
Age of consent: 16
Electricity: 220 Volts AC 2-pin
International Dialing Code: +54

Currency: Peso (AR$)
Exchange Rate:
UK£1 = 5.4 peso
US$1 = 2.9 peso
1EURO = 3.6 peso

Driving Guide
All vehicles drive on the right hand side of the road
Speed limits:
40kph cities
60kph other built-up areas
80kph highways
120kph motorways
Emergency
Ambulance - 107
Fire - 100
Police - 10
Tolls
Toll booths on motorways.
Documentation
Must have an international drivers licence & passport if hiring a car

Time Zone
GMT/UTC -3 hours

Argentina Snowboard Association
Doblas 14 - 1st floor
Buenos Aires
ARG-1425
Tel: +54 1 490 29209

CHAPELCO

5 OUT OF 10 — Okay basic resort

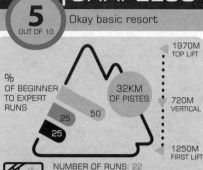

%
OF BEGINNER
TO EXPERT
RUNS

25
50
25

32KM
OF PISTES

1970M
TOP LIFT

720M
VERTICAL

1250M
FIRST LIFT

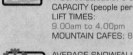

NUMBER OF RUNS: 22
LONGEST RUN: 4.3 miles (7km)
TOTAL LIFTS: 10
1 Gondolas/cable, 5 chairs, 4 t-bars
CAPACITY (people per hour): 11,600
LIFT TIMES:
9.00am to 4.00pm
MOUNTAIN CAFES: 8

AVERAGE SNOWFALL
Unknown
SNOWMAKING
none

WINTER PERIODS
none
SUMMER PERIODS
July to Sept
Lift Passes
1 Day pass - 49-86 pesos
6 Day pass - 278-484 pesos
Heli Boarding
No
Hire/Board Schools
Yes/Yes

FREERIDE 50%
Some trees and off-piste
FREESTYLE 30%
1Terrain park
CARVING 20%

FLY
to Buenos Aires and then inland to
Bariloche and then take a bus or taxi to
Chapelco
TRAIN
to Bariloche with a two hour transfer
time to the resort with onward travel by
bus or taxi to Chapelco.
CAR
Via Bariloche, head north to San Martin
de Los Andes on highway 234 and then
take the bumpy dirt road Hwy 19 to
reach the resort.

Tourist office Chapelco
Cumbres de Chapelco
233 Suipacha LOC 20.
Tel: ++54 (0) 1 350 021
Web: www.cerrochapelco.com
Email:chapelco@fibertel.com.ar

Pic - Chapelco resort

J ust above the town of **San Martin De Los Andes** lies the resort of **Chapelco** which despite being a small resort still offers a big variety of terrain for all types and levels of rider. The arrival of a new resort director has led to the development of a number of snowboard friendly policies on the mountain, including the construction of a permanent halfpipe accessed from the Palito drag lift, and a programme of snowboard demos and freestyle classes. A low elevation means unreliable snow cover at the base area but up at the mid station things are usually fine. The resort has a good reputation among Argentine boarders, but due to its North facing aspect suffers unreliable snow conditions at times. The slopes are equipped with a modern lift system and a number of mountain cafes. But note, food and drink on the mountain is expensive.

FREERIDERS will find, that when the lower section has snow cover, it offers a rolling terrain of fast cruising dotted with cat track hits.The moss shrouded Lenga trees are well spaced for excellent tree riding off the sides of the mid and lower pistes, but lack pitch in places. Steeps are found on the faces of Cerro Teta and the La Pala face (40 degree) which remain unpisted and are fed by a speedy quad and poma drag respectively. Although short these faces provide the buzz that the freerider is looking for with 3-10m cliff bands laying down the gauntlet between the Teta and the La Puma areas. The back bowl offers superb powder if you're willing to do the one hour hike back out.

FREESTYLERS have a permanent halfpipe accessed from the Palito drag lift which the locals session all day long.

CARVERS may find that due to the lack of good piste grooming, the runs are bumpy and rutted, making this place not so ideal.

BEGINNERS have an mountain with 40% of the terrain graded to suite their needs, but its not all ideal or super easy.

THE TOWN is small enough to be able to walk everywhere. **Accommodation** can be found in San Martin 18 miles from the base. The Poste del Caminero Hostel has bunks from $10 a night and there is a helpful tourist office to get you sorted. Check out the 'Deli' by the lake for cheap snacks and the best priced beer in town. There are also a couple nighclubs and laid back bars.

41

LAS LENAS

7 OUT OF 10

Very good resort when its snows, otherwise it can be very frustrating.

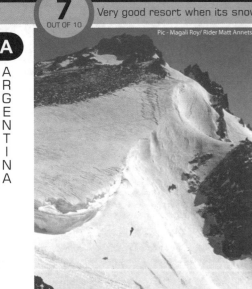

Pic - Magali Roy/ Rider Matt Annets

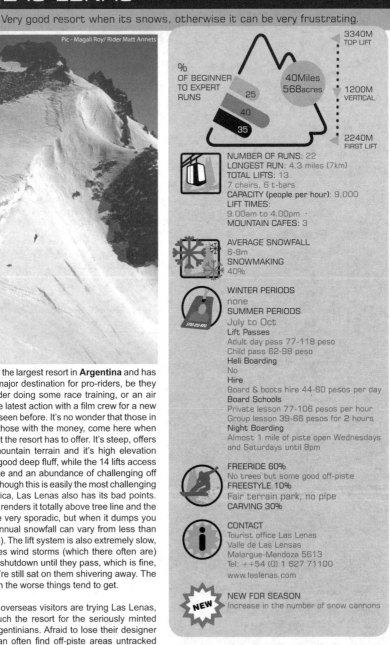

3340M TOP LIFT

% OF BEGINNER TO EXPERT RUNS
25
40
35

40Miles
568acres

1200M VERTICAL

2240M FIRST LIFT

NUMBER OF RUNS: 22
LONGEST RUN: 4.3 miles (7km)
TOTAL LIFTS: 13
7 chairs, 6 t-bars
CAPACITY (people per hour): 9,000
LIFT TIMES:
9.00am to 4.00pm
MOUNTAIN CAFES: 3

AVERAGE SNOWFALL
6-8m
SNOWMAKING
40%

WINTER PERIODS
none
SUMMER PERIODS
July to Oct
Lift Passes
Adult day pass 77-118 peso
Child pass 62-98 peso
Heli Boarding
No
Hire
Board & boots hire 44-60 pesos per day
Board Schools
Private lesson 77-106 pesos per hour
Group lesson 39-66 pesos for 2 hours
Night Boarding
Almost 1 mile of piste open Wednesdays
and Saturdays until 8pm

FREERIDE 60%
No trees but some good off-piste
FREESTYLE 10%
Fair terrain park, no pipe
CARVING 30%

CONTACT
Tourist office Las Lenas
Valle de Las Lensas
Malargue-Mendoza 5613
Tel: ++54 (0) 1 627 71100
www.laslenas.com

NEW FOR SEASON
Increase in the number of snow cannons

Las Lenas is the largest resort in **Argentina** and has become a major destination for pro-riders, be they a sponsored rider doing some race training, or an air head getting the latest action with a film crew for a new video we've all seen before. It's no wonder that those in the know, and those with the money, come here when you look at what the resort has to offer. It's steep, offers the rider big mountain terrain and it's high elevation should ensure good deep fluff, while the 14 lifts access 40 miles of piste and an abundance of challenging off piste terrain. Although this is easily the most challenging area in S.America, Las Lenas also has its bad points. Its high altitude renders it totally above tree line and the snowfall can be very sporadic, but when it dumps you get feet of it (annual snowfall can vary from less than 1m to over 10m). The lift system is also extremely slow, and when theres wind storms (which there often are) the lifts can be shutdown until they pass, which is fine, but usually you're still sat on them shivering away. The later the season the worse things tend to get.

Although more overseas visitors are trying Las Lenas, its still very much the resort for the seriously minted and famous Argentinians. Afraid to lose their designer shades, you can often find off-piste areas untracked for days, weeks if you're lucky enough to get on the snowcat. You'll also find the nightlife different, clubs don't get going until midnight and stay open to 5am and people are remarkably sober, but the ladies are truly to die for. The exchange rate means that whilst its extremely expensive for Argentinians, you'll be able to

enjoy yourselves no matter what budget.

FREERIDERS willing to do the short hikes can get to 50 degree faces and big ball cliff drops making this place a freerider's dream. When its open, the Marte chair delivers you to terrain that is possibly the best that the Southern Hemisphere has to offer. Ask in the wine bar about a guide and examine the off-piste maps on the walls for all the runs you'll need. From the top of the Marte head down toward the Iris t-bar, once the patrol have made you sign your life away, you can drop into one of the many chutes that will end up at the top of the Vulcano lift. For AR$25 peso you can take a ride in the snowcat, where you'll be almost guaranteed in getting fresh tracks for the next couple of hours. You'll find it next to the first aid hut on the Apolo run.

FREESTYLERS will find a park at the base which is the setting for the Reef big air comps. Its very snow dependant, but when theres snow theres a good variety of jumps and some rails.

CARVERS can have a great time with some well groomed fast trails and some great steep un-groomed runs. The Vulcano and Apolo runs have good long wide pistes.

BEGINNERS may struggle a little here with most of the slopes geared towards intermediates. Venus is one of the few beginner runs but due to its flatness, people coming from the Marte will try and fly down it, and you can find your self skating if you take a tumble. There are lessons available, and some of the instructors do speak english but often not fluent.

THE TOWN

The village is small but has a number of plush hotels and some cheaper apartments available. There is a supermarket selling most things, but if you want any thing fresh then bring it with you. Theres a cash machine, a couple of board shops, restaurants and the usual tourist trappings in the mall, but thats about it. The nearest town is Malargue about an hours drive away.

ACCOMODATION in Las Lenas is pricey (4 star hotels), though it is often easy to get a bed in the 'workers' dormitory for US$10 per night. There are a number of apartments available if you can't quite stretch to the Piscis or Otherwise the nearest 'affordable' beds are in Malargue, a small town down the valley, where you'll find hotel rooms from US$20 a night.

FOOD wise the 5* Piscies do a good AR$50 peso 3 course meal at one of their 2 restaurants and the food at the Aries can be very good. Apart from hotels, El Refugio do a reasonable fondue and Huaco some good steaks. If its burgers then the Innsbruck is ok, and the UFO Point do great pizzas. A good way to end the day is a meal at La Cima, situated at the top of the Eros lift. They serve authentic Argentinian grills including a parrillada, a mixed grill or rat on stick depending on your viewpoint. The place really kicks off once the eatings finished and the band start playing. If you're eating on a budget then you'll find a restaurant in the workers accomodation, open to all its AR$15 peso for a 3 course meal including wine. The local supermarket stocks everything you'll need if you're self catering, however fresh vegtables are rare so make sure you stock up before arriving.

NIGHTLIFE starts late and finishes early, so its just as well the lifts don't close till 5pm. Do what the locals do and grab a beer or a chocolate, sit outside or in the Innsbruck or UFO point until about 6pm then take a break. Around 9pm the restaurants will start to open up, grab some food then head to one of the late bars. The BU bar above the Corona Club is a good place to hang, and they often have bands playing. UFO Point and Corona Club take alternate nights, things don't start getting lively until its past midnight and theres usually a cover charge to get in. They certainly know how to party, but you wont find many people drinking so at least you'll always get served quickly. For a change in atmosphere the tiny wine bar's a good place to chat to locals whilst you sup a good Malbec.

FLY: to Buenos Aires and then inland to Mendozas, transfer to resort takes 5hrs. One flight a week to Malargue airport from Jorge Newbury Airport (Buenos Aires), transfer to resort takes 1 hr.

COACH: Overnight coach services available from Buenos Aires. Resort buses free and operate 24hrs

TRAIN: to Malargue, 40 miles from Las Lenas and will take 1 hour to reach Las Lenas.

CAR: 450 km away from Mendozas, head south on highway 40, and Provincial 222 to Las Leñas, 20 km after the city of Los Molles

1782M
TOP LIFT

% RUNS

12miles
200hect

720M
VERTICAL

20

50

30

1050M
FIRST LIFT

Runs: 21 Longest: 5km
Total Lifts: 10 - 5 chairs, 5 drags
Lift Capacity PH: 5,700
Av Snowfall: unknown
Snowmaking: 10%

Open June to Sep
Lift Passes Day AR$42, 3 Days AR$133,
Week AR$300, Season AR$1450

Fly Buenos Aires (BA) & Bariloche 2 hrs away.
Drive (BA) RN 22, RN 237 and RN 231
Bus From BA following companies run
coach services: Chevallier, the Valley, the Star, TAC

CERRO BAYO

Cerro Bayo is a resort with a local hill feel and some wicked scenery across the lakes of **Patagonia**. The area has 10 lifts giving access to an assortment of treelined pistes with an upper T-bar extending the last 300m above the trees to the summit. Freeriders can ride a 720m vertical off piste bowl before heading back into the trees to pick up a chair or continue to the base. Lodging and eating can be found in the village of **Villa La Angostura**, which is a small and very friendly place. Services are limited and not really geared towards winter holiday makers. However, it's a cool place with a few restaurants and places to kip in. Access to and from the slopes is made easy by either driving up yourself or taking the shuttle bus or taxi (pricey).

 WEB: WWW.CERROBAYOWEB.COM
EMAIL: INFORMES@CERROBAYOWEB.COM

CRAN CATEDRAL

lies west of San Carlos de Bariloche. The resort is spread across three peaks and gives rise to the second most extensive resort in S.America. Although a low elevation prevents snow cover to the base for the whole season, cover is usually good higher up with a variety of terrain. Best freeriding areas include the off piste from the Piedra del Condor peak. Accommodation is available at the base, but expensive. Its cheaper and better for nightlife and food, to stay in Bariloche.

In total $23million is being invested over the next few years. This year theres 5 new babylifts, and 6 new chairs are planned over the next 2 years, along with re-development of the base and an increase in terrain.

 WEB: WWW.CATEDRALALTAPATAGONIA.COM
EMAIL: INFO@CATEDRALALTAPATAGONIA.COM

Top: 1057m Bottom: 195m Vert: 772m
Runs: 19 Total Lifts: 3 chairs, 3 drags
Easy: 30% Intermediate: 30% Advanced: 40%

Fly
to Ushuaia 26km away
Main town is Tierra del Fuego

Web: WWW.CERROCASTOR.COM
Email: CONTACTO@CERROCASTOR.COM

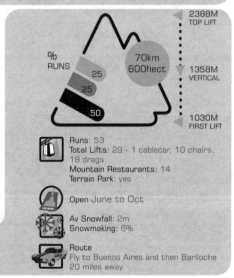

2388M
TOP LIFT

% RUNS

70km
600hect

25

25

50

1358M
VERTICAL

1030M
FIRST LIFT

Runs: 53
Total Lifts: 29 - 1 cablecar, 10 chairs,
18 drags
Mountain Restaurants: 14
Terrain Park: yes

Open June to Oct

Av Snowfall: 2m
Snowmaking: 6%

Route
Fly to Buenos Aires and then Bariloche
20 miles away.

CERRO CASTOR

Only in its 5th season. 2 new runs added this year. Lessons available from the base, private expect to pay between 63-70 pesos an hour, group lessons 35-42 pesos (2 hours). Board & boots available to hire at 42 pesos per day.

RESORT ROUND-UP

LA HOYA

La Hoya is decent size resort by South American standards, located a short distance from the town of **Esquel**. The notable point about this place is the amount of **advanced level terrain** on offer that will suite hard core freeriders 100%. Some of which will entail hiking and a few thigh burning traverse sections. Theres no halfpipe for freestylers. The area has good intermediate trails as well as okay novice runs at the lower sections. **Accommodation** and other facilities are available at the base area.

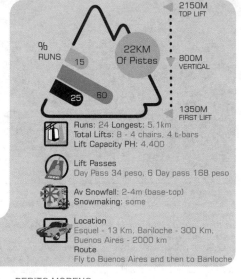

Runs: 24 Longest: 5.1km
Total Lifts: 8 - 4 chairs, 4 t-bars
Lift Capacity PH: 4,400

Lift Passes
Day Pass 34 peso, 6 Day pass 168 peso

Av Snowfall: 2-4m (base-top)
Snowmaking: some

Location
Esquel - 13 Km, Bariloche - 300 Km,
Buenos Aires - 2000 km
Route
Fly to Buenos Aires and then to Bariloche

Web: WWW.CAMLAHOYA.COM.AR
Email: CAMLAHOYA@CAMLAHOYA.COM.AR

Top: 1450m **Bottom:** 1000m **Vert:** 450m
Runs: 2 **Total Lifts:** 5 drags
Easy: 20% **Intermediate:** 60% **Advanced:** 20%

Fly
to Buenos Aires and then Bariloche 2 1/2 hours away.

PRIMEROS PINOS

is not really a resort as such. What you have here is a mountain area operated by a local company, with a few portable lifts, placed wherever the best snow is, which on occasions is non existant. However, when the place is able to tow punters up, the decents are for one style and one level of ride only. Beginners, nothing else. Truly, if you can ride and have two hours experience don't bother with this place. Some beds at the base, but main services down in Zapala.

Top: 1450m **Bottom:** 1000m **Vert:** 450m
Runs: 2 **Total Lifts:** 5 drags
Easy: 20% **Intermediate:** 60% **Advanced:** 20%

Fly
Fly to Buenos Aires and then Rio Gallegos 1 1/2 hours away

PERITO MORENO

is a tiny resort with more lifts than runs. This tiny outpost is located about 16 miles from the town **El Bolson**. You have a mountain area covered with densely spaced trees, with the piste cut out in a straight trail and a thin stretch of wood in the centre of the main Pista de Mario. **Freeriders** will find that although the piste is limited there is good backcountry with great powder, but be prepared to hike. Basic lodging at the base, and down in El Bolson.

Top: 1870m **Bottom:** 1600m **Vert:** 270m
Runs: 5 **Total Lifts:** 3
Easy: 90% **Intermediate:** 10%

Fly
to Buenos Aires and then Bariloche 1 1/2 hours away.

VALDELEN

is located way down in the southern tip of the country and the bottom of the Andes. As well as being Argentina's smallest resort, it is also one of the busiest ,attracting large numbers of skiers on a regular basis. It's a bit hard to see why because there is naff all here, no decent piste or off-piste just a few intermediate and beginner areas. There is little else here to please, especially if you're an advanced rider or freestyler. All local services are found down in the town of Rio Turbio.

45

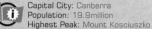

Australia has some nine resorts located on the eastern mountain ranges on the state borders of **New South Wales** and **Victoria**. There are also places to ride on the separate southern island of **Tasmania**. All the main resorts are easy to reach from the two major ports of entry, Melbourne and Sydney. Overall Australian snowboarding opportunities are no where near as good as what is available in Europe, North America or at nearby New Zealand. Still to make up for dull mountains with below average slopes, the aussies have a reputation for being party animals.

Road travel in Australia is good but with the draw back of having to pay high toll charges at the entry gates to some mountain ski areas. Once through the entrance gate, snow chains must be carried at all times. It is illegal not to have them and could result in a A$200 fine. There are internal **flights** from Melbourne and Sydney to airports closer to the resorts, but prices are pretty steep. If a **train** ride through the countryside is what you seek enroute to a resort, then central station in Sydney or Spencer Street in Melbourne is where to head for. Melbourne doesn't have any direct train line going to any of the apline regions, however theres a train service direct from Sydney to Jindabyne, the major station for NSW resorts. **Bus** companies run daily trips from the major cities to the bigger resorts. Costs vary, but for around you A$55 you can kick back and watch a video while some one else does the driving.

Accomodation will vary depending on your budget. Five star chalet lodges, club lodges and hostels can be found above the snowline but it may be cheaper if a bed is sought in a nearby town.

If you want to spend a season in Australia, it would be best to get here in late April, as this is when resorts start advertising job vacancies. The normal Australian winter season is between June and mid September.

Capital City: Canberra
Population: 19.9million
Highest Peak: Mount Kosciuszko 2229 m
Language: English
Legal Drink Age: 18
Drug Laws: Cannabis is illegal
Age of consent: 16
Electricity: 240 Volts AC 3-pin
International Dialing Code: +61

Currency: Australian Dollar (A$)
Exchange Rate:
UK£1 = A$2.6
1 EURO = A$1.7
US$1 = A$1.4

Driving Guide
All vehicles drive on the left hand side of the road
Speed limits:
110km/h Motorways
100km/h normal
60km/h built up areas
Emergency
For police,fire and ambulances dial 000
Tolls
A few, on some motorways . more info www.hillsmotorway.com.au
Some resorts have toll roads to acess them.
Documentation
Driving licences and permits must be carried at all times
Seatbelts
It is illegal to travel without a seat belt on

Time Zone
Victoria & New South Wales UTC/GMT +10 hours

Ski & Snowboard Australia (SSA)
Level 1, 1 Cobden Street
Sth Melbourne, 3205
Tel: (03) 9696 2344
Fax: (03) 9696 2399
Email: info@skiandsnowboard.org.au
Web:www.skiingaustralia.org.au

MT BULLER

7 OUT OF 10

Very good resort

Mt. Buller is 400 hectares of riding pleasure, with 26 lifts that would, in a perfect world, whisk 39,500 snowboarders per hour up the 400m vertical rise so they could make the best of Victoria's largest trail system. 'Buller' as it is affectionately known is the closest major resort to **Melbourne** so weekend riding is not recommended, unless you enjoy lift lines and busy slopes. The terrain mix at Buller will keep all levels of rider amused for

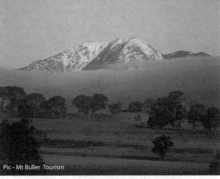

Pic - Mt Buller Tourism

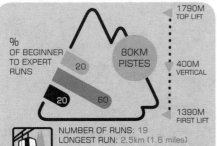

% OF BEGINNER TO EXPERT RUNS

20
20   60

80KM PISTES

1790M TOP LIFT

400M VERTICAL

1390M FIRST LIFT

NUMBER OF RUNS: 19
LONGEST RUN: 2.5km (1.6 miles)
TOTAL LIFTS: 25
13 chairs, 12 drags
CAPACITY (people per hour): 40,000
LIFT TIMES: 8.30am to 5.00pm

AVERAGE SNOWFALL: 1.5m
SNOWMAKING: 15%

WINTER PERIODS: June to October
Lift Passes
Day pass A$82, 3 Day A$225
5 Day A$360, Season pass A$1150
Nightboarding
No

FREERIDE 55%
A few trees and good off-piste
FREESTYLE 25%
2 parks & a half-pipe
CARVING 20%

Mt Buller Resort Management
Mt Buller, Victoria, Australia 3723
Tel: +61 3 5777 6077
Fax: +61 3 5777 6219
Web: www.mtbuller.com.au
Email:info@mtbuller.com.au

Fly
Fly to Melbourne international airport which is 248 miles away and will take 5 hours by bus to reach
Car
Via Melbourne, take the Maroondah highway route 153 north to Mansfield and then follow signs for Mt Buller.

NEW New for 04 season
new earth-shaped FIS spec 100m halfpipe, and $750k of new snow cannons

sometime, with an even spread between all levels.

FREERIDERS who like their terrain with a side serve of steeps, should head for the summit and try to tame **Fannys Finnish** or **Fast One** which are Bullers most notorious black diamond runs. If you have conquered Fannys then it must be time to head backcountry with the best reached by hiking out past the fire hut on the summit to a place known as **Buller Bowls**. The bowl is serious terrain that will avalanche if given the chance, so it is best to check conditions with the ski patrol. If tree runs take your fancy then slip off the side of Standard and make tracks between the snowguns. If you are early it is possible to get fresh tracks in the powder stashes in this area.

FREESTYLERS have an abundance of natural hits which makes the trails resemble a spread out fun-park. Theres a terrain park located at **skyline**, the halfpipes over at **Boggy Creek** and a separate rail park at **BB2**

CARVERS, the runs can often be a bit rutted, but with some good early morning grooming, speed freaks can cut some nice fast tracks down a number of well spaced trails to suit all levels.

BEGINNERS will manage perfectly well at Buller, with a good selection of easy slopes that are crowd free on weekdays but crowd drenched on weekends. Rookies should go and get a lesson from one of the professional instructors at the ski school, which also offers a 'Discover Boarding' lift ticket.

THE TOWN
Off the slopes Mt Buller is a equipped resort with great options for doorstep riding. Buller has the most on-mountain **accommodation** in Victoria, so guests can stay above the snowline and take full advantage of the fact that Buller has the largest number of alpine restaurants and night-spots in the state with partying up here going on until day light hours. But note this is an expensive resort that attracts Aussie's finest.

PERISHER BLUE

5 OUT OF 10 Good freeriding

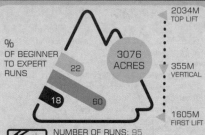

% OF BEGINNER TO EXPERT RUNS

22

18 60

3076 ACRES

2034M TOP LIFT

355M VERTICAL

1605M FIRST LIFT

NUMBER OF RUNS: 95
LONGEST RUN: 3km (2 miles)
TOTAL LIFTS: 50
12 chairs, 34 drags, 4 ski carpets
CAPACITY (people per hour): 52,903
LIFT TIMES: 9.00am to 5.00pm
MOUNTAIN CAFES: 18

AVERAGE SNOWFALL: 2.5m
SNOWMAKING: 95 acres

WINTER PERIODS: June to October
Lift Passes
1 Day A$73, 3 Day A$205,5 Day A$315
Nightboarding
Tuesdays and Saturdays 6:30 to 9:30
on the front valley. Halfpipe is floodlit on
saturdays.

FREERIDE 50%
Trees and good off-piste
FREESTYLE 25%
4 parks & 2 half-pipes
CARVING 25%

Pershier Blue Tourist Office
Po Box 42, Pershier Valley, NSW
Tel: +61 (02) 64 59 44 21
Web: www.perisherblue.com.au

Fly
Snowy Mountain Airport (Cooma) 1hr from
sydney, and 1hr from resort. Fly to Sydney
airport with a 6 hour transfer time.
Car
From Sydney, head south to Jindabyne
and then take the Kosciuszko road to
reach Perisher Blue (about 6hrs).
Jindabyne to Perisher is 20miles (33km).
Bus
SnoBus Snowscene Express from Brisbane/
Gold Coast Tel. 07 3392 1722. Valley Bus
and Coach Services operate from Sydney
and Canberra Tel. 02 6297 6300.
Train
to Jindabyne station, 45 minutes away.

New for 04 season
new superpipe will have walls 4.5 metres
high with a transition radius of about
5.2 metres. Increased snow making
facilities , new 8 seater chairlift The
Village 8 Express. New terrain parks and
snowdeck park.

Perisher Blue is in the **Kosciusko National park** in the Snowy Mountains. **Mt Kosciusko**, the highest point in the country is called Australia's 'Super Resort' as it has come about through the amalgamation of a number of resorts including, Perisher, Blue Cow, Guthega and Smiggins. There are 1250 hectares of rideable terrain with an elevation to 2054m. However the vertical descent is only about 350m. Nevertheless they have installed 50 lifts and the Australians make the most of the terrain available. Another plus is the huge amount of encouragement for snowboarders. There is a fun-park, a separate Board Riders school a woman's snowboard programme, a Board rider's guide and the Addiction Snowboard store where they will tune and groom your stuff. The mountain itself has a good range of difficulties but unfortunately the black runs are few and far between. Also if you stick too much to pisted areas you will find little to challenge riders above intermediate standard. Most of the black runs are accessible by T-bar only and it really is a drag.

FREERIDERS should check out the **Guthega** and **Blue Cow** areas. There are winding creek beds and some nice little rock drop offs. For powder try out the **Burnum, Eyre** and **Leichhardt** runs, thought don't bother in September as it's all gone.
FREESTYLERS have 3 parks for different abilities and a dedicated rail park. They've made big improvements over the last few years, and theres even a snowskate park. The superpipe often play host to events, running alongside is a beginners pipe. The parks run the full gammet of toys from a boardercross style series of quarter pipes to plastic picnic tables, barrels and rails.
BEGINNERS will find plenty of open easy slopes. However, although there are 50 lifts most of these are T-bars and J-bars which are slow and not very snowboarder friendly.

THE TOWN
Hotels in the resort cost at least $130-A a night. However you can stay just outside the resort for around $65 for bed, brekie and a huge supper. Don't worry about getting around because there is a free bus service between Perisher and **Smiggins** every ten minutes. There are no hostels or lodges for riders on a tight budget but if you ask around you could secure some floor space with a local rider. **Night life** here comes as standard grade Australian, very boozy and very basic with Ozzy girls flashing their tits.

MOUNT HOTHAM

Australias most snow sure resort with enough to keep you happy for a good few days.

Mount Hotham is Australia's highest resort and thus is the most snow sure area. The slopes area is a mixture of easy to negotiate beginners runs to tricky fast steeps that often cross between the more gentle slopes, so

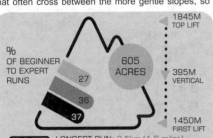

1845M
TOP LIFT

%
OF BEGINNER
TO EXPERT
RUNS

605
ACRES

27

36

37

395M
VERTICAL

1450M
FIRST LIFT

LONGEST RUN: 2.5km (1.6 miles)
TOTAL LIFTS: 13
10 chairs, 3 drags
CAPACITY (people per hour): 24,485
LIFT TIMES: 8.30am to 5.00pm

AVERAGE SNOWFALL: 1.5m
SNOWMAKING: 40 acres

WINTER PERIODS: June to October
Lift Passes
1 Day $82AU, 5 Day $359AU
Season $1076AU
Nightboarding
Wednesday & Saturday 6.30pm to
9.30pm at the Big D Quad Chair

FREERIDE 50%
Trees and okay off-piste
FREESTYLE 15%
A park & a half-pipe
CARVING 35%

Mount Hotham skiing company
PO Box 140, Bright
VIC 3741, Australia
Phone - (03) 5759 4444
Fax - (03) 5759 3692
Web:www.mthotham.com.au
Email:groups@hotham.albury.net.au

Fly
Hotham airport 20 miles away from resort
fly from Sydney or Melbourne.
Car
From Sydney take Hume Highway to
Albury-Wodonga and follow the snow
signs to Yackandandah then turn off to
Myrtleford. At Myrtleford turn on to
the Great Alpine Road to Bright, then
Harrietville and Mount Hotham.
Bus
Coach services from Sydney, Melbourne
and overnight from Adelaide
Train
From Sydney the XPT connects with
Trekset Coaches at Wangaratta and Hoys

novice beware, one minute you could be riding down a simple blue and the next minute hurtling down a steep black trail (study your piste map). Generally this is a resort that will suit intermediate freeriders with a number of very good trails that take you off the piste and in and out of open bowls and wide snow fields.

FREERIDERS. Some of the best freeride trails can be found off the **Heavenly Valley** chair lift which will give you access to some short but steep blacks that although may not take too long to do, they will however, test you to the limits. Over the last few years the resort has expanded its terrain cover which now includes some double diamond runs that are seriously steep and not for wimps. They are reached by the **Gotcha chair** lift which also takes you over to some nice blue out back trails.

FREESTYLERS who like fly high off natural hits will find loads of cool drop offs and lots of natural lips to gain air from. There is also a cool halfpipe and okay terrain park to check out.

CARVERS will love this place as it will suite your style of riding with twisting fast trails that take you over the whole area.

Total BEGINNERS only have a couple of green trails which are located right up at the top of the Summit chair, however quick learners will soon be able to tackle the array of blue trails with some of the most interesting to be found off the Village quad chair lift.

THE TOWN
Generally this is an expensive resort but it offers lots of things to do, all of which are well appointed for both on the slopes and the slope side village. **Off the slopes** visitors will find an abundance of resort facilities with a large selection of well placed hotels, lodges and other **accommodation** outlets that collectively can sleep over 4000 holiday makers. The village has a good selection of places to get a meal in and a number of good late night drinking outlets.

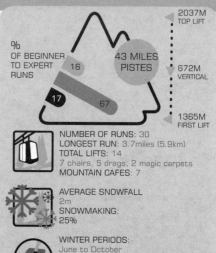

THREDBO TRAIL MAP

%
OF BEGINNER
TO EXPERT
RUNS 16 43 MILES PISTES

17 67

2037M TOP LIFT

672M VERTICAL

1365M FIRST LIFT

NUMBER OF RUNS: 30
LONGEST RUN: 3.7miles (5.9km)
TOTAL LIFTS: 14
7 chairs, 5 drags, 2 magic carpets
MOUNTAIN CAFES: 7

AVERAGE SNOWFALL
2m
SNOWMAKING:
25%

WINTER PERIODS:
June to October
Lift Passes
Day Pass - $83, Child $43
6 Day Pass - $432, child $238
Nightboarding
Friday flat every Thursday night and
Crackenback Supertrail on saturday.
6:30 – 9:30pm through July and August
Hire
Board and boots - $63-74 per

FREERIDE 60%
Trees and some off-piste
FREESTYLE 20%
A park & 2 half-pipes
CARVING 20%

Kosciusko Thredbo Pty Limited
P.O. Box 92, Thredbo Village, NSW 2625
Tel: (02) 6459 4100
Fax: (02) 6459 4101
Web:www.thredbo.com.au
Email:reservations@thredbo.com.au

Fly
daily flights into the Snowy Mountains
Airport (Cooma) from Sydney - 1.5 hours
transfer. Cooma from Sydney
Car
Sydney CBD to Thredbo – Once on the
M5 there are only 3 sets of traffic lights
to Thredbo. Melbourne to Thredbo – the
Kosciuszko Alpine Way is now fully sealed.
Bus
Most major cities are linked by daily service
to Thredbo. Greyhound operated a Sydney
service, Suimmit Coaches from Canberra.
Clipper coaches operate a regular service
from and to Sydney (Prices start from
$134 per adult return).

NEW

New for 04 season
new $500,000 winch cat and $500,000
spent upgrading hire equipment and
facilities

Thredbo is a large resort that has the highest lift access slopes and longest trail in **Australia**. Extensive use of snowmaking and good piste grooming make this a cool place for a weeks stay. The terrain here is equally matched for all levels and styles of riding with much of the mountain suited to intermediates. Although there are a number of steep advanced runs to keep hardcore freeriders happy for a good few days.

FREESTYLERS will also be pleased to find that there are a number of places to gain air from some big natural hits. There is also a good halfpipe and terrain park which has a series of man made jumps.

CARVERS have some really nice runs to excel on including a rather long trail that measures almost 6km (the longest trail in Australia).

BEGINNERS. The beginner slopes here are ideal for first timers with easy runs on the upper sections as well as on the lower areas making the whole mountain accessible.

THE TOWN
The nearest accommodation and local facilities are located at the base of the slopes with a selection of hotels restaurants, sporting attractions and shopping. Nightlife is very lively but basic.

CHARLOTTE PASS

Charlotte Pass is located some 310 miles (500 km) south of Sydney. The resort is the highest in New South Wales and provides a rather small amount of rideable terrain with only five access lifts. Overall the area will suit slow learning beginners and carvers without a brain. Still the slopes are crowd free and will do for an afternoons fun. But forget about staying for more than a day or two (dull is the word).

Accommodation is conveniently located near the slopes at the *Kosciusko Chalet*, which offers mid priced beds, eating and a bar.

Ride Area: 50 hectares
Number of Runs: 19
Top Lift: 1954m
Bottom Lift: 1760m
Vertical Drop: 189m
Total Lifts: 5 - 1 Chair, 3 Drags, 1 portable tow
Lift Capacity (People per Hour): 2600

FALLS CREEK

Falls Creek is a well developed modern resort that will make a weeks stay well worth it, but any longer a bit tedious. The 90 or so marked out trails are evenly split between beginner and advanced level, but although there are a lot of runs none are that long. Still the terrain is good and expert riders will find a selection of steep runs off the Ruined Castle chairlift which also gives access to some open sections and a route down to the terrain park. The terrain park has a 120m superpipe, the first in Australia. Carvers who like to go fast, will be able to down the fast blacks of the Internation t-bar, while beginners will find the Eagle chair gives access to good nursery slopes.

Lots of **accomodation** exists at the base of the slopes in Falls Creek village where you will find shops, bars and restaurants.

New for 04 season: new high speed fixed grip quad lift siituated in the Towers/Panorama area of Sun Valley. Will add a previously untracked 7.4 hectares to the resorts' terrain. 120m superpipe launched last season

Ride Area: 75km
Number of Runs: 92
Easy 17%
Intermediate 16%
Advanced 23%
Top Lift: 1780m
Bottom Lift: 1600m
Vertical Drop: 360m
Total Lifts: 15
Lift Capacity (People per Hour): 20,000

MOUNT BAW BAW

Mt Baw Baw is a small resort and the closest to the city of Melbourne. Overall nothing grabs you about this place unless you are a total beginner with a few hours to kill. The eight lifts cover a mixture of uneven terrain with a splattering of trees and gentle pistes that will suite carvers.

Local facilities are basic but very good with a choice of lodges and holiday apartments although not all that affordable apart from the Youth Hostel ++64 (0) 65 1129.

New for 04 season: extension of Hut Run Platter , increase in snowmaking, new magic carpet lift.

Ride Area: 30 hectares
Number of Runs: 14
Easy 25%
Intermediate 64%
Advanced 11%
Top Lift: 1564m
Bottom Lift: 1460m
Total Lifts: 5 - all drags

MOUNT BUFFALO

Mount Buffalo is not only a well established resort with a long history as a ski resort, but also a dull boring novices hangout that will bore the tits off any advanced freerider within an hour of being here

Ride Area: 15km
Number of Runs: 14
Easy 50%
Intermediate 40%
Advanced 10%
Top Lift: 1695m
Total Lifts: 5 - 2 Chairs, 3 Drags
Lift Capacity (People per Hour): 20,000

MOUNT SELWYN

Mount Selwyn is a small resort that is the ideal family ski resort, but is totally dull for any advanced snowboarder. The small amount of terrain on offer is best suited to piste loving, slow going carvers. The nearest accomodation and local facilities are to be found in the town of Adaminaby

Ride Area: 45hectares
Number of Runs: 10
Easy 40%
Intermediate 48%
Advanced 12%
Top Lift: 1614m
Bottom Lift: 1492m
Vertical Drop: 122m
Total Lifts: 12 - 1 chair, 7 drags, 4 tows
Lift Capacity (People per Hour): 9.500

Pic - Austrian Tourist Board

Capital City: Vienna
Population: 8.2million
Highest Peak: Grossglockner
3797m
Language: German
Legal Drink Age: 18
Drug Laws: Cannabis is illegal and
frowned upon
Age of consent: 16
Electricity: 240 Volts AC 2-pin
International Dialing Code: +43

Currency: Euro
Exchange Rate:
UK£1 = 1.5
US$1 = 0.8
AU$1 = 0.6
CAN$1=0.6

Driving Guide
All vehicles drive on the right hand
side of the road
Speed limits:
Motorways-130kph (81mph)
Highways-100kph (62mph)
Towns-50kph (31mph)
Emergency
Fire - 122
Police - 133
Ambulance - 144
Tolls
Payable on motorways and some
bridges. Austrian vignette for driv-
ing on the motorways costs 7.6
euros for 10 days, available from
most garages.
Documentation
carry driving licence, vehicle regis-
tration document and certificate of
motor insurance. Photo ID needed
Seatbelts
Seatbelts front & back must be
worn.

Time Zone
UTC/GMT +1 hour
Daylight saving time: +1 hour
(March - December)

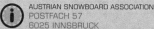

AUSTRIAN SNOWBOARD ASSOCIATION
POSTFACH 57
6025 INNSBRUCK
fax. 0043 512 34 38 48 / 31
Email: info@powdern.com
Web:w ww.powdern.com

The Austrian National Tourist Office
Vienna, Margaretenstr. 1
A-1040 Wien
Phone: +43 (0)1 / 588 66-0
Fax: +43 (0)1 / 588 66-20
www.austria-tourism.at

Austria is known as the snowboard capital of Europe with great resorts and a cool attitude. Austrian resorts aren't stretched out like the mega-sized places found in the French Alps and apart from being far more affordable than France, the slopes here are far better laid out with excellent mountain facilities, modern lift systems, easy access to the slopes, coupled with great traditional local services.

Of all the areas in Austria the most famed and the largest winter destination is the **Tirol**, which apart from being at 'the heart of the Alps' is also an area of outstanding beauty and home to some fantastic snowboard resorts that offer something for everyone. The Tirol also plays host to some of the most important snowboard events held in Europe, i.e. Air and Style, Lord of the Boards and the Brit Games.

The Austrian's don't go in for the purpose-built style resorts so common in other parts of Europe. What you do find are old traditional villages adapted to accommodate modern tourists. Standards are extremely high, with hotels, Guest House's and B&B's being main form of lodging. Apartment blocks are very rare.

Austrian is basic consisting of dishes like *Tafelspitz* (boiled beef), or various cured hams and German-style sausages. If you're a veggie (vegetarier), you're in for a hard time - the Austrian's don't go in for rabbit-food. *Goulash* soup in this part of the world is also wicked. But one thing Austria does lack is fast food joints.

An important and useful thing to note about Austria is that credit cards are not that widely accepted: cash, traveller's cheques or Euro-cheques are the norm.

Austrian Tourist Board

Flying to the resorts is easy via the international airports in Austria, Switzerland or Germany, then taking onward travel via the excellent rail or road services. Only a small percentage of resorts have **train** stations, however, connections from cities and gateway airports is made very easy by the fact that Austria has a first class **bus** service, which is on time, clean and inexpensive.

Driving in Austria is convenient and easy, with the roads and resorts being well sign-posted. In some parts, snow-chains are required. Austria has an autobahn tax called the Vignette which can be purchased at petrol stations or border crossings. If you are caught without the tax, you'll be liable to a costly on-the-spot fine.

If you are planning to do a working season in Austria, then EU nationals don't need either a visa or work permit and can stay for as long as they want. But if you want to teach snowboarding, you may need to have the relevant Austrian snowboard instructors teaching qualifications.

Innsbruck is not actually a resort but a gate way city to dozens of resorts. Five of the resorts on the city's doorstep are, **Axams, Igls, Seegrübe, Mütters** and **Stubai Glacier**. The resort areas around Innsbruck (apart from Stubai Glacier), are low altitude resorts and all with easy reach of the city. None of Innsbrucks resorts are very big or boast loads of lifts, however, they all offer a good level of diverse terrain. You can buy a special pass that covers you for all five resorts and the bus to each place. However, although local bus services are excellent, it may be an advantage to have your own car so you can travel around the resorts or further afield. All the road links are superb so you won't have any problems, but remember to carry some snow-chains in your car at all times. *Burton Snowboards* set up their first non-American headquarters in Innsbruck in 1992.

Innsbruck, may not be New York or London, but it still has a good scene and is home to a big snowboard culture. There are loads of things to do: you could visit the Olympic ice-rink, hang out and skate at loads of good spots, or simply party.

Innsbruck also holds the annual 'Air 'N' Style snowboard event up on the **Bergisel**, which is an Olympic ski jump stadium located on the outskirts of the city. The event is a big attraction and apart from snowboarding, loads of pop bands perform for the crowds (mind you only to boost their record sales - *scumbags*).

Innsbruck has simply loads of restaurants. There's a *McDonald's* which pumps out its cardboard crap, and a *Wiener Wald*, a version of *Kentucky Fried Chicken*.

Night-life in Innsbruck is particularly good, simply because there are no stupid aprés-ski crowds. There are plenty of late night bars - check out *Limerick Bills,* a cool Irish pub or *Jimmy's* Bar a very popular hangout and the club.

Accommodation is well located: you can bed down cheaply within walking distance of the city centre. Prices are extremely reasonable. *Pension Paula* the local backpacker's place, is only five minutes from the town centre and is without doubt the best place to stay in the city, with rates from 300sch a night. There is also a hostel and numerous hotels. *Hotel Central* is a budget place that also has a bar, and is only two minutes from the city centre.

Pic - Austrian Tourist Board

GETTING THERE
FLY to **Innsbruck International** airport which is 10 minutes from the city centre.
TRAIN. **The** nearest train station is in the centre of the Innsbruck.
DRIVING from Munich, head south on the A8 and A12 Autobahn routes direct to Innsbruck. The drive time from **Calais** is 11½ hours

Pic - Austrian Tourist Board

7 OUT OF 10

Overall Alpbach is a nice place, just a bit bland.

A

1850M TOP LIFT

% OF BEGINNER TO EXPERT RUNS

45KM PISTES

820M VERTICAL

30

10

60

1030M FIRST LIFT

LONGEST RUN: 8km
TOTAL LIFTS: 19
2 Gondolas, 7 chairs, 10 drags
CAPACITY (people per hour):19,000
LIFT TIMES: 8.30am to 4.00pm

AVERAGE SNOWFALL:
6m
SNOWMAKING:
70%

WINTER PERIODS:
Dec to April
Lift Passes
1 Day pass - 26,50 euros
6 Day Peak pass - 122 euros
6 Day Off Peak pass - 108 euros
Season Ticket - 252 euros
Hire
Schischule Alpbach charge 44 euros for a day lesson (4hr) or 5 days for 120.
Private lessons 145 euros for 4hrs

FREERIDE 40%
Trees and a bit of off-piste
FREESTYLE 20%
A park & a half-pipe
CARVING 40%

Alpbach 311
6236 Alpbach
Osterreich
Tel - +43-5336-5233
Fax - +43-5336-5234-24
snowphone - +43-5336-5233-25
Web:www.alpbacher-bergbahnen.at
Email:info@alpbacher-bergbahnen.at

Fly
to Innsbruck (60km), 50 minutes transfer time. Munich 170km, Salzburg 150km
Car
From Innsbruck head east along the A12 and exit at junction 32 for via Brixlegg and on to Alpbach
Drive time from Calais is 11 1/2 hours, 676 miles (1088 km).
Bus
direct from Innsbruck airport.
Train
fast trains to Wörgl or Jenbach then change to local railway for Brixlegg

Alpbach is a cool, all-Austrian alternative to some of its more famous nearby cousins. This perfect picture postcard resort, decked out with traditional chalets dotted in and around a gently rising mountain, is one of those places beloved by skiers in one-piece ski-suits who seem to spend more time sunning themselves outside mountain restaurants than checking out the slopes. However, this small and easy-going resort has been host to part of the ISF World Pro Tour, so it's not all bad news. Alpbach is without doubt, an intermediate's resort and one that won't take too long to conquer; you wouldn't spend more than a week here, and certainly not a whole season, unless you're easily pleased and like an unadventurous mountain.

FREERIDERS have a small area to explore, with some interesting terrain to ride. On the upper sections, you can check out some wide, open powder fields that eventually descend through trees en route to the base area. Advanced riders will find that the few black runs are not to be treated with arrogance. Unpisted routes from **Loderstein** back to the gondola station, give freeriders in soft boots a great time, as do the runs around the **Wiedersbergerhorn**, which often have excellent powder.
FREESTYLERS fed up with looking for natural hits, should make their way to the halfpipe and fun-park, located on **Gahmkopf**, where grommets can take their frustrations out in this average play area.
CARVERS with a good pair of boots will love Alpbach. It's a full-on carver's resort, with wide pistes devoid of any trouble spots. Although there isn't an abundance of pisted runs, what is available is well looked after, and easily negotiated.
BEGINNERS have a great learner's mountain. There are some perfect flats around the base areas to start out on, with excellent wide, open novice trails up in the **Skiweg** area.

THE TOWN
Alpbach offers some slope side **accommodation** with the bulk of beds available within easy reach of the village a two minute bus ride from the base lifts. Being a resort used by package tour operators means that on the one hand, the place can become very busy, but on the other, some cheap package deals are available. The village is a relaxed affair offering a number of restaurants, swimming and skating. As for **night-life**, apart from a few bars, you won't find much to shout about.

AXAMER LIZUM

great resort that will appeal to freestylers and intermediate freeriders

Pic - Axamer Lizum

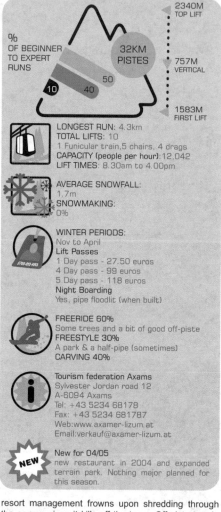

2340M
TOP LIFT

%
OF BEGINNER
TO EXPERT
RUNS

32KM
PISTES

757M
VERTICAL

50

10 40

1583M
FIRST LIFT

LONGEST RUN: 4.3km
TOTAL LIFTS: 10
1 Funicular train, 5 chairs, 4 drags
CAPACITY (people per hour): 12,042
LIFT TIMES: 8.30am to 4.00pm

AVERAGE SNOWFALL:
1.7m
SNOWMAKING:
0%

WINTER PERIODS:
Nov to April
Lift Passes
1 Day pass - 27.50 euros
4 Day pass - 99 euros
5 Day pass - 118 euros
Night Boarding
Yes, pipe floodlit (when built)

FREERIDE 60%
Some trees and a bit of good off-piste
FREESTYLE 30%
A park & a half-pipe (sometimes)
CARVING 40%

Tourism federation Axams
Sylvester Jordan road 12
A-6094 Axams
Tel: +43 5234 68178
Fax: +43 5234 681787
Web:www.axamer-lizum.at
Email:verkauf@axamer-lizum.at

NEW New for 04/05
new restaurant in 2004 and expanded
terrain park. Nothing major planned for
this season.

Axamer Lizum may not be the biggest of resorts, nor is it the chosen resort for holiday package tour operators, and yes the ski press may slag the place off, but then what would that clueless lot know. Built in 1964 for the winter Olympics, Axams is a full-on no nonsense great natural freeride-freestyle snowboarder's paradise. The resort has everything you could possible ask for and although not extensive, the terrain in places is as natural as it gets with top-to-bottom riding from Axams to Gotzens possible when snow permits. Axams may be a small place but don't be fooled Axamer Lizum, is the playground for the Innsbruck crowd that includes Max Plotzeneder and top racer Christine Rauter - and it's easy to see why. Axams is a quiet place, free of holiday ski crowds (although weekends are very busy), big on air and short on lift queues. Having twice hosted Olympic disciplines, the runs are obviously of a decent standard, with something to suit all. Freeriders and freestylers are going to get the best out of the slopes, with loads of great hits, big banks, and gullies that form natural pipes to drop in and out of and tight trees to weave through. The atmosphere on the slopes is really cool, and on certain days snowboarders actually out-number skiers, especially when competitions are on.

FREERIDERS wanting off-piste and trees won't be disappointed, although it should be pointed out that the

resort management frowns upon shredding through the spruce since it kills off the trees. Off-piste terrain is limited, but if you get the conditions, great powder can be ridden without a trek. There's a great area if you go right at the exit point off the funicular train, and follow the line of reds, Trail 4 and 3. Theres also a cool powder run back under the funicular. Riders already past the novice stage and with a few bruises under their belts will be able to collect a few more down Trails 5 and 5a. Experienced riders can go for it down the blacks on Piste 10 where the trail is on a bumpy, steep run, and is not the greatest descent in the world.

Pic - Axamer Lizum

THE TOWN

Off the slopes, this is one of those places where you will have to put yourself out, and having a car may also be a preferred option. There is some accommodation at the base of the slopes consisting of a couple of B&B pensions and hotels, but that's it. Staying slopeside is not recommended, unless you're a hermit. The village of Axams is only a few miles away and has a decent selection of local services, which include a few shops and a sports centre. However, the best option is to stay down in Innsbruck, (the biggest and best snowboard resort-city in Europe). There are regular transfer buses to get you there, and once there you are bombarded with services, shops galore, an Olympic ice ring, swimming pools, concert halls, the list is endless. What's more, Innsbruck is an inexpensive and friendly place.

Food. Innsbruck is the place for food with loads of cafes and restaurants at budget to suit all. Theres a good number of restaurants in the old town; obvious tourist traps but still pretty good. Around the same area are a couple of take away kebab and pizza places, and the standard McD's.You'll find a few Chinese and Indian restaurants and loads of Austrian restaurants serving dishes such as Tafelspitz (boiled beef).

Night-life in Axams is dull, without much happening. Off Limits is Axam's main hangout. Innsbruck, on the other hand, is a different story with simply loads going on and a large choice of cafe bars. There's an Irish bar called Limerick Bills and a club under Jimmy's Bar that rocks until very late.

SUMMARY

A great resort that will appeal to freestylers and intermediate freeriders spoilt only by the weekends queues. Some might find a full week stay to long
On the slopes: Excellent
Off the slopes: The best in Europe
Money wise: Great value resort with low price lift tickets and cheap accommodation deals available near the slopes

FREESTYLERS looking for the best hits should take the funicular train to the top, then follow the Number 1 blue run off to the left, which will bring you out onto a really cool mixture of red runs, with the best hits on Run 2. The terrain park and halfpipe are located at the base area and reached from the beginner's T-bars or by hiking up. The terrain parks been upgraded but still not huge, and the pipe is not up to much, but with such good natural terrain, you don't need man-made hits.

CARVERS will look and feel a little out of place here, as this is not long, wide autobahn territory. Saying that, there is room to crank some big carves, especially on piste Numbers 1 and 2.

BEGINNERS having their first go at snowboarding can loosen up and get to grips with the basics, on easy trails located at the base area just up from the ticket booths. The only drawback is that the easy slope is serviced by two T-bars, which may cause shy ones a few problems at first, but not for long.

FLY: to Innsbruck International transfer time 25 mins. Munich 2 1/2 hrs away
BUS: Ski buses from Innsbruck train station hourly for Axams and back again (45min journey). Bus services also from Munich to Innsbruck.
TRAIN: to Innsbruck International transfer time 25 mins. Munich 2 1/2 hrs away
CAR: Drive to Innsbruck via motorway A12. Axamer Lizum = 15 miles (24Km). Drive time is about 20 minutes
*From Calais, 646 miles (1039 Km) Drive time is around 11 1/2 hours.

A

A
U
S
T
R
I
A

% OF BEGINNER TO EXPERT RUNS

24

14

62

200KM PISTES

2230M TOP LIFT

1150M VERTICAL

1080M FIRST LIFT

NUMBER OF RUNS: 66
LONGEST RUN: 8km
TOTAL LIFTS: 48
7 Gondolas, 1 cable-car, 18 chairs, 15 drags, 2 handle tows
CAPACITY (people per hour):23,400
LIFT TIMES: 8.30am to 4.00pm

AVERAGE SNOWFALL:
6m
SNOWMAKING:
30%

WINTER PERIODS:
3rd Dec to 10th April 2005
Lift Passes
2 Day Pass 57 euros
6 Day Pass 165 euros
Night Boarding
Yes

FREERIDE 40%
A few trees and a bit of off-piste
FREESTYLE 20%
A park & a half-pipe
CARVING 40%

Tourismusverband Bad Gastein
Kaiser Franz Josef Str. 27
5640 Bad Gastein
Austria
Tel: +43 06434 2531-0
Web:www.boardgastein.com
Email:info@skigastein.com

Fly
to: Salzburg - 2 hours away
Car
From Salzburg head south along the A10 to junction 46 and then take the 168 route until signs for Badgastein along the 167.
Bus
Bus services on a daily basis from the airport to the resort

Bad Gastein is an old Austrian spa town that is located in the middle of the **Salzburg** region along the **Gastein Valley** and perched up at a height of some 1080 metres a short distance from the village of **Bad Hofgastein**. What you have here is a relatively unknown but large ridable area which is basically split into four resorts that although each are similar, they never the less offer something different. Collectively you have over 200km of marked out piste to ride though it should be pointed out that not all the areas or pistes are linked up by lifts. So study the local piste maps to ensure that you don't have any problems finding slopes and lifts. Overall this is an area that predominantly favours intermediate riders with an excellent choice of cruising runs to enjoy. Bad Gastein gives direct access to the slopes on the **Stubnerkogel**, **Sportgastein** and higher up to the summit of **Kreuzkogel**. You can also gain access via Bad Gastein to the half dozen or so runs on the **Gravkoel** where you will find some decent trees to shred. Bad Hofgastein and the area known as **Dorfgastein** are two other locations where you can do some cool riding.

FREERIDERS can basically pick and choose from any one of the areas in order to have a good time. The collection of slopes on the **Dorfgastein** are okay for freeriding.
FREESTYLERS might not embrace this place with its rather dull freestyle appeal. However, you will still be able to find some good hits and be able to catch some big air. There is also a pipe and terrain park up on the **Dorfgastein** slopes. The FIS hold boardercross competitions here in February
CARVERS will possibly like this place the most no matter which area you select. The whole area is littered with good pisted cruising runs, especially the runs up on the **Stubnerkogel** area.
BEGINNERS should think about choosing another resort as this is not really a hot place for learning snowboarding at.

THE TOWN
Off the slopes, Bad Gastein is a glamorous joint with okay services but dull night-life. **Off the slopes**, hotels chalets and other local facilities are in abundance but

not very convenient to all the slopes and other areas. Having a car around Bad Gastein may be a good idea, local transport is not hot. **Accommodations** options within the area are not overpriced and cheap budget priced lodgings are easy to find. **Eating** out options are not mega in terms of the types of places, what you have is a lot of hotel restaurants selling much the same style of food. As for a good lively night out, forget it.

A

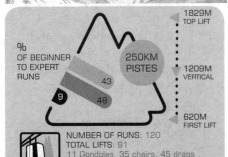

%
OF BEGINNER
TO EXPERT
RUNS

250KM PISTES

9 43 48

1829M
TOP LIFT

1209M
VERTICAL

620M
FIRST LIFT

NUMBER OF RUNS: 120
TOTAL LIFTS: 91
11 Gondolas, 35 chairs, 45 drags
CAPACITY (people per hour): 130,000
LIFT TIMES: 8.30am to 4.00pm

AVERAGE SNOWFALL:
Unknown
SNOWMAKING:
70%

WINTER PERIODS:
Dec to April
Lift Passes
Day pass 32 euros
6 Days 157.50 euros
Season 475 euros

FREERIDE 50%
A few trees and some off-piste
FREESTYLE 20%
A park & a half-pipe
CARVING 30%

Bergbahnen Hohe Salve
Meierhofgasse 29
6361 Hopfgarten im Brixental, Austria
Tel +43(5335)2238
Fax +43(5335)3085
Web:www.skiwelt.at
Email:bergbahnen.hopfgarten@skiwelt.at

Fly
1 1/2 hours from Salzburg (100km) airport.
Munich 150km, Innsbruck 70km
Car
via Munich (100 km) - exit Kufstein Süd
towards Innsbruck. via Innsbruck (70 km)
- exit Wörgl Ost - to Brixental
Train
via Munich, Kufstein and Wörgl to
Hopfgarten main station or Hopfgarten
Berglift

Hopfagarten in Brixental is a resort that forms part of Austria's largest linked area known as the **'Ski Welt'** and is located just 50 miles (80km) from **Innsbruck**. Collectively the resorts that make up Ski Welt have over 250km of marked out pistes and lots more off-piste terrain. The area is linked across a series of mountain slopes by a staggering array of over 93 lifts which are mainly chair lifts. Getting around all the areas will take some careful piste map reading, as you can easily get lost around here. Thankfully though the local piste map is well laid out and shows what is actually on the ground. The piste are also well marked, so you should have no excuse for ending up miles from where you started. Like all the resorts of the Ski Welt, Brixental, which sits across the valley floor from **Westendorf**, is a low laying resort with a high point of 1674m. In the past there has been a problem with a lack of real snow, however, the area has over 135km of snow-making facilities which helps to keep the runs open when the real stuff is in short supply. Brixental is a spread out affair and depending on where you stay, it may mean having to catch the ski bus to reach the slopes, not all the accommodation is close the runs.

FREERIDERS who plan to take a weeks holiday in the Ski Welt could do a lot worst than this area, and although Brixen on its own would be a bit tedious after a few days if you are a competent rider, but the fact that you have easy access to a lot more of well connected terrain, means a 7 days stay will not be wasted time. The expanse of this area means that provided the snow is good and plentiful, you will be able to ride each day on a new selection of pisted slopes aided by the fact that lift queues are never that long meaning you will be able to roam freely with ease.

FREESTYLERS have a number of options for getting air. Most of the resorts in the Ski Welt have either a halfpipe or fun park; some even have both, as does Brixental. However, it should be pointed out that not all the resorts maintain the pipes and parks unless there is an event being staged, which is often the case around here.

CARVERS should feel at ease here, the area offers a vast number of well groomed pistes to suite all levels making this a cool place for laying out turns on or simply a place for improving your technique.

BEGINNERS will find the slopes of Brixental are easy to get to grips with. There are some nice low down nursery slopes and once you have mastered Brixental the Ski Welt offers lots of easy opportunities to learn on.

THE TOWN
Off the slopes Brixental offers a good choice of accommodation, restaurants, and bars and what's more this is not an expensive resort.

Pic - Ellmau Resort

.%
OF BEGINNER
TO EXPERT
RUNS

250KM
PISTES

43

9

48

1829M
TOP LIFT

1209M
VERTICAL

620M
FIRST LIFT

NUMBER OF RUNS: 120
TOTAL LIFTS: 91
11 Gondolas, 35 chairs, 45 drags
CAPACITY (people per hour): 130,000
LIFT TIMES: 8.30am to 4.00pm

AVERAGE SNOWFALL:
Unknown
SNOWMAKING:
70%

WINTER PERIODS: Dec to April
Lift Passes
Day 32 euros, 6 Days 157.50 euros
Season 475 euros

FREERIDE 50%
A few trees and some off-piste
FREESTYLE 20%
A park & a half-pipe (in Soll)
CARVING 30%

Web: www.skiwelt.at
Tourismusverband Ellmau
Dorf 35, A-6352 Ellmau, Austria
Tel +43(5358)2301
Fax +43(5358)3443
email: info@ellmau.at

Tourismusverband
HNr. 202, Ortsmitte,
im Postamtsgebäude, A-6351 Scheffau
am Wilden Kaiser, Austria
Tel +43(5358)7373
Fax +43(5358)7373 7

Fly
to Salzburg - 1 1/2 hours away.
Car
From Salzburg head south on routes 21
and 312 to Ellmau on the left. This is a
45 mile (70km) journey
Drive time from Calais is 11 1/2 hours,
692 miles (115 km)
Bus
direct from Salzburg airport.

Ellmau forms part of the massive **Ski Welt** which is said to be Austria's largest linked ridable area located in the **Tirol** and only 90 minutes from **Salzburg**. 250km of linked piste covered by 92 lifts should mean utopia, but unfortunately this place is not that hot. The resorts low altitude means that good annual snow is not a feature of this place although to be fair the place has a good snowmaking set up to help when the real stuff is lacking. As for the slopes this is mountain that tends to suffer from a good selection of advanced freeriding areas, come to that, it lacks good natural freestyle terrain as well. The biggest let down here or the most annoying thing are the hordes of novice ski groups clogging up the place and littering the slopes with ski and poles as they fall over all over the place. This is a very popular ski resort which on the one hand means long lift queues but on the other hand, and in the resorts defence, this is also an affordable destination.

FREERIDERS who know their stuff, won't find the offerings here to their general liking. You can have a good time but nothing is that testing or to prolonged in terms of long runs and although the Ski Welt offers a lot of riding opportunities, a weeks trip would be better spent at a more adventurous resort. However, an okay to check out is the trail down from **Brandstadl** to **Scheffau**. FREESTYLERS should make the trip back down to the resort of **Soll**, to check out their halfpipe and terrain park because it's about the best place to get any big air from as this is not a freestylers resort whether you want natural hits of man mad offerings. But like any resort, if you look hard enough, you will find something to leap off.
CARVERS of limited experience can have a great time at **Ellmau** or at any of the nearby linked resorts. The area boasts a lot of wide and well groomed runs that will let you cruise with ease for hours on end. Check out the Hohe Salve for some fun.
BEGINNERS are the one group who should have no problems with this resort even if the place is a bit fragmented. There are plenty of easy to reach nursery slopes to seek out.

THE TOWN
Ellmau may be a quaint Austrian village, but it is also a bit of a mishmash of a place. **Off the slopes**, there's plenty of good Austrian hospitality on, or close to the slopes, with affordable pensions. Getting around can be a real pain in the arse and local transport services are poor. **Accommodation** is affordable and there are lots of hotel restaurants to get a meal in. **Night life** is super dull, unless you're in to après ski games.

FIEBERBRUNN

6 OUT OF 10

Up and coming resort with good snow and a superb pipe

Pic - Fieberbrun Resort

2020M TOP LIFT

%
OF BEGINNER
TO EXPERT
RUNS

35KM PISTES

34

16   50

1190M VERTICAL

830M FIRST LIFT

LONGEST RUN: 7km
TOTAL LIFTS: 13
3 Gondolas, 3 chairs, 7 drags
CAPACITY (people per hour):20,000
LIFT TIMES: 8.30am to 4.00pm
MOUNTAIN CAFES: 2

AVERAGE SNOWFALL:
Unknown
SNOWMAKING:
40%

WINTER PERIODS: Dec to April
Lift Passes
Day pass 26 euros
6 Days Schneewinkel area 149 euros
6 Days Kitzbuler Alpen area 170 euro
Night Boarding
Yes, pipe illumintated until 11pm

FREERIDE 45%
A few trees and fair bit of off-piste
FREESTYLE 15%
A park & a half-pipe (lit)
CARVING 40%

Fieberbrunn Tourism
Doffplatz 1
A-6391. Fieberbrunn
Tel. ++43 (0) 5354 563 04-0
Web:www.schneedorado.at
Email:office@schneedorado.at

Fly
to Salzburg - 1 1/2 hours away.
Car
from Salzburg, head west along route
312. St Johann, then turn right along
the 164 to Fieberbrunn. (44 miles).
Drive time from Calais is 11 1/2 hours.
696 miles (1119 km)
Bus
Bus services with links from Salzburg.

Fieberbrunn is a rather strange tale in terms of its popularity with snowboarding. It's not a high resort, nor is Fieberbrunn an adventurous place, and most good riders will have had enough after three or four days. Its snowboard status must be something to do with either the fantastic halfpipe, or else someone at the International Snowboard Federation has got a thing going with a local chick. The area lies in a natural snow pocket receiving 50% more snow than nearby **Kitzbuhel** over a course of a season. Sandwiched either side of the night illuminated half-pipe are the **Doischberg** and **Streuboden** gondolas which whisk you up from the car park to mid station. Fieberbrunn has never really attracted tour operators, the result being that the slopes are mainly inhabited by either locals or their cousins from Germany. Like most resorts, the well-prepared slopes do have busy periods (mainly at weekends and holidays), but don't be put off as this is a cool snowboard-friendly place.

FREERIDERS will find that the terrain is not the most testing, with only a couple of black runs that offer nothing much for advanced riders. The main runs on **Streuboden** are reached via a short journey on an unusual gondola system that arrives at two levels: the first of which will bring you out on easy terrain around trees, whilst the second takes you to open reds and a black run.
FREESTYLERS looking for an endless supply of natural hits will be disappointed with Fieberbrunn. This is not the place to seek big air, but the extremely well-shaped halfpipe is superb and is open until 11 o'clock each night!
CARVERS will find that the slopes appeal very much to intermediate hard booters, especially if you like well pisted and easy flats.
BEGINNERS have a very good choice of beginner-friendly areas for learning the basics. As a decent novice's resort, you can avoid the drag lifts by riding the runs down off the first gondola station.

THE TOWN. **Fieberbrunn** is a small village. Hotels, pensions and rooms in private houses are the main form of accommodation. Some of which are very close to the slopes. Prices vary, but in general the place is affordable. **Night-life** is definitely not one of Fieberbrunn's strong points. Night action is very quite compared to more commercial resorts but the town centre (Dorfplatz) with its new 'village-square' is cool. The *Rivershouse* is a good place for beers, guinness and snacks. There is a pool table and live music most weekends. The *Londoner* became the *Cheers* pub many years ago and stripped out all the tat that was on the walls, its the most expensive place for a beer in town but cheaper than most resorts. *Biwak* is a at the bottom of the slopes which looks out onto the halfpipe and plays more up to date sounds than the oompah band in nearby *Enzianhutte*. *Tenne* nightclub is the place for a late beer or dance, but avoid until 1 am when the under 16s are booted out (unless this is your sort of thing). **All in all** - a rapidly up and coming resort with great snow and off piste but lacking the nightlife in low season. Still if you're with a good crowd of people, who cares and **St Johann in Tirol** is only a ten minute taxi ride away which is home to the legendary *Bunny's Pub*.

7 OUT OF 10

Good freeriding resort

Pic - Galtur Resort

2292M TOP LIFT

%
OF BEGINNER
TO EXPERT   10
RUNS

47KM PISTES

700M VERTICAL

30   60

1584M FIRST LIFT

LONGEST RUN: 3,2km
TOTAL LIFTS: 12
4 chairs, 8 drags
CAPACITY (people per hour):15,000
LIFT TIMES: 8.30am to 4.00pm
MOUNTAIN CAFES: 4

AVERAGE SNOWFALL:
5.28m
SNOWMAKING:
10%

WINTER PERIODS: Dec to April
Lift Passes
1 Day pass 30 euros
6 Days 137.50 euros
Night Boarding
2 lit slopes (2.2 km total)

FREERIDE 35%
A few trees and okay off-piste
FREESTYLE 5%
No park or half-pipe
CARVING 60%

Galtur Tourism
Postfach 10, PLZ 6563, A-6563, Galtur.
Tel. +43 (0) 5443 8521
Fax. +43 (0) 5443 852176
web:www.galtuer.com
Email:info@galtuer.com

Fly
to Innsbruck airport 2 hours away.
Car
From Innsbruck, head west along the
A12 to Landeck and then the 316 to
Ischgl and the A188 to Galtur
* Drive time from Calais is 11 1/4 hours,
620 miles (998 km)
Train
nearest train is at Landeck, 30min away

Galtur is the less famous cousin of **Ischgl**, 20 minutes away at the head of the **Paznaun Valley**. Although a small resort, Galtur proves that size doesn't always matter. Whilst Ischgl gets all the attention Galtur is left relatively alone, making it a far quieter place to ride. Galtur is a very Austrian resort, with all the usual trappings. The terrain doesn't measure to mega status and pistes are fairly ordinary. However, it is possible to buy a lift ticket for the **Silvretta** area (of which Galtur is a part), that includes Ischgl, opening up some 155 miles of terrain. You can also do night riding here, which is not a common thing in Austria.

FREERIDERS in softs looking for interesting terrain should check out the Innere **Kopsalpe** area. It won't test advanced riders too much, but should keep intermediates happy for a few days.
FREESTYLERS won't love Galtur as it doesn't offer any real big air opportunities - though like any resort there are hits to be found if you look. The best thing to do is either take the 20 minute bus journey to Ischgl to ride their amazing fun-park, or check out the halfpipe at **Samnaun**, a small neighbouring Swiss resort.
CARVERS will find this a good place, but not exhausting. The well-pisted runs allow carvers to progress with ease, and the red and black runs on the **Saggrat** should give you a rush.
BEGINNERS are the one group of riders who will really like Galtur. The flats are easy to reach from the village and riders should have no real problems, unless they are scared of using the drag lifts that serve many of the runs (including the easy ones). Still, as the lift lines are non-existent and quiet, you'll be able to keep trying without too much hassle from irate skiers. The local ski-school, which caters mainly for beginners, will help you out.

THE TOWN
Everything is within easy access of the slopes and for such a small resort, there are plenty of things to do. Galtur is a typical Austrian village with normal **accommodation** offerings, from pricey hotels to well priced pensions. **Eating out** is all Austrian, which is average but bland. There is, however, way too much après-ski which will appeal to some sad types, but not the hardcore rider who likes to party hard.

HINTERTUX

Great open pistes

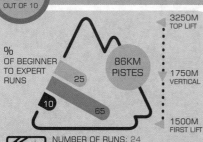

% OF BEGINNER TO EXPERT RUNS

86KM PISTES

- 3250M TOP LIFT
- 1750M VERTICAL
- 1500M FIRST LIFT

25
10
65

Pic - HintertuxResort

NUMBER OF RUNS: 24
LONGEST RUN: 12km
TOTAL LIFTS: 21 - 3 Gondolas, 2 cable-cars, 6 chairs,10 drags
CAPACITY (people per hour):30,000
LIFT TIMES: 8.30am to 4.00pm
MOUNTAIN CAFES: 5

AVERAGE SNOWFALL:
Unknown
SNOWMAKING:
20%

WINTER PERIODS: Dec to April
SUMMER PERIODS: May to Nov.
Lift Passes
Day pass 35 euros
6 Day pass 165 euros
Covers Ski & glacierworld Zillertal 3000 linked area
Night Boarding
No

FREERIDE 40%
A few trees and fair bit of off-piste
FREESTYLE 20%
A park & a half-pipe
CARVING 40%

Hintertuxer Gletscher
Zillertaler Gletscherbahn GmbH & Co KG
A-6294 Hintertux 794
Tel. 0043 / 5287 / 8510 - 0
Fax: 0043 / 5287 / 8510 - 380
Web:www.hintertuxergletscher.at
Email:info@hintertuxergletscher.at

Train
nearest train stop is Mayrhofen, 20 mins away. Express train stop is Jenbach, taxi service availble to tux for 18 euros pp
Fly
to Innsbruck (90km), 1 1/2 hours away. Munich 230km away.
Car
from Innsbruck, go west on the A12. Exit at B169 along the Zillertal Valley past Mayrhofen and onto Hintertux

NEW
New for 04/05
Hintertux now linked with Mayrhofen as part of the Ski Zillertal ski pass, giving you access to 230 km of pistes.

The base of Hintertux sits at a height of 1,500m at the far end of the **Zillertal valley**, which is also home to the resorts of **Mayrhofen** and **Eggalm**. It now forms part of the **Zillertal 3000** area offering 230km of pistes. Hintertux has a number of advantages and disadvantages: on the plus side, it's a glacial resort, and apart from being one of the best summer snowboard resorts in Europe, it also has an enviable snow record in winter. However, in winter the same pluses mean that when the lower altitude resorts of the valley are suffering from a lack of snow, Hintertux can become very busy. Still, the open expanse of freeride terrain provides some excellent powder fields that are seldom tracked out by the morning ski masses. In summer the extent of snow cover over the length of the runs is often more than many resorts get during the winter season. Slopes are always crowd-free and riding in a t-shirt is the norm

FREERIDERS have the pick of the slopes with various terrain on and off-piste. There are huge open expanses and loads of gullies and natural walls to ride. There's no tree riding as the altitude deters their growth, but it's no big loss as the terrain is more than sufficient, especially if you take a look at what's available to ride off Number 3 chair. FREESTYLERS have loads of hits to check out, which include a few cliff drops and a number of wide, natural gap jumps. If you're still not content, there's a fun-park and two halfpipes which they maintain all year round, although it's not always possible in July and August. CARVERS can feel as much at home here as anyone else. The pistes are really good for laying out big turns, and tend to be long with a few sharp turns here and there. BEGINNERS may find Hintertux a bit too daunting, especially if you're a total novice. There are some easy runs, but in truth you may be better off at another resort.

THE TOWN

Hintertux has a lot going for it on the slopes, but off the mountain, the place is totally crap with little or no real local services. . It's not that cheap either, with only a few restaurants and decent drinking holes. If its après-ski you're after though, you must check out the bar at the bottom of the gondola called *Hohenhaus Tenne*. Its full on, and has got the most bonkers toilets you've ever seen. The best thing is to stay down the valley at Mayrhofen, which is about a forty minute bus ride away. **Mayrhofen** is a cool place with loads of places to stay, lots of restaurants and heaps of other things going on.

A

AUSTRIA

Pic - Ischgl Tourism

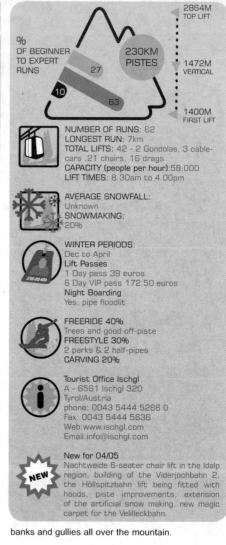

% OF BEGINNER TO EXPERT RUNS

10

27

63

230KM PISTES

2864M TOP LIFT

1472M VERTICAL

1400M FIRST LIFT

NUMBER OF RUNS: 62
LONGEST RUN: 7km
TOTAL LIFTS: 42 - 2 Gondolas, 3 cable-cars ,21 chairs, 16 drags
CAPACITY (people per hour):58,000
LIFT TIMES: 8.30am to 4.00pm

AVERAGE SNOWFALL:
Unknown
SNOWMAKING:
20%

WINTER PERIODS:
Dec to April
Lift Passes
1 Day pass 39 euros
6 Day VIP pass 172.50 euros
Night Boarding
Yes, pipe floodlit

FREERIDE 40%
Trees and good off-piste
FREESTYLE 30%
2 parks & 2 half-pipes
CARVING 20%

Tourist Office Ischgl
A - 6561 Ischgl 320
Tyrol/Austria
phone: 0043 5444 5266 0
Fax: 0043 5444 5636
Web:www.ischgl.com
Email:info@ischgl.com

New for 04/05
Nachtweide 6-seater chair lift in the Idalp region, building of the Viderjochbahn 2, the Höllspitzbahn lift being fitted with hoods, piste improvements, extension of the artificial snow making, new magic carpet for the Velilleckbahn.

Ischgl has gained a reputation as being one of Austria's best resorts - and it's a worthy reputation at that. Mind you, it's also one of Austria's more snobbish areas and can be very expensive. Ischgl may not be the most testing place, but it offers something for everyone, with well groomed slopes serviced by fast modern lifts. Snowboarders have been coming here for years to sample the excellent selection of wide, open, long runs which suit all standards and styles of rider. The *International Snowboard Federation* regularly stage slalom and halfpipe events here, so it must have something to offer. If what you find at Ischgl is not enough, then you can ride into the neighbouring Swiss duty-free resort of **Samnaun**. It can be reached by connecting lifts and is covered by the **Silvretta** lift pass, which can be used at three other resorts, **Galtur, Kappl** and **See**.

FREERIDERS have a high altitude mountain that ensures a good annual snow record, providing excellent wide open powder fields. For some easy freeriding, check out the stuff in the **Idjoch** area, which has a good mixture of blues and reds to play around on. Advanced riders will find plenty of stuff to keep them busy, although you won't be tested too often. **Pardatschgrat**, a black run leading back into the village (with the lower section cutting through some trees), is well worth a go, and you'll also find good off-piste freeriding down the runs off **Palinkopf.**

FREESTYLERS are probably going to be the most pleased with Ischgl for one reason, and one reason only - the **Boarder's Paradise** fun-park is the dog's bollocks. It is without doubt, one of the best parks in Europe and is equipped with all sorts of interesting obstacles with marked areas such as Freeride, New School, and Mogul, which starts at the top. At the bottom there is a well-shaped halfpipe. The whole area is designed with the intention of satisfying air heads of all levels (there's also a halfpipe at **Samnaun**). However, freestylers who are still not content will find plenty of natural hits to get that extra air fix off, with big drop ins,

banks and gullies all over the mountain.

CARVERS, especially hard boot riders, will love this resort, with its wide, motorway pistes where you can put down big arcs and easily make those 360° snow turns. Ischgl often hosts top slalom and giant slalom events so there must be good quality, fast carving terrain. The runs are so well-marked and pisted, that carving up Ischgl is a total pleasure, no matter what is on your feet.

Pic - Ischgl Tourism

down. There is a number of bars and late night hangouts. But the problem is that most places are full of sickly aprés-ski bores, wearing silly coloured lipsticks and face paints.

Accommodation is of a very high standard but with high rates to match. There are plenty of typical Austrian hotels, pensions and a number of Austrian-style apartment suites, with self-catering sleeping 6 or more. Nothing is more than a few minutes from the base lifts, with many of the places located in areas where cars are banned. Many tour operators come here offering package deals for weekly and two week stays.

BEGINNERS will soon see the benefits of learning here. The novice-marked runs are just that, being well located and offering some long, easy-to-negotiate trails. The only drawback is the amount of drag lifts that beginners need to use, but you've got to learn some time. The local ski school has a lot of snowboard instruction and lesson programmes are very reasonable.

THE TOWN

Ischgl is a modern resort, rather than an old traditional Austrian hamlet. However, this is a resort popular with the ski tour groups who come here by the coachload, so it can get very busy both on and off the slopes. Ischgl is also not the cheapest of places, so skint or budget-conscious riders will need to do some serious scamming to see a seven day trip through. Around the village there are a number of attractions from the adventure swimming pool, squash courts and a number of shops (selling tack mostly). There is a few snowboard hire outlets, with prices much the same from where ever you go.

Food. Depending on what you're into may have a lot do with how you eat here. There are quite a lot of restaurants in Ischgl, mostly hotel restaurants. However, they are nearly all Austrian style, offering a lot of bland menus. Fast food around here is a shop-lifter running out of the supermarket with a packet of biscuits. The Pizzeria is good, so it's not all bad news.

Night-life in Ischgl is dire and really lets the place

SUMMARY

Ischgl has one of the best fun-parks in Europe and offers some excellent all-round terrain for all levels. However, off the slopes things are a bit poncy.
Money wise: Very expensive resort, with over priced accommodation.

Pic - Ischgl Tourism

FLY: Fly to Innsbruck (100km) International transfer time to resort is 2 hours. Munich/Salzburg 300km-
BUS: Buses from Innsbruck, can be taken via Landeck to Ischgl on a daily basis. Landeck is 55 mins.
TRAIN: Trains go to Landeck , then take bus to resort (55 mins)
CAR: Drive to Innsbruck via motorway A12 to Ischgul, 178miles (286km). Drive time is about 2 hours
*From Calais = 639 miles (1028Km, Drive time is around 11 1/2 hours.

65

7 OUT OF 10

Good riding to be had

Pic - San Tang

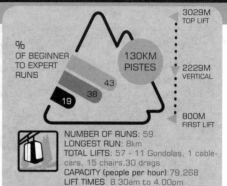

% OF BEGINNER TO EXPERT RUNS

130KM PISTES

43
38
19

3029M TOP LIFT

2229M VERTICAL

800M FIRST LIFT

NUMBER OF RUNS: 59
LONGEST RUN: 8km
TOTAL LIFTS: 57 - 11 Gondolas, 1 cable-cars, 15 chairs, 30 drags
CAPACITY (people per hour): 79,268
LIFT TIMES: 8.30am to 4.00pm

AVERAGE SNOWFALL:
10m
SNOWMAKING:
30%

WINTER PERIODS:
Dec to April
SUMMER PERIODS:
May to Oct
Lift Passes
1 Day pass 34.50 euros
6 Days 181 euros
Board School
1 day 50 euros, 3 days 120 euros
Private lesson 180 a day
Night Boarding
No

FREERIDE 50%
No trees and a bit of off-piste
FREESTYLE 20%
A park & a half-pipe
CARVING 30%

KAPRUN INFORMATION
Salzburger Platz 601, A 5710 Kaprun
Telephone: +43/6542/770-0
Fax: +43/6542/72032
Web: www.europasportregion.info
Email: welcome@europasportregion.info

Train
nearest at Zell an See 10 minutes away.
Fly
to Salzburg, 1 1/2 hours transfer.
Car
from Salzburg head south on the A10 to exit 46. Then head south west along the 168 via Taxenbach before turning left up to Kaprun (56 miles).

Winter or summer, Kaprun cuts it big style. The ride area is located on one of Austria's best glaciers, the **Kitzsteinhorn Glacier,** which reaches an altitude of 3,203 metres, making it a perfect place to ride. Being a glacier resort, you can ride here all year and no matter what month you visit, riders of all levels will find something to shred. It has to be said however, that much of what is here (or at nearby **Zell am See**), is best suited to intermediate freeriders and carvers

FREERIDERS wanting to gain access to Kaprun's best terrain and main runs, should head to the **Kitzsteinhorn.** Further up, you can reach good off-piste powder stashes, which can often still be found in the summer months of June and July.
FREESTYLERS are provided with a halfpipe at Kaprun all year round, and there's another one down in Zell am See during the winter. Kaprun's pipe is not the world's best but it still allows for some okay riding. The fun-park has an array of hits, but really freestylers should search out Kaprun's natural hits.
CARVERS will be at ease whether they ride at Kaprun or Zell am See, as both resorts have some great, open carving runs. At Kaprun you can access some excellent carving spots from the **Alpencentre.**
BEGINNERS can get going on a number of easy runs on the **Maiskogel mountain,** which is reached by a drag lift from the centre of the village. If you can't handle a drag lift, take the cable car at the north end of the village to reach the east slopes. Beginners are spoilt when it comes to snowboard instruction; Kaprun was the first Austrian resort to have an independent snowboard school. If you get bored with Kaprun, Zell am See is only a ten minute bus ride away, which gives you access to an extra 50 miles of piste covered by the same pass.

THE TOWN. **Kaprun** is a fairly large and stretched out affair. Having a car may save a lot of walking but there

is also a good and regular local bus service. Around town, you get a mixture of the old and new with a typical Austrian flavour. **Accommodation** options are excellent and Kaprun will satisfy both rich and skint snowboarders alike. **Evenings** in Kaprun are laid back - check out the Austrian Pub, Bauber's, or the Fountain bar. Nothing great about any of them, but there are worse places.

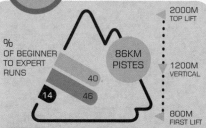

KITZBUHEL

6 OUT OF 10

Way overated and cheesy

% OF BEGINNER TO EXPERT RUNS

86KM PISTES

14 / 46 / 40

2000M TOP LIFT

1200M VERTICAL

800M FIRST LIFT

NUMBER OF RUNS: 58
LONGEST RUN: 10km
TOTAL LIFTS: 53
6 Gondolas, 27 chairs,18 drags
CAPACITY (people per hour):77,589
LIFT TIMES: 8.30am to 4.00pm

AVERAGE SNOWFALL: 1.8m
SNOWMAKING: 45%

WINTER PERIODS:
Dec to April
Lift Passes
Day 35 euros,6 Days 165 euros
Season pass 435 euros
Board School
Many companies to choose from.
Day lesson 60 euros, half-day 35, 6 days
135. Private lesson half-day 140 euros
Night Boarding
Thursday & Friday 6:30pm to 9:30pm.
Gaisberg quad chairlift open in Kirchberg.
13 euros

FREERIDE 45%
A few trees and some off-piste
FREESTYLE 10%
A park & a half-pipe
CARVING 45%

Kitzbühel Tourism
Hinterstadt 18
A-6370 Kitzbühel
Tel.: +43 (0) 5356 777
Fax: +43 (0) 5356 777-77
Web:www.kitzbuehel.com
Email:info@kitzbuehel.com

Train
Kitzbuhel has its own train station
Fly
to Salzburg ,1 3/4 hours transfer
Car
Via Salzburg, head south via the route
312 and 161 all the way to Kitzbuhel. 50
miles (82km).

NEW

New for 04/05 season
new pant filling 2.5km, 30 person gondola
connecting Hahnenkamm/Pengelstein and
Jochberg/Resterhöhe areas, completely
spanning the valley.

Pic -Kitzbuhel Tourism

The chances are that if you know **Austria**, you'll know about **Kitzbuhel**, famed for the **Hahnenkamm** (a World Cup ski downhill course), and noted for the billions of ski-package tour groups. Yep, Kitzbuhel is Austria's Benidorm, due to the hoards of skiers cluttering up the slopes and making fools of themselves in the bars and around town. A shame really, for apart from the long lift queues and the fact that it is a low-level resort, which doesn't guarantee snow cover on the bottom runs, it is a cool place to ride. Still, when the snow has dumped, no rider should get bored as there is enough room to ride without constantly bumping into skiers.

FREERIDERS should look under **Bichlam** in order to ride some cool powder, while advanced riders will find the more testing runs on **Ehrenbach** (part of the Hahnenkamm) & down the steeps of Ehrenbachgraben. The **Jochberg** area has some easy bowls to hunt out. The best way to cut the off-piste is to seek out the assistance of a local guide at the off-piste school.

FREESTYLERS are attracted to Kitzbuhel for its extensive amounts of natural hits, like the stuff found on **Pegelstein**, or those hits dotted around Safari, which starts at Pegelstein. The park and pipe also provide plenty of air time, even if they're not that well looked after.

CARVERS are primarily drawn to Kitzbuhel by the thought of tackling the **Hahnenkamm**. The rest of the area has plenty of good advanced and intermediate terrain that also allows for some fast carving descents.

BEGINNERS in particular are well suited to these slopes, as there's the chance of riding some long, easy runs serviced by chair lifts, and not just drags, offering the nervous T-bar virgin good, alternative options for getting around. The long **Hagstein** run is ideal for first timers; the only problem with this area is that it is often littered with fallen down skiers.

THE TOWN. Lodging in a town like **Kitzbuhel** is no problem, with heaps of beds at average prices in pensions and apartments. Mercifully, it has loads of cheap eating joints. **Boozing** goes off in a number of places, allowing drinking into the early hours of the morning. But beware, skiers apres all over the place, although most are in bed by 9pm having had their two glasses of gluhwein. Popular hangouts are *Take 5* & the *Londoner* bar (no points for names). A cheaper option is to head to **Kirchberg**, about 10km away. Its got less glitz but some good bars, and a good range of facilities.

A
AUSTRIA

Pic -Kufstein Tourism

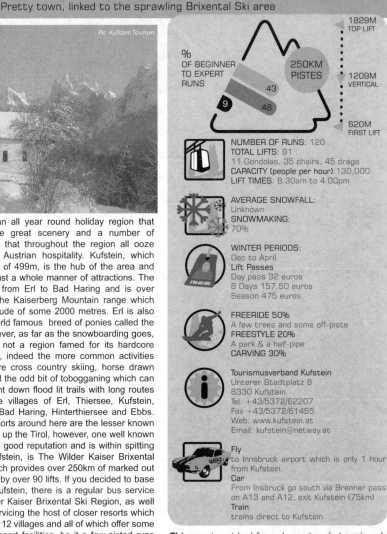

%
OF BEGINNER
TO EXPERT
RUNS

250KM
PISTES

43

9

48

1829M
TOP LIFT

1209M
VERTICAL

620M
FIRST LIFT

NUMBER OF RUNS: 120
TOTAL LIFTS: 91
11 Gondolas, 35 chairs, 45 drags
CAPACITY (people per hour):130,000
LIFT TIMES: 8.30am to 4.00pm

AVERAGE SNOWFALL:
Unknown
SNOWMAKING:
70%

WINTER PERIODS:
Dec to April
Lift Passes
Day pass 32 euros
6 Days 157.50 euros
Season 475 euros

FREERIDE 50%
A few trees and some off-piste
FREESTYLE 20%
A park & a half-pipe
CARVING 30%

Tourismusverband Kufstein
Unterer Stadtplatz 8
6330 Kufstein
Tel. +43/5372/62207
Fax +43/5372/61455
Web: www.kufstein.at
Email: kufstein@netway.at

Fly
to Innsbruck airport which is only 1 hour
from Kufstein.
Car
From Insbruck go south via Brenner pass
on A13 and A12, exit Kufstein (75km)
Train
trains direct to Kufstein

Kufstein is an all year round holiday region that boast some great scenery and a number of small hamlets that throughout the region all ooze with traditional Austrian hospitality. Kufstein, which sits at a height of 499m, is the hub of the area and a town that boast a whole manner of attractions. The area stretches from Erl to Bad Haring and is over shadowed by the Kaiserberg Mountain range which rises to an altitude of some 2000 metres. Erl is also home to the world famous breed of ponies called the Haflinger. However, as far as the snowboarding goes, in general this not a region famed for its hardcore skiing or riding, indeed the more common activities around here are cross country skiing, horse drawn sleigh rides and the odd bit of tobogganing which can be done at night down flood lit trails with long routes down in to the villages of Erl, Thiersee, Kufstein, Langkampfen, Bad Haring, Hinterthiersee and Ebbs. Many of the resorts around here are the lesser known ones that make up the Tirol, however, one well known area that has a good reputation and is within spitting distance of Kufstein, is The Wilder Kaiser Brixental Ski Region which provides over 250km of marked out pistes serviced by over 90 lifts. If you decided to base your self in Kaufstein, there is a regular bus service up to the Wilder Kaiser Brixental Ski Region, as well as a ski bus servicing the host of closer resorts which number around 12 villages and all of which offer some form of winter sport facilities, be it a few pisted runs with a couple of short drag lifts, or a village boasting long cross country trails.

Kufstein is the main town in the area which offers a full programme of down hill ski facilities and will suite mainly beginners and basic intermediates.

Langkampfen is a tiny place with only a few nursery slopes that will suite mums and dads that want to appear cool and with it (man).

Thiersee is not bad for a day or two, but again only best for novices and slow intermediate riders.
Hinterthiersee, is a stones throw from Kufstein, and another small place with a couple of decent pisted runs, some of which can offer a bit of speed and okay riding.

Landl is a cross country haven and no good for snowboarding.**Kiefersfelden** is yet another cross country skiers retreat. **Ebbs**, more cross country skiing. **Erl** is the place to go walking. **Bad Haring** is the Spa village. **Niederndorf** is close to the boarder with Germany.

LECH

Slopes Yes - Village No

The Arlberg, in the far eastern section of **Austria**, is home to all the top classy resorts that the country has to offer. Lech is just one of them, along with its close neighbours **Zurs, Stuben, St Christoph** and **St Anton**. More closely linked with Zurs, Lech sits at the back of St Anton, and is without doubt Austria's number one poncy retreat. Year in, year out, this high altitude resort attracts numerous royals along with the finest from the film and pop world - and all the arse-lickers they can muster to join them. Skiers come here to be seen, not to ski. But Lech is a great place to ride, for all levels and styles, with some major freeride terrain and excellent off-piste powder. So although you may have to push past a fur coat or two, you can ride happily on a mountain where the management have been keen to make Lech a snowboard-friendly resort.

2444M TOP LIFT

% OF BEGINNER TO EXPERT RUNS

110KM PISTES

994M VERTICAL

40
20 40

1450M FIRST LIFT

NUMBER OF RUNS: 32
LONGEST RUN: 5km
TOTAL LIFTS: 32
4 Gondolas, 18 chairs,10 drags
CAPACITY (people per hour):44,668
LIFT TIMES: 8.30am to 4.00pm

AVERAGE SNOWFALL:
2.6m
SNOWMAKING:
10%

WINTER PERIODS: Dec to April
Lift Passes
Day pass 39 euros
6 Days 184
Heliboarding
take-off from Kriegerhorn / Oberlech and from Flexenpass (Zürs) to two peaks: Mehlsack, Orgelscharte
Night Boarding
No

FREERIDE 50%
Some trees and good off-piste
FREESTYLE 20%
A park & a half-pipe
CARVING 30%

Lech-Tourismus
6764 Lech
Tel: +43 (0)5583 2161-0
Fax: +43 (0)5583 3155
Web:www.lech-zuers.at
Email:info@lech-zuers.at

Train
station Langen am Arlberg 17 km away
Fly
to Innsbruck (110km) , 2hrs transfer. Friedrichshafen, 120km. Altenrhein, 100km. Zurich, 200km. For about 2000 euros, you can get a helicopter from Zurich to Lech ...
Car
via Innsbruck, head west on the A12 to Landeck then take the 316 via St Anton to reach Lech

Pic.-Lech Tourism

FREERIDERS will love this place, with large amounts of steeps and deep powder. The runs off **Kriegerhorn** are the total dog's 'B's, as are the powder trails down from **Zuger Hochlicht,** which can take you from top to bottom free of any piste-loving pop star.

FREESTYLERS have a fantastic 300 metre long fun-park area, located on **Schlegelkopf**. The park is loaded with gaps, quarter-pipes and a decent halfpipe, which like all the best areas here, are free of posing image junkies.

CARVERS who turn up here with hard boots should have their balls boiled while still attached. This is soft boot heaven; only the poser patrol have hards here, and their boots are just for show.

BEGINNERS have a perfectly acceptable series of novice runs and good trails to progress on, making Lech a good first timer's resort. The only drawback is sharing the easy slopes with moaning no-hopers from the pop world, or a public school kid who thinks he's street wise (stick a finger in his eye and see what he thinks then).

THE TOWN

The town at the base of the slopes is expensive and dripping with sad people in fur coats and gold, so expect to pay highly for everything. Even the pensions cost an arm and a leg; you may find that a stay here is beyond the reach of most. Try lodging in one of the nearby hamlets. If you do give Lech the one night treatment, remember that night-life is dull and super poncy. However, to spruce things up, try seeing how many dickheads in fur coats you can cover with yellow spray paint.

wsg

MAYRHOFEN

8 OUT OF 10

Good all-round resort

Pic -Mayrhofen Tourism

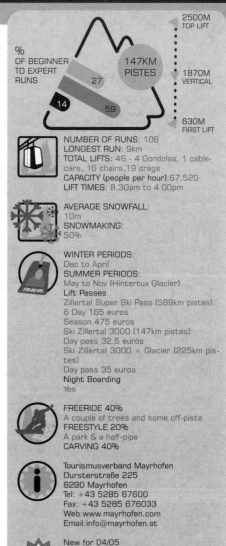

% OF BEGINNER TO EXPERT RUNS

147KM PISTES

14   27   59

2500M TOP LIFT

1870M VERTICAL

630M FIRST LIFT

NUMBER OF RUNS: 109
LONGEST RUN: 9km
TOTAL LIFTS: 46 - 4 Gondolas, 1 cable-cars, 16 chairs,19 drags
CAPACITY (people per hour):67,520
LIFT TIMES: 8.30am to 4.00pm

AVERAGE SNOWFALL:
10m
SNOWMAKING:
50%

WINTER PERIODS:
Dec to April
SUMMER PERIODS:
May to Nov (Hintertux Glacier)
Lift Passes
Zillertal Super Ski Pass (589km pistes):
6 Day 165 euros
Season 475 euros
Ski Zillertal 3000 (147km pistes):
Day pass 32.5 euros
Ski Zillertal 3000 + Glacier (225km pistes)
Day pass 35 euros
Night Boarding
Yes

FREERIDE 40%
A couple of trees and some off-piste
FREESTYLE 20%
A park & a half-pipe
CARVING 40%

Tourismusverband Mayrhofen
Dursterstraße 225
6290 Mayrhofen
Tel: +43 5285 67600
Fax: +43 5285 676033
Web:www.mayrhofen.com
Email:info@mayrhofen.at

NEW

New for 04/05
new 6-seater chair lift replaces the old 2-seater chairlift Eggalm-Nord, extension of the artifical snow making.
2003/4 season saw linking of Mayrhofen and Tux via the 150 person cable car, creating the Ski-Zillertal 3000 linked area.

This quaint Tyrolean village, framed by beautiful mountains, is located just 43 miles from **Innsbruck** and welcomes many British package holiday makers every year. It offers the largest ski area in the **Ziller valley** now it is linked with **Hippach, Finkenberg** and **Eggalm/Rastkogel**. Although it is picturesque, unfortunately the highest peak is only 2500 metres, and thus the snow conditions can sometimes suffer. In order to counter this, many snow making machines have been installed, covering 96 hectares of the terrain. The 146km of pistes are split into 40 km of blues, 86 km of red runs and 20 km of blacks.

For those staying in the centre of Mayrhofen, the only way up and down is the **Penken bahn gondola** as unfortunately it is not possible to board back into Mayrhofen. Even though the lift is high speed, there can still be big queues early in the day. To avoid the crowds you can take the free ski bus to the **Finkenberg** or **Ahorn** lifts, which are popular with locals or the new Horbergbahn which is to the east.

Once you exit the Penken, there is a short stroll and a drop off down to a learner t-bar and the Penken Express. The red runs on this side are good fun and have a few short tree runs, but can get quite crowded.

Drop down into the other valley for some more testing runs like the Black 14 which is fairly steep and icy but good fun. For here you can access the **Burton terrain park** which has been used for the British Championships and has some BIG jumps! The park also incorporates a halfpipe, rails and a chill out area. It is serviced by the Sun Jet chairlift so no walking is required.

Nearby the new 150 person cable car, the 150er-Tux, whips you up to the **Horberg peak**. From here you can turn right off the lift and take the Blue 6 piste then

-Mayrhofen Tourism

Another nice place for a day trip is the small resort of **Kaltenbach**. This place often has lots of untracked powder after a dump because no one goes there! You can also take the same train to **Zell am Ziller**, and then a bus or taxi to their lift. Unfortunately your Super Zillertal pass isn't valid here, but it is still worth a visit as it is a large area linked to **Gerlos** and **Konigsleiten**, which is famous for its tree runs.

THE TOWN

There is an old tradition in Mayrhofen which states after a day's boarding you must visit the *Ice Bar* as soon as you step off the Penken and drink a Grolsch. This bar sells the most Grolsch is Europe and is only open 4 hours a day! It gets heaving but can be

drop off the edge into the **Horbergtal** and go off-piste back to the terrain park. Work out where you are going to cross the river before dropping into the valley!

In this area this is also a nice wide blue learner slope next to the **Tappenalm lift**, which leads to the **Schneekar lift**. Ascend this and visit the Schneekarhütte restaurant at the top of a nice black run (Route 17). It stilll has a big log fire and good food which can be washed down with all sorts of organic schnapps. Take Black 17 or Red 7 down which is also pleasant.

After a few days you may have seen most of these mountains so it is well worth buying the Super Zillertal lift pass as it costs only slightly more than the standard pass and includes other resorts in the valley. With this pass you can take the old rickety Zillertalbahn mountain train or the bus for free to other resorts from the station at the bottom of town.

From here the **Hintertux Glacier** is only half an hour. This is an amazing place but at 3250 metres the conditions can be extreme, with wind chill factor down to -30 so make sure you wrap up! White outs can occur suddenly too. On a sunny day though, this place is very close to heaven. It is not often that busy, and there is lots of off-piste available but beware of crevasses and blue ice. After a day ripping it up, you must visit the *Hohenhauste* and go to the toilets. They cannot be explained, just make sure you drink a beer then nip to the loo!

great fun. In 2003 they also build a Kebab shop in the bar, so you don't even have to stumble outside for refreshment.

After après boarding, late beers can be drunk at the chilled and friendly *Scotland Yard pub*, and then you can dance til dawn at *Arena*. *Moe's Bar* serves decent food and good cocktails too. Other tips are the restaurant under *Sport Garni Strauss Hotel* which serves nice Austrian food, or there is a good Chinese near Scotland Yard.

In brief, visit Mayrhofen, have a great party but be sure to shred Hintertux too.

FLY: Fly to Innsbruck (65km), 1 1/4 hours transfer. Salzburg airport (170km) about 2 1/2 hr transfer.
TRAIN: Jenbach railway station is about 35 km away. Take the Zillertalbahn train or bus to Mayrhofen.
CAR: Drive from Innsbruck and go west on the A12. Exit at B169 along the Zillertal Valley to Mayrhofen. ° Drive time from Calais is 12 hours, 692 miles (1113 km).

5 OUT OF 10

Useful as a base for visiting Stubai

Pic -Neustift Tourism

Neustift is the small gate way village for a number of small ridabe mountain areas that link directly with the village as well as being the last out post for one of Austria's most popular, and in the eyes of some, best all the year round ridabe glaciers. '**Stubai Gletscher**'. During the winter months when many of the low lying resorts are struggling for snow, you can be sure to find a good snow cover up on Stubai. However, be warned, Stubai can become very busy when outlying resorts are struggling for snow cover, skiers from as far as **Munich** flock here in the bucket load. That aside Neustift its self is ideally suited to novices and slow learning intermediates and in general this area has a good annual snow record, so you won't always need to take the 20 minute drive and 15 minute cable car ride up to Stubai's slopes. Located close to Neustift are the runs on the **Elferhutte,** which rises to 2080m. Although not extensive, the runs on the Elferhutte are perfect for intermediates and easy going carvers with mainly red runs and the odd blue trail to master, but riders who rate them self's as experts will need to travel up to the Stubai Glacier to find some adventurous terrain. If you decided to hangout around Neustift, access to the slopes is easily done from the village.

FREERIDERS who like adventurous slopes with long scary drops will find plenty to please them at Stubai, but not a great deal around Neustift. What you find around the village are basic short and rather narrow runs that lend them self's perfectly well for a few days simple riding with out any hassles or crowds. Riders who want to learn how to carve at a gentle level will find the place okay, especially if you are a middle aged rider who likes to take it easy and doesn't want to ride with the pack. FREESTYLERS have little or nothing to go for on the **Elferhutte** slopes. Yes you can leap over a few uneven spots and there's always the odd obstacle to grind, but in the main, freestylers will need to head up to Stubai where there is a large halfpipe and a basic terrain park with snow sculpted hits. Locals from Innsbruck are always up at Stubai getting airs of their own hits and will be happy to show you around. CARVERS will be able to get something out of the slopes around Neustift but nothings to long making a trip up to Stubai a must for speed freaks.

% OF BEGINNER TO EXPERT RUNS

60KM PISTES

26
39
38

2080M TOP LIFT
1080M VERTICAL
1000M FIRST LIFT

NUMBER OF RUNS: 26
LONGEST RUN: 10km
TOTAL LIFTS: 20 - 4 Gondolas, 7 chairs,7 drags, 2 magic carpets
LIFT TIMES: 9:30 to 16:30

AVERAGE SNOWFALL: 5m
SNOWMAKING: 20%

WINTER PERIODS: Dec to April
Lift Passes
Elfer: Day Pass 19.5 euros, 6 days 96.5
Board School
Skischule Neustift
Day lesson 50 euros, 5 days 129
Private lessons 40 euros per hour
Night Boarding
Monday, Wednesday and Friday Rodelbahn "ELFER" open from 19:30 - 21:00

FREERIDE 50%
Some trees and good off-piste
FREESTYLE 20%
A park
CARVING 30%

TOURISMUSVERBAND NEUSTIFT IM STUBAITAL
Dorf 3,A-6167 Neustift im Stubaital
Tel.: + 43 / 52 26 / 22 28
Fax: + 43 / 52 26 / 25 29
Web:www.neustift.at
Email:tv.neustift@neustift.at

Train
to Innsbruck, then take bus
Bus
Local buses available from Innsbruck
Fly
25 minutes from Innsbruck airport.
Car
from Innsbruck over Brenner highway (Europa bridge), exit Schönberg. Go past Mieders, Telfes, Fulpmes and then Neustift

NEW

New for 04/05 season
new 8 person gondola in Elfer

BEGINNERS may find Neustift is a bit too limited and it won't take novices to long to conquer this place.
THE TOWN. **Neustift** is a well appointed village with a good local services. There is a good selection of hotels, guest house's and pension. You can even get a room in a farm house. Prices are very reasonable and standards high. The choice of restaurants are limited in terms of what is on offer and most are hotel outlets.

OBERGURGL

Very good carvers resort

Obergurgl sits at the head of the **Otzal Valley**, a mere 90 minutes form Innsbruck and only 20 minutes from the bigger resort of **Solden**. Although Obergurgl and Solden are located along the same valley and both are base locations for summer snowboarding up on the **Tiefenbach glacier**, the similarity ends

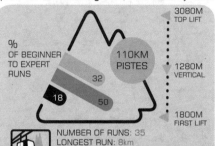

3080M
TOP LIFT

%
OF BEGINNER
TO EXPERT
RUNS

110KM
PISTES

32

1280M
VERTICAL

18

50

1800M
FIRST LIFT

NUMBER OF RUNS: 35
LONGEST RUN: 8km
TOTAL LIFTS: 23
4 Gondolas, 12 chairs,7 drags
CAPACITY (people per hour):37,000
LIFT TIMES: 8.30am to 4.00pm

AVERAGE SNOWFALL:
1.5m
SNOWMAKING:
45%

WINTER PERIODS: Dec to April
SUMMER PERIODS: May to Oct (Solden)
Lift Passes
Day pass 36 euros
6 day pass 167 euros
Night Boarding
8km of pistes open

FREERIDE 30%
No trees but some off-piste
FREESTYLE 10%
A park & pipe
CARVING 60%

Tourismusverband Obergurgl-Hochgurgl
Hauptstrasse 108
A-6456 Obergurgl-Hochgurgl, Austria
Tel +43 (5256) 6466
Fax +43 (5256) 6353
Web:www.obergurgl.com
Email:info@obergurgl.com

Train
train to Innsbruck or to Ötztal Bahnhof
Bus
bus from Innsbruck (4 times a day) or Ötztal-Bahnhof (8 times a day)
Fly
25 minutes from Innsbruck airport.
Car
From Innsbruck head along the A12 and turn off on to the B186 down the Ötztal Valley to Obergurgl.

there. Obergurgl, with its linked neighbouring resort **Hochgrugl**, is far smaller and less diverse than Solden especially when it comes to freeriding. Where Obergurgl shines and gets top marks is as a carver's resorts. The resort's high altitude also scores highly in its favour, this place has a very good annual snow record with heaps of the stuff falling every year. Mind you, being a high altitude resort means that prices are also high. On the slopes what you have is a wide open plateau that is completely void of any trees and is in general a tame mountain to ride. However, don't be put off, Obergurgl is still worth a visit. You could stay in Solden and visit this place for a day's riding by taking the local bus up or driving yourself. What ever, the runs are set out neatly and conveniently serviced by a series of lifts that go to a staggering summit elevation of some 3080 metres. Most of the runs are of an intermediate level with a series of reds, a few easy blues and only a couple of advanced black trails to check out.

FREERIDERS who like jagged and rough mountain slopes with big chutes and long gullies may find things around here a little on the tame side. There are no tree runs but there are some good off-piste and powder areas that can be ridden at speed.
FREESTYLERS will largely be wasting their time up here, this is not an air head's retreat. There are of course a few natural hits as with most mountains covered in snow, but they are few and far between. Still, the resort does have a pipe and terrain park.
CARVERS are the ones in for a treat. Obergurgl is dream for those who want to arc over in style on well groomed runs that are wide and free of obstacles.
BEGINNER should have no real problems with this place. The mountain is nicely laid out and novices can ride from the mid point all the way to the base via the number 5 and 6 trails.

THE TOWN
Off the slopes **Obergurgls** local services are excellent and very convient for the slopes. There is a good choice of hotels and guest house along with shops and sporting facilities. A number of the big hotels have indoor swimming pools and gyms. **Night life** is a tad tame with only a handfull of bars to choose from.

9 OUT OF 10

Together these two resorts make any snowboard trip worthwhile

Pic.-Saalbach-Hinterglem

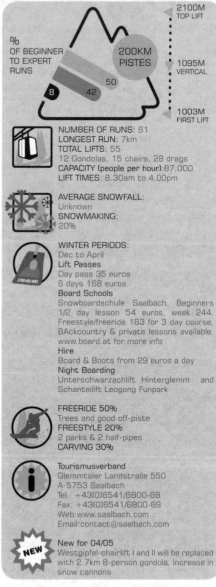

2100M
TOP LIFT

%
OF BEGINNER
TO EXPERT
RUNS

200KM
PISTES

50
8 42

1095M
VERTICAL

1003M
FIRST LIFT

NUMBER OF RUNS: 61
LONGEST RUN: 7km
TOTAL LIFTS: 55
12 Gondolas, 15 chairs, 28 drags
CAPACITY (people per hour):87,000
LIFT TIMES: 8.30am to 4.00pm

AVERAGE SNOWFALL:
Unknown
SNOWMAKING:
20%

WINTER PERIODS:
Dec to April
Lift Passes
Day pass 35 euros
6 days 168 euros
Board Schools
Snowboardschule Saalbach. Beginners
1/2 day lesson 54 euros, week 244.
Freestyle/freeride 163 for 3 day course.
BAckcountry & private lessons available.
www.board.at for more info
Hire
Board & Boots from 29 euros a day
Night Boarding
Unterschwarzachlift Hinterglemm and
Schanteilift Leogang Funpark

FREERIDE 50%
Trees and good off-piste
FREESTYLE 20%
2 parks & 2 half-pipes
CARVING 30%

Tourismusverband
Glemmtaler Landstraße 550
A-5753 Saalbach
Tel.: +43(0)6541/6800-68
Fax: +43(0)6541/6800-69
Web:www.saalbach.com
Email:contact@saalbach.com

NEW

New for 04/05
Westgipfel-chairlift I and II will be replaced
with 2.7km 8-person gondola. Increase in
snow cannons

Saalbach-Hinterglem are two closely linked villages. They lie along a valley floor where the mountain slopes rise up on both sides of each village. The first village you arrive at is **Saalbach** with **Hinterglem** a few minutes up the road. Together they become one large snowboard area that covers 124 miles of piste, and forms a massive and good rideable area. Over the years, this has become a very popular place for visiting snowboarders, but it's not so favoured by many Austrian riders. This has nothing to do with the terrain since the area boasts some of the best in the country, with excellent advanced freeriding and fantastic beginner areas. It has more to do with the fact that this is a very busy tourist retreat, which can often see stupidly long lift lines and way overcrowded slopes, especially at weekends and holiday periods. Mornings can be stupidly busy, especially the first lifts up via the **Schattberg** cable car, but mercifully, once up, things get a lot better. For a resort to host world ski events you would expect some great terrain - and that is exactly what you get at Saalbach-Hinterglemm. There are trees, steeps, powder and natural hits, not to mention eight miles of snowboard-only runs for freeriders and carvers, as well as two halfpipes and a fun-park to suit all levels and styles of freestyler. If you get bored here or can't handle it, take up brass rubbing as it will suit you better.

FREESTYLERS will find a large amount of natural hits dotted all over the place, many of which are favourite spots of the locals. The eight mile snowboard-only area, has a good fun-park loaded with a series of hits

and gaps, is well maintained and a pleaser. Saalbach and Hinterglem also have separate halfpipes; the one at Saalbach on the **Bernkogel** area is the better of the two; the pipe at Hinterglem is more tame and will

Pic -Saalbach-Hinterglem Tourism

suit mainly novice air heads, having a less scary vert, and lower walls.

FREERIDERS wanting off-piste powder will find some good stuff on the slopes of the north side of the valley, where you can gain access to some great runs which are not messed up by skiers. There's also a boardercross circuit for freeriders to shred.

CARVERS of all grades will do well here - the place is a carver's dream. Those at advanced level, who want a testing black run, should take the **Schattberg** cable car, from where you'll find what you're looking for. Those less adventurous carvers will find the red run named **Limberg-Jausern,** a nice long treat.

BEGINNERS will quickly see improvements in their riding, with ample slopes that are easy to reach and negotiate; but note this place is littered with drag lifts, so expect a bit of T-bar tackling. The numerous ski-schools all offer snowboard tuition and will soon help you sort out any T-bar problems.

THE TOWN
Being a popular tourist place, the area can sometimes feel tacky and overpopulated - but don't let that put you off. Whichever village you choose to stay in, you'll find a high level of service and plenty of off-slope things to do, from shopping for tourist toys, pigging out, drinking or body fitness. It should be mentioned though, that nothing comes cheap as this is an expensive place. Spread out between the two villages you'll be able to

find an indoor swimming pool, a bowling alley, numerous saunas and fitness gyms. Ice skaters also have an ice ring to perform on. Snowboard hire is available in both villages, with prices the same wherever you go. You need a passport as security when hiring.

Accommodation ranges from cosy chalets to schilling-hungry hotels. Prices are mainly on the high side, but you can find pensions with rates from 21 euros a night. Pension Montan or Pension Scharnagl are both good, while Bergers Sporthotel is a good choice.

Food. There are many eating holes, with all the hotels serving typical Austrian dishes. There's also a number of pizza joints so getting a meal around here should pose no real problems, however, you should remember that this is not a cheap place. Riders on low funds may have to resort to supermarket offerings.

Night-life is very lively, spoilt by the fact that most places go in for après-ski for some very sad groups, who don't know how to party on their own. The Ice Bar is a popular hangout and stays open late. The stupidly named Londoner bar is also popular; both are après haunts, so be warned.

SUMMARY
Together these two resorts make any snowboard trip worthwhile, with a good selection of all-round and all-level terrain. Good off-slope services.
On the slopes: Really good **Off the slopes**: Okay but snobbish

Pic -Saalbach-Hinterglem Tourism

FLY: to Salzburg International (90km) transfer time to resort is 1 1/2 hours
TRAIN: to Zell am See (12 miles), then taxi
BUS: from Salzburg, can be taken to Zell am See, then transfer by local bus to Saalbach.
CAR: From Salzburg via motorway A10 & 311. Saalbach is 59 miles (94Km), Drive time is about 1 1/2 hours

75

7 OUT OF 10   Good all-round resort

Pic -Sshladming Tourism

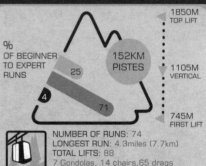

%
OF BEGINNER
TO EXPERT
RUNS

152KM PISTES

25

4

71

1850M
TOP LIFT

1105M
VERTICAL

745M
FIRST LIFT

NUMBER OF RUNS: 74
LONGEST RUN: 4.3miles (7.7km)
TOTAL LIFTS: 88
7 Gondolas, 14 chairs,65 drags
LIFT TIMES: 8.00am to 4.00pm

AVERAGE SNOWFALL
5m
SNOWMAKING
30%

WINTER PERIODS
Dec to April
SUMMER PERIODS
May to Nov
Lift Passes
1 Day pass 32 euros
6 Day pass 165 euros
Season pass 380 euros

FREERIDE 40%
A few trees and limited off-piste
FREESTYLE 20%
A park & 2 pipes (1 all year)
CARVING 40%

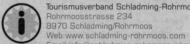

Tourismusverband Schladming-Rohrmoos
Rohrmoosstrasse 234
8970 Schladming/Rohrmoos
Web:www.schladming-rohrmoos.com
Email:info@schladming-rohrmoos.com

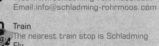

Train
The nearest train stop is Schladming
Fly
to Salzburg, 1 hour away.
Car
Drive via Salzburg, head south on the A10
and exit at junction 63 in the direction of
Radstadt, along to 146 to the Schaldming
turn off. ° Drive time from Calais is 12 1/2
hours, 741 miles (1192 km).

NEW

New for 04/05 season
improvements to the pistes and snowmaking. New shaper for the terrain park on the
Dachstein glacier

Schladming is an all year-round resort, with summer riding on the **Dachstein Glacier,** and is a popular snowboard haunt. The riding is spread out over a number of areas which offer basic intermediate terrain, and perfect beginner stuff. **Schladming** is not a hardcore or advanced rider's destination, but that's not to say there aren't any testing runs. There are actually seven different mountains, but not all of them are connected by lifts. The **Hauser Kaibling** mountain has lots of intermediate terrain, with a series of long reds that are ideal for carvers. There are excellent novice trails, with the option to ride a long blue all the way down to the base at the village of Haus, just up the road from Schladming. **Hochwurzen**, which rises up to 1,850m, has lots of trees for freeriders to drop through, and a number of reds at the top that base out into simple blues, with easy runs back to Schladming. The **Planai** mountain holds the main trails and is reached from the edge of Schladming by gondola. Planai's runs offer something for everyone, with some interesting intermediate freeriding terrain. The Reiteralm area is much the same as Hochwurzen and although it has a bigger riding area, it's less convenient for Schladming.

FREERIDERS will find that any of the areas listed above can suit their needs, with some cool tree runs to be found on the Planai, and favourable powder to be found at **Hauser Kaibling**.

FREESTYLERS will find natural hits in most areas, with the Planai and the **Dachstein Glacier** having the best spots. There are also now three halfpipes and a fun-park to catch air on. One of the pipes is also well maintained during the summer months.

CARVERS will find all seven areas great, with some of the best pistes on the Hauser Kaibling mountain.

BEGINNERS will find the **Rohrmoss** area at 869m is flat and boring, but should still appeal to novices. Snowboard instruction is very good, and they even have a children's snowboard school.

THE TOWN

Accommodation is spread out around a large area, but the old town of Schladming has the biggest selection and offers the best facilities. Prices vary throughout the area, but as there is a youth hostel with cheap bunks, life is made easy for riders on a budget. Some good restaurants like Giovanni's. **Night-life** is okay but nothing outstanding. The area offers a vast amount of sporting facilities.

Seefeld is a tiny picture post card resort and every thing you imagined an Austrian village to be. This low key retreat is only 20 kilometres from **Innsbruck** and can be reached with ease along the A12 Autobahn via **Zirl**. Seefeld is noted more in the winter for being a cross country ski retreat and in the summer a popular holiday destination attracting visitors to sample the beauty and the tranquillity of the area. The German resort of **Garmisch** is only a short distance away across the Austrian German boarder and both resorts can be ridden with the one ski pass called the 'Happy Card',

Pic -Seefeld Tourism

which can be used in other resorts in various countries. On its own Seefeld is not noted for its hard-core down hill skiing or snowboarding, but nevertheless this is still a fun mountain with riding possible up to an altitude of 2100 metres and descends back down to the village outskirts. The ride area is split across two separate areas that of the **Gschwandtkopf** and the **Rosshutte**. The smaller of the two, being the Gschwandtkopf, is rather limited with only a few easy slopes for novices to try out. However, its still easy to get around and is a good spot for beginners to spend a few days learning on. The Rosshutte is a little more extensive with longer trails and wider slopes, but nothing that adventurous.

FREERIDERS will find riding here is done at sedate pace. Nothing is going to take you to long to conquer and good intermediate and expert riders will have this place licked within a day or two at the most. Still, there is a few spots to make a visit here a worth the while. The top section of the **Seefelder Joch** gives access to a few interesting spots which includes a few trees that line the lower parts of the main run down to the base area and the village.

FREESTYLERS are offered the delights of the halfpipe and fun park located on the Rosshutte area and reached by taking the funicular train that takes you up to 1800m. The halfpipe is well looked after with nice walls and good transitions for take off's. The fun park is also well maintained and has a decent assortment of man mad hits from which to gain some quality air time from. However, out of the pipe and park, good natural hits are hard to come by.

CARVERS are the ones who can shine the most here. The open wide runs of the **Rosshutte** area are superb for laying out fast turns on.

BEGINNERS have a resort that is in the main all theirs. Very little of the place is out of bounds to novices.

THE TOWN
Off the slopes Seefeld is quaint village with superb local facilities. Five star hotels and well appointed guest houses make up this almost car free hamlet. There are also good sporting attractions as well as decent restaurants and okay bars.

%
OF BEGINNER
TO EXPERT
RUNS

30KM PISTES

5 20 75

2100M
TOP LIFT

900M
VERTICAL

1200M
FIRST LIFT

NUMBER OF RUNS: 36
LONGEST RUN: 6km
TOTAL LIFTS: 25 - 3 Gondolas, 5 chairs,18 drags
LIFT TIMES: 9am to 4pm

AVERAGE SNOWFALL:
3m
SNOWMAKING:
90%

WINTER PERIODS: Dec to April
Lift Passes
Day pass 28 euros, 2 Days 54

FREERIDE 40%
Some scattered trees and ok off-piste
FREESTYLE 15%
A park & pipe
CARVING 45%

Office Seefeld
A-6100 Seefeld
Tel: +43(0)5212/2213
Fax: +43(0)5212/3355
Web:www.seefeld-tirol.com
Email:info@seefeld.at

Train
take the Karwendelbahn from Innsbruck to Garmisch
Fly
Innsbruck 21km away, Munich 138, Zurich 300
Car
East: Highway A12 / Exit Zirl east, head 12km in a northerly direction following the signs for Garmisch Partenkirchen
West: Highway A12 / Exit Telfs east + 12 kms

Pic -Woody

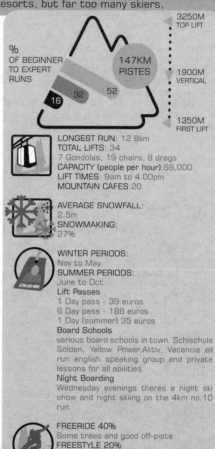

%
OF BEGINNER
TO EXPERT
RUNS

16 32 52

147KM
PISTES

3250M
TOP LIFT

1900M
VERTICAL

1350M
FIRST LIFT

LONGEST RUN: 12.8km
TOTAL LIFTS: 34
7 Gondolas, 19 chairs, 8 drags
CAPACITY (people per hour):66,000
LIFT TIMES: 9am to 4.00pm
MOUNTAIN CAFES:20

AVERAGE SNOWFALL:
2.5m
SNOWMAKING:
27%

WINTER PERIODS:
Nov to May
SUMMER PERIODS:
June to Oct
Lift Passes
1 Day pass - 39 euros
6 Day pass - 188 euros
1 Day (summer) 35 euros
Board Schools
various board schools in town. Schischule
Solden, Yellow Power,Aktiv, Vacancia all
run english speaking group and private
lessons for all abilities.
Night Boarding
Wednesday evenings theres a night ski
show and night skiing on the 4km no.10
run

FREERIDE 40%
Some trees and good off-piste
FREESTYLE 20%
2 parks & a half-pipe
CARVING 40%

Solden Tourism
Otztal Arean, Postfach 80
Solden A-6450. Tirol
General info: +43 (0) 5254 2120
Reservations: +43 (0) 5254 22120
Avalanche info: +43 (0) 512 1588
Web: www.soelden.com
Email: info@soelden.com

This World Class Resort is located 90 km (56 miles) from **Innsbruck** and 40 km (25 miles) from **Ötztal**, and is just down the road from the better known resort of **Obergurgl**. The area consists of "The Big 3" mountains, **Schwarze Schneide, Gaislachkogel** and **Tiefenbachkogel**, which are all over 3000 metres and serviced by high speed lifts with stunning views into Italy from their summits. At the top are 2 glaciers offering Austria's biggest glacial ski area and the mountains offer 147km of pistes, which are all perfectly groomed when the lifts open at 8am. More importantly, there is least double this distance in easily accessible off-piste terrain. One night a week the **Gaislakogel** opens in the evening and you can go nightboarding on a few of the slopes. There is also a big ski / snowboard and firework show on the same night which is worth a look. The **Giggijoch** gondola serves the other end of town and both are linked with a frequent bus service. Every Friday there is a big party at the top of the gondola with bands playing. **Rettenbach** also hosts the Hannibal outdoor musical in April which is a re-enactment of his mission to cross the Alps with an elephant, incorporating 500 actors, a 20 metre snow pyramid, lasers and fireworks. At the bottom of the piste there is the **Salomon station** with a really cool bar upstairs.

FREERIDERS. The **Gaislakogel** mountain is quite limited in terms of high altitude pistes, but there is a large area of off-piste right underneath the gondola in the **Wasserkar valley**. However, this is avalanche prone, so check the risk level before you shred it. There are also routes off the side of this peak down to the **Ski Route**, but it is easy to end up at the top of some very big cliffs so it is advisable to go with a guide ! Off piste under the **Giggijoch** gondola through trees, come to road, walk for 20 minutes,

or you can stop short and join back to the piste at the *Sonnblick bar* and drink a beer before descending. On the way to the glacier from the Giggijoch, be sure to try the **Schwartzseekogl** and make some tracks in the powder on either side. It can be a great run as it is steep and fast but look out for rocks. There is also a large mountain restaurant at the bottom of the run which gets the sun on its huge terrace all

SOLDEN

afternoon. The red run on the **Rettenbach Glacier** is used every year for the opening event of the World Cup Skiing Championship. At the top it is quite steep, which makes it a great place to duck the ropes for overhead powder spray turns, but stay close to the ropes as there are a lot of crevasses here. At least one boarder a year disappears down a crevasse here so remember: don't board off-piste alone, especially on a glacier. Another nice ride is the longest route in the resort which consists of the 12 km run from the top of Rettenbach Glacier onto the Ski Route, past *Phillip's bar* on Route 7 and ending at the **Gaislakogel gondola** station. With snow conditions permitting, it is possible to do most of this trek off-piste and far from the madding crowds. Check out the tracks as you take the **Golden Gateway** gondola to the Glacier to see possible routes down.

FREESTYLERS. There is a large terrain park underneath the Silverstrass Express with 3 different lines of jumps and rails for differing abilities. This is relocated to the Rettenbach glacier in summer for the BASE Boardcamp in June.

BEGINNERS. The main runs at the top of the **Giggijoch** get very mogulled late in the day, but this is where most of the board schools will take you. For the best beginners pistes, proceed through the ski tunnel to reach the Tiefenbach glacier and its huge, wide, cruising blue run which is great for learners or trying out new ground tricks. There are also 2 T bars feeding quiet red runs and some steeper off-piste opportunities.

THE TOWN
Very few English people stay here as there is only one UK package operator servicing the resort, so the place is filled with Dutch and Germans who like to board and party. In contrast to some French resorts, the locals are extremely friendly and very helpful. The town stretches out along the main road for a couple of miles with the 2 main gondolas at the each end of the town. The **Gaislakogel** gondola is in the West, and the **Giggijoch** is in the East. The queues at both of these gondolas can get quite bad, so miss the ski school rush at 9am, or take the small, slow, but tranquil single chair lift hidden away just to the west of the Giggijoch. A swim in the massive pool at the **Freizeital Arena** and a mixed naked sauna there are other evening options. The only amenity this town doesn't have is a laundrette !

Accomodation. Almost 20,000 beds, but it can be extremely difficult to get accommodation here so it is

better to book through the Tourist Office before arriving. If Solden's full then try nearby **Vent** or **Obergurgl**, but you might need a car as the buses finish early. Visit **www.soelden.com** or **www.tiscover.at** for available accomodation.

Night-life. After the lifts close at 4pm, the party

Pic -Woody

commences with most of the après ski bars full of people wanting to do some serious drinking. It is possible to board right to the door of *Marco's bar* which is near the Post Office. This is a great spot to sit outside next to a heater and watch the sun set over the peaks. For more serious partying and dancing on tables there is the *Bla bla Bar* and *Hinterherr* which is opposite the Dutch bar, *Alm Rausch*. These three bars get crowded but the waitresses are highly efficient and manage to constantly ply you with ale. Once you have eaten dinner enjoy a digestif at the *Grizzly bar* which is very chilled with log fires, then go onto the *Lavina* nightclub and dance til 6am or for the best music in town, visit the *Stamperl bar,* which is popular with locals and open to 8am.

Food. There are plenty of restaurants in the town. Those definitely worth visiting are the *Alm Haus* with its wooden exterior and traditional Austrian fodder, the *Nudeltopf* for great pizzas and pasta or *Monty burger* (the only take-away) for fast food so you can carry on partying.

SUMMARY. Sadly the glaciers are regressing fast in the summer due to global warming, and may totally disappear in only twenty years. Therefore you really should go and check it out this season, but please try and keep it our WSG secret !

FLY: Fly to Innsbruck International (85km), transfer time to resort is 1 1/4 hours. Munich (223km) possible, take train to innsbruck, then change for Otzal

BUS: Buses from Innsbruck go direct to Solden with daily return services from Innsbruck train station.

TRAIN: Trains to Otztal (20 minutes).

CAR: Drive via motorway A12 from to Innsbruck to Solden, approx 50 miles (80Km), drive time is about 1 1/4 hours. *From Calais 654 miles (1052 Km). Drive time is around 12 hours.

6 OUT OF 10   Okay for beginners

Pic -Soll Tourism

%
OF BEGINNER
TO EXPERT
RUNS

250KM PISTES

1829M TOP LIFT

1209M VERTICAL

620M FIRST LIFT

9   43   48

NUMBER OF RUNS: 120
TOTAL LIFTS: 91
11 Gondolas, 35 chairs, 45 drags
CAPACITY (people per hour): 130,000
LIFT TIMES: 8.30am to 4.00pm

AVERAGE SNOWFALL:
Unknown
SNOWMAKING:
70%

WINTER PERIODS: Dec to April
Lift Passes
Day 32 euros, 6 Days 157.50 euros
Season 475 euros

FREERIDE 50%
A few trees and some off-piste
FREESTYLE 20%
A park & a half-pipe (in Soll)
CARVING 30%

Web: www.skiwelt.at
Tourismusverband Söll
A-6306 Söll, Dorf 84
Austria
Tel. +43 5333 5216
Fax +43 5333 6180
Web:www.soell.at
Email:info@soell.com

Fly
to Salzburg airport 90 minutes transfer
time.
Car
From Salzburg head south on the routes
21 and 312 to Ellmau on the left, a
45 mile (70km) journey. Drive time
from Calais is 11 1/2 hours. 692 miles
(115km).
Bus
direct from Salzburg airport.

Soll can be summed up in a few simple words: 'traditional appealing village with excellent slopes for beginners'. This is one of Austria's most popular resorts for package tour operators who send ski groups here en-masse. Soll is located a short distance from the resorts of **Ellmau, Scheffau, Going** and nearby **Brixen, Hopfgarten** and **Westendorf**, all of which form part of Austria's largest linked ski and snowboard area, known as the **Ski Welt**. All the resorts are similar in style and character yet still have something different to offer whether it be on the slopes or around one of the traditional styled villages. Soll has two distinctions, one, it's a pretty lame mountain for advanced riders and two, the so called picturesque village offers a high level of good services. The 34km of slopes here are ideal for no hopers and cross-over skiers (those with an identity crisis who don't really want to snowboard but feel they should try it just once so they can boast about there endeavours when they get home). Getting to this resort is very easy from either Salzburg (only 90 minutes away) or Innsbruck; however, trying to appreciate the opportunities on the slopes when you arrive is a different matter. Expert riders will soon tire of the resort while slow carvers and beginners will love it. This is also a cool place if you're on a tight budget and planning to take a cheap package holiday.

FREERIDERS will find this place a bit limiting. However, the black graded slope that runs down from the **Hohe Salve** is not a bad trail and not to be treated too lightly, same goes for the slope under the **Brixen Gondola**.

FREESTYLERS have a halfpipe and terrain park to practice tricks in, but that's about all as the natural freestyle terrain is poor.

CARVERS not wanting to be tested will be happy apart from the fact that the well groomed slopes can often be so busy with skiers that it's impossible to link up more than a few turns.

BEGINNERS are the ones who will appreciate Soll the most.

THE TOWN
Soll is a small village that offers high quality services. The lay-out is not the most convenient for the slopes, you may find your-self staying a fair distance from the base lifts. There are lots of **restaurants** and surprisingly **nightlife** around here can be very good. There is a good choice of bars and a few night spots which are not over-priced just over full with sad skiers doing après crap.

Best resort in Austria, but very snobby

Pic -St Anton Tourism

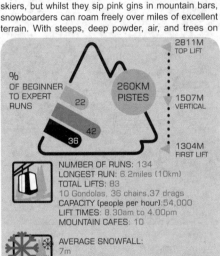

Those who know about where to ride would have to agree that **St Anton** has the best terrain in Austria, making this place an absolute must. This is a resort that has it all and will suite all styles of riding, though favouring freeriders the most. Honestly, the place will suite whether you're a freestyle freak, a piste carving poser, a freeride speed king or simply a nappy-wearing new kid. The area does have the reputation for being expensive and attracting the fur-clad, Ferrari-owning skiers, but whilst they sip pink gins in mountain bars, snowboarders can roam freely over miles of excellent terrain. With steeps, deep powder, air, and trees on

2811M TOP LIFT

%
OF BEGINNER
TO EXPERT
RUNS

22

260KM PISTES

42

36

1507M VERTICAL

1304M FIRST LIFT

NUMBER OF RUNS: 134
LONGEST RUN: 6.2miles (10km)
TOTAL LIFTS: 83
10 Gondolas, 36 chairs,37 drags
CAPACITY (people per hour):54,000
LIFT TIMES: 8.30am to 4.00pm
MOUNTAIN CAFES: 10

AVERAGE SNOWFALL:
7m
SNOWMAKING:
20%

WINTER PERIODS
Dec to April
Lift Passes
1/2 day 29.5 euros
1 Day pass - 39 euros
5 Day pass - 160 euros
Board School
4hr group lesson 53 euros
Private 4hr lesson 209 euros
Hire
Board & Boots around 35 euros a day

FREERIDE 40%
Lots of trees and great off-piste
FREESTYLE 20%
A park & pipe
CARVING 40%

Tourismusverband
A-6580 St.
Anton am Arlberg
Tel. +43 (5446) 2269-0
Fax +43 (5446) 2532
Web:www.stantonamarlberg.com
Email:info@stantonamarlberg.com

all sides of the mountain slopes, it's hard to beat. The **Arlberg ski pass** allows you to ride the linked areas of **St Christoph** and **Stuben**, which also both offer great snowboarding terrain, with amazing amounts of powder.

FREERIDERS are best suited to St Anton as it's the perfect playground, with a little of everything: steeps, powder, trees and big drop offs. Riders who know what they're doing should worm their way up to **Kapall** where they'll find loads of great freeriding terrain, with good natural hits. Alternatively, head to the summit of **Valluga Grat** via the Galzig cable car to reach some major off-piste, with long runs back down to St Anton and St Christoph. Intermediates just getting it together will find loads to ride, especially on **Gampen** and **Kapall**. The runs on **Galzig** are easier, but tend to get busy with skiers. Advanced riders will love Rendl, a separate mountain on the opposite side of St Anton across to the Gampen runs. Whenever there's a fresh dump, expect to find the locals and ski-bums cramming into **Rendlbahn** for first tracks. This area is absolutely amazing for full-on freeriding terrain with tight and open trees and crowd-free slopes.

FREESTYLERS spending a month or two here will never find every natural hit - the resort is simply littered with great take off points and drop ins. It's a great freestyler's place, and if you're not content with the natural stuff, then there's a park and pipe at **Rendl Beach** to play on. Although the pipe is not really that good, it is improving with each new season.

CARVERS are much in evidence on St Anton's slopes. Some are obviously rich Germans who have the kit because they think it's cool, whilst others have heard how good the terrain is for laying big arcs. You can perform here with no trouble on countless well groomed runs like **Osthang**, but in truth, any rider spending more than an hour in hard boots here should have his balls hacked off, since this is a true soft boot resort.

BEGINNERS with a little adventure will be able to handle St Anton, but wimps may have trouble if they stray too far from the easy runs. A learner's slope at Nasserein provides a good starting point for a number of easy blue trails.

THE TOWN
St Anton is with out doubt one of Europe's most prestigious resorts with a reputation for attracting the rich and famous. The place positively stinks with money drenched posers who haven't got the slightest interested in the slopes, they simply come to rub shoulders with their ilk. It should also be pointed out that this is a very expensive resort, infact St Anton is probably the most expensive winter sports destination in all Austria. That said, you at least pay for quality and good local services. For those with the cash, there is a host of local attractions, with numerous shops, banks and sporting facilities.

Accommodation: There's plenty of lodging but nothing cheap and anyone on a low budget will find it hard going. B&B's are available in the hamlets of Bach, St Jakob and Nasserein, all are less expensive than St Anton, there's also a free regular ski-bus linking them.

Food. Got a gold credit card? If yes, proceed to one of the many restaurants, if the answer is no, then Opps' because eating out daily will be beyond most. However, there are some relatively cheap options in the centre of town like the Funky Chicken or Pizzeria Pomodora.

Night-life is lively. Taps which is located on the Gampen home run is where riders chill after a day's ride. Bar Cuba, formerly known as Amadaeus, is a soulless bar with mock terracotta bits and bobs, a cocktail menu and over-excited staff while at the end of the night most end up in either the Platz'l bar or the Postkeller.

Pic -Palmer Snowboards

SUMMARY
The best resort in Austria, with great freeriding for advanced and intermediate riders. The biggest problem is the stuck up snobbery of the place.

FLY
to Innsbruck International, transfer time to resort is 1 1/4 hours
BUS
from Innsbruck go direct to St Anton with daily return services from Innsbruck.
TRAIN
direct to St Anton center
CAR
Drive to Innsbruck via Landeck. St Anton is 61 miles (98Km), Drive time is about 1 1/4 hours.
*From Calais 618 miles (994 km), Drive time is around 11 hours.

St Johann in Tirol is **Austrian** through and through, read any one of the numerous ski guides and see how this place is often described as 'quaint, charming, traditional, lovely and picturesque. And while these points are true, the important factor is, what has this traditional

Pic : St Johann Tourism

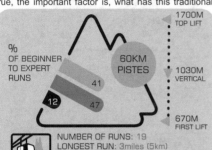

% OF BEGINNER TO EXPERT RUNS

1700M TOP LIFT
1030M VERTICAL
670M FIRST LIFT

60KM PISTES

41
12
47

NUMBER OF RUNS: 19
LONGEST RUN: 3miles (5km)
TOTAL LIFTS: 17
2 Cable-cars, 6 chairs,9 drags
CAPACITY (people per hour):20,000
LIFT TIMES: 8.30am to 4.00pm

AVERAGE SNOWFALL:
5.6m
SNOWMAKING:
45%

WINTER PERIODS
Dec to April
Lift Passes
1/2 day 24 euros
1 Day Pass - 29 euros
6 Day Pass - 149 euros
Board School
Full day lesson 50 euros, 6 days 141 euros
1/2 day 30 euros

FREERIDE 30%
Trees but no decent off-piste
FREESTYLE 20%
A park & pipe
CARVING 50%

St Johann Tourist Office
Poststraße 2
A-6380 St.Johann in Tirol, Austria
Tel +43(5352)63335 0
Fax +43(5352)65200
Web:www.bergbahnen-stjohann.at
Email:info@stjohanntirol.at

Bus
services run regulary from the airport daily.
Fly
to Salzburg - 90 minutes away
Car
From Salzburg head south on the route 312 direction Worgl to reach the resort. Drive time from Calais is 11 3/4 hours. 672 miles (1082km).

village to offer visiting snowboarderds?. Well St Johann has some 60km of well groomed and well marked out pistes to ride serviced by a modern lift system comprising of 3 gondolas, 4 chair lifts and 10 drag lifts. An important point to note about St Johann is that this is a very popular resort with a large number of British and German visitors. The resort is usually buzzing through the winter months especially over the Christmas and new year periods and from mid January through to the end of March. Although this is not a high altitude resort, St Johann can still boast a decent annual snow record of over 780cm a season and should the real stuff not fall, the resort has snowmaking facilities that cover over 47% of the marked out slopes. In terms of terrain, an advanced rider will have this place licked within a matter of two days, intermediates four days while beginners will enjoy a full week exploring the slopes, which are collection of reds, a handful of blacks and a load of easy blues. Still slope facilities are very good and the unusually for a place of this size, there are some 15 mountain cafes and bars. Another plus side for St Johann is that this is a cheap resort and very affordable resort.

FREERIDERS, if you are a basic intermediate freerider then this mountain will suit you and should provided you will a number of intresting options that should easily take a week to muster. The best thing for advanced riders to do is check out the offerings at the nearby resorts of **Kitzbuhel** or **Saalbach-Hinterglem.**
FREESTYLERS have fairly decent halfpipe and terrain park to play in. Whilst around the slopes riders will be able to find plenty of good natural hits to get air from. But by any stretch of the imagination this is not an adventrious freestylers place.
CARVERS, are presented with a number of well pisted trails on which some fast carving can be had.
BEGINNERS who holiday with their parents and don't plan to do a lot of riding in their lives will love this place as its perfect for novices.

THE TOWN
Around the town you will find lots of hotels, Pensions (B&B's) and other local services close to the slopes and at affordable prices. Nightlife options are excellent with a good choice of bars and restaurants to choose from.

83

7 OUT OF 10

Good open flat runs, but can get crowded at weekends

Pic: Doppelmayr/Bohler

% OF BEGINNER TO EXPERT RUNS

3200M TOP LIFT

110KM PISTES

1500M VERTICAL

23 54

23

1721M FIRST LIFT

NUMBER OF RUNS: 22
LONGEST RUN: 6miles (10km)
TOTAL LIFTS: 19 - 5 Gondolas, 8 chairs,9 drags,3 Magic carpets
CAPACITY (people per hour):36,000
LIFT TIMES: 8.00am to 4.45pm
MOUNTAIN CAFES: 9

AVERAGE SNOWFALL:Unknown
SNOWMAKING:10%

WINTER PERIODS: Dec to April
SUMMER PERIODS: May to Nov
Lift Passes
1 Day 34.5 euros ,6 Days 172.7 euros
Board Schools
1 day 60 euros,4 days 139 euros
Hire
board & boots 24-37 euros for 1 day

FREERIDE 35%
A couple of trees and some off-piste
FREESTYLE 15%
A park & a pipe (not all year)
CARVING 50%

Staubi Gletsvherbahn
A-6167 Neustiff im Stubaital
Tel. +43 (0) 52 26 81 41
Web:www.stubai-gletscher.com
Email:info@stubai-gletscher.com

Train
The nearest train station is Innsbruck.
Fly
to Innsbruck airport, 40 mins away.
Car
Drive Via Innsbruck, head south on the A13 toll road until the Staubi turn off at Mieders. Then head up the B183 to Staubi.
Bus
Free buses daily between Schönberg & Stubai

NEW

New for 04/05 season
new 8 seater cable car from top station 'Eisgrat' to the 'Top of Tyrol', the highest point on the glacier ski area at 3,165m

Stubai Glacier is the biggest resort under the Innsbruck area. It's also the only **Innsbruck** resort that has summer snowboarding. Stubai is a great mountain to try and offers the chance to ride fast on wide, open runs that are well groomed and serviced by a set of efficient, modern lifts. The only drawbacks are that, being a high glacier resort, it can be stupidly cold in the winter where the temperature can make it almost impossible to ride, and there's very little tree cover. The other problem is that because Stubai nearly always guarantees snow when lower areas are short on the stuff, the masses head here, making the place very busy, especially at weekends. Munich is only two and a half hours away and so the place also gets a regular German overload. Access to the slopes involves a twenty minute cable car ride, but once up, you're presented with a great selection of runs. There's 2 rental places at the top of the eisgrat and gamsgarten gondolas, they promise a 20 minute service while you take a beer.

FREERIDERS will find an abundance of trails to ride, but none of them are too demanding and lack a bit of variety. The 4 black runs on offer are pretty short, but trail 8 should keep you on your toes. The majority of the resort is above tree level, the only trees are below the **Mittelstation**, just watch out for crevaces and avalanches. From the gondolas you should be able to pick a few nice decents and drops without hiking. The **Wilde Grubn** is a 10k run back to the base, its not always properly marked so make sure you know where you're heading.

FREESTYLERS have a park & halfpipe but its not particularly well maintained and a little hit and miss. You'll find plenty of natural hits all over the place though. CARVERS; you'll love this place; there's plenty of nice wide, well maintained pistes available. The management take great care in preparing the slopes; they don't just piste bash at night, but throughout the day, so there's plenty of opportunity to cut the corduroy. BEGINNERS are well taken care of with a number of perfectly well-appointed, easy, flat blue runs. But watch out for the drag lifts. For the tots and the seriously bad, they've added a number of magic carpet lifts, and they're even covered.

THE TOWN
Theres many small villages on the road to Stubai, the main one of note being **Neusift**, a 20 minute drive from the glacier. There you'll find a good selection of hotels and pensions, some bars and restaurants. Probably the best place to stay is in Innsbruck, although it takes about an hour by car to get there.

WILDESCHONA VALLEY

Beginner and intermediate area

The Wildschonau Valley, which is located in the **Kitzbuheler Alps**, is home to a number of tiny and traditional Austrian resorts. **Niederau, Oberau, Thierbach** and **Auffach** may all seem on the surface to be to small to bother with, but first impressions are often deceptive. Okay none of the resorts that make up this part of the **Tirol** are extensive or in any way adventurous. However, what this collection of novice and intermediate mountain retreats do provide, is an area that's relaxed, void of any crowds, very laid back and with out any of the hustle and bustle of the bigger and more popular destinations favoured by the tour operators and ski crowds. This collection of resorts would be idea for a family group on a weeks holiday, but would not appeal to hard-core riders in terms of the mountain or larger louts looking for an action packed resort bustling with night life. The majority of visitors here are either cross country skiers or middle aged downhill skiers. But

Pic -Wildschona Tourism

with most things, there's always something that will appeal to most and although there are only a couple of black graded runs, proficient riders will be able to take advantage of the reds that are open planed and free of crowds. No one queues up long around here, and although none of the resorts link up on the slopes, getting around them is easy.

AUFFACH is the larger of the four resorts with around 20km of marked piste set out on the **Schatzberg** mountain slopes. Auffach offers the highest altitude riding in the area with a nice series of red runs set out over a wide open plateau. This is also the home to the areas main halfpipe and fun park, which are located up on the upper regions. One point to note about Auffach is that 99% of the lifts are drag lifts, so be warned novices.

NIEDERAU is the second largest with just 14km of piste and is the first resort you come to along the valley floor. The slopes have one black run and some okay reds and all in all this place can be ridden with ease in day.

OBERAU is basically a place for total beginners with only 10km of piste and just 8 runs. There is simply nothing here for intermediates of advanced riders to really try out.

THIERBACH is much the same as Oberau, and really only of interest to first time skiing grannies and grand dads. Even novices may even have this place licked after a few hours.

THE TOWN
Off the slopes you are presented with typical Tyrolean hospitality. All the resorts have accommodation close to slopes and offer good quality hotels, chalets, farm accommodation and pensions. Everything about this area is laid back and basic, so don't expect a large amount of facilities. There are a few restaurants, but night life is extremely tame, although still very good and affordable.

1900M
TOP LIFT

%
OF BEGINNER
TO EXPERT
RUNS

47KM
PISTES

40

590M
VERTICAL

5

55

828M
FIRST LIFT

NUMBER OF RUNS: 39
LONGEST RUN: 3.1m(5km)
TOTAL LIFTS: 28
2 Gondolas, 24 chairs, 2 drags
LIFT TIMES: 8.30am to 4.00pm

AVERAGE SNOWFALL
Unknown
SNOWMAKING
20%

WINTER PERIODS
Dec to April
Lift Passes
1 Day 30 euros

FREERIDE 40%
Scattered trees and limited off-piste
FREESTYLE 10%
A park & pipe
CARVING 50%

Wildschonau Tourism
A-6311 Wildschonau.
++43 (0) 5339 8255-0
Web:www.Wildschonau.com

Fly
to Innsbruck airport, 50 mins away.

ZELL AM SEE

Not a bad resort but too busy

Pic -Ride Snowboards

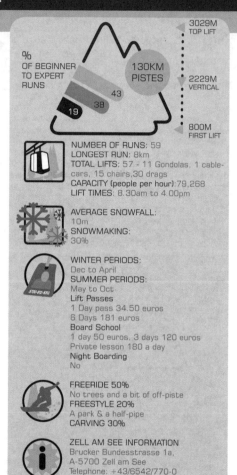

%
OF BEGINNER
TO EXPERT
RUNS

130KM PISTES

43
38
19

3029M
TOP LIFT

2229M
VERTICAL

800M
FIRST LIFT

NUMBER OF RUNS: 59
LONGEST RUN: 8km
TOTAL LIFTS: 57 - 11 Gondolas, 1 cable-cars, 15 chairs, 30 drags
CAPACITY (people per hour): 79,268
LIFT TIMES: 8.30am to 4.00pm

AVERAGE SNOWFALL:
10m
SNOWMAKING:
30%

WINTER PERIODS:
Dec to April
SUMMER PERIODS:
May to Oct
Lift Passes
1 Day pass 34.50 euros
6 Days 181 euros
Board School
1 day 50 euros, 3 days 120 euros
Private lesson 180 a day
Night Boarding
No

FREERIDE 50%
No trees and a bit of off-piste
FREESTYLE 20%
A park & a half-pipe
CARVING 30%

ZELL AM SEE INFORMATION
Brucker Bundesstrasse 1a,
A-5700 Zell am See
Telephone: +43/6542/770-0
Fax: +43/6542/72032
web: www.zellamsee.com
Email:welcome@europasportregion.info

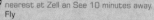

Train
nearest at Zell an See 10 minutes away.
Fly
to Salzburg, 1 1/2 hours transfer.
Car
from Salzburg head south on the A10 to exit 46. Then head south west along the 168 via Taxenbach before turning left up to Kaprun (56 miles).

Zell am See is located close to a large lake and not far from the glacier resort of **Kaprun**. Zell offers over 130km of marked out piste, much of which is treelined. A third of the runs are covered by snowmaking facilities, which is a good thing, as this resort doesn't have the greatest annual snow record. This resort has long been popular with snowboarders in Austria and has always been welcoming. The management do frown when it comes to riding in the trees, as you are not allowed to snowboard through the wooded sections. In general this is a pretty good snowboarders resort with the added advantage of a glacier at Kaprun just down the road should the snow here turn out to be crap or you simply fancy a change. Zell's main disadvantage is its own popularity as it's high on tour operators lists and therefore very crowded. Each Saturday the resort sees a fresh intake of thousands of two plankers in their new holiday clothes ready to make a mess of the overnight grooming of the pistes. Whatever level of a rider you are or whatever style of riding you do, this place will give you the opportunity to practice your skills, and most people will be able to make a 5 day trip well worthwhile

FREERIDERS have a varying selection of runs to choose from. Advanced riders may want to take the cable car up to the **Berghotel** where you will be able to gain access to a couple of good steep sections. There are also a number of cool runs down the **Sonnkogel**. If you are looking for deep powder and open bowl riding, then head on up to the glacier at **Kaprun**.

FREESTYLERS can choose to ride the pipe and park at Zell or try out the same at Kaprun, which has a pipe all year round. Around Zell locals often build their own hits but if you can't be bothered, you will be able to find lots of stuff to fly from.

CARVERS have an ordinary mountain to cut up with plenty of well groomed trails to try out, more so at Zell than at Kaprun.

BEGINNERS have lots of nursery areas as well as spots that allow for easy progression making this a good novice resorts.

THE TOWN

Zell am See is a busy village with a lot going on and plenty of accommodation at all price ranges. The village is a lively one and as well as having loads of restaurants, mainly hotel ones. **Night- life** here is also quite good with some okay bars to check out.

ZELL AM ZILLER

Okay beginners & intermediates area

Zell am Ziller is situated in the spectacular **Zell Valley** which is a mere 40 miles from **Innsbruck**. What you have here is a traditional Austrian village set out over the valley floor with ridable slopes that rise to a respectable high point of 2480m. Zell am Ziller forms part of what is known as the **Zillertal Arena** which along with resorts such as **Gerlos** and **Konigsleiten/Wald** offers some 450km of terrain, and although the 150 plus lifts are not all linked on the slopes, they are linked by a single lift ticket which costs from E115 for 5 days. All the resorts that form part of the arena have something different to offer but in general this area can best be described as suiting intermediate freeriders and piste loving carvers. Zell and its neigh-

bouring resorts are all well designed and spread out giving a nice sense of open space but note, this open space attracts quite a lot of weekend skiers, although in general lift lines are not very big apart from the early morning first gondola ride up from the village. Zell's terrain is spread out above the tree line offering some wide open runs and some nice off-piste powder areas. Most of the upper runs are graded red, but some of them are a bit over rated and there's not a great deal for expert riders to ride down.

FREERIDERS can spend a week here and still not ride half of what is available through out the Zillertal Arena. With much of the terrain best suited to intermediates, what freeriders can achieve is a fun easy time that will allow them to explore some cool off-piste areas that on occasions has some deep powder stashes. You will also be able to shred down some decent gullies and through some open tree sections. The **Krimml Express** chair gives access to a really cool long red trail that can be ridden either back to **Zell** or down into the connecting resort of **Gerlos.**

FREESTYLERS are best provided with facilities at **Gerlos** under the name of **'Boarders Town'. Gerlos** has a 400 metre fun park which is packed with obstacles and shaped by a modern pipe draggon. There is also a boardercross circuit and a decent halfpipe.

CARVERS have mountain that should keep then happy for the duration of their stay be it a week or two. The pistes are well maintained and there are some nice long trails.

BEGINNERS are the ones who should appreciate this area the most because this is a first class beginners resort and any novice spending a week here will leave a competent intermediate rider.

THE TOWN
Off the slopes Zell has good local services with affordable accommodation, shops, restaurants, a post office and sporting facilities all next to the slopes. Nightlife is very quite but there is a disco should you want to strut your stuff.

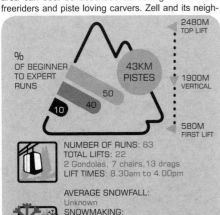

%
OF BEGINNER
TO EXPERT
RUNS

43KM
PISTES

10
40
50

2480M
TOP LIFT

1900M
VERTICAL

580M
FIRST LIFT

NUMBER OF RUNS: 63
TOTAL LIFTS: 22
2 Gondolas, 7 chairs, 13 drags
LIFT TIMES: 8.30am to 4.00pm

AVERAGE SNOWFALL:
Unknown
SNOWMAKING:
2%

WINTER PERIODS:
Dec to April
Hire
Board & boots 24 euros per day
Board School
3 day 2hrs per day lesson 80-94 euros
Private lesson 35 euros per hour

FREERIDE 50%
A few trees and some okay off-piste
FREESTYLE 40%
A park & a half-pipe
CARVING 10%

Zell im Zillertal
A-6280 Zell im Zillertal
Tel: + 43 05282 2281
Web:www.zell.at
Email:info@zell.at

Fly
to Innsbruck airport which is only 50 minutes from Zell. You can also take a train into Zell am Ziller.

8 OUT OF 10

Great freeriding resort

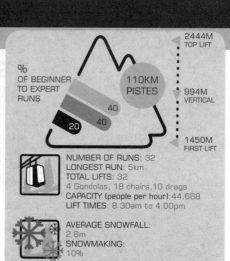

Pic Lech/Zurs Tourism

%
OF BEGINNER
TO EXPERT
RUNS

40
40
20

110KM
PISTES

2444M
TOP LIFT

994M
VERTICAL

1450M
FIRST LIFT

NUMBER OF RUNS: 32
LONGEST RUN: 5km
TOTAL LIFTS: 32
4 Gondolas, 18 chairs, 10 drags
CAPACITY (people per hour): 44,668
LIFT TIMES: 8.30am to 4.00pm

AVERAGE SNOWFALL:
2.6m
SNOWMAKING:
10%

WINTER PERIODS: Dec to April
Lift Passes
Day pass 39 euros
6 Days 184
Heliboarding
take-off from Kriegerhorn / Oberlech and
from Flexenpass (Zürs) to two peaks:
Mehlsack, Orgelscharte
Night Boarding
No

FREERIDE 50%
Some trees and good off-piste
FREESTYLE 20%
A park & a half-pipe
CARVING 30%

Lech-Tourismus
6764 Lech
Tel: +43 (0)5583 2161-0
Fax: +43 (0)5583 3155
Web:www.lech-zuers.at
Email:info@lech-zuers.at

Train
station Langen am Arlberg 17 km away
Fly
to Innsbruck (110km) , 2hrs transfer.
Friedrichshafen, 120km. Altenrhein, 100km.
Zurich, 200km. For about 2000 euros, you
can get a helicopter from Zurich to Lech ...
Car
via Innsbruck, head west on the A12 to
Landeck then take the 316 via St.Anton
to reach Lech

Who knows or cares what Zurs means in Austrian; what we can tell you is that in plain English, Zurs stands for super-sad, super-rich, super ponces, and the worst level of stuck-up skiers known to man. This relatively small resort is in the same locality as that other fur-dripping hangout, **Lech**. However, on a more positive side, the slopes are surprisingly free of champagne-drinking 'wa wa's', which means that riders can roam freely over some excellent slopes. Zurs is without doubt, one of Austria's most spectacular resorts and could rival any in Europe when it comes to the type of terrain it has to offer. Its diverse and interesting slopes make it a great place to snowboard, offering powder fields and miles of pistes

FREERIDERS will literally be able to pick a line as they travel on a chair lift over vast areas of untracked mountain. You're never far away from marked areas and the lifts, so no hiking is involved with this side of the mountain. There are so many ways down that there aren't really any no-go areas; just be careful and pay attention to the avalanche warnings. Alternatively, the other side of the valley which makes up the resort, has plenty of long, steep pistes, gullies and chutes - take a piste map with you.
FREESTYLERS would do well to check out the 300 metre pipe and park area on Lech's slopes. However, Zurs has a lot of good natural terrain for grabbing big air. There are loads of cliff drops of various sizes, and plenty of banked walls to pull off tricks.
CARVERS will find lots of challenging terrain. The marked-out slopes are groomed to perfection, and perfect corduroy tracks are left just waiting to be sliced up at Mach 6.
BEGINNERS-although Zurs is primarily an intermediate/advanced freeriding area, some of the lower slopes offer perfect conditions for learning. The lifts are slow, but redeemed by the generally patient and friendly lift attendants (yes, they do exist!).

THE TOWN
Lodging, eating and drinking in **Zurs** is classicly Austrian, and will burn a big hole in your wallet. You can stay out of Zurs in neighbouring villages that are far cheaper and have a better local feel to them, offering a more relaxed atmosphere. In Zurs, the streets are littered with poodle-carrying idiots in search of posh hangouts, but you'll be surprised at how many snowboarders you'll come across, so don't be too put off by the hideous reputation. Zurs is definitely worth a visit.

AUFFACH

Auffach is a tiny, relatively boring resort, that will please family ski groups. Auffach has a joint lift pass with neighbouring areas, which is a good thing because there's a nothing here for riders with any know-how. However, Auffach is good for beginners. About town, theres okay slopeside lodging available

BAD HOFGASTEIN

Bad Hofgastein is located centrally in the Salzburg region, and forms part of one of Austria's largest rideable areas. Intermediate carvers are well suited to these slopes, with a nice long seven mile run to practice some wide carves. Total beginners will love it, and its not bad for freestylers with a good pipe. There is plenty of slopeside lodging and good local services

BAD MITTENDORF

Bad Mittendorf is a spa town that likes to shroud itself in strange old tales. What isn't fiction is that this is not the greatest of snowboard destinations. The 15 miles of piste rarely allows an adrenalin rush, although there are a couple of okay black trails and the odd red that's worth a look. Crap for freestylers but perfect for beginners.
Off the slopes you will find simple and affordable slopeside accommodation and services.

Ride Area: 16miles of pistes
Total Lifts: 20

IGLS

Igls is perched high above Innsbruck, 3 miles from the city centre. There's nothing here,

especially for competent riders. This is a beginner's area with half a dozen trails easily accessed by a cable car.

Ride Area: 120miles
Easy 20%
Intermediate 50%
Advanced 30%
Top Lift: 2247m
Total Lifts: 35
Contact:
Igls Tourist Office
Hilberstra'e 15
Postfach Igls, PLZ 6080
A-6080 Igls, Austria
Tel: ++43 512 377101
Fax: ++43 512 3771017

KAUNERTAL

Kaunertal is a glacial resort open all year round. Overall, the terrain is great for novices but a bit dull for advanced riders. What you get is a mixture of easy freeriding with powder areas and excellent carving terrain. K Freestylers have one of the most perfectly shaped halfpipes on the planet. What you get is a mixture of easy **freeriding** with powder areas and excellent carving terrain. **Freestylers** have one of the most perfectly shaped halfpipes on the planet.
Lodging and local services can be found at Feichten, 16 miles down the valley, so a car is a must

Ride Area: 12miles
Easy 20%
Intermediate 50%
Advanced 30%
Top Lift: 3160m
Total Lifts: 7
Contact:
Kaunertal-Kauns-Kaunerberg tourist information office
Feichten 134
A-6524 Kaunertal,Austria
Tel: +43 5475 2920
Fax: +43 5475 2929

MUTTERS

Mutters is a small rideable area nestled between Innsbruck and Axamer Lizum. But this is no match for Axams, which can be reached with a backcountry hike. There are only a few runs, mainly suited to beginners and intermediates. Mutters attracts a lot of cross-country skiers. Great local facilities in Innsbruck, 20 mins.

Ride Area: 6miles
Top Lift: 1800m
Total Lifts: 8
Contact:
Mutters Tourist Board
Kirchplatz 11
A-6162 Mutters,
Austria
Tel: +43 512 548410
Fax: +43 512 5484107

NIEDERAU/OBERAU

Niederau/Oberau are two tiny hamlets with little interest for snowboarders.g Freeriders have nothing of real note, although the blacks under the gondola are not for the squeamish. **Freeriders** have nothing of real note, although the blacks under the gondola are not for the squeamish. **Carvers** who can ride will have this place done by lunch. Perfect for **beginners**. Good slope side local services.

Ride Area: 25miles
Top Lift: 1600m
Total Lifts: 28
Contact:
Schmiedeweg 10
82496 Oberau
Tel - +49-(0)8824 / 93973
Fax - +49-(0)8824 / 8890

OBERTAUREN

Just when you thought that Austria was all the same, along comes Obertauren, noted for its excellent snow records.h The terrain here is very much freeride-orientated with lots of areas to check out suited to all levels. The terrain here is very much **freeride**-orientated with lots of areas to check out suited to all levels. **Freestylers** have a pipe.Advanced riders have plenty

89

of good, testing blacks where **carvers** can leave some nice lines. **Novices** have good areas. Excellent lodging and local facilities are at the base of the slopes.

Contact:
Obertauern Tourist Board
A-5562
Obertauern,
Austria
Tel: ++ 43/6456/7252 or 7320
Fax: ++ 43/6456/7515
www.obertauern.com
Getting there:
Fly to: Salzburg - 1 1/4 hours away

PITZAL

Pitzal is a high altitude resort, allowing for summer riding on the Pitztal Glacier. The glacier is reached by an unusual funicular train that travels through the mountain, and gives access to good, intermediate **carving** runs and off-piste **freeride** areas. Set aside is a 4 mile snowboard-only area with a good **pipe** and **fun-park**. There's even a kid's park! Local services in **St Leonard** are in a basic Austrian format

Ride Area: 97km
Top Lift: 3440m
Bottom Lift: 1600m
Total Lifts: 12
Lift pass: 1/2 Day Pass - $25 Day Pass - $31.50
Lift times: 9.00am to 9.00pm
Hire: Board & Boots $33
School: Private lesson $30 per hour
Group lesson $20 per hour
Contact:

Pitzal Tourist Office
Pitztaler Stra?e
6473 Pitztal
Austria
Tel: +43 5414 86999
Fax: +43 5414 86999 88
Getting there:
Fly to: Salzburg - 20 minutes away

SCHRUNS

Schruns is a tiny resort close to the Swiss boarder. The slopes make for an okay one day visit if you can ride or a week if you can't. The place only has one noted black trail but it also has a long 8 mile run which will keep an intermediate **freerider** happy. Great place for **begiunners** but crap for freestylers.
Very basic but good local facilities at the base of the slopes.

Ride Area: 13miles
Top Lift: 2400m
Total Lifts: 13
Contact:
Tel - ++43 (0) 556 721 660
Fax - 0043 (0)5556/72554
Getting there:
Fly to: Innsbruck - 2 hours away

SERFUS

Serfus is a cool place with a decent mountain. Overall, the area provides good all-round snowboarding, no matter your style or standard. Well appointed and affordable local services.

Ride Area: 50miles
Top Lift: 1427m
Total Lifts: 21
Contact:
Serfaus Tourist Board
Untere Dorfstra'e 13
A-6534 Serfaus,
Austria
Tel: +43 (0) 5476 / 62390
Fax: +43 (0) 5476 / 6813
Getting there:
Fly to: Zurich - 120 minutes away

ST CHRISTOPH

St Christoph is a small, glitzy outpost in the Arlberg close to its far more famous cousin, **St Anton**, and like its neighbour, this is a money mountain that provides great slopes with miles of

backcountry freeriding, and natural freestyle terrain. **Advanced riders** have enough runs to keep them occupied for a week, while **carvers** have more than enough to last them a month. Great for **beginners**. **Off the slopes** you'll pay dearly for everything

Ride Area: 40miles
Top Lift: 2811m
Total Lifts: 86
Getting there:
Fly to: Innsbruck - 11/2 hours away

ST WOLFGANG

St Wolfgang put simply, is not a good snowboarding resort. There is nothing much here, not even for beginners. Granny may manage a few turns, but others will soon tire of it. Freestylers do have a small park and pipe, but don't blink or you'll miss it. In truth, this is a family-orientated, beginner's ski resort. On the slopes theres lots of close by accommodation

Ride Area: 24km
Top Lift: 1600m
Bottom Lift: 1200m
Total Lifts: 9
Contact:
St Wolfgang Tourist Office
Postfach 20
A-5360 St. Wolfgang
Austria
Tel: +43 6138 2239
Fax: +43 6138 2239 81
Getting there:
Fly to: Salzburg - 45 minutes away

WAGRAIN

As a base to reach any one of a dozen other ride areas, offering over 200 miles of linked cool, freeriding terrain, with a number of good parks and pipes, then this is a great place to be. Piste-hugging **carvers**, are also spoilt for choice here with dozens of well groomed trails. **Beginners** are spoilt for choice. **Off the slopes**, it's Austrian picture postcard stuff, but dull.

Top Lift: 2109m
Bottom Lift: 850m
Total Lifts: 9
Contact:

Bergbahnen AG Wagrain
Markt 59,
A-5602 Wagrain
Tel - ++43 6413 8238
Fax - ++43 6413 8238 11
Getting there:
Fly to: Salzburg - 60 minutes away

WALDRING

Waldring is a dull, geriatric heaven, and of interest only to those who are brain-dead. Its only saving grace is that the place is close to other resorts so you can at least escape the tedium of the place. Anyone planning more than an hour's stay here needs to see a shrink.
Local services consist of a few old people's homes and a morgue.

Ride Area: 16 miles
Top Lift: 1900m
Total Lifts: 12
Contact:
Ferienwohnungen & Komfortzimmer Mitterer
Pillerseestra_e 33
A-6384 Waidring
Tel: ++43 (0) 5353 5616
Getting there:
Fly to: Salzburg - 60 minutes away

WESTENDORF

Westendorf is all but the same as its nearby neighbours, Soll and Ellmau.7 There are a couple of black trails for advanced riders._ Unlike Ellmau, however, there is at least a decent halfpipe and park for air heads to try out. e Carvers also have a good choice of trails on which to practice the art of signing snow with an edge. There are a couple of black trails for **advanced** riders.Unlike **Ellmau**, however, there is at least a decent halfpipe and park for air heads to try out. **Carvers** also have a good choice of trails on which to practice the art of signing snow with an edge. Good **beginner's** areas.
Local services at the base of the slopes are cheap and cheerful.

Ride Area: 25 miles
Top Lift: 1865m
Total Lifts: 14
Contact:
Michaela Zass/Christl Beihammer

Pfarrgasse 1
PLZ A-6363
A-6363 Westendorf
Austria
Tel: +43 5334 6230
Fax: +43 5334 2390
Getting there:
Fly to: Salzburg - 120 minutes away

WINDISCHGARSTEN

Forget it totally. This place is crap

Ride Area: 4 runs
Getting there:
Fly to: Salzburg - 120 minutes away

ZAMS

Zams is a relatively unknown and small resort. There's a grand total of eight runs, all suited to beginners going backwards. The best thing to do is pass by and check out the **Kaunertal Glacier** which is far better. **Off the slopes** forget it, the place may be traditionally Austrian, but it is dull.

Ride Area: 26km
Runs: 16
Top Lift: 2212m
Bottom Lift: 780m
Total Lifts: 8
Easy 50%
Intermediate 40%
Advanced 10%
Contact:
Zams Tourist Board
Hauptplatz 6
A-6511 ZAMS
Tel - +43-(5442)633 95
Fax - +43-(5442)633 95 15
Getting there:
Fly to: Salzburg - 90 minutes away.

Capital City: Sofia
Population: 7.5 million
Highest Peak: Musala 2925m
Language: Bulgarian
Legal Drink Age: 18
Drug Laws: Cannabis is illegal and frowned upon
Age of consent: 16
Electricity: 240 Volts AC 2-pin
International Dialing Code: +359

Currency: Lev (BGL)
Exchange Rate:
UK£1 = 2.9
EURO = 2
US$1 = 1.25

Driving Guide
All vehicles drive on the right hand side of the road
Speed limits:
60 kph - towns
80kph - main roads
120kph - motorways
Emergency
Police - 166
Fire - 160
Ambulance - 150
Tolls
All 4 lane motorways have tolls of 2 leva per km
Documentation
Driving license, insurance and vehicle registration, along with your passport.

Time Zone
UTC/GMT +2 hours
Daylight saving time: +1 hour

Bulgaria Snowboard Federation
Sofia 1606
51 Skobelev blvd.
Phone / Fax:++359 2 9522 015
Web: http://bgsf.dir.bg/dynamic.html
Email: bgsf@mail.orbitel.bg

Throughout Eastern Europe there are loads of amazing snowboard destinations located in high mountain areas. However, the biggest problem in this part of the world is who's shooting who in order to be president. One minute you have a top resort and the next it's a battle ground. Still if you decide to try out the east then remember that on the whole, travel can be a nightmare and most places have bugger all services with undeveloped resorts. But the big plus for this part of Europe are the costs, cheap to the extreme is the easiest way to put it, with prices so low it's worth ducking and diving from the odd stray bullet.

Bulgaria (which is not a war torn part of eastern) is ahead of its neighbours in attracting westerners to sample its winter hospitality with a number of resorts which provide a good and a far cheaper alternative to many of the resorts in the Western Europe. Travelling to Bulgaria should pose no real problems with international flights arriving at the capital of Sofia. Note for entering Bulgaria visitors from EU member countries don't need a visa Another point, forget about credit cards, although there are not widely accepted, you're better off with hard cash, US Dollars are the best currency for changing into Lev's. On the slopes, piste preparation is not hot and mountain facilities are primitive but prices are very low and the pistes are un-crowded. A number of tour operators offer package tours to Bulgaria with great budget deals available.

Freeriders will enjoy the unpredictable and uneven terrain features found in most rideable places but freestylers will be left a little disappointed if big pipes and man made terrain parks are your thing. Such things are almost none existent however lots of natural freestyle terrain is available along with some very big cliff jump areas.

The best way of travelling in Eastern Europe, is to hire a car or bring your own reliable vehicle. Always check with the national embassy to get the latest facts about travel in Bulgaria or any other part of Eastern Europe. Overall, resort's services are very basic with low key primitive accommodation, restaurants and amenities. Locals in many parts of the east have never seen westerners and on the whole are very friendly and will look after you, especially if you flash a few dollars.

5 OUT OF 10

Basic but cheap resort

%
OF BEGINNER
TO EXPERT
RUNS

2543M
TOP LIFT

40KM
OF PISTES

32

4

64

1226M
VERTICAL

1317M
FIRST LIFT

NUMBER OF RUNS: 20
LONGEST RUN: 6km
TOTAL LIFTS: 15
1 Gondola, 2 chairs, 12 t-bars
CAPACITY (people per hour): 9750
LIFT TIMES:
8.30am to 4.30pm

AVERAGE SNOWFALL
Unknown
SNOWMAKING
some

WINTER PERIODS
Dec to April
SUMMER PERIODS
None
Lift Passes
1 Day pass - 12BGL
3 Day pass - 20BGL
6 Day pass - 60BGL
Hire/Board Schools
Yes/Yes
Night Boarding
Yes

FREERIDE 40%
Few trees and no good off-piste
FREESTYLE 10%
1 halfpipe
CARVING 50%

FLY
Fly to Plovdiv airport 71 miles (115 km)
BUS
Bus services from Sofia are possible
direct to Borvets with a transfer time of
around 2 1/2 hours.
CAR
Via Sofia, take the route 82 south out of
the city via the town of Pancharevo and
Samokov to reach Borovets.

Tourist office Borovets
Balkantourist, Borovets 2010, Bulgaria
Tel: ++359 (0) 2 835 219
Web: www.borovets-bg.com
Email: rila@borovets-bg.com

New for 2004/5
2 new 4-chair lifts replacing a drag & one
of the older 2 man lifts. New 12km ski-
run, increase in snowmaking.

Pic -Bulgaria Tourism

Borovets is the best known of the Bulgarian Resorts, with a wide range of facilities and on one of the highest rideable areas in Eastern Europe. Locals say that the season comes late in Borovets: mid-February often sees only half the runs open, but riders in the know say that April has the best snow. The terrain is mainly suited to intermediate carvers, with nothing too challenging for the experienced. The 23 miles of piste is split into three areas, offering open runs and lines through trees. Hard packed snow and ice frequently make the runs tough work and with small rocks sticking out when there's poor snow cover, a little vigilance is essential. Some of the best riding can be found on the runs above the 2500m point. The 6 person gondola ride to the top station takes about 25 minutes and to avoid queues avoid the period between 9am and 11am. A tip for those on a package trip is to buy your lift ticket before you arrive, it could save you $20.

FREERIDER'S favourite spot is an off-piste run down under the gondola pylons. The small cluster of trails off the Sitnyakovska chairlift are ideal for intermediate riders but they are a bit short.
FREESTYLERS will be glad to know that it's not frowned upon if you want to build kickers. There is a halfpipe off the Martinovi Baraki 4 chairlift
CARVERS will find enough wide areas to put in a few turns, but overall this is not a very good carving resort.
BEGINNERS have only one official blue marked run, but you should soon master some of the reds. Take note, the French designed lift system caters well for skiers, but it's not hot for novice boarders. The main problem is some of the lift take-offs are quick with deep rutted tracks that will throw you off with ease. One particular lift is so bad that it's not uncommon to see bodies dropping like flies.

Borovets is a is a small place set around 1400 metres. The main hotels are the Rila, Samokov and the Olympic. Everything here is cheap. Evenings can be very boozy, with cheap beer available every where. It's worth noting that most places don't accept credit cards or travellers cheques. Food is basic, filling and mainly based on pork and chicken. Evenings are okay and go on until the early hours of the morning and with booze so cheap be prepared for serious drinking and wicked hangovers.

4 OUT OF 10 — Small and basic

Pic - Bulgaria Tourism

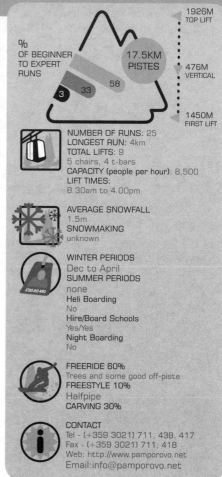

%
OF BEGINNER
TO EXPERT
RUNS

3 33 58

17.5KM PISTES

1926M TOP LIFT

476M VERTICAL

1450M FIRST LIFT

NUMBER OF RUNS: 25
LONGEST RUN: 4km
TOTAL LIFTS: 9
5 chairs, 4 t-bars
CAPACITY (people per hour): 8,500
LIFT TIMES:
8.30am to 4.00pm

AVERAGE SNOWFALL
1.5m
SNOWMAKING
unknown

WINTER PERIODS
Dec to April
SUMMER PERIODS
none
Heli Boarding
No
Hire/Board Schools
Yes/Yes
Night Boarding
No

FREERIDE 60%
Trees and some good off-piste
FREESTYLE 10%
Halfpipe
CARVING 30%

CONTACT
Tel - (+359 3021) 711, 438, 417
Fax - (+359 3021) 711, 418
Web: http://www.pamporovo.net
Email:info@pamporovo.net

Pamporovo is a small un-assuming resort that is set amongst the **Rhodope Mountains** which are located in the south of Bulgaria. This is also a resort that claims to be the sunniest in Europe and the home to the mythical singer 'Orpheus'. Pamporovo is only an hour or so away from Bulgaria's second city Plovdiv which makes this a popular destination for weekend city dwellers. The mild winters in this part of the country give rise to two distinctions, great sunny mountain but not always great snow capped slopes, due mainly to the weather patterns coming from the nearby Aegean sea. However when the mountain is covered in snow Pamporovo becomes the ideal place for beginners with a nice selection of easy slopes; along with a number okay trails to please intermediate riders. But this is not a resort for hard-core freestylers or riders of an advanced level, although fast carvers will find a number of cool runs to take at speed, notably the area of The Wall which is often used for major ski events. But the dominating feature at this the 500 ft giant TV tower and restaurant which sits on the summit of Snezhanka at 1926m.

FREERIDERS have a mountain that doesn't offer a great deal in terms of exciting or varied terrain if you like to ride hard and fast. But that said there are some tight trees to check out and a few natural uneven spots to hit.
FREESTYLERS who crave natural wind lips and big cliff jumps will be disappointed, however, the guys from the Smolyan snowboard club regularly build and maintain a decent halfpipe which measures over 100 metres.
CARVERS have a couple of good carving runs to check out but note, piste grooming is not hot here, resulting in runs being left rutted and often uneven.
BEGINNERS are the ones who will like Pamporovo the most. The terrain is ideally suited to novices with a selection of easy to reach green and blue runs serviced by drag and chair lifts. Snowboard hire and instruction

is available on the slopes.
THE TOWN
Off the slopes Pamporovo is a purpose built but relaxed resort with a good level of resort facilities located close to the slopes. There is a shopping complex, hotel swimming pool, sauna, a number of bars and the odd disco all within easy reach of the slopes and all with a common theme, cheap. Every thing is affordable and booze is almost a give away. Around the resort there are a number of well appointed hotels offering cheap nightly room rates and good weekly packages. Hotels Perelik and Mourgavets are both popular place to stay and have pools, bars, restaurants and even a bowling alley. For those wanting self catering then the Malina Village is the place to stay with a number of well equipped chalets for hire.

VITOSHA

Okay for a few days

Pic - Bulgaria Tourism

Vitosha, which is Bulgaria's highest resort and one that boasts a long season, is located just half an hour from the capital of city **Sofia** and set amid the **Vitosha National Park.** This is a small resort that attracts hordes of punters form the nearby capital especially at weekends. The village is perched high up at a level of 1800 metres with lifts travelling up to a top station of over 2290 metres. The season here generally runs from December to mid April with the mountain best described as suiting beginners and slow learning intermediates. The 20 or so marked out trails are serviced by 11 lifts, which is almost one lift to two runs, thus helping to keep lift lines to a minimum. Overall Vitosha is a simple place resort that should keep you amused for a couple of days if you are an advanced rider or entertained for a week should you be a novice. The mountain boasts a number of interesting slopes, a long 5km run and some nice wooded areas. But if your the sort of rider who looks for something different at every turn and doesn't like riding the same runs more that twice, then you won't enjoy this place.

FREERIDERS will be pleasantly surprised with some of the slopes especially if you head up the highest point of the **Cherni Vrah peak**. from here you will be able to gain access to a number of challenging runs which includes the **Vitoshko Lale area** which has a mixture of un-even red and black runs but one thing this place is not noted for is off-piste or backcountry riding. Although there are some trees to check out, there's no back bowls of deep powder spots.

FREESTYLERS won't fall in love with Vitosha as this is not a place for getting big natural airs. Yes there are a few natural hits, and local are always building kickers, but there isn't any big launch pads or permanent terrain parks or halfpipes to ride.

CARVERS have a mountain that on one hand provides some decent fast spots, but on the other hand the choice of good carving sections are limited to just a few runs.

BEGINNERS have the best of things here with 10 out of the 20 runs graded as easy, with the largest cluster of novice runs found around the **Stenata** area. The long green off the **Romanski** chair is a nice easy run.

THE TOWN

Off the slopes you will find that Vitosha is a bit low key with not a lot going on. The resort has a number of convenient hotels with cheap rates. Around the resort you will find a few night spots, but in truth this sleepy place is not a hot spot. The best night spot is the Hotel Prostor. For a far greater selection of locals services you should visit the city of Sofia which is 23 km away reach.

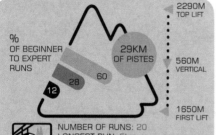

%
OF BEGINNER
TO EXPERT
RUNS

12 28 60

29KM
OF PISTES

2290M
TOP LIFT

560M
VERTICAL

1650M
FIRST LIFT

NUMBER OF RUNS: 20
LONGEST RUN: 5km
TOTAL LIFTS: 9
1 Cable car, 2 chairs, 6 t-bars
LIFT TIMES:
8:30am to 4:00pm

AVERAGE SNOWFALL
1.5m
SNOWMAKING
none

WINTER PERIODS
none
SUMMER PERIODS
Dec to April

FREERIDE 60%
Some trees and some good off-piste
FREESTYLE 5%
No terrain park or pipe
CARVING 25%

FLY
Fly to Plovdiv airport which is around 52 miles (83 km) away with a 2 hour transfer time.
BUS
Bus services from either Plovdiv or Sofia are possible.

C

Capital City: Ottawa
Population: 32.5 million
Highest Peak: Mt Logan 6050m
Language: English & French
Legal Drink Age: 18/19
Drug Laws: Cannabis is illegal but attitudes are changing
Age of consent: 16
Electricity: 110 Volts AC 2-pin
International Dialing Code: +1

Currency: Canadian Dollar (CAD)
Exchange Rate:
UK£1 = 2.4
EURO = 1.6
US$1 = 1.3

Driving Guide
All vehicles drive on the right hand side of the road
Speed limits:
Motorways-100kph (62mph)
Highways-90kph (55mph)
Towns-50kph (31mph)
Emergency
911 for police/ambulance/fire
Tolls
Some tunnels & a few roads
Documentation
Must carry drivers license
Info
Driver & Passengers must wear seatbelts. Frequent drink driving checks in place, and its illegal to have an opened alcohol container in your vehicle.

Time Zone
6 time zones in Canada
GMT +4 to +8

Canadian Ski and Snowboard Association
Suite 200, 505 8th Avenue S.W.
Calgary, AB T2P 1G2
Tel: (403) 265-8615
Fax: (403) 777-3213
www.canadaskiandsnowboard.net

Canada has around 270 resorts, located on either the west or east coast of the country with a few resorts in the central provinces. There is even a snowboard only resort known as 'The Snowboard Ranch' which is located 18 miles from the town of Peterborough in the province of Ontario.

The western provinces boast Canada's best mountainous areas, Alberta and British Columbia (BC). Both regions have resorts that are a match for any in Europe. The gateway cities for flights to the west coast areas are Calgary in Alberta, and Vancouver in BC.

On the east coast there are a number of areas to ride, the majority being in the French speaking province of Quebec. The 100+ resorts on the east coast of Canada resemble much of what is found on the east coast of America - low level, wooded, and often windswept terrain. Canadians treat their visitors with respect and provide a very high level of resort services to meet customer requirements. There are good slope facilities in most places, along with an abundance of places to eat and sleep close to the slopes. Prices are generally higher than those in the US but lower than in Europe. Canadians also like a beer and a good night out, so expect to party hard.

Accommodation facilities in Canada include condos and high quality hotels, as well as B&B's, lodges, hostels or dorms. Prices vary from place to place and are generally quite high wherever you go, (unless you can bunk on a floor and overload with people).

Getting around Canada by train is easy on VIA Rail, the Canadian national rail network, or Amtrak which runs across the Canadian/US border. Greyhound buses are another cheap option. Entry into Canada is liberal but you will need a passport and be advised, you can't work in Canada without a work permit as rules are strict. If you get caught scrubbing dishes in a

Pic -Marmott basin Resort

Elks in Marmott basin Resort, Alberta

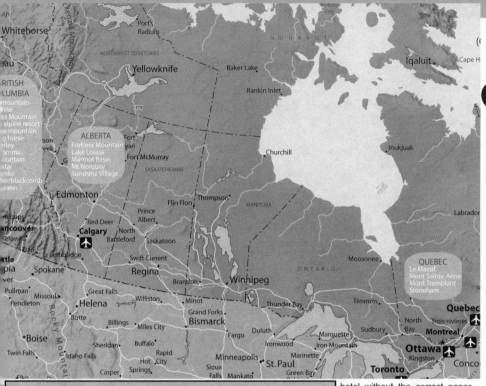

hotel without the correct paper work, you'll soon be on your way home.

If you wish to teach snowboarding in Canada, you will need the Canadian Association of Snowboard Instructors (C.A.S.I.) Level 1 certificate. For details on the course, which costs from C$294, contact C.A.S.I. on 001-514 748 2648 or visit www.casi-bc.com

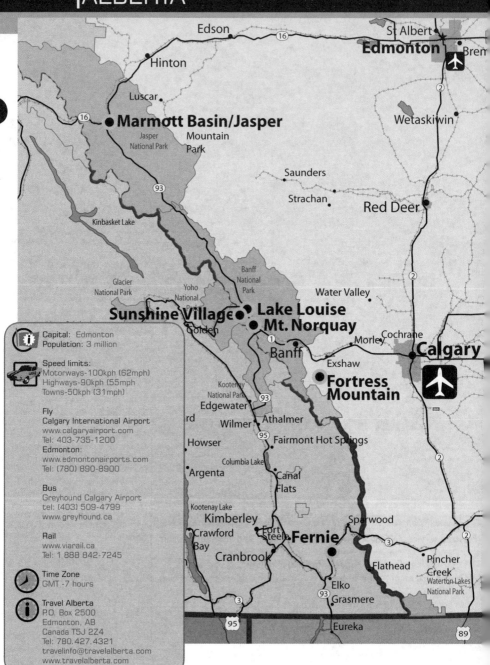

C
A
N
A
D
A

A
L
B
E
R
T
A

Edson

16

St Albert
Edmonton
Bren

Hinton

Luscar

16

Wetaskiwin

Marmott Basin/Jasper

Jasper
National Park

Mountain
Park

93

Saunders

Strachan

Red Deer

Kinbasket Lake

Glacier
National Park

Yoho
National

Banff
National
Park

Water Valley

2

Sunshine Village
Golden

Lake Louise
Mt. Norquay

1

Banff

Morley

Cochrane

Calgary

Exshaw

Capital: Edmonton
Population: 3 million

Speed limits:
Motorways-100kph (62mph)
Highways-90kph (55mph)
Towns-50kph (31mph)

Fly
Calgary International Airport
www.calgaryairport.com
Tel: 403-735-1200
Edmonton:
www.edmontonairports.com
Tel: (780) 890-8900

Bus
Greyhound Calgary Airport
tel: (403) 509-4799
www.greyhound.ca

Rail
www.viarail.ca
Tel: 1 888 842-7245

Time Zone
GMT -7 hours

Travel Alberta
P.O. Box 2500
Edmonton, AB
Canada T5J 2Z4
Tel: 780.427.4321
travelinfo@travelalberta.com
www.travelalberta.com

Kootenay
National Park

93

Edgewater

rd
Wilmer

Athalmer

Fortress
Mountain

Howser

95

Fairmont Hot Springs

Columbia Lake

Argenta

Canal
Flats

2

Kootenay Lake

Kimberley

Sparwood

Crawford
Bay

Fort
Steele

Fernie

3

2

Cranbrook

Flathead

Pincher
Creek

Waterton Lakes
National Park

Elko

3

93

Grasmere

95

Eureka

89

FORTRESS MOUNTAIN

7 OUT OF 10

Not bad for a weekend

Fortress Mountain is a decent but small resort that lies in the shadow of some very impressive rock faces. Located only 40 miles from **Calgary**, Fortress attracts a fair amount of weekend city dwellers, but don't be put off, as it's a cool place to ride. There are great off-piste areas and full on tree-riding, whose marked trails cover three sides of the mountain. Even though it's rated as more of an intermediate's resort, beginners and advanced

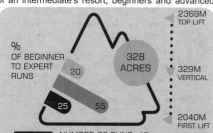

%
OF BEGINNER
TO EXPERT
RUNS

20
25
55

328 ACRES

2369M
TOP LIFT

329M
VERTICAL

2040M
FIRST LIFT

NUMBER OF RUNS: 47
LONGEST RUN: 1.25 miles (2km)
TOTAL LIFTS: 6 - 4 chairs, 2 drags
CAPACITY (people per hour): 8,620
LIFT TIMES: 9.00am to 4.00pm

AVERAGE SNOWFALL:
6.3m
SNOWMAKING:
60%

WINTER PERIODS:
Nov to April
Lift Passes
1 Day pass - $30
5 Day pass - $131
Night Boarding
No

FREERIDE 55%
Trees & good backcountry
FREESTYLE 20%
No Terrain park but a halfpipe
CARVING 25%

Fortress Mountain
Box 208
Kananaskis Village, Alberta
Phone: 403-264-5825
Web:www.skifortress.com
Email:info@skifortress.com

Bus
services direct from Calgary &
Edmonton.
Fly
to Calgary with a 1.5 hour transfer to
Fortress Mountain.
Drive
From Calgary, via Highways 1 & 40
towards Kananaskis. Fortress is 50
miles north of Banff. Calgary to resort
will take 1 1/2 hours.

riders should not feel left out. Those who can handle themselves at speed have plenty of hard-core riding to go for, especially on Backside, where you can find a nice double diamond black trail to test you. The mountain's layout helps to maintain a good snow covering, as well as providing some excellent powder terrain, which can be ridden into May.

FREERIDERS should come away from Fortress as professional tree-riders as the glades are awesome. Backside has some of the best freeride terrain, offering a great time shredding through the spruce and hitting off some sweet banks. The off-piste opportunities are very impressive, provided you seek the knowledge of a local rider who can show you where to ride. The boundary lines are not strictly adhered to, which makes a trip to the Fortress area all the more fun, though be careful and make sure you've studied the piste map.

FREESTYLERS have a halfpipe located between the 2nd and 3rd Chute slopes, but at the moment there is no fun-park. The pipe is shaped with the aid of a Pipe Dragon.

CARVERS are not spoilt for choice since there are few long flats, but there is still some reasonable carving terrain. The **Jolly Jester** is a cool long haul on the Backside, whilst on the front, **Friars** is the place to carve at speed.

BEGINNERS may not find Fortress the most convenient mountain to learn on, but it's certainly not the worst. There are a number of easy trails to tackle, aided by the boys at *Fortress Snowboard School*, who offer novice and beyond programmes.

THE TOWN
Off the slopes, basic accommodation is available on and around the mountain, but is limited to a few chalets or a bed at the ski dorm. A greater selection of local services is provided in the village of **Kananaskis**, which is 25 minutes away. Kananaskis has a number of hotels and a good choice of places to eat or drink in. It's not very cheap or the most happening place for night-life, but is still worth a visit.

LAKE LOUISE

9 OUT OF 10

Excellent freeriding on four mountain faces

Pic: Lake Louise Resort

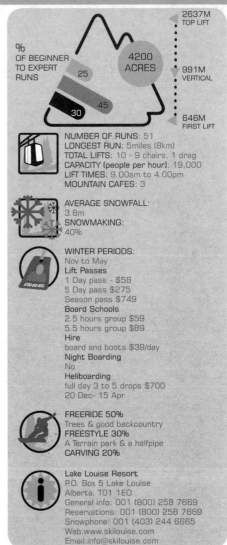

%
OF BEGINNER
TO EXPERT
RUNS

4200 ACRES

25

30

45

2637M
TOP LIFT

991M
VERTICAL

646M
FIRST LIFT

NUMBER OF RUNS: 51
LONGEST RUN: 5miles (8km)
TOTAL LIFTS: 10 - 9 chairs, 1 drag
CAPACITY (people per hour): 19,000
LIFT TIMES: 9.00am to 4.00pm
MOUNTAIN CAFES: 3

AVERAGE SNOWFALL:
3.8m
SNOWMAKING:
40%

WINTER PERIODS:
Nov to May
Lift Passes
1 Day pass - $58
5 Day pass $275
Season pass $749
Board Schools
2.5 hours group $59
5.5 hours group $89
Hire
board and boots $39/day
Night Boarding
No
Heliboarding
full day 3 to 5 drops $700
20 Dec- 15 Apr

FREERIDE 50%
Trees & good backcountry
FREESTYLE 30%
A Terrain park & a halfpipe
CARVING 20%

Lake Louise Resort
P.O. Box 5 Lake Louise
Alberta. T01 1E0
General info: 001 (800) 258 7669
Reservations: 001 (800) 258 7669
Snowphone: 001 (403) 244 6665
Web:www.skilouise.com
Email:info@skilouise.com

Lake Louise is widely rated as one of Canada's best resorts and by far the biggest and most popular resort in **Alberta**. Being a popular place has however, led to an area that is often unbearably busy, both on the slopes and around town. In the past year or two, the resort has undergone a lot off changes on the slopes with the inclusion of the new **Glacier Triple Chair** which starts at the base area. The resort has also done much to improve the slopes with new piste groomers and a new Super Pipe Grinder.

The terrain on offer here is spread out over four mountain faces, Front Side/South Face, the Ptarmigan, Paradise and Back Bowls and the Larch area that collectively provided slopes to suit all levels and styles of rider. The well-connected lift system includes a high speed quad that can whisk you to The Top of the World in under ten minutes, from where you can access the Back Bowls with unlimited long tree-lined powder runs lying in wait at every turn, and with new runs and lifts planned for the Wolvern and Richardsons Ridge areas, there's always new ground to explore. Lake Louise is also located close to the smaller resorts of Sunshine and Mt Norquay with all three sharing a joint lift pass.

FREERIDERS should note that it is illegal to ride in the marked out avalanche danger areas. If you're caught expect to be ejected from the hill with your pass confiscated, and even prosecuted. However, if you have the balls and fancy some out of bounds, the **Purple Bowl** in the **Larch Area** is a mega place to check out, offering a mixture of extreme and easy terrain. If you don't mind a knee-deep hike, trek up to the double black at **Elevator Shaft** where you'll find a host of black runs, cornice drops and rock jumps to try out. The steep blacks on the **Summit Platter** will test the best, but be warned: don't go outside the marked boundary into the West Bowl unless you know what you are doing.

FREESTYLERS have a superb fun park known as the '**The Jungle**' and reached off the Olympic chair. At 650 metres long and loaded with hits, the Jungle boasts being the largest terrain park in North America. There is also a competition standard halfpipe located on the Larch area.

LAKE LOUISE

Pic - Lake Louise Resort

visitors prefer to stay in **Banff** which is only 30 miles from Louise and offers a far greater choice of services and much lower prices.

C

CANADA

ALBERTA

Accommodation in Lake Louise is very expensive with a number of classy hotels and lodges to chose from. Self catering is also possible with some reasonable deals available for groups. If you have the cash, the *Post Hotel* is excellent. However, Banff offers the best selection of affordable places. The *Blue Mountain* has nightly rates from $50 for B&B. The *High Country Inn* has rooms from $70 a night while the Youth Hostel has bunks from $20 per night per person.

CARVERS can opt to weave down a large number of well groomed pistes or try out some of the fast off piste slopes. For a long easy run try the **Wiwaxy Trail** on the front side of the South facing slopes, which at 8 kms, is the longest run in the area. Alternatively, for less crowded riding, check out a run known as Larch.

BEGINNERS will find Louise a particularly good place to start out, with a host of easy to reach runs starting at the base area. The runs off **Eagle chair** are the best and allow you to have a long cruise home down trails such as 14 and 1, which are also in a speed restricted area. The Lake Louise Snowboard School is excellent and offers loads of beginner to advanced programmes.

THE TOWN
Lake Louise's holiday complex is located five minutes from the slopes and can be reached by local shuttle bus.The village, which is dominated by the **Chateau Lake Louise** has a good selection of local facilities and caters well for dot.com millionaires but not for budget conscious snowboarders. The truth is, Lake Louise has become far too overcrowded with holiday punters and charges excessive prices for everything. Many

Food, Around Lake Louise the choice of restaurants is excellent, but very pricey. The *Chateau* is criminally expensive. However, in Banff the *Hard Rock Cafe* offers good food, while *Bumper's* has the biggest steaks you've ever seen. The licensed cafe at the youth hostel has the best value food.

Night-life. Evenings in Louise are simply lame although *Charlie's* or *The Grill* are good for a beer and a game of pool. Banff offers more street-wise entertainment and goes on well into the early hours. The *Rose and Crown* is a popular pub that gets very crowded on occasions.

SUMMARY
Excellent freeriding on four mountain faces although slopes can get very busy. Facilities in Louise are a bit on the dull side, but overall with Banff as an alternative this is a great destination for all.
Money Wise: Very expensive lodging and eating out but extremely good value

CAR
Calgary via Canmore/Banff. Lake Louise is 115 miles (185km). Drive time is about 2 1/4 hours.
FLY
Fly to Calgary International. Transfer time to resort is 2 1/4 hours.
BUS
A bus from Calgary takes 2 1/4 hours. Info: (403) 762 6700, a return is $99, and buses run every other hour. A local shuttle bus runs daily to Lake Louise from Banff.

101

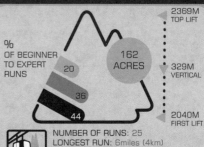

5 OUT OF 10   Not a bad hangout

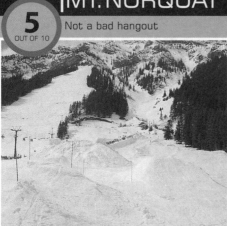

Pic: Mt Norquay Resort

% OF BEGINNER TO EXPERT RUNS

2369M TOP LIFT
162 ACRES
20
36
44
329M VERTICAL
2040M FIRST LIFT

NUMBER OF RUNS: 25
LONGEST RUN: 6miles (4km)
TOTAL LIFTS: 5 - 3 chairs, 2 drags
CAPACITY (people per hour): 7,000
LIFT TIMES: 9.00am to 4.00pm

AVERAGE SNOWFALL:
3m
SNOWMAKING:
90%

WINTER PERIODS:
Dec to April
Lift Passes
1/2 Day $37, 1 Day pass $49
Night Boarding
4.00pm to 9.00pm, pass $24
Hire
Board & Boots 1 day - $32
5 Days $150

FREERIDE 50%
Trees but no backcountry
FREESTYLE 30%
A Terrain park & a halfpipe
CARVING 20%

Mt Norquay
P.O. Box 1520
Banff, Alberta, Canada, T1L 1B4
Tel: (403) 762-4421
Fax: (403) 762-8133
Web: www.banffnorquay.com
Email:info@banffnorquay.com

Bus
services direct from Calgary &
Edmonton via Banff.
Fly
to Calgary 1 1/2 hours transfer to
Mount Norquay.
Drive
From Calgary, via Highway 1 head
towards Banff via Canmore. Mt Norquay
lies north of Banff and south of Lake
Louise alongthe Norquay road. Calgary
to resort is 68 miles.

Mount Norquay is the nearest boarding area to Banff via a ten minute bus ride (costing C$9 leaving regularly from the main hotels). With just 6 lifts, it is the smallest resort in the area, but not without a lot of varied terrain to ride. Since 90% of the runs have snow-making machines, you shouldn't have any problem with the white stuff, even late in the season. Some of the steepest terrain in the **Banff** area can be found at **Norquay** on either side of the North American chair, which the locals claim can be superb after a heavy dump. Norquay has night riding from 4pm to 9pm. A night ride ticket costs $24

FREERIDERS should take the high speed Mystic Ridge lift to ride the best boarding area on the mountain. It gives you access to six long blue runs through the trees, with **Imp** and **Knight Flight** being favourites. There are some steeper options from this lift, like **Black Magic**, and the interestingly named **Ka-Poof**, which can either be great after a heavy fall of snow, or awful with icy hardpack late in the season.

FREESTYLERS have a good halfpipe and fun-park, both of which are shaped by the Rockies first turbo Pipe Grinder. Below the pipe is a full on fun-park with all types of hits, including a massive quarter-pipe, gap jumps and table-tops. The great thing is that it's nearly always deserted and there's even a new tow rope that runs adjacent to the beginner pipe. A discounted lift pass is available for riders using the park via the **Cascade** lift at just $27.

CARVERS will warm to Norquay even though none of the runs are particularly long. The easy flats of the **Spirit Quad** chair is the place to head first before cranking it down **Excalibur**, a decent black run off the **Mystic Quad**.

BEGINNERS have very easy access to tame pistes from the base station. The green runs next to the slow **Double Cascade** chair are a great place to learn some linked turns although there is a lack of easy graded terrain.

THE TOWN
There are no local facilities at **Norquay** apart from *Timberline Inn* at the bottom of the ride-out (tel: (403) 762 2281). The Timberline Inn has a bar and restaurant with nightly rates from $88 for a single. **Banff** is the better option, here you'll find all the local services that you could possibly want. Banff is only ten minutes away and is served by a regular bus that runs seven days a week to and from the slopes.

8 OUT OF 10

Excellent terrain

Pic - mike moynihan/Sunshine Resort

Sunshine and **Goat's Eye Mountain** are amongst the oldest resorts in **Alberta** as well as being one of the best places in the Banff area for deep snow. The area receives serious amounts of snowfall every year and is a good alternative

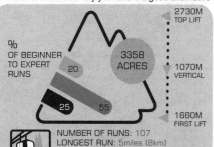

2730M TOP LIFT

% OF BEGINNER TO EXPERT RUNS

20

3358 ACRES

1070M VERTICAL

25   55

1660M FIRST LIFT

NUMBER OF RUNS: 107
LONGEST RUN: 5miles (8km)
TOTAL LIFTS: 12
1 Gondola, 9 chairs,2 magic carpets
CAPACITY (people per hour): 20,000
LIFT TIMES: 9.00am to 4.00pm
MOUNTAIN CAFES: 5

AVERAGE SNOWFALL:
9m
SNOWMAKING:
none

WINTER PERIODS:
Nov to May
Lift Passes
1 Day pass - $60 CDN
Season pass - $799 CDN
Board School
Group full day $80
Private full day $469
Hire
Board and Boots $34/day
5 Days $137

FREERIDE 60%
Trees & backcountry
FREESTYLE 25%
A Terrain park but no halfpipe
CARVING 15%

Sunshine Village
Suite 400,550, 11th Ave SW. Alberta
Tel: 001 (403) 762 6500
Web:www.skibanff.com
Email:comments@skibanff.com

Bus
services direct from Calgary &
Edmonton via Banff.
Fly
to Calgary, with a one hour transfer to
Sunshine Village.
Drive
From Calgary, via Highway 1 head
towards Banff via Canmore. Sunshine
lies north of Banff and south of Lake
Louise. Calgary to resort is 70 miles.

C

C
A
N
A
D
A

A
L
B
E
R
T
A

to its neighbour, Lake Louise. Sunshine's high speed quad on Goat's Eye Mountain gives you the chance to ride 34 runs including some severely steep, double black diamond runs such as **The Wild Side, Hell's Kitchen** and **Freefall**.

FREERIDERS will find Sunshine very pleasing with excellent terrain, loads of trees and plenty of virgin powder to be had. The best and most challenging areas can be found on **Goat's Eye Mountain**. Steeper runs through the trees include **Little Angel, Ecstasy** and **Slim Pickin's** where you may find powder. From the Standish chair lift you can ride down a frozen waterfall on the aptly named **Waterfall run**. If you head out to Trail 87, you'll find some excellent freeriding. However, be careful not to enter the avalanche-prone, closed area, which is well marked.

FREESTYLERS here have it good, with a cool halfpipe under the **Strawberry chair** and a sizeable terrain park reached off the **Standish chair**. You can also pull some big air and spin until you're dizzy, on the lots natural hits dotted all over the place. Sunshine also has a Boardercross trail down the Birdcage run.

CARVERS will find lots of groomed runs to tackle. From the top of **Lookout Mountain** you can ride a long, lazy green down to the day lodge, whilst under the **Angel Quad** you can test your skills on some steep blacks. You can also find some okay cruising trails on **Sunshine Coast** and **Wild Fire**, but make sure you have plenty of speed for the long traverse back to the lift station.

BEGINNERS and intermediate riders are well catered for on runs that include The **Red 90, South Divide** and **Green Run**. If you can handle riding the T-bar, the **Wawa** drag lift gives access to some excellent novice freeriding.

THE TOWN
You can stay in **Sunshine Village**, at the *Sunshine Inn* which offers the only ride-in, ride-out accommodation in the **Banff** area. However, it's not particularly cheap plus there's very little to do in the evening making it unsuitable if you want to party. Banff is only 15 minutes away along Route 93 and a regular local bus services operates between Banff and Sunshine.

103

wsg

MARMOT BASIN

8
OUT OF 10

Great freeriding mountain with excellent challenging runs

Pic : Hugh Lecky//Marmot Basin

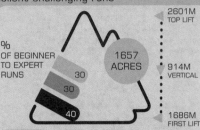

2601M
TOP LIFT

%
OF BEGINNER
TO EXPERT
RUNS

1657
ACRES

914M
VERTICAL

30
30
40

1686M
FIRST LIFT

NUMBER OF RUNS: 84
LONGEST RUN: 3.5miles (5.6km)
TOTAL LIFTS: 9
6 chairs, 2 drags,1 magic carpet
CAPACITY (people per hour): 11,931
LIFT TIMES: 8.30am to 4.00pm
MOUNTAIN CAFES: 3

AVERAGE SNOWFALL:
4m
SNOWMAKING:
40%

WINTER PERIODS:
Nov to May
Lift Passes
1 Day $55 , 5 Day pass - $268
Season Pass - $729
Board Schools
$60 inc 2 hour beginners lesson day pass
and board
group $28/hour
Hire
board and boots $33/day
Snowmobiles
Snow Farmers is a skidoo-ski operation
about an hour west of Jasper
Heliboarding
Wiegele's HeliSki, CMH, & Robson
Helimagic all operate within 1-2 hrs drive
of Jasper, on the BC side of the border.

FREERIDE 60%
Trees & good backcountry
FREESTYLE 20%
4 Terrain parks & 2 halfpipes
CARVING 20%

Marmot Basin
Box 1300
Jasper, ALberta, Canada
TOE 1EO
Phone: 1-(780)-852-3816
Fax: 1-(780)-852-3533
Web:www.skimarmot.com
Email:info@skimarmot.com

NEW

new for 04/05 season
1 new magic carpet for beginners and new
terrain adding more double-black diamond
boarding. The approach to "Murray's" is
accessible by hiking from the top of the
Knob chair and will allow for some amazing
descents.

Marmot Basin, or other wise known as **Jasper**, is an absolute gem of a resort and highly rated by those in the know. Just driving to this place through **Jasper National Park** in the **Rockies** is a pleasure in its self with some stunning scenery en-route. Marmot is a resort that attracts snowboarders and skiers who like their slopes hassle-free and despite being a popular haunt, no one spends more than a few minutes queuing in lift lines, the lifts here can shift over 10,000 people an hour uphill. Recently Marmot, has opened up even more terrain with two new mountain faces known as the **Eagle Ridge** which provide a further 20 runs of steep double black diamond slopes and intermediate trails. Overall the terrain here is evenly split between all levels and styles of riding, with good backcountry areas to explore, nice bowls and trees to dip into and fast carving slopes.

FREERIDERS looking for powder should check out **Eagle East** where the bowls are full on. If you take the Triple chair lift and the **Kiefer drag**, you will eventually arrive at **Caribou Ridge** which offers an abundance of testing terrain with bumps and hits for both the freerider and freestyler. Intermediates who know what they are doing will also like this area and can ride most of the mountain one way or another. If you have the energy, advanced freeriders can hike up to **Marmot Peak** which yields an amazing ride down through powder bowls. The trees in the lower sections are pretty cool, but if you have the balls, check out **Knob Bowl** off Knob Chair for a taste of heaven.

FREESTYLERS have plenty of good natural terrain for catching air, but check out **Rock Garden** for some of the best hits. There are lots of trees here and if you look out, you will find the odd log to slide. Alternatively, the fun-park decked out with a number of hits and a halfpipe is the place to head for, although it's not the most testing. Here, grommets can catch air all day without bothering anyone else.

C
CANADA
ALBERTA

MARMOTT BASIN

- Hugh Lecky/Marmot Basin

CARVERS have some good opportunities to lay out nice, big arcs on the kind of prepared piste that carvers delight in. For some demanding riding, Exhibition is the place to visit, while the more sedate carver will like **Dromedary** trail.

BEGINNERS will note one clear thing about Marmot Basin and that is how good it is for cutting their first tracks. The slopes are accessible with the easy stuff at the bottom and some good progression runs found higher up, which allows for long and gentle riding back to base. What's more, novices can get around the slopes without having to use any T-bars thanks to the way the chair lifts have been set out. Snowboard instruction services are good with a number of tuition packages available for all levels and styles of riding. There are even lessons available with video analysis to quicken your progression. A two hour group lesson costs from C$50 with lift pass and full equipment hire.

THE TOWN
Marmot Basin doesn't offer any slopeside accommodation or full local services other than the new *Caribou Chalet* at the base of the slopes. However, the town of Jasper is only 10 miles away and although it isn't as big as its more famous cousin

Banff, Jasper is less crowded and you shouldn't have any problem finding good quality lodging at prices to suit all. There is a regular ski bus that runs all day stopping at many of the hotels en-route from Jasper to the slopes.

Accommodation in Jasper ranges from the usual selection of lodge-style hotels to B&B's or hostels which are widely spread out. Places like The Amethyst Lodge offer a selection of well equipped rooms with rates from C$70/night per person, while *The Astora,* located in central Jasper, has winter rates from C$40/night per person. The *Marmot Lodge,* also centrally located, offers self catering style accommodation for groups or couples as well as having an indoor swimming pool and fitness centre.

EATING options in Jasper are much the same as in any of Alberta's towns. If you want a slap up feast, then dine at the expensive *Edith Cavell,* or the *Tonquin Rib Village* where you can get a damn fine steak. If you like pizza, then visit *Papa George's* or *Jasper Pizza Place.*

Night-life in Jasper is best described as very low key and a bit boring. *Pete's Bar* seems to be the in-place to check out, where you can mix with a lively crowd boozing and playing pool. The *Whistle Stop* is also a cool hang out with pool and on screen sports action. *O'Shea's* is a typical Irish pub, while the *Atha-Bar* is the place for live music and a dance

SUMMARY
Great freeriding mountain with excellent challenging runs on crowed free slopes. However, the resort is let down by the lack of slope side facilities, although what is on offer in Jasper is first class
Money wise: Generally an expensive resort but great value for money

CAR
Edmonton via Jasper. Marmot Basin is 270 miles. Drive time is about 4 1/2 hours.
FLY
to Edmonton International, transfer time to resort is 4 1/2 hours. Local airport is Hinton 38 miles.
BUS
A daily bus service run by Greyhound, operates 4 times a day from Edmonton to Jasper and takes around 5 hours.
TRAIN
run direct into Jasper

105

BANF TOWN

Banff is the link town for Lake Louise, Norquay and Sunshine. Although the resorts don't link on the slopes they all share a joint lift pass. Getting around Banff and the other resorts is easy via the regular daily bus service. Lake Louise is the most popular of the three, so it's best to get up early and catch the first bus if you want to cut first tracks. The bus starts at one end of town and stops at various hotels until there is no more room. Norquay is the nearest resort to Banff and takes 10 minutes; Sunshine is 10 miles out of Banff, whilst Lake Louise is 32 miles away and takes 45 minutes. If you miss the bus and don't have a car, hitching is a popular way to get to the resorts. Banff has a number of good snowboard shops. The main ones are Rude Boys, Unlimited, and Frozen Ocean. Skaters will find a skate-park in Canmore which is only 15 minutes outside Banff.

CANADA OLYMPIC PARK

If you're hanging out in Calgary and fancy an afternoon's play, then try the Canada Olympic Park. But don't expect too much. This is a blip of a hill which doesn't offer much in the way of snowboard terrain other than having some flat, easy areas for novices and a fun-park for freestylers.

CANYON SKI AREA

Ride Area: 70 acres
Number of Runs: 12
Easy 30%
Intermediate 40%
Advanced 30%
Top Lift: 899m
Bottom Lift: 753m
Vertical: 146m
Total Lifts: 5 - 2 chairs, 3 drags
Lift pass: 1/2 Day Pass - $25 Day Pass - $31.50
Lift times: 9.00am to 9.00pm
Hire: Board & Boots $33
School: Private lesson $30 per hour
Group lesson $20 per hour
Contact:

Red Deer Ski & Recreation Area Ltd RR2,
Site 8, Box 26 Red Deer
Alberta T2N 5E2
Telephone: (403)346-5580
Fax: (403)347-0009
www.canyonski.net
info@canyonski.net

EDMONTON SKI CLUB

Non profit organisation, with a few runs

Ride Area: 25 acres
Number of Runs: 6
Easy 17%
Intermediate 66%
Advanced 17%
Longest run: 183m
Vertical Drop: 91m
Average Snowfall: 9.1m
Total Lifts: 4 - all t-bars
Lift Capacity (People per Hour): 9.500
Lift pass: 1/2 Day Pass - $9 Day Pass - $11
Contact:
Edmonton Ski Club
9613 - 96 Avenue
Edmonton, Alberta T6C 2B3
Tel: 465-0852
www.edmontonskiclub.com

CASTLE MOUNTAIN

Castle Mountain is a small resort located in the southern part of the province. The 36 trails are carved out through trees with a mixture of simple freeriding, nice powder bowls, and fast carving runs. It is also good for freestylers and novices.

Main local services can be found in the town of Pincher Creek, a 40 minute drive away.

Pic - Castle Mountain Tourism

Ride Area: 250 acres
Number of Runs: 59
Easy 15%
Intermediate 40%
Advanced 35%
Expert 10%
Longest Run: 5km
Top Lift: 2273m
Bottom Lift: 1410m
Vertical: 863m
Total Lifts: 5 - 2 chairs, 3 drags
Lift pass: 1/2 Day Pass - $35 Day Pass - $45 Season $674
Hire: Board & Boots $30 per day
School: Private lesson $45 per hour
Group lesson $32 all day (4hrs)
Contact:
Castle Mountain Ski Resort
Box 610 Pincher Creek,
Alberta,
Canada T0K 1W0
General: (403)627-5101
Fax: (403)627-3515
www.castlemountainresort.com
info@castlemountainresort.com

Pic - Castle Mountain Tourism

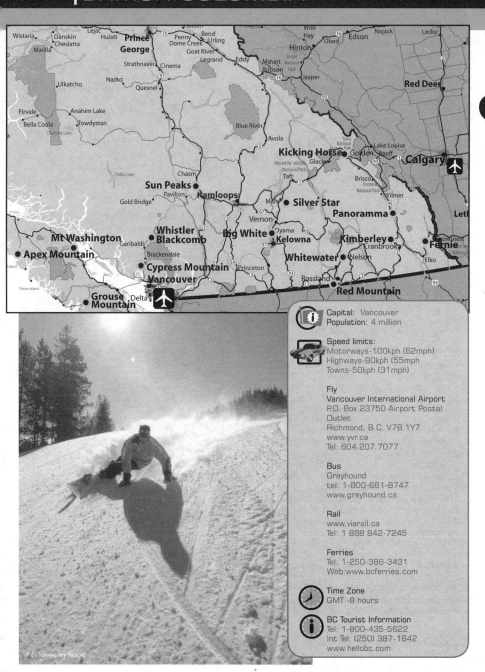

C

CANADA

BRITISH COLUMBIA

Capital: Vancouver
Population: 4 million

Speed limits:
Motorways-100kph (62mph)
Highways-90kph (55mph)
Towns-50kph (31mph)

Fly
Vancouver International Airport
P.O. Box 23750 Airport Postal
Outlet
Richmond, B.C. V7B 1Y7
www.yvr.ca
Tel: 604.207.7077

Bus
Greyhound
tel: 1-800-661-8747
www.greyhound.ca

Rail
www.viarail.ca
Tel: 1 888 842-7245

Ferries
Tel: 1-250-386-3431
Web:www.bcferries.com

Time Zone
GMT -8 hours

BC Tourist Information
Tel: 1-800-435-5622
Int Tel: (250) 387-1642
www.hellobc.com

Pic - Kimberley Resort

107

APEX MOUNTAIN

7 OUT OF 10 Great riding

Photo: Apex Mountain

2187M
TOP LIFT

% OF BEGINNER TO EXPERT RUNS 16

550 ACRES

605M
VERTICAL

36 47

1575M
FIRST LIFT

NUMBER OF RUNS: 60
LONGEST RUN: 3miles (5km)
TOTAL LIFTS: 5 - 3 chairs, 2 drags
CAPACITY (people per hour): 8,700
LIFT TIMES: 9:00am to 3:30pm

AVERAGE SNOWFALL:
6m
SNOWMAKING:
40%

WINTER PERIODS:
Nov to April
Lift Passes
1 Day pass - $48, 5 Day pass - $220
Season pass - $599
Board Schools
Group $60 for 3 hours, Private $55/hr
Hire
Board & Boots $38/day , extra days $29

FREERIDE 50%
Trees & backcountry
FREESTYLE 20%
No Terrain park but a halfpipe
CARVING 30%

Apex Mountain Resort
PO Box 1060
Penticton BC
V2A 6J9
Phone (250) 292-8222
Fax (250) 292-8100
Web:www.apexresort.com
Email:info@apexresort.com

Bus
services direct from Vancouver takes
around 5 hours.
Fly
to Vancouver. Domestic transfers
possible to Penticon.
Drive
From Vancouver, use higway 1 via Hope
and Manning Park.

NEW new for 04/05 season
Board cross track in terrain park

Apex Mountain may be a small resort, but with it's down-to-earth atmosphere and great riding opportunities, it's no wonder that Apex is a popular place. Located in the sunny **Okanagan Valley**, Apex is known for its great natural terrain: bowls, gullies, glades and groomed cruising runs radiate from the rounded top of the resort's main peak, **Mt Beaconsfield**. If you're a novice or intermediate, head for the wide boulevards off the Stocks Triple chair, where you'll find half a dozen nicely graded, rolling descents. Notice how the trail names evoke the area's mining history - **Motherlode, Gambit** and **Sluice Box**.

FREERIDERS looking for some decidedly 'darker blue' cruising should head on up to **Mt Beaconsfield** and try **Ridge Run** and **Juniper** where a search for more challenging terrain won't take long. Alternatively, check out the whole series of wicked runs plunging down Apex's North Side. Wind your way through the woods and, if you dare, peer down **Gunbarrel**, a chute that's just 'one turn wide', and drops straight down the fall-line for 366 double black diamond vertical metres (1,200 ft).
FREESTYLERS who expect facilities to be laid on should forget Apex, as there is no park or pipe. However, a bit of hunting will reveal some good natural gullies and hits on **Mt Beaconsfield**.
CARVERS will fair well on Apex's short, but challenging trails. There are enough steep blacks for the advanced alpine rider to carve, while the novice can practice on some nice, flat blues.
BEGINNERS should find that Apex allows for an easy time, as in general, this is a good mountain to learn on and allows for quick progression. **Grandfather's** Trail is a nice green that allows you to ride from the summit to the base with ease. The local snowboard school offers various learn to ride packages with a one day lesson, lift and full hire costing form C$57 per person.

THE TOWN
The *New Inn* at **Apex** offers ride-in accommodation and some good value bed and lift ticket deals, from C$60/night mid-week. If you're planning on staying a while there are apartments available to rent, otherwise

there are plenty of beds in the town of Penticton, forty minutes away. When the sun goes down on Apex Mountain, The *Gunbarrel Saloon* is the main place to eat and enjoy all sorts of entertainment. Other good food haunts are *The Rusty Spur* and *Longshot Bar*.

8 OUT OF 10

Excellent freeriding on crowd free slopes

Big White is a genuine snowboarders mountain that has it all. Snowboarders in search of good mountains have been cruelly misled by the world's slack ski press for years, since **Big White** has been

%
OF BEGINNER
TO EXPERT
RUNS

18

2565 ACRES

26   56

2319M
TOP LIFT

777M
VERTICAL

1755M
FIRST LIFT

NUMBER OF RUNS: 118
LONGEST RUN:4.5miles (7.2km)
TOTAL LIFTS: 15 - 1 Gondola, 9 chairs, 3 drags,2 Leitner Tube Lifts
CAPACITY (people per hour): 25,400
LIFT TIMES:8.45am to 8.00pm
MOUNTAIN CAFES: 7

AVERAGE SNOWFALL:
7.50m
SNOWMAKING:
none

WINTER PERIODS:
Nov to May
Lift Passes
1 Day pass $60, 5 Days pass $276
Season pass $859
Board Schools
2 Hour Group $42
Private 2 Hours $157
Hire
board and boots $36/day 5 days $142
Snowmobiles
1 to 4 hour tours
Night Boarding
Tuesday to Saturday Free with any multi-day pass

FREERIDE 45%
Trees & good backcountry
FREESTYLE 45%
2 Terrain parks & 3 halfpipes
CARVING 10%

Big White resort
PO Box 2039 Stn. R
Kelowna B.C.
Canada, V1X4K5
Tel: (250) 765-3101
Web:www.bigwhite.com
Email:bigwhite@bigwhite.com

new for 04/05 season
Huge $127.9 investmet for 04/05 season but $123.1 million of that is on accomodation, leaving 4mil on a new terrain park, lift, new runs & a grooming machine

Pic - Big White

C
C
A
N
A
D
A

B
R
I
T
I
S
H

C
O
L
U
M
B
I
A

hardly mentioned at all in the numerous ski guides and magazines. Knowledgeable Canadians have had a freeride paradise with an annual 24 feet of champagne powder largely to themselves, at one of the country's best resorts. Over recent years, large amounts of money have been spent on the resort, but this year surpasses all that's gone before with **$127.9 million** going into the resort. Two new chairs lifts, access to another 200 acres of terrain, 6 new pistes, grooming machines, more beds taking the resort total up to over 14,000, a café with sun deck at the bottom of the spanking new $2.5 million Terrain Park. The result is a modern, super efficient resort which won't remain a secret for long.

Big White is located in the **Okanagan Valley**, an hour from the town of **Kelowna**. The mountain is best described as a winter skate-park, with over 2,000 acres of natural terrain features spread over two mountain faces that will leave you breathless. The terrain at Big White is split evenly between freeride and freestyle, suiting beginner and intermediate riders, as well as providing some very good expert trails. The initial access to the slopes begins from the village area, with lifts taking you up the South face slopes, home to an array of green and blue runs that criss-cross each other.

FREERIDERS now get the chance to ride 200 new accessed acres down some impressively large powder bowls. Riders with balls (or equivalent) should take the **Alpine** T-bar and test their extreme riding on one of the double black diamond runs that are found on the Cliff, but only if you can ride and ride well. Likewise, the black runs off the Powder chair are not for the squeamish. For those not quite up to the same standard, the blue runs off the **Ride Rocket** chair are worth a blast, as is the **Blue Ribbon** over in the **West Ridg**e area.

FREESTYLERS are going to wet themselves. A new $2.5 Million 50 acre Park will open this season. Two 450 feet pipes, an Olympic Board Cross, a whole shed load of jumps and rails, snow making throughout,

109

C

C
A
N
A
D
A

B
R
I
T
I
S
H

C
O
L
U
M
B
I
A

gates and a high speed chair lift just for the park which takes you over the pipes so you can check everyone out on the way up. The pipe will be used for national snowboard events. Big White also provides a small pipe for novice riders so that learners can gain their first airs and can learn the basics of pipe-riding with ease. The 8 plus acre terrain park, which is housed on the **Freeway area**, is designed for all levels of freerider and comes loaded with spines, gaps, and a monster quarter pipe.

CARVERS will love Big White as the terrain is perfect for laying big turns. By taking any of the main lifts, such as **Ridge Rocket** or **Bullet**, you gain access to great carving slopes. **Cougar Alley** is full on and for a long carve you should crank it from the summit of the **Alpine** T-Bar, down to the base.

BEGINNERS won't be disappointed with Big White as it is totally accessible and has a good selection of easy trails. First timers can ride from the summit to the base, but study your lift map first. Instruction is good and well priced, with a one day lesson, equipment hire and lift pass costing from C$55.

THE TOWN
Off the slopes, **Big White** is a friendly and affordable place that is well set out and has the image of a laid back, sleepy mountain town with an Alpine feel. Weekends usually see an influx of extra punters from surrounding towns and cities, but the place is never so busy as to be annoying - there is room for all. Local amenities are basic, but offer everything you may need during your stay, with shops and other services being well located and within walking distance of each other. Riders with too much money can throw it away at the casino, whilst families can prance around on the 7500 squ,ft, ice rink. And if that's not enough, then perhaps a snowmobile tour will suite, with over 70 miles of tracks to explore.

Accommodation in Big White is very good with much of it on, or close to the base slope areas, which allows you ride to your door. There are a couple of classy hotels to choose from and a few chalets. For groups, there is a choice of condominiums with prices to suit even budget riders. The *White Crystal Inn* is a quality hotel located close to the slopes. It has a bar, restaurant, and fitness room, but note, it's not cheap.

Pic - Sang Tan

Eating choices are numerous and of an extremely good standard. For a hearty breakfast, check out the *Ridge Day Lodge* which opens from 8.30am daily. *Snowshoe Sam's* has a great reputation and food to match. *Dom's* serves up tender chicken while *Loose Moose* is the joint for a burger.

Night-life: By no means mad cap or hardcore drinking, but you can make it lively. The *Loose Moose* is the place to get on the dance floor, while *Raakels* is the place to chill and listen to some live music. For a bigger selection of night-life, check out the action in **Kelowna**. It is only 45 minutes away but you will need your own transport at night.

SUMMARY
Excellent freeriding on crowd free slopes, with great terrain for all levels. Local facilities are very basic but good. Night life is tame but okay.
Money Wise: Expensive lodging and eating out but overall good value

CAR
Vancouver via Merrit & Kelowna. Big White is 278 miles (447km), drive time is about 5 hours.
FLY
to Vancouver International. Transfer time to resort is 5 hours. Local airport is Kelowna 45 mins.
BUS
A bus from Vancouver takes around 5 hours. Local buses run daily from Kelowna to Big White and take just 45 minutes.

CYPRESS MOUNTAIN

5 OUT OF 10 — Okay for a few days

Pic - MArk Gunter

Cypress Mountain is one of three local mountains in the **Vancouver** area (the other two being **Grouse Mountain** and **Mt Seymour**). Situated 30 minutes drive from **West Vancouver**; Cypress Mountain caters largely for people living in the city. It's a relatively small resort with

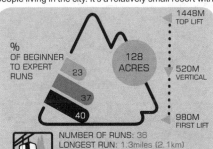

1448M
TOP LIFT

%
OF BEGINNER
TO EXPERT
RUNS

23

128 ACRES

37

40

520M
VERTICAL

980M
FIRST LIFT

NUMBER OF RUNS: 36
LONGEST RUN: 1.3miles (2.1km)
TOTAL LIFTS: 5 - all chairs
LIFT TIMES: 8.30am to 10.00pm

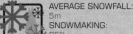

AVERAGE SNOWFALL:
5m
SNOWMAKING:
85%

WINTER PERIODS:
Dec to April
Lift Passes
1 Day pass $42
Night $34
Board School
2 Hours $40
Hire
Board and Boots $37/41 Day
Night Boarding
Between 15 Dec to 28 Mar

FREERIDE 50%
Trees & backcountry
FREESTYLE 20%
A Terrain park and a halfpipe
CARVING 30%

Cypress Mountain
P.O. Box 91252
West Vancouver, B.C. Canada
V7V 3N9
Tel: 604-926-5612
Web:www.cypressmountain.com
Email:contact@cypressmountain.com

Bus
services direct from Vancouver takes
around 30 minutes
Fly
to Vancouver 30 minutes transfer to
Cypress Bowl
Drive
From Vancouver, use highway 1
westbound, direction Horseshoe Bay.
Leave at exit 8 for Cypress Bowl

only four chair lifts and one drag lift, all of which are a bit outdated. The terrain on offer is very much beginner to intermediate level, but that doesn't deter the large number of 'Vancouverites' who flock here. Nightboarding is one of the biggest draws at Cypress Bowl, offering uncrowded riding for the true enthusiasts until 11pm every night.

FREERIDERS may find the best riding to be had on **Mt Strachan** in the east, which has two chair lifts, Sunrise and Sky that take you to the top of the best black runs. On a clear day, the view is absolutely stunning, with the enormous **Mt Baker** dominating the horizon down to **Washington**, USA. Snowboarding on this side of Cypress Bowl is better than anywhere else in the resort due to the steep and variable terrain, and because of the altitude, there is also more snow. There are some truly top class off-piste tree runs to contend with (although a little short by European standards), and some more challenging black runs too.

FREESTYLERS have a snowboard park called the 'BoardZone' that is well maintained by the owners and a few local riders who are constantly changing the set-up. There is also a big halfpipe and if that's not enough, there are two awesome 12 foot quarter-pipes.

CARVERS in search of loads of fast and extreme slopes will be a little disappointed but the runs are nicely groomed.

BEGINNERS have it best at Cypress Bowl. The Eagle chair on **Black Mountain** gives access to some easy/intermediate winding runs; alternatively, the flats on **Mt Strachan** and the **Sunrise chair** are ideal for learning the basics. *Cypress Bowl Snowboard School* offers courses to suit all, with a one week course that includes full equipment hire, costing from C$290.

THE TOWN
There is no accommodation on the mountain as the city of Vancouver is so close. In downtown **Vancouver,** there is an excellent hostel which has friendly staff, awesome facilities and runs daytrips to the mountain. Alternatively there are all the normal types of hotels that any large city can offer. There is plenty happening in Vancouver at night, particularly downtown on Granville St. Watch out for *Fred's Tavern* or *Roxy's.*

C
A
N
A
D
A

B
R
I
T
I
S
H

C
O
L
U
M
B
I
A

111

FERNIE ALPINE RESORT

8 OUT OF 10

Excellent open bowl freeriding on crowd free slopes

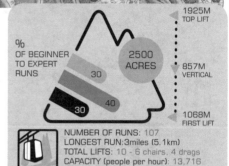

Pic -Fernie Resort

Fernie Alpine Resort deservedly has a reputation for being a powder paradise. With an average annual snowfall of 875cm and enough steep gladed terrain to keep you entertained for the longest of stays, it is not surprising that it has become so popular, especially with the Antipodean snowboarding contingent. Since the take over by **Banff** and **Lake Louise** the ski area has doubled in size. The two new chairs have opened the doors to three bowls, **Timber, Currie** and **Siberia** that offer some of the mountains most challenging terrain. Beginners, intermediate and advanced riders will feel equally at home on the slopes and if for some reason you decide to leave your board at home for the day, there are a number of activities from dog sledding to snowmobiling that will entertain you.

FREERIDERS, this is what Fernie is all about. Advanced Riders looking for steep tree runs could do worse than heading up to **White Pass**, then traversing around **Currie Bowl** to **Stags Leap** and the surrounding area. Or, at the top of the **Timber quad**, a quick two-minute walk will take you to the top of **Siberia Ridge**, where you can pick your line and charge through the well spaced trees. Unfortunately due to its increasing popularity you may have to fight for your fresh lines. Once the ski area is tracked out, there are a number of 30-40 minute hikes that are worth every lung-bursting step. Make sure that you are not the one to put the boot pack in. Head to **Mongolia Ridge** for more trees, **Polar Peak** for stunning panoramic views, clear powder fields or chutes back into **Currie Bowl** or **Fish Bowl** for a more cruisy ride.

FREESTYLERS, Fernie does have a terrain park and halfpipe, but both are of poor quality and the **Deer chair** that accesses them both is frustratingly slow. Pipe etiquette is unheard of, so it can be a hazardous place with skiers and boarders dropping in left right and centre and ski schools regularly snowploughing their way down the middle, toddlers snaking

1925M
TOP LIFT

%
OF BEGINNER
TO EXPERT
RUNS

30

2500
ACRES

857M
VERTICAL

30

40

1068M
FIRST LIFT

NUMBER OF RUNS: 107
LONGEST RUN:3miles (5.1km)
TOTAL LIFTS: 10 - 6 chairs, 4 drags
CAPACITY (people per hour): 13,716
LIFT TIMES:8.30am to 3.30pm
MOUNTAIN CAFES: 8

AVERAGE SNOWFALL:
8.75m
SNOWMAKING:
none

WINTER PERIODS:
Nov to April
Lift Passes
1 Day pass - $58
3 Day Pass - $174
5 Day pass - $280
Season pass - $779
Board Schools
Lesson, lift and equipment - $43
Hire
Board and boots - $25 (Kids - $20)

FREERIDE 50%
Trees & good backcountry
FREESTYLE 25%
A Terrain park & a halfpipe
CARVING 25%

Ski Area Road, Fernie, BC
Canada, V0B 1M6
Tel: 001 (250) 423-4655
Fax: 001 (250) 423-6644
Web:www.skifernie.com
Email:info@skifernie.com

NEW new for 04/05 season
3 areas have been gladed for easier access.
DayLodge will be upgraded, new cat has been added to the grooming fleet. New access from Currie Bowl to Bear Chair.

THE TOWN & GETTING THERE

Web Rider Simon

of attractions which include ice skating, a cinema, swimming pools and other sporting facilities. Fernie is also a top summer destination.

Accomodation. There is plenty of budget accommodation to choose from. The *Raging Elk* is one of two conveniently located hostels downtown and there is any number of hotels and motels. *Canadian Powder Tours* is a beautiful log cabin 15 minutes walk from the centre of town. Here you'll find gourmet food, transport to and from the mountain and optional guided tours of the ski area or the backcountry. On the mountain hotels and self catering apartments include The *Wolf's Den* and *Lizard Creek Lodge* are more expensive but offer ride to your doorstep convenience.

Food. The choices for eating out are extensive and cater for every pallet and every price range. If you wish to dine out in style then you should check the *Lizard Creek Lodge* dining room. *Gabriella's* is the place for Italian dishes while *Rip & Richard's* is noted for its local cuisine. *Smitty's* Restaurant is noted for its pancakes, breakfasts and light lunches.

Night-life in Fernie is rather tame but still enjoyable. There are a number of bars but they all seem much the same. Check out *Eldorados* for live music, The *Central* or the imaginatively named *The Pub* which has pool tables and table football.

SUMMARY
Excellent open bowl freeriding on crowd free slopes and a mountain with a good annual snow record. Good for beginners and ideal for freestlye riding.

behind. Instead, why not head to **Lost Boys** in **Siberia Bowl** or the area below the **Face lift** traverse, both being ideal places to build your own kickers to huck yourself off into deep, soft powder.

CARVERS, for those of you who like to wear hard boots and stay on piste, Fernie has plenty of wide open runs that are groomed regularly. After a fresh dump of snow, what is better than laying out some big carves on that packed powder corduroy. Try the **Bear, North Ridge** or **Falling Star**.

BEGINNERS will enjoy learning to ride at Fernie. Instructors are of high standard and will have you up and going in no time. Once you have enough confidence to leave the confines of the **Mighty Moose** beginner area you will find plenty of empty, tame runs off the **Deer chair**, before trying the **Bear** and **Elk** runs which link together to give a long ride down to the Day Lodge.

THE TOWN
The town of **Fernie** has developed from the coal and lumber trade and is situated on the banks of the **Elk River** and beneath the impressive Lizard mountain range on which the ski area lies. Accommodation and local services can be found a few minutes down the valley in the old town of Fernie. Here plenty of affordable places to eat, sleep and drink are offered with a real Wild West feel. Lodging is available nearer the slopes, but it can be expensive. There is a shuttle bus service that operates to and from the mountain on a daily basis, costing around $4CDN for a return trip. Fernie offers a high level of services with a host

Pic - Henry George Fernie Resort

CAR
From Calgary drive to Okotoks & then Sparwood. Calgary to resort is 188 miles (300km). 5 3/4 hours drive time.
FLY
to Calgary International. Transfer time to resort is 3 hours. Local airport is Cranbrook (Air Canada fly into) about 1hr away
BUS
A bus service from Calgary runs twice daily and is operated by Greyhound Bus Lines . (3 1/2 hours). Shuttle bus runs around town $3 one way.
TRAIN
run by Amtrax only go as far as Whitefish, Montana USA.

GROUSE MOUNTAIN

5 OUT OF 10 — A nice day out

Pic: Grouse Mountain

% OF BEGINNER TO EXPERT RUNS

212 ACRES

1250M TOP LIFT

384M VERTICAL

274M FIRST LIFT

40
20   40

NUMBER OF RUNS: 25
TOTAL LIFTS: 6 - 4 chairs, 2 drags
LIFT TIMES: 9.00am to 10.00pm
MOUNTAIN CAFES: 4

AVERAGE SNOWFALL: 7.5m
SNOWMAKING: 75%

WINTER PERIODS: Nov to April
Lift Passes
1 Day $42, Night Pass after 4pm $32
Season Pass $675, Season Night $395
Board School
Group $38, Park Clinic 5hours $89, 5 day
park clinic $420
Hire
Board and Boots $39/day, 5 Days $166
Night Boarding
13 runs 113 acres

FREERIDE 50%
Trees & some backcountry
FREESTYLE 25%
2 Terrain parks
CARVING 25%

Grouse Mountain Resorts Ltd.
6400 Nancy Greene Way
North Vancouver, BC, V7R 4K9
Tel: 604.984.0661
Web:www.grousemountain.com
Email:info@grousemtn.com

Bus
regular services to the base of Grouse
Mountain every half hour. (Bus 232 from
Phibbs Exchange/Bus 236 from Lonsdale
Quay) http://www.bctranslink.com
Fly
to Vancouver
Drive
15 minutes from downtown Vancouver.
Follow Georgia Street westbound through
Stanley Park and across the Lion's Gate
Bridge. Take the North Vancouver exit to
Marine Drive, then left up Capilano Road
for 5 km (3.1 miles).

Grouse Mountain is a small resort that is located on the very northern outskirts of **BC's** capital **Vancouver**. Along with a mountain top multi-media theatre, **Grouse Mountain** has a good selection of trails that will keep the average grade snowboarder content for a day or two, satisfy an expert rider for an afternoon and totally please a beginner for a 5 day period. Regular night riding on Grouse's flood lit slopes is very popular with townies from Vancouver, who take to the slopes in the evenings after a day in the office. However, Grouse doesn't attract mass crowds due largely to the poor and unreliable snow conditions. Still, when the 22 well marked trails are covered in snow then this is a mountain that provides some good fun riding with a little for everyone. Apart from a couple of double black diamond extreme runs, however, much of the terrain is rated intermediate and overall is tame.

FREERIDERS will find that much of what is on offer here at will suit them so long as they are not looking for major long steeps covered in knee deep powder. There are however, some areas where the average rider can show off on runs such as the **Devil's Advocate**. This is a short but fast steep trail that winds its way down through some tress before linking up with a long intermediate run known as the **Inferno**. With all or most of the runs carved out of trees, there are ample opportunities to slice through the trees and grind the odd fallen log.

FREESTYLERS will soon realise that **Grouse** is not what one would call a freestyle's destination. Neither the halfpipe or the fun park are up to much or that extensive, and to be honest, the natural terrain features here will provide for a more pleasing time than any man-made hit.

CARVERS have a reasonable selection of trails to choose from with some excellent wide carving to found off the **Peak Patio** and **Peak** chair lifts. Both lifts give access to some basic runs.

BEGINNERS may not have dozens of novice trails to choose from, but nevertheless, the easy runs are well appointed and most first timers should have no bother negotiating the nursery areas before progressing up on up to more challenging terrain. The local ski school offers a number of snowboard programmes.

THE TOWN
Off the slopes the place to stay is in Vancouver, where you will be able to find just about anything to suite you're fancy. vancouver is a fantastic city loaded with tourist attractions. Vancouver Tourist Office tel: 001 (604) 683 2000.

Three hours west of **Calagary** and close to the town of Golden, lies the resort of Kicking Horse, which changed its name from **Whitetooth** a few years back when it was a small sleepy resort. With large sums of dollars being spent

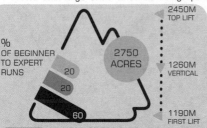

% OF BEGINNER TO EXPERT RUNS

2750 ACRES

2450M TOP LIFT

1260M VERTICAL

1190M FIRST LIFT

20
20
60

Rider: Ryan J/Photo:Mike McPhee

NUMBER OF RUNS: 96
LONGEST RUN: 10km
TOTAL LIFTS: 5
1 Gondola, 3 chairs, 1 drags
CAPACITY (people per hour): 1,400
LIFT TIMES: 8.30am to 3.30pm
MOUNTAIN CAFES: 2

AVERAGE SNOWFALL: 7m
SNOWMAKING: none

WINTER PERIODS: Dec to April
Lift Passes
1 Day $53, 6 Days $305, Season $697
Board School
Private lesson $425 (6rs), Group $50 (2hrs). Beginner package $80 full day inc equipment, lesson & lift pass
Hire
Board & Boots $31 per day
Snowmobiles
Yes
Heliboarding
See client services at the base lodge

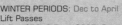

FREERIDE 40%
Trees & some backcountry
FREESTYLE 10%
No Terrain park or pipe
CARVING 40%

Kicking Horse Mountain Resort
P.O. Box 839,1500 Kicking Horse Trail
Golden BC,VOA 1H0
tel: 250-439-5400
fax: 1-250-439-5401
Web:www.kickinghorseresort.com
Email: guestservices@kickinghorseresort.com

Bus
services to Golden from Calgary, takes around 3 hours. Snow shuttles run from Golden to Kicking Horse (15mins)
Fly
to Calgary, transfer time to is 3 hours.
Drive
From Calgary take Trans-Canada Highway 1 west to Golden, 9 miles from highway,Goldens 15 mins. 164 miles, 3 3/4 hours.

on development, the resort is staking its claim as one of the biggest resorts around trying to be a match for the likes of Fernie and Lake Louise. All the lower trails are hacked out between thick lines of ferns and suit novices, although there are a couple of notable advanced runs such as **Pioneer** and **Grizzly**. The top half of the mountain is of more interest to the better boarder with some decent black runs and a couple of double-diamonds to keep you smiling.

FREERIDERS can either take advantage of a few good pisted runs or if cash is no problem, take a heli-board trip to some more challenging areas. The trail marked out as **Porcupine** is a cool run that can be done at speed, but only if you know what you are doing. For the intermediate freerider, check out **Kicking Horse**, which starts out fairly mellow before dropping away more steeply mid-way down. For the advanced, get straight up the gondola to the top of the mountain and drop into either of the bowls off the ridge. If you fancy a short hike then pop over the top of the **Blue Heaven peak** for 5-10 mins and get yourself down the newly opened **feuz bowl**.

FREESTYLERS may be forgiven for thinking that kicking horse is not for them, its splattering of natural hits and the occasional log won't keep your attention for long.

CARVERS are best served here. The tree-lined trails run in a straight line down to the base area. **Pioneer** and **Grizzly** are notable carvers' trails where you can lay out some fast lines at speed, but this is an advanced rated run so be warned.

BEGINNERS might look at the piste map and think that the place is made up of runs not suited to their ability, but on the ground it's a different story. Some of the runs are a little over-rated and could be tackled by a novice within a few days. Trails marked out as **A, C, D** and **F** offer easy flats at the lower areas, with the **Waitabit** run higher up being a nice progression trail.

THE TOWN
Theres been a significant investment in mountain side accommodation but most of it outrageously priced; *Vagabond lodge* is the cheapest and has rooms from $160pppn. A better range is found in the town Golden, 15 mins away. The *Kicking Horse Hostel* (www.kickinghorsehostel.com) Station Avenue, tel (250) 344-5071 has beds for $25. Although not the most happening place, Golden is free of marauding crowds, very affordable and is still okay.

8 OUT OF 10

Good resort that will suit all levels of riders especially beginners

Kimberley Resort

1982M TOP LIFT

% OF BEGINNER TO EXPERT RUNS

20

1800 ACRES

751M VERTICAL

45

35

1230M FIRST LIFT

NUMBER OF RUNS: 67
LONGEST RUN: 4miles (6.4km)
TOTAL LIFTS: 10
5 chairs, 4 drags, 1 magic carpet
CAPACITY (people per hour): 5,500
LIFT TIMES: 9.00am to 9.00pm

AVERAGE SNOWFALL:
4m
SNOWMAKING:
65%

WINTER PERIODS:
Dec to April
Lift Passes
1/2 Day Pass $38, Full day $48
Board School
Private lesson $55 per hour
Group lesson $30 2hrs
Beginner package lift pass, lesson & hire $49
Hire
Board and boots - $39/day
Night Boarding
North Star Express High Speed Quad
open from 5.30 to 9pm, $19

FREERIDE 40%
Trees & good backcountry
FREESTYLE 20%
A Terrain park
CARVING 40%

Kimberley Alpine Resort
PO Box 40, 301
North Star Blvd
Kimberley, BC
V1A 2Y5 Canada
Tel: (250) 427 - 4881
Web:www.skikimberley.com
Email:info@skikimberley.com

Kimberley Alpine Resort, to give the place its full title, is on the up and up and is currently in the middle of a multi million dollar expansion plan that has incorporated new mountain facilities as well as a new slope side village. Kimberley's history, like many old Canadian towns, stems from the days of mining. However, you would be forgiven for not knowing this when you arrive as the area has been developed into an all year round quality outdoor recreation centre. First impressions of the place are not one of a sleepy old mining town, instead you are left feeling like you've just landed in a sausage-munching Bavarian town. Still, this strange fusion of Canada and Germany seems to work well as Kimberley is growing rapidly and is presently the fourth largest resort in British Columbia. Kimberley is owned by the same company that owns Lake Louise in Alberta, but that's about the only connection between two. Located 3 hours from **Lake Louise**, Kimberley is a resort that will appeal to everybody with a good selection of all level trails. The large percentage of easy and intermediate runs may be one reason that the slopes here attract a lot of skiers, however, snowboarders in the know are not left short changed with a good choice of fast black runs.

The runs are spread out over two faces and cut through a lot of thick spruce trees providing some great tree-riding. Although advanced riders are not going to be pushed much here, there are a are a couple of notable double black diamond runs that deserve full attention in order to avoid a broken collar bone.

FREERIDERS will find that Kimberley offers them some really cool tree-riding and some fairly good powder days. The runs off **Buckhorn chair** take you to some nice terrain, while the **Easter triple chair** lends access to the double black Flush run, which descends through trees that will either make or break you.

FREESTYLERS are presented with a fairly ordinary halfpipe and funpark which are located on the **Rosa** and **Main** trails just up from the base area. There are also a few good natural hits located off the Rosa chair,

THE TOWN & GETTING THERE

which also gives access to some gentle terrain interspersed with wooded sections where you can practice some grinding skills on downed logs.

CARVERS get the best look-in on Kimberley's slopes with some decent wide open runs allowing for big arcs. The run marked **Main** is a fast long burner which brings you out at the main base area, while **Flapper** is a shorter but faster pleaser.

BEGINNERS who plan to spend a week here should leave far more competent than when they arrived. This is a particularly good resort for beginners with some excellent novice trails that cover the whole mountain and some nice long green runs that allow easy riding from the top to bottom.

THE TOWN

Downtown Kimberley is only five minutes from the slopes and offers a very good selection of facilities as well as what is said to be Canada's biggest cuckoo clock. Overall Kimberley is not a cheap resort in terms of accommodation and general local services. However, what is not in question is the way you are looked after; the locals are very friendly. Kimberley is also an all year round holiday destination offering a host of sporting attractions form golf to white-water rafting and water skiing.

Accommodation in Kimberley is very good with easy access slope side lodging in condo units or chalets. The *Rocky Mountain Condo* and Hotel centre

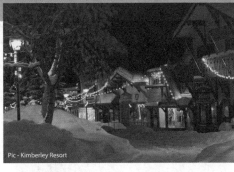

Pic - Kimberley Resort

is located at the very base of the slopes just a short walk from the North Star Express chair lit. The hotel offers everything you could want during your stay with units sleeping up to 14 people. Downtown Kimberley has the biggest selection of lodging with cheap B&B's and motels.

Food. Around Kimberley you will find a good mix of eateries with something for everyone to sample whether on the mountain or in the village. The *Day Lodge Cafeteria* serves up a good breakfast while *Mingles' Grill* specialise in killer grills. *Kelsey's* Restaurant and the *Steamwinder Pub* offer a good selection of bar food, although both are a bit cheesy going in for apres ski.

Night wise, Kimberley is a bit dull and definitely not a hot action town. Nothing really stands out or captures your attention. The place has a number of bland bars that all seem to go in for far too much stupid apres ski rubbish. Still, you can get very messy and drink on until the early morning hours.

SUMMARY

Kimberley is good resort that will suit all levels of riders especially beginners with lots of easy to handle green runs. Excellent friendly local services.

Kimberley Alpine Resort

Pic - Kimberley Resort

CAR
From Calgary, travel via Memoral Drive and the P2 / P3 and P95A routes all the way to Kimberley. Calgary to resort is 281 miles, 8 hours drive time.
FLY
to Calgary/Vancouver with daily domestic flights to Cranbrook (15 mins away).
BUS
Greyhound bus leaves Calgary at 6:15 pm and arrives 12:15 am, tel 1-800-661-8747

MT. WASHINGTON

5 OUT OF 10

Basic but still cool

Pic:

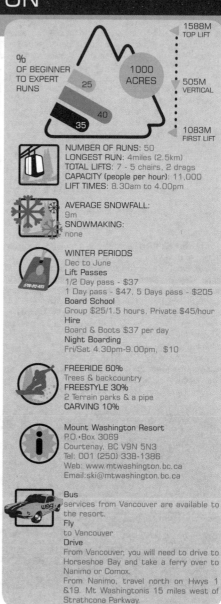

%
OF BEGINNER
TO EXPERT
RUNS

25

40

35

1000 ACRES

1588M
TOP LIFT

505M
VERTICAL

1083M
FIRST LIFT

NUMBER OF RUNS: 50
LONGEST RUN: 4miles (2.5km)
TOTAL LIFTS: 7 - 5 chairs, 2 drags
CAPACITY (people per hour): 11,000
LIFT TIMES: 8.30am to 4.00pm

AVERAGE SNOWFALL:
9m
SNOWMAKING:
none

WINTER PERIODS
Dec to June
Lift Passes
1/2 Day pass - $37
1 Day pass - $47, 5 Days pass - $205
Board School
Group $25/1.5 hours, Private $45/hour
Hire
Board & Boots $37 per day
Night Boarding
Fri/Sat 4.30pm-9.00pm, $10

FREERIDE 60%
Trees & backcountry
FREESTYLE 30%
2 Terrain parks & a pipe
CARVING 10%

Mount Washington Resort
P.O.•Box 3069
Courtenay, BC V9N 5N3
Tel: 001 (250) 338-1386
Web: www.mtwashington.bc.ca
Email:ski@mtwashington.bc.ca

Bus
services from Vancouver are available to
the resort.
Fly
to Vancouver
Drive
From Vancouver, you will need to drive to
Horseshoe Bay and take a ferry over to
Nanimo or Comox.
From Nanimo, travel north on Hwys 1
&19. Mt. Washingtonis 15 miles west of
Strathcona Parkway.

Just off the west coast of Canada and floating in the Pacific Ocean is **Vancouver Island**, which is home to a number of resorts. The most notable and indeed the biggest is Mt Washington, which is located in the middle of the island. Over recent years large amounts of money has been spent on upgrading the whole area to make it modern and more fashionable. The amount of terrain available here is pretty cool offering a good mixture of off-piste, powder, trees and well groomed runs. As Mt Washington grows, so do the crowds, therefore be warned that the slopes can get busy at peak times.

FREERIDERS up to advanced status have a good selection of steep blacks reachable off the top of the **Eagle Express** chair. Here you can head down trails like Hawk, a fast run that starts out wide before dropping down through trees. Less adventurous but still as good is the cluster of runs off **The Gully**, such as **Scum's Delight.**
FREESTYLERS head here en-masse to ride some great natural terrain and take advantage of the clean hits in the park. Located by the **Coaster run** off the **Whiskey Jack** chair, the park is loaded with table-tops, gaps, hits and a good halfpipe.
CARVERS who only want a series of straight, fast slopes to cut up, will not be disappointed. If you're up to the grade, check out **Chimney** - it will prove whether you are a man or a mouse. Alternatively, **Whisky Jack** is a gentle but excellent carver's run, especially if you are still mastering the art.
BEGINNERS will have to do introductory courses on how to cope with bruises on the lower slopes, before heading up higher. Based at the lower sections, the **Green chair** and **Discovery** lift gives rise to some easy novice terrain.

THE TOWN
In resorts that are constantly growing and developing, one is bound to find differences each time you visit.
Local facilities are a bit sparse but what is on offer is good. If you can't find what you're after, then check out the offerings in **Courtney**, 25 minutes away. This is where you will also get the best night-life. **Accommodation** options are fairly extensive with 4,000 tourist beds available in a variety of condos and chalets, many of which are on, or very close to, the slopes. Lodging is not overpriced here - you can get a decent condo for C$70/night or a chalet from C$100.

8 OUT OF 10

Great heli-boarding

Located 3 hours from **Calgary, Panorama** is an absolute gem of a resort that is growing in popularity every year. The resort is constantly improving every aspect of the

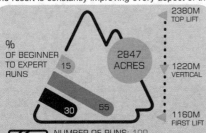

% OF BEGINNER TO EXPERT RUNS

15

2847 ACRES

30   **55**

2380M TOP LIFT

1220M VERTICAL

1160M FIRST LIFT

NUMBER OF RUNS: 100
LONGEST RUN: 5.5km
TOTAL LIFTS: 9
1 Gondola, 5 chairs, 3 drags
CAPACITY (people per hour): 7,000
LIFT TIMES: 9.00am to 10.00pm

AVERAGE SNOWFALL:
4.8m
SNOWMAKING:
40%

WINTER PERIODS
Dec to May
Lift Passes
1 Day pass $59, 5 days $249
Season $799
Board School
Group $49/1.5hr, Private $109/1.5hr
Hire
Board & Boots $35 per day, 5 days $140
Snowmobiles
2 hours $110
Heliboarding
Yes
Night Boarding
Thu-Sun Till 9.00pm inc Terrain parks

FREERIDE 60%
Trees & backcountry
FREESTYLE 20%
2 Terrain parks & a pipe
CARVING 20%

Panorama Resort
Panorama. V0A 1K0. B.C
Tel: 001 (250) 342 6941
Web:www.panoramaresort.com
Email:paninfo@intrawest.com

Bus
direct from Calgary takes around 2 hrs.
Fly
to Calgary, 2 hours transfer
Drive
From Calgary, use highway 1 and P93 to Radium Hot Springs, then Hwy 95 to Invermere, which is 11 miles from Panorama. Calgary to resort is 184 miles. 4 3/4 hours drive time.

Pic - Panoramma

place. 2000/2001 saw the opening up of an extra 700 acres of backcountry terrain while down in the village a number of new lodging properties were added. Panorama is a retreat style resort: very quiet and uncrowded with virtually no day-trip skiers unlike many other resorts. The big news about Panorama is that it offers some of the most convenient heli-boarding around. *R.K. Heli-ski* offers hourly, daily or weekly trips that include excursions into the **Purcell Mountains**. Heli-boarding is not restricted to expert freeriders but no matter what your standard is, it's not cheap. *R.K. Heli-ski* offers various daily or weekly trips which cover 6 major mountain areas where you can ride over 700 square miles of terrain taking in massive snow bowls. Three heli-trips with a guide, breakfast and lunch cost from C$520 and is well worth the cost. Five days heli-boarding with accommodation will sting you some C$4000, but you will never forget the experience.

FREERIDERS will soon notice how well this resort lends itself to powder-hunting, tree-riding and natural hits. Overall, much of the terrain suits intermediate and advanced freeriders, but there is plenty for novices to get their teeth into. For a freeride rush you should check out the **Extreme Dream Zone**, located off the **Summit** T-bar, where you will find a series of black and double black steeps, trees and cliff jumps.

FREESTYLERS have a good fun-park which is well designed and there are also loads of natural hits all over the slopes.

CARVERS will find this a very good resort for laying out big turns, particularly for intermediate carvers. A couple of blue runs to the right of the **Horizon** chair are excellent.

BEGINNERS will find Panorama perfect. The easiest runs are located on the lower sections and provide some good novice riding.

THE TOWN
Off the slopes, accommodation is offered in a number of well-located lodges, although they are not that cheap. There are a number of eating haunts ranging from expensive restaurants to pub fare and fast food. The *T-Bar* is worth mentioning as is the *Black Forest* if you like Schnitzel. **Night times** are very tame with *The Glaciers* and the *Jackpine* being the places to spend the evenings in.

119

RED MOUNTAIN

8 OUT OF 10

fantastic resort that offers great riding on crowd free slopes

Pic -Red Mountain

%
OF BEGINNER
TO EXPERT **10**
RUNS

1585 ACRES

2073M
TOP LIFT

813M
VERTICAL

45

45

1185M
FIRST LIFT

NUMBER OF RUNS: 83
LONGEST RUN: 4.5miles (7km)
TOTAL LIFTS: 6 - 5 chairs, 1 drag
CAPACITY (people per hour): 6,150
LIFT TIMES: 8.45am to 3.30pm
MOUNTAIN CAFES: 2

AVERAGE SNOWFALL:
7.6m
SNOWMAKING:
none

WINTER PERIODS:
Dec to April
Lift Passes
1 Day pass $48
6 Day pass - $264
Season Pass - $759
Board Schools
Private lessons $55 (1hr) $135 (3hrs)
Group lessons $32 (2hrs)
Hire
Board & Boots $32 a day
Heliboarding
Yes

FREERIDE 65%
Trees & good backcountry
FREESTYLE 25%
A Terrain park & a halfpipe
CARVING 10%

Red Mountain
P.O. Box 670,
Rossland. V0G 1Y0. BC
General info: 001 (250) 362 7384
Reservations: 001 (800) 663 0105
Snowphone: 001 (250) 362 550
Web:www.ski-red.com
Email:info@ski-red.com

NEW

new for 04/05 season
Sold to an investment group in June 2004.
Plans this season include installation of
magic carpet lift & improvements to the
terrain park. 385 acres of new boardable
terrain.

Red Mountain and the town of **Rossland,** located just north of the US/Canadian border, go back in history to the days of the Canadian gold-rush of 1896. One of the oldest resorts in Canada, Red Mountain has been operating as a ski resort since 1947 when its first chair lift was installed. Red was seen by many for a long time as a bit of a dark horse. However, as time has progressed, so has Red's reputation. As a powder heaven and home to some of the best extreme riding in Canada, Red Mountain has freeriders wetting themselves when they see what awaits them. Although this may not be in the super league of resorts, it nevertheless has a lot going for it with excellent, crowd-free runs and early powder unspoilt by morning masses. Old school riders will remember the Burton video 'Board with the World' where riders are seen at Red Mountain shredding everything in sight, coverways, table tops, downed skiers etc.

Grante Mountain and **Red Mountain** make up 1,100 acres of terrain. Both offer a variety of runs that mainly suit snowboarders who ride well. First timers are going to have their work cut out. The trail map lists many of its runs with a star to mean extreme, and that's exactly what the runs live up to. Grante is the bigger of the two areas and is easily accessed from the base lodge. Once at the top you can head off in a variety of directions, but note that most of the runs at the top are for advanced riders, although **Ridge Road** will take novices off to easier slopes.

FREERIDERS should check out **Buffalo Ridge** which takes you down one side of Grante into bowls, natural hits and lots of trees. **Sara's Chute**, a double black, takes you down steeps, through trees and eventually brings you out onto **Long Squaw**, a green trail that leads back to the base area.

FREESTYLERS will find Red's **Rhythm Method** halfpipe located under **Red's Face**, while the well maintained fun-park is reachable from **Boardwalk**. Alternatively, there are plenty of natural hits, especially

on **Grante Mountain**, to gain air from.

CARVERS will find loads of good pisted runs although not all are regularly groomed. On the **Paradise** side of the mountain, the terrain will suit those wanting tamer stuff and carvers can lay out big lines on runs such as

RED MOUNTAIN

Pic -San Tan

first time needs, by offering a number of tuition programmes that will soon have you shredding **Red Mountain** with ease.

THE TOWN

Red Mountain has a good but basic selection of lodging properties and facilities at the base of the slopes. Prices vary but staying close to the slopes is generally more expensive than staying down the road in the town of Rossland. **Rossland** is an old town that offers a variety of good local services from cheap eating haunts to boozy late night hangouts. Board and boot hire is available at a number of slopes or in **Rossland**, check out *Powder Hounds* for all your needs. **Job Seekers** should call (250) 362 7384 or email: jobs@ski-red, to get the latest details.

Food. Rossland is not noted for its restaurants, but what you find is very good, and at prices to suit all pockets. *Sunshine Cafe* has a good menu while *Elmer's* serves great veggie food. *The Flying Shovel* dishes up good pub grub. *Mountain Gypsy* is the spot for pizzas and pasta.

Night-life in Rossland is not exactly the most happening, but it's still cool. It offers a number of good night-time hangouts where you can drink to jazz music or boogie to pop. Most bars play decent tunes and have pool tables. The *Flying Steamshovel* is bar, as are *The Powder Keg* and *Rafter's*. (Local talent is also good)

Accommodation is as you'd expect from any resort. At the slopes there is a selection of Lodges, Chalets and Condo's. Places such as the *Red Mountain Cabins*, a short walk from the slopes, is pricey but very good. However, the best option is to stay in the town of **Rossland** which is only 2 miles from the slopes. The options include cheap B&B's and a hostel which are all close to the night-time action. Check the web site for accommodation and the latest prices.

SUMMARY

A fantastic resort that offers great riding on crowd free slopes, especially just after a fresh dump of snow. Low key but great local services

Southern Comfort. Other notable trails to check out are **Doug's Run** and **Maggie's Farm**.

BEGINNERS may be a bit put off when they first see the terrain level ratings and although the slopes are rated intermediate/advanced, it doesn't mean novices can't ride here. There is ample terrain to play on at the **Upper** and **Lower Back** trails, before riding the **Long Squaw** trail that runs back to the base lodge. The staff at the local snowboard school cater well for all your

C

CANADA

BRITISH COLUMBIA

CAR
Vancouver via Osooyos & Rossland. Red Mountain is 371 miles. Drive time is about 10 hours.
TRAIN
to Spokane in the US
FLY
Fly to Vancouver International. Transfer time to resort is 7 hours. Local airport is Castlegar 20 mins.
BUS
A bus from Vancouver takes around 7 hours. A Local bus run sdaily from Rossland to Red Mountain.

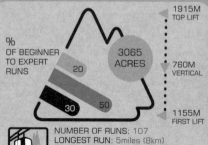

SILVER STAR

7 OUT OF 10 — Good all-round resort

Pic - Silver Star

%
OF BEGINNER
TO EXPERT
RUNS 20

3065 ACRES

30 50

1915M TOP LIFT

760M VERTICAL

1155M FIRST LIFT

NUMBER OF RUNS: 107
LONGEST RUN: 5miles (8km)
TOTAL LIFTS: 10 - 4 chairs,4 drags, 2 Dopplemeyer Tube Lift
CAPACITY (people per hour): 13,800
LIFT TIMES: 8.30am to 9.00pm
MOUNTAIN CAFES: 13

AVERAGE SNOWFALL:
7m
SNOWMAKING:
none

WINTER PERIODS:
Nov to April
Lift Passes
Half Day $46, 1 Day $60, 5 Days $236
Board Schools
Group $69 four hours
Private $99/hour Full day $399
Hire
Board & Boots $36/day , 5 days $186
Night Boarding
Thu to Sat 3.30pm - 8.00pm, $22

FREERIDE 60%
Trees & backcountry
FREESTYLE 20%
A Terrain park & a halfpipe
CARVING 20%

Silver Star Mountain Resort
Box 3002
Silver Star Mountain, BC
Canada V1B 3M1
Tel: (250) 542-0224
Fax (250) 542-1236
Web:www.silverstarmtn.com
Email:guestservices@skisilverstar.com

Bus
services from Kelowna, can be arranged on request.
Fly
to Vancouver, and then onto Kelowna, (40 mins).
Drive
From Vancouver, use as a map reference the town of Vernon, which is 12 miles from Silver Star along Hwy 97.

NEW — new for 04/05 season
More lifts, expanded terrain park, boarder cross, new beginners area and some base facility improvements

---

Silver Star is pure Canada and damn good at that. Any place that can boast an average snowfall of 700cm should be given a platform, and Silver Star has earned its title as a rider's paradise with stupidly large amounts of powder on an annual basis. There is plenty of good off-piste terrain, with big bowls and heaps of trees to shred. The 1,200 acres of marked runs are spread out over two faces - the **South Face** on **Vanace Creek** and the North Face on **Putman**, collectively suiting advanced freeriders.

FREERIDERS who know the score have a number of double black diamond runs to check out. The first port of call should be the **South Face** runs before heading over to the North. **Vanace Creek Express** lift takes you up to the summit where you'll find open terrain and the option of dropping down to some wide open blacks. The more gentle stuff is reached via **Sundance**. **Christmas Bowl** is really cool and if you have the bottle, try the **Attridge Face** run. **Putnam Creek** tests everybody - steeps through trees with pure freeriding territory.
FREESTYLERS looking for air will be pleasantly surprised with the natural hits. However, with a two acre fun-park, you don't need to look far to find places to hit. The park is located below **Big Dipper trail**, off Yellow chair lift.
CARVERS who can ride will find this a challenging resort. The **Milky Way** is an excellent open area where big arcs can be accomplished with ease. The steepest carving is on the North Face slopes where you'll be put to the test.
BEGINNERS will appreciate Silver Star with its well connected green and blue runs. The local snowboard school runs daily programmes as well as weekly camps offering video analysis.

THE TOWN
Off the slopes, Silver Star's old-fashioned Victorian theme offers **accommodation** for all budgets, with comfortable lodges available at the base of the slopes. **Eating** options are not only good, but also cheap and as with the evening hangouts, they are all within walking distance of the slopes. Silver Star's **night-life** may not be major, but it's still cool with a couple of drinking holes to check out. The town of **Vernon** is located only a short distance from Silver Star and offers a greater selection of facilities. Vernon is the place to go for a lively Saturday night out and to eye up some local skirt.

C
CANADA
BRITISH COLUMBIA

122

SUN PEAKS

7 OUT OF 10

A really good resort

Sun Peaks is a resort that hopes to knock Whistler off the top spot. Situated about 40 miles from **Kamloops**, in the interior of the Rockies, this is a resort that has come of age. Over the past few years, huge expansion plans have been put into operation with fast modern lifts and

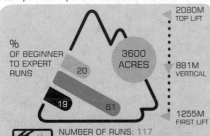

% OF BEGINNER TO EXPERT RUNS

20

3600 ACRES

2080M TOP LIFT

881M VERTICAL

19   61

1255M FIRST LIFT

NUMBER OF RUNS: 117
LONGEST RUN: 5miles (8km)
TOTAL LIFTS: 9
5 chairs,3 drags, 1 magic carpet
CAPACITY (people per hour): 9,000
LIFT TIMES: 8.30am to 3.30pm

AVERAGE SNOWFALL:
5.29m
SNOWMAKING:
65%

WINTER PERIODS:
Nov to April
Lift Passes
1/2 Day pass $46
1 Day pass $56
Season pass $799
Board Schools
2Hours Group $49/69
Private $52/hr

FREERIDE 45%
Trees & backcountry
FREESTYLE 30%
A Terrain park & a halfpipe
CARVING 25%

Sun Peaks Resort Corporation
1280 Alpine Road
Sun Peak
British Columbia, Canada V0E 1Z1
Phone: (250) 578-7222
Fax: (250) 578-7223
Web:www.sunpeaksresort.com
Email:info@sunpeaksresort.com

Bus
services from Vancouver takes 5 1/2 hours
Fly
to Vancouver with domestic flights to Kamloops
Drive
From Vancouver, take Hwy 1 east via Kamloops, then via Hwy 5 exit to Jasper for Sun Peaks.

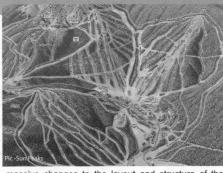

Pic -Sun Peaks

massive changes to the layout and structure of the village. The overall results mean a damn fine mountain to ride that is not overpopulated with holiday masses. Sun Peaks is a large resort with a large vertical descent. The marked-out terrain isn't super-varied, but what is on offer is still good and well prepared with riding to suit all levels and styles.

FREERIDERS looking for long, wide straights with trees galore will find this mountain ideal, keeping you well occupied for a week or more. Take the long **Burfield Quad** to the top and you can gain access to some great terrain. If you plan to go outside the marked boundary, you are required to register with the ski-patrol. For some cool in-boundary riding, **Head Wall** is the place to bust a gut, with a series of short but demanding double diamond blacks. For something a little less daunting, try out the long and sweeping 5 mile trail off the **Ridge**, which can be tackled by intermediate riders.

FREESTYLERS have a massive 30 acre fun park area located off the **Sunrise chair**, which is loaded with hits and a pipe. Around the slopes you also find numerous natural hits to launch off.

CARVERS Sun Peaks should appeal to you in a big way; some of the runs here are superb, and just right for laying the board over an edge at speed. If you have the balls, try the steep **Expo**; if not, try your luck down **Spillway**.

BEGINNERS who don't appreciate the novice slopes here or manage to progress with style should give up snowboarding and take up train spotting. This is an excellent beginner's resort with some perfect novice tracks off **Sundance**.

THE TOWN
Accommodation and all other amenities can be found in **Sun Peaks** or in the small hamlet of **Burfield**. Whichever you choose, both offer good facilities that compliment those on the slopes. Mind you, it should be pointed out that this is not a budget rider's destination as it can get expensive. There's a good choice of restaurants, bars and shops to choose from, but night-life is very tame with *Masa's* the favoured evening hangout for booze, music and meeting the locals.

10 OUT OF 10

Major riding for all styles but busy

%
OF BEGINNER
TO EXPERT
RUNS

20

7071
ACRES

25   55

2284M
TOP LIFT

1609M
VERTICAL

675M
FIRST LIFT

NUMBER OF RUNS: 230
LONGEST RUN: 7miles (11km)
TOTAL LIFTS: 33
3 Gondolas, 18 chairs, 12 drag
CAPACITY (people per hour): 59,000
LIFT TIMES: 7.00am to 3.30pm
MOUNTAIN CAFES: 17

AVERAGE SNOWFALL:
9.14m
SNOWMAKING:
35%

WINTER PERIODS:
Dec to May
SUMMER PERIODS:
June to August (Blackcomb Glacier)
Lift Passes
1 Day $65 , 6 Day pass - $345
Season pass - $1519
Board Schools
Half day Group $135 Full day $205
Private Half day $399 Full day $599
Hire
Board & Boots 1 Day $36,5 Days $150
Heliboarding
3 runs of 1400/2300M $640pp
6 runs of 2700/4600M $940pp
Snowmobiles
$99 for begginers trip
full day @$229
Night Boarding
Yes & Superpipe illuminated this season

FREERIDE 50%
Trees & awesome backcountry
FREESTYLE 30%
2 Terrain parks & 3 halfpipes
CARVING 20%

Whistler and Blackcomb Mountains
4545 Blackcomb Way,
Whistler, B.C. VON 1B4, Canada
Tel: 604.932.3434
Web:www.whistler-blackcomb.com
Email:wbres@intrawest.com

new for 04/05 season

NEW

The west side of Whistler Mountain
officially opens this season with 400
acres of new terrain. The resort
boundary will be extended to include
Flute Bowl providing 700 acres of new
patrolled backcountry terrain. Creekside
base reopens after 4 years with much
improved servives. Ready for the 2005
Snowboard World Championships a new
150m night lit Superpipe will be built on
Lower Cruiser in the Base II area

C

CANADA

BRITISH COLUMBIA

Pic - Whistler

Whistler & Blackcomb, which has the longest snow
season of any resort in North America, has been
continually been voted the No.1 resort in North America, and
after you spend a day on the mountain it is pretty easy to
see why. The reason people come here is simple: the riding
on offer here is unbelievable. There is so much in terms
of different terrain that if you get bored here, you must be
a loser. You can choose from great bowls, terrain parks or
tree runs. The two mountain areas offer over 230 marked
runs with seven alpine bowls on Whistler and five bowls
on Blackcomb. There are three halfpipes, 2 terrain parks, a
bordercross track and some seventeen mountain restaurants.
Lifts normally open at 8.30am, but early birds can take to the
slopes at even earlier. Fresh Trax queues start at 7am with
lifts to the top of Whistler and with as much breakfast as you
can eat, you can ride the virgin trails before the rest of the
public for an extra C$16 on your lift pass. If you can't make
it here during the winter, don't fret as Blackcomb is the only
real summer snowboard area in North America. A number of
snowboard camps are held here on an annual basis during
the summer months and are open to anyone wishing to pay
the camp fee. The courses are tailored to all levels.

FREERIDERS in search of powder have twelve bowls to pick
from. **Symphony** and **Bagel** bowls on Whistler are a couple
of favourites. While on Blackcomb, the **Couloir Extreme**, a
double black diamond trail, will test the best. **Ridge Runner**
and **Slingshot** are two more of Blackcomb's pleasers, but
they are seriously extreme. For a real fix, speak to a local
and ask them to direct you to '**Kyber Pass**', which is an off
piste two hour trail.

FREESTYLERS looking for air will have endless days of
fun, with a major fun park on Blackcomb and a lesser one
on Whistler **Blackcomb** is the main hangout, where you will
find a massive halfpipe pipe with 14ft walls and a resident
DJ blasting out tunes (mind you it's mostly crap techno stuff).
Whichever mountain you choose, you will find plenty of great
natural terrain to air off.

CARVERS (those without big beards) wanting to lay out
some big arcs should check out the **Dave Murray** run on
Whistler. Novice carvers who are just finding out what it's
like to hold an edge, can practice with ease down the wide

place that attracts the rich and famous. This place can be hellishly expensive, even for a burger and fries. However, In its favour, services are of a very high standard and locals are very friendly and do their best to help you. All the main amenities are located in **Whistler's** smart village, which is loaded with high profile expensive retail shops and restaurants. The village also has a host of sporting attractions from swimming to ice skating, to racquet sports in the Meadow Park sports centre.

Accommodation in the main is expensive. There are budget options such as one of the ski dorms or hostels, but you will need to book in advance in order to get a bed. Condos are a good option for groups of riders. Lodges and hotels are of a super high standard but then so are the costs. The *Blackcomb Lodge*, *Chateau Whistler* or *Pan Pacific* all come highly recommended.

Food is served from an array of restaurants, some of which attract sad Hollywood stars and disposed royals, while others cater for the more normal amongst us. For a cheap meal try *Subway* or *Tex-Mex*. For those without morals there's a *McDonald's* and a *KFC* in the market place. If steaks are your thing then check out *The Keg*. The *Longhorn* right at the base of the slopes offers reasonably priced food.

Nightlife here is possibly the one thing that lets the resort down slightly. Not that it's bad, but most places are geared towards the over 30's. That said you can have a laugh in the likes of *Garfinkel's* bar. The *Longhorn* is also a good place to get tanked up in and the staff are real cool. For clubbing check out *Tommy Africas* or *Maxx Fish*.

open **Springboard** or **Grundy** runs, which are on the Blackcomb mountain.

BEGINNERS are spoilt when it comes to snowboard instruction programmes. On **Blackcomb** mountain you can get lessons for any age, including classes for **Junior Jibbers** (aged 7-12) and **Kiddie Rippers** (aged 5-6). Both mountains offer plenty of good novice trails, with some of the best being at the base of Blackcomb, aided by beginner lifts. Budding young *Terjes* can also get freestyle instruction and find out just how to ride a pipe and hit a big jump with style and in safety.

THE TOWN
Whistler is an all year round fashionable and buzzing

SUMMARY
Major riding for all styles and all levels, especially backcountry. But take note of the fact that lift queues can be very long. Great summer riding.
Money Wise:
Stupidly expensive with prices forevery thing way over the top

C A N A D A B R I T I S H C O L U M B I A

CAR
Vancouver via Squamish. Whistler is 75 miles (120km), drive time is about 2 1/4 hours.
TRAIN
direct to Whistler
FLY
to Vancouver International. Transfer time to resort is 2 hours
BUS
from Vancouver takes around 2 hours. A local bus runs daily around Whistler and Blackcomb.

WHITEWATER

5 OUT OF 10 Fun for a few days

Pic-Whitewater

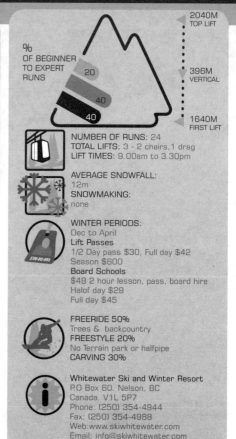

% OF BEGINNER TO EXPERT RUNS

20
40
40

2040M TOP LIFT
396M VERTICAL
1640M FIRST LIFT

NUMBER OF RUNS: 24
TOTAL LIFTS: 3 - 2 chairs,1 drag
LIFT TIMES: 9.00am to 3.30pm

AVERAGE SNOWFALL:
12m
SNOWMAKING:
none

WINTER PERIODS:
Dec to April
Lift Passes
1/2 Day pass $30, Full day $42
Season $600
Board Schools
$49 2 hour lesson, pass, board hire
Halof day $29
Full day $45

FREERIDE 50%
Trees & backcountry
FREESTYLE 20%
No Terrain park or halfpipe
CARVING 30%

Whitewater Ski and Winter Resort
P.O Box 60. Nelson, BC
Canada. V1L 5P7
Phone: (250) 354-4944
Fax: (250) 354-4988
Web:www.skiwhitewater.com
Email: info@skiwhitewater.com

Bus
services from Vancouver, go to the town of Nelson.
Fly
to Vancouver, with a transfer time of around 12 hours.
Drive
From Vancouver, use as a map reference the town of Nelson along Hwy3 of Hwy 6. Calgary to resort is 478 miles, 12 hours drive time.

Whitewater is located close to the town of **Nelson** and is a very good bet for riding, even when other resorts are begging for snow. Whitewater receives 1,200cm of snow each winter and due to the area's stable winter temperatures, the snow lasts and lasts. The lifts access some of the best high altitude in-bounds terrain in Canada. Whitewater is a huge bowl, contained by two ridges that join at the apex to form the 2,440m (800 ft) **Ymir Peak**. Ymir (pronounced 'why-mur') is named after a Norse legend and traps any westerly storm. Water vapour sucked off nearby **Kootenay Lake** is turned into consistently dry champagne powder that fills the bowl. Admittedly a 'high end' resort, with a majority of expert and intermediate terrain, Whitewater still has a lot of room for those lovers of groomed run cruising with long, easy beginner runs off the **Silver Ling** lift.

FREERIDERS should take the **Summit chair** to access the opposite ridge which offers steeper, groomed, intermediate runs and the most challenging off-piste through bowls and trees. Try **Dynamite**, **Catch Basin** and **Glory Basin**, and lay down one powder track next to another. Get up early to challenge Blast, a steep fall-line under the chair lift.

FREESTYLERS need to roam over the whole area to find places to get air, as there is no permanent pipe or park. However, there is plenty of great natural freestyle terrain.

CARVERS wanting fast groomed terrain will enjoy Whitewater's trails which offer every level of hard booter something to tackle.

BEGINNERS will find that Whitewater is the kind of area that doesn't really have beginners - just learners who progress in powder by riding steeper and deeper lines. A new beginner park called The Hunter has been created near the day lodge. However, most people who have mastered the basics choose to head for the hills and carve up snow where groomers never reach.

THE TOWN

There is no in-resort accommodation available at present, but there is a wide range of places to sleep in the town of Nelson. **Nelson** has good local facilities and is very affordable, if only a bit dull and basic. The *Dancing Bear Inn* has beds from C$19/person and Stay and Ride specials from C$45. During the day there is great food in *Shucky's Eatery* (even the soups are made with wine), and offers everything from fries to a full course lunch. *Coal Oil Jonny's* offers Nelson brewed beer on tap.

FAIRMONT SPRINGS
Small family resort, about 40 miles from Banf

Pic -Fairmont Springs

Number of Runs: 13
Longest run:1mile (1.6km)
Info: Has a terrain park (nothing big) & beginners pipe
Top Lift: 1585m
Bottom Lift: 1280m
Vertical: 304m
Total Lifts:2 - 1 chairs, 1 drags
Lift pass: 1/2 Day Pass - $25
Day Pass - $34
Lift times: 4.00pm to 10.00pm
Hire: Board & Boots $20
School: 1 Hour lesson - $44
Contact:
Fairmont Hot Springs Resort
Box 10, Fairmont Hot Springs,
British Columbia, Canada, V0B 1L0
Phone:1-800-663-4979 or
Tel: 250-345-6311
www.fairmontresort.com
info@fairmonthotsprings.com
Location: Hwy. 93/95, 3 hours west of Calgary

HARPER MOUNTAIN
A decent size family resort, near Kamloops.
Ride Area: 400 acres
Number of Runs: 15
Easy 25%
Intermediate 50%
Advanced 25%
Info: Has a terrain park
Top Lift: 1524m
Bottom Lift: 1097m
Vertical: 427m
Total Lifts:3 - 1 chairs, 2 drags
Lift pass: 1/2 Day Pass - $21
Day Pass - $29
Lift times: 9.30am to 10.00pm
Hire: Board & Boots $34 a day
School: Full day inc hire, lift pass & lessons $215
Contact:
Snow Phone 250-573-4616
Office 250-372-2119

Lodge 250-573-5115
www.harpermountain.com
info@harpermountain.com

HEMLOCK VALLEY

Pic -Hemlock Valley

Number of Runs: 34
Info: Has a terrain park
Top Lift: 1524m
Bottom Lift: 975m
Vertical: 397m
Total Lifts:4 - 3 chairs, 1 drags
Lift pass: 1/2 Day Pass - $32
Day Pass - $39
Night Pass - $15
Lift times: 9.30am to 10.00pm
Hire: Board & Boots $36 a day
School: Beginners all in day lesson, lift, hire $59.00
Private lesson $56 per hour
Contact:
20955 Hemlock valley road.
Agassiz B.C. Canada V0M-1A1
Phone: (604) 797-4411
Fax: (604) 797-4440
www.hemlockvalleyresort.com
info@hemlockvalleyresort.com

MOUNT SEYMOUR RESORT
30 minutes from Vancouver with 3 terrain parks & a halfpipe

Ride Area: 60 acres
Number of Runs: 21
Longest run:1.6km
Info: Well setup up for freestylers with 3 terrain parks and a halfpipe
Snowfall: 17m
Top Lift: 1265m
Bottom Lift: 1020m
Vertical: 330m
Total Lifts:5 - 2 chairs, 2 magic carpets
Lift pass: Day pass $34
Lift times: 8.30am to 10.00pm
Night Boarding: 11 slopes lit, pass $15
Hire: Board & Boots $37 a day

School: Day lesson, lift & hire $45
Contact:
Mount Seymour Resort
1700 Mt Seymour Rd
North Vancouver, BC
V7G 1L3
General Information 604.986.2261
24-Hour Snow Phone
604.718.7771
Resort Fax 604.986.2267
www.mountseymour.com
guestservices@mountseymour.com
Location: 30 minutes from downtown Vancouver. Heading west on Hwy #1, cross the Second Narrows Bridge, take the 3rd exit (#22) on to Mount Seymour Parkway and follow the signs to the Provincial Park. Turn left at Mount Seymour Road (at MohawkStation) and arrive at the base area in 15 minutes.

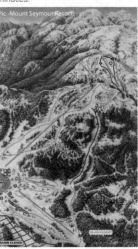
Pic -Mount Seymour Resort

Capital: Quebec City
Population: 7.3 million

Speed limits:
Motorways-100kph (62mph)
Highways-90kph (55mph)
Towns-50kph (31mph)

Fly
Quebec Airport
www.aeroportdequebec.com
Tel: (418) 640-2700

Montreal Airport
www.admtl.com
Tel: (514) 394-7200

Bus
Greyhound
tel: 1-800-661-8747
www.greyhound.ca

Rail
www.viarail.ca
Tel: 1 888 842-7245

Ferries
Tel: 1-250-386-3431
Web:www.bcferries.com

Time Zone
GMT -4/-5 hours

Quebec Tourist Information
Tourisme Québec
P.O. Box 979
Montréal (Québec)
H3C 2W3 Canada
Tel: 1 (514) 873-2015
www.bonjourquebec.com

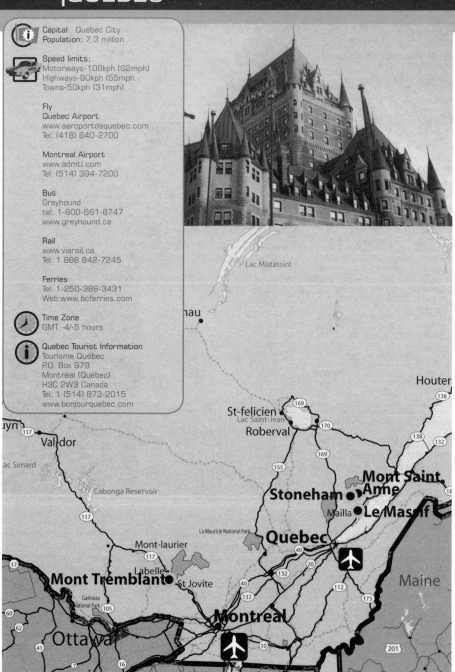

Lac Mistassini

Houter

St-felicien
Lac Saint-Jean
Roberval

Val d'or

Lac Simard

Cabonga Reservoir

Stoneham

Mont Saint Anne

Mailla

Le Massif

La Mauricie National Park

Quebec

Mont-laurier

Labelle

Mont Tremblant

St Jovite

Gatineau National Park

Montréal

Maine

Ottawa

LE MASSIF

4 OUT OF 10

Small resort on the up

Le Massif is an unassuming and rather un-adventurous small mountain resort that lies just 45 minutes north of **Quebec City**. In recent years the resort has undergone a number of major re-developments spending in excess of 25 million dollars on facilities that will greatly

Pic -Le Massif Resort

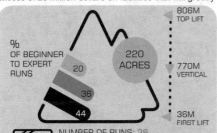

806M TOP LIFT

% OF BEGINNER TO EXPERT RUNS

20

220 ACRES

36

44

770M VERTICAL

36M FIRST LIFT

NUMBER OF RUNS: 36
LONGEST RUN: 2.3miles
TOTAL LIFTS: 5 - 3 chairs,2 drags
CAPACITY (people per hour): 6,500
LIFT TIMES: 8.30am to 4.00pm

AVERAGE SNOWFALL:
6.5m
SNOWMAKING:
63%

WINTER PERIODS:
Dec to April
Lift Passes
Half day $33,One day $41
Five days $170,Season $759
Board Schools
Group $45 two hours
Private $40/hour
Hire
Board & Boots $32day

FREERIDE 40%
Lots of trees but very limited backcountry
FREESTYLE 20%
No Terrain park but a halfpipe
CARVING 40%

Le Massif
1350 Principale, C.P.47,
Petite-Riviere-Saint-Francois. Quebec.
Web: www.lemassif.com

Bus
services from Quebec City go Le Massif and take around 45 mins.
Fly
to Montreal with a transfer time of 3.5 hours to the resort.
Drive
Driving from Quebec City, head north along hwy 138 past Mont-Sainte-Mane.

NEW
new for 04/05 season
$5 Development inc 6 new trails, a high speed quad chair lift 90 new snow guns and plans for summer boarding.

improve not only the number and type of mountain runs, but also access to the resort and local facilities. It was also taken over in 2004 and its new owners are spending a further $5million on improvements.You can now travel from Quebec City along route 138 to the top of the slopes, as well as the base. What you will find on your arrival is a mountain that offers most grades something to try out although it has to be said that a week here would become very boring after a few days. Still the resort can now boast up to 36 marked out trails which are tree lined up to the summit which is also the location of the new Day Lodge. All 36 runs are serviced by just 5 lifts including a new fast quad chair, which Le Massif boasts at being the longest high speed chair lift in **Quebec Province**. And that's not the only boast they make around here, as they also claim to have the most extensive snowmaking facilities on the east coast. What ever the legitimacy of such claims, Le Massif can claim to be an okay place to ride if you are a total beginner or basic intermediate rider.

FREERIDERS have a fairly ordinary mountain to ride that allows for some basic freeriding down mixed ability slopes which are sandwiched between lots of dense wooded sections. However, this place is not hard-core and forget about any decent back-country terrain or powder bowls.
FREESTYLERS should be able to have fun here. There are plenty of spots where you can pull some natural air with banks of snow lining many of the tree lined slopes. You will also find the odd log to grind over, (should you not mind wrecking your boards base). Man mad hits are short in supply however, there is a pipe and on occasions they do build other obstacles.
CARVERS who come to a resort looking for loads of super fast steeps, should go else where. That said Le Massif does have a number of nicely groomed carving trails to ride along.
BEGINNERS have the best chance to shine here with a good selection of easy runs to choose from which can all be reached with ease and with out needing to use drag lifts all the time.

THE TOWN. Off the slopes Le Massif's local facilities are basic to the extreme. All your accommodation and eating needs can be found down in Quebec City which is 45 minutes away.

C

CANADA QUEBEC

129

Okay but not hot

Pic Mt Tremblant

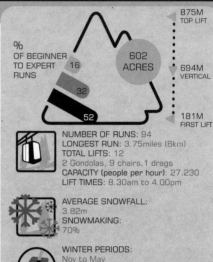

% OF BEGINNER TO EXPERT RUNS

16
32
52

602 ACRES

875M TOP LIFT

694M VERTICAL

181M FIRST LIFT

NUMBER OF RUNS: 94
LONGEST RUN: 3.75miles (6km)
TOTAL LIFTS: 12
2 Gondolas, 9 chairs, 1 drags
CAPACITY (people per hour): 27,230
LIFT TIMES: 8.30am to 4.00pm

AVERAGE SNOWFALL:
3.82m
SNOWMAKING:
70%

WINTER PERIODS:
Nov to May
Lift Passes
6 Days peak season $335, low season $242
Board Schools
90 minute group lesson $55 CAD
Hire
Board & Boots $28 per day

FREERIDE 40%
Trees snd some backcountry
FREESTYLE 20%
A Terrain park & a halfpipe
CARVING 40%

Mont Tremblant Resort
PO Box 240, 2001 ch. Principal
Mont-Tremblant, Quebec,
Canada J0T 1Z0
Information: 001 (819) 425-8681
Fax: 001 (819) 425-9604
Web:www.tremblant.com
Email:info@tremblant.com

Bus
services from Montreal, go to the town of Tremblant.
Fly
to Montreal, with a transfer time of around 2 hours.
Drive
From Montreal, travel north along Hwys 15 &117, direction Ste Jovite, turning of at signs for Mont Tremblant. Montreal to resort is 91 miles, 2 hours drive time.

Tremblant is one of the largest boarding areas in **Canada** and forms part of what is believed to be one of the oldest mountain ranges on the planet. Tremblant's organisational connections with Blackcomb, Panorama and also mighty Stratton in the US, helps them lay on a good time. The mountain's layout is excellent and extremely well planned, covering two sides, the South and the North which also has a new beginner slope running from the top to the bottom. The **South side** gives initial access to the runs which are all carved out of thick forest. The **North side** is a little smaller, but offers the same degree of cool riding. Both sides make up an area suited to carvers and freeriders, especially intermediate and advanced riders.

FREERIDERS have a really good mountain to explore, with plenty of white knuckle trails with drop offs, trees and powder. For some excellent tree-riding, go to **Emotion**. This area is graded a double black diamond trail, so it's not for the weak-kneed.
FREESTYLERS have a decent size halfpipe and park, located under the **Express Flying Mile** chair on the South side, and only takes a few minutes to reach. The park is well looked after and you also get to listen to some tunes blasting out of the P.A.
CARVERS buckle up tight as you'll be able to show off in style on well-pisted trails with 'carve me up' written all over them. **Geant**, a long wide black run on the North side, is really fun, while **Zag-Zag** on the South side is a killer double black that tames out lower down.
BEGINNERS Tremblant offers more than enough for first timers, with easy green and blue runs on the South side. Take the **Express Tremblant chair** and novices can ride from top to bottom, via **La Crette** and Nansen green trails. If you're a starter (in the day) starter then you may wish to have a late lesson; for around C$20 you can have an evening instruction session.

THE TOWN
The village of Tremblant is only a few minutes from the slopes, although there are some slopeside facilities with a good selection of condos and hotels to choose from. Getting around is easy on foot,

alternatively there is a daily local bus service. **Food** and drinking options are okay and night-time can be pretty rowdy, rocking 'til the late hours. But note this is not the cheapest of places, so expect to notch up some credits on your card.

6 OUT OF 10

A bit tedious, but okay for a few days

Mont Sainte-Anne is a decent resort and will certainly keep an intermediate rider content for a few days and a beginner satisfied for a week with ease. With its proximity to Quebec City, the tree lined slopes here attract hoards of city dwellers at weekends, making

Pic Mt Saint Anne Resort

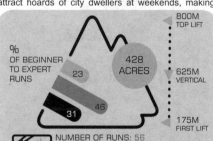

% OF BEGINNER TO EXPERT RUNS

800M TOP LIFT

428 ACRES

625M VERTICAL

23

46

31

175M FIRST LIFT

NUMBER OF RUNS: 56
LONGEST RUN: 3.8miles (5.7km)
TOTAL LIFTS: 13
1 Gondolas, 6 chairs,6 drags
CAPACITY (people per hour): 18,560
LIFT TIMES:8:30am to 3:45pm (or 9:45 pm)

AVERAGE SNOWFALL:
4m
SNOWMAKING:
80%

WINTER PERIODS:
Dec to May
Lift Passes
1 Day $48.60, 5 of 6 days $206.91
Board Schools
2hr workshop $43.45, 5 days $199.95
Hire
board and boots $29/day
helmet $7/day
Night Boarding
4 p.m. - 9:45 p.m.,17 pistes lit, $22.60

FREERIDE 50%
Trees snd some okay backcountry
FREESTYLE 25%
3 Terrain parks & a halfpipe
CARVING 25%

Mont-Sainte-Anne
2000, boul. Beau Pré
Beaupré (Québec) Canada,G0A 1E0
Phone: (418) 827-4561
Fax: (418) 827-3121
Web:www.mont-sainte-anne.com
Email:info@mont-sainte-anne.com

Bus
services from Montreal, go to resort
Fly
to Montreal, 2 1/2hrs from the resort.
Drive
From Montreal, take Hwy 40 and drive north in the direction of Quebec. Exit at the junction for route 138 and then take the R-360 to the resort. Montreal to resort is 180 miles. Quebec is 25 miles.

this a busy place to ride and while the resort can boast lots of rideable terrain, this is not the highest of resorts. Any resort close to a large city is often busy and suffers long lift queues, but thanks to the fast, high-tech lift system, these are greatly eliminated. Spread out on three facing slopes, **South, North** and **West**, the trails cut through thick trees that stretch to the summit. The **South Face** offers the most challenging terrain, with a number of decent black and extreme runs, which will test both freeriders and carvers alike.

FREERIDERS of all levels should like **Mont Saint-Anne,** however, if you like to ride fast, you could get round this place in a day or two. All the slopes are carved out of closely knitted trees providing for some bumpy trails, but lacking in wide, open powder bowls. The south side slopes offer the most challenging runs with a cluster of fast double black diamond runs down the middle, one of which runs from the top all the way to the base and will burn up your thighs or make your eyes water if you bail.

FREESTYLERS are free to roam the whole mountain, but they may wish to stay in the approximately 300,000 square foot fun-park which is located up on **La Grande Allee** trail. Here there is a good series of man made hits and a well shaped 75 metre halfpipe with walls cut by Quebec's first *Pipe Dragon*. The fun park, which is a good one, is unfortunately fully opened to skiers, who often wreck the the walls with their four edges.

CARVERS may feel most at ease here. The pisted runs are well-suited to cranking over at speed. The most testing trails, including double black diamond runs, can be found on **South Face**.

BEGINNERS are provided with gentle green runs that allow riding from top to bottom on some very tame descents. If you stay here for a week, you should be very competent by the time you leave (a two-week trip might be a bit much, even for a novice).

THE TOWN
Mont Sainte Anne offers a very good selection of local services both at the base of the slopes or 25 miles away in down town Quebec City. Local lodging options are extensive with some 3000 visitor beds within a 3 mile stretch of the slopes. The main village is well set out and pleasant place to stay. There are a number of shops to serve your needs from boutiques to basic snowboard shops all mainly geared towards the casual visitor. The area also offers loads of other sporting attractions.

C
CANADA QUEBEC

131

STONEHAM

Okay resort all round

Pic -Stoneham Resort

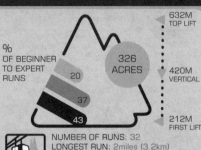

%
OF BEGINNER
TO EXPERT
RUNS

20
37
43

326 ACRES

632M
TOP LIFT

420M
VERTICAL

212M
FIRST LIFT

NUMBER OF RUNS: 32
LONGEST RUN: 2miles (3.2km)
TOTAL LIFTS: 10
5 chairs,4 drags,1 Tubing Lift
CAPACITY (people per hour): 14,200
LIFT TIMES: 8.30am to 4.00pm

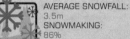

AVERAGE SNOWFALL:
3.5m
SNOWMAKING:
86%

Stoneham is one of the largest resorts in **Quebec** which forms part of the 'Resorts of the Canadian Rockies Group' who also own the likes of Lake Louse, Fernie and Kimberley amongst others. With such a pedigree one would expect Stoneham to have something good to offer, and indeed it does, as well as playing host to the FIS Snowboard World Cup. The 30 plus trails are spread out over a group of mountain faces with the slopes carved out of tightly knitted trees that grow over the whole area form the base up to the summits of each mountain area. Initial access to **Stoneham** is via route 73 from **Quebec City**, which is only 20 minutes away. As you drive into the resort you are presented with a series of mountains peaks set out in a horse shoe like fashion that all base out together. In general Stoneham offers mostly simple slopes to suite beginners and intermediates. However, expert and advanced riders will find some okay terrain with a least six double diamond black trails to ride down. The 322 acres of terrain is serviced by 9 lifts with the highest area achieved by a quad chair up to 630 metres. The mountain faces are not exactly lift linked but you can easily travel around all the areas by the series of interconnecting trails. 183 acres of terrain, which equals 16 runs, is also used for night riding.

WINTER PERIODS: Nov to April
Lift Passes
Half day $32, Full day $40, 5 days $160
Board Schools
Half Day lesson $36.51, Full Day $56.51.
Specialist park & pipe 3 day courses
Hire
Board & Boots $29 per day
Night Boarding
16 trails open, tickets $23

FREERIDE 40%
Lots of trees & some nice backcountry
FREESTYLE 30%
4 Terrain parks & 2 halfpipes
CARVING 30%

Stoneham Mountain Resort
1420, Hibou Road,Stoneham (Québec)
Canada G0A 4P0
Phone: (418) 848-2411
Web:www.ski-stoneham.com
Email:info@ski-stoneham.com

FREERIDERS will find that Stoneham offers a number of decent challenges making a weekend stay worth while. There are a series of double black runs that will provided a few white knuckle rides with trees and other obstacles to negotiate en-route down. However, Stoneham is not a powder mountain.

FREESTYLERS should note that Stoneham is not a mountain paved with loads of natural freestyle terrain however, the management have decided to address the balance by building a host of features which includes four large terrain parks loaded with all sorts of toys, including a boarder-cross run. The resort also has a Super-Pipe with 17 foot walls, located down a steep black slope on mountain 4.

CARVERS have a resort that should appeal with a good selection of well groomed trails to choose from.

BEGINNERS will find that this is a good place to learn the basics of snowboarding. There are a number of novice runs that run from the highest points down to the base area.

Bus
routes to Québec City. Then, a shuttle service links up Québec City to the resort.
Fly
to Montreal with a transfer time of 3 hours to the resort. You can also fly to Quebec City from Montreal.
Drive
20 minutes from Québec City. Take Highway 73 North and exit at Stoneham. Follow road signs to the resort (6 km)

THE TOWN. **Stoneham** offers a choice of condos and hotels beds at the base of the slopes. The *Stoneham Hotel* has double bed rooms from $83 per night and comes with a bar and restaurant. As for **night life**, forget it. Although there are half a dozen good restaurants and a couple of okay bars, none are that hot and nothing rocks. For a full range of services you will need to stay down in **Quebec City**.

BELLE NEIGE

Number of Runs: 19
Easy 29%
Intermediate 28%
Advanced 43%
Top Lift: 305m
Bottom Lift: 150m
Vertical: 115m
Total Lifts:4 - 2 chairs, 2 drags
Lift pass: Day pass $28
Contact:
Nos coordonnées
6820, Route 117
Val-Morin (Qc) JOT 2RO
Tel: (819) 322-3311
www.belleneige.com
info@belleneige.com

BROMONT

New for 04/05 season;new Quad
Lift will serve the Mont Soleil area

Ride Area: 202 acres
Number of Runs: 52
Easy 25%
Intermediate 23%
Advanced 23%
Expert 20%
Info: Has 3 terrain parks
Top Lift: 565m
Bottom Lift: 180m
Vertical: 385m
Total Lifts:5 - 4 chairs, 1 magic
carpet
Lift pass: 1/2 Day Pass - $36
Day Pass - $44
Night Boarding: 30 trails open
Hire: Board & Boots $33 per day
Contact:
150, Champlain

Bromont (Quebec)
1 866 BROMONT • [450] 534-2200
www.skibromont.com
operations@skibromont.com
Location: From Montreal. On
Highway 10, take Exit 78 towards
bromont. Cross the traffic light on
Boulevard Bromont and turn right
on Champlain to SkiBromon, takes
45 minutes

CAMP FORTUNE

Number of Runs: 17
Total Lifts:5
Contact:
Camp Fortune
300 ch. Dunlop,
Chelsea, QC J9B 2N3
Tel - 819.827.1717
Fax - 819.827.3893

CLUB TOBO

Number of Runs: 6
Total Lifts:2
Contact:
Tel: (418) 679 5243

COTES 40-80

Number of Runs: 6
Total Lifts:2
Contact:
Tel: (514) 229 2921

EDELWEISS VALLEY

Has a terrain park & night
boarding

Ride Area: 150 acres piste, 1300
acres total
Number of Runs: 18
Easy 33%
Intermediate 48%
Advanced 17%
Expert 2%
Longest run: 1mile (1.6km)
Night Borading: 12 out of 18 trails
Top Lift: 343m
Bottom Lift: 152m
Vertical: 191m
Total Lifts:5 - 4 chairs, 2 drags,1
Magic carpet
Lift pass: Weekday Pass - $32

Weekend Pass - $34 Night $23
Lift times: 8.00am to 10.00pm
Board School: Private lesson (1hr),
lift pass & rental $65 for day
Hire: Board & Boots $28 per day
Contact:
Mont Saint-Sauveur 350 Saint-Denis Saint-Sauveur,
Québec, JOR 1R3
Telephone : (450)227-4671
www.edelweissvalley.com
Directions:
From Ottowa-Hull - 5-15 miles
via routes 105, 307, & 366 to
Edelweiss Valley.

GRAY ROCKS

Number of Runs: 22
Easy 19%
Intermediate 45%
Advanced 36%
Vertical: 189m
Annual Snowfall: 4.2m
Total Lifts:5 - 4 chairs, 1 Magic
carpet
Lift pass: 1/2 Weekday Pass - $20
Weekday Pass - $25 1/2 Day
Weekend Pass - $25 Weekend Pass
- $35
Lift times: 8.00am to 10.00pm
Board School: weekend lessons
$105 for 2 days inc 6hrs lessons,
lift & hire 1/2-day (2hrs) lesson
$40, full day (4hrs) $60
Hire: Board & Boots $30 per day
Contact:
Gray Rocks Resort & Convention
Center
Mont Tremblant, Quibec.
Tel - 1-800-567-6767
www.grayrocks.com
Directions:
FLY: Fly to Montreal 1 1/2hrs away
BUS: Shuttles from Montreal
Airport, tel: 1-800-471-1155
DRIVING: From Montreal (by car
: 90 minutes / 120km / 75 miles)
Take Autoroute 15 North until it
merges with route 117 North at
Ste-Agathe. Continue along route
117 and take the first exit for St-Jovite. At the first traffic light in
St-Jovite, turn right on route 327
North for 5 km to Gray Rocks (on
your right).

C

CANADA

SASKATCHEWAN

BLACKSTRAP

Blackstrap has just 8 runs with only 88 metres of vert with the longest run just making 450m. , This small mountain is best for novices and slow intermediates. The resort also, provides a cool fun park with a few table tops and a halfpipe. . No slope side lodgings exist, the nearest accommodation and services can be found at Dundurn, Hanly and Saskatoon.

Location: DRIVING: Located 32km south of Saskatoon via Hwy 11 and Hwy 211
Contact:
Blackstrap Winter Sports Park
Blackstrap Provincial Park
Box 612 Mailing Address:
Dundurn,
Phone: (306) 492-2400
Fax: (306) 492-2401

BLUE MOUNTAIN

Located 32km south of Battleford, Blue; Mountain is a very small retreat that offers a host of sporting activities including some limited snowboarding. There is some basic accommodation on site as well as other basic amenities.

Location: DRIVING: 1 1/2 hours west from Saskatoon via Highway #16 and Grid # 687 north at the town of Denholm (which eventually turns into Highway # 378).
Contact:
Blue Mountain Outdoor Adventure Center R.R.
#1 North Battleford
Saskatchewan CANADA S9A 2X3
Phone (306) 445-4941

CUDWORTH SKI AREA

Located south on 6thAve, Cudworth consists of just one 230 metre trail with just 24 metres of vertical with one tow. Accommodation and other facilities are available in Cudworth.

Contact:
tel- (306) 256 3281

LITTLE RED RIVER PARK

Located 3km east of Prince Albert via Hwy 5, Little Red River Park consists of just two runs and two lifts. One slope is of beginner level while the other is an intermediate trail. The are also ski patrol, snowboard Instruction and a halfpipe. Accommodation and other facilities are available in Prince Albert

Contact:
1084 Central Ave, Prince Albert SK tel- (306) 953

MISSION RIDGE SKI AREA

Located 2km south east of downtown Fort Qu'Appelie Mission Ridge, is a mountain with 8 runs, 92 metres of vert and 4 lifts. This small resort is a popular destination and can get busy. The area boasts a funpark and also provides night riding with special rates. **Freestylers** will find a 3.5 acre park featuring hip jumps, rails. Accommodation and other facilities are available close by in Fort Qu'Appelie

Number of Runs: 35
Easy 10%
Intermediate 60%
Advanced 30%
Top Lift: 6,770 ft
Bottom Lift: 4,570 ft
Vertical: 2,200 ft
Annual Snowfall: 4.2m
Total Lifts:6 - 4 chairs, 2 drags
Lift pass: Day pass $40 Night Pass $10
Lift times: 9 AM to 4 PM (4PM to -9PM select days in Jan & feb)
Location: FLY: Fly to seatle (140 miles away), local airport is Pangborn Memorial Airport
TRAIN: Amtrak serves Wenatchee, 12 miles away
DRIVING: From Seattle, Take U.S. Hwy. 2 east to Wenatchee and follow the signs to Mission Ridge, 138 miles.
Contact:

Mission Ridge P.O. 1668, Wenatchee, WA 98807-1668 Phone (509) 663-6543

PASQUIA SKI SLOPE

Located 12km south east of Zenon. Pasquia is a tiny hangout with 4 slopes, 1 tow and only opens for afternoon riding with private bookings. Accommodation and other facilities are available in Zenon.

Contact:
RR Tisdaie, SK tel- (306) 767 2682

SKI TIMBER RIDGE

Located 5km south of Big River on Hwy 55, Ski Timber Ridge provides 5 trails, with the longest run at 800 metres and the max vert at 90 metres. You can also get snowboard hire and instruction at the slope with daily lessons and privates. Main accommodation and other local facilities are available in Big River which is only 2 km away and has a number of okay lodging options, good places to eat as well as a host of

sporting activities
Number of Runs: 6
Top Lift: 2600ft
Bottom Lift: 1400ft
Total Lifts:2
Hire:Boards available from rental shop on slopes
Board School:Board instruction available
Location: DRIVING: Located 32km south of Saskatoon via Hwy 11 and Hwy 211
Contact:
Ski Timber Ridge
Box 741 Big River,
Saskatchewan (Canada) S0J 0E0
Phone: 469-4545

SASKATCHEWAN

STURGIS ASSINIBOINE

Located 1km south of Sturgis off Hwy 49, Tiny area offers five trails with a maximum vert of 36 metres and one drag lift. Very basic and limited local facilities are available in Sturgis 1 km away

TABLE MOUNTAIN PARK

Located 29km west of Battleford off Hwy 40. Eight trails, 107 metres of vert and 4 lifts make up this small hangout that also has night riding and a fun park. Local services and lodging available in North Battleford and Cut Knife

Contact:
Box 343, North Battleford, SK
tel. (306) 937 2920

TWIN TOWERS SKI AREA

Only 3km south of Stranraer off Hwy 31, Twin Towers has six slopes, the longest being 853 metres, 91 metres of vertical and 2 lifts with a snowboard area and rentals on site. All local services availible in Herschel, Rosetown (58km), Kindersley and Plenty.

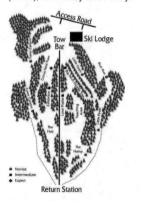

Number of Runs: 9
Lift pass: Day pass $20 Half Day $17 Season $£240
Lift times: 10:00 am - 4:30 pm
Total Lifts: 1
Hire: Board & boots $27
Location:
DRIVING: Located 3kms South Of Stranraer on Highway 31 . 45 minutes from Biggar, Rosetown, Kindersley & Kerrobert

WAPITI VALLY

Wapiti Valley is located 47 kms north of the City of Melfort and 24 kms south of Choiceland on Highway #6 to Codette Lake and the Saskatchewan River Valley.

Number of Runs: 11
Easy 36%
Intermediate 55%
Advanced 9%
Longest run: 0.7miles (1.2km)

Verical Drop: 90m
Total Lifts: 3 - 1 chair, 2 drags
Lift times: 9:00 am - 4:30
Lift Pass: Day Pass - $20 1/2 Day Pass - $15 Season $199
Hire: Board & Boots $25 per day
Board School: Private lesson 1hr $25
Group lesson 1hr $12-16
Location: DRIVING: Wapiti Valley is located 47 kms north of the

City of Melfort and 24 kms south of Choiceland on Highway #6 to Codette Lake and the Saskatchewan River Valley.
Contact:
Wapiti Valley Regional Park
P.O. Box 181 Gronlid,
Saskatchewan, Canada, S0E 0W0
Telephone: (306) 862-5621
Fax: (306) 862-5621

WHITE TRACK

Located 27km from Moose Jaw in Buffalo. Its nine slopes are evenly split between 3 drag lifts and a maximum vert of 70m. All local services available in Moose Jaw, Chamberlain and Regina

Contact:
Box 702, Moose Jaw, SK
Tel (306) 691 0100

135

C
H
I
L
E

Pic - Scott Needham

Valparaiso
PORTILLO
Mendoza
Santiago LA PARVA
VALLE NEVADO
EL COLORADO
San
Rafael
TERMAS DE CHILLAN
Concepcion
ARGENTINA
ANTUCO
Valdivia
Neuquen
PUCON
San Carlos
Puerto Montt **ANTILLANCA**
Raw
Coihaique
:ao
ula
Comodoro
Rivadavia
Puerto Santa Cruz
Puerto
Rio Gallegos

Capital City: Santiago
Population: 15 million
Highest Peak: Cerro Aconcagua
6962m
Language: Spanish
Legal Drink Age: 18
Drug Laws: Cannabis is illegal and
frowned upon
Age of consent: 16
Electricity: 240 Volts AC 2-pin
International Dialing Code: +56

Currency: Chilean Peso (CLP)
Exchange Rate:
UK£1 = 1,165
EURO = 775
US$1 = 620

Driving Guide
All vehicles drive on the right hand
side of the road
Speed limits:
Motorways - 120kph
Highways - 100kph
Towns - 50kph

Time Zone
UTC/GMT -4 hours
Daylight saving time: none

Chilean Snowboard Association
Vitacura 5534, Vitacu
CHI- Santiago
Tel:+56 (0) 2 2182 879

Servicio Nacional de Turismo
Avenia Providencia 1550,
P.O. Box 14082,
Santiago, Chile
Tel:+56 (0) 2 236 1416

5 OUT OF 10 Okay resort

Pucon is a friendly and laid back place situated on the slopes of the **Villarica Volcano** in the **Lake District** region. It provides the rider with a perfect natural funpark for freestylers and cool freeriding destination. It should keep all snowboarders no matter what your ability, busy and content for a good seven days or more, although the volcano is still live and smoking. The resort is made up of four old creaking chairlifts and

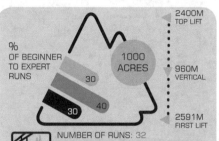

% OF BEGINNER TO EXPERT RUNS

- 30
- 30
- 40

1000 ACRES

2400M TOP LIFT

960M VERTICAL

2591M FIRST LIFT

NUMBER OF RUNS: 32
TOTAL LIFTS: 9 - chairs,6 drags
CAPACITY (people per hour): 5380
LIFT TIMES: 9.00am to 4.00pm

AVERAGE SNOWFALL:
Unknown
SNOWMAKING:
Unknown

WINTER PERIODS:
June to Sept
Lift Passes
1 Day pass - 13,500
Season pass - 150,000
Board Schools
Private lessons US$25 for 55mins
Group lessons US$15 for 90mins

FREERIDE 50%
Lots of trees & some nice backcountry
FREESTYLE 30%
A Terrain park
CARVING 20%

Tourist office Pucon
Pucon. Villarica
Tel: ++56 (0) 1 350 021
Web:www.puconchile.com
Email:snowboard@puconchile.com

Bus
services from Santiago are possible with a change over, and will take around 12 hours.
Fly
to Santiago, 492 miles from Pucon.
Drive
Via Santiago, head south on highways 5 and 119 via Temuco and Villarrica and then on up to Pucon.

three drags, all but one of which are above tree line. Plans are afoot to install a further lift above the long left hand chair to access the steeper higher terrain. The feeling of riding the mountain is unique. The previous volcanic eruptions and lava flows have left behind a terrain of rollers and deep gullies. While the lift-accessed area is not particularly large and the lift positioning unimaginative, it contains some excellent freeriding/freestyle terrain with never ending hits, cornices and huge natural halfpipes that easily compensate for the lack of steeps. In short it's a playground. Snow quality varies due to the lower elevation and local climate factors. Storms roll in from the Pacific and drop their load, or the mountain may become fogged in. Winds quite often affect the operation of the old lifts.

FREERIDERS should check out the gullies on the left, and the cliff banks on the far right of the area. Steeper freeriding can be found by hiking from the tops of lifts, and guides (essential) can be hired in town to hike to the crater if you long to stare into the fiery bowels of Earth before riding back to the base for a coco.
FREESTYLERS are now presented with an okay halfpipe, when conditions permit. However, whether there is a pipe or not, the area has so much natural terrain for getting air, that it's not really needed. There are some major cliff jumps and big banks here.
CARVERS don't bother; piste bashing it's not the thing here.
BEGINNERS will manage here but in truth there are better places.

THE TOWN
Access to the resort is by hitching at the foot of the access road or by minibus taxi ($6 per person return) from agencies in town. Adventure tourism is big in Pucon. Rafting ($20-35) is a buzz; take the upper trip as the lower one is for wusses. The nearest **accommodation** is found in Pucon 1 mile away where you can get a cheap bed from as low as $8 a night. Good **night time** hangouts include *Mamas and Tapas* where local girls strut their stuff, and *Piscola*.

137

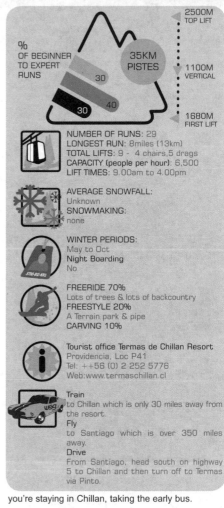

2500M
TOP LIFT

%
OF BEGINNER
TO EXPERT
RUNS

35KM
PISTES

30

30   40

1100M
VERTICAL

1680M
FIRST LIFT

NUMBER OF RUNS: 29
LONGEST RUN: 8miles (13km)
TOTAL LIFTS: 9 - 4 chairs,5 drags
CAPACITY (people per hour): 6,500
LIFT TIMES: 9.00am to 4.00pm

AVERAGE SNOWFALL:
Unknown
SNOWMAKING:
none

WINTER PERIODS:
May to Oct
Night Boarding
No

FREERIDE 70%
Lots of trees & lots of backcountry
FREESTYLE 20%
A Terrain park & pipe
CARVING 10%

Tourist office Termas de Chillan Resort
Providencia, Loc P41
Tel: ++56 (0) 2 252 5776
Web:www.termaschillan.cl

Train
to Chillan which is only 30 miles away from
the resort.
Fly
to Santiago which is over 350 miles
away.
Drive
From Santiago, head south on highway
5 to Chillan and then turn off to Termas
via Pinto.

Termas De Chillan is a small resort positioned on the south facing slopes of a dormant volcano and boasts the longest season of any of the S. American resorts. Despite a good snow record the resort has done little to make the most of it and offers only three ageing chairlifts and three drags. Most of the terrain is above treeline with the lower chair retrieving adventurous boarders from the trees and depositing them back at the base. The upper chair, **Don Otto**, not only accesses the best freeriding terrain on the mountain, but also holds the record for being the longest chairlift in S. America (2.5 Km). It is also one of the oldest and slowest and its frequent closure whenever the wind blows, means it's long overdue for replacement. The alternative when this chair is down is to ride a succession of three drags, (the middle poma holding the record for 'most blokes rendered infertile') to access some neat gullies with big banks. Plans have been made to extend the top drag further into the higher terrain which otherwise is rewarding but the hike-to country.

FREERIDERS will find what is regarded by locals as the best on offer, is accessed via a 10 minute hike from the top of the temperamental **Don Otto** chair. Hiking right from the top of this the rider is rewarded with 890 vertical meters of open bowls that exit into a series of 35-45 degree chutes back into the base. With pisting operations seemingly unheard of here the area is a freeriders dream. Beware though, avalanche control is also almost unknown of and you'd be lucky to ever see the ski patrol.
FREESTYLERS have a well constructed snowboard park and pipe reached off the middle poma.
CARVERS who require pisted corduroy tracks, Mickey Mouse is really an Elephant, get the picture!
BEGINNERS, if it were not for the way the lifts are laid out, then this would be an ideal novices haunt, but it's not.

THE TOWN
Without your own transport access to the base is dependant on either hitching (relatively easy) or if you're staying in Chillan, taking the early bus.

With the nearest 'town' being 50 miles away the resort has developed a complex of hotel and condo's below the base, mainly catering for affluent Chilean and visiting westerner. This accommodation is far out of reach of the average boarders pocket making finding somewhere to sleep nearby a problem. Four bed apartments ($25 per-person) can be rented at **Las Tranoas** 10 km from the base.

CHILE

ANTILLANCA

Antillanca is yet another volcano based resort. However, unlike similar hangouts there is at least some good backcountry tours you can take and without too much hiking or traversing, though you'd better be tooled up incase you get lost on one of the many other volcanos in the area. The pisted areas provide some basic freeriding above and amid trees. Nothing is laid on for freestylers but there are rocks to get air from. Good facilities are available at Antillanca's base area

Number of Runs: 13
Easy 20%,Intermediate 30%
Advanced 30%,Expert 20%
Top Lift: 1534m
Bottom Lift: 1070m
Total Lifts:5 - 1 chairs, 4 drags
How to get there: Fly to Santiago, then bus which will take over 10 hours

ANTUCO

Antuco is one of Chile's resorts that can easily be over looked, simply because there is not much to look at. Located on a volcano (like so many other resorts in this part of the world). Antuco is a place best left to locals in the area. It's certainly not worth going out of you're way to visit. The two runs wouldn't hold the attention of a nat beyond 30 seconds. Beginners can have fun, but freestylers forget it as should piste loving carvers.
Best lodging are local and local services can be found at Los Angeles (not the US city), 40 minutes away
Number of Runs: 2
Easy 20%,Intermediate 50%
Advanced 30%
Top Lift: 1850m
Vertical Drop: 450m
Total Lifts:2
How to get there: Fly to Santiago, then bus via Los Angeles 40 mins away

EL COLORADO

30 miles, or 40 minutes from the capital is El Colorado, Chile's biggest resort. Being so close to Santiago has its draw backs as the slopes can often get very busy with Chile's high earning city dwellers who have been coming to the resort for skiing, since the thirties.u The 25 marked

out trails cater for everyone's needs especially advanced riders although the off-piste is a bit naff. However, this is a good resort for piste carvers and novices. Expensive lodging, restaurants and bars are all slopeside
Number of Runs: 25
Easy 40%,Intermediate 20%
Advanced 30% ,Expert 10%
Top Lift: 3333m
Bottom Lift: 2430m
Vertical Drop: 903m
Total Lifts:18 - 4 chairs, 14 drags
Lift pass:Day Pass - $29
How to get there:
FLY: Fly to Santiago, then bus, which will take 40 minutes.
BUS: Bus service from Santiago, US$13 round trip.
DRIVING: 39km east of Santiago

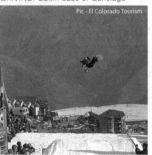
Pic - El Colorado Tourism

LA PARVA

La Parva is another resort in the throws of Santiago, and another popular modern affair loaded with all the razzmatazz and trappings found at many big foreign resorts. However, this is not big resort, but rather a good two days and its an all done sort of place . Still what is available is extensive, well set out and caters well for piste lovers and fast riding freeriders with some nice blacks and expert trails to try out. Lots of good local facilities are provided at the base area of the slopes, but nothing comes cheaply.

Number of Runs: 20
Easy 15% ,Intermediate 55%
Advanced 30%
Top Lift: 3630m
Vertical Drop: 960m
Total Lifts:14
How to get there: Fly to Santiago, then bus, which will take 50 minutes

LLIAMA

Visitors could be excused for getting a bit confused when they arrive here. Nothing to do with the slopes, but more to the fact that there are to Lliamas here with both using the same name and both similar in character, with much the same terrain, number of runs and lifts that serve them. Another common feature about this place is that for any fast riding thrill seekers, pick somewhere else, as this place is very flat and basically boring. Best lodging and local facilities are in Temco, 5 minutes away.

Number of Runs: 7
Easy 20%,Intermediate 60%
Advanced 20%
Top Lift: 1800m
Total Lifts:5
How to get there: Fly to Santiago and then to Ladeco 55 minutes away

PORTILLO
new $1.4 million quad chairlift to access the Plateau side of the resort quickly
Portillo is a world renowned American run resort located at the foot of Aconcagua. Its high elevation provides it with plenty of dry snow making for good powder. 12 lifts access some 22 pistes and an abundance of steep off piste faces._ Heli operations will take those with flexible enough plastic to higher elevations and descents. Heli operations will take those with flexible enough plastic to higher elevations and descents. The resort is distinctly up-market offering expensive accommodation and eating in its ugly complex of posh hotels, condos and slightly cheaper 'dormitories'

Ride area: 800 acres
Number of Runs: 22
Easy 10%,Intermediate 70%
Advanced 20%
Top Lift: 3348m
Total Lifts:12 - 7 chairs, 5 drags
How to get there:
Fly to Santiago and then bus 2 hours away.
DRIVING: Access Portillo by hitching from Los Andes, via the access road. 100 miles northeast of Santiago

C
C
H
I
L
E

Finland produces some of the best young freestylers in the world. You may ask how such a small country, with a small population, can do this, well the answer must lie in the fact that Finnish resorts offer so little in terms of terrain that the main challenge is the halfpipes. Finlands resorts are small. Max drop of runs is 50-120m (for southern Finland) depending on the resort. There are usually 5-6 runs per resort (although they claim more - if there's a tree on the piste, that makes it 2 runs)

All resorts have ski/snowboard hire and a restaurant. Many also have lessons available in English.

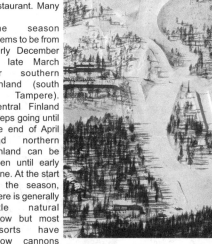

Pic - Ruka Tourism

Capital City: Helsinki
Population: 5.2 million
Highest Peak: Haltia 1328m
Language: Finnish and Swedish
Legal Drink Age: 18
Drug Laws: Cannabis is illegal and frowned upon
Age of consent: 16
Electricity: 240 Volts AC 2-pin
International Dialing Code: +358

Currency: Euro
Exchange Rate:
UK£1 = 1.5
US$1 = 0.8
AU$1 = 0.6
CAN$1 = 0.6

Driving Guide
All vehicles drive on the right hand side of the road
Speed limits:
Motorways-120kph (74mph)
Highways-100kph (80mph)
Towns-50kph (31mph)
Emergency
Police - 10022
Fire and Ambulance - 112
Tolls
None
Documentation
carry driving license, insurance certificate and vehicle registration, along with your passport

Time Zone
UTC/GMT +2 hour
Daylight saving time: +1 hour

Finnish Snowboard Federation
Radiokatu 20
00240 Helsinki.
Finland
tel- ++358 400 414 587
www.fsa.fi

Finnish Tourist Board
Head Office: P.O. Box 625,
Töölönkatu 11,
00101 HELSINKI, FINLAND
Tel.: +358 (0)9 4176 911
www.visitfinland.com

The season seems to be from early December to late March for southern Finland (south of Tampere). Central Finland keeps going until the end of April and northern Finland can be open until early June. At the start of the season, there is generally little natural snow but most resorts have snow cannons and they do a good job. From early March (in southern Finland), the snow starts to melt and the conditions are not particularly reliable. The easy runs tend to be closed first with most resorts only half open by the end of March.

Temperatures vary quite a lot. In the south, -5 to -10 is the typical winter daytime temperature but -15 to -20 is not uncommon.

Travelling: Fuel is actually cheap (around 1 euro/litre or 60p/litre). If you are based in Helsinki, there are buses to most of the local resorts. Language: Although the official languages are Finnish and Swedish, almost everyone speaks very good English. Finns are also friendly and very reserved (except when drunk, which is quite often).

Crowds: The Finns are fair-weather skiers and boarders. If it's a nice sunny afternoon, they flock to the resorts and it gets rather busy (although nowhere near as bad as the Alps). If it's a bit too cold or dull or it's late in the day, some of the places are practically empty.

Resorts are usually open from around 10am to 8 or 9pm. Since it's dark by 4pm in the winter, most runs are floodlit although some places only keep a few runs open, particularly if it's not busy.

Costs do vary a bit but in general 4 hours equipment hire cost 30 euros. A lift pass will set you back 25 euros.

HIMOS

Over all, rather dull

Most resorts in **Finland** are tiny blips spread over rolling hills and although Himos is small, it is by no means the smallest resort in the country. But compared to elsewhere in central Western Europe, it's almost a joke that only Scotland could match. Located in the southern part of the country and three hours by road from the Finnish capital of Helsinki, Himos is a very popular resort with

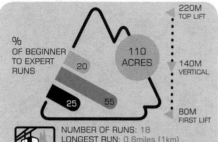

% OF BEGINNER TO EXPERT RUNS
20 · 25 · 55 · 110 ACRES

220M TOP LIFT
140M VERTICAL
80M FIRST LIFT

NUMBER OF RUNS: 18
LONGEST RUN: 0.6miles (1km)
TOTAL LIFTS: 12 - 9 chairs,3 drags
CAPACITY (people per hour): 11,200
LIFT TIMES: 9.30am to 5.00pm

AVERAGE SNOWFALL:
80cm
SNOWMAKING:
100%

WINTER PERIODS:
Nov to May
Lift Passes
1 Day pass - 27 euros
4 Day pass - 91 euros
Board Schools
private 50min 35euro
Hire
Board and boots 30euros
helmet 6euros

FREERIDE 25%
Poor trees & no backcountry
FREESTYLE 50%
2 Terrain parks & 2 half-pipes
CARVING 25%

Himos Information Cnt
Himosvuri 42100 Jamsa. Finland
Tel: ++358 42 786 1051
Web:www. himos.fi
Email:markkinointi@himos.fi

Bus
services direct from Helsinki airport.
Fly
to Helsinki, 3 hours transfer time.
Drive
Drive via Helsinki, head north on motorway 4/E75 direction Lahti and then Jamsa to reach Himos which is a distance of 140 miles (225 km).

F
FINLAND

a large number of Finnish snowboarders, especially freestylers. The resort opened in 1984 and first impressions will have you wondering what the hell you are doing there. The tiny hill that rises above the shores of the frozen lake is split into two slope areas, both offering the same terrain: a mixture of flat, unadventurous trails.

FREERIDERS are not going to find this place up to much as there's nothing really to excite. The longest trails are on the north slopes, with one black and a couple of red runs on offer. The runs on the west slope offer a few more challenges, with some blacks that weave through the trees, but don't expect powder.

FREESTYLERS are provided with two half-pipes and a fun park, which they call '**The Street**', comprising of hits and rails which at least make up for the boring terrain. Locals often build the odd hit and you may even find a few logs to session in the trees.

CARVERS who don't ask for much in life will probably get the best out of the slopes here, although the longest trail only just manages about 1000m, equalling at best 3 or 4 good carves. The slopes on the west hill give you the chance to shred at speed down some well prepared black trails and the short red runs are good for carvers who want progress.

BEGINNERS have only a few, very short green trails to get started, but as the blue trails and even the reds are overrated difficulty-wise, novices have more on offer than it first seems. To help total first timers, there is a slope with a free lift. Most novices should have this place sorted in three days, if not, take up cross country skiing as you'll be more in tune with that.

THE TOWN
Accommodation, which is spread out but within easy reach of the slopes, is offered mainly in chalet form with a number of hotels, but nothing is cheap!
Don't expect any happening **night life**: the main place is the *Himos Hotel* which is dull to the extreme. The place isn't totally crap, it just doesn't offer very much.

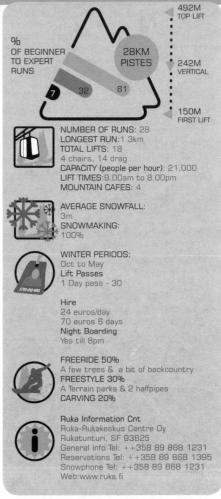

%
OF BEGINNER
TO EXPERT
RUNS

7 | 32 | 61

28KM
PISTES

492M
TOP LIFT

242M
VERTICAL

150M
FIRST LIFT

NUMBER OF RUNS: 28
LONGEST RUN: 1.3km
TOTAL LIFTS: 18
4 chairs, 14 drag
CAPACITY (people per hour): 21,000
LIFT TIMES: 9.00am to 8.00pm
MOUNTAIN CAFES: 4

AVERAGE SNOWFALL:
3m
SNOWMAKING:
100%

WINTER PERIODS:
Oct to May
Lift Passes
1 Day pass - 30

Hire
24 euros/day
70 euros 6 days
Night Boarding
Yes till 8pm

FREERIDE 50%
A few trees & a bit of backcountry
FREESTYLE 30%
A Terrain parks & 2 halfpipes
CARVING 20%

Ruka Information Cnt
Ruka-Rukakeskus Centre Oy
Rukatunturi, SF 93825
General info Tel: ++358 89 868 1231
Reservations Tel: ++358 89 868 1395
Snowphone Tel: ++358 89 868 1231
Web: www.ruka.fi

Finland is generally a flat country with lots of lakes and the Kusamo region, where this typical Finnish resort is located, is no exception. The journey to **Ruka** involves no great uphill climbs or winding mountain passes, you simply arrive to see the hill popping out of the landscape like a volcano. Ruka is just about Finland's largest resort and has hosted some major snowboard championships, indicating that the place has something to offer. Don't get too excited though as this is not hardcore freeriding territory and you can explore the whole area in half a day. However, the mainly intermediate slopes do offer carvers some nice flats to carve up and the slopes can be accessed with ease from any of the 5 car-parks dotted along the road that circles most of the hill. Trees cover much of the mountain, so all the trails are cut through the forest giving you the feeling you are on a different run every time, rather than just riding 100 metres across from where you were originally. All the slopes are well groomed and pisted constantly, so bumps don't get a chance to build up. Most of the area has blue and easy red runs, with only a couple of blacks down the front side.

FREERIDERS will find some interesting terrain to explore, although it won't take too long. There are some nice areas to ride including open and tight tree sections, especially round the side of the ski jump. Ruka is also known for having some good powder stashes. Although it's never super deep, it's still good fluffy stuff.

FREESTYLERS have two fun park areas and three halfpipes, all serviced by T-bars. Both parks have a good range of gaps and table tops of all sizes and are groomed daily, so you won't need to hike up with your own shovel to shape hits. One of the parks and pipes are located up off lift number 17, where it gets cold but you will find a shelter with a wood fire burning to warm you up between runs. Don't leave your gloves drying above the fire though, as a pair of $200 smoked Fishpaws are not as trendy as you may think.

CARVERS are provided with flats and well spaced out trails, allowing for some interesting carving, most of which needs to be done on a series of red runs. The runs off the 7 lift are nice, long descents which allow novice carvers the option to move across from some tamer blue trails. Lift 15 also gives access to a good tree-lined carving trail that can be taken at speed.

BEGINNERS are presented with plenty of gentle runs that allow for long descents from the summit, making Ruka a good place to learn the basics. Lifts stay open with the help of flood-lights until 8 pm most nights, so you can get loads of riding in if early mornings aren't

THE TOWN & GETTIN THERE

Pic - San Tang

F

FINLAND

your thing. Instruction facilities are very good here and you can get tuition for riding the flats or the halfpipe.

THE TOWN

Ruka is an all year round tourist destination, so add that to the fact that Finland is an expensive country, and what you get is a super expensive but good resort. Ruka, which is only half hour bus ride from **Kuusamo** airport, has a good selection of well appointed local facilities which include a damn fine sports centre and a number of shops. If Ruka is not your thing, Kuusamo is the nearest big town with a far greater selection of everything with slightly lower prices, which will help the budget conscious rider.

Accomodation. The choice of accommodation is extremely good, both at the slopes and back along in Ruka. Options range from very expensive hotels to very expensive shared chalets. If you find staying in Ruka or at the slopes is just too expensive then the town of Kuusamo is only 20 miles away and offers a greater selection of places to stay with a wider price. You will have to commute to the slopes however.

Food. The options for eating out are fairly good, with a choice of restaurants around town and near the slopes, but it hurts having to pay so much money even for a burger. Still The *Ampan* is well known for serving up a good pizza, while *Ali-Baba* does great grills to order, burnt or rare, it's your call.

Night life in Ruka is tame and not bright lights and disco style. However, things are very lively and the Fins know how to party hard (mind you how they manage to get drunk with the cost of booze in this place is a mystery). The only main night time hang out is *Ruka Mesta Club*, forgetting how much things costs, will initially take a while and it won't be until you're drunk that you can loosen up.

SUMMARY
Not a bad place with terrain that allows for freeriding and some really good carving. Great for novices. Good but expensive slope side facilities.

Pic - San Tang

CAR
Drive to Helsinki via Kuusamo. Ruka / Kuusamo is 20 miles, drive time is about 14 hours.
TRAIN
to Taivalkoski (50 miles).
FLY
Fly to Helsinki international, transfer time to resort is 14 hours. Local airport is Kuusamo, 20 miles.
BUS
Buses from Helsinki can be taken via a change over at Kuusamo with a jouney time of around 14 hours.

wsg

TAHKO

4 OUT OF 10 Not up to much

Pic - Tahko Resort

% OF BEGINNER TO EXPERT RUNS

65KM PISTES

50

50

210M TOP LIFT

200M VERTICAL

10M FIRST LIFT

NUMBER OF RUNS: 17
LONGEST RUN: 1.2km
TOTAL LIFTS: 10
1 chairs,8 drags, 1 children's lift
CAPACITY (people per hour): 12,000
LIFT TIMES: 10.00am to 4.00pm
MOUNTAIN CAFES: 4

AVERAGE SNOWFALL:
0.66m
SNOWMAKING:
100%

WINTER PERIODS:
Nov to May
Snowmobiles
600km of routes
Night Boarding
5 slopes 11km

FREERIDE 15%
Poor trees & poor backcountry
FREESTYLE 20%
A Terrain parks & 2 half-pipes
CARVING 65%

Booking Centre Tahkovahti
Nilsiantie 79, 73300 Nilsia, FINLAND
Tel: ++358-17-481 400
Fax: ++358-17-481 401
Web:www.tahko.com
Email:tahkovahti@tahko.com

Bus
services with transfers will take around 10 hours.
Fly
Fly to Helsinki 445km transfer.
Kuopio airport 40km
Drive
Drive via Helsinki, head north on motorway 4/E75 to Lahti and then take the M5 to Heinola and then A5 to Siilinjarvi via Kuopio before
taking the B75 to Tahko.

Tahko is regarded by many Finnish snowboarders as their premier resort, which when compared with what else is on offer in the country, is easy to see why: even the ISF liked Tahko enough to sanction snowboard events here. Tahko is a resort that attracts many cross-country skiers, but these strange creatures that dress in spray-on clothing set off into the trees and thankfully aren't seen again until the later hours of the day. Lucky, as the terrain is not very extensive and can easily become clogged up with two plankers of all types. The riding on the **Tahkovuori** hill is not going to excite you for very long: a few hours and you have done the lot. Still, the terrain is not bad and the pistes are well looked after, with full snowmaking facilities to help when the real stuff is in short supply. All the runs are cut through trees, offering slopes to suit intermediate and novice riders, but absolutely nothing for advanced riders to get their teeth into.

FREERIDERS have nothing to write home about. There are some tree areas which most of the runs are carved out of, but most are unrideable. However, on a good day there are some okay powder spots , but don't get up late they're all gone within an hour.

FREESTYLERS have a well shaped halfpipe located at the lower section alongside the tree line. Apart from the pipe, locals like to build their own hits, but as for big natural hits, forget it. There are a number of banks to ride up, however.
CARVERS who dare to be seen in hard boots here will find some decent trails, with a couple of good red pistes to cut big wide turns on. But you won't be putting in too many before you hit the bottom and are being stared at again by everyone else in the lift queue who will be in soft boots for certain.
BEGINNERS have an ideal resort with half of the runs suited to novices, even if all the lifts are drags. Snow Valley is an area set aside for kids and first timers, but if you're a 300 pound, hairy arsed learner with no sense of control, stick to the main beginner runs as wiping out three year olds is not funny, and not on.

THE TOWN
Tahko has a small, but good selection of **accommodation** options near the slopes. You can opt to sleep in a hotel, chalets or a bungalow. Alternatively if you're driving here, and on a tight budget, you could park up in a caravan spot, but it will be freezing in mid winter. **Night life** is quite sad and expensive, but there are worse haunts

ROUND-UP

ISO-SYOTE

Iso-Syote is one of Finlands biggest resorts with a total of 21 runs. What you have here are two small mountains, offering you an area of gentle snowboard terrain that allows for some okay freeriding with some fantastic novice trails from top to bottom. There is a good halfpipe and some of the trails are flood lit for late riding! Lots of very basic lodging is available near the slopes in cabins and chalets. You can also party late but not hard.

Runs: 21, Total Lifts:5
Top Lift: 432m How to get there: Fly to: Helsinki- 14 hours away by car

KALLI

Ultra boring ride area
Runs: 1, Total Lifts:1

KALPALINNA

Okay ride area located 2 hours from Helsinki
Number of Runs: 18

KASURILA

Very boring ride area located 9 hours from Helsinki
Runs: 8,Total Lifts:3

KAUSTINEN

Small halfpipe, Located 10 hours from Helsinki
Runs: 5 ,Total Lifts:4

KOLIN HIIHTOKESKUS

Flat and very dull. Located 7 hours from Helsinki
Runs: 6 ,Total Lifts:4

LAKIS

Not worth the effort. Located 10 hours from Helsinki.
Runs: 3 ,Total Lifts:3

LEVI

Levi is a small resort that boasts 140 miles of trails although 125 of them are for oldies on cross country skis. The terrain is set out over a stump of a hill and offers freeriders a little bit of uneven rough to ride, including some trees. **Freestylers** have a natural halfpipe and a 100 metre man made version. **Carvers** have a few good trails.Levi is also ideal for **beginners**. Local facilities are well located

Ride area: 29km
Number of Runs: 45
Easy 41%,Intermediate 51% ,Advanced 8%
Top Lift: 530m
Bottom Lift: 200m
Vertical Drop: 325m
Total Lifts:26 - 1 Gondola, 25 drags
Night Boarding;13 slopes and halfpipes illuminated
How to get there:
FLY: Fly to Kittila airport Transfer time to resort = 20 minutes Buses from Helsinki can be taken via Rovaniemi to Levi on a daily basis. Rovaniemi is 1h 45 mins. Trains go to Rovaniemi – 1h 45 min and to Kolari – 1h.. DRIVING: From Helsinki via Rovaniemi to Levi its a 20 hours drive by car (1028km)

MERI - TEIJO

Small halfpipe, 8 hours from Helsinki
Runs: 8 ,Total Lifts:3

MESSILA

Ok slopes & halfpipe, 7 hours from Helsinki
Runs: 9, Total Lifts:9

MIELAKKA

Very flat ride area,2 hours from Helsinki
Runs: 3,Total Lifts:2

MUSTAVAARA

Small halfpipe,6 hours from Helsinki
Runs: 4,Total Lifts:3

MYLLYMAKI

Small halfpipe,7 hours from Helsinki

OLOS

Flat area with a pipe, 1 hour from Rovanemi
Runs: 6,Total Lifts:4

OUNASVAARA

Tiny area with a pipe, Located 1hour from Kittila
Runs: 9,Total Lifts:4

PAASKYVOURI

Flat dull area, 8 hours from Helsinki
Runs: 4,Total Lifts:2

PALLS

Very boring ride area, Located 20 hours from Helsinki
Runs: 9, Total Lifts:2

PARNAVAARA

Small halfpipe, 8 hours from Helsinki
Runs: 3, Total Lifts:1

PEURAMAA

Good for carvers, 10 hours from Helsinki
Runs: 5,Total Lifts:6

PUKKIVUORI

Small halfpipe,8 hours from Helsinki
Runs: 15,Total Lifts:2

PYHA

Phya is as small as they can possible get, with just eight or so runs and nothing longer than two turns on a long carving board. However, it is a snowcovered hill that has a half-pipe and a couple of fairly steep runs. A good intermediate will manage quite easily, but an advanced rider really shouldn't bother with this place. Actually, only novices should give it a go, if you live locally because its not worth trekking up other-wise.

SALLA

Salla seems a rather remote resort but it's no more remote than any other Finnish outback. This place is located in the mid to northern section of the country and on the Russian border, infact you can take a snowcat trip in to the Russian side to ride back down.Y The 9 runs on the Finnish side are basic but an easilypleased freerider may find it okay. At the base are there is a hotel and not much more

SAPPEE

Sappee is one of the closest resorts to Helsinki and a place that attracts a few weekend city dwelling snowboarders. However never to the point of bursting, which is surprising because this place is small, half a dozen riders giving it shit at mach 6 would crowd the slopes as well as clear them. Great for novices and ideal for freestyles who like man made hits, crap for any one else. Expensive but okay lodging and local services are in easy reach

YLLAS

Yllas is much in keeping with what is found at most Finnish resorts and while it is bigger than many places, it's not mega. It is also linked with Levi. What you get is a hill rising above the tree line, which allows for some okay intermediate freeriding, as well as some powder spots and decent carving terrain. Freestylers are usually found in the halfpipe, or pulling air off one of the many natural hits. Ideal for novices. Local facilities can be found in two small villages nearby

145

Mont Blanc

Sixty million French people are the lucky owners of some of the best snowboard resorts in the world, (Chamonix and Serre Chevalier should be on the calling card of all snowboarders) and without doubt, have the most extreme and largest areas in Europe.

Resorts vary from the old to the new, but what makes them stand out is the variety of resorts themselves. Some are ugly, semi-modern dumps, whilst others are olde worlde hamlets. What is common however, are the facilities on offer. Fast-food and good bars are plentiful and all help to create a good snowboard scene.

Getting to French resorts is no problem; most are reached by road, although please note that motorways have expensive tolls. Flying to France offers a number of routes, with the principal airports to resorts being Grenoble, Lyon, Chambery and Geneva in Switzerland.

Train services in France are affordable, excellent and fast. Furthermore, during the winter months there is a direct train service from London's Waterloo station to Bourg St Maurice station, a short five minute walk to the funicular that

Capital City: Paris
Population: 60 million
Highest Peak: Mont Blanc 4808m
Language: French
Legal Drink Age: 18
Drug Laws: Cannabis is illegal and frowned upon
Age of consent: 16
Electricity: 240 Volts AC 2-pin
International Dialing Code: +33

Currency: Euro
Exchange Rate:
UK£1 = 1.5
US$1 = 0.8
AU$1 = 0.6
CAN$1 = 0.6

Driving Guide
All vehicles drive on the right hand side of the road
Speed limits:
Toll Motorways - 130 kph
Motorways - 110kph
Main Roads - 90kph
Towns - 50kph
Emergency
Fire 18 / Police 17 / Ambulance 15
Tolls
Payable on motorways & some bridges
Documentation
Driving licence must be carried along with motor insurance.

Time Zone
UTC/GMT +1 hour
Daylight saving time: +1 hour

French Tourist Board
178 Piccadilly, W1J 9AL, London
Tel : 09068 244 123 (60p/min)
Fax : (020) 7493 6594
E-mail : info.uk@franceguide.com
Web: www.franceguide.com

French Snowboard Association
Route du Parc du Souvenir
06500 Menton, France
tel+33 492418000
web:www.afs-fr.com
Email:afs@afs-fr.com

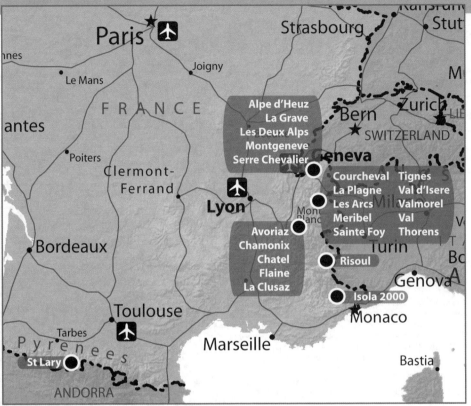

F

serves the resort of Les Arcs. Most resorts can be reached indirectly by train and bus. EU nationals won't need a visa to work in France; however, France is the worst country in the world to get a job as a snowboard instructor. The authorities are very protective of their own. If you're caught teaching on the slopes and don't hold the French ski instructor's certificate. You will be arrested and jailed. However, more mundane forms of work such as bar work are permitted. Many opportunities do exist, especially at the bigger resorts.

Accommodation in most places consists of apartment blocks sleeping any number from 1-21, which are usually quite easy to overload with floor scammers, provided they pay up with some beers.

On the money side, France is expensive, but you can get by if you eat fast-food or buy in supermarkets (where alcohol is really cheap). Avoid the overpriced discos as late night bars are just as good.

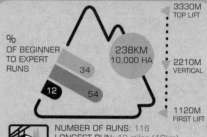

7 OUT OF 10 Really good slopes

% OF BEGINNER TO EXPERT RUNS

238KM 10,000 HA

3330M TOP LIFT

2210M VERTICAL

1120M FIRST LIFT

34
12
54

NUMBER OF RUNS: 116
LONGEST RUN: 10 miles (16km)
TOTAL LIFTS: 87
10 Gondolas, 6 cable-cars, 24 chairs, 45 drags, 2 magic carpets
CAPACITY (people per hour): 98,000
LIFT TIMES:
8.30am to 4.30pm

AVERAGE SNOWFALL
Unknown
SNOWMAKING
20%

WINTER PERIODS
Dec 4th to April 30th 2005
SUMMER PERIODS (late)
Oct to Nov
Lift Passes
1 day 35.2 euros, 2 days 68.5 euros
6 days 182 euros
Board Schools
ESF do a 2 1/2 hr/day over 6 days free-style and freeride courses for 115 euros
Night Boarding
Tues & Thurs, Signal Slalom Stadium piste. 8.5 euros/free if 2 day pass +

FREERIDE 50%
No trees but some off-piste
FREESTYLE 20%
2 terrain parks and a half-pipe
CARVING 30%

Car
via Grenoble, head south on the N75 and turn off at Le Pont de-Clax on to the N91 turning off for Alp d'Heuz.
Fly
to Lyon, 2 hour transfer
Bus
Direct from Lyon airport to the resort.

Office du Tourisme
Place Paganon
38750 - ALPE D'HUEZ
FRANCE
web: www.alpedhuez.com
email: info@alpedhuez.com

new for 04/05 season
new Funitel, the Marmottes III connects the Marmottes II to the Herpie Cable car on the Sarenne glacier. Built to improve early and late season boarding.

Anyone planning a two-week trip to **Alpe d'Huez**, will not have enough time to ride all the amazing and varied terrain that this place has to offer. Each year, this high altitude resort offers amazing amounts of great powder days covering some fantastic backcountry and wide open plateaus. The terrain is as much for the advanced rider as it is for the novice. Due to its location and mostly south-facing slopes, the runs here get a lot of annual sunshine. This has the benefit of letting you ride in great sunny conditions and also helps to soften up certain areas early on in the day. There's heaps of snow here so don't be worrying if the odd bit thins out early. The resort has a well-equipped and fast lift system that can shunt almost 100,000 punters up the mountains per hour. Unfortunately, its popularity with overseas holiday crowds means that Alpe d'Huez can get a bit clogged up, especially at weekends. Holiday periods are absolutely crazy, so avoid this time at all costs if you want to escape millions of day-glow two-plankers. However, during normal periods you can ride freely all week long from top to bottom, on and off-piste, without having to cross-track your own path or that of another skier.

FREERIDERS can be forgiven for thinking that they are in heaven. Alpe d'Huez is a backcountry freeride gem with miles of off-piste powder, in areas such as Gorges de Sarenne and Glacier de Sarenne. Please note that, riding without a guide is total folly. For assistance seek out the services of a local guide through one of the ski-schools or via Planet Surf snowboard shop.

FREESTYLERS are provided with a fun-park with pipe that in many ways isn't necessary. There are loads of natural air spots you'll feel spoilt for choice.

CARVERS are teased with so many well groomed trails, that picking one as a favourite is just not possible.

BEGINNERS are bombarded with a easy green runs at the lower areas, the only bug being that these areas are usually very busy.

OFF THE SLOPES the whole place is cheesy and very tacky. On the other hand it provides great all-round affordable local services close to the slopes. You can dine very affordably with cheap pizza restaurants in abundance. Night-life ranges from a cinema to loud partying which is brash and full-on, although this place does go in for a lot of apres crap.

F
R
A
N
C
E

AVORIAZ

Great resort for freeriding and carving; watch the lift queues.

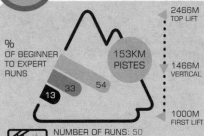

%
OF BEGINNER
TO EXPERT
RUNS

13 33 54

153KM
PISTES

2466M
TOP LIFT

1466M
VERTICAL

1000M
FIRST LIFT

Pic -Avoriaz Tourism

NUMBER OF RUNS: 50
LONGEST RUN: 3miles (5km)
TOTAL LIFTS: 37
2 Gondolas, 1 cable-cars, 18 chairs,
16 drags
CAPACITY (people per hour): 47,000
LIFT TIMES:
8.30am to 4.00pm

AVERAGE SNOWFALL
9m
SNOWMAKING
17%

WINTER PERIODS
Dec to April
SUMMER PERIODS
none
Lift Passes
day/23euro
snowboard park area 16 euros
Ports du Soleil day 35euro,
6 days 171 euros
Heli Boarding
minimum of 4 people, from 230 euros/pp
excluding guide (nearby in Italy)
Board Schools
lessons from 35euros/hr
6 days from 150 euros

FREERIDE 40%
A few trees and good off-piste
FREESTYLE 30%
2 terrain parks and 2 half-pipes
CARVING 30%

Avoriaz Tourist Office
Place Centrale
74110 Avoriaz
France
Tel: + 33 (0)4 50 74 02 11
Fax: + 33 (0)4 50 74 24 29
Web:www.avoriaz.com
Email:info@avoriaz.com

NEW

NEW FOR 04/05 SEASON
new Zore 4-seater chairlift. Zore and
Tétras runs improved, new training area
and an extension of Gazex; the avalanche
triggering system.
Portes du Solei area has an additional 3
new 6-seater chairlifts.

Avoriaz is easily one of the top French snowboard resorts and is seen by many as the snowboard capital of Europe. The management have been very positive in promoting snowboarding here since day one. For instance, Avoriaz was one of the first areas to have a snowboard-only section, including a pipe, a park-and-ride area and its own lift. Furthermore, the resort has been producing a snowboarder's passport, covering all aspects of Avoriaz, for a number of years. 153km of piste in Avoriaz links up with **Les Portes du Soleil**, a group of areas straddling the French/Swiss border, creating one of the largest circuits in Europe with some major off-piste to shred. The terrain on offer in Avoriaz is more than amazing and will suit every level and style of rider: trees, big cliff drops, powder bowls and easy, wide flats - it's all here. And as everybody gets the odd off day and fancies doing something other than riding, Avoriaz puts on a choice of services that are normally found only in US resorts: quad-bike riding, snowmobiling and climbing are all an alternative buzz.

FREERIDERS with bottle will find the steep blacks on Hautes Forts well worth the effort, where you can cut some nice unspoilt terrain at speed and in style. However, riders who really want to explore the major off-piste terrain can do so by going heli-boarding, since Avoriaz is one of the few resorts in France that allows this pursuit.

CARVERS This resort is as much suited to you as any other rider, with plenty of wide, open slopes for Euro's to lay out big turns. The reds down **Chavanette** and **Arare** are good carving lines.

BEGINNERS should find Avoriaz no problem. There are plenty of easy flats around the base area to try out your first falls, before progressing up to the higher blues and reds reachable by chairs (which will help those who can't get to grips with T-bars and the Poma button lifts). One note of caution is that a lot of ski classes use the easy runs, which means they can be

THE TOWN & GETTING THERE

very busy at times, so expect congestion.

FREESTYLERS flock here for the natural hits and big air opportunities, of which some of the best are found around the tree-lined Linderets area. Avoriaz's fun-park has been established for years now and can be found near the Arare piste, off the **Lac du Bleu** drag lift. The park has a great selection of hits including a buried Beetle car. The halfpipe is deep and long, with sounds that blast out to accompany you on your way down. And if the pipe and park areas on Avoriaz slopes were not enough, then there is another terrain park with its half pipe located at **Les Crosets**, on the Swiss side of the resort area.

Pic - Avoriaz Tourism

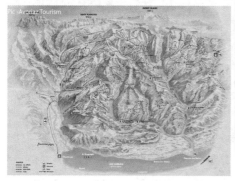
Pic - Avoriaz Tourism

TOWN

As for the local services, what you get is a wonder of contemporary architecture - a purely purpose-built, dirty and ugly sham, perched way up the mountain with most of the buildings being made of wood - tons of it. However, whatever your opinion on the looks, the resort provides excellent access from all accommodation to the slopes, with riding to your door the norm. Overall Avoriaz caters well for snowboarders and is not too fancy (in fact its pretty damn cheesy and down market). There are heaps of local attractions with a number of sporting complexes and cinemas to help while away your evenings, although most people just party the night away.

Accomodation. There are loads of wooden apartment blocks, with self-catering being the main choice. Prices vary but you can get great deals.

Food. Avoriaz can feed everyone so long as they're not too choosy. The main menu is based around two-week old pieces of cardboard pizza costing a few euros or costly 3 course French cuisine which could sting you for 50 euros a throw. *Marie Brech* is very good eatery while *Us1* serves an okay grill.

Nightlife here resembles what you would find in a sea side resort on the south coast of England. Pure holiday camp designed for the world's dole cheats making the place pretty lively and often rowdy. Booze flows freely all day and all night. The Place is a main hangout as is *Le Choucas* and *Les Ruches*, which all play cool sounds and have plenty of holiday talent to check out.

SUMMARY

Good value resort with excellent freeriding and carving areas. The main problem with Avoriaz are the crowds and long lift queues.

CAR
From Geneva, drive to Avoriaz = 52 miles (80km)
Calais 554 miles (891 Km). Drive time is around 9 1/2 hours
FLY
Fly to Geneva international, 2hr transfer
TRAIN
Trains stop at Clues (20 mins).
BUS
Bus services from Geneva airport in Switzerland, are available on a daily basis to Avoriaz via Clues

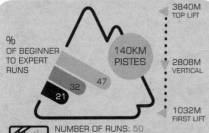

3840M TOP LIFT

% OF BEGINNER TO EXPERT RUNS

140KM PISTES

2808M VERTICAL

47

32

21

1032M FIRST LIFT

NUMBER OF RUNS: 50
LONGEST RUN: 13miles (21km)
TOTAL LIFTS: 62
6 Gondolas, 7 cable-cars, 16 chairs, 33 drags
CAPACITY (people per hour): 47,000
LIFT TIMES:
8.30am to 4.30pm

AVERAGE SNOWFALL
9.6m
SNOWMAKING
47 snow cannons

WINTER PERIODS
Dec to April
SUMMER PERIODS
none
Lift Passes
1 Day pass - 40 euros
6 Days pass- 176 euros
Heli Boarding
No
Board Schools
Group lessons 3 x 3 hr 100 euro
Group Freeride Freestyle 5 x 3 hr 135 euros. Private 2hr 80 euro
Full day 230 euro
Board Hire
Beginners 1 day 20 euros, 6 days 105
Pro 1 day 23 euros 6 day 150 euros

FREERIDE 65%
Got the lot; trees & amazing off-piste
FREESTYLE 25%
2 terrain parks and 2 half-pipes
CARVING 10%

Tourist Office Chamonix
85 Place du Triangle de L'Amitie
F74400 Chamonix, Mont Blanc
General info: ++33 (0) 450 53 00 24
Reservations: ++33 (0) 450 53 23 33
Avlanche info: ++33 (0) 836 681 020
Web: www.chamonix.com
Email:info@chamonix.com

F

F
R
A
N
C
E

As you drive into the Chamonix valley on a two lane elevated road your stomach empties, not from the bad food on the plane or the tight bends of the road, but from that tingle of anticipation the very name Chamonix excites even the most hardened of pro's and it doesn't disappoint. On your right towers above Europe's highest mountain, **Mont Blanc**, (don't tell the French about **Mt Elbrus**) the blue ice from a brimming glacier tumbles towards the road threatening to break off and take you out. Once in the town you pick up on the hardcore vibe of the place. Early morning there's skiers and boarders stuffing a pastry into their mouths whilst rushing to get first lift, a rope over one shoulder a transceiver over the other and a waist full of carabineers. Chamonix was a town long before anyone thought of making purpose built ski resorts and unlike most French resorts it's an all year round destination, with climbers flocking here when the snow melts like migrating geese. The place benefits from this with loads of bars, cheep eats and all kinds of shops. The lift system is antiquated and should have been sold to the Hungarians years ago. The pistes are unkempt and the queues for the bus home can be a joke, but that's the Chamonix experience it's not polished like some of it's neighbours it's infrastructure is rough and so are it's slopes, great. The valley is really a collection of ski areas Le Brevent out of Chamonix town. **La Flegere** out of **Les Praz** and at the head of the valley are Argentiere and Le Tour, both with great terrain. The best way to deal with Chamonix is to have a car if not there is a bus service and a train.

Pic -Chamonix Tourism

FREERIDERS Chamonix can be heaven and hell. With good snow it's the big one when it come to hard core riding. You've got it all steep faces, glacial runs, trees and couloirs. With little snow you may find yourself spending more time on the lifts and in the pub than on

151

F

F
R
A
N
C
E

the slopes. With a 6 day pass you get 2 rides on the **Grands Montets** cable car (after that you've got to get your hands in those pockets) from it's top there are two black pistes **Point de Vue** and **Pylones**, with heaps of off-piste alternatives, including skirting the impressive **Glacier d'Argentiere**. From the top of the Bochard bubble you can head into the **Combe de la Pendant bowl** for 1000m of unpisted descent. The runs down are amazing with loads of cliffs, hits and chutes, but the area can be avalanche prone. Out of **La Tour** are some fun tree runs towards the Les Esserts chair with small drop offs just big enough to make you keep your wits about you, don't get carried away and head down to far as you'll end up walking back up to the lift. The world renowned Vallee Blanche is great it takes 4/6hrs, involves a cable car ride, a few uphill sections and sphincter testing ridge walk. Although the 20km decent isn't the most challenging of terrain, the surrounding ice and scenery are fantastic. You'll need to stump up for a guide as there's crevasses to fall into and it's best to do it early on a week day as it's less crowded.

FREESTYLERS don't need a fun-park here as there's lots of natural hits and drop off's La Tours a good place to head. It seems that the attitude is to build a pipe for competitions and then leave it to melt, and after last years late cancellation and future move of the chamjam to the Pyrenees who knows when that will be. The parks also neglected here and anyway

Chamonix is a mountain resort, so if you stay in the park you'll never see what the resorts all about.

CARVERS will be out of luck as the pisters here spend more time drinking pastis and smoking gauloises than grooming the slopes.

BEGINNERS will find Chamonix's slopes a little sporadic, there are greens and blues but they are so spaced out that it's best to learn to ride elsewhere and then come here when you've got it nailed.

THE TOWN
One of the plus sides of Chamonix being a real town is the fact that there's no attitude. The locals are used to visitors all year round and know that's where the cash comes from. You'll see people skateboarding to work something you'd never see in the more stuck up French resorts. There are also plenty of things to do in Chamonix with a large sports centre, swimming

Pic -Chamonix Tour

TOWN & GETTING THERE

pool, climbing wall, arcades and a bowling alley. Argentiere at the head of the valley has a good choice of bars and restaurants and is a great place to stay as it's close to the two best board areas. Le Praz is very quite with little on offer, if you are going to walk into Chamonix town take a torch as the French drive like white van man.

Accommodation is varied you can get a bed in a bunk house for £10 or get yourself a nice hotel room. The tourist office are really helpful if you arrive needing a bed. Go to www.chamonix.net for a good range of accommodation. There's lots of self-catering apartments particularly in Chamonix sud. For an all inclusive snowboard centred chalet holiday and also training weeks go to www. mcnab.co.uk. If you've got a car there's a great bunk house at the head of the valley on the road towards Italy near Le Tour.

Food choice is good here, there's the French norm of pizzas and melted cheese but there's also a whole choice of pub food and cellar restaurants. In the main pedestrian area is a great hole in the wall fast food joint, which always has a fast moving queue outside try their Americana sandwich.

Pic - Chamonix Tourism

Nightlife. It can be a real party town with lots of **bars** having happy hours and cheep jugs of beer. The centre of town has a bar for most and a few late night clubs like *Dicks Tea Bar* and the *Jeckyl and Hyde*. There's lots of English bars, some popular with the Swede's there's even a *Queen Vic* a good night can be had at the Cantina. The *Office bar* in Argentiere is good for a beer and has a tex-mex menu which is reasonably priced. There are also a few French bars which are a little cheaper. Le Praz has a couple of very local bars.

SUMMARY

Chamonix offers some truly excellent freeriding and great natural freestyle terrain. It's not great for beginners and can suffer if there's not much snow. It's rough round the edges but that's its charm. If you can wait till there's fresh snow then jump in your car.

CAR
from Calais drive to Geneva. From Geneva, Chamonix is 50 miles away, approx 1 hour drive.
*From Calais 551 miles (886 Km Drive time is around 9 hours.
FLY
Fly to Geneva international.
TRAIN
Trains stop in Chamonix. TGV sometimes available to nearby Saint-Gervais Le Fayet station.
BUS
Bus services from Geneva airport in Switzerland, are available on a daily basis to the centre of Chamonix.

153

Good for families or day board from Geneva.

F

F
R
A
N
C
E

Chatel, part of the **Portes du Soleil** area, has the heart of a traditional village and is surrounded by new flats and chalets, all of which have the compulsory wood cladding to give it that alpine feel. While other resorts suffer from lack of snow Chatel can get more than it's fare share. Due to it's proximity to **lac Leman** (the French for lake Geneva). The water of the lake evaporates and if the wind is favourable falls on the nearest mountain as snow Chatel. You get some great view over the lake when you're up on the slopes of Super Chatel the main pisted area. It's accessed by an over crowded gondola which then gives way to a series of lifts allowing you easy access to Morgins and with a short walk through Morgins town Champoussin, remember your passport as both are in Switzerland. It's been known for customs officers on skis to stop people and search their backpacks. A drive up the valley from Chatel leads you to Linga and Pres la Joux there's a free bus. From Pres la Joux it's a couple of chairs to Avoriaz or Les Crosets. It's not the best placed resort within the Portes du Soleil to explore the 680km of piste but you almost feel like your in a traditional French alpine village, well almost.

FREERIDERS could find it hard to get the most from Chatel but if you take a real close look and don't mind a bit of a walk in or out you may just find some truly great off piste runs. There are some easy pitch tree runs from Tour de Don towards Barbossine. From the top of Col-des-Portes you can take a long sometimes tricky route down the Morgins Valley into Morgins village and if you're up for a walk try Pointe de Chesery and head down to Les Lindaretts. Head to Pre-la-Joux if you fancy some steep blacks.

FREESTYLERS - although there are some natural hits and plenty of places to build a kicker your better off going to nearby Avoriaz, which has a big fun park.

CARVERS will enjoy Chatel with its groomed intermediate piste and access to the miles of Portes du Soleil. You can get off on trying to get as much done before racing the lifts home.

BEGINNERS will find Chatel ok. The draw backs are not the runs as there are plenty of blues and greens, although some are a bit flat which leads to a bit of hopping. The main problem is the drag lifts up high, there's loads of them and the runs down into resort are often over crowded. Having said that it's possible to board from near the top all the way into resort on a blue, snow permitting.

OFF THE SLOPES there's little to do, there is a cinema which shows films in English (look for VO or version original on the advert) and in nearby Val d'Illez there's a Thermal Bath **Accommodation** is mainly chalets a lot of which have been brought by the Swiss as property is

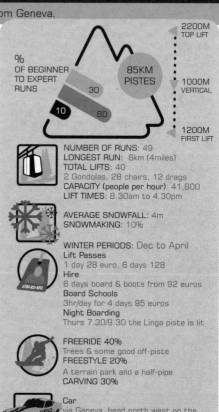

%
OF BEGINNER
TO EXPERT
RUNS

2200M
TOP LIFT

85KM
PISTES

30

10   60

1000M
VERTICAL

1200M
FIRST LIFT

NUMBER OF RUNS: 49
LONGEST RUN: 6km (4miles)
TOTAL LIFTS: 40
2 Gondolas, 28 chairs, 12 drags
CAPACITY (people per hour): 41,600
LIFT TIMES: 8.30am to 4.30pm

AVERAGE SNOWFALL: 4m
SNOWMAKING: 10%

WINTER PERIODS: Dec to April
Lift Passes
1 day 28 euro, 6 days 128
Hire
6 days board & boots from 92 euros
Board Schools
3hr/day for 4 days 95 euros
Night Boarding
Thurs 7.30/9.30 the Linga piste is lit

FREERIDE 40%
Trees & some good off-piste
FREESTYLE 20%
A terrain park and a half-pipe
CARVING 30%

Car
via Geneva, head north west on the N2 turning on to the D902 at Thonon. Chatel lies along the D22
Fly
Fly to Geneva, 1 1/2 hours drive away.
Train
to Thonon les bains, 45 minute away.

Chatel tourist Office
F-74390 Chatel-Haute Savoie,FRANCE
Tel: ++33 (0) 450 73 22 44
web: www.chatel.com
email: touristoffice@chatel.com

cheaper in France than Switzerland. For hotels there's a limited choice but a lot of British tour operators sell holidays here. **Food wise** its Pizzas, pizzas, pizzas. The best place for a pizza with a friendly group of staff and a vibe of Ben Harper music washing your food down along with the wine is *Basse Cour* on the lower road of the main village.

Chatel's **night life** is a little limited the Tunnel and Avalanche are two very English bars and have happy hours the L'is bar is a small French bar but if you can get a little booth is a good place to warm up after a long days boarding.

Courchevel is one of France's premier resorts, and part of the world renowned Trois Vallees ski area. It offers a complete range of terrain, a fantastic modern lift system, an ok park and a reasonable snow record. All that comes at a cost; it's one of the most expensive resorts in Europe, full of very rich French in Versace ski suit and furry boots closely followed by wannabe Brit snob. At the end of the week you won't think

Pic: Courchevel Tourism

twice about paying £1.50 for a bag of crisps and washing it down with a £5 pint of euro fizz. There are four stations all named after their altitude. 1850 home to flash hotels, luxury chalets and Michelin star restaurants with a good connection over to Meribel. 1650 has had a lot of money spent replacing most of the drag lifts, which means all those hidden spots have been opened up. It's almost a resort to itself with a new very slow second hand chair added to a couple of old chairs linking it to 1850. 1550 with direct access to 1850 has lots of chalets, which can be a long walk from the lifts. 1300 (le praz) the only alpine style village is good if you want to chill out at night but is sometimes short of snow early and late season. There's two bubble lifts one going direct to the fun park, there's also an Olympic ski jump if you fancy breaking your legs. If you've got loads of the green or manage to get a cheep chalet deal then Courchevel can be a fantastic resort, but don't go during school holidays as the place is mobbed.

FREERIDERS will love this place; there's everything from wide rolling pistes of 1650 to steep rock shoots under the saulire cable car. Theres so much piste that it doesn't get chopped up and they have a huge fleet of piste bashers to flatten it out each night. There's some good off-Piste straight off the lifts, under the Vizelle bubble and Dou des Lanche chair, besides the Chanrossa chair and down through the trees to Le Praz a must in bad visibility. If you don't mind a walk check out the back of the Creux Noirs. One great spot which must be treated with the utmost respect in the Vallee des Avals which is prone to a slide but has a great refuge and is stunningly beautiful, access is from the Chanrossa chair and a short walk.

FREESTYLERS will find the big snow-park under the Plantrey chair, there's some good hits and two pipes. If the suns out get there early as by

---

Stats

%
OF BEGINNER
TO EXPERT
RUNS

25
11
64

160KM PISTES

2700M TOP LIFT
1400M VERTICAL
1300M FIRST LIFT

NUMBER OF RUNS: 275
LONGEST RUN: 5km (3miles)
TOTAL LIFTS: 65
10 Gondolas, 1 cable-cars, 16 chairs, 38 drags
CAPACITY (people per hour): 68,000
LIFT TIMES:
8.30am to 4.00pm
MOUNTAIN CAFES: 10

AVERAGE SNOWFALL
6m
SNOWMAKING
26%

WINTER PERIODS
12th Dec - 24th April 2005
Lift Passes
1 Day pass 37 euros
6 Days pass 182 euros
Heli Boarding
In Italy
Night Riding
In 1650
Board Schools
Group lessons 15 hr 195 euros
12 hr 165 euros
private 2 hr 120 euros, 3 hr 165 euros
Board Hire
Board & Boots 6 days 150 euros

FREERIDE 40%
Trees & off-piste
FREESTYLE 20%
2 terrain parks and 2 half-pipes
CARVING 40%

Tourist Office Courchevel
La Croisette - Bp 37
73122 Courchevel. Cedex
General info Tel: ++33 (0) 4 79 08 00 9
Web: www.courchevel.com
Email: pro@courchevel.com

F

F
R
A
N
C
E

155

afternoon one walls slush and the others bullet, there's a free drag. The top of the Verdon's got some man made dunes and some good kickers. A small drop off can be found by the Bel air and Signal drags 1650. Go to the top of the Suisses if your looking for some big drop offs.

CARVERS will be in hard boot heaven. They reputedly spend £20,000 a night grooming the pistes, so get up for first lift and you can carve your way down the Saulire racing the cable car. When everyone else gets up, head over 1650 for motorway wide runs.

BEGINNERS should head for the Biollay and Bellecote both have a good sustained pitch, the Biollay even has a travelator at the bottom for total beginners. 1650 has some great wide runs but still a lot of drag lifts so watch out. If looking for a lesson, check out rtmsnowboarding.com a British board school who hold beginners, freestyle and carving clinics.

Pic -Robbie A

THE TOWN
Everything but Le Praz is a purpose built 70's nightmare, although they've stuck up some wood to try to add some charm it's still an ugly place. The lift access from most accommodation is great, and there's plenty to do with ice rink, climbing wall cinema, bowling and gyms. If you've got strong pants you can organise a tandem freefall, flying out of the tiny airport (March only). But remember to bring those Euros in Courchevel as cash is king.

Accommodation. If cash is short the best thing to do is get a half board chalet, so you don't do all your cash on food. You can get some great last minute deals on the web. If your wallet is fat then there are some great French hotels and some amazing chalets with under ground swimming pools and huge fire places. All the big tour operators have chalets/hotels. If you've got kids try Le Praz.

Food. If you are catering for yourself then it's pizza, melted cheese in various guises or raw meat cooked at the table on a hot stone. If you've loads of dough then get out your Michelin guide. The D'Arbeilo in Le Praz is good rustic place.

Night-life has been slowly dieing as the French reclaim the resort, leaving people with little choice, there are a few English bars or some rip off French clubs. 1850 it's the Jump bar and the tiny TJ's. Both hot and packed with bad rugby tops and chalet girls with pearl earings. In 1650 the Bubble, which looks like an airport departure lounge, is cool and run by attitude free staff. If you're staying in 1550 the Tavernas a good place for a pint.

SUMMARY
Good all-round resort. Miles of groomed piste and natural terrain. An excellent intermediate/advanced resort but expensive. If you're a beginner save you money and come here when you can utilise the resort properly. **Money Wise**: Hellishly expensive resort but worth it if you have the cash.

CAR
From Geneva via the A40, approx 50 miles.
FLY
Fly to Lyon international, transfer time to resort = 2 1/4 hours or 3hr transfer from Geneva
TRAIN
snow train and euro star to Moutiers, 15 miles on from station by road.
BUS
Bus services from Lyon or Geneva airport in Switzerland, are available on a daily basis to the centre of Courchevel.

6
OUT OF 10

Okay slopes, dire off

Flaine is a purpose-built, 1960's mess, whose architects must have designed the resort in the space of five minutes, then built it with five million tonnes of waste concrete. Ugly? Yep, and designed purely for hordes of skiers. However, as far as snowboarding is concerned, Flaine offers some great and varied terrain for different abilities. Flaine sits in a big bowl and forms part of **Le Grand Massif** area, which includes the linked resorts of **Samoens, Morillon**, and **Les Carroz**, offering good off-piste.

Pic - Flaine Tourism

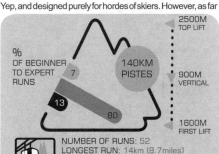

% OF BEGINNER TO EXPERT RUNS

2500M
TOP LIFT

140KM
PISTES

900M
VERTICAL

7

13

80

1600M
FIRST LIFT

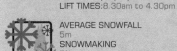

NUMBER OF RUNS: 52
LONGEST RUN: 14km (8.7miles)
TOTAL LIFTS: 28
1 Gondola, 1 cable, 9 chairs, 17 drags
CAPACITY (people per hour): 28,000
LIFT TIMES:8.30am to 4.30pm

AVERAGE SNOWFALL
5m
SNOWMAKING
5%

WINTER PERIODS
13th Dec - 25th April 2005
Lift Passes
1 Day 32 euros, 6 Days 160 euro
Night Riding:No
Heli Boarding
Yes, email info@mdh.fr min 4 people
Snow mobiles
Check out flainesnowski.com
Board Schools
private lesson 1hr 32 euros
group 3hr/6 days 118 euros
Board Hire
Board & Boots 100-150 euros for 6 days

FREERIDE 50%
Trees & off-piste
FREESTYLE 20%
A terrain park and a half-pipe
CARVING 30%

Flaine Tourist office
Galerie des Marchants, 74300 Flaine
Tel: ++33 (0) 450 90 80 01
web: www.flaine.com
email: welcome@flaine.com

Car
Via Geneva, head south on the A40 to Cluses and then take the B road on the left up to Flaine.
Fly
to Geneva 90km, about 1hrs transfer to Flaine. Also Annecy 80km & lyon 190km
Train
to Cluses which is 10 mins away.

FREERIDERS have some great opportunities for off-piste riding, with long, interesting runs to tackle. The area above the Samoens lift is pretty good, but alternatively, you should check out the trees in **Les Carroz**, where you will get a good lesson on how to treat wood at speed. Advanced riders should check out **Combe de Gers**, which is a steep back bowl that drops away with 700 metres of vert (don't bail this one). To get the best off-piste riding, hire a guide, which will cost about 60 euros for two hours. Heliboarding is also possible here.

FREESTYLERS may at first feel they are invading a Euro-carver's hangout, but air heads have a good two mile long fun-park area, loaded with big hits to get high. There's even a kid's halfpipe called the **Fantasurf**. The park is supported by a reduced lift pass, so check at the ticket office for the latest deals.

CARVERS are certainly at home here: Flaine was one of the first carving capitals in France and like most of the country, there are many good areas for Alpiners to show off.

BEGINNERS have a number of very easy flat runs which are serviced by a free lift located a short walk from the village area. However, to progress, you will need to buy a pass and head up to the more interesting runs. There are a couple of long blues leading away from the top of **Les Grandes Platieres** cable car, that will allow novices to find out what linking turns are like.

Flaine is not a massive or happening village, nor is it the most expensive, but it's hell on earth in terms of the way it is presented as a holiday camp on a mountain. The Brits that have come here over the years have done a good job in turning it into a tacky hole. Lodging is basic, and apartments are the main accommodation with most either next to the slopes, or within a short walk. Evenings are noisy with Brits and lots of apres-ski

F

F
R
A
N
C
E

157

ISOLA 2000

4 OUT OF 10

Okay but a little bit cheesy

Pic.- Isola 2000 Tourism

% OF BEGINNER TO EXPERT RUNS

120KM PISTES

11   35   54

2610M TOP LIFT

810M VERTICAL

1800M FIRST LIFT

NUMBER OF RUNS: 47
LONGEST RUN: 4km (2.5miles)
TOTAL LIFTS: 25
1 Gondola, 12 chairs, 12 drags
CAPACITY (people per hour): 20,000
LIFT TIMES:
8.30am to 4.30pm

AVERAGE SNOWFALL: Unknown
SNOWMAKING: 15%

WINTER PERIODS
Dec to April
Lift Passes
1 day 22 euros, 6 days 102 euros
Hire
110 euros for 6 days
Board Schools
private: 1hr 37 euro
group: 5 day mornings 100 euros

FREERIDE 40%
Trees & some good off-piste
FREESTYLE 20%
A terrain park and a half-pipe
CARVING 40%

Car
Via Nice, head north on the N202, then the D2205 to Isola turning left on to the D97 for Isola 2000. 1.30hr from Nice
Fly
Fly to Nice, 50 miles away.
Train
to Nice, which is a 50 minute transfer.
BUS
17.50 euros one way from Nice 2hr
Tel: 0033 (0)493859260

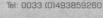

Tourist bureau
2000 INSULATED
06420 2000 Insulated
Tel: 04 9323 1515
Web: www.isola2000.com
Email: info@isola2000.com

Isola 2000, situated in the south of France, has more to offer than you'd expect. A calculated and very purpose-built resort, the French seem to have got their sums a bit wrong in the early days when they built this rather cheesy and tacky mess, whose original plan was to pack in hordes of cheap package tour groups. However, things have changed a little, and the place is losing its poor reputation and gaining a lot of respect. The resort has easy access to lifts, and the area offers plenty of varied terrain to keep even the most adventurous rider busy for a week or two, a season here would be pushing it.

FREERIDERS scoping the land will touch the piste only to hop between tree runs, or to get back on the lift. Isola has ample tree coverage over the mid to lower areas. Natural gullies can be hit near Melezes, plus look out for the drop offs in the trees as you're going up the chair lift - they're all over the place. Turn to the north-facing slope when conditions are good, above Grand Tour, as it is well worth hiking the ridge for freshies. Do watch your run out though as you come to a severe drop off onto a flat piste below.
FREESTYLERS Isola 2000 is home to the Back to Back Snowboard Club, and a dedicated and maintained snowboard park. They don't have a residential Pipe Dragon yet, but with the experienced locals, you can be sure of a park with table-tops, spined tombstones and gaps. The locals are good to watch and know how to take a good line
CARVERS. The whole area was planned to make runs long, well groomed and easy to return to base, with good cruising and carving on both sides of the mountain. BEGINNERS have a massive designated area near the base lift station. This keeps them out of trouble on a good area for progression, before they take on the higher grade runs, allowing quick learners the chance to ride the whole resort.

THE TOWN
The easiest option with accommodation would be to stay in one of the apartment blocks - comfortable, unfussy and just a stone's throw away from the lift station and amenities. If you're after a bit more style and want to impress your other half, take up space in one of the chalets available. For food, why not try the Crocodile Bar, which serves up some decent Tex-Mex. It's also a good local snowboard hangout and stays open long into the early hours, with good measures and good sounds.

5
OUT OF 10

Limited terrain and can get very busy

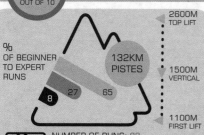

2600M
TOP LIFT

%
OF BEGINNER
TO EXPERT
RUNS

132KM
PISTES

1500M
VERTICAL

8   27   65

1100M
FIRST LIFT

NUMBER OF RUNS: 83
LONGEST RUN: 3km
TOTAL LIFTS: 55
4 Gondola, 2 cable-cars, 14 chairs, 35 drags
CAPACITY (people per hour): 53,000
LIFT TIMES:
8.30am to 4.00pm

AVERAGE SNOWFALL
5m
SNOWMAKING
10%

WINTER PERIODS
Dec to April
Lift Passes
1 Day 26 euros, 6 Days 138 euros
Board Schools
Group lessons, 1 day 30 euros, 5 days 125 euros
Board Hire
Board & Boots 22-26 euros for 1 day
115-140 euros for 6 days

FREERIDE 50%
Some trees & good off-piste
FREESTYLE 20%
A terrain park and a half-pipe
CARVING 30%

Tourist Office
74220 LA CLUSAZ
Tel. +33 (0) 450 32 65 00
Fax +33 (0) 450 32 65 01
Web:www.laclusaz.com
Emai:infos@laclusaz.com

Car
Via Geneva 50 km, head south on the A40 and exit at Bonneville on to the D12 via Borne to La Clusaz
Fly
to Geneva (50km) , then 1.5 hour transfer time. Lyon airport 150km away, nearest airport is Annecy 30km away.
Train
Train services go to Annecy which is 30km away. More info www.sncf.com
Bus
3 coaches /day from Geneva airport (8am, 1pm, 5pm). Takes 1hr 45, from 50 euros return.

Pic - La Clusaz Tourism

F
R
A
N
C
E

La Clusaz is located in the distant shadow of Mont Blanc and is only an hour-and-a-half from Geneva. La Clusaz is a cluster of five low-level rideable areas, linked by a series of lifts. The two very noticeable problems with La Clusaz are a) the low altitude, which can mean poor snow levels, and b) the French disease of overpopulation by ski-tour groups. Collectively, snowboarding can be described as poor. It lacks anything of great interest, unless you're a carver who likes to pose alongside lift lines on blue runs. Advanced riders will have this place licked in a few days, with the only decent challenge being a long black on the Massif de Balme area. You can ride four of the five areas via a network of connecting lifts, while the fifth, the Massif de Balme, can be reached by road or chair lift. Here you ride down a red or black before taking the gondola back up.

FREERIDERS will like the less crowded area of the Massif de Balme, where a series of red runs and a long black lead to open slopes which allow you to ride off-piste, hitting some powder stashes. The Combe du Fernuy is the area that descends a red section, down a tree line onto a cool run, en route to the Massif de Balme area. There are lots of trees, but no great challenges.
FREESTYLERS have a halfpipe and park on the Massif de Balme slopes, but neither are shit hot or particularly big. The way the area is spread out means that there is a lot of okay natural terrain for catching air, but this is not a great freestyle place.
CARVERS are very well matched to all five areas. The slopes allow for some good, wide arcs on intermediate terrain; the longest run is on the Balme slopes, whilst on Massif de Beauregard, there's an interesting long run to tackle at speed.
BEGINNERS can achieve a lot here, with slopes that are excellent for finding out what snowboarding is like at the early stages. The Beauregard and L'Etale areas have good, easy slopes; the only potential problem is that they are mostly serviced by drag lifts.

OFF THE SLOPES, the village has everything you would expect from a tourist trap. There's a good selection of beds ranging from expensive chalets to cheap, shared apartments, set in a traditional French-style village. Accommodation, shops, and restaurants are located within easy reach of the slopes, with many slope side hangouts. Evenings are dull and uneventful, unless you're a brain-dead apres fan

159

LA PLAGNE

5 OUT OF 10

Okay slopes but cheesy town

Pic - La Plagne Tourism
OT la Plagne/D.Schmitt

F

F
R
A
N
C
E

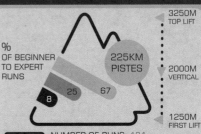

% OF BEGINNER TO EXPERT RUNS

225KM PISTES

8 25 67

3250M TOP LIFT

2000M VERTICAL

1250M FIRST LIFT

NUMBER OF RUNS: 134
LONGEST RUN: 15km
TOTAL LIFTS: 86 - 7 Gondola, 2 cable-cars, 35 chairs, 61 drags, 2 carpets
CAPACITY (people per hour): 120,899
LIFT TIMES: 8.30am to 4.30pm

AVERAGE SNOWFALL: 5.2m
SNOWMAKING: 95 hectares

WINTER PERIODS:Dec to April
Lift Passes
1 Day 38 euros, 2 Days 71 euros
6 Days 181 euros, Season 650
Hire
Loads of local shops to choose from
Board Schools
17 schools to take your pick from

FREERIDE 40%
A few trees & some good off-piste
FREESTYLE 10%
3 terrain parks and a half-pipe
CARVING 50%

Car: From Lyon/Albertville (196km) take Motorway A43 and A430.
Fly: to Lyon which is 2 hours away. Others:Geneva, Chambery, Grenoble & Annecy
Train: Daily from Paris (4hrs 15min) to Aime ,10 minutes transfer. From UK take Eurostar direct on saturdays to Aime.
BUS:Bus services available from most towns.Tel: 04 79097227

Office de Tourisme de la Plagne
73211Aime Cedex
Tel 33(0)4 79 09 79 79
Fax : 33(0)4 79 09 70 10
Web: www.la-plagne.com
Email: bienvenue@la-plagne.com

NEW

New for 2004/5: 2 new 6 seater chair-lifts at Bijolin and La Salla, increased snow making, and first phase of their electronic lift access plan.

There are 10 resorts that compose the **La Plagne** boarding area, ranging from traditional villages to modern purpose high altitude resorts built resorts, some of which are horrible such as Aime la Plagne, a single great apartment block. La Plagne is mainly suited to intermediate boarders as theres not much steep terrain and few challenging runs. There are some good wooded areas which can be a blessing in white outs, especially around the areas of *Les Coches* and *Champagny en Vanoise*. This resort is ideally suited to the Euro carver with mile after mile of motorway cruising. In 2003 the **Vanoise Express** opened which links La Plagne with **Les Arcs**, creating the **Paradski** area with access to 238 runs totally 425km. Vertigo sufferers be aware its 2km long, holds 200 people, with 380m between you and the ground, so keep your eyes closed for the 4 minutes it takes.

FREERIDERS there are some great advanced runs down from the *Bellecote glacier*, which goes up to 3250m, so there shouldnt be a shortage of snow here even at the end of the season. You can also head off piste down to *Peisey- Nancroix* to link up to the Les Arcs area. Another great long piste run runs from the top of Les Verdons down to Champagny en Vanoise, with a vertical drop of 1250m. It has some sweet trees to cruise through at the bottom, but you will have to catch it on a good day to get the best snow. Whenever you get bored, just jump on the Vanoise Express and head over to Les Arcs.

FREESTYLERS won't find many natural hits in La Plagne, but there are 3 terrain parks to keep you happy. One in Plagne Bellecôte under the Blanchets chairlift, with a 120m halfpipe. A second at Montchavin-Les Coches, accessed from the Dos Rond chairlift. The Champagny en Vanoise's park is accessed from the la Rossa chairlift. Full of kickers, spines, tabletops, rails, and benches with lines for all levels. CARVERS are very well matched to all five areas. The slopes allow for some good, wide arcs on intermediate terrain; the longest run is on the Balme slopes, whilst on Massif de Beauregard, there's an interesting long run to tackle at speed.

BEGINNERS can achieve a lot here, with slopes that are excellent for finding out what snowboarding is like at the early stages. The Beauregard and L'Etale areas have good, easy slopes; but they are mostly serviced by drag lifts.

OFF THE SLOPES
the village has everything you would expect from a tourist trap. Accommodation, shops, and restaurants are located within easy reach of the slopes, with many slope side hangouts. There's a good selection of beds, from expensive chalets to cheap shared apartments. Evenings are dull and uneventful, unless you're a brain-dead apres fan.

A cheaper option for the Trois Vallees, but can suffer from poor snow cover

La Tania is an off shoot of the Albertville Olympics built to house the spectators, it's steadily grown ever since, popular with the Dutch and Brits. The resort built in between Courchevel and Meribel has good access to the Trois Vallees. It's got a couple of drags, one just for total beginners and a big bubble with bench seats that aren't big enough to get half your arse on. At the top of the bubble you've got two choices, take the Praz Juget drag to access Courchevel or the Dou Des Lanches chair for

Pic - La Tania Tourism

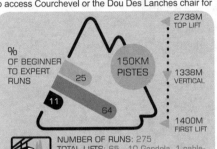

% OF BEGINNER TO EXPERT RUNS

150KM PISTES

25
11
64

2738M
TOP LIFT

1338M
VERTICAL

1400M
FIRST LIFT

NUMBER OF RUNS: 275
TOTAL LIFTS: 65 - 10 Gondola, 1 cable-car, 16 chairs, 38 drags
CAPACITY (people per hour): 70,000
LIFT TIMES:
8.30am to 4.30pm
MOUNTAIN CAFES: 10

AVERAGE SNOWFALL
Unknown
SNOWMAKING: 26%

WINTER PERIODS
Dec to April
Lift Passes
1 day 40 euros, 6 Days 198 euros
Board Schools
4x3hrs 150 euros, 3x3hrs 135 euros
Board Hire
Board & Boots 81-116 euros for 6 days

FREERIDE 40%
Lots of trees & good off-piste
FREESTYLE 20%
2 terrain parks and 2 half-pipes
CARVING 40%

La Tania Tourist Office
73125 Courchevel Cedex, France
Tel - ++33 (0)4 79 08 40 40
Fax - ++33 (0)4 79 08 45 71
Web: www.latania.com
Email: info@latania.com

Car
A43N to Albertville, N90 to Moutiers follow direction Courchevel
Fly to Lyon and Geneve 2 hours away.
St Etian and Chambery also close
Train to Moutiers access by Euro Star and Paris
Bus from Moutiers 30 mins

Meribel, if you don't do drags you can get to Courchevel off the Dou Des Lanches but the runs flat and you'll be walking. If heading for Meribel make sure you've got a Trois Vallees pass, and best to endure the flattish path to reach Meribel proper as if you drop down to soon you'll end up at the altiport and the only way out is a flat track or a slow drag.

FREERIDERS have got two great runs down, the blue Folyeres a rolling run through the trees with some great drop off hits or the red Moretta Blanche good for a full speed hack. Off Piste access is good the trees are ok at the top but they get real tight as you near the resort. Under the Dou Des Lanches can be fantastic but don't go near it without a transceiver as it's prone to sliding. Also good is between Loze and Dent de Burgin chairs. FREESTYLERS will find lots of natural hits and loads of areas up high to build a big kicker. If you want pre made then head for Courchevel or Meribels fun parks. CARVERS, for the two main runs into resort, best to head down towards the altiport as the pitch is good and the width ok.
BEGINNERS will find a short drag lift out of resort, but not the best place to learn. Beginners will find the best slopes link with Courchevel.

THE TOWNS basically a collection of chalets and a couple of blocks of flats, in typical French purpose built style, but its a good place to sit, look up the hill and have a beer. Other than a few French bars Le Pub gives all there is to give, affordable filling lunches on a big sun terrace, live music a few times a week and doesn't mind a loud piss up. Which is a good job as it's all there is to do, and the Dutch do it all. Food wise its Pizza, cheese and meat, savoie style.

Pic - A - Snowboards

%
OF BEGINNER
TO EXPERT
RUNS

3226M
TOP LIFT

241KM
PISTES

50

17 33

2026M
VERTICAL

1200M
FIRST LIFT

NUMBER OF RUNS: 121
LONGEST RUN: 7km
TOTAL LIFTS: 76
1 Funicular, 3 Gondolas, 1 cable-car, 30 chairs, 40 drags, 1 Telebenne
CAPACITY (people per hour): 68,000
LIFT TIMES: 8.30am to 4.30pm
MOUNTAIN CAFES: 14

AVERAGE SNOWFALL:
5m
SNOWMAKING:
25%

WINTER PERIODS: Dec to May
Lift Passes
Les Arcs:
1 Day 36.5 euros, 6 Days 176 euros
Paradiski: 6 Day pass 220 euros
Nightboarding
Yes, half-pipe lit
Snowmobiles
Yes

FREERIDE 40%
Trees & fantastic off-piste
FREESTYLE 40%
A terrain park and a half-pipe
CARVING 20%

Tourist Office Les Arcs
105 place de la Gare
73700 Bourg Saint Maurice
Tel. 33(0)4 79 07 12 57
Web: www.lesarcs.com
Email:lesarcs@lesarcs.com

NEW
Vanoise Express opened in December 2003 linking Les Arcs with La Plagne. New for 2004/5: 2 new 6 seater chair-lifts Les Marmottes, and Bois de l'Ours. Cabriolet cablecar between Arc 1950 and Arc 2000

Most people delight in telling you that Les Arcs is a massive, concrete carbuncle on the arse of the **French Alps** - but these people probably haven't been here, let alone spent any sort of time in the place. Ignore such comments, come with an open mind, and ride one of the best sets of mountains in the world. Les Arcs itself is split into five distinctive resorts - 1600, 1800, 1950, 2000 and **Bourg-St-Maurice**. Each place has a different feel to it, so choose wisely. **1600**, where most of the chalets are situated, is quite chilled out with loads of trees. **1800** is the party place, while **2000** is a bit hideous and isolated, but has good access to some amazing terrain. The latest village is **1950**, next to a 60m waterfall which opened in 2003 and has been created by those Intrawest people. Despite having a huge riding area, Les Arcs has managed to retain a cosy feel as its dead easy to get from one area to another and you are only likely to run into heavy lift queues during the height of the French holidays. On the mountain, Les Arcs has it all, from mellow beginner slopes to some of the most challenging runs anywhere in France, with hardly any moguls. What Les Arcs does have however, is a lot of punters as this is a very popular resort, but with such a vast expanse of snow to explore, the slopes are left fairly quite. The **Vanoise Express** opened in Dec 2003 and now

THE TOWN & GETTING THERE

links the resort up with **La Plagne** creating the **Paradiski** area.

FREERIDERS it's all here and it's all good! If there is fresh snow on the ground, you can be guaranteed an amazing day through trees in **Peisey** or above 1600, off cornices in 2000, or just straight lining anything all day long. The area off the **Trans Arc** cable car gives access to some great off-piste riding

FREESTYLERS might not see a lot of jumps on first arrival, and in truth, there aren't many natural jumps waiting to be hit. However, there are plenty of kickers all over the place, especially in Peisey, 2000 and high above 1800 - use your eyes and feel the force when you get up there. The hits on an area known as **Les Clocherets** are also worth a visit. If you're into man-made jumps, then there's a park above the **Altiport** restaurant, which should keep everyone happy from the grommet learning to jump, to the seasoned pro. However, it's true to say that the park is not well maintained, even though locals help out.

CARVERS are in hard boot heaven here, with amazingly well groomed, wide open pistes that are generally crowd free most of the time especially the higher grade runs. Les Arcs piste lends itself perfectly for big slashing turns. The **Mont Blanc** piste on 1600 is ideal for intermediate carvers, and the Belette and Myrtille runs are good for advanced carvers who can handle a board at speed.

Pic -Les Arcs Tourism

BEGINNERS are sorted here and it shouldn't be long before you're riding all over the place aided by the quality of the piste and the fact that most areas are connected by fairly easy trails and

F

F
R
A
N
C
E

lifts. There are a lot of drag lifts, so expect a bit of embarrassment as you fall off after the first two yards.

THE TOWN
The five areas of **Les Arcs** are somewhat spread out, although they link up by both lift and road. Each area has quick access to the slopes, making riding back to your **accommodation** the norm at the end of the day. 1800 is the most popular place to stay, where there is a good selection of apartment blocks and hotels. The best thing about all the areas is that prices for accommodation, eating out and partying are largely the same throughout, with something to appeal to everyone. The general feel to the whole area is one of a gigantic, spread-out holiday camp that rocks 'til late, looks tacky, but has heaps going on with all manner of sporting facilities and shopping. Many operators run package holidays using chalets, hotels and apartments throughout the resort. Prices vary however - you can rent an apartment for four people for a week from 400 euros, loading in at least four more bodies, and then split the cost. Most lodging is next to the slopes, with nothing involving a long trek. No matter what area you base yourself in, you will be able to find somewhere that serves up food to your liking. The place is littered with **restaurants** with cheap and chearful offerings being the favoured selection. 1800 has the best offerings with places like *Mountain Cafe,* where they serve huge portions of everything including Tex-Mex. The *Red Rock Bar* is also noted for grills etc.

CAR: via Lyon to Les Arcs, 210 km (130 miles), approx 2 hours. Take motorway to Albertville, dual carriageway to Moûtiers then the RN 90 to Bourg Saint Maurice
*From Calais 709 miles (1140 Km) Drive time is around 11 1/2 hours.
FLY: to Lyon international Transfer time to resort is 2 hours. Contact Satobus Alpes on +33 (0)4 37 255 255 to arrange transfer. Chambéry-Aix & Geneva airports available.
TRAIN: to Bourg-St-Maurice. Eurostar snowtrain takes 8hrs from London Waterloo.
BUS: from Lyon airport, are available on a daily basis via Bourg St Maurice to Les Arcs.

Pic - Les Deux Alpes Tourism

F

FRANCE

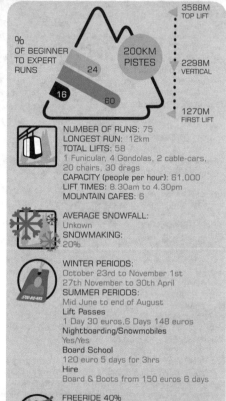

%
OF BEGINNER
TO EXPERT
RUNS **24**

16 **60**

200KM PISTES

3568M
TOP LIFT

2298M
VERTICAL

1270M
FIRST LIFT

NUMBER OF RUNS: 75
LONGEST RUN: 12km
TOTAL LIFTS: 58
1 Funicular, 4 Gondolas, 2 cable-cars,
20 chairs, 30 drags
CAPACITY (people per hour): 61,000
LIFT TIMES: 8.30am to 4.30pm
MOUNTAIN CAFES: 6

AVERAGE SNOWFALL:
Unkown
SNOWMAKING:
20%

WINTER PERIODS:
October 23rd to November 1st
27th November to 30th April
SUMMER PERIODS:
Mid June to end of August
Lift Passes
1 Day 30 euros.6 Days 148 euros
Nightboarding/Snowmobiles
Yes/Yes
Board School
120 euro 5 days for 3hrs
Hire
Board & Boots from 150 euros 6 days

FREERIDE 40%
No trees but some off-piste
FREESTYLE 20%
Terrain park and half-pipe's open all year
CARVING 40%

Tourist Office Les Deux Alpes
BP 7-38860, Les Deux Alpes
General info: ++33 (0) 4 7679 2200
Web: www.les2alpes.com
Email:les2alp@les2alpes.com

Les Deux Alpes ranks amongst France's biggest and most friendly resorts. Not just friendly, but snowboard-friendly. Home to world class performers like Alexis Parmentier, the resort has plenty of testing and rider-friendly terrain. As a glacial resort, when other areas are suffering from a lack of the white stuff, Les Deux Alpes has no such problem. The 23-25th of October 2004 sees the now legendary **Mondial**, a huge event that attracts most of the world's snowboard equipment manufacturers, holding a 'come and try it' session of next season's kit. Hand in your passport, and ride off on next year's board! Five thousand boarders, a Big Air jump comp, a boardercross and full-on night-life, makes it a wild time. A great time to vist this place is summer, as the glacier allows for some fine summer riding in T-shirts. A lot of camps are held here in June and July, with camp programmes mainly aimed at freestylers. Last season the finals of the Orange Brits were held there, a full week of partying and competions featuring the top UK riders from the AIM series.

FREERIDERS While skiers with poor imagination brand it a motorway resort, the same is not true for boarders. When there is a fresh dump, you can ride almost everywhere you can see - the off-piste is huge and challenging. The only terrain missing is that of trees, but with a free day on the lift pass in nearby Serre Chevalier, tree huggers should feel catered for. Check out the Dome for a powdergasm, and routes off the new 6-man chair, La Fee, for steep, deep and testing riding. The resort of **La Grave** is connected via the Dôme de la Lauze ski tow, and its a renowned freeride wilderness.

FREESTYLERS can pipe and park ride all year round. Winter sees the park located at the mid-station with a well prepared pipe and a permanent boardercross course. In the summer, the park is on the glacier, which features in virtually every European snowboard video, such is its reputation. Summer sees the addition of two pipes serviced by a separate drag lift and the funicular train under the glacier.

CARVERS This is an alpine rider's dream retreat, with nicely pisted runs like the Roch-Mantel and the Signal for a warm up. The glacier itself is great for ballistic speed. The Sandri run at the foot of the glacier to the mid-station is a warp factor 9, if you adhere to the essential turn only rule. So, for those of you who think turning is to admit defeat, tuck 'em away and go for it.

LES DEUX ALPES

THE TOWN & GETTING THERE

BEGINNERS starting out couldn't ask for a better place to make steady progress. The only problem is that the home runs down the front face are amongst the steepest in the resort, but there is a winding green run as an alternative. A real bonus is that the gentlest terrain is at the very top of the resort, where you can find the best snow. Due to the layout of the lift system, other than your first morning on the beginner's slope, you need never take a drag for the remainder of your stay. The chairlifts, gondolas and other lifts make the whole uplift problem easier to sort out than a wonderbra, which should please the wimps.

THE TOWN

Off the slopes and at the base of the runs, Les Deux Alpes sits conveniently for most local services, but being a large town, not everything is within walking distance. The resort is a mix of old school and purpose-buildings, with accommodation ranging from quaint chalets, ritzy hotels, to apartment blocks that wouldn't look out of place in a New York suburb. There are loads of off-slope services, including a cinema, bowling alley, sports complex and an outdoor climbing wall. There are lots of the usual shopping outlets, and a mini-mall selling the usual tourist junk and pricey snowboard gear. It should also be pointed out that this is a busy package tour destination.

Accommodation: Standard grade apartment blocks, and a number of traditional-style chalets and modern hotels at prices that won't always hurt.

Food-wise, this place caters well for people on a budget, as well as those who want to splash out. There are some reasonably priced pizza and burger bars that are very good indeed. The Thai takeaway is much better than the disappointing Chinese. For a Tex-Mex, visit Smokey Joes or Saxo - also home to some of France's loveliest bar staff (top french tottie).

Night-life goes off seven nights a week, and it's common to see apres-ski idiots throwing up all over the place early on, having had a glass of gluwein at a poxy teatime bonding session. Okay for a laugh is the Brazilian Bar, while Mike's and the Dutch Bar are for those who just want to get wasted.

EVENTS

October 23-25th 2004
Mondial du Snowboard
Pro competitions, free board tests, major partying

F

F
R
A
N
C
E

Pic - Les Deux Alpes Tourism

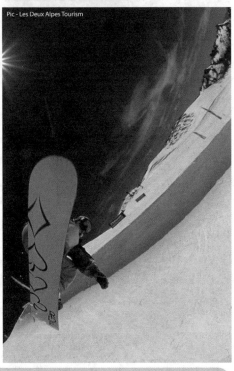

CAR
Drive via Lyon to Les Deux Alpes via Grenable, approx 106 miles (170 km), about 2 hours
*From Calais 571 miles (950 Km) Drive time is around 9 3/4 hours.
FLY
Fly to Lyon international Transfer time to resort is 2 hours. Local airport is Grenoble
TRAIN
Trains to Grenoble (25 minutes)
BUS
Bus services from Lyon airport, are available on a daily basis via Grenoble.

wsg

MERIBEL

6 OUT OF 10   Over hyped resort. Good park though.

F

F
R
A
N
C
E

Pic - San Tang

% OF BEGINNER TO EXPERT RUNS

150KM PISTES

14   28   58

2952M TOP LIFT

1552M VERTICAL

1400M FIRST LIFT

NUMBER OF RUNS: 76
LONGEST RUN: 4km (2.5 miles)
TOTAL LIFTS: 60
16 Gondolas, 18 chairs, 18 drags, 8 Telebabies
CAPACITY (people per hour): 50,000
LIFT TIMES: 8.30am to 4.30pm

AVERAGE SNOWFALL:
5m
SNOWMAKING:
26%

WINTER PERIODS:
Dec to April
Lift Passes
1 Day pass 37 euros
6 Days 182 euros
Nightboarding
Yes
Board School
Around 150 euros for 5 days of 3hr
Hire
Board & Boots 120-170 euros a week.

FREERIDE 40%
Trees & some off-piste
FREESTYLE 20%
A terrain park and a half-pipe
CARVING 40%

Office du Tourisme de Meribel
73551 Meribel Cedex - France
Tel: 04 79 08 60 01
Fax: 04 79 00 59 61
Web: www.meribel.net
Email: info@meribel.net

Meribel at 1450m is a favourite for the Brits. Set in the middle of the Trio Vallees it's a good base to explore this massive area. So good in fact the French want it back. The Brit's have been slowly buying this resort and you can spend a week here without the need to speak a word of French, which is a good job as most of the bar staff wouldn't understand you anyway. This resort has enough varied terrain to keep everyone in a mixed ability group happy. Because of it's altitude the runs into resort can suffer from lack of snow and are often rock hard ice. They do have good snow making capabilities but as we all know its no replacement for the real thing. Meribel can be busy it's over priced and full of British skiers but has some great boarding.

FREERIDERS have a massive area to explore with well maintained pistes and lots of powder faces. From the **Saulire** are some long reds down to **Mottaret** which it turn will allow you to gain access to the **Mont Vallon** area the highest point in the Meribel Valley. Under the **Plan de Homme** chair are some well spaced trees with an easy pitch but a lot of rocks. Get off the **Olympic Express** chair and keep going straight and you drop into a 845 meter decent towards **St Martin de Belleville**, keep left as you may run out of snow early or late season. A short walk between two peaks off the **Mont Vallon** bubble will lead you

to a huge bowl with some big drop offs, **take care** avalanche is a real possibility here. If you do leave the valley don't miss the last lift home as taxis are ridiculously expensive.

FREESTYLERS have a good fun park which is reached by the **Plattieres bubble** get of at the second stage. The Pipe is good and wide and was used one year for the British championships, following the pipe are a number of graded hits which could do with steeper and longer run outs but are fine. The second and smaller park with some small hits and a mini boardercross is next to the Arpasson drag.

Pic - Meribel Resort

Mottaret which is more of a purpose built village but is better placed for access to Mont Vallon the main fun park and Val Thorens.

Meribel is package deal central, and as such the bars are full of pissed Brit's in silly hats waiting for dinner, or later on really pissed Brit's after buckets full of cheep wine they got free with their chalet dinner. Before the days board is over you can sink a few in the lively *Rond Point*. *The Pub* has pool and a few tv's, opposite is *La Taverne* which is often mobbed and of course where there's Brit's there's a *Dicks Tea Bar*. All the bars are way over priced so if you are in a chalet ask them to chill the red wine so you don't have to hold your nose to get it down your throat.

CARVERS will find some really sweet runs. The pistes are not as well maintained as in Courchevel but are plentiful and wide. Meribel has red runs with a vertical drop of almost 1300m if you cant find somewhere to carve on a run that long give up.

BEGINNERS have lots of opportunities to master those linked turns around the Altiport area, although some of the lifts are very old and slow. If heading for the **Mont Vallon** area be prepared for some flat spots on the way home.

THE TOWN

Meribel is tainted by the Brit's, the bars have imaginative names like *Le Pub*. It's a big spread out resort as they sensibly won't allow high rise developments so its grown out rather than up. The two main streets are full of bad clothes shops, board/ski hire, bars and restaurants. On the slopes away from the board you can take a tandem paraglide or ride a snow-mobile. Just up from **Meribel** is the village of

All the big tour operators come here. You should be able to get a deal as there's chalet after chalet to choose from. Don't stay in **Brides-les-Bains** however cheep it is (see trio vallees)

Tex-mex, pizza and burgers to be had in the pubs. As for the restaurants *The Tremplins* good and if you want it there's a Michelin star at the *Cassiopee*.

CAR
Via Lyon, head south to Moutiers via A432, A43, N90 and then the D915 to Meribel.
*Drive time from Calais is 9 3/4 hours, 585 miles (941 km).
FLY
Fly to Lyon, which has a 2 1/4 hour transfer time. St Etienne is also close
TRAIN
Train services go to Moutiers which is 10 minutes away.
BUS
Coach from Lyon airport

F
FRANCE

167

MONTGENEVRE

4 OUT OF 10 — Okay but basic

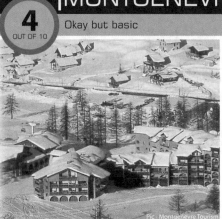

Pic - Montgenevre Tourism

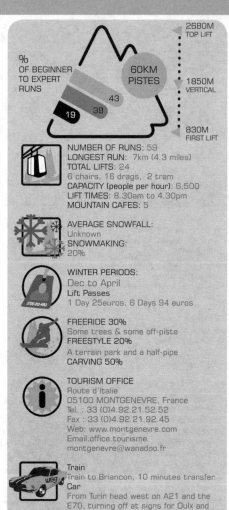

%
OF BEGINNER TO EXPERT RUNS

19 38 43

60KM PISTES

2680M
TOP LIFT

1850M
VERTICAL

830M
FIRST LIFT

NUMBER OF RUNS: 59
LONGEST RUN: 7km (4.3 miles)
TOTAL LIFTS: 24
6 chairs, 16 drags, 2 tram
CAPACITY (people per hour): 6,500
LIFT TIMES: 8.30am to 4.30pm
MOUNTAIN CAFES: 5

AVERAGE SNOWFALL:
Unknown
SNOWMAKING:
20%

WINTER PERIODS:
Dec to April
Lift Passes
1 Day 25euros, 6 Days 94 euros

FREERIDE 30%
Some trees & some off-piste
FREESTYLE 20%
A terrain park and a half-pipe
CARVING 50%

TOURISM OFFICE
Route d'Italie
05100 MONTGENEVRE, France
Tel. : 33 (0)4.92.21.52.52
Fax : 33 (0)4.92.21.92.45
Web: www.montgenevre.com
Email:office.tourisme.
montgenevre@wanadoo.fr

Train
Train to Briancon, 10 minutes transfer
Car
From Turin head west on A21 and the
E70, turning off at signs for Oulx and
precede down the B24 to Montgenevre.
Fly
Turin in Italy is 1hr away. Grenoble is
145km away

Montgenevre forms the only French part of a circuit known as the **Milky Way**: a collection of resorts that extends along a number of valley floors and criss-crosses over into Italy. Montgenevre is basically at the opposite end to its more famous relation, the Italian resort of **Sauze d 'Oulx**. Collectively, the circuit offers over 250 miles of rideable terrain on slopes that have a good, reliable snow record, thanks to the average height of each area. Montgenevre's own 60km of marked out trails are an interesting mixture of mainly intermediate trails and some poor advanced terrain, rising from the village which is at an altitude of 1850m. Although this is a popular tourist resort, it is not as tainted with package tours as some other resorts in the region. Easy access to the slopes is made possible by a number of base lifts that will take you up to the main slopes of the **Les Anges** and **Le Querelay** areas, or in the opposite direction to **Le Chalvet**.

FREERIDERS can cut decent off-piste powder and ride some nice tree lines, although you won't find much of it a great challenge. The trails on Le Chalvet, located in what tends to be the quietest area to ride, give access to some cool freeride terrain and has a nice big powder bowl.

FREESTYLERS are presented with what they call a fun-park, but in truth it is a dire pipe, with only a few man-made hits. The best options for air are to seek out the natural terrain features.

CARVERS are a common sight here, with boy wonders in hards posing on Les Anges and Le Querelay, which are both popular and easy. The two blacks down the Pian del Sole en route to the village of Claviere, are a little more interesting and worth a blast.

BEGINNERS are well catered for here, with a host of easy trails that can be reached (having first studied the piste map), without needing to ride a drag lift. Fast learners will soon be able to ride from the summit of Les Anges to the base, via a mixture of blue and green trails.

LOCAL FACILITIES are based conveniently for the slopes with a mixture of apartment blocks, chalets, shops, sporting facilities and restaurants, styled in a sober manner but aimed at the package tour ski groups. The village is okay, although there isn't a great deal to get excited about. Lodging is very affordable. Evenings can be very lively, with a number of bars that have young crowds partying every night all night.

F
FRANCE

6 OUT OF 10

A low, basic resort, but part of the huge Portes du Soleil

Morzine is a long established pretty French resort. Its location at 1,000 metres (3,300 feet) can turn snow to rain fairly quickly, so temperature is crucial to this resort. With a good snow fall, however, Morzine and the nearby resort of Les Gets, can suffice for the snowboarder.

Pic - Morzine Tourism

MORZINE-LES GETS
See Avoriaz pages for details on the Morzine-Avoriaz section

2466M TOP LIFT

% OF BEGINNER TO EXPERT RUNS

11

110KM PISTES

1466M VERTICAL

43

47

1000M FIRST LIFT

NUMBER OF RUNS: 66
LONGEST RUN: 3miles (5km)
TOTAL LIFTS: 48
2 funiculars, 3 cable-cars, 22 chairs, 18 drags
LIFT TIMES:
8.30am to 4.00pm

AVERAGE SNOWFALL
9m
SNOWMAKING
unknown

WINTER PERIODS
Dec to April
Lift Passes
day 26 euros , 6 days 131.8
Just Terrain park access 15,50 a day
Board Schools
6 half-days 100 euros
Private lesson 33 euros per hour
Night Boarding
On Boule de Gomme and Stade slopes

FREERIDE 40%
A few trees and good off-piste
FREESTYLE 20%
A terrain park
CARVING 40%

Morzine's tourist office
B.P. 23 - 74110 Morzine - France
Tel: 00 33(0) 450 74 72 72
Fax: 00 33(0) 450 79 03 48
Web:www.morzine-avoriaz.com
Email:info@morzine-avoriaz.com

NEW

NEW FOR 04/05 SEASON
new Zore 4-seater chairlift. Zore and Tétras runs improved, new training area and an extension of Gazex; the avalanche triggering system.
Portes du Solei area has an additional 3 new 6-seater chairlifts.

The terrain varies from the long, tree lined, wide slopes of Morzine, to a board park in Les Gets, to the more challenging slopes of **Mont Cherry** and **Chammossiere**.

FREERIDERS.These mountains can be less busy than the slopes on the Avoriaz and Swiss side. Hence, you'll find more room for carving and it's prettier too, with tree-lined slopes and the odd café dotted around.

FREESTYLERS. The board park in Les Gets comprises of a boarder x, quarter pipes and spines. Don't forget that this massif links to Avoriaz (although the links are a bit flat in places) which has excellent board parks (see section on Avoriaz).

BEGINNERS.Mainly chair lifts on these slopes so the poma or t bar does not have to tackled. The green slopes will be too flat for the snowboarder, but there are some easy blues and reds in Morzine for the beginner. The Pleney slope, which heads back to the town, is a steep red.

THE TOWN
For those who need to take a break from the slopes there is plenty of shopping available in the town ranging from equipment to fashion. There is a swimming pool, bowling alley, pool tables, cinema, ice skating and ice hockey games.

Food. Providing you are not allergic to cheese, Morzine has plenty of restaurants at reasonable prices. Morzine is typified by the Haute Savoyard specialities of tartiflette (bacon and potatoes), raclette and fondue.

Nightlife. Not après ski as such – but if an evening out in the pubs, doubtless mixing with people from Clapham, floats your boat, then Morzine is perfect . Lots of English and Dutch frequent the 15 bars and 2 main nightclubs, with friendly, and generally drunken, behaviour. The *Dixie bar* is in the centre of town and the *Boudda Bar, The Cavern* and *Le Crepuscle* are closer to the Morzine slopes. Bars are open until 2am, Nightclubs until 3-4 am – *Opera Rock* and *Le Paradis*.

Accommodation. A good range of accommodation is on offer from self catering apartments (there is a reasonable supermarket in the town centre), to guesthouses and hotels.

Cool place to ride, with the largest half-pipe in France

Pic - Risoul Tourism

F

FRANCE

Risoul is located between Gap and Briancon, and combined with the neighbouring resort Vars, the whole area offers about 160 km of terrain. The big men of the resort are more than happy to have snowboarders here, since the image of non-conformity fits in nicely with the way the resort is run - clearly with the young in mind. Risoul 1850 offers everything from easy slopes for beginners, to double black diamond runs for extreme freaks.

FREERIDERS tend to show up here around New Year in search of decent terrain, which they can find on Pic de Razies, Melezet and Platte De La Nonne, or Pic De La Mayt. Ride in these big powder bowl areas, and you can forget about sex being the best thing in the world. One warning - you won't decide on which is your favourite run for days or even weeks, as there are so many damn good ones.

FREESTYLERS should take De Cezier chair to reach Surfland, where the jibbing begins. This playground (which is akin to paradise), offers a complete boardercross run, rails, several quarter-pipes, small practice kickers, a pro-jump over a bus, and one of the best, and reputedly the longest halfpipe in France. 150m long, 20m wide and with 5m walls, this pipe will probably offer you more air-time than you actually want. Every Friday night there's a high-jump contest, with local riders jumping to World Pro Tour levels (there's also a barbecue in the evening).

CARVERS All the slopes are designed and prepared for hardcore edge-to-edge activities, and there are even special slopes for race practice (poles available at the ski school).

BEGINNERS If you take the cabin lift named Accueil, you'll find the area that Risoul has set aside for its snowboard kindergarten - the short and easy run is perfect for your first try on a board. There are also two small, slow drag lifts to practice on, before going up into the real snowboard world.

THE TOWN
Risoul is a small village where the inhabitants still treat you as a guest. There is a good selection of slope side **accommodation**, with seven suplits in an apartment costing around 120euros per rider. **Eating out** is cool at places like *Snack Attack*. For **night-life**, head to the *Yeti* (little Holland), where you must drink more booze than the Dutch dude, then leave him on the floor and take off with his girlfriend.

% OF BEGINNER TO EXPERT RUNS

161KM PISTES

11   34   55

2750M TOP LIFT

1100M VERTICAL

1650M FIRST LIFT

NUMBER OF RUNS: 122
LONGEST RUN: 8km (5 miles)
TOTAL LIFTS: 55
1 Gondola, 13 chairs, 41 drags
CAPACITY (people per hour): 41,000
LIFT TIMES: 8.30am to 4.30pm

AVERAGE SNOWFALL:
Unknown
SNOWMAKING:
10%

WINTER PERIODS: Dec to April
Lift Passes
1 Day 25 euros, 6 Days 135 euros
Board Schools
ESI run a 6 day snowboard school
Hire
Board & Boots 120 euros for 6 days
Night Boarding
Yes & pipe is somtimes lit

FREERIDE 40%
Some cool tree runs & good off-piste
FREESTYLE 20%
A terrain park and a 150m half-pipe
CARVING 40%

TOURISM OFFICE
05600 Risoul 1850
Tel.: 04 92 46 02 60
Fax: 04 92 46 01 23
Web: www.risoul.com
Email:o.t.risoul@wanadoo.fr

Train
to Montdauphin, 20 minutes away.
Car
Via Grenoble head south east along
route 91 via Briancon, 117 miles.
Fly
Fly to Grenoble, 2 1/4 hr transfer time.

8 OUT OF 10

Fantastic freeriding when theres fresh snow.

Sainte-Foy who told them? The word is out, but there's still time. Ten years ago if you asked someone about Sainte-Foy a blank look would greet you. If you'd driven there you would've missed it, if it hadn't of been for the fact the road ended. The home of mushroom loving David Vincent has changed, ask now and a gleam will light up the eyes of those who've been and the answer of no but I'd love to from those unlucky others. Towards Val d'Isere and Tignes from Bourg St Maurice there's a small turning to the left. Up it's 8km of once potholed tarmac lies the hamlet of Saint Foy. Not a place to spend a weeks holiday but if you're nearby, have use of a car and it's just dumped GO. This place with good snow has a hallucinatory feel, you won't be asking your mates to pinch you, you're going to need a twat round the head

Pic - Sainte Foy Tourism

with their board to believe what you're seeing. A boarders dream, but who knows for how much longer? The road in is smooth, the building of chalets is changing the vibe from ramshackle farm house to modern resort. Gone are the days of being greeted by goats looking at you from their barns, lets hope they leave the slopes alone.

FREERIDERS, its what snowboards were invented for. There are basically 3 slow lifts, they run one after the other to take you from 1550m to the *Col de L'Aiguille* at 2612m. From here you have a myriad of choices but be careful each brow you come over leads to another untouched field and the next thing you know your ollieing your way over fences and the bottom lift will be a hitch hike away. On the way up you can look for the line you want to take. Be it wide open face, rock shoots or into the trees this place is a wide open mountain with only a few runs winding their way down under the lifts. If you can handle a walk and a long flattish path then you can drop down over the back side of Rocher d'Arbine. **WARNING** to get the best of this place get a guide; not just to show you the way, but to advise about safe routes and snow conditions.

FREESTYLERS need to discover how to seek out natural hits, since that's all you're going to get - but that's all you're going to need! Why bother making pipes in a natural heaven - they're better left to the tourist traps. Riding will never be as free or as natural as in this place. There's loads of drop offs and plenty of banked walls just waiting to be hit, but novice air heads must take care and ride only with a competent rider who can pre-spot for you, as who knows what may lie under that flat blanket of soft looking snow.

CARVERS will soon whish they'd headed for Val d'Isere or Tignes, with only 25km of marked pistes. BEGINNERS have some fine rolling runs under the first 2 chairs and won't have the crowds of bigger resorts to contend, and cheaper lift passes.

On the slopes are some great little mountain restaurants, off the slopes, you will find a resort with little to offer. There are chalets, but they are spread out with no connections to night-life or eateries. But then, if you stay here it's for the riding not for anything else. Nightlife is a beer in the British run pub or a glass of wine in your chalet. Sainte-Foy is small and let's hope it stays that way.

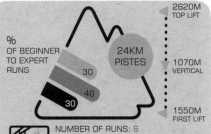

2620M TOP LIFT

% OF BEGINNER TO EXPERT RUNS

24KM PISTES

30

40

30

1070M VERTICAL

1550M FIRST LIFT

NUMBER OF RUNS: 6
LONGEST RUN: 7km (4.3 miles)
TOTAL LIFTS: 5 - 3 chairs, 2 drags
CAPACITY (people per hour): 12,000
LIFT TIMES: 8.30am to 4.30pm

AVERAGE SNOWFALL: Unknown
SNOWMAKING: none

WINTER PERIODS: Dec to April
Lift Passes
1 Day 17.5 euros, 6 Days 96 euro

FREERIDE 80%
A few trees & amazing off-piste
FREESTYLE 10%
Just natural hits
CARVING 10%

Tourist office Sainte-Foy
73640 Sainte-Foy-Tarentaise
Tel: ++33 (0) 4 79 06 95 19
Web: www.saintefoy.net
Email: stefoy@wanadoo.fr

Train
Euro star, snow train and tgv go to Bourg-St-Maurice, 20 minutes away.
Car
Via Bourg-St-Maurice, take the N90 direction Tignes/Val d'Isere for saint -Foy.
Fly
Fly to Geneva, 2 1/2 hours transfer time. Same from Lyon.

F
R
A
N
C
E

171

Pic - St Lary Tourism

%
OF BEGINNER
TO EXPERT
RUNS

100M PISTES

2515M TOP LIFT

915M VERTICAL

1600M FIRST LIFT

14 12 74

NUMBER OF RUNS: 40
LONGEST RUN: 4km (2.5 miles)
TOTAL LIFTS: 32
2 cable-cars, 9 chairs, 22 drags
CAPACITY (people per hour): 25,000
LIFT TIMES: 8.30am to 4.30pm

AVERAGE SNOWFALL:
Unknown
SNOWMAKING:
10%

WINTER PERIODS:
4th Dec 04 to 10th April 05
Lift Passes
1 Day 27.5 euros, 6 Days 150 euros
Board Schools
2 ski schools with board instructors
Hire: hire shops at all elevations
Night Boarding: No

FREERIDE 40%
Tree runs but poor off-piste
FREESTYLE 10%
A terrain park and a half-pipe
CARVING 50%

TOURISM OFFICE
37 rue Vincent Mir – BP 39
65170 SAINT-LARY Cedex
Tel : (0033)5.62.39.50.81
Fax : (0033)5.62.39.50.06
Web: www.saintlary.com
Email: st-lary@wanadoo.fr

Train
to Lannemezan, 20 minutes transfer.
Car
Via Tarbes, head south on the D935 and
D929 towards the Spannish Border to
Reach St Lary.
Fly
to Tarbes airport in Spain 2 hours away.

NEW
New for 04/05 season
new Glacier ski-lift in old glacial cirque
increases vertical by 300m, increasing
board area to 700ha/100km slopes

The main village of Saint Lary lies at 630 metres in the Aure Valley; above here there are two small villages, **Saint Lary La Cabane** at 1,600 metres, and **Saint Lary Pla D'Adret** at 1,700 metres. All three are connected by a series of lifts, with the upper villages reachable by road, or from Saint Lary by the cable car which takes you to the slopes. This relatively small resort lies in the **French Pyranees** and goes back to the 1950's. If you think that French ski resorts are massive purpose-built shams, this place will make you think again. What you get is a resort that is very snowboard-friendly, with good terrain that can be tackled by novices and riders with only a few days under their belts. However, this is also a popular resort which results in a number of long lift queues, especially at weekends.

FREERIDERS looking for vast powder bowls are not going to get them here. Advanced and hardcore riders wanting major long steeps are going to find this place a bit easy without too many challenges. The cluster of black runs off the Tortes chair offers some opportunities for freeriders to excel on fairly featureless terrain. Alternatively, the area known as Bassia is pretty cool, and will suit riders looking for trees to shred.
FREESTYLERS will find the snowboard park on Vallon Du Portet interesting, with its long boardercross circuit, an improved pipe, and a series of decent hits.
CARVERS looking for fast, wide piste to lay out big turns on will find the few reds that are available are basic but okay. They should also provide novices who are getting to grips with a hard boot set up, some early learning opportunities.
BEGINNERS will certainly find the easy blues spread out across the resort perfect for learning, with a mixture of chair lifts and drags to ferry you around. The short easy stuff reached from Saint Lary Pla D'Adret will sort you out, before taking the runs over on Vallon Du Portet. The Corniche is a long, easy blue that freeriding novices will soon be able to handle.

THE TOWN
An old Pyrenean village, St Lary is laid out along a main street where you'll find chalets and hotels. Services are extremely good here, without the hustle and bustle of tourist traps. Although somewhat limited, most facilities are found in Saint Lary, rather than the other two villages. Eating and night-time hangouts are okay: quiet and tame, and inexpensive.

F
FRANCE

ST GERVAIS

6
OUT OF 10

Some good freeriding from this little known Chamonix cousin.

Despite its proximity to Mont Blanc and the ever popular Chamonix, St Gervais is not a very well known resort, probably due to the fact that no major tour operators go there. St Gervais itself is fairly small, but the lift pass (Evasion Mont-Blanc) covers 6 ski areas comprising of over 450km of slopes and some easily accessible off piste areas. It is also one of the areas covered on the Ski Pass Mont Blanc which allows access to the whole of the Mont Blanc region, (12 areas).

Pic - St Gervais Tourism

F

F
R
A
N
C
E

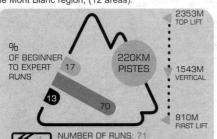

%
OF BEGINNER
TO EXPERT
RUNS

17

13

70

220KM
PISTES

2353M
TOP LIFT

1543M
VERTICAL

810M
FIRST LIFT

NUMBER OF RUNS: 71
LONGEST RUN: 3km (1.9 miles)
TOTAL LIFTS: 41
2 Gondolas, 13 chairs, 24 drags, 1 tram
CAPACITY (people per hour): 23,920
LIFT TIMES: 8.30am to 5.00pm

AVERAGE SNOWFALL: Unknown
SNOWMAKING: 20 cannons

WINTER PERIODS: Dec to April
Lift Passes
1 Day 31.5 euros, 6 Days 151 euros
Board School
group 2.5hrs 23 euros, 6 days 94 euros
private 1 hr 30 euros
Hire
Board & Boots from 90 euros a week

FREERIDE 45%
A few trees & some off-piste
FREESTYLE 35%
A terrain park, dodgy half-pipe
CARVING 20%

Tourist office St Gervais
115 av. du Mont-Paccard. F-74170 St Gervais
Tel: ++33 (0) 450 47 76 08
Web:www.st-gervais.net
Email:welcome@st-gervais.net

Train
Train services are possible all the way to Le Fayet, just 2 minutes away.
Bus
Bus from Geneva airport daily
Car
Via Paris, head down the A6 to Macon then take the A40 to St Gervais.
Fly
Fly to Geneva airport 50 minutes away.

FREERIDERS should check out the huge wide open bowls at Les Contamines, where there is varied off piste riding almost everywhere you look. It's best when visibility and snow are good though, as if it is cloudy you will just get frustrated that you are missing all the best lines and hitting all the hidden cat-tracks. Mont-Joy has some good steep off-piste riding. It is possible to ride right down to Les Contamines, but taking a guide to avoid accidental cliff drops is highly recommended.

FREESTYLERS have a fun park at Mont Joux, although it is not very impressive and seems to be rather neglected, particularly the halfpipe. The few jumps range from a small table top to a 30ft gap jump. It also gets very busy at times, especially weekends.
CARVERS will find plenty of wide pistes, although some of them do tend to get chopped up by the end of the day. There are slalom courses at Mont Joux and across Megeve at Rochebrune.
BEGINNERS can save money by getting a lift pass for just the Bettex area, which has a few nursery slopes, including one chairlift. However, the slopes on the other side of the mountain tend to get more sun and are less icy. The areas around the Mont d'Arbois and Ideal lifts are recommended as there are a variety of easy runs as well as some easily reached harder ones for when you start feeling brave. The low points for beginners are the flat bits on the runs back down to Bettex.

LOCAL SERVICES are good and include ice skating, ice climbing, a cinema, loads of shops and a large number of restaurants. Around the mountain there is a good choice of accommodation in St. Gervais, with over 30 hotels, chalets, lodges and apartments. A lot of these are located below the St. Gervais-Bettex gondola, so theoretically you can ride to your door, snow permitting. Night life, however, is tame and limited to one club which is crap, plays dull French music and is expensive.

10
OUT OF 10

Without doubt one of the best resort in France, pricey but worth every euro.

Pic - Serre Chevalier Tourism

F
R
A
N
C
E

Serre Chevalier is one of the best places to ride in France. This great resort has heaps of major terrain, tight, open trees to weave, extreme drop offs to get the adrenaline going, big bowls with silly amounts of good powder, countless banks and gullies, super-fast flats to push the hair back, hits everywhere, and a giant, natural fun-park - all located next to an unassuming, old-fashioned French village (with a hint of the new here and there). As one local rider once put it 'who needs fun-parks, when this place is a complete fun-park at every level and distinction!' Serre Chevalier is suitable for everyone, with an area that links up with Briancon and Le Monetier, to provide 230km of terrain. Serre Chevalier is the largest of the three areas, and also the place for the best terrain and action. However, being a great resort does have its drawbacks as this is a major destination for package tour operators. This has the result of causing some long lift lines first thing in the morning, but once up, things become a lot better.

FREERIDERS get to shred plenty of open, tight trees, gullies and deep bowls, as well as some long steeps, where advanced riders can busy themselves for weeks on end. Serre Chevalier is perfect soft boot territory, and those riders wanting wide expanses of powder without having to hike, should check out the stuff off the Balme chair lift.

FREESTYLERS should basically session the whole mountain as there are too many hits to mention - it will take most riders at least a season to hit each jump only once. The place is a super-big, natural fun-park, with lots of logs to grind, and loads of big jumps everywhere. There's also a man-made pipe at the lower section of the Yret chair on Le Monetier's slopes should you need it.

CARVERS are presented with as much alpine terrain as they could possibly need. If you have the bottle, the Olympique trail is a fast, black race run that bases out in the village of Chantemerle, and will certainly get the adrenaline pumping. You can get some serious speed down the Olympique trail, and although

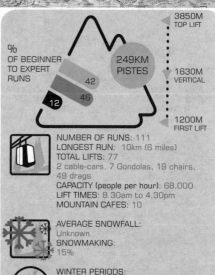

3850M
TOP LIFT

%
OF BEGINNER
TO EXPERT
RUNS

249KM
PISTES

42

46

12

1630M
VERTICAL

1200M
FIRST LIFT

NUMBER OF RUNS: 111
LONGEST RUN: 10km (6 miles)
TOTAL LIFTS: 77
2 cable-cars, 7 Gondolas, 19 chairs, 49 drags
CAPACITY (people per hour): 68,000
LIFT TIMES: 8.30am to 4.30pm
MOUNTAIN CAFES: 10

AVERAGE SNOWFALL:
Unknown
SNOWMAKING:
15%

WINTER PERIODS:
4th Dec 04 to May 1st 2005
Lift Passes
Grand Serre Che linked area:
1 Day 33 euros, 6 Days 160
Just Serre Chevalier:
1 Day 29 euros, 6 days 137
Board Schools
A number of board schools. Private lessons from 31 euros an hour. Group 4hrs for 6 days 102 euros.
Night Boarding: Yes

FREERIDE 60%
Lots of tree runs and good off-piste
FREESTYLE 30%
A terrain park and a half-pipe
CARVING 10%

Tourist Office Serre Chevalier
BP 20-05240 La Salle Les Alpes
General info: ++33 (0) 4 92 24 74 43
Web: www.serre-chevalier.com
Email: contact@ot-serrechevalier.fr

THE TOWN & GETTING THERE

advanced riders and competent intermediate boarders will manage, novices should give this run a miss (unless they have a death wish).

BEGINNERS should find the runs around Frejus more suited to their needs, with a number of long, easy runs that bring you back down the mountain into the village of Villeneuve, via some tree-lined trails. Serre Chevalier has a lot of drag lifts - some of which can be a nightmare, often travelling a long way at speeds suited to riding down, not up. Watch out for the sharp turns that some of the drag lifts make through the trees. If you can master Serre Chevalier's drag lifts, you shouldn't have any trouble in the rest of the world.

THE TOWN
Serre Chevalier provides a number of options for lodging and other local services. These are situated along a stretched-out valley road, set back from the base lifts. Briancon is the largest place to stay, but is not so convenient for the main slopes, whereas the villages of Chantemerle and Villeneuve (a few miles apart, linked on the slopes and by road), offer the best facilities nearer the slopes. There are plenty of shops as well as good watering holes, but there is one small blip on Serre Chevalier's otherwise shining record: it's a tourist trap that attracts a number of British and Italian tour companies, who bring in far too many package groups.

Accommodation: 30,000 visitors can be bedded around here. The choices range from a bunk house and modern apartment blocks for groups on the cheap, to classy hotels.

Food. Your dietary needs are well sorted here, with a vast selection of restaurants and fast-food outlets to choose from, including a number of creperies. Le Frog (please), is known for its French cuisine, as is the *Yeti*, *Nocthambule* and *Le Refuge*. For a decent fish meal, *La Bidulle* is highly recommended and is located in Villeneuve. *L'Amphore* is the place for a slab of pizza

Night-life is somewhat mixed here, with some happening and lively bars but also a few sad and very expensive disco's, Night life rocks until late in most

Pic - Serre Chevalier Tourism

bars so you don't need the clubs. Check out the likes of the Iceberg or Yeti Bar, where they often have live music. The White Hare is a cool hangout.

SUMMARY
Without doubt, one of the best resort in France. Great freeriding with powder and full-on, freestyle terrain. The one bug is the hordes of skiers.
On the slopes: Fantastic - best in France
Off the slopes: Very, very good
Money Wise: This is not the cheapest of resorts, but its worth every euro.

CAR
From Grenoble, Lyon or Paris take Motorway A51, exit Pont de Claix at 80 km from the resort via Lautaret Pass
FLY
Fly to Lyon (200km) airport 3 hour transfer. Nearest airport is Turin (108km), Marseille (250km) has a free bus saturdays 2pm to the resort.
TRAIN
to Briancon, 10 minutes away.
BUS
Buses are available from Lyon airport.

F

FRANCE

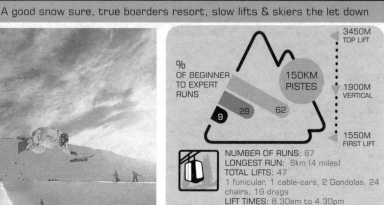

Pic - A-Snowboards

%
OF BEGINNER
TO EXPERT
RUNS

150KM
PISTES

9 29 62

3450M
TOP LIFT

1900M
VERTICAL

1550M
FIRST LIFT

NUMBER OF RUNS: 67
LONGEST RUN: 6km (4 miles)
TOTAL LIFTS: 47
1 funicular, 1 cable-cars, 2 Gondolas, 24
chairs, 19 drags
LIFT TIMES: 8.30am to 4.30pm
MOUNTAIN CAFES: 10

AVERAGE SNOWFALL:
5m
SNOWMAKING:
40%

WINTER PERIODS:
Nov to May
SUMMER PERIODS:
June to Oct
Lift Passes
Espace Killy:
1 day 38 euros, 6 days 181 euros
Tignes only:
1 day 32.5 euros, 6 days 154 euros
Board Schools
Huge (too many) number of ski & board
schools in the resort
Hire
loads of hire shops, all over priced.
Board and boots start around 150
euros for 6 days.
Night Boarding: No
Heliboarding
from nearby Italian resort; 2 drops
Miravidi-Ruitor (3300 vertical drop) 225
euros. Contact Snocool.com, tel: 06
1534 5463

FREERIDE 50%
A couple of trees and huge off-piste
FREESTYLE 25%
A terrain park and a half-pipe (all year)
CARVING 25%

Tignes Information
BP 51 - 73321 Tignes cedex
Tel: +33 4 7940 0440
Web: www.tignes.net
Email: information@tignes.net

Tignes is very snowboard friendly; long before the other French resorts welcomed snowboarders, Tignes opened it's arms wide and said come here and slide down that, jump over that, and listen to this while your at it. If Carlsberg made snowboard resorts they would have made Tignes. Set at 2100 meters and part of the 290km of pistes that is the Espace Killy, it has a very good snow record, a glacier, a lake and a lot of varying terrain; Tignes can almost guarantee everyone leaves satisfied. You drive up to the resort on the same road towards Val D'Isere from Bourg Saint Maurice accessible by euro star and the snow train. A painting of Hercules holding back the water greets you as you cross over the high dam, and as you pass a church on your right you can see Jesus, who has freed his arms from the crucifix pointing towards the old submerged village, eerie man eerie. Tignes is one of the major resorts in France, and has long been hosting national and international events, their web site even has a Japanese translation. BASI runs some of it's snowboard instructors courses here. Snowboard teams and manufacturers also use Tignes to host training camps and events. The main lifts open early September and close late May and with summer boarding on the Grande Motte Glacier from mid June to September you can almost board every day of the

TIGNES

THE MOUNTAIN

Pic - J. Mitchell

year. This year they even had a summer fun park. If you are up for it you can dive under the ice of Tignes-Le-Lac and look up at the ice distorted mountains.

FREERIDERS have loads of choice, there are some really long off piste runs some great reds and blacks and the wide Grande Motte Glacier. If you are lucky with the snow there's the 1200 meter decent from Aiguille Percee to Tignes Les Brevieres on a choice of runs, with help you can find a very long off piste route. To the sides of Les Lanches you can find good little rock shoots and bowls. Tignes is set in a wide open valley so you can see all the lines you'd love to take, it's just working out how to get to them. From the Toviere area there's some great spots of snow between the runs and two long blues into Val Claret. The Funiculaire and Cabel Car take you to the Glacier at 3456 meters for more or less guaranteed good snow. From the top a choice of Reds and off piste routes await you, but watch out for crevasses. Always a good side trip is the Vallee Perdue in the Val D'Isere valley just make sure you have a espace killy lift pass and you make the last lift home. Take it easy in Tignes especially after a fresh dump, as it doesn't take much to trigger off avalanches and it's no fun stuck in an upside down world of blue light. If you want to go off piste take a guide, Snocool offer freeride and freestyle lessons. If you've got the cash and a group of four they'll drop you and a guide out of a Helicopter in Italy, 2 drops cost around 200 Euros.

Pic - Tignes Tourism

FREESTYLERS will love the newly moved fun park which has two pipes some rails, a boardcross, and a number of hits ranging from spines to kickers and of course the grosse table pro, a big mother off a table top. There's always a bit of French hip-hop blasting from the bottom of the pipe and when the locals are there it realy goes off. Tignes has a very high standard of freestyle boarders, even the purest Freerider will be impressed, but don't be put off just get down there check out the small hits and move on up in size as your confidence improves. Don't go to the park and wipe out on a huge kicker probably chopping up the hit at the same time as putting an end to your holiday. If you've never jumped before build a small hit somewhere soft before hitting the park, or find a natural hit and session it, and remember no silly hats ever they just aren't funny. The new park is next to the Les Lanches chair lift and walkable from Val Claret.

CARVERS of all abilities are provided with slopes of all widths and pitch. The Grande Motte Glacier although sometime wind swept and cold is normally pisted flat. It's great for cranking it over at full speed it's long enough to give even the hardest carver leg burn.

BEGINNERS have plenty of blue runs and loads of schools to choose from. Although not as good for the complete novice as Val D'Isere for someone on week 2 or 3 it's fine and you can always head out of the valley to ride the runs under the Marmottes chair. Kebra Surfing in Le Lac, which is Tignes oldest snowboard shop and school, and Surf Feeling in Val Claret offer a number of teaching programmes for freestyle or freeriding. It's around 150 euros for a weeks lesson.

F

F
R
A
N
C
E

THE TOWN

tignes is a relatively ugly place it consists of two main areas Le Lac which is the main hub and Val Claret a split level town joined by a urine stinking lift, both joined by a free bus. Le Lac is strangely enough next to a lake which is normally frozen over. The areas mobbed with apartment blocks, hotels, and an array of bars, restaurants and shops all of which are expensive. At the head of the valley within an easy walk of the funicular is Val Claret smaller than Le Lac but of a similar ilk. It has better slope access and good parking next to the slopes, if you're on a day trip and has a few piste side cheep eats. Wherever you choose to stay, prices are much the same in both high. Tignes is an expensive resort whether you visit in winter, or come for summer snowboarding. Summer is actually a great time to visit as so much goes on, from snowboarding to water sports on the lake there's even a skate park.

ACCOMODATION

With over 28,000 visitor beds, this place has something for everyone, although there is not a wide selection of cheap accommodation. However, there are plenty of apartments for self-catering groups. The Tignes web site has a good listing of accommodation. Tour companies use this place big style, which means last minute package deals are always available at budget prices. www.tignes.net

EATING

French food is full fat all butter croissants followed by melted cheese. If you're on a diet when you arrive, then this place will kill it dead and you'll go home fatter than ever. Every type of fast-food is available along with a large selection of restaurants serving expensive French dishes with heaps of garlic. None of it comes cheap so it's probably best to sort out catered accommodation before arriving.

NIGHTLIFE

Night-life starts early and ends late - in fact, for some it never ends. This is a major party resort, with a wide choice of English and French bars, but you will never have enough funds to keep going in the bars or clubs as beer prices are shocking, at around 6 euros a pint. The best thing to do is tank up on supermarket carry-outs or the cheep plonk they give out with your chalet dinner. Minesweepers will be able to compare their pint nicking skills with some of the best in the industry. Le loop and the Angel bar in Le Lac are pretty good bars to get you started.

Pic - Tignes Tourism

SUMMARY

Great all-round resort with something for everyone, no matter what your ability. However, watch out some for long lift queues and crowds during school holidays and weekends.

On the slopes: Fantastic
Off the slopes: Very good
Money wise: This is an expensive resort in all aspects but not as bad as some of the unfriendly French resorts. Well worth the cash.

CAR
Drive via Lyon to Tignes, about 102 miles (165 km). Drive time is about 2 hours.
*From Calais 593 miles (995 Km) Drive time is around 12 hours.
FLY
Fly to Lyon or Geneva international, 2 1/2 hour transfer to resort. Local airport = Chambery.
TRAIN
Trains to Bourg-St-maurice, 30 min drive away
BUS
Bus services from Lyon airport, are available on a daily basis direct to Tignes.

VAL D'ISERE

8
OUT OF 10

Great mountain, crap town.

Pic - Val D'Isere Tourism

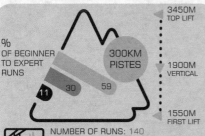

3450M
TOP LIFT

%
OF BEGINNER
TO EXPERT
RUNS

300KM
PISTES

11 30 59

1900M
VERTICAL

1550M
FIRST LIFT

NUMBER OF RUNS: 140
LONGEST RUN: 5.5km
TOTAL LIFTS: 97
2 funiculars, 4 Gondolas, 4 cable-cars,
46 chairs, 41 drags
CAPACITY (people per hour): 120,000
LIFT TIMES: 8.30am to 4.30pm

AVERAGE SNOWFALL
6m
SNOWMAKING:
15%

WINTER PERIODS:
November 27th to May 8th 2005
Lift Passes
1 Day 39 euros, 6 days 187 euros
Board School
ESF and some Brit based schools
Hire
lots of hire shops
Heliboarding
In Italy but can fly out of val d'isere

FREERIDE 50%
Trees & some excellent off-piste
FREESTYLE 20%
2 terrain parks and 2 half-pipes
CARVING 30%

Tourist office
BP 228 - 73 155 Val d'Isère cedex
Tel.: + 33 4 79 06 06 60
Fax : + 33 4 79 06 04 56
Web: www.valdisere.com
Email: info@valdesere.com

Val d'Isere would be the best resort in France if it wasn't for all the stuck up twats. It's got a great lift system a reliable snow depth and some fantastic riding with loads of off piste only a short hop from the lifts. They are trying a little harder to make snowboarders welcome, holding events like The Big Day Out, but are way behind Tignes which together make up Espace Killy. The resort is set along one road starting with La Daille a few ugly blocks of flats, mostly full of resort staff, time shares and self catering apartments. You may find you'll start or finish your day here as it's only a short free bus ride from the resort proper and home of the Funival funicular which will whip you to the top of the mountain faster than Bush could invade any oil producing state. The main village has been tastefully developed using a lot of the local stone. The main streets full of designer shops, restaurants and British bars, set back from the road are loads of hotels and chalets ranging from affordable to ridiculous.

FREERIDERS will want to come back again and again, there are miles of piste, 200 in fact (inc Tignes) and more off piste than you'll be able to do in a week. There's terrain here for all, from motorways like Ok and Orange to the steep and tight of piste S. After a dump it's an off piste playground with fresh tracks to be had all day on the les Marmottes face or try the Vallee Perdue which is a mad track only a few feet wide in places with blind bends and a couple of board off scrambles. In bad visibility head for the trees of Le Fornet. Warning you want to be on that flight home so follow resort advice on Avalanche risk and if you are not sure don't do it.

FREESTYLERS can find endless natural hits. The fun park under the Mout Blanc chair has a few hits and a mini board-x but stupidly finishes below the adjacent slalom drag a sign of the resorts prejudice to our two plank friends. Best to head for the fun park at Tignes.

CARVERS in softs can tear the place up in-between hits, and those of you in hards will be well in with the

179

French euro cavers who lay it over when ever they can.

BEGINNERS on their first ever day will find the two free slopes, located in the centre of the village, perfect. Once confident of putting together a few turns, there are plenty of easy slopes and you can always get the bubble down at the end of the day. As most of the runs into resort are steep and at the end of the day packed.

THE TOWN
Off the board, there's husky dog sledging, ice climbing, ice karting, Snowmobiles, paragliding, cinemas and loads of bars full of merchant bankers and red faced blonde haired Swedes and maybe a few French. Like Courchevel the main draw back is the cost.

ACCOMODATION
Watch out for where your accommodation, most is close to the slopes. If your not then there's the free buses which are sometimes quicker than going by board if you want to get somewhere specific, but at night after a skin full you may be in for a cold wait for that bus home.

EATING & NIGHTLIFE
The Pacific bar is good to watch English football, Cafe Face is a cool place but has that bull shit French thing about putting your coat in the cloakroom at a fee. Bananas has a good vibe but can get packed and the Moris pub has live music. For a fry up breakfast go to the Billabong café, if you want a meal in the evening take a stroll with the fur clad poseurs along the main street and choose from sausage to sushi.

SUMMARY
Overall, Val d'Isere has something for everyone there's varying terrain for all abilities some great off piste and a good snow record but be ready to pay for it, they take card and cash don't you worry.

Pic - Val D'Isere Tourism

Pic - Val D'Isere Tourism

CAR
Drive via Bourg-St-Maurice, take the N90 direction to Tignes and then on to Val d'Isere.
*Drive time from Calais is 101/2 hours. 597 miles (960 km).
FLY
Fly to Geneva, 21/2 hours transfer time.
TRAIN
Train services go to Bourg-St-Maurice, 20 minutes away.

3
OUT OF 10

the place is dull, crap, and comes at a price

As a relatively new resort, established around 20 years ago, **Valmorel** has grown into a family/group ski-centre. This is by no means an adventurous place - indeed it's best described as dull. Nevertheless, it is a well planned

Pic - Valmorel Tourism

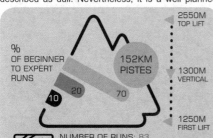

2550M
TOP LIFT

%
OF BEGINNER
TO EXPERT
RUNS

152KM
PISTES

1300M
VERTICAL

10   20   70

1250M
FIRST LIFT

NUMBER OF RUNS: 83
LONGEST RUN: 4km
TOTAL LIFTS: 54
2 Gondolas, 15 chairs, 37 drags
CAPACITY (people per hour): 51,000
LIFT TIMES: 8.30am to 5.00pm

AVERAGE SNOWFALL
4m
SNOWMAKING:
10%

WINTER PERIODS:
Dec 18th to April 24th 2005
Lift Passes
1 Day 23 euros, 6 Days 159 euros
snowpark 15 euros per day
Board School
ESF and IFS have schools
Hire
7 sports shops with ok hire kit

FREERIDE 20%
A few trees but poor off-piste
FREESTYLE 20%
1 terrain parks and 1 half-pipe
CARVING 60%

Tourist office Valmorel
la maison de Valmore, Bourg-Morel,
F-73260
Tel: +33 (0) 4 7909 8555
Fax: +33 (0) 4 7909 8529
Web: www.valmorel.com
Email: info@valmorel.com

Bus
Lyon airport, tel: +33 4 37 255 255,
Geneva airport tel: +41 22 798 2000
Train
Train services are possible all the way to
Moutiers, about 10 minutes away.
Car
via Albertville, take the N90 and turn
right on to the D95 to reach Valmorel
Fly
to Lyon (180km) or Geneva (125km)

and well set out resort, with slopes that are ideal for simple piste-riding. Valmorel, on its own, boasts 50 or so pistes which are not always that well maintained. When linked to *St Francois Longchamp*, the ride able terrain increases to a respectable 100 miles (152km). Getting around the slopes should pose no problems, although you might have to queue for lengthy periods of time with skiers who sing nursery rhymes to their offspring. Valmorel is not noted for having the best snow record, especially on the lower slopes. Still, once you get away from the idiots in the lift lines and hit the slopes, things only get better. Keep an eye open, however, for ski-classes cluttering up certain slopes

FREERIDERS are not going to get too excited with what's on offer here, but there is some alright off-piste riding around the *Mottet* area. Although Valmorel is a tame resort, some challenging riding is possible on a couple of black trails, though a good rider would rate them more as red runs.
FREESTYLERS are going to be most disappointed. There is a so-called fun-park, but it's toss. By virtue of being a mountain, all resorts should have some natural freestyle terrain to catch some air, but this place doesn't. What there is, isn't up to much, so try mowing down ski families, and practice leaping over them as they lie on the ground screaming in fear (bliss).
CARVERS who don't manage to hold an edge here, should give up snowboarding immediately and become a skier. Valmorel is a perfect resort for edging a board over at speed, or for general riding on intermediate trails.
BEGINNERS, this area is littered with easy trails, but novices need to learn quickly to avoid sharing the same slopes with so many novice skiers.

THE TOWN
Valmorel's village is dull, boring, expensive and full of some of the worst ski groups around (families). Accommodation options are good, but evenings aren't. Nothing happens, and there aren't any good bars of note, or come to that, places to eat. Well, there is Pizzaria du Bourg which serves up great slices.

F

F
R
A
N
C
E

F

FRANCE

Pic - Val Thorens Tourism

High, high, high; Val Thorens is the highest resort in Europe, it's a load of purpose built block of ugly flats, a few shops and a line of bars with nothing to do at night but drink and at a height of 2300m it's painfully cold when walking for that drink. Who cares with a lift system that whisks you up to 3200m, north facing slopes, a 900cm average snow fall and a connection to the Trois Vallees you can stick the bad points where the sun don't shine. Furthermore, although not noted as a summer resort, you can still ride here right up until early August. Like the rest of the Trois Vallees it's full of package deal holiday makers. Lots of Brit's but not as many as Meribel or Couchevel, it's also popular with the Dutch and Swedes. Many of the apartments will give you instant slope access; some have a high rise chair going past your window so keep an eye out when leaving the shower. They've made Val Thornes a car free zone so at least you don't have to look out for motors when running for the pub, but you will have to make parking arrangements if driving. It's a rip off 58 Euros a week if you book in advance more if not. It's a board friendly place with a Fun Park and without the stuck up attitude of some of the Trois Vallees resorts, it also has the best web site of this area by far with routes web cams and more www.valthorens.com.

FREERIDERS have much choice, take a trip up to the Cime de Caron for the best view in the Trois Vallees and then drop down the back side or follow the long sweeping red or black down. Intermediates should try the long, wide red runs around Fond 1, Boismint or the Peclet Glacier. The expert will relish the sheer volume of challenges on offer, from powder snow on the glaciers of Peclet and Chaviere, to world class, mogul-bashing on the long, steep Cime de Caron black run. If you have a head for heights, then visit Le Plein Sud, where you can cut some nice couloir descents. If you can handle a walk get a guide and head up left from the top of the Col Chair, over the col de Gebroulaz and ride the Glacier de Gebroulaz down into the Meribel Valley a truly amazing run. The resort height gives good snow but no trees so if you want to pretend to be

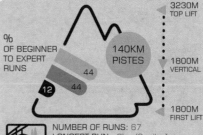

3230M
TOP LIFT

%
OF BEGINNER
TO EXPERT
RUNS

140KM
PISTES

44

12   44

1800M
VERTICAL

1800M
FIRST LIFT

NUMBER OF RUNS: 67
LONGEST RUN: 3km (2 miles)
TOTAL LIFTS: 47
2 cable-cars, 3 Gondolas, 16 chairs,
8 drags
CAPACITY (people per hour): 53,000
LIFT TIMES: 8.30am to 4.30pm
MOUNTAIN CAFES: 6

AVERAGE SNOWFALL:
10m
SNOWMAKING:
25%

WINTER PERIODS:
1st Nov to May 8th 2005
Lift Passes
1 Day pass 37 euros, 6 days 182 euros
Board Schools
ski schools with snowboard sections
Hire
lots of choice
Night Boarding: No
Snowmobiles
alone 70 euros an hour
2 people 80 euros an hour

FREERIDE 40%
A couple of trees and good off-piste
FREESTYLE 20%
A terrain park and a half-pipe
CARVING 40%

Val Thorens Tourist Office
Maison de Val Thorens
F-73440 VAL THORENS
Tel : 33 (0)4 7900 0808
Fax : 33 (0)4 7900 0004

THE TOWN & GETTING THERE

James Bond head for Meribel.

FREESTYLERS have a dedicated snowboard park near the Funitel lift, which has a boardercross circuit and a 110 meter long halfpipe. However, these are only kept in tip-top condition during a competition, rather than on a regular basis. There are some good natural hits but mainly drop offs. Look out for the Val Thorens board week in early December

CARVERS have a stupid amount of pistes to mince down. The Cime de Caron is a well-established black run that tests the best speed-freaks and race heads, it's also possible to have snowboard slalom training with poles ask at the tourist info.

BEGINNERS have a variety of easy runs leading into the resort, which allow for easy access and steady progression. You don't have to travel far from the resort base before getting to a novice trail, but be advised there are heaps of little kids in bash hats that take up space while snaking down behind their all in one red suited ESF instructor. If you want lessons try one of the independent ski schools which should have a board specialist if they don't go elsewhere.

THE TOWN

Val Thorens is the archetypical purpose built resort. No one would have built a thing here if it wasn't for alpine sports, not even a cow shed. A sheltered valley and an almost flattish spot have turned into high rise central. The obvious remit when planning this place was, 'get them in, pile them high, and don't worry about how the place looks or feels'. The outcome is a place that looks dire, but serves its purpose which is beer shelter and food in that order. Around the resort, you'll find

Pic - Val Thorens Tourism

Pic - Val Thorens Tourism

a number of shopping complexes and places to eat. There is also a comprehensive sports centre, with a swimming pool and artificial climbing wall.

Accommodation: 20,000 visitors can sleep soundly here, all within spitting distance of the slopes. There are loads of self-catering apartment blocks, sleeping up to eight people, and a number of good hotels and serviced chalets, many actually on the slopes and next to a lift.

Food is plentiful here with a selection of restaurants more than 45 ranging from the normal selection of resort-style, expensive French restaurants, dodgy fast-food stands, to the normal offerings of a supermarket. For a cheap slap-up meal, try *El Gringo's*, or for something more classy, *Chalet Glaciers*. The *Scapin Pub* is also noted for its quick and affordable dishes which include pizza and garlic overdose food.

Night-life comes in the form of drunken Dutch après skiers. There are some ok bars at the top of town. Check out The Frog, The Malaysia, or The Underground. It's a great place for New Years Eve with fire works and music in the streets, even the firemen get in on it.

CAR
Drive to Lyon via Albertville, approx 130 miles (209 km). Drive time is about 2 hours.
*From Calais 600 miles (965 Km). Drive time is around 11 hours.
FLY
Fly to Lyon international. Transfer time to resort is 2 1/2 hours
TRAIN
Trains to Moutiers from Paris hours. Resort 37 km from station.
BUS
Bus services from Lyon airport are available on a daily basis direct to Val Thorens.

183

ALPE DU GRAND SERRE
Good riding here, 2 hours from Lyon airport
Runs: 35, Total Lifts:20

AURON
Some thick wood, 1 hour from Nice airport
Runs: 70, Total Lifts:21

BAREGES
Okay for novices, 45 minutes from Lourdes airport. Has a terrain park
Number of Runs: 18

LA FOUX D'ALLOS
La Foux d'Allos, a purpose-built resort, is located way down in the southern section of the French Alps, 50 miles from the village of Digne. On its own, La Foux d'Allos offers a ride area of 70 miles, but linked with nearby resorts, the combined range gives freeriders of all levels 150 miles of terrain, with a good selection of advanced and novice runs. Local services are slopeside and very affordable, if only a tad dull
Ride area: 12km
Top Lift: 2600m
Bottom Lift: 1800m
Total Lifts:22
How to get there:
Fly to: Nice 2 hours away

LA GRAVE
La Grave is secretly stashed away in the Oisans. When the snow falls, this mountain has 7,100 vertical feet of drops, couloirs, cliffs, gullies, chutes, steeps, trees and crevices. This mountain isn't child's play so never ride alone. This is basically home to only die-hard extremists, with a few snowboarders who can hold their own. Still, the lack of skiing tourists simply quarantees 'no

battle of the freshies' with untracked powder for days.

Pic - La Grave Tourism

Freeriders will find above the only gondola, two T-bars that lead to the Glacier de la Girose. If La Grave hasn't seen snow in weeks, this mountain gets mogul madness. Therefore, the 15 minute hike over the top to Les Deux Alpes should entice the pipe and park enthusiast. If it does dump snow, cruise down the glacier, but be pre-warned of the numerous, unmarked crevasses. Contact the area's tourist office to find out about free guided tours. The community would like to put more safety into their terrain, where death by ignorance isn't an uncommon occurrence. Further down Glacier de la Girose, lies many steep cliffs and unavoidable gullies. Once past these gullies, stay on the traverse to the skier's right and keep an eye out for the gondola station at P1. Do not become bewitched by the untracked powder through the trees and river beds, or you will find yourself plummeting off 100m cliffs. Ruillans, spread out like curtains,

are four couloirs to be explored. This gives you the chance to ride top to bottom. Further down, are some great natural quarter-pipes and tree runs. Take warning of the cliffs and the river near the bottom. This side of La Meije has held The Derby for the past ten years. In the world of snow racing, The Derby has the largest vertical drop of 2,150 metres on snowboard, ski, monoski or telemark.

Local facilities at La Grave are as basic as you can get. There are a few shops, and only a few lodging options to choose from (your neighbours will be cows and sheep). Riders spending a season here will find that rent and a season's lift pass is cheap. On the social scene, you will have to make your own. This isn't a beer swigging party hangout because the only pub closes early.

Ride area: 12km
Top Lift: 3568m
Vertical Drop: 2150m
Total Lifts:4
How to get there: By air : Lyon Satolas or Grenoble Saint-Geoirs airport and from there by VFD coach or taxi to La Grave. By train : to Briancon and from there by VFD coach or taxi to La Grave. By road : motorway A 48 to Grenoble, then RN 91 to Bourg d'Oisans and Col du Lautaret.

LA JOUE DU LOUP
South of Grenoble and a stone's throw for the Veynes, lies the almost unheard of resort of La Joue du Loup, a tiny place place providing a mere half dozen trails. However, when linked with the resort of Superdevoluy, there's

a more respectable 60+ miles to ride and explore. If you're an adventure seeker, nothing here is really that daunting. Great for first timers on a family outing

Ride area: 97km
Top Lift: 2750m
Vertical Drop: 1040m
Total Lifts:32
Night Boarding:13 slopes and halfpipes illuminated
How to get there: By air: 126 km from the airport of Grenoble-Saint Geoirs. By train: 28 km from the train station of Veynes-Divoluy. By car: Superdivolue is located 640 km from Paris, 216 km from Marseille and 190 km from Lyon

LA NORMA
La Norma is yet another unspoilt tourist spot, although it does get its fair share of weekenders. They who are attracted to the open trails that offer some steep and fast, although rather limited, riding with only a couple of black graded trails and nothing that will require many turns before you're back in a lift line. In truth this is a novices retreat where first timers can learn to ride without all the hassles associated with the big tourist resorts. Affordable slopeside services are available but are best described as dull

Ride area: 97km
Runs: 27
Top Lift: 2750m
Bottom Lift: 1350m
Total Lifts:18
How to get there: Air: Lyon or Geneva Airports - 2 hrs 30 mins transfer by hire car . Train: Modane station (overnight train from Paris), then 6km by bus or taxi to resort. Car: To Chambery (A43) and on to St Jean de Maurienne, then take the N6 to Modane (direction of Torino - Tunnel of Frejus).

ROUND-UP

LA ROSIERE
On its own, La Rosiere is a tiny outpost, with an even balance of terrain that any rider worth their salt will have licked in a day or two. However, as La Rosiere crosses the border with Italy and is lift linked to La Thuile, the 80+ miles poses a different question. Add the 900+ miles of the Aosta Valley, and suddenly we are into a whole new ball game, which will take the best of the best years to conquer.
Ride area: 55km
Runs: 32
Top Lift: 2642m
Bottom Lift: 1850m
Total Lifts:19
How to get there: Fly to: Geneva 2 hours away.

LES ANGLES
Les Angles is definitely not one of your normal ski tourist traps. Located in the Pyranees, it shares a non-lift linked pass with a few neighbouring resorts, with 200 miles of average rideable terrain for all styles. It is, however, crowd-free, and an alternative to the massly populated areas further north. There's a pipe for air heads, but in truth most runs are for novices. There are plenty of slopeside services but most things around here are boring and dull and not the cheapest.
Ride area: 40km
Top Lift: 2400m
Total Lifts:20
How to get there: Fly to: Perpigan 1 1/2 hours away.

LES GETS
Linked to the 450kms of the Port du Soleil, Les Gets sits at 1172 meters to the south of Morzine. It's a small Savoyard village escaping the all too typical high rise developments that blight Avoriaz across the valley. It's possible to buy a Les Gets/Morzine pass which includes Le Mont-Chery, les Chavannes, Nyon and Le Pleney this adds up to 110km of red and blue pistes, which is fine for a weekend but if you're here for a week you should stump up the cash for the Port du Soleil Pass. It's an annoying walk across Morzine Village or a ridiculous mini train ride to access the lifts up to Avoriaz, but well worth it to both freeriders and freestylers as it opens up not only a great fun park but also another 340km of piste. Les Gets has spent more than 24 million Euros over the last two summers upgrading the lift system and creating a new access point outside the village, with a huge car park so as to keep the traditional vide to the village. **Freeriders** will enjoy the slopes around Chamossiere and Le Ranfolly as they lead to some little gullies and tree runs. **Freestylers** will be best off heading for Avoriaz although there's a good little park on Mount-Chery's with hits and rails, accessible with the Les Gets/Morzine pass. **Carvers** have a lot of well suited terrain if fact almost all of it. **Off the slopes** there's not much in the way of lively night life with only a few bars. There is Bowling and a Cinema

METABIEF
Metabief is slap bang on the border with Switzerland, which is probably why it is a cool and very friendly snowboard hangout. Although there are only 26 miles of piste and just a couple of black runs to entice hardcore freeriders, the place is still worth a visit. Laid back, unpopulated, with good slopes for all, and plenty of lodging and night-time action, although hangouts are some distance from the slopes.
Ride area: 40km
Runs: 23
Top Lift: 1430m
Bottom Lift: 880m
Total Lifts:22
How to get there: Fly to: Geneva 1 hour away

MONTCHAVIN
Linked to the tourist trap of La Plagne, this small resort suddenly seems a better option.On its own slopes, Montchavin has nothing to offer advanced riders, but plenty to entertain intermediate carvers and total beginners - they will find the place seemingly designed for them by Mother Nature. **Freestylers** are also presented with a park and pipe, but they are crap.Slopeside **lodging** is plentiful and okay

Ride area: 200km
Runs: 16
Top Lift: 3250m
Vertical Drop: 2000m
Total Lifts:22
How to get there: Fly to: Geneva 2 hours away

PRA LOUP
Spread over two areas, Pra Loup and Molanes are not that bad to try, although being popular with weekenders and package tours, means clogged-up blues and busy lift lines. Par Loup is more or less a beginner's and intermediate piste-lover's hangout. Advanced riders will want

more than what's on offer. **Accommodation** is provided in a selection of affordable, tacky apartment blocks
Ride area: 80km
Top Lift: 2500m
Total Lifts:31
How to get there: Fly to: Toulouse 2 1/2 hours away.

SAMOENS
Good fun park

Pic - Samoens Tourism

Runs: 38
Total Lifts:16
How to get there: 30 minutes from Geneva airport

VARS
Ok advanced runs
Runs: 60
Total Lifts:30
How to get there: 140 minutes from Marseille airport.

VILLARD DE LANS
Linked resort with Correncon en Vencours. Okay advanced runs.

Ride area: 130km
Runs: 32
Total Lifts:27
How to get there: 40 minutes from Grenoble airport.

185

Not many people think of Germany as a snowboard destination and although it's no match for its close alpine neighbours, Germany can still boast plenty of rideable terrain. The dozen or so resorts are all located in the southernmost parts of the country, with some crossing over into Austria. The thing that seems to be consistent amongst about German resorts is the efficient way things are set out and how you're looked after. Most places are expensive and often stupidly overcrowded at weekends.

Travelling by car is a good idea, with resorts reached on one of the best road systems in the world. Unlike many other European destinations, there are no road tolls so you aren't hit with extra costs

Capital City: Berlin
Population: 82.4 million
Highest Peak: Zugspitze 2963m
Language: German
Legal Drink Age: 16 beer, 18 spirits
Drug Laws: Cannabis is illegal and frowned upon
Age of consent: 16
Electricity: 240 Volts AC 2-pin
International Dialing Code: +49

Currency: Euro
Exchange Rate:
UK£1 = 1.5
US$1 = 0.8
AU$1 = 0.6
CAN$1 = 0.6

Driving Guide
All vehicles drive on the right hand side of the road
Speed limits:
50kph (31mph) Towns
81kph (62mph) Highways
130kph (recommended) Autobahns
Emergency
Fire - 112
Police and Ambulance - 110
Tolls
None
Documentation
A driving lisence must be carried as well as insurance.

Time Zone
UTC/GMT +1 hours
Daylight saving time: +1 hour

German Snowboard Association
Zizelsbergerstrasse 3,
81476 Munchen
Tel - ++49 (0) 89 7544 7320
Web: www.gsahome.de

pic - Bayerische Zugspitzbahn Tourism

Munich is the most convenient gateway airport for all the resorts with good onward travel facilities. It is possible to take a train across Austrian, Swiss and French borders direct to many resorts making train travel a good option.

For those thinking about doing a season in Germany, work is possible but you will need to speak the language (or have a good grasp of it). EU nationals can stay as long as they want without a work permit.

Accommodation is similar to that in Austria, from affordable pensions to way overpriced hotels. It's often cheaper to stay in a nearby town. **Night life** in Germany is pretty cool, Germans like to party hard and the beer is pure nectar. Clubs and discos are not bad, although far too many bars allow Euro pop. Overall, Germany is not the cheapest place, but is highly recommended.

4 OUT OF 10

Okay beginners resort

Feldberg is located in the south west of Germany in the Black Forest and a stones throw from the French and Swiss borders. The town of Feldberg is a sprawling affair and offers its visitors a mass of attractions all year round. As a winter destination, this adequate resort is regarded by many in Germany as the countries number one resort even though in terms of terrain its 50 kms of piste are half of what is available over in Garmisch, which is south of Munich and Germany's most famous resort. Feldberg's location means that

pic - feldberg tourism

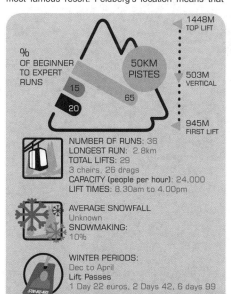

%
OF BEGINNER TO EXPERT RUNS

15
20
65

50KM PISTES

1448M
TOP LIFT

503M
VERTICAL

945M
FIRST LIFT

NUMBER OF RUNS: 36
LONGEST RUN: 2.8km
TOTAL LIFTS: 29
3 chairs, 26 drags
CAPACITY (people per hour): 24,000
LIFT TIMES: 8.30am to 4.00pm

AVERAGE SNOWFALL
Unknown
SNOWMAKING:
10%

WINTER PERIODS:
Dec to April
Lift Passes
1 Day 22 euros, 2 Days 42, 6 days 99

FREERIDE 50%
A few trees & a bit of off-piste
FREESTYLE 20%
1 terrain park#
CARVING 30%

Feldberg Tourist Information
Kirchgasse 1
79868 Feldberg
Tel - ++49 (0) 7655 / 8019
Fax - ++49 (0) 7655 / 80143
Web:www.liftverbund-feldberg.de
Email:info@liftverbund-feldberg.de

Train
Train services go direct to Feldberg.
Car
From Zurich head north along the B315 and travel via Schaffhausen.
Fly
Stuttgart, Basel and Zurich airports approx 1hr drive away.

if you are planning to visit by air then the easiest way to get here is to fly into Zurich in Switzerland and then hire a car and drive up or catch a bus. In terms of skiing and snowboarding, Feldberg is a resort that attracts a lot of families as the two main mountain areas are made up largely of novice trails with a few intermediate slopes. All the runs are laid out over wide open spaces with a splattering of trees here and there namely on the Grafenmatt-Hochst mountain. This mountainis the one and only area that has anything difficult to ride with a few interesting black trails to check out. The runs on the Seebuck mountain are mostly intermediate trails while the Gafenmatte is home to the best novice slopes. Overall this is not a place that you would want to spend more than a few days at. The size and pace of what is going on here will make it a bore after three days, unless you are brain dead or a child in nappies.

FREERIDERS who want for a simple day's riding and are not too adventurous, will find Feldberg an ideal place to spend some time at. There is an okay mixture of terrain with the best and most challenging freeriding to be found off the letter K drag lift.
FREESTYLERS should stick to riding in the terrain park located off the letter E drag lift. This is the only place to get any air time.
CARVERS have a good resort for cruising with a number of well groomed trails to check out, especially those on the Seebuck.
BEGINNERS have a mountain that is perfect for learning on with a number of easy blue trails that cover all the areas, but note that all the easy runs are served by drag lifts.

Feldberg is a large town with a very good choice of local services that include hotels, pension homes and chalets. There is also a good choice of bars and restaurants, the only draw back being that this is an expensive resort.

5 OUT OF 10

Average resort with some decent intermediate/beginner terrain.

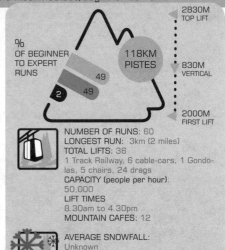

pic - Garmisch Tourism

% OF BEGINNER TO EXPERT RUNS

2830M TOP LIFT

118KM PISTES

49

2   49

830M VERTICAL

2000M FIRST LIFT

NUMBER OF RUNS: 60
LONGEST RUN: 3km (2 miles)
TOTAL LIFTS: 36
1 Track Railway, 6 cable-cars, 1 Gondolas, 5 chairs, 24 drags
CAPACITY (people per hour):
50,000
LIFT TIMES
8.30am to 4.30pm
MOUNTAIN CAFES: 12

AVERAGE SNOWFALL:
Unknown
SNOWMAKING:
15%

WINTER PERIODS:
Dec to April
Lift Passes
1 Day 40 euros, 6 Days 180 euros
Board Schools
6 days with 3 hour lessons from 110 euros
Hire
Board & boots 20 euros a day
Night Boarding: Until 8:30pm

FREERIDE 45%
Some tree runs and okay off-piste
FREESTYLE 15%
A terrain park and a half-pipe
CARVING 40%

Garmisch Tourist office
Verkehrsamt, Richard Strauss-Platz 2
D-82467 Garmisch-Partenkirchen
Tel - +49 (0) 8821-180-700
Fax - +49 (0) 8821-180-755
Web: www.garmisch-partenkirchen.de
Email: tourist-info@garmisch-parten-
kirchen.de

Garmisch is Germany's most popular resort, although some say the resort of Feldburg has more claim to the favourite title award. What ever the merits of this, Garmisch certainly the countries biggest resort which is located in the southernmost part of the country a short distance from Munich and Innsbruck in Austria. This very German of German places is in fact an extremely popular all year round holiday destination that attracts thousands of visitors. The area offers loads of out-door sporting attractions as well as putting on lots of top sporting competitions. The ski world hosts all sorts of world ranking ski events here which includes ski jumping. Garmisch even played host to the 1936 Winter Olympics, although to be fair, the world was a bit messed up during that period of time, so anyone boasting about such a role should be viewed with a bit of contempt. All said and done, this is a resort where you can have a good time, located beneath Germany's highest mountain, the Zugspitze, where a cable car goes to the rocky 2964m summit (no rideable descent is possible). The five resort centres dotted around the village are all connected by buses and trains. On the mountain, the slopes are divided into four areas and are serviced by around 50 lifts. The pistes will appeal mostly to intermediate riders looking for easy descents but expert riders will soon get bored.

FREERIDERS coming here for the first time may be a bit disappointed if they arrive thinking that they will find a mountain blessed with loads of hardcore freeride terrain. They will find a big mountain with a number of steep sheer unrideable faces, and a number of okay rideable slopes that will allow advanced riders to blast around at speed for at least two days, but bore them after three. Snowboarders in general favour the Zugspitzplatt slopes, which is the only area not directly linked on snow with the other sections. Although this is not an adventurous place, there are opportunities to ride through trees and on a good day a few stashes of powder can be cut.

FREESTYLERS will find quite a few good natural hits as well as those built by local grommets. You'll also be able to grind a few downed logs around the tree areas, but in the main, this is not a great place for getting any serious air. However, there is a halfpipe but don't expect it to be maintained all the time.

ic - Garmish Tourism

THE TOWN

Garmisch is an all year-round holiday destination which caters extremely well for it's visitors. There is a huge selection of places to stay with services spread out over a wide area. Numerous events are held in the town all year round, so not only is this place a very expensive town, it can also be very busy. The area also has loads of sporting attractions and if you are feeling lucky there is even a casino to try your hand in.

The area can **accommodate** over 20,000 visitors with a number of places in the main town area or spread out into the countryside. Prices are not cheap and no real budget options exist even though there is a large number of pension's and self catering places. Still one thing is for sure, most places are of a very high standard and hotels come loaded with restaurants, bars, pools, and sporting centres.

Restaurants are plentiful and cater for all tastes, if not all budgets. Most places serve up a variety of disgusting sausages and potato dishes. However, you can get some decent chicken and fish meals. Veggies should pay a visit to the Grand Cafe. If you do want to taste a local dish and don't mind sucking on bland pieces of horse meat, then check out the Max Cafe.

Nightlife here is pretty good and very lively set to a Bavarian theme. An excellent choice of German beers are available in a number of okay bars where the booze flows fast and well into the early morning hours, mind you, the music in most places is enough to make you want to leave. Check out the *Irish Bar* or the *Rose and Crown*.

CARVERS who want to carve around on gentle, short slopes will favour the areas off the Alpspitzbahn cable car, but there is other carving to be found up on the Zugspitz slopes. Whatever area you ride, you'll have fun spotting how many mullets with head bands there are riding around with ski-boot set ups.

BEGINNERS are well catered for with a number of spots ideally suited to novices. There is a number of easy options for riding up high and back down through the trees to the village and car parks.

ic - Garmish Tourism

CAR
From Munich, head south on the A95 Autobahn and then route 23 direct to Garmisch (140km)
*From Calais 575 miles (925 Km), drive time is around 10 hours.
FLY
Fly to Munich airport about 120km (1 1/2 hours) away or Innsbruck (Tyrol) 60km.
TRAIN
Train services are possible all the way to the centre of Garmisch.
BUS
Bus services from Munich airport are available on a daily basis direct to Garmisch

SCHLIERSEE

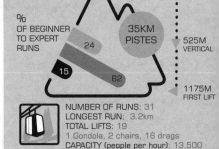

Rather basic but okay

pic: Schliersee Tourism

Frequented by Munich's high-society kiddies and some cool riders, Schliersee is also home to the living snowboard legend Peter Bauer (you still meet him riding here). What you get are two areas, interconnected by a free shuttle-bus: the Taubenstein is less crowded and is the place to be on a fresh powder day but you'll get bored pretty quickly in the days in-between! Most of the runs are intermediate and nothing will keep you excited for long. At the parking lot you jump on the shuttle that takes you to the Stumpfling-an-Sutten area at the other side of the Spitzingsee, where the whole area lies in front of you, waiting to be ridden

FREERIDERS if there's enough snow, take the Brecherspitz lift, opposite the Firstam, to gain access to a freerider's paradise: long, steep tree-runs that remind you of Canada. On this mission you should follow the locals because there's a 25 metre cliff, with a flat and rocky landing hidden in the trees.

FREESTYLERS have a good mountain to practice getting air at various points around the slopes. The Osthanglift T-bar takes you to a good freestyle area. If you stay on the slope-side of the lift on the way down, you'll find some good natural hits and spines decorated with some nice rollers. The Firstalm is where the funpark is but it doesn't get shaped too often.

CARVERS have a very good mountain to ride, with well groomed runs that will intrigue the hopeless novice, but bore the tits off most advanced riders. However, the pistes are open enough to allow for some wide carves and to be fair, a decent amount of speed can be achieved. The longest run is the 3200m Sutten, which is good for screaming down in under 3 minutes.

BEGINNERS have a cool first timer's resort, although there's a limited amount of slopes and a lot of weekend ski crowds cluttering up the place. Easy access is possible to all the beginner trails.

THE TOWN

Local facilities are located in two areas, Schliersee in the east and Rottach-Egern in the west which has the best night-life and some cheap B & B's. Both places offer good local services but be prepared to pay for it because this is not a cheap hangout, no matter what you're after.

Eating spots are good and evenings begin at the Braustuberl Bar, but watch out for the big waitresses who eat snowboarders for supper. Later, head for the Moon-Club where you are bound to find a nice fraulein.

190

% OF BEGINNER TO EXPERT RUNS

35KM PISTES

24

15

62

1700M TOP LIFT

525M VERTICAL

1175M FIRST LIFT

NUMBER OF RUNS: 31
LONGEST RUN: 3.2km
TOTAL LIFTS: 19
1 Gondola, 2 chairs, 16 drags
CAPACITY (people per hour): 13,500
LIFT TIMES: 8.30am to 4.00pm

AVERAGE SNOWFALL
3m
SNOWMAKING:
none

WINTER PERIODS:
Dec to April
Lift Passes
1 Day 37 euros, 3 Days 105, 6 days 17

FREERIDE 40%
A few trees & some okay off-piste
FREESTYLE 20%
1 terrain park & a half-pipe
CARVING 40%

Schliersee Tourist Office
Schliersberg Alm
D- 83727 Schliersee
Tel: ++49/ +8026 / 6722
Fax: ++49/ +8026 / 6685
Web: www.schliersbergalm.de
Email: info@schliersbergalm.de

Train
services possible to the centre of Schliersee
Car
Via Munich, head south on the A8/E45 Autobahn and turn off at Kolbermoor on to rot
472 via Hausham & the 307 to Schliersee
Fly
to Munich airport , 1 1/2 hours away.

BALDERSCHWANG
Intermediate's place. Overall this is a boring place with a small and badly kept halfpipe.

How to get there:120 minutes from Munich airport

FELLHORN
Fellhorn is the mountain, Obersdorf is the town that serves it and together they are rated by many nationals as the best on offer in Germany. What you get is a mountain area that has a series of open trails with a few tree lines and a couple of decent steeps They regularly stage top events in the competition standard halfpipe. Whereever you ride here, expect to bump into a lot of skiers as it's a popular hang out.; **Freeriders**, check out the Kanzelwand trail for a good ride. **Freestylers** have a well maintained fun-park to play in. **Carvers**, have a good series of pisted trails from top to bottom.4 **Beginners** this place is perfect for all your needs. There are good **facilities** 10 minutes from the slopes.

Ride area: 44km
Top Lift: 1967m
Total Lifts:30
How to get there: Fly to: Munich 1 1/2 hours away.

MITTENWALD
Mittenwald is located in the Isar Valley and is an okay freeriders destination. It is famous for its steep Dammkar run which is served by a cable car that climbs 1311 vertical metres with only one tower

(sufferers of vertigo take note). **Freestylers** have a halfpipe. **Beginners** have plenty of easy slopes. Local **services** are convenient but not cheap

Ride area: 22km
Top Lift:2244m
Total Lifts:8
How to get there: Fly to: Munich 1 1/2 hours away

METABIEF
Metabief is slap bang on the border with Switzerland, which is probably why it is a cool and very friendly snowboard hangout. Although there are only 26 miles of piste and just a couple of black runs to entice hardcore freeriders, the place is still worth a visit. Laid back, unpopulated, with good slopes for all, and plenty of lodging and night-time action, although hangouts are some distance from the slopes.

Ride area: 40km
Runs: 23
Top Lift: 1430m
Bottom Lift: 880m
Total Lifts:22
How to get there: Fly to: Geneva 1 hour away

OBERAMMERGAU
Oberammergau is a happy go lucky sort of place but certainly not the most adventurous of resorts. On the Laberjoch area the runs offer more testing and challenging terrain. For those freestylers wanting to get big air, the halfpipe is your best option, but it's not the best nor well kept. The west side of the valley, on the Kolben, is the place for novices and intermediate riders looking for gentle and simple terrain to shred.

Okay expensive local services exist, but not near the slopes
Ride area: 10km
Top Lift:1700m
Total Lifts:10
How to get there: Fly to: Munich 1 1/2 hours away

OBERSTAUFEN
Oberstaufen is a collection of seven small rideable areas. The main offerings are to be found on the Hochgrat mountain which offers some good off-piste and challenging runs. Intermediate carvers will also find the slopes worth the effort while beginners have access to some okay areas. **Off the slopes**, this place is by no means cheap as it is a very popular German tourists town.

Ride area: 20km
Top Lift: 1340m
Total Lifts:12
How to get there: Fly to: Munich 2 hours away

WILLINGEN
Willingen is a northern low key resort which is virtually unheard of. The area is spread over two large hills with mainly nursery slopes. The main hill has some decent runs with the option of cutting through the trees but lacks any great length. Note also that this place inhabited by lots of skiers (the older generation) and sledgers, so the few slopes that there are, are often very, very crowded, especially at weekends. Freeriders have very little to keep them interested beyond an hour, but there are a few trees to drop through. Freestylers haven't got a chance here unless you

dig your own hit. Carvers will find the number 11 trail about the only thing of worth. Beginners aged 1 or 100 will love it here as the slopes are so slow and easy you'll be able to change your nappy as you ride.

There are lots of small villages close by but they're all pricey
Top Lift: 830m
Total Lifts:14
How to get there: Fly to: Munich 1 hour away

WINTERBERG
Winterberg, is situated southwest of Dortmond in the Sauerland mountain range which not many snowusers have heard of. The runs are spread over 5 hills with 25 slopes, but nothing too testing, the longest barely making 2 miles. **Freeriders** have lots of trees to weave through and with many runs interlinking, there are a few nice freeride spots to check out. **Freestylers** don't have a pipe or park but many of the runs have natural hits formed en route at the sides and there's also a number of ski jumps that you can air off. **Carvers** could do worse, but if you know how to carve at speed then you won't want a week here. **Beginners**, this place is great for you, however, only for a one off trip before going to Austria for your next snowboard holiday. Very good and lively local **facilities** slope side or close by

Ride area: 40km
Top Lift: 809m
Total Lifts:11
How to get there: Fly to: Dortmund 1 hour away

191

Italy is somewhat different from the rest of Europe; a little more temperamental it might be said. Rather sad mountain dress sense is quite obvious, with a love for the all in one day-glow colour ski suits. That said, Italy is a great place to snowboard and one of the cheapest European countries to visit. Italian resorts (which vary more off

Capital City: Rome
Population: 58 Million
Highest Peak: Mont Blanc de Cour-mayeur 4,748m
Language: Italian
Legal Drink Age: 18
Drug Laws: Cannabis is illegal and frowned upon
Age of consent: 16
Electricity: 240 Volts AC 2-pin
International Dialing Code: +39

Currency: Euro
Exchange Rate:
UK£1 = 1.5
US$1 = 0.8
AU$1 = 0.6
CAN$1=0.6

Driving Guide
All vehicles drive on the right hand side of the road
Speed limits:
50kph (31mph) Towns
90kph (55mph) Highways
130kph (80mph) Motorways
Emergency
Fire - 115
Police - 113
Ambulance - 118
Tolls
Payable on motorways using the Autostrada system
Mont Blanc tunnel charges approx 20 euros each way
Documentation
A driving lisence must be carried as well as insurance.

Time Zone
UTC/GMT +1 hours
Daylight saving time: +1 hour

Italian Snowboard Association
Piazza Regina Elena,
12 - 38027 MALE
Tel 045 8303277
Fax 045 8389129
Web: www.fsi.it
Email: fsi@iol.it

the slopes than on) are stretched across the northern part of the country, with many linking with neighbouring countries.

If you're intending to drive in Italy, remember: Italians can't drive; the term 'giving way' refers more to bowel movements than it does to other road users! But due to the fact that Italy has loads of small, remote resorts tucked away off normal public transport routes, driving is often the only option. Italian resorts are not always well located for airports as most places require an average of three hours transfer.

Train services are not too convenient, but you can get fairly close to many places. Rail fares are cheap and so it's a good option. Bus fares are also cheap, but services are not very reliable and understanding the time tables is an art form in itself.

Riders looking to work should have no real problems, lots of winter tour operators include Italy in their programmes and are always hiring catering staff and the normal array of tour reps etc. Italy is a member of the EU so normal visa rules apply.

Accommodation is on the whole basic and cheap. Around resorts, facilities are not as intense as in France, but the over indulgence in aprés ski behaviour and stupid face painting is still the same. That aside, however, Italy is well worth a visit.

FAR FLUNG

INTRO

To some it's a one week holiday, to others it's a life. Many people spend years and all their cash chasing the winter around the world. To lots it's a living, some lucky people make a living riding fantastic terrain, others make their dollar by helping beginners link a few turns. What ever snowboarding is to you and however much you've put into it, be it time, money or blood there's one thing that's true to all of us who snowboard. There's always another mountain to ride. The Alps and Rockie's are great but what about putting a few virgin lines down in India and finishing the day with a Vindaloo or carving it up in Cyprus before heading for the beach. Where there's a mountain with snow, you can ride.

We at WSG want you to broaden your horizons Bosnia? Lebanon?? Algeria??? Yes you can board in all these places, some may not be snow sure and yes some may have a lift system that looks like it was made during the industrial revolution, but snowboarding and travelling to a far flung place with food and a culture you've never experienced, what an adventure.

pic - Pete Coombs

ALGERIA

...he ...ason is ...ecember ... March. ...eres one ...sort called ...nsea, the capital is Algiers 3hours ...ght from the UK

CHSEA
1860 to 2508m
Runs: 4km pistes
50% beginners
50% Intermediate
Lifts: 2

ARMENIA

Reportedly has 2 resorts. Capital Yerevan, Currency Dram

BOLIVIA

Chacaltaya is highest resort in the world with the fastest and hardest to mount drag lift. Its 30km from La Praz, resort height 5420 meters, vertical drop 200 meters, 1 rope tow, 1 run, season Nov-March

BOSNIA AND HERZEGOVINA

...as 16 small resorts, Capital Sarajevo. ...ain resorts **Bjelasnica** 20 mins from ...arajevo hosted some events of 1984 ...inter Olympics. Other main resorts ...e **Ingman** and **Trebevic**

CHINA

11 resorts for 1.3 billion people. Largest resort is **Nanshan** , 62km from Beijing, 10 pistes, 1 half pipe, snow making, 2 chair lifts and 9 drags, a Burton LTR board school, lift pass 220/360RMB/day

CROATIA

Resort **Sljeme Mountain medvednica**, 6 runs, 4.5km of slopes, has snow making and night boarding, 1 days pass 70,00kn (about £7)
Capital Zagreb
Currency Kuna 10-£1

CZECH REPUBLIC

...as 22 resorts, capital Prague, ...rrency Koruna. ...ghest point Snezka 1602 meters

Spindleruv Mlyn
Lifts: 4 chair lifts & 12 drags
Runs: 20, 22km of pistes
Longest Run: 2.7km
Night Boarding: 1 run 6pm to 9pm
Lifts: 2

FAR FLUNG

CYPRUS

Right slap in the middle of the Mediterranean island of **Cyprus** towers **Mt.Olympus**. At just under 2000m its able to collect enough snowfall from late December to March to have its own resort. Originally built and operated by the British army after the Second World War, the 60's saw the **Cyprus Ski Club** take over the resort and have since installed more lifts and expanded the terrain. Its about an hours drive from **Nicosia** and **Limassol** and a short drive from **Troodos village**. Not surprisingly the season is very hit and miss; the snow doesn't tend to last too long once on the ground, with rocks showing through after about 4 days without snow. However when the snow is good there are a few trees to board through. The 4 drag lifts are old but seemed to keep going all season without a hitch, but they seem to have lost the keys to the piste basher as it's seldom used. The slopes can be busy at the weekends and holidays, but its normally extremely quiet during the week with just a few people on the slopes. Locals only just beginning to recognise snowboarding and up till now only skis are available to rent from the store situated next to the cafe adjacent to the 'sun valley' run. Boards can be purchased from **Force Eight Sports** in Limassol. During heavy snowfall, the local police will stop vehicles from reaching the slopes unless you're a 4x4 or using snow chains. For 2 or 3 days you can have some fun, get your board legs for the season, get some weird looks from the local (pink all-in-one wearing) skiers, and in the afternoon you can sit on the beach.

FREERIDERS. When theres snow the double black diamond (pah) slopes of the jubilee and racing run are as steep as it gets. Theres plenty of trees to shred though.

FREESTYLERS. No much fun for the freestylers with no Park and very few natural hits.

CARVERS will find the slopes narrow (20/25 m) and badly maintained.

BEGINNERS.Good for beginners to learn the basics.

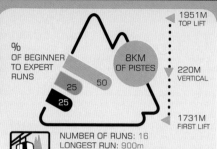

%
OF BEGINNER TO EXPERT RUNS
25 / 25 / 50

8KM OF PISTES

1951M TOP LIFT
220M VERTICAL
1731M FIRST LIFT

NUMBER OF RUNS: 16
LONGEST RUN: 900m
TOTAL LIFTS: 4 - all t-bars
MOUNTAIN CAFES: 1

AVERAGE SNOWFALL
Unknown
SNOWMAKING
none

WINTER PERIODS
Jan to March
Lift Passes
Day pass CYP 9.5
Week pass CYP 33
Hire
Board & Boots 7.5CYP per day at the resort. Mavros Sports & ThreeSixty in Nicosia and Force 8 Sports in Limassol also hire gear.

FREERIDE 70%
Some trees and off-piste
FREESTYLE 10%
No man made hits
CARVING 20%

FLY
Fly to Larnaca airport
CAR
From Limassol or Nicosia follow signs for Troodos, through Moniatis village to troodos square, then follow signs to Mt. Olympus . After 1.3km take steep left for Sun Valley area (1km) or continue for 1km to reach North Face area

Cyprus Ski Federation
Diagorou & Panteli Katelari 21
Office 101 Libra House
P.O.Box 22185
1518 Nicosia, CYPRUS
Phone: +357 (22) 675340
Fax: +357 (22) 669681
Web: www.skicyprus.com
Email:info@CyprusDestinations.com

GEORGIA

Gudauri , 3000m
Runs: 16km
Lifts: 2
1 1/2 hours from Tbillisi

Bakuriani, 1800m
Lifts: 2
Located on the Minor Caucasian Mountains about 1 1/2 hours from Tiblisi

FAR FLUNG

GREECE

et this, Greece the hot spot where bodies bare all on countless drenched beaches, scattered ound numerous islands, also has winter sports industry? Not well ow, and come to think of it not en thought of by most. Never the s you can snowboard at one of een recognised ski resorts, though ne are very dubious. There are umber of mountain ranges where ow falls on an annual basis allowing chance to shred it. Athens may be historic home of the Olympics but t 2 1/2 hours away is the resort of rassos, where you can ride some runs. Although the Greeks allow owboarders on to the slopes they're totally sure about the whole scene and may at times seem a bit nd-offish but they're cool enough. ece is definitely not a freestyler's yground; forget about half-pipes or -parks. Some of the areas may have idly short runs and be equipped t 2 1/2 hours away is the resort of an antique single lift system located ngside the resorts only building, and e the terrain is not that great. It's erally flat, not well groomed and not y adventurous, but what the heck

you're riding in Greece.

If you fancy giving Greece a go remember to contact the resort prior to leaving, to see if the place is actually open and check the latest snow forecasts. The resorts are unbelievable basic, many without any facilities. You won't find dozens of places to eat, sleep or drink in, and as for hard-core partying, forget it. The walkman and duty free territory. Be well advised to take your own snowboard because hiring options are zero. Getting to the resort is best done by driving yourself as public transport is poor.

Agio Pnevma , 1720m
Runs: 3
Lifts: 2
Contact: 051 835952
Agio Pnevma is located 43km from Drama

Kaimaktsalan, 2050m -2480m
Runs: 13,
Lifts: 6
Contact: 0381 82169, 22073
Kaimaktsalan has the highest lifts in Greece and is located 45km outside Edessa. Has a small terrain park.
www.edessacity.gr/VORAS/

Orphea Valley, 1750m
Runs: 1
Lifts: 1
Contact: 051 835952
Orphea Valley is located 44km from Kavala

Seli, 1500m
Runs: 8
Lifts: 4
1 chair, 3 t-bars
Contact: 0332 71234
Mountain Vermio, Maccedonia

Tria-pente Pigadia,1402m to 2005m
Runs: 4, Longest 2km
Lifts: 4
1 chair, 3 t-bars
Contact: 0332 44446
Mountain Vermio, Maccedonia

Vasilitsa ,1750m
Runs: 3,
Lifts: 2 drags
Contact: 0462 26100

Vigla , 1650m
Runs: 3
Lifts: 2
Contact: 0385 22354
Vigla is located 18km from Florina

HOLLAND

reputidly 51 dry slopes and a number indoor real snow slopes, including opes longest real snow slope.

wPlanet is about 45 mins outside sterdam, and featires a 230m and m real snow slopes.
wPlanet Spaarnwoude

Heuvelweg 6-8,
1981 LV Velsen-Zuid,
phone: +31 (0)255-545848,
fax: +31 (0)255-545840,
www.snowplanet.nl

SnowWorld is part owned by the Austrian resort, Solden. Theres 2 different locations. For more info look at www.

snowworld.nl , prices are around 15 euros an hour.
SnowWorld Landgraaf have the worlds largest indoor slopes at 500m and 520m. Located in the Strijthagen nature park
SnowWorld Zoetermeer has 3 slopes and 8 lifts. Located in the Buytenpark nature park

ICELAND

eportedly has 12 resorts which allow snowboarding both in the ter and summer months. None of resorts are big or offer extensive untain services. What you have are ic low level mountains with poor d access to them. On the slopes s tend to be short and not that l kept. However, Iceland Is a very ndly snowboard country and resorts more than happy to provide hits for stylers to get air off. Visitors to Iceland notice that apart from the short day light rs, that this is a very expensive country. n requirements for entry in to the country very liberal but you will need to have n flight tickets on arrival.

Kerlingarfjoll is no longer in operation and dismantled, but boarders still welcome whenever theres snow

Hlidarfjall, 1000m
Reputedly have a terrain park and pipe.
Runs:14
Lifts: 4 - 1 chair, 3 drags (2930 ph)
Lift pass: Day 1000/1400 ISK weekday/ weekend
Season pass 14,000 ISK
Hire: Board & Boots 2,500 ISK per day from resort
Board School: Lesson, lift & rental 3000 ISK per day
Private lesson 5000 ISK for 3hrs
Contact: www.hlidarfjall.is tel: 462-2280
Location: 10 minute drive from the town of Akureyri

Skálafell
Reputedly has a terrain park and pipe.
Lifts: 5 - 1 chair, 4 drags
Night Boarding: Yes
Contact: www.skidasvaedi.is tel: 354 566 7095

Blafjoll
Runs:20
Lifts: 11 - 2 chair, 9 drags
Lift times:Monday - Friday from 14:00-21:00. Weekends and public holidays from 10:00-18:00
Night Boarding: Yes
Contact: www.skidasvaedi.is tel: +354 561 8400
Location: 20 minutes from Reykjavik. Buses run from most towns to resort.

195

FAR FLUNG

INDIA

One of the best areas to ride is said to be at the resort known as **Auli**, near **Joshimath** in the **Garhwal Himalaya's**, where snowboarding expeditions have taken place. **Manali** is a place that offers some major heli-boarding while the areas known as **Narkanda** and **Kufri** are only suitable for total beginners and as they have very little in terms of facilities they are not recommended. The Indian season is best from mid- December to the end of March. All the areas offer a variety of terrain with a lot of freeriding and backcountry hikes possible, although you should only go backcountry riding in India with a knowledgeable mountain guide.

Gulmarg - is in the Kashmir region 32 miles from Srinagar and has 5 lifts and heli-boarding. US8million has been invested in a new Gondola which should open for the 2004/5 season.

Auli - is in the Uttar Pradesh on 10 miles from Joshimath with 12 miles of wooded piste.

Kufri - is in the Himachal region 9 miles from Shimla and is a flat place to suite beginners.

Narkanda - is in the Himachal region 40 miles from Shimla with the top lift at 3143m.

Manali - is in the Himachal region just 35 miles from Kullu.

Rohtang - is in the Himachal region just 30 miles from Manali.

All the Indian resorts provide very basic local facilities but are very cheap indeed.

Israel has one major resort Mt. Hermon, located in the Golan Heights near the border between Israel and Syria. The resorts has had

ISRAEL

US$1million spent recently updating the lifts and other facilities. Theres 4 funiculars and 5 chairs covering 45km of pistes, but no sign of any terrain parks

IRAN

Check official travel advice for current conditions before heading there, but Iran is cheap, the food is excellent, you can drink the tap water, and most importantly there are some excellent snowboard resorts.

The Germans, who were building much of Iran's railroads in the early 1930's introduced Iranians to skiing, and the building on the resorts begun. In 1947 the Iranian Ski Federation were formed, and in 1951 the first chair lift was built.

It may be surprising to hear that 30% of all people on Iranian slopes are snowboarders. The ski lifts are well maintained and there have been no accidents in the past twenty years.

Iran has two big ski resorts; Shemshak and Dizin. Both resorts are within 2 hours drive from the capital, Tehran. There are a total of 20 resorts in Iran, although most of them will have little more than a couple of tows.

How to get to these resorts
You will have no problems arriving at Tehran airport with your own snowboard equipment, however, make sure it is in a snowboard bag, It is best to get a taxi from the airirport into Tehran - it will cost $6 maximum and will take half an hour. You cannot rent cars in Iran so it is best to organise a bus tour from Tehran up to the ski resort you want to go to. This only costs $6-$7. Either you can go up for the day or you can leave the tour and stay in the resort for the week then catch a tour bus back down. Go to one of the many sports/ski shops in Tehran to organise a tour.

General information about all resorts
The season is from the beginning of December to the end of March. You can easily go off piste, and there are vast fields of powder. However, there are no ski patrols recording the avalanche risks and triggering off avalanches where needed to reduce the risk. It is possible to hire a guide to go off piste for $5-6 per day. The guides are reliable and are usually trained in Austria or Switzerland. There are also reliable mountain rescue teams. There are no heliboarding facilities. Most of the time the weather is reliable so you are sure to get a good weeks riding whenever you go. There are a variety of lifts in these resorts ranging from gondolas and chairlifts to button lifts. Also, it is wise to take your own food to the resorts. Look out for a town called Fasham on the Way to Shemshak – you can buy all your basics there.

Accommodation
The concept of bed and breakfast accommodation is non-existent in Iran. However, because accommodation is cheap why not stay in a 4 star hotel for $50 per night for a double room. Head to the north of the city; this is the safest and has upmarket hotels like the Hilton and Sheraton. You can contact the Iranian tourist board and ask them to organise accommodation for you in Iran.   What to wear On the slopes it is fine to wear your normal snowboard gear. However, if you are a girl make sure you are wearing a beanie, If it is sunny and you are boiling it is not advisable to strip off to your t-shirt on the slopes if you are male or female. At all other times, women have to cover their hair and body but you do not need to Wear a black cloak or chador, Instead it is fine to wear a colourful thin silk scarf tied under your neck and wear loose trousers, shirts with long sleeves, and a loose thin jacket

that reaches down to your knees. It is fine to smoke anywhere except while walking along the street. Guys should nor wear shorts and it is best to wear long sleeved shirts.

The food

The food is unbelievably tasty – with fresh kebabs, amazing rice based dishes, fresh cheese, a lot of vegetarian dishes, amazing sweets, and an array of fruit to choose from. Things you do have to be careful about are eating salads and herbs that haven't been washed properly. However keep it in mind it is absolutely safe to drink the tap water. Also check out Arak – Iranian vodka made with raisons and dried apples containing 35-45% alcohol. It is illegal for Muslims to drink Arak, but not for Armenian Christians to drink it. Therefore as tourists, you can buy Arak from the Armenians for approximately $3 for 2 litres.

More Info

The tourist board can organise accommodation for you, work out an itinerary, give advice on prices and give telephone numbers for places, and its ok, they speak English. Contact Iran Tourism and Touring Organisation by email at info@itto.org

Iran Ski Federation,
Shahid Shirodi Sports Complex,
Varzandeh St., Shahid Mofatteh Ave.,
Tehran, I.R. Iran.
Web: www.skifed.ir

Email: office@skifed.ir
tel: +9821 8825161-2

DIZIN
If you continue along the road for another 30mins after **Shemshak** you will reach **Dizin**. At an altitude of 12,900 feet this is the highest snow resort in Iran and attracts the most amount of snow. Iran gets powder snow by the bucket loads, it is not

uncommon for 50cm to land overnight during a dump in Shemshak, and more in Dizin. However, because of the huge amount of snow there are a lot of avalanches, and Iranians just let them happen naturally. There is no dynamite bombing, therefore theres a risk that the road to Dizin might be blocked with snow. However, in the past three years the road has been open most of the time. To be on the safe side check at Shamshak before driving along.

 2650m to 3600m
Runs: 16
25% Easy
44% Intermediate
31% Advanced
Lifts: 13 - 3 Gondolas, 2 chairs, 8 drags
Location: Tehran 123km away and Shemshak is 71km

Dizin is a completely different resort to Shemshak. The views are amazing, you can see unending mountain ranges and there is a clear view of the highest mountain in Iran, the semi-active volcano, Mount

Damavand. Also, it is possible in this larger resort to see all the nine runs. Like Shemshak, the runs are wide, long and interconnecting and there are no trees. However, the slopes are not as steep attracting beginners through to advanced riders. The price for ski pass and hired equipment is the same as in Shemshak. It is also

easy to find accommodation here.

Shemshak is only a 45-minute drive from **Tehran**. The route is stunning, there are interesting towns to stop at on the way, and if you are hungry try out the amazing kebabs. Shemshak is well known as a resort for advanced skiers and snowboarders. The slopes are steep and funnily enough, have names such as The Wall. There are approximately eight extremely long runs with access to off piste slopes. Iranian slopes are generally long, wide, interconnect and there are no trees. This resort is undulating so it is hard to see all the different slopes. This is the most popular resort. There are cafes on the slopes and hotels and chalets at the bottom of the slope. It is extremely easy to find accommodation since a lot of people come here for the day or they stay at their own chalets. A one day ski-pass costs a measly $12 for an adult. It is also very easy to hire snowboard equipment. A whole setup for a day will cost $15, and don't worry its not second hand Russian stuff, a lot of it is brand new.

 2550m to 3050m
Runs: 16
Lifts: 7 - 2 chairs, 5 drags
Location: 57 kilometers north-east of Tehran

If you want to have good apres-snowboard sessions this is the place to be. A lot of the Persians who come here are young, rich students studying in America or Europe and are probably on holiday seeing their parents. So practically all of them speak English, they are very western in their outlook and they are up for a damn good party. Shemshak is known as the party resort. So, look out for a group of snowboarders that look friendly and go up and chat, mention that you have heard that this is the party resort and they are sure to tell you what's going on.

KAZAKHSTAN

Kazakhstan a former part of the Soviet Union is known for its vast flat steeps and home of the soviet space program. In its far south-east corner lies part of the **Tien Shan** mountain range known as the celestial mountains, an absolute gem of a place. **Khan Tengri** at 7010 M supposedly the worlds most beautiful mountain and Mecca to many a climber its best known peak. The place has still got all the hang ups of the old Soviet Union with a big police presence, road blocks to look for capitalist spies from the west and a need to carry your passport everywhere you go. If you travel independently you will get hauled of the bus at every check point, by police with bigger hats than a New Orleans pimp.

Alma-Ata pronounced almarty is the capital, a mix of Russian and Kazakhs people which has been described as a huge knocking shop no ones heard off. Its a great place to drink vodka and check out the locals, also a good base for the only real resort Chimbulak, home to the soviet ski team and the highest and largest ice ring in the world.

Heli boarding is the real pull of Kazakhstan, using old soviet military helicopters which will seat up to 20 people. The choice of terrain is endless and being the only helicopters with the ability to land and more importantly take off again, at altitudes of nearly 6000 meters you really can just choose the hill you want. The main draw back other than cost is the cold, with temperatures of -10 a winter norm in Alam-Ata the high peaks can easily drop below -30. Having said that with hundreds of peaks higher than Mont Blanc you can forget about January and go in the summer. The cheapest and easiest way is to stay at **Karkara** base camp (you will need a Kyrgyzstan visa) and take a short 20min flight into the mountains. If you don't fancy a tent or being stuck with only the base camp bar and stories of the days riding then you could stay in Alma-Ata but it's an hours flight and at around £1000/hr to keep the thing in the air the cash could be better spent than flying back to the knocking shop. A flight to **Inylchek Glacier** to see **Khan-Tengri** and **peak Pobedy** is a must, you can sleep at the climbers base camp but take a good sleeping bag. Check out www.khantengri.kz.

CHIMBULAK
An hours drive from **Alma-Ata** at 2200 meters is the village of Chimbulak which has hotels, board hire, bowling and vodka fuelled Russians. A good little resort to get your legs ready for that helicopter your going to get. Other than a few rope drags there's three chairs that can handle up to 900 people/hr, they run in a straight line one after the other to take you from 2200 m to 3160 m. The resorts is sheltered by imposing peaks on it's flanks, which helps with the temperature, there's also some trees to head for if the visibility is bad. The fun park has some hits and a few slides. It's open from 10 till 5 and you can sort out transport to resort with one of the many agents in Alma-Ata. To save cash take a Lada taxi but make sure you've sorted out the return price before you leave town or once your up there it'll cost the price of a new Lada to get back.

KYRGSZSTAN

Kyrgyzstan is a place for boarders who like a hike or have loads of cash for a helicopter. The neighbour of **Kazakhstan**, Kyrgyzstan is a lot more laid back and cheaper. You won't get stopped by the police but you might get taxed by a local if you walk trough the parks alone at night. **Bishkek** the capital has wide tree lined streets from which you are surrounded by huge snow covered peaks. 80% of this country is mountainous and most of the other 20% is lakes. During the soviet rule most of Kyrgyzstan was out of bounds to foreigners, due to missile testing in lake Issyk Kul and its boarder with China. Home to felt hats, headless goat polo and wrestling on horse back while covered in goose fat, the Kyrgz are a hospitable lot. The main drink in the countryside is fermented

mares milk, which tastes like off yogurt and turns the local men into giggling kids. The food is mostly meat based with horse a favourite, in the countryside you see herds of horses waiting for the pot. Since the brake up of the soviet union the Kyrgz have embraced independence, setting up there own currency and welcoming investment from the west and lorry loads of plastic junk and rip off clothes from China.

HELI-BOARDING
Is basically the same as in Kazakhstan but a little cheaper. You may find that you'll stay in Karkara camp and use the same helicopter as you would if you booked it in Kazakhstan. The main advantage along with cost is if you start your trip in Kyrgyzstan you will only need a Kyrgyz visa.

ALA-ARCHA
A 30 km Lada drive from Bishkek is the Ala-Archa national park a steep sided treed valley with a small resort at its top. The accommodation is a few km after the park gate a modern A frame hotel. Last spring the road in was taken out by a huge land slide but they've been working really hard to rebuild it and a temporary routes been set up. The valley is lined with 5000 meter plus peaks and cascading glaciers. There's 4 lifts drag lifts starting at 3400 meters going up to 4000 meters there's 4 runs, but its basically go anywhere you want. The whole resort is on the Ala-Archinsky glacier so watch out for crevasse. The best thing to do is leave the lifts alone and get your board on your back and get some real fresh lines. There's loads of slopes to choose from with shed loads of snow but there no reliable mountain rescue so your on your own.

FAR FLUNG

LATVIA

Valmiera is the main snowboarder's hangout in **Latvia**, and is located 80 miles (130km) north of the Latvian capital Riga. What you get here are two slopes, with longest measuring a mere 170 metres and serviced by two basic lifts and one snow-cannon the (only one in Latvia). You couldn't split this place into styles and levels; suffice to say that novices alone will have half an hours fun. The winter allows for some limited riding on real snow while the summer sees an influx of boarders to ride the only sliding carpet, (better known as a Dry Slope'), in the Baltics. During the summer a lot of BMX riders also turn up to ride the BMX dirt track, while others simply come to chill out and take the occasional boat trip on the river Gauja.

Valmiera is happy to have snowboarders try out its hill, but as yet they haven't been able to provide a halfpipe or fun-park However, plans are being put forward and it's hoped that for this coming season some kickers will be built for air heads to get high. You can now get snowboards and boots for hire at the base and snowboard instruction is also now available on request.

Lodging and other local services at the slopes are not for wimps or for those looking for all the creature comforts of an Alpine resort. You can choose to stay in one of the small camping style houses located behind the slopes, which use old wood stoves for heating. Alternatively in the town of Valmiera you will find hotels and other basic cheap lodgings.

night-life, it's do it yourself with a Walkman. Or check out, Multi Klubs, Tirgus iela 5, ph 42 32114 for a **party**.

Fly to Riga International airport 80 miles away. **Bus:** transfers takes 2 /2 hours. **Trains:** via Riga take 2 /2 hours. **Driving:** via Riga, head north on the A2 for 50 miles travelling via Sigulda and turning north via Cesis to reach Valmiera.

LEBANON

Reportedly has 6 resorts spread along the high snow capped mountains of the country. Lebanon's most famous resorts are Cedars and Faraya.

Cedars is located in the northern half of the country about 80 miles from Beirut. The slopes are small with, only a couple of runs and five lifts.

Faraya, which only 30 miles from Beirut, is the biggest of Lebanon's resorts, although it is still relatively small compared to European destinations. Faraya has a dozen lifts and about 40 runs covering 60km that are rated mainly as intermediate standard with a couple of advanced runs and some very basic beginner's trails.

Entry in to Lebanon by foreign nationals is allowed but be careful as it wasn't n that long ago when the country was at civil war with its self, and there are repoortidly still terrorist activity in some parts of the country. All visitors need a passport and a visa to entry the country. UK visitors will be issued with a visa on arrival. The country is made up of Muslims and Christians, which was the main cause of the civil war. People are very friendly but don't take things for granted and don't stray off in to unknown areas.

LIECHTENSTEIN

This tiny country is situated between the borders of Switzerland and Austria. The main resort is Malbun which is just over 2 hours from Zurich irport. The resort is not pariculary big, with 20km of pistes and 6 lifts

Malbun

Not the biggest, but does have a terrain park with a few rails & kickers
Lifts: 6 - 2 chair, 4 drags (6800 ph)
Lift pass: Day pass 37 CHF
6 Days 155 CHF, Season 380 CHF
Board School: Ski school Malbun offer 3 day beginners course 120 CHF (2hrs lesson per day), 5 day 170 CHF. Private lessons CHF 60 per hour
Contact:

Mountain railways, P.o. box 1063
9497 Triesenberg Malbun
Tel: + 423,265 40 00
Web: www.bergbahnen.li

Location: From Zurich (110 km) head to Valduz via coffin, approx 1 1/2 hours. Munich, 250km, Innsbruck 170KM. nearest airport is Zurich Kloten, 1 1/2 hr transfer

POLAND

These people have had some shit, the second world war started here and ended with 20 years of communist Russian rule. When you arrive in **Warsaw** or **Krakow** its grey even when the sun shines its grey and the taxi drivers will try to rip you off by about 1000%. Look a little deeper past the unsmiling faces and the bastard taxi drivers and what you'll find is real old spot. Renaissance buildings, cheep beer, beautiful people and enough vodka and gherkins to see out any post nuclear war fall out. In the **High Tatras** the bushes are full of wolfs and bears, in the city there full of suit wearing vodka heads who just couldn't make it home.

Zakopane, founded in the seventeenth century is now a collection of wooden chalets, soviet flats and western branded shops. 100km south of Krakow near the Slovak boarder it's the best known resort in Poland, it's really a town which services a collection of small resorts. Kasprow Wierch 3 km away has the best runs, it has a cable car built in that in two stages will take you up to 1985 meters and offers some long runs down, there's also two great treeless bowls to play in.

Gubalowka which is reached by tram has some shorter runs good for beginners except its mostly t-bar lifts, sometimes when they can be arsed there's a pipe here. Nosa has night boarding and artificial snow production it has a few chairs but is mainly t-bars.

If you're in Poland over the winter or on a road trip in eastern Europe then visit Zakopane, but if your sitting at home planning your one week this season away don't, unless you love vodka and gherkins

199

MOROCCO

Not known as a snowboarding destination Morocco could surprise some. It is home to the **Atlas Ranges** and the tallest mountain in North Africa **Jebel Toubkal**, at 4167 meters.

From the sun drenched streets of **Marrakech** you can have a breakfast of croissant and mint tea while your ears ring with the call to prayer, the buzz of street sellers and horse drawn carts. Through the morning haze of 2 stroke oil you can see the snow capped peaks of the central High Atlas. A 76km drive from the city is the resort of **Oukaimeden**. It claims a 663m vertical drop from 3258meters, there's 1 chair lift, 7 drags and 20km of piste. If you find any of this working or open then you're in luck. Most of the time its donkey or walk up. From the top there are great views of the Marrakech plane and with good snow a fun ride down. There are some posh hotels and also a few bunk houses. If you don't want to hire a board that's the shape of a bullet bring your own.

The High Atlas run from the Atlantic east towards the **Sahara**, and are home to the Berber Tribe a rock hard group of once nomadic herdsmen. Now semi nomadic and most with thicker skin on there hands then you have on your feet. When the Arabs from the east invaded they couldn't control them and instead persuaded them to take on the Spanish. They made it all the way over the Pyrenees before getting a slap in Martel. When the French were here they never got control of these beautiful mountains and there inhabitants are still on the wild side but really hospitable as most true mountain people are.

A two hour drive from Marrakech is the small Berber village of **Imlil**, the last port of call before heading up **Jebel Toubkal**. It's a good idea to spend the night here to organise a guide if you haven't done so in Marrakech. Best to crash down in a locals house and bung then a few £ in the morning. From Imlil you can hike up to the bloody cold **Toubkal Refuge**, to make it easy hire a porter or a mule. From here it's possible to hike the surrounding slopes and board back to the refuge. There's a good bowl directly behind the refuge. You will need a guide as well as all your own equipment and food, including a very good sleeping bag, ice axe and crampons. Remember to go slow and drink plenty of water to stave off altitude sickness and the best snow is normally late Jan early Feb.

In the Middle Atlas 81km south of **Fez** is **Michlifen** it's got 1 chair and 1 drag, 4 pistes, a top elevation of 2000m and a drop of 200m. With its low altitude and a strong African sun it's best to get up early before the snow becomes slush. The town of **Ifrane** is where all the accommodation is and if you hadn't of just driven though pine trees with monkeys in and all the men weren't in dresses you wouldn't think you where in Morocco. The kings got a mansion here and there's posh hotels with bell boys, it's a weird hybrid of France and Africa and it isn't cheap.

Morocco doesn't offer great boarding and if you're not prepared to hike it's awful. But it's a cool destination if you want to spice up a visit to Fez and Marrakech. Boarding in Morocco is about the whole experience meeting the locals eating the food and seeing some great mountains, not just the boarding. After all who do you know who's boarded in Africa?

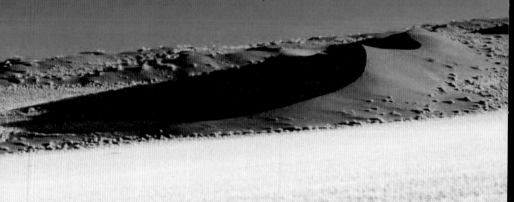

NEPAL

In 2003 permission was granted to the Himalayan Heli Ski Guides (HHMG) to become the first company to operate Heli Skiing in **Nepal**. Its possible to board in the Annapurna region and plans are now to open up the **Everest** region to trips. More info can be found on /www.heliskinepal.com

PAKISTAN

Malam Jabba is the only real resort in **Pakistan**, 300km from Islamabad. The resort is in the **Swat Valley**, at a height of 2896m. Its not the biggest resort in the world, with 2 chairs and a 200m vertical, but it does get a restactable 5m of snow a season. The resort was up for sale in 2002.

PERU

2 resorts **Pasto-Ruri/Huascaran** the second highest in the world at 4800 meters. The Cordillera Blanca area is the only area possible to board or ski, from the nearby town of Huaraz there are several places where you can hire gear, and organised trips are possible, or grab a local guide. **Pastoruri glacier** is the most recognised area

ROMANIA

Poiana Brasov is a small resort with just 9 miles of marked out terrain offering some limited advanced carving on the **Valea Lupului** trail to basic freeriding through trees up on the Postavarul area. Although the slopes are not noted for having long lift queues, some of the runs can be very busy, especially the beginner areas. Freestylers will have to make do with getting air by building hits and then hiking them as there is no halfpipe here or any good natural kickers.

Off the slopes the purpose built resort is suitable for a few days hangingout with a few cheap hotels and lots of cheap night-life. There are a few night clubs here and lots of... erm...'Gentleman's Bars'. If you know what I mean!

Szczawnik is the other most recognised resort, but at 520m its little more than a hill.

POIANA BRASOV
1020m - 1775m

Runs: 10 (12km of pistes)
34% EASY
34% INTERMEDIATE
33% ADVANCED
Lifts: 8
1 gondola, 3 cable-cars, 5 drags
Board School: yes, 120 instructors.
English spoken
Contact: www.poiana-brasov.com
Location: 13km from town of Brasov. Fly to Bucharest, 3 hours away

PORTUGAL

Portugal, believe it or not, has a mountain winter sports resort where you can snowboard, complete with uphill lift services. Although Sierra de Estrela is no match for the main European Alps it's still real snow and cheap to visit. It's worth noting that the summit manages over 2000m, higher than anything in Scotland and higher than many Scandinavian resorts. Portugal has a good snowboard following that stems from its influences and links with the big surf scene here. The riding style favour mostly freeride and free-style with only a few Alpine/Carvers around. The people are really friendly and if you do decide to do a.road trip or a two day visit in winter, remember that even if this snow is miserable, at least the people are not; they are warm and friendly and will show you a cool time, partying and chasing gorgeous women, while waiting for the white stuff to fall. Getting around in winter is best done with your own vehicle; local transport is not so hot.

SIERRA DE ESTRELA

Portugal's only resort is that of Sierra de Estrela, located in the mid-northern region of the country. Despite the area's altitude, conditions are not always that favourable. The warm winds that blow in from the Atlantic coast also make it impossible to have snowmaking facilities. Most riders only check the place out at weekends and if the locals want to ride any longer they tend to visit Sierra Nevada in Spain and Val D'isere or Isola 2000 in France. At present it only gives 10 hectares of lift serviced terrain, though there is more to explore if your willing to do some hiking.

Freeriders will find some amazing off-piste, that will appeal as much to inter-mediate riders as it will to advanced. If you take the lengthy hike over to the area called Covado de Boi at the opposite side of the main area, you'll gain access to a good share of couloirs to ride and some big hits to fly off. The only real draw back is that once at the bottom, if you have someone waiting with a car to take you back to the main area, you'll have to hike back. Still work hard, play hard! The other good place to check out is Lagoa Escura, a big slope where the best powder is to be had on a totally crowd free area that

bases out at an amazing lake.

Freestylers should also check out the Covado de Boi area, where there's a 300 metre natural half pipe, which on occasions has 3 metre walls banked up.

Carvers who like to ride only long wide runs, forget it. This place is not for you. That said though, there .are some open areas that allow for a few signatures in the snow with your edges.

Beginners this place is absolutely perfect for you, although hopelessly limited.

Because Sierra de Estrela is an eco-logical natural park, there are a lot of development restrictions on and around the mountain. Although some accommodation is available close by, the best option is in Covilha, 12 miles away where you'll find hotels, restaurants, shops to hire snowboards, bars, discos and places to simply hang out, all at afford- able prices.

RUSSIA

pics - Chris Homer

The West's influence has taken over and Russia is not the place it used to be. Although snowboarding is now on the scene it's still very much in its infancy here.

The capital city **Moscow**, where everything is freely available at the right price, has a few snowboarding areas. '**Moscow's 3 Hills**' are all within half an hour of the city centre via the extremely efficient Metro. Alternatively get on a suburban elektrichka train, pay less than a buck, and head out of the city for more resorts and enter a whole new Russia. The people are friendly and everything is dirt cheap. Okay you get basic lifts, food and accommodation, but you'll see the real Russia and snowboard on uncrowded slopes. The Caucasus Range to the south of Russia is home to Europe's highest mountain in **Elbrus**. At 5642m it's larger than the west's best by a few hundred metres.

Snowboarding is possible from mid-November to late April but be prepared for temperatures as low as -25c in mid February. At the resorts equipment hire is occasionally available but it is highly recommended to take your own. English is spoken by some Russians in Moscow, but very few in the southern mountains so learning a few words of Russian will make things a lot easier.

VISA INFO
All visitors to Russia must have a passport and a valid visa. The maximum visa time for a tourist is 30 days, however, various other visas are available, such as a business visa which can last for up to 60 days. A transit visa only lasts for 24 hours and is used for individuals who intend only to pass through the country en-route to another. There is a charge for visas and delays brought about due to too much bureaucracy. Contact national embassies for full details.

HEALTH
A helpful point to note is that most UK visitors can get free emergency medical care provided the individual has a valid passport.

Capital City: Moscow
Population: 143.8 million
Highest Peak: Gora El'brus 5633 m
Language: Russian
Legal Drink Age: 18
Drug Laws: Cannabis is illegal
Age of consent: 16
Electricity:220 Volts AC 2-pin, 50hz
International Dialing Code: +7

Currency: Euro
Exchange Rate:
UK£1 = 53
EURO = 36
US$1 = 29

Driving Guide
All vehicles drive on the right hand side of the road
Speed limits:
60km (37mph) towns
90km (55mph) outside towns
Speeding fines payable, "unofficial" payment not uncommon
Emergency
01 - Fire
02 -Police
03 - Ambulance
Info
Very few car hire companys rent cars without a driver for you. Some very dodgy roads, less than half of roads are sealed
Documentation
Home driving licence and a russian translation of it. Passport.

Trains
Train services around the country are okay and very affordable. The metro trains in Moscow are superb with stations that are a work of art. It is also possible to take trains from the west to the east, but you will need to change trains on route as Russia uses a different rail gauge.

Bus
Buses services in Russia are cheap and on the whole good but they are also notoriously slow and time tables are a myth.

Fly
Gateway international airport is,Moscow (Sheremetevo). The airport is 18 miles out of the city.

Approximate global air travel times to Moscow:
from:
London 5¹ᐟ² hours
Los Angles 17¹ᐟ² hours
New York 14 hours

Time Zone
UTC/GMT +3 hours
Daylight saving time: +1 hour

Russian snowboard federation
Ananyevskiy pereulok, 5/12, office 161
Moscow 125502
www.snbrd.ru

DOMBAI - RUSSIA

Very interesting place with a very pioneering feel to it.

Set amongst the **Caucasus Mountains** near the **Georgian** border is **Dombai** with its unique atmosphere and visited by your average Russian tourist, many of whom are from the surrounding towns and villages, who tend to go up the mountain to eat, view the peaks and drink Vodka as opposed to boarding. The riding is good with plenty to suite all. The lower slopes provide some runs through the trees which are gentle and ideal for beginners. Even though the mountain has three piste bashers grooming is infrequent and piste markings generally range from poor to non-existent. There are lots of hiking options available although Russians are not big on going off-piste. The chair lifts and cable cars are from the bygone era and nothing is new. You will see some of the most ingenious repair work undertaken. Take for instance the broken perspex windows of the gondola car, they've had drilled holes either side of the crack and then sewn it together. The lifts are interesting with a "pay as you ride" system. When lifts are down, some of the piste basher drivers charge each person to ride on a Cat Track tour. Safety is not high on the list of priorities, but it has to be remembered that this is Russia and anything goes.

Freeriders will find that this is mainly their destination. Due to the limited number of snowboarders (about 5%) when the powder falls it can be ridden for days with no chance of being tracked out.

Off the slopes accommodation is basic, cheap and widely available. Food is filling, service of a Russian standard and don't expect to see a menu when you are here! Try the **Georgian** hot cheeseboard called 'Khachapuri. To get the very most out of a trip would require a translator as foreign languages are generally not spoken. The locals are friendly and are very pleased to meet foreigners, especially English speakers, as they like to practice their language skills and love to share their drink with you. Night time madness is best sampled in the *Hotel Vershiny*. There are two disco/bars and a few places to eat. The ground floor disco is generally more locals with a mixture of European and old Russian *"Pop"*. Snowboard videos are shown behind the DJ's stand and the place has a distinct 70's feel purely by accident. A swimming pool and a sauna is also available in the hotel but you may need a health card to get in. Overall the place is very interesting and has a very pioneering feel to it. If you are planning a trip to Russia bring your snowboard with you and have an adventure in the **Caucussus**.

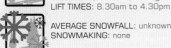

3050M TOP LIFT

%
OF BEGINNER
TO EXPERT
RUNS

35

25   40

1450M VERTICAL

1650M FIRST LIFT

NUMBER OF RUNS: 22
LONGEST RUN: 3.2miles (5km)
TOTAL LIFTS: 11
1 Gondolas, 4 chairs, 6 drags
LIFT TIMES: 8.30am to 4.30pm

AVERAGE SNOWFALL: unknown
SNOWMAKING: none

WINTER PERIODS:
Nov to May
Lift Passes
1 Gondola ride - 25
Cost per lift - 2
Cat rides - 20
Heli boarding
yes

FREERIDE 80%
Trees & lots of backcountry
FREESTYLE 15%
No pipe, no park
CARVING 5%

Tourist Office Dombai
Dombai
Tel: +7 (0) 86522 78168
Accommodation Tel: +7 (0) 865 58 279
Web: www.dombai.ru
Email:mail@dombai.ru

Car
Via Mineral nye, you need to head south for a few kms along the M29, cutting off at Essentuki on to the A157 and the A155 via Teberda and to Dombi.
Fly
Fly to Moscow and then fly inland to Mineral nye Vody which is 62km from Dombai.

KANT

Kant is located within an industrial estate to the south of **Moscow**, 20 minutes from Red Square, this is Moscow's most accessible hill. From the metro it's only a five minute walk. Generally it is regarded as a club field, with hourly rates of $3 US, available to non-members. One of the most bizarre hills ridden, it has 270 degree views of drab old apartment blocks. It started life as a dump and is classed as an artificial hill. The disused dump was filled with earth, had grass planted on it, and to increase its gradient and length, rubbish was transported from surrounding building sites. This can cause problems with your base when there is limited snow coverage so to counteract this, management often sprinkle sawdust over the thin areas.

The Kant Sports Club has four lighted slopes with four Russian type 'Boogie System' lifts to serve them. This system requires the rider to hire a boogie and regardless of whether you are goofy or regular the lifts are equally difficult.

The runs are generally about 200 metres long and suited to beginners or intermediates who want to mess around. There are some hits available but the landings are pretty sketchy. Still there is plenty of fun to be had

and three piste bashers do their best to keep the slopes in good condition. Near the slopes there is also a cheap cafe and a few shops.

The nearest metro is **Nagornaya** (on the Grey Line)

KRYLATSKOYE & SPARROW HILLS

Krylatskoye is **Moscow's** best local resort with 12 lifts located on two hills and is very small. Runs are 250 to 350 metres long and uncrowded. The slopes are gentle and can be taken at an easy pace for beginners or flat out by intermediate riders. There are also some small natural drop offs and a few hits available.

The lifts, which is an assortment of a boogie system, button lifts and water ski type pullies. are operated by three different companies. A "pay as you ride" token system operates with tickets being purchased from the kiosk at about 29US cents a go. Piste bashers are not used on the slopes but the runs are often to be found in good condition. The resort, as most things in Russia, is old fashioned and outdated, but has a real fun feel about

it. At the bottom of the slopes is a red London bus which has been converted into a cafe.

KRYLATSKOYE

slopes are a 20 minute walk, from the Metro station and well worth a visit.

The nearest metro is at Krylatskoye (on the Blue Line).

SPARROW HILLS

is situated in the south-west of Moscow on the only high ground near the city, it is the smallest of the "Moscow's 3 Hills". There are two simple slopes, about 250 metres in length, which form a backdrop to the very impressive ski jumps located here. Two boogie lifts serve the runs. The resort is close to the New Moscow State Circus so you can double up on your day with a bit of fun.

PARAMONOVO

Paramonovo, from **Savyolovsky** train station in Moscow, is a one hour journey north on an elektrichka surban train to the Tourist Station. From the desolate station platform take a 10 minute walk back down the railway line from the direction the train has just come to the main road. From here a taxi can take you the remaining 7km to the Paramonovo slopes. The fare will be about $5US, but be prepared to wait a while as there are few cars around. The resort, a local hunt for the rich Moscovites, is set amongst pine trees in the fresh air and

countryside. The advertising literature boasts '10 boogie lift systems covering 10km of piste'. This may actually be true but generally as few as 3 lifts operate intermittently which can cause queues at weekends. The runs are similar length to the 'Moscow's 3 Hills' but provide a lot more possibilities for tree riding and sizeable hits. They even have spotters on the main jumps. Boogies cost around $5US (or £3UK) to hire for a day and then all lifts are free. Cheap accommodation is available near the slopes.

SLOVAKIA

Slovakians drink more beer per capita than any other country in the world and at 50p a pint who can blame them. It's home to the **High Tatras mountains** (see Poland) part of the **Carpathian range**. Its best resort is **Jasna** in the Low Tatras. Slovakia the eastern half of the former **Czechoslovakia** is a beautiful place and is well cheep. The towns are made up of Renaissance architecture and grey commie high-rise tower blocks. **Bratislava** the capital has an international airport, and makes a great place to start your trip. It's a 3 hour train ride to the hills, through some breathtaking scenery. You can also fly to Kosice or the closest to Jasna Tatry-Poprad.

As well as great beer and beautiful woman it has some good riding. If you're an experienced rider and like a road trip then it's a cool place to tour it's also a good place to learn. The instruction is ok and board hire is available, Burton have a hire shop in Jasna. If you're a complete beginner then why spend loads of money on a lift pass for a huge area when your going to spend days on the same slope. A weeks pass is around £50. Most resorts have a lot of drag lifts but you've got to learn them. There's nothing worse than seeing your mates heading off to that hidden spot while your on your belly being dragged up the hill holding on for dear life.

Bratislava the capital has an international airport, and makes a great place to start your trip. It's a 3 hour train ride to the mountains through some breathtaking scenery. You can also fly to Kosice or the closest to Jasna Tatry-Poprad. Most resorts have really old ski lifts and there's always a few closed, when you get up the hill they look like they've not worked in years. But there all boarder friendly most with loads of rail slides and a few wonky hits.

JASNA
Up a dead end road you find Slovakia's best resort Jasna sometimes referred to as Chopok the name of the mountain. A tree laden resort although a little tight for a full speed tree run it makes for picture postcard scenery. It can get over loaded at weekends and school holidays with snow ploughing Ukrainians, but has a good choice of terrain for beginners and intermediates. The top is susceptible to high winds and is often closed, and don't believe the map that makes out the resorts of Jasna and Trangoska are linked, it's a good hours walk after the top lift to get up and over. There's plenty of cheep eats on the hill as long as you like goulash, fried cheese or corn on the cob, beer is available and drunk everywhere. The fun park which you can walk to is loads of rail slides and not much else. Two of the nursery slopes are open at night and frequented by one piece suits bent double, with arses pointed to the havens and eyes fixed on the tips of there skis. Accommodations in hotels and for £18 a night you can get half board in a small room. If you want to live it up there's the newly built hotel Grand where the Burton hire and board schools is. The resort is really just a collection of hotels so for a beer it's the hotel bar. On a Friday night they put up a marquee near the grand and fill it with cheeky girl look-alikes and thump out house music.

SERBIA

KOPAONIK 1770M TO 2017M
Located on Mt Kopaonik. Nato fired Cruise Missiles at Transmitters on Mt Kopaonik in March 1999.
Runs: 23
20% beginners
70% intermediate
10% advanced
Longest run: 3.5 km
Lifts: 22 lifts - 8 chair, 14 drag
Getting there: 275 km from Belgrade 3hrs flight from London

SOUTH AFRICA

Capital: Pretoria - CapeTown
Travel is not the most convenient and be carefull, crime is rampant, some of the worst in the world.
Time Zone: GMT + 2 hours
Top peak: MtAuxSources 4165m

TIFFINDELL 3001M
is the only place in South Africa with snow making facilities. Southern drakensberg Mountains on Mt Ben Mc Dhui
Season:May to September
Lift: 1 lift, 2km piste
50% beginners
50% Intermediate

In Gauteng there's an artificial indoor slope.

SOUTH KOREA

Capital Seoul, Currency Won
17 resorts

Best known Seoul Ski Resort with 3 lift 4 runs,

Bear Town 11 slopes 8 lifts,
Cheonmasan 4 slopes 7 lifts,
Daemyeong Vivaldi 13 slopes 10 lifts
Gangchon 9 slopes 6 lifts,
Jisan 7 slopes 4 lifts,
Muju 26 slopes 13 lifts,
Phoenix Park 13 slopes 9 lifts,
Seongwoo 21 slopes 9 lifts,
Yangji 7 slopes 6 lifts
Yongpyeong 31 slopes 15 lifts

TURKEY

If Turkey's human rights record wasn't as bad as it is, it would be far easier to recommend a visit to this little talked of winter sports destination. Most people who visit this massive country do so only in the summer months, and most never venture from the main tourist destinations. Outside the normal tourist traps Turkey can be a hostile place. However, Turkey is an amazing country with spectacular mountains. What you will experience in Turkey is a mixture of good freeriding on mountain slopes that will offer all levels something to take on. Advanced riders will need to find out from locals where the best off piste is and see if you can hire the services of a local mountain guide. Like all mountains, Turkeys peaks can be very dangerous so extreme caution should be taken. Ski or snow- board patrols are not common and especially not in remote areas. Still for those who can afford it, there are options to go heli-boarding

with a guide. Turkey's resorts, which although they're great value for money are also very primitive and not big with only a few marked out trails and poor mountain facilities Off the slopes resorts services are very basic. Where there are slope services, they are surprisingly very good with hotels, restaurants, and bars on the slopes allowing for plenty of doorstep snowboarding. The one big feature about Turkey and what it has to offer is the cost of things, 'Cheap', making Turkey better than many parts of Europe. Travel to Turkey should pose no real problems. It would be a good idea to check with your local travel centre to see which companies offer winter package deals. Onward travel from airports and train stations may prove to be the trickiest of all your tasks. But give it a go as Turkey, despite its well documented faults, is well worth a visit for a snowboard holiday.

ULUDAG

Located south east of the Istanbul, is the biggest resort in Turkey boasting high altitude riding, heli-boarding and a good lift system. This small resort is also the playground for Turkeys rich. The 16 miles of pistes are well located to the resort with a number of hotels on the slopes allowing for convenient doorstep riding on a daily basis. In general this is a resort that offers mainly inter- mediate easy going freeriders a simple time. And although there are a number of black steeps up on the Zivre Peak area, Uludag will not hold the attention of adrenaline seekers for too long.

Freeriders are presented with a mountain that offers the chance of riding some okay off piste On the **Kusaklikaya** area, reached off the Kusaklikaya chair lift. There's also the chance 10 shred through trees and ride some decent red runs at speed especially the trail that descents from the Zirve summit. Here the runs start out as a fast open black before descending into a red and tamer blue to the base, but be prepared for a 400 metre hike.

Freestylers will have to make do with getting air from the natural hits, as no permanent pipe exists. However, there are some really good gully's to ride up. Log freaks will also find some wood to grind.

Carvers will be able to stretch themselves on wide open pisted runs which offer a mixture of fast reds on the Kusaklikaya area and blues on the Beluv area.

Beginners are best staying on the Beluv area, which has some good novice runs reached by chair or drag lift. Note, that the easy slopes can get busy at weekends but like the rest of the mountain, are crowd free on week days.

Uludag is a match for many foreign resorts, boasting good slope side hotels and a number of okay places to eat and drink. Although this is a place that caters for Turkeys high earners, it's still a very affordable place that has a lively night scene and is well worth a visit.

TAIWAN

Invented grass skiing, so lets leave them to it. They also produce hi-Tec boarding wear, goggles etc

UKRAINE

5 resorts, capital Kiev, currency Hryvnia

VENEZUELA

Capital Caracas, Currency Bolivar,
Resort **Merida** 4765 meters, 4 lifts, runs 2km

5 OUT OF 10

No hype, just a relaxed place to ride

pic - Andalo Tourism

I
ITALY

2150M
TOP LIFT

%
OF BEGINNER
TO EXPERT
RUNS

60KM
PISTES

29

1100M
VERTICAL

4

67

1050M
FIRST LIFT

NUMBER OF RUNS: 24
LONGEST RUN: 5km (3.1miles)
TOTAL LIFTS: 18
1 Gondola, 16 chairs, 1 drags
CAPACITY (people per hour): 24,000
LIFT TIMES: 8.30am to 4.00pm
MOUNTAIN CAFES: 10

AVERAGE SNOWFALL:1m
SNOWMAKING: 90% of slopes

WINTER PERIODS: Dec to April
Lift Passes Day 29 euros, 2 Days 51.5
euros, 6 Days 135.5 euros
Board Schools
Altopiano ski schools has snowboard
lessons

FREERIDE 50%
Lots of trees & good off-piste
FREESTYLE 10%
A Terrain park & a half-pipe
CARVING 40%

Andalo Tourism
Piazza Paganella, 2,
Andalo. I38010
Tel: ++39 (461) 585836
Web: www.paganella.net
Email: info@paganella.net

Bus
Trento (32 km) or Mezzocorona (17 km)
Train
Trento (32 km) or Mezzocorona (17 km)
Car
Highway A 22 - Brennero Modena, take
San Michele All'Adige exit (km 18)
Fly
90 minutes from Verona airport.

NEW

New Stuff
2003/4 New Chairlift "Teresat"

Andalo lies at the base of the **Brenta Dolomite** mountain range just north of the city of Verona, which is also the gateway city for air transfer being only an hour and a half away. The towns of **Andalo**, **Fai della Paganella** and **Molveno**, form the **Paganella ski area** with over the 60 kilometres of marked out runs. It may not have the greatest annual snow record when the snow does fall; it provides a mountain that allows for some fine off-piste riding which includes lots of tight tree runs. Should the real snow not fall, then the resort boasts at least 90% snowmaking coverage on its pistes. The fact that this place is not the most famous resort may be its saving grace, because while some of the bigger and more popular destinations attract hordes of piste lovers, Andalo is left relatively crowd free and un-spoilt. The resorts history dates back many years yet this place is not an old fashioned out dated dump, on the contrary, the resorts management are constantly spending large sums of money keeping the mountain facilities up to date. In general the resort is split between being good for novices and intermediate riders. Advanced riders are not blessed with to many steep sections but that said, there are a number of hair raising descents to test the best. All the slopes are easily reached from the village via the main gondola. Once up the slopes you will be able to get around with ease, and for those who hate drag lifts, you'll find most of the runs are reached by chair lifts with a chair possible to the top section at 2125m.

FREERIDERS will be pleased to find that Andalo is actually a good place to ride with a number of riding options on offer. There are lots of tight trees to shred as well as a number of scary drops and fast steeps. FREESTYLERS will also find Andalo a cool place. There is a halfpipe on occasions but its not always maintained. Local riders often construct their own hits and session them before moving on to try out some of the natural air terrain which is in abundance all over the mountain. CARVERS have lots of wide open spots where it is possible to lay out some big turns on runs that are well pisted on a daily basis. BEGINNERS can start out on the easy slopes around the village area before heading up the mountain where you will find some excellent novice trails from the top station down

to the mid section. The local ski school offer snowboard lessons and board hire is available in the village.

THE TOWN. **Andalo** is a basic and simple village that offers its visitors a high standard of good facilities. There are a number of good hotels with **accommodation** available next to the slopes. Around the village you will find shops, a sports centre, an ice ring and a swimming pool. There is a **night-club** and a couple of bars but don't expect a lot of action as night times are relaxed and basic.

Bardonecchia is not only a small fashionable mountain town and not only a popular all year round holiday destination, but also rated in the top ten of Italy's resorts. Skiers have been flocking to these slopes for many years bringing with them all the razzle dazzle of the Italian ski world, indeed one of Italy's past Kings was said to be a regular visitor to this part of the Susa valley. As a town, this place has been around since the time of the Romans and although a lot of what you find here is old, clapped out and in need of immediate repair, the place can still cut the mustard with a well set out series of mountain slopes that are connected by some twenty nine lifts. The 140 kilometres of marked out

pic - Bardoncchia Tourism

I
I
T
A
L
Y

pistes cover a series of mountain faces that are split either side of the valley floor, and take in the hamlets of Campo Smith, Melezet and Jafferau. The main runs on the slopes of Bardonecchia will suite all levels but in the main are best for intermediates. Campo Smith and Melezet are pretty evenly split between beginners and intermediates, but one thing that is common with all the areas are the lift queues, which at weekends and over holidays can be stupidly long.

FREERIDERS will find that this is a fairly ordinary place to ride with nothing much to entice you back. However, up on the Jafferau area, which is only five minutes bus shuttle bus from Bardonecchia, you will find a nice big snow bowl and some cool backcountry spots along with some fast steeps.

FREESTYLERS. first impressions of the terrain and the opportunities for getting air, will not be good. There is a pipe and park, but it's not well maintained unless there's a competition running, so its best to look out for more natural hits for getting air.

CARVERS are the ones who should be most at home here, especially if you are only looking for gently descents on which to lay out some easy lines. Most of the slopes are well pisted and make for good carving, some of which can be done at speed.

BEGINNERS have a resort that is well suited to their needs. At Campo Smith and Melezet there are two large nursery areas but be warned, they do get very busy with novice skiers. Note also that this area operates a lot of old drag lifts.

THE TOWN

Bardonecchia is a mountain town that provides a high level of good services although not a cheap place. There is a good choice of hotels, apartments, chalets and B&B's to choose from with rates that are mostly on the high side. Around the town, or within close proximity, there are varying attractions from skating to bowling; the town also has a good selection of shops and banks. Restaurants are also plentiful but night life is some what lame.

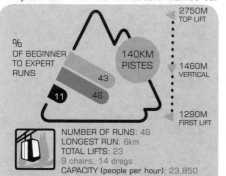

%
OF BEGINNER
TO EXPERT
RUNS

2750M
TOP LIFT

140KM
PISTES

1460M
VERTICAL

43

11   46

1290M
FIRST LIFT

NUMBER OF RUNS: 49
LONGEST RUN: 6km
TOTAL LIFTS: 23
9 chairs, 14 drags
CAPACITY (people per hour): 23,850
LIFT TIMES: 8.30am to 4.30pm

AVERAGE SNOWFALL
Unknown
SNOWMAKING:
15%

WINTER PERIODS:
Dec to April
Lift Passes
1 Day 27, 2 Days 47.5, 5 Days 118

FREERIDE 40%
A few trees & ok off-piste
FREESTYLE 10%
1 dodgy terrain park & pipe
CARVING 50%

Piazza Europa 15.
Bardonecchia
Tel - ++39 (0) 122 99137
Fax - ++39 (0) 122 902266
Web: www.bardonecchiaski.com
Email: colomion@bardonecchiaski.com

Train
Turin (Torino-Bussoleno-Bardonecchia)
Car
A32 Turin to Bardonecchia to Frejus
exit ss24
Fly
Turin 1 1/4 hours away 90km.

211

5 OUT OF 10 — Basic but okay

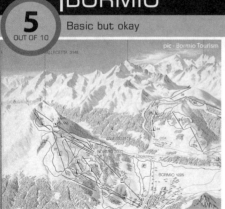

pic - Bormio Tourism

% OF BEGINNER TO EXPERT RUNS — 37, 45, 18

50KM PISTES

3012M TOP LIFT
1787M VERTICAL
1225M FIRST LIFT

NUMBER OF RUNS: 11
LONGEST RUN: 6km
TOTAL LIFTS: 17 - 3 Cable-cars, 7 chairs, 6 drags, 1 Magic carpet
CAPACITY (people per hour): 13,500
LIFT TIMES: 8.30am to 4.30pm

AVERAGE SNOWFALL:3m
SNOWMAKING: 40% of slopes

WINTER PERIODS: Dec to April
Lift Passes
Alta Valtellina ski area:
Day 31 euros, 5 day 154
Season pass 472 euros

FREERIDE 45%
Lots of trees & good off-piste
FREESTYLE 5%
No terrain park & a half-pipe
CARVING 50%

Tourist Office Bormio
Via Roma 131-B. Bormio 123032
Tel: ++39 (0) 349 903 300
Web: www.bormioonline.com
Email: info@bormioonline.com

Bus
From Millan take the A801 bus operate by Società Trasporti Pubblici Sondrio, tel: 0342/511212. Takes 4 hours.
Train
Train services are possible to Tirano which is 20 minutes away.
Car
Drive via Milan, head north via the towns of Lecco, Sondrio and Tirano, along the A38 to Bormio.
Fly
Fly to Milan airport, 4 hours away. Ryanair have flights to Bergamo, 170km away (its 50km from Milan, but its sold as Milan)

Bormio dates back hundreds of years and it's quite possible that the Romans who built an ancient spa town near here could have actually been the first to shred the slopes in their tin hats. However, Bormio as we know it today is rated very highly in Italy, with it's modern roots going back to the early sixties when the resort started dragging punters up its mainly intermediate all-round terrain. Bormio is a fairly busy place, with overkill in some very sad all in one ski suits. The ski world does a lot of racing on the slopes here; Bormio hosted the 1985 World Championships, and is doing the same in 2005 which suggests that there must be something on offer. Italian skiers like this place a lot, as do Germans and quite a lot of Brits. This means the slopes do become very clogged up at weekends and over holiday periods. Lift passes also provide access to the resorts of Santa Caterina (40km pistes) and San Colombano (30km pistes) creating the Alta Valtellina ski area, but the areas are only linked via ski-buses.

FREERIDERS have a mountain that is not extensive especially for advanced riders. There is some good off piste freeriding with powder bowls and trees to check out. The best stuff reached from the Cima Bianca, where the runs start off steep and mellow out to test the best. Don't bother hitting this stuff in hards, you'll regret it as this section is soft boot only terrain.
FREESTYLERS wanting to get big air will not find a great deal, but there are plenty of natural hits. The resort doesn't have a pipe or park, the nearest is 10 minutes away at Passo Dello Stelvio (linked by a shuttle bus). The Stelvio glacier, the largest in Europe, offers the opportunity to snowboard during the summer.
CARVERS will find that Bormio is an excellent place for any level and the 9 mile run from the top station down to the village provides plenty of time to get those big carves in. It's perfect for riders who want to see what it's like linking turns and by the time you hit the bottom, you'll know for sure.
BEGINNERS will find the slopes at Bormio ideal for basics and excellent for progression. What's more, all the easy stuff can be reached without tackling a drag lift.

THE TOWN
Bormio is a rather strange affair, but nevertheless a very rustic and Italian place. **Accommodation** is offered in a range of locations, with the choice of staying on or near the slopes. **Around town**, you soon notice how glitzy things are however, staying here can be done on a tight budget if you leave out dining in fancy restaurants: seek out one of the cheap pizza joints. Night-life is nothing to get excited about; in fact it's pretty dull but still boozy.

CANAZEI

Big linked area in Fassa Valley.

Canazei forms part of what is know as the **Dolomiti Superski**, which is said to the largest ski area in the world providing over 1200 kilometres of ridable terrain. What ever the merits of this claim one thing is for sure, and that is this place has got a lot going for it and will make a two weeks stay well worth the effort. Located along the **Fassa Valley**, of the Sella Ronda, Canazei is the largest of the cluster of villages that make up this area, with lifts that link it to **Campitello, Mazzin, Alba** to name but a few. Canazei, which is a sizeable town, sits at the base of the mountain with access up to the

pic - Canazei Tourism

slopes having to be made by gondola and then on up by a large cable car. The first gondola ride up is often only possible after a long wait, as it's the only lift out of the town up to the slopes, unless you are in Campitello where they have a cable car to take you up. Generally this is a place that suits intermediate riders but, with such a vast area to explore, every level of rider should find something to test them. The terrain features are a mixture of rugged gullies to wide berth carving slopes on a mountain that has a fairly average annual snow record and at a resort which the operates between December and April, which is a tad short when one thinks of the vast size of the area in general.

FREERIDERS are in for a bit of a treat here simply by the very fact that there is so much terrain to explore. If you can't have a good time here you should think about becoming a monk. The area is riddled with interesting terrain from chutes to trees to powder stashes. However, one major disappointment is the lack of challenging steeps for expert riders to perform on.

FREESYLERS should be able to enjoy this place as much as any other style of rider. There a lots of big drop off's and plenty of natural hits for gaining maximum air. The resort also builds a halfpipe, but it's not very well maintained nor is there a decent terrain park to play in.

CARVERS have acres and acres of well groomed tracks to speed down with some sizeable runs that allow for carving from the top to the bottom. The longest run in the area is over six and a half miles long (11km) which will get the thighs pumping.

BEGINNERS can't fail here, the place has lots of good nursery slopes and plenty of easy to negotiate intermediate runs to try out once you have mastered the basics. Note though that Canazei may only have a few drag lifts, but the Dolomiti Superski area has over a 130.

THE TOWN
Canazei is town that has over 10,000 tourist beds with loads of hotels and apartments to choose from, and although there is plenty of lodging close to the slopes, this is not a cheap place. However, the town has loads of restaurants and bars offering some very lively nightlife.

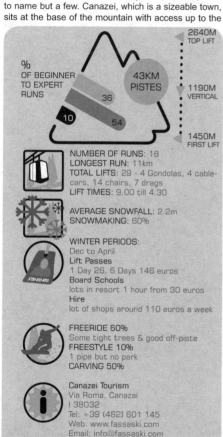

% OF BEGINNER TO EXPERT RUNS

43KM PISTES

36
10
54

2640M TOP LIFT

1190M VERTICAL

1450M FIRST LIFT

NUMBER OF RUNS: 18
LONGEST RUN: 11km
TOTAL LIFTS: 29 - 4 Gondolas, 4 cable-cars, 14 chairs, 7 drags
LIFT TIMES: 9.00 till 4.30

AVERAGE SNOWFALL: 2.2m
SNOWMAKING: 60%

WINTER PERIODS:
Dec to April
Lift Passes
1 Day 26, 6 Days 146 euros
Board Schools
lots in resort 1 hour from 30 euros
Hire
lot of shops around 110 euros a week

FREERIDE 60%
Some tight trees & good off-piste
FREESTYLE 10%
1 pipe but no park
CARVING 50%

Canazei Tourism
Via Roma, Canazai
I 38032
Tel: +39 (462) 601 145
Web: www.fassaski.com
Email: info@fassaski.com

Bus
daily bus from train station
Train
Trento,Bolzano and Ora are the nearest
Car
Main road to resort is the A22
Fly
3 hours from Munich airport. also close is Verona

ITALY

213

5 OUT OF 10

Beter food than boarding, unless you're fond of skating

Cervinia is set under the 4478 meters that is the Matterhorn. Truly one of the worlds most beautiful mountains, and if you can handle a walk you can board on its flanks. The town has a pleasant feel with a few poseurs mincing up a down the main street but nothing to bad. The resort is placed at the top of the Aosta Valley and links up with the extortionate resort of Zermatt, so if you want to board an exclusive resort without the cost then Cervinia's for you. Although it's never been anti board it has been slow in making boarders feel at home, last year they opened a new park and even sell a cheaper day pass just to access the park area 21 euros. Overall it's a fine place to take a group holiday and if you've only boarded in France before then you'll find it a laid back place with some friendly locals, well you're in Italy after all.

pic - Cervinia Tourism

FREERIDERS Cervinia is a good place to board for the intermediate, it's a little flat in places to get the heart thumping of an advanced rider, and the novice may find themselves hopping along the flat a little to much to put up with. Seeing your mates disappear over that rise while you come to a halt is a quick way to piss off even the calmest of beginners. The pistes are well maintained and are easily viewed, so you can see the best spots from the lifts. If you want off piste then get your thinking head on and you can find some good routes. There's some great little spots and if you can't find them ask a local. If you get bored head over to Zermatt, or if you have the cash get a Helicopter.

FREESTYLERS will find the new Indian Park good for some big hits, the pipes ok and there's a few small hits to learn on. If you have a good look round you will find some good rock drops, find the right one and you could get a photo of you flying across the Matterhorn.

CARVERS will get a little moist when they sit in their first chair over these slopes. There wide and flat and the 22 km red run, Valtournenche, is the place to carve long and hard, while the blacks down into the village are cool. The pistes are never packed although they are busy during holidays.

BEGINNERS, the place to get your first bruises is up at the Plan Maison, which is reached by a cable-car. Be prepared to tackle some drag lifts in order to get to the easy flats, which also come with a heavy dose of ski schools. The runs rise up from the village at three main points and apart from a few areas, the lower sections are not beginner friendly, although there is a blue that leads down giving novices the chance to ride home.

THE TOWN

With fresh snow it almost feels like a real alpine town but as the snow melts so does its charm. There are some really uninspired concrete blobs which they call hotels but on the whole it's a pleasant enough place to stay. Cervinia has plenty of affordable apartments and hotels to stay in, with easy access to the slopes a common feature. Italians know their so theres a big choice of affordable restaurants and mountain cafes. Theres some lively bars and a few reasonable piste side café bars, check out the *Dragon* for a beer or the *dodge L'Etoile* disco to check out the rich Italian skirt. Large tour groups do stay here but it has a good mix of nationalities so never feels mobbed.

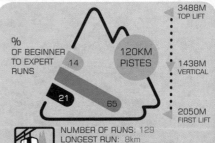

%
OF BEGINNER
TO EXPERT
RUNS — 14

120KM PISTES

21 — 65

3488M TOP LIFT
1438M VERTICAL
2050M FIRST LIFT

NUMBER OF RUNS: 129
LONGEST RUN: 8km
TOTAL LIFTS: 20 - 2 Gondolas, 2 Cable-cars, 10 chairs, 6 drags
CAPACITY (people per hour): 28,500
LIFT TIMES: 8.30am to 4.30pm

AVERAGE SNOWFALL:10m
SNOWMAKING: 25% of slopes

WINTER PERIODS: Oct to May
SUMMER PERIODS: June to Sept
Lift Passes
1 Day 32 euros, 6 days 170 euros
with zermatt 42 euros and 206 euros
Board School
Private around 30 euros hour
Hire
Board & Boots around 150 euros a week

FREERIDE 55%
Lots of trees & good off-piste
FREESTYLE 15%
A terrain park & a half-pipe
CARVING 30%

Cervina Tourist Office
Via Carrel 29, I11021, Breuil-Cervinia.
Asota
Tel: ++39 (0) 166 949 086
Web: www.cervinia.it
Email: info@sportepromozione.it

Train
to Chatillon, which is 20 minutes away.
Car
via Geneva, head south on the A40, via the Mont Blanc Tunnel. Take the A5 and turn off at Chatillon on to 406
Fly
Fly to Geneva airport, 2 1/2 hours away
Or Turin which is 200km away

ITALY

CLAVIERE

7
OUT OF 10

Okay linked area.

Claviere is said to be Italy's oldest resort, and judging by its appearance its easy to see why, not that is look is a mark of what is on offer here. Because this happens to be a decent and popular resort that is just ten minutes away from the French resort of Montgenevre. Both resorts also form part of the ski circuit known as the **Milky Way** which offers over 400km of marked out pistes and takes in the resorts of **Sauze D'Oulx, Sansicario, Sestriere** and **Cesana** all of which are linked by an array of lifts totalling some 91, with a lift access height of over 2820 metres possible at Sestriere. Claviere has long been a

pic - Claviere Tourism

% OF BEGINNER TO EXPERT RUNS

50KM PISTES

26

14

60

2300M
TOP LIFT

950M
VERTICAL

1350M
FIRST LIFT

NUMBER OF RUNS: 19
LONGEST RUN: 6km
TOTAL LIFTS: 11
4 chairs, 7 drags
LIFT TIMES: 9.00 till 4.30

AVERAGE SNOWFALL: 8m
SNOWMAKING: 10%

WINTER PERIODS:
Dec to April
Lift Passes
6 days 123 euros
Board Schools
Plenty of Italian ski schools
Hire
Board & Boots from 18 euros a day

FREERIDE 55%
Some tight trees & good off-piste
FREESTYLE 20%
A terrain park & a half-pipe
CARVING 25%

Claviere Tourism
Claviere I 10050
Tel: +39 (122) 878 856
Web: www.claviere.it

Bus
Everyday from Turin to Claviere and during weekends to Briançon
Train
Oulx statio then take a bus
Car
A32 Turin to Bardonecchia to Frejus exit Oulx
Fly
90 minutes from Turin airport. 97 km

popular resort and one that attracts a large number of skiers from all over Italy and from neighbouring France. This often makes the place very busy, especially at weekends, however, don't let that put you off, because once you get up on to the slopes, time spent in lift queues are generally minimal. Claviere, and its French neighbour **Montgenevre**, are just minutes apart and you can easily board between the two resorts on the same lift pass, which can also be used for the rest of the Milky Way circuit. The type of terrain is much the same where ever you choose to ride and in the main will favour intermediate freeriders the most.

FREERIDERS would be hard pushed to ride all of the terrain on offer here during a weeks visit. The slopes offer a good mixture of trees, off-piste powder and pisted runs. Advanced riders may only find a few decent black runs at Claviere, however, within the Milky Way circuit, there is an abundance of expert level terrain to try out.
FREESTYLERS will now be pleased to hear that there is now a snowboard park and half pipe here, which has only come about in the last few seasons. However, the area boast lots of good natural freestyle terrain where air heads can go high off banks and rollers dotted all over the place.
CARVERS looking for long and wide open slopes will be happy to find that this place has lots of them. With the vast majority of the runs graded red or blue carvers who like to glide around at a leisurely pace will love both Claviere and the rest of the Milky Way. But note, there are a lot of flat spots and some traversing is called for between runs, so expect some thigh burning moments.
BEGINNERS will have no problem coping with this place. Blue runs stretch from the summit's to the base areas allowing for some fine easy riding. But with seven drag lifts to contend with, getting around can be a bit tricky for drag lift virgins.

THE TOWN
Off the slopes the resort is full of character and duty free shops. The village is not big and getting around the place is easy. The choice of lodgings is rather small, but options to sleep near the slopes are plentiful. Nightlife is very tame with only a few restaurants and bars to chose from.

ITALY

5 OUT OF 10 — Okay but dull village

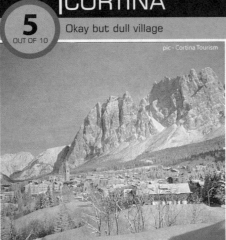

pic - Cortina Tourism

%
OF BEGINNER
TO EXPERT
RUNS

140KM PISTES

33

5

62

3243M TOP LIFT

2020M VERTICAL

1224M FIRST LIFT

NUMBER OF RUNS: 52
LONGEST RUN: 9km
TOTAL LIFTS: 51 - 6 Cable-cars, 29 chairs, 16 drags
CAPACITY (people per hour): 60,000
LIFT TIMES: 8.30am to 4.30pm

AVERAGE SNOWFALL:4m
SNOWMAKING: 90% of slopes

WINTER PERIODS: Dec to April
SUMMER PERIODS: None
Lift Passes
1 Day pass 32 to 37 euros
6 Days 160 to 182 euros
both super ski pass's
Board School
private from 36 euros/hr
6 morning lessons from 300 euros

FREERIDE 50%
Some trees & off-piste
FREESTYLE 10%
No terrain park or half-pipe
CARVING 40%

Cortina Tourist Board
Pizza San Francesso,
8 Cortina d'Ampezzo
Tel: +39 (0) 436 3231
Web: www.dolomitisuperski.com/cortina
Email: cortina@dolomiti.org

Train
to Calalzo Pieve, 20 minutes away.
Car
Drive via Venice, head north on the A27 via Ponte Nelle Alpi. Then take the 51 via Tai di Cadore and onto Cortina. 96 Miles.
Fly
Venice airport 2 hours away 162km.

I T A L Y

Every country has a place that the rich, famous and Royals head for, just to be seen 'on the piste' and to get a picture wearing sad clothing for the cover of Hello! Magazine. Enter Cortina, for this is one of those places, with so many balcony posers lying around outside restaurants that the slopes are left quiet. This allows snowboarders space to roam and explore the terrain. Cortina, located in the northern reaches of the Italian **Dolomites**, is an ex-Olympic resort, whose area is made up of two large mountain plateaus that rise up around the village. On one side you have an area called Faloria, which connects up to Forcella, and rises to a height of 2950m. On the other side of the village lies the slopes of Tofana. **Tofana** is not connected by lift to the other areas, but can be reached via a cable car from the town or by the local bus to **Pocol**. The terrain here is pretty good and will suite all. Advanced riders get a mountain to challenge them to the limit and keep them interested for a week or even two, while intermediates will have ample opportunity to brush up on their skills and to progress nicely on a series of good slopes.

FREERIDERS will find that the most challenging runs are located down from the Tofana, which rises to 3243m and is accessed by cable car. From the summit you'll find plenty of stuff to check out, offering some good powder riding.

FREESTYLERS may not get man-made hits, but not to worry as there are plenty of natural ones with some cool drop offs and big banks to catch air from on both mountain sections. The Tofana area has the best stuff though.

CARVERS; the Sella Ronda trail is definitely worth a visit, as is the Canellone which is a two planker's race run and the area to cut the snow in style, but not for wimps.

BEGINNERS can progress here on good easy slopes, with the best stuff around the mid section of the Tofana. These can be reached by chair (rather than drag) lifts.

THE TOWN
Cortina is a large place, with silly priced hotels and apartment style accommodation located mostly near or on the slopes. You can always try the Bobsleigh ride for 75mph fun. Around the village are various food joints offering the usual Italian fare. The evenings are pretty boring here and the rich only make it very glitzy. However, it's not all gloom as you can spend the evening mocking the rich and mine sweeping their drinks: they won't even notice because they're too busy posing.

7 OUT OF 10

Great resort, as long as you're not a very adventurous boarder

Courmayeur lies on the opposite side of the Mont Blanc valley and only a stone's throw away from the top French resort of Chamonix which is a short drive back up through the Mont Blanc Tunnel. Courmayeur, a high level resort gives access to slopes that can be ridden by all and generally, this is a good place to spend a week or two. However, with its mixture of traditional Italian architecture and its modern resort offerings, Courmayeur is a destination that attracts millions of British skiers and other foreign nationals every year. They then copy their Italian counterparts by cladding themselves in horrid expensive ski wear and clogging up the slopes to often bursting point. The village is well spread out, but there is no real chance of leaping out of the nest, ollieing over a balcony and landing in a lift queue: you are going to have to do a bit of walking in order to take the cable car up to the slopes. The terrain will please intermediate carvers, but bore advanced freeriders. Be warned, every man and his dog hits the slopes at weekends and holidays. The main thing you notice is the amount of plate bindings and ski boots that there are about, as this is a carver's pose place, although many don't know what to pose in (ski boots are a no-no people). Top Italian female pro Martina Magenta hails from Courmayeur and can often be seen carving up the slopes. If you ride here in summer, the best time to come is in May or June when the snow is still good and not too rutted or over slushy.

ITALY

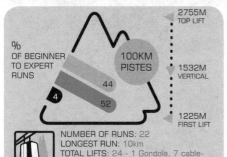

% OF BEGINNER TO EXPERT RUNS

100KM PISTES

44
4
52

2755M TOP LIFT

1532M VERTICAL

1225M FIRST LIFT

NUMBER OF RUNS: 22
LONGEST RUN: 10km
TOTAL LIFTS: 24 - 1 Gondola, 7 cable-cars, 8 chairs, 8 drags
LIFT TIMES: 8.30am to 4.30pm
MOUNTAIN CAFES: 10

AVERAGE SNOWFALL:
7m
SNOWMAKING:
15%

WINTER PERIODS: Dec to April
SUMMER PERIODS: June to Oct
Lift Passes
1 Day 32 euro, 6 Days from 150 euros
Board Schools
5 days of lessons 110 euros
Hire
Board & Boots from 25 euros a day
Heliboarding
Contact Societa delle Guide de Courmayeur

FREERIDE 40%
Some tight trees & good off-piste
FREESTYLE 10%
Just natural stuff
CARVING 50%

Tourist Office Courmayeur
Monte Bianco, Pizzale 3
Courmayeur. I11013
General info: ++39 (0) 165 842 060
Web: www.courmayeur.net
Email: info@courmayeur.net

FREERIDING here is pretty damn good, with some cool terrain to hit and the possibility of some trees to cut in the lower section. If it's powder and off piste riding you want, then Courmayeur is not the mega outlet like it's close French neighbour, but there is some good stuff to be had on steeps and trees down from the Cresta D'Arp. If you take the Mont Blanc cable car, you can gain access to the Vallee Blanche and ride into Chamonix. Although you will need to get the bus back, it'll be worth it.

FREESTYLERS here make do with the natural hits as there is no park or pipe to ride. You can however, get big air and find enough to jib off, eg snow cannons, logs, stair rails, ski instructors, there's plenty. You'll also find plenty snow built up in lumps pushed to the side of runs or covering small trees and small mounts etc.

CARVERS who like to stay on the pistes will find loads of well pisted runs to content themselves with, especially the areas under the Bertolini chair lift.

BEGINNERS who decide to give Courmayeur a try won't be disappointed; it's a perfect place to learn,

217

although the slopes can often be far too busy, leading to a few collisions. Novices should head for the runs off the Checrouit cable car, where you'll find some nice easy slopes to try out your first toe and heel side turns amongst the ski crowds, taking out the stragglers as you go.

THE TOWN

Off the slopes, Courmayeur is a busy, stretched out place, with a lot going on. Most of the time the village plays host to package tour groups and although this helps to keep prices realistic, it does mean you have to rub shoulders with a lot of idiots. The village has a host of sporting attractions with the usual resort style swimming pools, ice rinks and fitness outlets. There is also an overdose of Italian style boutiques, selling expensive designer wear, but alas, there are no decent snowboard shops.

Accommodation is very good here. The town can sleep 20,000 visitors with lodging close to the slopes and in the town centre. You can choose to bed down in one of the hotels, or stay in one of the self catering apartment blocks which can accommodate large groups of riders. There is also a number of reasonably priced bed and breakfast homes to choose from.

Food wise, Courmayeur does a good job fattening up its visitors with the usual option to pig out in a few pizza restaurants. There are also a number of basic holiday tourist style eateries offering funny sounding traditional Italian dishes. However, you can eat reasonably if you stick to the lower end pizza joints such as La Boite, but if you're feeling flush and want to dine, check out Pierre Alexis.

Night life in Courmayeur is late, loud and very boozy. Italians party hard here, but unfortunately so do a lot of apres skiers, who give the place a rowdy and low life feel to it. Popular places to check out are the Popas Pup, Bar Roma or The Red Lion, all of which are lively watering holes with a young party style crowd.

pic - Michael Vechi/Courmayeur Tourism

SUMMARY

Not a bad place, with some good carving but basic freeriding. Great for beginners apart from over crowded novice slopes. Good local services. Overall this is an expensive resort but also a good value one.

On the slopes: Very good
Off the slopes: Okay
Money wise: Overall this is an expensive resort but also a good value one.

5 OUT OF 10

Okay alpine style resort, with a pretty good half-pipe

Folgarida is a fairly ordinary purpose built resort that links closely with the more famous resort of Madonna di Campiglio and the less famous resort of Marilleva. Collectively the area boasts over 260 kilometres of lift linked piste, however, on its own Folgarida accounts for a small portion of the total area. Unlike many purpose built resorts in France and Italy, this place is not an ugly sham crammed with mountain tower blocks. What you get here is a well balanced alpine style retreat nestled between trees and great scenery. This is also a place that attracts riders who like things easy and with out the hustle and bustle of the rather more stuck up neighbour of Madonna di Campiglio. Folgarida doesn't have a great choice of runs with only a few north facing easy slopes and almost nothing for expert riders apart from one black trail that runs down from the main gondola at the mid section. However, what this resort does have is a very good modern lift system that is able to whisk thousands of visitors up to its slopes and onto the neighbouring areas, all of which share a joint lift pass. This resort on its own, would only take two days of your time, but as the place links nicely with its neighbours, a two week stay would be well worth it.

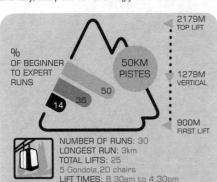

% OF BEGINNER TO EXPERT RUNS

50KM PISTES

2179M TOP LIFT

1279M VERTICAL

900M FIRST LIFT

50 · 36 · 14

NUMBER OF RUNS: 30
LONGEST RUN: 3km
TOTAL LIFTS: 25
5 Gondola,20 chairs
LIFT TIMES: 8.30am to 4.30pm

AVERAGE SNOWFALL:
Unknown
SNOWMAKING:
86%

WINTER PERIODS: Dec to April
Lift Passes
1 day from 22 euros
6 days from 118 euros
Board Schools
2 ski schools will give boarding lessons
Hire
a few shops, arond 20 euros a day

FREERIDE 45%
Some tight trees & good off-piste
FREESTYLE 10%
Terrain park & Halfpipe
CARVING 45%

Folgarida Tourism
38025 Folgarida di Dimaro
Tel. 0463/988400
Fax 0463/988450
web:www.ski.it

Bus
Dolomitibus tel 0039 437217111
Train
Trento 28 km Rovereto 18 km both with bus conections
Car
A22 Brennero Motorway exit Trento Centro, then along Fricca ss349
Fly
2hrs minutes from Verona airport. North is Bolzano airport.

pic -Folgarida Tourism

FREERIDERS don't have a great deal of adventurous terrain to explore directly at Folgarida, however, close by there is plenty of scope for shredding in and out trees or for riding across good off-piste powder fields and down some bumpy slopes. Unfortunately expert riders are the ones who are mostly let down the most here with only a few of the slopes graded as black or difficult. Intermediates on the other hand have the largest share of runs to ride, with an array of red runs that crisscross all over the slopes of Folgarida and Madonna di Campiglio and a couple of long ones on Marilleva area.

FREESTYLERS can either elect to ride the pipe and park located off the Bambi chair, or simply choose to ride around going off natural hits. Madonna's pipe is of a high standard especially when a competition is on.

BEGINNERS can come here knowing that they won't be disappointed. The resort is ideal for novices with an excellent selection of easy runs to try out, including good nursery areas that can be easily reached but are serviced by drag lifts.

THE TOWN
Folgarida is low key alpine resort with a good choice of local facilities all within walking distance of the slopes. There are affordable hotels, apartment blocks and chalets as well a few shops and an outdoor ice rink. Eating out and night life are both very low key but enjoyable none the less.

ITALY

219

FOPPOLO

5
OUT OF 10

Small and mixed

Foppolo is a simple resort that will appeal to visitors who like crowd free slopes but slopes with good annual snow fall. Like many purpose built resorts, Foppolo, which dates back as a ski resort many many years, is located at the foot of the mountain. As a purpose built resort, access to the slopes is easy and convenient with riding spread out over a number of connecting mountain areas with riding up to the summit of Montebello at 2100m and down to the small hamlet of Carona at 1100m. Much of the terrain on offer here is rated evenly between beginners and intermediates with only small amount of black advanced grade slopes. Despite the lack of challenging terrain, this is still a cool Italian hangout with out to many ski crowds messing up the slopes. Foppolo, has some 20 pisted runs serviced by a dozen lifts which are mainly drag lifts. The resort also links up with that of San Simone, but you need to take the 15 minute shuttle bus to reach its slopes as it doesn't link directly on snow. However, all the areas share a lift pass. Where ever you ride, what you will notice is the simplicity of the place and the ease in which to get around. You will also notice that the resort staff work hard at keeping the slopes well pisted and covered in artificial snow, when its needed, which is quite often.

FREERIDERS should be advised that this is not the most interesting place in terms of the diversity of terrain features. Much of the riding is set well above the tree line, however, there are some really nice bowls to shred through and a few okay off-piste spots to try out. From the summit point of Montebello, which is reached after a long drag lift ride, you can ride down a number of fast black trails that wind down a steep mountain face and are not to be taken lightly or you will end up in pain. At the bottom you can either elect to go back towards Montebello, or head on up in the opposite direction to the slopes of Carona where you will be able to try out a few more black runs.

FREESTYLERS won't enjoy this place that much. With no park or pipe air heads are left to either make their own hits or finding natural ones.

CARVERS who like long and wide open runs will find a number to keep them occupied with a few nice reds to check out and some long easy blues.

BEGINNERS have lots of easy runs to learn on starting with the nursery slopes which rise up directly from the resort centre. The first main cluster of blue runs are reached via a long chair lift which can be used to reach most of Foppolo easy runs. Access to Carona on snow is not possible for total novices.

THE TOWN

Accommodation in the resort is basic but convenient with lodging close to the slopes. The resort has a few shops, an ice rink, a few restaurants and a splattering of bars, but don't expect any happening nightlife.

pic -Foppolo Tourism

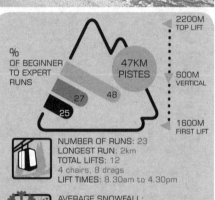

2200M
TOP LIFT

%
OF BEGINNER
TO EXPERT
RUNS

47KM
PISTES

600M
VERTICAL

27   48

25

1600M
FIRST LIFT

NUMBER OF RUNS: 23
LONGEST RUN: 2km
TOTAL LIFTS: 12
4 chairs, 8 drags
LIFT TIMES: 8.30am to 4.30pm

AVERAGE SNOWFALL:
Unknown
SNOWMAKING:
25%

WINTER PERIODS:
Dec to April
Lift Passes
1 day 23 euros, 6 days 100 euros
Board Schools
4 ski schools in town
Hire
Available in town

FREERIDE 50%
Few tree runs & little off-piste
FREESTYLE 5%
No park or pipe
CARVING 45%

Foppolo Tourism
web: www.foppoloski.it
Email: info@bremboski.it

Fly
2hrs from Verona or Milan airport.

pic - La Thuile Tourism

I T A L Y

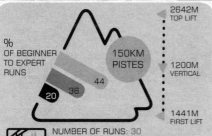

2642M
TOP LIFT

%
OF BEGINNER
TO EXPERT
RUNS

150KM
PISTES

1200M
VERTICAL

44
20 36

1441M
FIRST LIFT

NUMBER OF RUNS: 30
LONGEST RUN: 11km
TOTAL LIFTS: 17
1 cable-car, 10 chairs, 6 drags
LIFT TIMES: 8.30am to 4.30pm

AVERAGE SNOWFALL:
5m
SNOWMAKING:
23%

WINTER PERIODS: Dec to April
Lift Passes
1 day from 22 euros
6 days from 113 euros
Board Schools
1hr private from 26.5 euros
10 hours within one week 330 euros
Hire
Board & Boots 15 euros a day
or 65 euros 6 days
Heliboarding
Scuola di la Thuile 4-7 people you go to
Testa del Rutor @ 3486 meters and
board down to 1200 meters

FREERIDE 30%
Some tight trees & good off-piste
FREESTYLE 30%
Terrain park & Halfpipe
CARVING 40%

Tourist Office La Thule
Via Marcello Collomb, 3
11016 La Thuile, Italy
Tel. +39 0165 883049
Fax +39 0165 885196
Web: www.lathuile.it
Email: info@lathuile.it

La Thuile nestles a few miles down the road from its more famous cousin Courmayeur, but unlike it's neighbour, it is a far quieter resort. This is despite the fact that it has a good 53 miles plus of piste and even more off piste for all snowboarding styles and abilities. There is plenty to keep you occupied for a week or two. La Thuile is located in the Aosta Valley and links with La Rosiere. Collectively they provide over 100 miles (160km) of marked out and pisted terrain. This is not just a hard boot carvers resort, the wide open pistes, steeps and trees are there for everyone. The terrain lies at a height that helps to ensure good snow conditions prevail all season, backed up by snowmaking facilities if it does get thin. For those who like powder, there can be fresh snow on the high, north facing slopes even in April. For those who like tree runs, you'll find perfect snow conditions throughout the season. An important aspect of the resort is that it is very well served by chairlifts, which makes waiting in line extremely rare. Most of all, it gives the rider the possibility of reaching the most remote parts of the resort (where skiers are few and the fresh snow is untouched) without having to hike steep slopes, with your board. La Thuile offers all snowboarders a vast range of possibilities that include long off-pistes in fresh powder, black runs with steep vertical drops, large perfectly prepared slopes for those who love carving and a variety of cliffs, natural jumps and virgin slopes.

FREERIDERS have some good black runs to try out: the Diretta (which runs through the trees) is full on and will test those who think they know it all. There's also some cool freeriding to be had on the La Rosiere side, while those looking for off-piste will find it off the San Bernardo chair. However the real off-piste is best tackled by going heli-boarding which is offered here.

FREESTYLERS have a good pipe, which the local snowboard club help to look after. However, you may find that the abundance of natural hits dotted around both La Thuile and La Rosiere offer better air time.

221

wsg

LA THUILE

THE TOWN & GETTING THERE

CARVERS have a variety of great pisted slopes for laying out big carves on and most can be tackled at speed without having to negotiate too many sightseeing skiers.

BEGINNERS need to know that apart from a couple of small nursery slopes at the base, the main easy runs are located above the Les Suches area, which is served by chairlifts rather than all drags. However, slow learners will not be riding back into the village at the outset. To help get to grips with what snowboarding is about, why not take a few lessons with the local ski school? After all, they have been teaching snowboarding here for years and know their stuff.

THE TOWN
La Thuile is finally reached after a short drive up twisting and winding mountain road. On arrival, you are presented with a scenic and old Italian village with a hint of the new here and there. The main happenings are conveniently at the base of the slopes and straddle a large river. Visitors are made very welcome in La Thuile and local services cater very well for all your needs. Around the village you will find a few shops, places to pig out and one or two hotels with their own sporting facilities, such as a hotel swimming pool, gym and saunas. But other than that there is nothing major going on. Snowboard hire is best done from Ornella Sports +39 (0) 165 844 154.

Accommodation La Thuile is a relatively small resort with around 3000 beds, bunks or other things on which to kip on. However, what there is quite sufficient for a weeks stay with the option to lye out horizontally in bed on the slopes or within a short walk of the first lifts. A number of tour operators offer full holiday packages here, so some good package deals are available.

Food.As for eats, you can get all the usual Italian dishes here along with a selection of standard grade euro nosh. However, your choice of where to eat out is a bit limited on the whole. Still, that said, what is offered is good and you can eat very well here on a low budget. Restaurants of note are that of La Rascards for a choice of local dishes, or La Grotta which is known for its slices of pizza and pasta, although not the cheapest of places.

pic - La Thuile Tourism

Night life in La Thuile is very tame by Italian standards, so if you're the sort that likes to party hard all night long, this is not your resort. La Thuile is a very relaxed place and there is nothing much going on. Any so called action seems to be as the lifts close when there is a flurry of apre nonsense. Still you can enjoy a beer in the La Bricole bar.

pic - La Thuile Tourism

SUMMARY
An okay freeriders resort with some nice powder spots and trees to ride. Also good for carving but the slopes can be a bit tricky at the lower sections.
On the slopes: Very good
Off the slopes: Basic
Money wise: Not cheap but overall very affordable and well worth the money.

CAR
Drive to Geneva via Mont Blanc Tunnel. La Thule is 76 miles (122 km), about 2 1/4 hours.
*From Calais 583 miles (939 Km). Drive time is around 10 hours.
FLY
Fly to Turin and take a bus. Geneva international. Transfer time to resort 2 1/4 hours.
TRAIN
Trains to Pre-St-Didier (3 miles).
BUS
Bus services from Geneva airport are available on a daily basis as well as from Milan.

I
T
A
L
Y

LIMONE

Relatively quiet resort, some good freeriding when it snows.

Limone is located south of **Turin** and only a short distance from the French and Italian border. Limone is a traditional Italian town with a past that involves the railways. Today however, this relatively unknown holiday destination is a simple place that attracts summer and winter tourists all year round to sample its holiday attractions which include great mountains. The old sprawling town sits at the base of an impressive set of high peaks, with the 2344 metre summit of the **Cima Pepino Mountain** well within sight. The place is not widely known as a ski or snowboard destination outside of Italy which

pic-Limone Tourism

I T A L Y

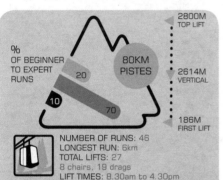

| 2800M TOP LIFT |
| **%** OF BEGINNER TO EXPERT RUNS |
| **80KM PISTES** |
| 20 |
| 2614M VERTICAL |
| 10 |
| 70 |
| 186M FIRST LIFT |

NUMBER OF RUNS: 46
LONGEST RUN: 6km
TOTAL LIFTS: 27
8 chairs, 19 drags
LIFT TIMES: 8.30am to 4.30pm

AVERAGE SNOWFALL:
Unknown
SNOWMAKING:
15%

WINTER PERIODS: Dec to April
Lift Passes
1 Day 29 euros, 3 days 76

FREERIDE 60%
A few trees & some off-piste
FREESTYLE 15%
No park or pipe
CARVING 25%

Assessorato al Turismo
Comune di Limone Piemonte
Via Roma 30
Tel. 0171 92.95.15
Fax 0171 92.95.05
Web: www.limonepiemonte.it
Email: iat@limonepiemonte.it

Train
Train services are possible to Limone Piemonte.
Car
from Turin (Torino) head south via Carmagnola, Cuneo, and Borgo S.Dalmazzo on the route 20 until you reach Limone.
Fly
Turin airport is 1 1/2 hours away.

can be a bit of a blessing as the place is not tainted with mass package ski tour groups. But on the down side, not being the most popular of places can often mean a lack of on-going resort development. Still, this may not be a big fancy resort boasting loads of steep challenging slopes, but you can nevertheless have a great time riding on slopes that can fill up with weekend visitors but are empty during the mid week periods. This is a simple resort that is suited to intermediate riders with very little to offer expert riders. Advanced riders will find some interesting terrain, but it won't take more than a few days to ride-out. The one big draw back about Limone is its annual snow record. Its fairly close proximity to the Mediterranean Sea means that this is not a resort blessed with heaps of regular snow.

FREERIDERS have a cool mountain to explore and should find Limone a pleasant surprise. There is a good choice of areas to ride that offers, tree riding, lots of gullies and uneven trails to descend down. Expert riders will find the Olimpica run a pleaser.

FREESTYLERS don't have any laid on facilities as such, the poor snow record prevents the annual building or maintaining of parks.

CARVERS who usually prefer miles of perfect well groomed trails, may be a bit disappointed. Most of the main runs are a bit choppy and not great cruising trails; that said you can still carve here.

BEGINNERS might well find that this resort is not for them. There are some good novice slopes but they are very limited and serviced by a host of drag lifts.

THE TOWN
Limone is an old town located within easy reach of the slopes. The town offers basic but affordable facilities with a good choice of hotels, apartment blocks and some bed and breakfast homes.

Good overall resort

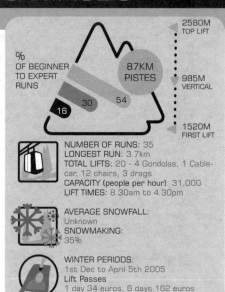

2580M
TOP LIFT

%
OF BEGINNER
TO EXPERT
RUNS

87KM
PISTES

985M
VERTICAL

16   30   54

1520M
FIRST LIFT

NUMBER OF RUNS: 35
LONGEST RUN: 3.7km
TOTAL LIFTS: 20 - 4 Gondolas, 1 Cable-car, 12 chairs, 3 drags
CAPACITY (people per hour): 31,000
LIFT TIMES: 8.30am to 4.30pm

AVERAGE SNOWFALL:
Unknown
SNOWMAKING:
35%

WINTER PERIODS:
1st Dec to April 5th 2005
Lift Passes
1 day 34 euros, 6 days 162 euros

FREERIDE 50%
Few tree runs & good off-piste
FREESTYLE 25%
Terrain park & a half-pipe
CARVING 25%

Madonna di Campiglio-Pinzolo-Val Rendena
Azienda per il Turismo S.p.A.
via Pradalago, 4
38084 Madonna di Campiglio (TN)
tel: +39.0465.442000
fax: +39.0465.440404
Web: www.campiglio.to
Email: info@campiglio.net

Fly
Verona airport 2 1/2 hours away 150km.
Train
Trento, a 25 minute transfer.
Car
via Verona, go north on A22 to the Mezzocorona Jct. Then take the A43 north and A42 south turning off at Dimaro and on to Madonna along the A239.

NEW

New for 04/05 Season
new 6-seat chairlift in Grostè area replaces the 2 old 2-seater chairlifts Grostè 1 & Grostè 2

Madonna Di Campiglio is one of the best resorts in the Dolomites and thankfully not tainted with too many cheap ski package tour groups, which helps to keep lift queues to almost zero. The pistes are relatively crowd free, although it should be said that Madonna does attract some of Italy's finest clientele. This well established ski haunt has now become a snowboarder's favourite, one that is trying really hard to satisfy boarders and it has to be said that it does a fairly good job. The old International Snowboard Federation used to stage a number of top events in Madonna, attracting many top riders. It's not just the snowboarding they come for, the parties go off as well, with top bands and DJ's playing at the side of the half-pipe. The ride area, which rises up around the resort, is linked with **Folgarida** and **Marillea**, giving a combined coverage of over 100 miles of extremely well groomed trails and some good off-piste. Much of the terrain will suit riders who are just getting to grips with their style and ability, but advanced riders with a few years under their belts will find it a little unchallenging in places, but still okay.

FREERIDERS should check out the areas at **Spinale**, where you'll find some good powder spots and some nice tree sections to blast through lower down. **Fortini** also offers a testing time.
FREESTYLERS like this place a lot and not just for the mega halfpipe (when an event is on) or the fun park and boardercross, located on **Groste area**. For those who like their hits natural, there are plenty of snow walls and steep hits to get air from.
CARVERS, the race run normally set aside for ski races, is the place for competent riders who want to show skiers how a mountain should be tackled at speed and with only two edges.
BEGINNERS will find Madonna is one of the best first timers resorts around, with lots of well set out easy runs, allowing for easy access and quick progression to more difficult terrain.

THE TOWN has plenty of eating and sleeping options, with affordable places to sleep close to the slopes. Around the town, there are heaps of things to do with a whole manner of attractions such as ice speedway circuit and waterfall climbs. **At night**, things can get very lively, going off big style and lasting well into the early hours of the morning. There is a good choice of bars and clubs but they are all a bit pricey.

I
T
A
L
Y

8 OUT OF 10

Small resort offering some fine intermediate but limited expert terrain.

Tonale is high altitude resort perched in a wide open expanse that is both snow sure and sunny. Without doubt this a cool place to visit, a resort that is both old and new in terms of the village and its development. The resorts is constantly improving and subsequently becoming more and more popular. But that popularity isn't a problem, lift queues are almost non existent and the piste never become cluttered up leaving lots of wide open runs to free of crowds. During the winter months

pic. Tonale 1200m

Tonale gets a good share of snow and should the real stuff be lacking then the resorts snowmaking facilities can cover over 40% of the marked out pistes. Should you want to do some summer riding then this place can also accommodate you with good riding possible up on the nearby **Presena Glacier** in the summer months. You can reach the glacier from Tonale by cable car, but the glacier only opens in the winter if the snow on the lower areas is lacking. Tonale offers great intermediate and beginner level riding with options to ride a long tree lined run between Tonale and the nearby resort of **Ponte di Legno**, although note that you can ride to Ponte di Legno, but you have to get a ski bus back. Both resorts share a joint lift pass, which is a modern hands free system whereby you pass through the lift gates with your pass still in your pocket. The lifts them self's are equally split between being chair lifts and drag lifts along with a cable car. All the lifts link well and even novices can get around with out having to use too many drag lifts.

FREERIDERS who like wide open pistes with long sweeping runs will love this place, but for those who crave steep gullies and like tight trees you will not be so impressed, but what ever your into, this is a good freeriders resort.

FREESTYLERS will need to make do with hitting natural jumps or building there own. There are however, lots of cool jumps including a number of drop ins of rock sections and lots of cool snow banks to fly high off.

CARVERS have a mountain that is simply fantastic. The wide open motorway style piste will let you ride fast and wide across runs that make carving a total joy. The 4 km trail to Ponte di Legno is a cool trail while the 3 km race runs will test the best.

BEGINNERS who can't learn how to ride here, can only be described as stupid because this place is one of the best resorts in Italy for novices. There are loads of easy to negotiate blue runs spread out over wide pisted areas with lots of nursery slopes all located close to the village centre.

THE TOWN. Tonale is a laid back resort with good hotels and apartment blocks. Around the village you will be able to get a cheap bed, a decent meal in one of the many restaurants, and have a simple but cheap night out.

I T A L Y

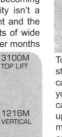

3100M TOP LIFT

% OF BEGINNER TO EXPERT RUNS

80KM PISTES

34

16

50

1216M VERTICAL

1884M FIRST LIFT

NUMBER OF RUNS: 29
LONGEST RUN: 4.5km
TOTAL LIFTS: 26 - 1 Gondola, 14 chairs, 10 drags, 1 other
LIFT TIMES: 8.30am to 4.30pm

AVERAGE SNOWFALL:
Unknown
SNOWMAKING:
40%

WINTER PERIODS:
Oct to May
SUMMER PERIODS:
June-Sep on the Presena Glacier
Lift Passes
1 Day 27.5 euros, 5 days 127

FREERIDE 65%
Lots of trees & good off-piste
FREESTYLE 15%
A Pipe but no real park
CARVING 20%

Passo Tonal Tourist Office
I-38020
Tel: 64 903 838
Web: www.passotonale.it
Email: tonale@valdisole.net

Train
to Male of the Trento-Mali Electric Railway. Passo Tonale can be easily reached by regular bus service. The nearest station of the State Railways is Mezzocorona.
Car
A22 super highway then SS43
From Milan or Turin A4 exit at Seriate then follow signs
Fly
Verona 163km 3 hours away.
Milan 250 km 4.5 hours

PRATO NEVOSO   ARTESINA
pic Prato Nevoso Tourism

I
T
A
L
Y

Prato Nevoso is a relatively unknown resort, yet this small and very friendly place has been operating as a ski resort since 1965, although not by any stretch of the imagination a big or adventurous hangout. Although Prato Nevoso is not a big or adventurous hangout, it is still good with some nice terrain that will please intermediate carvers and bring a smile to the face of all novices. Prato Nevoso is located close to the French border, only a stones throw from the **Mediterranean sea** in the southern part of the Alps. Despite its proximity to warm areas, this is an area with a good annual snow record with heavy snowfalls throughout the winter months. Since its birth the resort has constantly improved its facilities and is currently working on plans for new lifts which will greatly improve access and acreage of rideable snow. On its own, Prato Nevoso is tiny with only 30km of piste, however, being linked with the resort of **Aresina**, the rideable acreage rises to a respectable 100km plus. Lifts join to two resorts to form an area know as the **'Mondole Ski'** which offer a splattering of trees, some nice powder and wide open slopes.

FREERIDERS are presented with an area that will please those who like their mountains hassle free. There is option of going off piste by hiking with a pair of snow shoes and the resort publishes a 'Free Ride' map to help you find the best spots. You can get further advice from the local snowboard club (details available from the Surf Shop Prato Nevoso).

FREESTYLERS are well catered for with a good flood-lit terrain park, which packs in not only a series of killer hits, but also a halfpipe and a permanent boardercross circuit.

CARVERS will probably get the best out of the slopes here, with a selection of well maintained slopes. The runs are wide and sweeping free of any rocks and uneven obstacles.

BEGINNERS have a resort that is perfect for them in every way with a good number of easy to reach novice runs.

2100M
TOP LIFT

%
OF BEGINNER
TO EXPERT
RUNS

100KM
PISTES

730M
VERTICAL

50

10   40

1330M
FIRST LIFT

NUMBER OF RUNS: 16
TOTAL LIFTS: 30
10 chairs, 20 drags
CAPACITY (people per hour): 9,500
LIFT TIMES: 8.30am to 4.30pm

AVERAGE SNOWFALL: 6m
SNOWMAKING: 7 Snow Cannons

WINTER PERIODS:
Dec to April
Lift Passes
1 Day 25 euros, 6 Days 120 euros
Night boarding
Yes, and terrain park lit
Board Schools
Private 30 euros per hour
Group 2hr/6 days 120 euros

FREERIDE 20%
Few trees & some off-piste
FREESTYLE 20%
Terrain park & a half-pipe
CARVING 60%

Prato Nevoso Tourism
Piazza Mirtilli 25-12083
Prato Nevoso
Tel: +39 (0) 174 334 130
Web:www.pratonevoso.com
Email: associazioneturistica@pratonev
oso.com

Fly
to Turin airport which is 1 hour away.
Train
to Mondovi, 30 minutes from resort.
Car
via Turin, head south on the auto route
A6 and turn off at signs for Mondovi.
From here follow the signs to the
resort. Total distance 62 miles (100km).

THE TOWN
Lodging and local services are based around the mountain with a number of hotels offering direct slope access. Overall, this is not an expensive resort unless you want it to be. You can bed down in the pricey *Hotel Galassia* or flake out in one of the inexpensive apartments. The village has an array of amenities from a pharmacy, to a mini golf course. There is also a number of okay restaurants, bars and night-clubs to check out.

5 OUT OF 10

Overall okay, but basic

pic -Roccaraso Tourism

East of **Rome**, in the region of **Abruzzo**, lies the mountain range of the **Apennines**. This range is home to a number of small areas collectively titled Roccaraso which was moulded into a ski resort in the 1950s and has been something of a national secret ever since. This place doesn't show up in your average travel brochure and due to this you don't find many foreigners here. In fact, during the week you might find it very quiet on the slopes, but at the weekend, expect a deluge of Romans and Neapolitans sporting the most lurid all in one ski suits and large lift queues. There is nothing

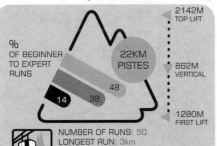

%
OF BEGINNER
TO EXPERT
RUNS

22KM
PISTES

2142M
TOP LIFT

862M
VERTICAL

48

14   38

1280M
FIRST LIFT

NUMBER OF RUNS: 50
LONGEST RUN: 3km
TOTAL LIFTS: 29 - 2 cable-cars, 10 chairs, 17 drags
CAPACITY (people per hour): 33,940
LIFT TIMES: 8.30am to 4.30pm

AVERAGE SNOWFALL:
1m
SNOWMAKING:
5%

WINTER PERIODS:
Dec to March
Lift Passes
1 Day 24 euros, 6 days 150
Board Schools
Private lessons 30 euros an hour

FREERIDE 40%
Lots of trees & no backcountry
FREESTYLE 25%
2 Pipes but no real park
CARVING 35%

Roccaraso Tourist Board
67037 Roccaraso (L'Aquila) via C. Mori
Tel: +39 (0) 864 62210
Web:www.roccaraso.net

Train
direct to Roccaraso from Rome.
Car
Via Rome, take the A24 towards Aquila, then the A25 towards Sulmona. Once past Sulmona, follow the signs for Roccaraso. Journey time 2 hours.
Fly
to Rome airport, 2 hours away.

I
T
A
L
Y

really challenging here, especially if the lack of altitude results in a lack of snow. However, the pistes are well maintained, and anyone who does find themselves in a lift queue can at least have fun mocking skiers in an array of sad outfits.

FREERIDERS will find a range of terrain to cover. Pistes are varied but will suffice more for those in the beginner or intermediate category than for advanced riders. There's little in the way of natural hits or off piste powder fields, but the low altitude means there are plenty of trees around (ie; Monte Pratello). Many of these are tightly packed though, and as such, inaccessible to many.

FREESTYLERS are blessed with two parks (off lifts 1 and 22) if there is enough snow out of which to build them or if the pisteurs can be arsed, whichever comes sooner. Otherwise take your shovel and build yourself a kicker or two.

CARVERS will revel in the knowledge that the pistes are kept well groomed and that there's not a mogul in sight. There are a few steep runs available and many of these are pretty wide.

BEGINNERS will find this a great place to get started. Plenty of easy runs on the lower slopes mean that you don't have to take the lift to the top to find what you need. There are gentle runs down from most of the lifts, however, the majority of the reds aren't over threatening so these will be handy as you progress.

THE TOWN
The good news is that it is not over expensive here. There is lift-side accommodation at Aremogna, but the town of Roccaraso, a short drive down the hill, is where most of the visitors stay. This is also where the very limited nightlife occurs. Italians are not big drinkers and this reflects in the town's social scene. There are a couple of nightclubs, *Bilba* and *Jambo*, but most of the activity goes on within the confines of the hotels.

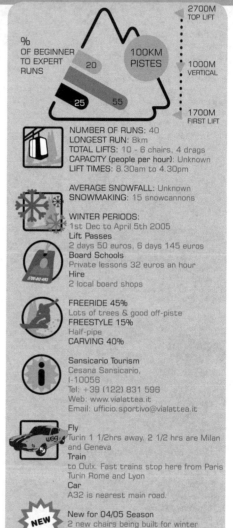

pic -Sansicario Tourism

I T A L Y

%
OF BEGINNER TO EXPERT RUNS

20

25 55

100KM PISTES

2700M
TOP LIFT

1000M
VERTICAL

1700M
FIRST LIFT

NUMBER OF RUNS: 40
LONGEST RUN: 8km
TOTAL LIFTS: 10 - 6 chairs, 4 drags
CAPACITY (people per hour): Unknown
LIFT TIMES: 8.30am to 4.30pm

AVERAGE SNOWFALL: Unknown
SNOWMAKING: 15 snowcannons

WINTER PERIODS:
1st Dec to April 5th 2005
Lift Passes
2 days 50 euros, 6 days 145 euros
Board Schools
Private lessons 32 euros an hour
Hire
2 local board shops

FREERIDE 45%
Lots of trees & good off-piste
FREESTYLE 15%
Half-pipe
CARVING 40%

Sansicario Tourism
Cesana Sansicario,
I-10056
Tel: +39 (122) 831 596
Web: www.vialattea.it
Email: ufficio.sportivo@vialattea.it

Fly
Turin 1 1/2hrs away, 2 1/2 hrs are Milan and Geneva
Train
to Oulx. Fast trains stop here from Paris Turin Rome and Lyon
Car
A32 is nearest main road.

NEW New for 04/05 Season
2 new chairs being built for winter Olympics-Turin 2006, should be open.

Sansicario is a low level and modern purpose built resort that forms part of the vast Milky Way circuit which includes the neighbouring Italian resorts of **Sauze D'Oux, Sestriere, Cesana, Claviere** and the popular neighbouring French resort of **Montgenevre**, all of which link fairly well on the slopes by lifts and via the pistes. They also share a joint lift pass should you want to venture farther than staying on the slopes available at Sansicario. In general what you have here is a popular resort which attracts a lot of Italians to its slopes through out the winter season period. And they are attracted to this place because of the diverse terrain, the sunny slopes good choice of challenging runs that includes some excellent off-piste riding much of which in and out of trees and across big powder bowls. Sansicario boast some 40 marked out trails which are mainly rated as red runs for intermediate riders. However, the **Milky Way** has hundreds of runs for all levels, so no one is going to feel left out here. You can ride with some ease from the top station all the way back down to the resort base, although total novices won't find it an easy thing to do, as the top runs are mainly all intermediate slopes with a couple of black trails here and there.

FREERIDERS will be able to come here knowing that this place will put them to the test in many ways, with a great choice of different terrain features to choose from. They will also be able to arrive knowing that a weeks visit here and across the Milky Way will not be enough to see all and ride out all the terrain laid out for you. If you're into trees and off-piste terrain then you will be well satisfied here.
FREESTYLERS may find the initially offerings around Sansicario a little tame. But first impressions can be deceiving, because if you look out you will find loads of good natural spots for getting big airs. There are some cool gullies to check out and loads of hits formed by some of the un-even terrain features that make up this mountain. The area also provides numerous pipes and man made hits.
CARVERS have a resort that is particularly good for their chosen style of riding. The abundance of fast and well pisted red runs that make up Sansicario slopes are idea for laying out big turns on.
BEGINNERS are the one group that may find this place a little off putting, as only a small percentage of the runs are rated for novices, and those runs that are grade blue for beginners are limited to a few sections at the lower areas off the dreaded drag lifts.

OFF THE SLOPES Sansicario is a good winter holiday destination with well appointed hotels and guest houses good restaurants and shops but alas rather dull night life

SAUZE D'OULX

Okay resort for all

Sauze d' Oulx is a resort that clubs together with a host of other areas to form one of the biggest rideable areas in Europe, known as the **Milky Way.** Located in the north west of Italy, Sauze doesn't have the greatest snow record, but does have a long history as a holiday camp style resort, the sort of place where certain low lifes come to get drunk near the snow. In truth, things aren't quite as bad as they sound and nowadays the place is inhabited by more Italians than package groups from afar. At one end of the Milky way is Sauze d' Oulx, perched at 1500m and at the other end is

pic -Sauze D'Oulx Tourism

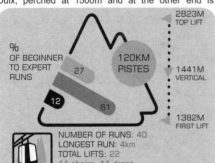

% OF BEGINNER TO EXPERT RUNS
27
12
61
120KM PISTES

2823M TOP LIFT

1441M VERTICAL

1382M FIRST LIFT

NUMBER OF RUNS: 40
LONGEST RUN: 4km
TOTAL LIFTS: 22
11 chairs, 11 drags
CAPACITY (people per hour): 18,000
LIFT TIMES: 8.30am to 4.30pm

AVERAGE SNOWFALL:
Unknown
SNOWMAKING:
40%

WINTER PERIODS:
Dec to April
Lift Passes
1 Day 27 euros, 6 days 145 euros

FREERIDE 50%
Lots of trees & some backcountry
FREESTYLE 15%
A Pipe but no real park
CARVING 50%

Tourist office Sauze d'Oulx
Piazza Assietta, 18
Tel. +39 0122 858 009
Web: www.comune.sauzedoulx.to.it
Email: info@comune.sauzedoulx.to.it

Train
to Oulx which is 5 minutes away.
Bus
Regular bus service from Oulx train station
Car
via Turin, head north west on the A32 to Oulx and then on to Sauze d'Oulx.
Fly
to Turin, 1hr away. Local airport is Torino

Montgeneve in France, which together offer over 285 miles of rideable terrain, linked by a hectic lift system covered by a single pass. This vast area that takes in the slopes of **Sauze, Sansicario, Borgata, Sestrieres, Claviere and Montgenevre** provides an area of mostly intermediate and beginner terrain, with enough stuff for advanced riders to take on. There are a few black graded knuckle rides up on the Borgata and Sestrieres area to test the best, particularly freeriders. The biggest cluster of runs are found on Sauze d' Oulx' own slopes, where intermediate freeriders will find loads of interconnecting red runs that weave through tight trees.

FREERIDERS looking for good off-piste won't be disappointed, with many runs leading through dense trees. The **Rio Nero** is a long favourite off piste trail that bases out at the road between **Oulx** and **Cesana**, but does entail a bus ride back to the lifts.

FREESTYLERS have loads of natural hits to get air from, but you wouldn't call this a freestyler's hangout.

CARVERS will find a staggering amount of good carving runs to ride in Sauze, making this a particularly good alpine resort.

BEGINNERS will get on well, but note that there are dozens of drag lifts and instruction is nothing to shout about.

THE TOWN
Resorts don't come much more basic than Sauze, although in a strange way, it all adds to the place and if you are out for a cheap time, this is where you'll get it. Lodging here is cheap in apartments and evenings are very lively, with pub upon pub and loads of good eating haunts making this place not so much a tacky hole but rather an okay place to visit. For a beer, check out the likes of *Paddy McGinty's* (full on Italian name or what!) or the *Banditos* disco for a late night drink, dance and some holiday skirt!

ITALY

229

VAL GARDENA

8
OUT OF 10

Good mix of terrain to suit most

pic/Val Gardena Tourism

2518M
TOP LIFT

%
OF BEGINNER
TO EXPERT
RUNS

175KM
PISTES

1458M
VERTICAL

30

10

60

1060M
FIRST LIFT

NUMBER OF RUNS: 55
LONGEST RUN: 10km
TOTAL LIFTS: 82 - 6 Gondolas, 2 cable-
cars, 34 chairs, 35 drags
CAPACITY (people per hour): 25,000
LIFT TIMES: 8.30am to 4.30pm

AVERAGE SNOWFALL: 2.5m
SNOWMAKING: 45%

WINTER PERIODS:
Dec to April
Lift Passes
1 Day 31-35 euros
6 days 154-175 euros
Hire
board from 16 euros /day
boots from 7 euros/day

FREERIDE 50%
Lots of trees & good off-piste
FREESTYLE 20%
2 Half-pipes & terrain park
CARVING 30%

Val Gardena Tourist Office
Str Meisules 21a3,
I-39048
Tel: ++39 (0) 471 795 122
Web: www.val-gardena.com
Email: info@val-gardena.com

Fly
to Verona airport 2 hours away.
Train
to Bolzano which is 30 minutes away.
Car
From Bolzano, head north on the A22
and turn off at Bressanone taking the
E66 towards Brunico and turning off on
to the B244 to the resort area

NEW
New for 04/05 Season
Gardena Express Patrol Funicular
basement

Val Gardena is located in the northern area of the **Dolomites** and forms a collection of resorts and mountain slopes that is said to be the largest snowboarding area in the world. There is a staggering 600 miles of marked trails and are serviced by some 460 lifts of all shapes and styles these can be utilised by the **Dolomiti Superski** pass. A limited pass called the Val Gardena still covers 175km of piste with 82 lifts. Val Gardena has the unfortunate history of being the place where a particularly sad Brit with a Russian name achieved a so called top ski result (who gives a toss). However, this is not a sad place to snowboard, it's actually very good, with something for everyone. Val Gardena is a huge valley, housing three main villages and a handful of satellite hamlets. And truly, if you can't ride here and enjoy yourself, then you must be a closeted synchronised swimmer or worse, a downhill skier with a nice shiny medal! The main villages here are **Ortisei** (the biggest town in the area) and **St Christina**. Wherever you choose to stay, you can move around the resort via a regular shuttle bus service. The well set out mass of lifts don't connect up everywhere, but with a piste map you can get around a very large portion of it without too many problems. Try the circuit ride known as the **Sella Ronda**, which takes you around 15 miles of lift connected runs.

FREERIDERS on the whole find Val Gardena a cool place to ride, with a good mixture of terrain features from trees to banks and wind lips. The best off-piste riding can be had in areas like **Passo Pordoi,** but its best tackled with the services of a local guide.
FREESTYLERS will find that the fun park and half-pipe, located on the area known as the **Selda** is the place to hang out and get some air. If you're there at the right time you could also be riding to tunes by top DJ's.
CARVERS of all levels will find millions of well pisted trails to get their fix from. Runs criss cross all over the area and no rider will see all of them in a week's trip, or even two.
BEGINNERS who can't learn to snowboard here must be clueless idiots; this place is a first timer's heaven.

The runs up above **Ortisei** are full-on, perfect nappy territory.
THE TOWN
Accommodation and evenings are very Italian, with loads of good options in the main villages or at one of the smaller hamlets, which will have cheaper places to sleep and hang out. **Eating** and other local happenings are much the same wherever you are: all are laid back and okay.

ITALY

ROUND-UP

CORNO ALLE SCALE

This is not a resort that many people would have heard of, but its worth a mention and even a visit, especially if you fancy a night out in the nearby town of Bologna. Corno Alle Scale has plenty of terrain to suit all standards with some gnarly off-piste for freeriders to bury themselves in. This is not a place for novices who like everything on hand, likewise freestylers looking for a host of man made hits be disappointed. The only draw back about this place is that **accommodation** is located way back down the road (about 10 km) and with no local bus service, you must have your own transport. What is on offer is very basic but at least affordable. There is also a cheesy disco bar and a number of small drinking holes.

Contact:
Corno alle Scale Tourist Office
P.zza Marconi,
6 -40042-Lizzano in Belvedere (Bo)
Tel - 0534 50105
How to get there: Fly to: Bologna 1 hour away

GRESSONEY

Located in the Aosta Valley, Gressony is the neighbour to nearby Champoluc, with heaps of pisted terrain between the two resorts. The large amount of off-piste terrain here, offers a lot of big drop-ins, gullies and wide open bowls to please all freeriders. For carvers, there are ample wide spaces. Beginners have loads of easy flats to get hold of. Local facilities are very good and close to the slopes with some cheap options for lodging, eating and partying late at night.

Ride area: 200km
Top Lift: 2661m
Total Lifts:46
Contact:
Tel - +39 (125) 307113
Fax - +39 (125) 307785
Snow Phone - +39 (125) 307113
www.gressoney.com
How to get there: Fly to: Turin 1 hour away

PIANCAVALLO

Piancavallo is a tiny purpose built resort and not unsightly. There is only a handful of runs that are split between beginner and intermediate level and nothing for advanced riders apart form a single graded black trail. Freestylers have a pipe. This is a simple piste loving carvers place through and through. Chalet accommodation and good services are slope side

Ride area: 24km
Top Lift: 1829m
Total Lifts:18
Contact:
Tourist Office
Piazzale,Della Puppa
Loc Piancavallo,33081 Aviano
Tel: 0434655191
Fax: 0434655354
www.piancavallo.com
How to get there: Fly to: Venice 3 hours away

PILA

Pila is fantastic resort located in the Aosta Region. What you will find here is a decent sized mountain with a series of pisted and unpisted trails that will keep any rider more than happy for a week. Although not extensive, the terrain offers advanced freeriders awesome off piste and trees areas. Freestylers have a pipe.Suitable for carvers as well. Novices have a great selection of easy runs. Local services are cheap, good and slope side

Ride area: 64km
Top Lift: 2750m
Total Lifts:13
Contact:
www.pila.it
How to get there: Fly to: Turin 3 hours away

SANTA CATERINA

Santa Caterina is a resort that will appeal to sedate riders. The resort is linked to Bormio as part of the Alta Valtellina ski area and gives you access to over 100km of pistes. The resort is being improved for the 2005 season, a new slope, Edelweiss is being developed especially for the FIS Alpine World Ski Championships

in January. **Freeriders** may be able to find some okay backcountry riding but its very limited and will only please intermediate riders. **Freestylers** have a half-pipe, but its not always looked after. **Carvers** just out for a simple day's piste riding will be at home, even granny could have a go. Fine for **beginners** but not a great choice of runs. Slope side services are good and affordable

Contact: www.santacaterina.com

SELLA NEVA

Sella Neva is a small resort in the north eastern corner of Italy bordering Slovenia and Austria. This is a popular carvers resort as well as offering some excellent freeridng and natural freestyle terrain. You can shred some trees at speed, go waste deep in powder or fly off endless cliffs. The fun park contains a half-pipe and is located off the Gilberti lift. This is also a good beginners resort. Sella Nevea is a good cheap resort with basic services.

SESTRIERE

Sestriere offers the potential for some great advanced riding both on and off piste, with a vast amount of terrain to explore in this part of the Milky Way.Freeriders will find a good choice of challenging runs and some excellent off piste. Freestylers are not well catered for but you will still find some interesting natural hits. Carvers have acres of good terrain. Beginners do not want for much more than you get here. Off piste services are affordable and close to the slopes

VAL DI SOLE

Large linked area of four skiing resorts, Folgarida, Marilleva, Pejo and Passo Tonale

VAL SENALES

Linked with Val Senales. The Schnals Valley Glacier guarantees snow year-round

Snowboarding has hit Japan, tsunami-like and swept away a lot of the discriminatory 'ski only' policies. Every year the situation improves and with the huge number of riders now around there are very few places that can afford to turn away their custom. Some places even cater specifically for riders, notably some of the smaller ones who have developed their terrain parks to attract freestylers. Snowboarding in Japan has been greatly influenced by the European scene. Most lift

Capital City: Tokyo
Population: 127.3 Million
Highest Peak: Fujiyama 3776 m
Language: Japanese
Legal Drink Age: 18
Drug Laws: Cannabis is illegal
Age of consent: 16
Electricity: 100 Volts AC 2-pin
International Dialing Code: +81

Currency: Yen (JPY)
Exchange Rate:
UK£1 = 196
EURO = 132
US$1 = 110

Driving Guide
All vehicles drive on the right hand side of the road
Speed limits:
40kmh towns,80kmh Expressways
Emergency
Police 110, Fire/Ambulance 119
Tolls
Expressways charge per km. Approximate cost from Tokyo to (near) Hokkaido 14,000 yen
Documentation
International Driver's Licence not required, but must carry home driving licence.

Time Zone
UTC/GMT +9
No daylight saving changes

Japan Snowboard Association
Nac Shibuya Building 4F
15-10 Nanpeidai
Shibuya-ku
Tokyo 150
Tel - +81 (0) 3 5458 2661
Web: www.so-net.ne.jp/jsba

Japan Tourist Information
10 Fl., Tokyo Kotsu Kaikan Bldg.,
2-10-1, Yurakucho, Chiyoda-ku,
Tokyo 100-0006
Tel:(03)3201-3331
Fax:(03)3201-3347
www.jnto.go.jp

Asahikawa
Takikawa
Furano
Hokkaido
Asahidake
Sapporo
Niseko Hirafu
Shiranuka
Muroran
Hakodate

Sambongi
Akita
Hanamaki
Sakata
Ichinoseki

Gala Yuzawa
Naeba
Sendai
Arai Mountain
Niigata
Muikamachi
Takada
Honshu
Omachi
Utsunmiya
Tokyo
Nagoya
Arai

systems are Swiss or Austrian in make and the term 'ski area' is known as the 'Ski Gelande' (taken from German). A lot of resorts, restaurants and shops also take French or German names. Night-riding is big in Japan and almost all resorts offer some kind of flood-lit runs. One of the reasons for the popularity of night riding must be the lack of a party scene.

Japanese snowboarders seem to have a lack of experience, a mix of intense reserve and a desire to be noticed by the opposite sex. You will see a lot of riders on their knees looking up-slope in semi-pose mode while wearing the latest gear. The majority of those you meet will be ready to try out their conversational English on you and most can say a few words although whether they can understand you is a different matter.

Lift passes generally cost between 4,000 yen (£20) and 5,000 yen (£25) per day and are only slightly discounted if you purchase more than a days worth. Passes can be bought with cash at the resort, or just as easily at convenience stores all over country. (Lawson, AM-PM, 7-Eleven and Family Mart are the main ones). These stores

usually produce a pamphlet listing the resorts they offer passes for. Their prices, which include 1,500 yen or so worth of lunch vouchers, are better value than buying at the resorts themselves.

TRAVELLING AROUND:

Train - Japan's train service is excellent (frequent, clean, on time) but expensive if you buy your tickets in Japan. The Rail Pass can be bought for 7, 14 or 21 day periods from your local tour operator before you travel to Japan. Prices are approximately £150, £220, £280. This is one of the best deals you will get so seriously consider this option. The pass includes unlimited travel on the world renowned bullet trains (shinkansen).

Car - If you want to hire a car you'll have to bring your International Driver's License. One difficulty will be the language, because working out the insurance terms will be a nightmare. The cheapest cars can be hired from large companies such as Toyota, Nippon and ORIX from 6000 yen a day but these are dinky toys big enough for only two.

Japan Travel: tel (03-3502-1461 (00 88 22-2800 from the UK) is an excellent English language phone service that can tell you anything you want to know concerning transport (fares and timetables) or accommodation. It will even help with language problems.

THE SEASON

Japan, especially the north island of **Hokkaido** gets plenty of snow. Its location puts it in the path of the cold air stream that comes off Hokkaido. Before reaching Japan, the air stream picks up its moisture over the Japan Sea then dumps when it hits the Japan Alps running up the west coast. From January through till March you can expect to have 3m base in most of the serious resorts. Several of the **Honshu** resorts boast a season from October till May, but it's only really in Hokkaido where you can expect to find any decent conditions as late as this. In fact none of the resorts are seriously running until mid-December but a few, in the name of good publicity, spend their money on creating a long strip of 'snow' on a shallow slope and declare themselves open at the end of October. At this time it's still pretty hot and humid.

Basically you have a good 3-4 month period to check things out although you are seriously advised to avoid the slopes at the beginning of January. During the first week of the year the Japanese have a long national holiday granted by most companies - it's as crowded as hell.

Riding off-piste: There are certain resorts, maybe a majority, in Japan where snowboarding is mainly a fashion statement and Tokyoites go for their one day on the slopes every year. These places tend to be pretty strict in the way they control boarding. Often some lifts are still (the number gets fewer every year) closed to boarders and any off piste will be fenced off and patrolled. On the other hand there are a few areas where the resorts really do cater for the more hardened rider and ski/board patrol will even tell you which backcountry areas are good/safe, and you may meet some locals to ride off with.

Wherever you go, those of you always looking to 'cut the fresh' will be pleased to know that you'll probably find yourself alone, carving the ivory. Japanese are very compliant, so 99% wouldn't dream of leaving the slopes for a little off-piste. There are ski-patrols of course but they are fairly inconspicuous, so the chances of you being whistled at are really slim.

ACCOMMODATION

Accommodation in Japan doesn't boast any great deals when it comes to somewhere to put your head for the night. Resort hotels are very popular with the Japanese, who will pay through the nose for a room with a view. The advise is to avoid the western style hotels and go for a traditional Japanese inn (**Ryokan**) or a family-run hotel (**Minshuku**). Both are usually reasonably priced (nice tatami-mat rooms for 7000 yen including evening meal and breakfast are possible) and you get the added feel of authenticity. Normally very small, these hotels are typically very Japanese in style-tatami-mat floors, table heaters, futon, yukata (traditional bath robe) and slippers all make up what can be a very pleasant cultural experience when you're off the slope. The Japanese are quiet lot and for the most part you'll find the staff are extremely welcoming and helpful.

FOOD

The food in Japanese inns is great and usually traditional, but you'll sometimes even find some western foods on your plate - omelette and ham often appear at breakfast time. If you can stomach fish, rice and natto (curdled soy beans) in the morning, all power to you- it's a great way to prepare the body for the day's onslaught on the slopes.

Resort food, is usually pretty varied although there seems to be a 'standard' menu which you'll find at pretty much every resort. Meals range from western snacks like hotdogs and fries to Japanese noodle and rice dishes. Recommended is the quintessentially Japanese ski lunch of curry, pork cutlet and rice, washed down with a can of Asahi Superdry, Japan's premium beer. All for about 1500 yen, usually obtained by exchanging a ticket bought at a vending machine (jidoo hanbaiki). Look lost and forlorn if confused - someone will help you! For those you like to pig out big style, will find that some resorts offer all-you-can-eat (viking) deals for around 1500-2000 yen, which allows you to stuuf down various strange fish and traditional noodle dishes.

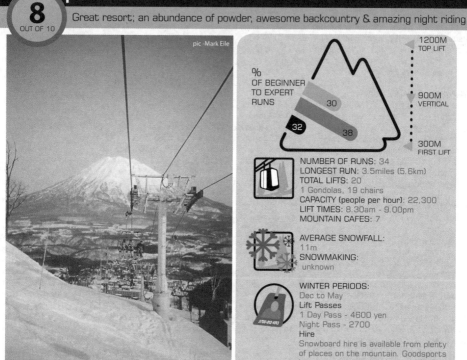

pic -Mark Eile

J

JAPAN

%
OF BEGINNER
TO EXPERT
RUNS

30

32

38

1200M
TOP LIFT

900M
VERTICAL

300M
FIRST LIFT

NUMBER OF RUNS: 34
LONGEST RUN: 3.5miles (5.6km)
TOTAL LIFTS: 20
1 Gondolas, 19 chairs
CAPACITY (people per hour): 22,300
LIFT TIMES: 8.30am - 9.00pm
MOUNTAIN CAFES: 7

AVERAGE SNOWFALL:
11m
SNOWMAKING:
unknown

WINTER PERIODS:
Dec to May
Lift Passes
1 Day Pass - 4600 yen
Night Pass - 2700
Hire
Snowboard hire is available from plenty
of places on the mountain. Goodsports
has a great range and is on the main
road half way up the hill to the lifts.
Board School
Half day 3,200yen, full day 4,800
Learner Day package 2hr lesson, hire &
lift 6,800yen
Snowmobiles
Snowmobile tours are available from
7800 yen . Deep powder riding available.
Night Riding
Night riding here is regarded as a must
do. Large ride area including tree runs
and terrain parks, till 9pm every day

FREERIDE 50%
Lots of trees & huge backcountry
FREESTYLE 30%
A Half-pipe & 3 terrain parks
CARVING 20%

NISEKO TOKYU RESORT
044-0081 Niseko kogen Hirafu
204 Kutchan cho
Abuta Gun Hokkaido ,JAPAN
TEL:0136-22-0109
FAX:0136-22-2821
Web: www.niseko-tokyu.co.jp
Email:hirafu@resortservice.co.jp

Located between a volcano and the Japan Sea, Niseko is the best of the Japanese resorts and compares well with resorts in North America and Europe. **Niseko** is mostly a freeriders resort and the main attraction has to be its big mountain terrain, however it also has 4 terrain parks incredible night riding and a modern lift system; definitely a great place to ride.

Niseko gets on average a good 11m of light dry powder, so during the months of January and February you can expect regular and major dumps and you can often still be riding in mid-April. Niseko is essentially one mountain although it is divided up into three linked areas covered by one mountain pass. This area does have avalanches so check with the ski patrols to get the latest info. The tops of **Annupuri**, **Higashiyama**, and **Hirafu** are all within a few hundred metres hike of the top of the mountain (1308m). From here you can ride down backcountry to **Goshiki Onsen** (hot springs) on the opposite side of the mountain. To get back you'll need a taxi or the infrequent bus.

FREERIDERS should head straight to the peak. After a 20min hike from the top chair you reach the peak of **Mt Annupuri**. From here your options are close to 360 degrees with views from volcano to sea. The terrain is endless with open powder bowls, trees and gullies. The length of your ride is governed by how far you want to hike to get back inbounds. The hike back is along a cat track however some runs off the peak can

THE TOWN & GETTING THERE

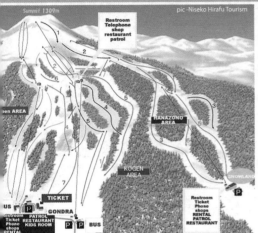

Summit 1309m

Restroom
Telephone
shop
restaurant
patrol

pic -Niseko Hirafu Tourism

get you back to a lift without hiking. The backcountry is sensational with plenty to choose from all within easy access of the resort. Backcountry tours are available from *Niseko Powder Connection* +81-136-21-2500 or the *Niseko Outdoor Adventure Sports* Club (www. noasc.com) tel +81 136-23-1688, which has a shop and office near the Hirafu base. A full day will set you back 7000-8000 yen

FREESTYLERS are well catered for with 1 halfpipe and 4 terrain parks. The terrain parks range from pro to beginner and are well made and maintained with a good variety of hits and rails. Also if you look hard enough you will find plenty of hits built by enthusiastic locals.

CARVERS can take advantage of the 900m of vertical Niseko-Hirafu has to offer. There are plenty of long wide runs especially heading towards the **Hanazono** area. The well groomed terrain provides awesome runs for everyone from beginner to experts.

BEGINNERS can start on their own slope without feeling in the way and then slowly graduate up the mountain at their own leisure. With easy runs available

from top to bottom beginners can also enjoy the 900m of vertical Niseko-Hirafu has to offer.

THE TOWN

Accommodation is found in the village directly below the lifts and ranges from five star hotels to family owned pensions. Most of the accommodation is fairly affordable, especially if you have a group of four or more.

Food in Niseko-Hirafu is excellent. There are some western style places and even a *KFC* if you feel the need. However most of the restaurants are Japanese. But the variety of local traditional places is superb with each one creating its own unique atmosphere. The bu-cha bar & restaurant is a great place to go for a meal or just to have a cheeky one off the wood. *Hank's* a cosy little cabin where Hank cooks up meals on an open fire and *Big Cliff* serves great food and is open late. There is also a couple of mini marts for groceries and alcohol. There are more options in the town of **Kutchan** (15 mins away)

Nightlife is rather laidback but can get amped up at certain times of the year if you know where the parties are. Plenty of bars to choose from and most are open to the early hours if you're feeling thirsty. *Fatty's bar* is two trucks parked together to create a unique bar.

J

J
A
P
A
N

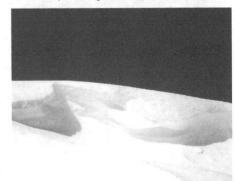

CAR
Sapporo to resort is 102.1km, approx 2 1/2hrs drive Take nakayama pass(route230) for 66km, then Kyougoku (route276) for another 30km, then (route 343) to resort
FLY
International flights available to and from Chitose Airport, Sapporo approx 2 1/2hrs from resort
TRAIN
To Kutchan station, 15 mins away take a bus or taxi to resort. Kutchan to Sapporo (Hakodate Line) approx 2 hours
BUS
Limousine Bus Service from Chitose Airport, Sapporo to Niseko-Hirafu. 3500 yen 9.00am - 4.30pm

ASAHIDAKE ONSEN

Other Hokkaido Hills, are Asahidake and its located in the centre of Hokkaido with two lifts and where you're free to make your own route down (a major draw point in regulated Japan). There are plenty of trees and with Hokkaido's excellent snow record there is usually plenty of powder

Ride area: 100acres
Top Lift: 660m
Bottom Lift: 140m
Total Lifts:6
Contact:
www.araimntspa.com
How to get there: Otaru train station is 30mins away

FURANO

pic -Furano Resort

Furano is a major summer and winter resort. It is run by the Prince Hotels Group, which offers the largest hotel slopeside. There is also plenty of accommodation to be had in the town. It can be reached by bus from either Sapporo or Asahikawa (the nearest airport). This place is one of Japan's most famous ski areas and has hosted World Cup ski events. There's a big night skiing area, plenty of trees and natural hits for freeriders and also long groomed runs for carvers. In the centre of Hokkaido it is known to get very cold in January which means the powder usually remains fine.

Runs: 12
Top Lift: 1209m
Bottom Lift: 250m
Total Lifts:17
Contact:
http://www.princehotels.co.jp/furano-e
How to get there: Furano station - 10 mins away

NISEKO KOKUSAI MOIWA

Niseko Kokusai Moiwa is a cheaper and much smaller resort on a lower peak just to the west of the main mountain. It is probably only worth a trip if you have more than 3 or 4 days in the area, but it is reputed to offer some great backcountry riding

Ride area: 8 runs

Top Lift: 800m
Bottom Lift: 330m
Total Lifts:4
How to get there: Niseko Station - 20 mins away

SAPPORO KOKUSAI

Sapporo Kokusai is 30 minutes from Sapporo, is well set up for boarders with both a park and pipe. You can find good freeriding and some excellent riders. Japanese who decide to do a season but don't want to move to a resort itself, often take a part time job in Sapporo and spend their free time riding here. Sapporo was one of the first in Japan to actively encourage riders. The run below the gondola is fun, while a hike to the top gives access to some backcountry.

Runs: 7
Top Lift: 630m
Bottom Lift: 140m
Total Lifts:5
Contact:
www.sapporo-kokusai.co.jp
How to get there: Sapporo Station - 90mins away

Arai Mountain piste map

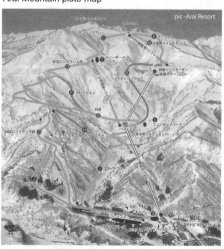
pic -Arai Resort

JAPAN - HONSHU ISLAND

ARAI MOUNTAIN

Arai Mountain Resort has been running for just over 10 years and was developed by the Sony Corporation. As a result the facilities are quality, and unlike a lot of other Japanese resorts the lifts are all new and fast. It's definitely one of the best resorts on Honshu and attracts some very good riders. It often hosts rider camps in the spring and international contests. The terrain is in a bowl and even allows for a little hiking (unfortunately banned by most resorts here). There are two very well kept pipes but the main attraction is the powder resulting from the big dumps because of its location in the first mountain range west of the Japan Sea. This could also be seen as its main drawback as it is a long way from Tokyo

Ride area: 100acres
Runs: 10
Top Lift: 1280m
Bottom Lift: 1280m
Total Lifts:5
Contact:
www.araimntspa.com
How to get there: To get to Arai, take the bullet train to Nagano (2 hours from Tokyo) then a local train (1hr 40mins) then a free shuttle bus (15-mins) to the slopes. All this will set you back about 90 USD in train fares, so it may be worth looking into bus tours if you don't have a rail pass

GALA YUZAWA

Conveniently located, it even has its own bullet train stop, (one along from Echigo Yuzawa) this is a modern set-up, especially popular with the younger day trippers. Here you don't have to endure a 10-minute bus journey but you will have to put up with higher prices and unfriendly staff (even a single locker costs #5).

Ride area: 126acres
Runs: 15
Top Lift: 1181m
Bottom Lift: 800m
Total Lifts:11
Contact: www.gala.co.jp
How to get there: Gala Yuzawa train station at resort

JOETSU KOKUSAI

Joetsu Kokusai is a little further afield (30-mins by bus). It has one of the largest terrain parks (i.e. more than 4 jumps) in Japan and two good pipes. These are both in front of the Edwardian looking hotel. For freeriders the Osawa slopes are best. This is a good resort for boarders, although some of the lifts are old and slow. It is not worth visiting the peak.

MUIKAMACHI HAKKAI-SAN

Muikamachi Hakkaisan can be a powder paradise in January and February. It is an hour further west from Echigo Yuzawa (30-mins by local train to Muikamachi, then 30-mins by bus). Because of this it is usually less busy but still managable in a day trip from Tokyo. The resort is especially popular with skiers out to enjoy the moguls, so there is usually plenty of terrain left for freeriding. Below the gondola is a 3km downhill course that will take it out of you. The No. 3 chairlift lets you enjoy a shorter workout. The Raku (easy) course allows you to cut through the thick forest and offers plenty of air points but there is no pipe or park. The area itself is one of the most famous in Japan for sake (rice wine) which you will no doubt get to taste if you stay here. In the winter 'Atsukan' (hot rice wine) is good for warming you up, it's available here and in all other resorts.

MYOKO KOHGEN

Seki Onsen is a resort, which understands the needs of the powder hounds. Near the west coast in Niigata Prefecture it has a great snow record, often with 1m plus dumps overnight in Jan/Feb. There's a decent pipe and some good natural hits and kickers. Locals or the patrol will advise you on back country riding - they'll also tell you that you have to take responsibility for yourself, although in the land of group culture it's cool to find somewhere that lets you do this. Seki Onsen is the home

resort for Masanori Takeuchi, a well-known Japanese rider.

NAEBA

Naeba is perhaps the most famous resort in Honshu and more like a western one in terms of the number of hotels and other things going on. It is a 45-mins bus journey from Echigo Yuzawa station. Snowboarding has been allowed all across the hill since the 98/99 season and they have now built their own mini park and regularly host air contests. However, there is no pipe and the resort is best for freeriders. Similarly to Niseko and Zao, you can happily enjoy three or four days here without getting bored. There are some excellent tree runs if you duck the ropes and because of the lack of Japanese who do this you're always able to make your own tracks. The best spots for doing this are below the No. 1 gondola, and of the No. 2 gondola.

Accommodation in Naeba is operated by the Prince Group, which offers a variety of modern slopeside accommodation (++81 (0) 257-89-2311). If you call in advance there

are usually special deals going, including lift pass. Oji Pension (0257-89-3675) is just 5 minutes walk behind the Prince Hotel, and is run by the friendly Mr. Sakamoto. He has a stock of new rental boards and a Brazil shirt signed by Pele. A futon, breakfast and evening meal should cost around 7500 yen, and he can sort you out with lift pass discounts

http://www.princehotels.co.jp/Naeba-e

237

J

J
A
P
A
N

Shot: Lake Matherson pics: WSG

New Zealand consists of two main islands, North and South. Whakapapa and Turoa are the only commercial resorts on the North Island, so most visitors will use Queenstown, Wanaka and Christchurch as a base for visiting the South Island resorts. Winter season generally lasts between June to October.

There are twelve commercially owned and operated resorts and a dozen or so 'Club Fields' run by non-profit club committees. Small, social and New Zealand made, they are a classic piece of Kiwiana and well worth while checking out. In recent years many people have rediscovered the charms and attractions of Club Fields. They are lured by the uncrowded slopes, with the spectacular setting of the Southern Alps, spread out as a back drop.

Taking a 'Snowboard Tour' is a good idea if you're visiting NZ for a short time, as it would help maximise your time on the mountain. There are a number of companies offering all inclusive boarding tours for New Zealand, shop around because prices are competitive.

New Zealand resorts tend to have very limited on-mountain accommodation, so you will be most likely staying in some nearby town. Naturally, these vary in size as does the night-life from the busy party towns to the quieter club fields. Queenstown has over 20 bars and clubs and is often referred to as the action and adventure capital of NZ.

NZ's international gateway airports are, Auckland and Wellington for North Island and Christchurch and Queenstowns for the South Island. The average flight time from London is 21 hours with a few stop overs.

Driving in NZ is an economical way to get around. Car hire services are available at all the airports and when hiring, ask about deals for road trips to the mountains, these can include discounts on accommodation and lift passes. Campervans are a cheap hire option with a five day hire costing from $460. As well as the usual hire companies, there are some that specialise in longer term rental for backpackers, with prices from $25 per day. More info take a look at *www.rentalz.co.nz*

Capital City: Wellington
Population: 4 Million
Highest Peak: Mount Cook 3764m
Language: English
Legal Drink Age: 18
Drug Laws: Cannabis is illegal and frowned upon
Age of consent: 16
Electricity: 230 Volts AC 2-pin
International Dialing Code: +64

Currency: New Zealand Dollar (NZ$)
Exchange Rate:
UK£1 = 2.8
EURO = 1.9
US$1 = 1.6

Driving Guide
All vehicles drive on the left hand side of the road
Speed limits:
50kph (31mph) Towns
100kph (60mph) Motorways
Emergency
Fire/Police/Ambulance - 111
Tolls
No tolls, but check if hiring a car that its allowed on all roads
Documentation
International Driver's Licence not required, but must carry home driving licence.

Time Zone
UTC/GMT +12
DST +1 hr (March - Oct)

New Zealand Snowboard Association
PO Box 18911
South New Brighton
Christchurch, New Zealand
Tel: +64 3 382 2206
Fax: +64 3 382 2106
Web: www.nzsba.co.nz
Email: nzsba@xtra.co.nz

Auckland

Rotorua

Whakapapa/Turoa

Cape Farewell

Westport

★**Wellington**

Cape Pallister

NEW ZEALAND

Mt. Lyford

Mt. Hutt

Porter Heights

Ohau mt. Dobson **Christchurch**

Cardrona

Treble Cone

Remarkables ●**Queenstown**

Snowpark Cornet Peak

Dunedin

N

NEW ZEALAND

Bus travel in NZ is cheap and convenient, either with a local bus company or one of the majors with most resorts covered. You can travel from Queenstown to Christchurch for around $40.

Most resorts can be reached by train which is not that expensive. However, you will need to transfer by local buses, in most cases under 12 miles.

Taking a 'Snowboard Tour' is a good idea if you're visiting NZ for a short time, as it would help maximise your time on the mountain. There are a number of companies offering all inclusive boarding tours for New Zealand, shop around because prices are competitive.

239

CLUB FIELDS ROUND-UP

In recent years many people have rediscovered the charms and attractions of Club Fields. They are lured by the uncrowded slopes, with the spectacular setting of the Southern Alps, spread out as a back drop.

Facilities at the club fields tend to be quite modest and basic, there are no club fields with chairlifts, but some do have T- bars or platter lifts. The most common lift is the rope tow. If you contact the club offices in advance and tell them the day you wish to come, they can help arrange a ride for you by putting you in touch with someone else who is driving there. Local Ski or Snowboard Shops will sometimes have booking sheets of people who are going or want to go to a club field.

All the club fields have on-mountain lodging available. This can range from dormitory cabin style, to double rooms with en-suite. If you are planning on staying overnight on the mountain, ring ahead to check there are vacancies because often they have large groups and clubs booked in or staying and may be full up, depending on bed numbers. There are package deals available which can include accommodation, an evening meal and breakfast, and discounted day passes (and sometimes transport). There are cheaper prices staying mid-week and for a week. This is a great time to go because there is usually no one else to share the slopes with.

For day visitors, there is a cafeteria or snack shop for food. It is a good idea to bring a few of your own munchies too. There is usually a communal dining and kitchen area where you can prepare and eat food.

At some club fields you can buy alcohol (mainly beer), but supplies can run out, so if you are staying a night of more it would be rise to bring your own, if you are one of those people who need a couple of cold ones to finish the day. Check with the ski area first about their policy on alcohol.

North Island

STRATFORD MOUNTAIN CLUB
Ride area: 100acres
Runs: 10
Easy 5%
Intermediate 30%
Advanced 65%
Top Lift: 1680m
Bottom Lift: 1260m
Total Lifts:4
1 t-bar, 3 rope tows
Contact:
PO Box 3271,
New Plymouth,New Zealand
Phone: +64 027 2800 860
snow.co.nz/manganui
Location:
20km from Stratford, take the sealed access road off highway 3 for 18km, 20 min walk from carpark

South Island
All the clubfields listed below, except Erewhon, are located in the Craigieburn Mountain Range. :To get there take highway 73, which goes from Christchurch to Greymouth via Arthurs Pass. Mt Cheeseman, Broken River, Temple Basin, Porter Heights (a commercial field) and Mt Olympus, have a combined sea son pass deal

HANMER SPRINGS
Easy 10%
Intermediate 60%
Advanced 30%

Hire: Available on slope
Lift passes: Day pass $5 for a member $40 otherwise
Accomodation $5 for a member, $25 otherwise.
Membership $120
Total Lifts: 2
Contact:
PO Box 66
Hamner Springs
Phone: (025) 341 806
Fax: (03) 315 7201
www.skihamner.co.nz
Location:
Take the access road Clarence Valley road from Hamner Springs. 155km from Christchurch & Kaikoura

BROKEN RIVER
Top Lift: 1820m
Bottom Lift: 1400m
Ride Area: 300 hectares
Board School: Private $42 per hour
Group lesson $20 per hour
Lift passes:Day pass $42

pic: Broken River Resort

Overnight accomodation:
$25 - White Star Chalet
$48 - Broken River Lodge
$70 - Lyndon Lodge
Total Lifts: 5 tows
Contact:
PO Box 2718
Christchurch,New Zealand
Phone / Fax: (03) 318 7270
www.brokenriver.co.nz
Location:
1 1/2 hours west of Christchurch on State Highway 73 (the Arthur's Pass Road approx 8km past Castle Hill Village). Follow 6km access road

CRAIGIEBURN
Top Lift: 1811m
Bottom Lift: 1308m
Ride Area: 101 hectares
Intermediate 55%
Advanced 45%
Total Lifts: 3 rope tows
Board School: Goup lesson $20 per hour. Private lesson $30 per hour
Hire: No hire equipment available
Lift passes:Day pass $25 member, $44 non-member
Accomodation $65 non-member
$2 tow belt hire per day
Contact:
Box 2152, Christchurch New Zealand
Tel: +64 3 365 2514
www.craigieburn.co.nz
Location:
From Christchurch take highway 73 to Craigieburn for 110Km, 1 1/2 drive time

then take 6km access roa

MOUNT CHEESEMAN

pic: Mt Cheesem

Top Lift: 1845m
Bottom Lift: 1552m
Easy 15%
Intermediate 50%
Advanced 35%
Total Lifts: 3 - 2 pomos, rope tows
Hire: Board & Boots $35 c
Lift passes:Group lesson $ per hour. Private lesson $ per hour. Beginners lesse hire & lift pass $58 per da
Contact:
PO Box 22178
Christchurch,New Zealan
Phone: +64 3 344 3247
www.mtcheeseman.com
Location:
located in the Craigieb Range, 112km (1.5h from Christchurch on 73, take the 12km unsea access road to resort s posted 1km past Castle Village

CARDRONA

7 OUT OF 10

Okay all round resort

Cardrona lies off the **Crown Range** road between **Wanaka** and **Queenstown**. Shuttle bus services operate from both towns, so it is accessible wherever you choose to base yourself. The last few seasons has seen the major NZ resorts really step up a gear in developing decent terrain parks and pipes. Cardrona being no exception with a 1000m terrain park and 4 half-pipes

pic Catdrona Resort

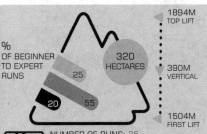

%
OF BEGINNER
TO EXPERT
RUNS

25
20   55

320 HECTARES

1894M
TOP LIFT

390M
VERTICAL

1504M
FIRST LIFT

NUMBER OF RUNS: 25
LONGEST RUN: 1.6km (1 mile)
TOTAL LIFTS: 7 - 3 chairs, 1 drag, 3 x Magic
Carpets in beginners area
CAPACITY (people per hour): 7,700
LIFT TIMES: 9.00am to 4.00pm

AVERAGE SNOWFALL: 2.7m
SNOWMAKING: none

WINTER PERIODS: late June to Oct
Lift Passes:
1 Day $68, 5 Days $305, Season $1049;
Early bird season passes before April 30th.
Hire:Board & Boots NZ$46 per day
Board School
Group lessons 2hrs $37-43
Snowboard instruction course; $600-700
10-days. Pipe camps $380 5-days +passes

FREERIDE 50%
No trees but extensive backcountry
FREESTYLE 30%
2 terrain parks & 4 Half-pipes
CARVING 20%

PO Box 117, Wanaka, New Zealand
Tel: +64 3 443 7341
Fax: +64 3 443 8818
Web: www.cardrona.co.nz
Email: info@cardrona.com

Fly
to Christchurch 3 1/2hrs transfer. ANZ Christchurch-Wanaka , once a day. Queenstown 60 mins ,Wanaka 35 minutes from Cardrona.
Bus
Pre book seats in Wanaka and Queenstown. leave 08:30 & return 16:00. $25 return.
Car
From Christchurch, take 1,8,8A and 89. 277 446km , 3 1/2 hrs.Queenstown is 58km

NEW

New for 04 Season
High-speed detachable quad chair replaced the La Franchi chair

which this year has attracted the likes of Burton to hold the NZ open there. Although this may not be in the super league of big resorts, the humble offerings here are never the less acceptable and will appeal to all levels and style of rider. If you are moved by the steep and deep then you won't be disappointed with such areas known as **Powder Keg** and **Arcadia** Chutes reached off the La Franch chair.

FREERIDERS will love it here. There is a fantastic variety of snow-gathering gullies and plenty of rocks to throw yourself off. Keg and Arcadia are the areas where Cardrona holds it's National Extreme Championships. Records have been set by dropping down the 30 metre plus Eagle Rock in Captain's Basin, so if you're feeling suicidal this one is for you. If the runs within the boundary don't satisfy you, you could go heli-boarding in Cardrona's expansive back bowls.

FREESTYLERS are provided with a 800m boardercross course and a cool 1000m terrain park that comes loaded with a large table top, spines, jumps and rails. There are also four halfpipes including 2 superpipes, reached off the Macdougall quad chair lift. The 90m beginner's pipe has a not too intimidating 3m high wall; at the other end is the 140m Johnny Holmes Superpipe with 5m high walls.

CARVERS will find either of the two main faces ideal for laying out some big turns on. The Sluce Box is a great carvers run.

BEGINNERS may find the novice slopes a bit overcrowded on weekends and during holidays. However, persevere as this is a resort that should appeal to first timers with nice beginners runs of the Macdougall quad, which allows for easy progression.

OFF THE SLOPES, life goes on in the town of **Wanaka** (20 miles), or **Queenstown** (35 miles). Wanaka is the quieter of the two and more relaxed place with a number of cool bars and plenty of cafes. Overall, prices for **accommodation** are good and affordable. If you get to know the right people you'll be able to join in on the popular past time of 'Keg' parties.

N
E
W

Z
E
A
L
A
N
D

241

CORONET PEAK

7 OUT OF 10

Good freeriding & park, cracking do anything town

pic -Coronet Peak Tourism

%
OF BEGINNER
TO EXPERT
RUNS

1690M
TOP LIFT

280 HECTARES

428M
VERTICAL

20

45

35

1200M
FIRST LIFT

NUMBER OF RUNS: 25
LONGEST RUN: 1.8km (1.2 miles)
TOTAL LIFTS: 6 - 3 chairs, 3 drags
CAPACITY (people per hour): 7,000
LIFT TIMES: 9.00am to 4.00pm
MOUNTAIN CAFES: 3

AVERAGE SNOWFALL:
Unknown
SNOWMAKING:
30%

WINTER PERIODS:
June to Oct
Lift Passes
1 Day NZ$77, 3 Day $204
Season pass - $1599
Hire
Board & Boots NZ$50 per day
Board School
Group lessons NZ$38-46 1hr50. New
freestyle lessons $85
Night Boarding
Mid July to mid September, Friday and
Saturday nights 4pm to 9pm (NZ$37)

FREERIDE 55%
A few trees & good backcountry
FREESTYLE 30%
A Terrain parks & Half-pipes
CARVING 15%

Coronet Peak
PO Box 359, Queenstown
New Zealand
Tel: ++0064-3-442 4620
Web: www.nzski.com/coronet
Email: service@coronetpeak.co.nz

NEW
New for 04 Season
30 snowguns adding 30% more snow to
selected trails

Located amid the Southern Alps and lakes of the **South Island**, Cornet Peak, on the shores of Lake Wakatipu, is only 30 minutes from the hustle and bustle of the town to **Queenstown**. Cornet which has a shared lift pass with the neighbouring resort of The Remarkables, has terrain suitable for snowboarders of all abilities, with slopes that offer a combination of wide open pistes and well groomed trails that drop to a vert of 428 metres. The ride area is serviced by six well set out lifts and to ensure good snow cover at all times, Cornet has a multi-million dollar snowmaking system that covers from top to bottom. The low altitude here gives Cornet natural, undulating terrain with great spines and gullies for some of the best-riding available. The Cornet Express high-speed, detachable quad takes you to the summit where you gain access to some hot back bowls so loved by hard core freeriders. Check they are open though, because if you catch an avalanche and survive, it could be a long hike out when there is powder. However, it is worth it and make sure you ride the Rocky Gully T-bar.

FREERIDERS will find the runs down from the summit pretty cool, especially the M1. Advanced riders should try out the series of blacks from the summit known as the Exchange Drop, which if you don't treat with respect will make your eyes water as you do DROP. Powder hounds looking for some steep, deep, fluffy stuff need to check out the back bowls or the terrain around the Sarah Sue run, but note riding down this area does entail a hike back up to the resort to get on the lifts again.

FREESTYLERS should try out Sara Sue off Greengates for some big spine jumps, banks and natural quarter-pipes. Cornet is continually developing its terrain parks with table tops and rails built into various strategic 'fun-parks' all over the mountain. But beware, Cornet gets pretty crowded so be careful. The patrollers, including some on snowboards, are serious about using look outs on blind jumps, especially down Exchange Drop,

where you would do well to obey the No-Hit/No Jump and slow down zones to avoid any trouble.

CARVERS will enjoy the long blue trail known as the M1 as well as the runs known as Greengates and Million Dollar, which are pisted to perfection and great for leaving some nice long lines on.

BEGINNERS will find the best stuff is off the Meadows

THE TOWN & GETTING THERE

chair and alongside the learners poma. But there isn't a mass of novice trails here, although what is available is still good. The local ski school offers a 'Snowboard Starter' package for $60 and is well worth the money as instructors know their stuff.

THE TOWN

After hard days riding, the next best thing is to be able to hang out in a place that offers you a good choice of accommodation, plenty of restaurants and loads of bars with varying price ranges to suite all pockets. And that is exactly what you get in **Queenstown**, a big town full of all the joys and spoils to make a week a month or even a year an eventful one. Queenstown has every possible holiday services you could want and a vast array of outdoor sport activities. You can take part in paragliding, rock climbing, go jet skiing or even have a game of golf (if you?re sad enough) or really bored.

Accomodation. The choice of lodging around here is very impressive, but forget about any beds slopeside. Queenstown is the best place to be as it has the biggest selection and best budget options, but its also close to all the off-slope action. Motels are a common form of accommodation around here as are bed and breakfast homes. Bungy Backpackers is a cheap hangout. Tel ++64 03 442 8725

Food. Being a big town, as one would expect, there is a massive choice of restaurants and cheap cafes in Queenstown. Every type of food is available with lots of options to eat cheaply. Notable places for a feed are; The Cow, which offers moderately priced pizza and spaghetti. Berkels Gourmet frys up a good burger, while Gourmet is good for breakfast.

Night life, in Queenstown rocks hard and late. Locals here like and know how to party hard, and if there's nothing laid on then guaranteed something will happen to set the evening off. The choice of bars is great with some good boozers, such as the Red Rock Cafe which also serves good bar food. The World Bar is also cool hangout.

SUMMARY
Good freeriding resort offering some very nice powder areas. The resort management has a healthy attitude towards snowboarding here.
On the slopes: Really good
Off the slopes: Very good
Money Wise: Overall this is an expensive resort but offers good value.

Coronet Peak Tourism

N

**N
E
W**

**Z
E
A
L
A
N
D**

CAR
From Christchurch, take routes 1,8,8A and 89. 277 miles (446km) . 3 1/2 hrs. Queenstown is 36 miles (58km).
FLY
to Christchurch 3 1/2 hours away. Flights available to Queenstown (10mins away)
BUS
A bus to resort from Queenstown (20 mins). From Christchurch, its 6 hours.

4 OUT OF 10

Basic and dull, but a beginners paradise.

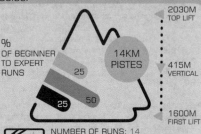

```
%
OF BEGINNER
TO EXPERT
RUNS
```

14KM PISTES

2030M TOP LIFT

415M VERTICAL

1600M FIRST LIFT

25 / 25 / 50

NUMBER OF RUNS: 14
LONGEST RUN: 1.5km (1.2 mile)
TOTAL LIFTS: 3
1 chairs,1 drag, 1 learner rope
CAPACITY (people per hour): 4000
LIFT TIMES: 9.00am to 4.30pm
MOUNTAIN CAFES: 1

AVERAGE SNOWFALL:
2m
SNOWMAKING:
none

WINTER PERIODS: late June to Oct
Lift Passes
1 Day NZ$50, 3 Day $135,5 Day $213
Hire
Board & Boots $40 per day
Board School
Group lessons $23
Private lessons $50

FREERIDE 50%
No trees but some backcountry
FREESTYLE 20%
No terrain park but a natural Half-pipe
CARVING 30%

Mount Dobson Ski Area
30 Alloway Street, Fairlie
South Canterbury, New Zealand
Tel: ++64 3 685 8039
Fax: ++64 3 685 8716
Web:www.dobson.co.nz
Email:mtdobson@xtra.co.nz

Fly
to Christchurch airport 90 mins away.
Bus
Bus services with change overs at the town Fairlie.
Train
to Timaru, 8 miles from the resort.
Car
From Christchurch, take highway 1 south and highway 8 to Fairlie and then on to Mt Dobson.

N E W Z E A L A N D

Mount Dobson is a small commercial resort located in the **Southern Canterbury** region of the country on the **South Island**. With a mere nine miles or so of rideable marked piste, Dobson boasts at having the largest beginner's slopes in New Zealand. Whatever the merits of such a claim are, Mt Dobson is a laid back place and has far less hassle about it compared to some of the bigger commercial resorts. The slopes here attract family groups and those out for a simple afternoons sliding around. Even though lift prices are a lot cheaper than other resorts, the slopes are not over populated with budget minded skiers. The terrain sweeps around a main face offering a mixture of very easy gentle slopes and a number of short fast tracks which are all serviced by drag lifts.

FREERIDERS of an intermediate level will find a day riding the slopes here is not a bad way to pass some time. The best of which will be the trails on the main face of the T-bar, and runs off the **West** and **East** trails. Riders, who like something to get stuck into and need a few challenges, may find Dobson a little repetitive and lacking in general interest. However, there is some nice challenging riding in the back bowls and the series of short blacks that drop down from the West and East runs, will give you something to think about. **The Bluff** is not a bad run and has a few humps en-route to the bottom of the Platter 2 drag lift.

FREESTYLERS will find it hard pressed to find anything man made to fling off. There is a natural half-pipe to be found off the west trail, but thats about it.

CARVERS who like to do big wide turns but don't like to do them for too long, will find Mt Dobson perfectly in tune with their thinking and liking. Nothing here takes that long to carve up, with only a couple of fast pisted tracks to choose from.

BEGINNERS will find the whole place a joy and even though a number of the runs graded "Difficult and intermediate" are a bit over rated and can be challenged after a short time by most.

OFF THE SLOPES, accommodation and other local facilities are offered in the towns of **Fairlie** or **Kimbell**. What you get in either, is very basic, affordable and sufficient for a few days stay. Night life is very tame and not up to much.

244

MT. HUTT

Worth the dodgy drive up, but not by much

Mount Hutt is the third resort in **Mount Cook** Line's 'Big Three', located 30 minutes from **Methven**. This is an early opening resort mainly thanks to its snowmaking facilities as well as the high altitude. You can enjoy some of the best snow cover for the longest season

pic Mt Hutt Tourism

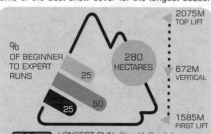

2075M TOP LIFT

%
OF BEGINNER
TO EXPERT
RUNS

280 HECTARES

25

25 50

672M VERTICAL

1585M FIRST LIFT

LONGEST RUN: 2km (1.2 mile)
TOTAL LIFTS: 9 - 2 chairs, 7 drags
CAPACITY (people per hour): 9,200
LIFT TIMES: 9.00am to 4.00pm
MOUNTAIN CAFES: 2

AVERAGE SNOWFALL:
1.8m
SNOWMAKING:
15%

WINTER PERIODS:
early June to late Oct
Lift Passes
1 Day $72, 5 Days $330
Hire
Board & Boots NZ$50 per day
Board School
Group lessons 2hrs NZ$38-46
Freestyle lessons 1hr50 $85

FREERIDE 50%
No trees but good backcountry
FREESTYLE 25%
1 terrain parks & 2 Half-pipes
CARVING 25%

Mt Hutt Ski Area
P.O. Box 14, Main St,
Methven,New Zealand.
Web: www.nzski.com/mthutt
Email: service@mthutt.co.nz

Fly
to Christchurch airport 90 mins away.
Bus
from Metven to Mt Hutt take 30 min.
Car
From Christchurch, take highways 73 &
72 trrough Tardhurst and Homebush to
Metven and then on up to Mt Hutt.

NEW

New for 04 Season
new 10,000m2 permanent earth formed
terrain park

in the **South Island**. The 9 lifts service an excellent expanse of terrain for everybody to take advantage off. Being one of NZ's biggest commercial resorts means that Mt Hutt can become very busy, attracting a lot of family ski groups. However, don't let that stop you, the resort is very snowboard friendly and there are plenty of good areas to ride with out crashing into two plankers all day. As with most of the NZ resorts access is via an ungraded road, which can be closed during snow or windy storms.

FREERIDERS who like the challenge of steep and extreme terrain, then the **South Face** is covered with double black diamond runs to test the cockiest of riders. Other great runs to check out, especially for ungroomed and touched powder, are Towers and Virgin Mile. Here you can ride free of crowds but remember that Mt Hutt is a very popular resort so move fast on powder mornings to get the best uncut stuff which there is plenty off on offer with no need to hike to.

FREESTYLERS will find that the crew have been busy building a new earth sculpted 10,000m2 terrain park that should become one of the best in NZ and available for most of the season. There are also 2 halfpipes. You will find plenty to jump and launch off down Exhibition Bowl, Morning Glory and through Race Hill, although exercise some caution on these blind jumps. If possible have someone spotting if possible especially if there are races or training in the area.

CARVERS gracing the slopes in hard boots will find some nice corduroy terrain around Broadway to carve up.
BEGINNERS. Mt Hutt is considered one of the best learning resorts in NZ with novice trails serviced by fixed grip tows.

OFF THE SLOPES you can base your self in **Methven**, **Christchurch** or **Ashburton**, all offering a variety of accommodation, food and nighlife. Methven is the closest, just 30 minutes away. Budget **accommodation** is limited so try to book ahead. There are plenty of restaurants and cafes serving a variety on dishes at varying rates. **Night life** is okay in the bars but avoid the cheesy discos.

N

NEW ZEALAND

245

MT. LYFORD

4 OUT OF 10

Overall rather boring

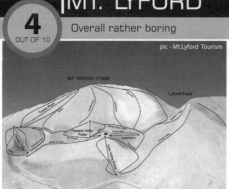

pic - Mt.Lyford Tourism

% OF BEGINNER TO EXPERT RUNS

305 HECTARES

1750M TOP LIFT

450M VERTICAL

1249M FIRST LIFT

30

40

30

LONGEST RUN: 1.9km (1.2 mile)
TOTAL LIFTS: 6 - All drags
LIFT TIMES: 9.00am to 4.30pm
MOUNTAIN CAFES: 1

AVERAGE SNOWFALL:
2.6m
SNOWMAKING:
unknown

WINTER PERIODS:
June to Oct
Lift Passes
1 Day NZ$45, Season $329
Hire
Board & Boots $40 per day
Board School
Group lessons $15 per hour
Private lessons $45 per hour

FREERIDE 60%
No trees but good backcountry
FREESTYLE 20%
No terrain park or pipe
CARVING 20%

Mt Lyford Alpine Resort
Private Bag, Waiau
North Canterbury, New Zealand
Tel: +64 3 315-6178
Fax: +64 3 315-6158
Web: www.mtlyford.co.nz
Email: lyfordski@xtra.co.nz

Fly
to Christchurch airport 2 hours away.
Bus
from Christchurch with changes at
Culverden and Waiau, tel 03 388 8987
Car
From Christchurch, take highway 7 north
and highway 70 via Culverden and Waiau
to reach My Lyford.

NEW

New for 04 Season
new t-bar, 2 new groomers

Located just hours from **Christchurch** and only 18 miles from the town of **Kailoura**, is the small and commercial resort of **Mount Lyford.** This totally privately owned mountain may not be the biggest resort in New Zealand, but by the same token it's not the smallest, and unlike some of the other commercial resorts, Mt Lyford is far more affordable and offers great value for money for any rider who can handle a few days. Mt.Lyford is a very snowboard friendly hangout and on occasions has boarders out numbering skiers. Still who ever is there, will tell you that its pretty dull for any more than a couple of days if you stick to the marked slopes but great if you go heli-boarding into the backcountry areas. The area gets good natural snow cover that is spread out over two areas which are somewhat different to each other. The **lake Stella** area is a short drive around the mountain, is the advanced riders spot while beginners will find the best slopes on the **Terako** field.

FREERIDERS should make their way to the top of **Mt Terako** via the Terako lift for some uneven terrain. From the top and after a short hike, you can either ride down the series of steep blacks such as **Die Hard**, or you can elect to take the slightly easier runs such as the **Thriller**. Riders who can afford it and want to ride some backcountry powder, will be able to experience the best stuff by taking a heli-board trip with Hanmer Helicopters.

FREESTYLERS may find Mt Lyford a little non-happening but still worth a visit to wile away a day with out the crowds. The slopes are not blessed with an abundance of natural hits. However, you will find a few rocks to leap over and one or two wind lips.

CARVERS will find the least to do here if your only desire is corduroy trails. However, an hour here will allow for some fun. Only 20% of the rideable area is groomed.

BEGINNERS will love Mt Lyford because you can practice your thing on some very tame slopes, which are free of large ski groups. The only thing is that all the lifts are drags.

OFF THE SLOPES the by word is, 'very basic and dull'. There is chalet **accommodation** along the access road but little else. *Keiths Cafe* is the place for breakfast while the *Lodge Hotel* will provide some evening madness.

7 OUT OF 10

Good overall resort

Some would say that you haven't truly snowboarded in New Zealand until you have spent a day at **Ohau Ski Area** and a night at the Ohau Lodge. Seemingly in the middle of nowhere, about half way between **Queenstown** and **Christchurch**, most people make the mistake of only visiting Ohau for a day en-route between other resorts. The views alone here are amazing with **Mount Cook,** NZ's highest mountain, in sight all around the area.

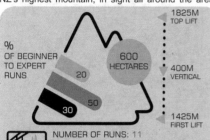

1825M TOP LIFT

%
OF BEGINNER TO EXPERT RUNS — 20, 30, 50

600 HECTARES

400M VERTICAL

1425M FIRST LIFT

NUMBER OF RUNS: 11
LONGEST RUN: 1.9km (1.2 mile)
TOTAL LIFTS: 3 - 1 chair, 2 drags
CAPACITY (people per hour): 1,400
LIFT TIMES: 9.00am to 4.30pm
MOUNTAIN CAFES: 1

AVERAGE SNOWFALL:
1.8m
SNOWMAKING:
none

WINTER PERIODS:
June to Oct
Lift Passes
1 Day pass - NZ$50
Hire
Board & Boots $40 per day
Board School
Group lesson $36 1.5 hours
Private lessons $70 per hour

FREERIDE 50%
No trees but good backcountry
FREESTYLE 30%
Just natural stuff
CARVING 20%

Ohau Snow Fields and Lake Ohau Lodge
PO Box 51, TWIZEL
South Island, NZ
Tel: +64 (0) 3 438 9885
Web: www.ohau.co.nz
Email: ohau@ohau.co.nz

Fly
to Christchurch airport 2 hours away.
Bus
from Christchurch, changes at Twizel or Omarama.
Car
From Christchurch, take highways 1 and 8 via Twizel.

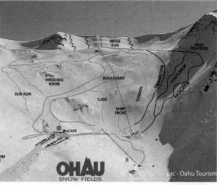

pic - Oahu Tourism

This internationally renowned snowboarders resort offers some excellent riding for all levels on amazingly crowd free slopes with a fair share of good powder days. Riders come here because they know that this place cuts it, without any hype of bull shit, just a damn fine mountain that will please hardcore freeriders with a good choice of steeps.

FREERIDERS are most at home here. Apart from the two learner areas at the base and the wide groomed Boulevard Run, the terrain is generally steep. Left of the T-bar, is the steepest part of the area with the **Escalator trail** being the steepest run on the mountain. The strong-nerved should consider traversing further than Escalator, past the **Rock Bluff** and ride down to the Platter lift. The face above the day lodge, with the **Sun Run trail** on it, offers some steep runs and because it gets sun early in the day, it's often the best place to ride in the morning. On the other face, the **Exhibition** and **Escalator** runs, remain in the shade until late in the day.
FREESTYLERS will have to make do with natural hits, if getting high on a board is you're type of fix, nothing is laid on here.
CARVERS may at first feel left out, however after some close examination, you will soon see that there is enough pisted carving trails to shine on, with runs like the **Shirt Front,** where you can give some style at speed.
BEGINNERS tend to hang out on the **Boulevard** run although it does get a little steep in places (below Top Flat). Boulevard does give less confident riders a good reign of the mountain and a few ski areas have such an easy run from there highest point.

STAYING
The Ohau experience is best enjoyed by staying at the **Ohau Lodge**, situated at the base of the mountain. Food and booze are available in the Lodge on back down in the town of **Twizel**. Wherever you decide to chill out, there's a good choice of cool hangouts with reasonable prices for booze.

N

N
E
W

Z
E
A
L
A
N
D

247

6 OUT OF 10

Good place to ride

pic - Porter Heights Tourism

%
OF BEGINNER
TO EXPERT
RUNS

15

35

50

365 HECTARES

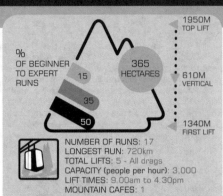

1950M
TOP LIFT

610M
VERTICAL

1340M
FIRST LIFT

NUMBER OF RUNS: 17
LONGEST RUN: 720km
TOTAL LIFTS: 5 - All drags
CAPACITY (people per hour): 3,000
LIFT TIMES: 9.00am to 4.30pm
MOUNTAIN CAFES: 1

AVERAGE SNOWFALL:
2.9m
SNOWMAKING:
10%

WINTER PERIODS:
June to Oct
Lift Passes
1 Day NZ$50, Season $700
Hire
Board and boots - $40
Board School
Lesson (2hrs), lift and equipment - $75
Group 2hrs $25, Private $55 per hour

FREERIDE 50%
No trees but good backcountry
FREESTYLE 30%
A terrain park & pipe
CARVING 20%

Porter Heights Ski Area
PO Box 15, Springfield,
Canterbury, New Zealand
Tel: +64 3 318 4002
Fax: +64 3 318 4008
Web: www.porterheights.co.nz
Email:ski@porterheights.co.nz

Fly
to Christchurch airport 1 hour away.
Train
to Springfield, 12 miles from the resort.
Bus
Bus services with change overs at the
town Springfield.
Car
from Christchurch (89km), take highway 73
via Darfield, Springfield & past Lake Lyndon

N

N
E
W

Z
E
A
L
A
N
D

Porters Heights is situated in the **Craigieburn Range** and is the closest boarding area to **Christchurch**. The whole area is likened to a large terrain park with heaps of runs that can't be beaten on a powder day with cool challenging chutes and hits. Legendary runs like **Big Mama** (one of the largest in the Southern Hemisphere) and **Bluff Face** (NZ's steepest) help to make this an extremely interesting and challenging resort for any snowboarder.

FREERIDERS should go to the top of the No 3 T-bar, because from here the mountain is yours. The view of **Lake Coleridge** and surrounding mountain ranges is spectacular. Don't hang around sightseeing for too long though - the first tracks on Big Mama aren't available all day. It is a reasonably easy traverse (with a little climbing) along a ridge line to the top of Big Mama, but it's not until you're standing at the top of the slope that you realise just how long the run is. It is a huge 620 vertical metres from top to bottom - one of the largest vertical drops in a lift accessed area in NZ. If you're fit enough to enjoy long powder runs, **Big Mama** is heaven. If you prefer chutes, traverse to the left from the top of lift No 3 T-bar to **Aorangi Chutes** and the Leapers, where the terrain is steep and the chutes are narrow. **Bluff Face** is another cool place to ride reached via a traverse down to McNulty's cat-track and hike up to the summit of Allison Peak. The **Powder Bowl** and **Crystal Valley** runs are both outside the ski boundary. There is a great boarding to be had on both, but the hike can be a mission. For reasons of safety, inform the ski patrol if you intend to go into any of these areas.

FREESTYLERS have a lot here to check out. There's an international size halfpipe in **McNulty's Basin** and heaps of good natural hits dotted around the whole area.

CARVERS will find the runs down either side of the No 1 T-bar have a reasonably consistent gradient and make excellent cruising runs for intermediate boarders

BEGINNERS will find the runs limited to a few short flats at the base area which are serviced by a couple of easy to use lifts.

THE TOWN
The best place to base yourself for local services, is in nearby **Springfield**, where there's some good lodging options, good eating out and great night time happenings shared with friendly locals.

REMARKABLES

Good place to ride!

The Remarkables lies within sight of the **Cornet Peak** resort. Higher in altitude, the car park is the same level as Cornet's

pic - WSG

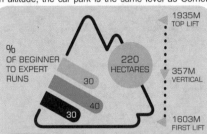

1935M TOP LIFT

% OF BEGINNER TO EXPERT RUNS

220 HECTARES

30

40

30

357M VERTICAL

1603M FIRST LIFT

LONGEST RUN: 1.6km (1 mile)
TOTAL LIFTS: 5 - 2 chairs, 3 drags
CAPACITY (people per hour): 3,000
LIFT TIMES: 9.00am to 4.00pm
MOUNTAIN CAFES: 1

AVERAGE SNOWFALL:
2.7m
SNOWMAKING:
10%

WINTER PERIODS:
June to Oct
Lift Passes
1 Day $72, 5 Day $330, Season $1599
Hire
Board & Boots NZ$50 per day
Board School
Group lessons 2hrs NZ$38-46
Freestyle lessons $85 1hr50
Night Boarding
Yes

FREERIDE 65%
No trees but good backcountry
FREESTYLE 25%
A terrain park & Half-pipe
CARVING 10%

The Remarkables Ski Area
PO Box 359, Queenstown
New Zealand
Tel: +64 (0) 64-3-4424615
Fax: +64 (0) 64-3-442 4619
Web:www.nzski.com/remarkables
Email:service@theremarkables.co.nz

Fly
to Christchurch or Queenstown.
Bus
Bus from Queenstown to the resort is available on an hourly basis $25 return.
Contact skishuttle@coachline.co.nz
Car
From Christchurch, take highways 1, 8, 8A and 89. Approx 6 hours.

NEW

New for 04 Season
new Xbox Terrain Park will triple size of existing terrain park, includes 150m superpipe

summit, with the result being that the mountain is very craggy and rocky. The Remarkables tends to be a lot quieter than Cornet Peak with fewer skiers. It also gets some incredible powder days and offers terrain for every style and grade of rider. The area is some what sheltered but still gives out plenty of sun and loads of natural snow. The **Homeward** runs are the place to shred some deep powder where you can ride some long floating turns with an amazing back drop. The Homewards take you right down to the access road to catch the shuttle bus back to the base building in order to do the whole thing again. The runs here are accessed by three chairlifts. The **Alta** double chair services the best intermediate terrain to suit carvers or freeriders. The **Sugar quad** is the lift to take to get access to some good advance terrain and competent intermediate stuff. However, advanced riders looking to cut it in style and be pushed to the fore should check out the runs found off **Shadow lift.**

FREERIDERS prepared to do some hiking, and after checking the snow conditions with the patrol, can reach some major dogs bollocks terrain with big chutes and scary steeps. Turn left off the Shadow and hike 20 minutes up to the ridge to access the area known as **Elevator** above **Lake Alta**. If you continue up along the ridge then the chutes get narrower and more extreme, so be bloody careful if you don't want this to be your last ever run. Go left off Sugar for the Toilet Bowl a freeriders heaven, which again takes you to the access road and the shuttle bus.

FREESTYLERS will find a new **Xbox Terrain Park** that has tripled the size of the old terrain park, and includes a 150m superpipe. Riders will find plenty of cliffs and rock drops to get air from, especially in areas around Sugar and Alta. There are also plenty of cat-tracks to drop off.

CARVERS will find a number of runs to laying out big super G turns on but in truth this is not a groomed piste lovers home.

BEGINNERS have two superb learner areas with fixed grip tows and an excellent snowboard school that will soon get you sorted out and cutting the mountain up in style.

THE TOWN. Read the **Queenstown** section in the **Coronet peak** review

6 OUT OF 10

Exactly what it says on the tin. If you like terrain parks, then its a must

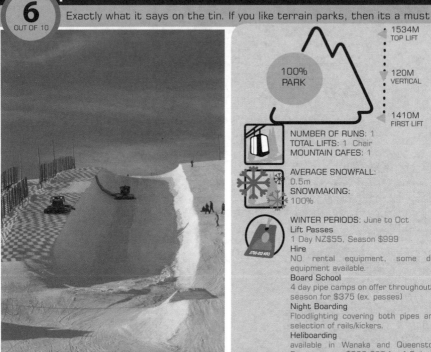

pic - Snowpark Tourism

1534M
TOP LIFT

100%
PARK

120M
VERTICAL

1410M
FIRST LIFT

NUMBER OF RUNS: 1
TOTAL LIFTS: 1 Chair
MOUNTAIN CAFES: 1

AVERAGE SNOWFALL:
0.5m
SNOWMAKING:
100%

WINTER PERIODS: June to Oct
Lift Passes
1 Day NZ$55, Season $999
Hire
NO rental equipment, some demo
equipment available.
Board School
4 day pipe camps on offer throughout the
season for $375 (ex. passes)
Night Boarding
Floodlighting covering both pipes and a
selection of rails/kickers.
Heliboarding
available in Wanaka and Queenstown.
Expect to pay $500-600 for 4-5 drops.

FREERIDE 0%
FA
FREESTYLE 100%
A terrain park & 2 pipes
CARVING 0%

Snow Park Ltd
Cardrona Valley, RD1
Wanaka 9192, New Zealand
Phone : +64 3 443 9991
Fax: +64 3 443 9990
Web: www.snowparknz.com
Email: info@snowparknz.com

Fly
to Queenstown (55km) or Wanaka (35km)
Train
to Springfield, 12 miles from the resort.
Bus
Daily from Queenstown to resort.
snowbus@paradise.net.nz, or Wanaka
email ewa@adventure.net.nz
Car
From Lake Wanaka its 35km up the Cardrona
Valley. From Queenstown its 1 hr.

NEW

New for 04 Season
NZ$3million investment in new chairlift &
30 snow guns improving coverage by 350%.
X -games shaper Frank Wells onboard for
the terrain parks.

N

N
E
W

Z
E
A
L
A
N
D

Snowpark is New Zealands latest resort, only opening a couple of seasons ago, and is the only one dedicated to freestyling. You'll find it on the **South Island,** about 35km from **Wanaka**. Natural terrain wise this place will not get your pulse racing, but natural is not was this place is. What you get is a resort packed with pipes, rails, hips, boxes the lot; and a team dedicated to making it happen and happen big. Theres no equipment hire so make sure you turn up with everything.

This place is packed with features, and is perfect for the pro as much as the novice taking their first steps into the park. Most of the major features are dug out of the landscape, so they should be open all season.

The Super Pipe is designed to full World Cup spec, and theres another suitable for beginners. Theres a 50x8m 1/4 pipe, this year they're looking at 40+ rails, boxes and hits of varying sizes for all abilities. To ease progression they have 3-4 sizes of each rail, and a similar setup for the boxes. Theres an increase in the number of beginners jumps this year, and its graded to get you ready for some of the monsters such as the 100ft kicker they built for Burton.

TREBLE CONE

Good overall resort

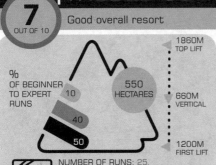

1860M
TOP LIFT

%
OF BEGINNER
TO EXPERT
RUNS

10

550
HECTARES

660M
VERTICAL

40

50

1200M
FIRST LIFT

NUMBER OF RUNS: 25.
LONGEST RUN: 3.5km (2.2 mile)
TOTAL LIFTS: 6
2 chairs, 3 drags, 1 Magic carpet
CAPACITY (people per hour): 6,200
LIFT TIMES: 9.00am to 4.00pm
MOUNTAIN CAFES: 1

AVERAGE SNOWFALL:
2.5m
SNOWMAKING:
10%

WINTER PERIODS:
June to Oct
Lift Passes
1 Day NZ$75, Child NZ$35
Hire
Board & Boots NZ$46 per day
Board School
Group NZ$45 ph, private from $75 ph

FREERIDE 60%
No trees but good backcountry
FREESTYLE 15%
Rail park, few kickers, good natural
CARVING 25%

Treble Cone Ski Area
PO Box 206, Wanaka, New Zealand
Tel: ++(03) 443 7443
Fax: ++(03) 443 8401
Web:www.treblecone.com
Email:tcinfo@treblecone.co.nz

Fly
to Christchurch or Queenstown or direct
to Wanaka (NEW direct Air NZ flight)
Bus
from Queenstown to resort available on
an hourly basis.Shuttles from Wanaka
by Edgewater Adventures and Alpine
Coachlines NZ$27 return
Car
From Christchurch, take highways 1, 8,
8A and 89 to Wanaka. The drive time is
around 5 hours.
30 minutes drive from Wanaka, 1.5hours
from Queenstown via Crown range

NEW

New for 04 Season
Over NZ$2million invested including new
bar & cafe and groomers

pic : Treble Cone Tourism

Treble Cone is half an hour from the town of **Wanaka** and provides some incredible terrain, on and off piste in a major scenic place. Some would say that Treble Cone gets more than its fair share of dry southern snow as well as the resort boasting a vert un-matched in the rest of the country. With 50% advanced terrain, Treble is known as one of New Zealand's more testing and challenging resorts that competent freeriders and freestylers should love and be able to go home with a few stories to tell after tackling some major steeps, long chutes and deep powder bowls on some gnarly black faces

FREERIDERS will like it here especially when there has been some fresh snow. A particular good area to drop into is **Powder Bowl**. A wide open slope leading into the lower gullies for some big powder turns and super floating glides. For the more adventurous the off-piste in the **Matukituki Basin** is the place to check out.
FREESTYLERS should head to the top and from the summit, drop into the **Saddle Basin** alongside the Saddle double chair, to take advantage of loads of natural hits and halfpipes to gain maximum air time. The **Gun Barrel**, which is also reached from the summit, is another legendary, long natural halfpipe where banked slalom events are regularly held. The terrain park is loaded with and if you're still not satisfied and in need of an adrenaline rush, there are loads of big drops offs and rocks of all sizes dotted all over the mountain.
CARVERS need not feel left out as Treble Cone has done lots of work developing a series of well groomed runs down the face of the mountain which are ideal for laying down some big wide arcs.
BEGINNERS may note that although Treble Cone is not known as a beginners mountain don't be put off, as there is still enough to try out without killing yourself on the first day. Its skiers who can't handle it here, not fast learning boarders.

THE TOWN
Away from the slopes local services are provided down in **Wanaka**, a quiet and relaxed place that provides good places to kip and a few bars popular with snowboarders. For some decent food why not try *Kai Ahaka* for a tasty treat and great coffee. The *Pot Belly Stove* also serves decent local food. Places to check out for a beer are the likes of the *Barrows*, which is the locals haunt, or *Outback bar* which has a pool table and serves booze until late.

N
E
W

Z
E
A
L
A
N
D

6 OUT OF 10

Simple but good resort

pic - Turoa Tourism

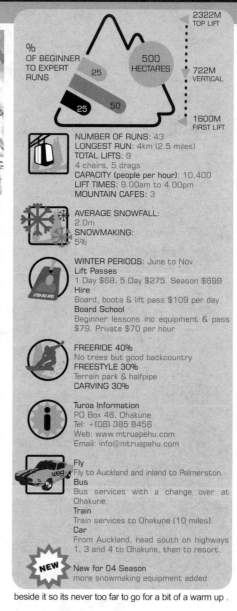

% OF BEGINNER TO EXPERT RUNS: 25 / 25 / 50

500 HECTARES

2322M TOP LIFT

722M VERTICAL

1600M FIRST LIFT

NUMBER OF RUNS: 43
LONGEST RUN: 4km (2.5 miles)
TOTAL LIFTS: 9
4 chairs, 5 drags
CAPACITY (people per hour): 10,400
LIFT TIMES: 9.00am to 4.00pm
MOUNTAIN CAFES: 3

AVERAGE SNOWFALL: 2.0m
SNOWMAKING: 5%

WINTER PERIODS: June to Nov
Lift Passes
1 Day $68, 5 Day $275. Season $699
Hire
Board, boots & lift pass $109 per day
Board School
Beginner lessons inc equipment & pass
$79. Private $70 per hour

FREERIDE 40%
No trees but good backcountry
FREESTYLE 30%
Terrain park & halfpipe
CARVING 30%

Turoa Information
PO Box 46, Ohakune
Tel: +(06) 385 8456
Web: www.mtruapehu.com
Email: info@mtruapehu.com

Fly
Fly to Auckland and inland to Palmerston.
Bus
Bus services with a change over at Ohakune.
Train
Train services to Ohakune (10 miles).
Car
From Auckland, head south on highways 1, 3 and 4 to Ohakune, then to resort.

NEW
New for 04 Season
more snowmaking equipment added

Turoa is now joined with **Whakapapa** creating, at 4,500 acres, New Zealands largest resort. Turoa is covered with gullies, bowls, walls and wide slopes: the type of terrain only found on a volcano. This can vary incredibly from year to year, depending on the amount of snow cover. Because the area is so large and conditions can vary so much, it is worthwhile spending time in the bars down in **Okakune**, meeting the locals first hand and finding out where the current best spots are. The runs marked on the trail map are really of little more than aesthetics value. There are countless possible routes and like Whakapapa on the other side of the mountain, the fun of riding at Turoa is finding them.

FREERIDERS of an advanced level should get to the top of the Bacardi T-bar. From here you can appreciate the scope of the place and get an idea of where you'd like to ride. The runs out to your right **(Limit, Solitude and Layback)** are long runs in wide open spaces, where the thrill of riding down an active volcano can be fully realised. The runs way out to your left (Speedtrack, Main Face and Triangle) are a little steeper. There is nowhere on Turoa where the urge to climb Ruapehu's Peak is stronger than when viewing **Mangaheuheu Glacier**, from the Glacier Entrance run. If you want to hike to the top, check with the ski patrol on the best route and do not go without telling them. They'll also appreciate it if you can report to them on your return. It doesn't matter which route you take from the peak back to the ski area, they are 475 of the most unforgettable vertical metres in New Zealand. FREESTYLERS have a decent park, however on a powder day, which don't occur with great frequency in the North Island, Turoa's walls and gullies beckon you to charge hard. There's nothing like launching off **Clays Leap** or the M**angawhero Headwall** and landing in the safe hands of powder.
CARVERS learn to freeride and get real! This is not a hard booters place.
BEGINNERS will find the Alpine Meadows area beside the car park the place to start out on. The cafeteria is right beside it so its never too far to go for a bit of a warm up .

THE TOWN. There is an abundance of local facilities in **Ohakume**, only 10 miles away. **Accommodation** is provided as cheap B&B's, inexpensive motels and pricey hotels. **Food** and drinking is plentiful, *Clinches Cafe* is the place for breakfast.

WHAKAPAPA

Good freeriding

pic - WSG

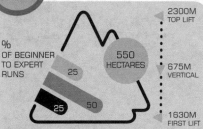

2300M
TOP LIFT

%
OF BEGINNER
TO EXPERT
RUNS

550
HECTARES

675M
VERTICAL

25

25   50

1630M
FIRST LIFT

NUMBER OF RUNS: 40.
LONGEST RUN: 2.8km (2.8 mile)
TOTAL LIFTS: 13
7 chairs, 6 drags, 1 learner rope
CAPACITY (people per hour): 23,000
LIFT TIMES: 9.00am to 3.30pm
MOUNTAIN CAFES: 6

AVERAGE SNOWFALL:
2.0m
SNOWMAKING:
10%

WINTER PERIODS: June to Nov
Lift Passes
1 Day $68, 5 Day $275. Season $699
Hire
Board & boots $47 per day
Board School
Beginner lessons inc equipment & pass
$79. Private $70 per hour
Night Boarding
6pm to 9pm in Rockgarden area

FREERIDE 50%
No trees but good backcountry
FREESTYLE 25%
Terrain park & halfpipe
CARVING 25%

Ruapehu Alpine Lifts Ltd
Private Bag, Mount Ruapehu
New Zealand
Tel: +64 7 892 3738
Fax: + 64 7 892 3732
Web: www.mtruapehu.com
Email: info@mtruapehu.com

Fly
to Auckland & inland to Taupo airport.
Bus
Bus services with a change over at
Ohakune.
Train
Train services to Ohakune (10 miles).
Car
From Auckland, head south on highways
1 to Taupo and then on to Whakapapa.

NEW
New for 04 Season
night boarding, extensive work on pipe.

Whakapapa is located near Tuora, on the slopes of Mount Rauapehu. The diversity of the terrain here is caused by the way the underlying volcano has formed over millions of years. As the largest recognised ski resort in the country, Whakapapa has something for everyone, with steeps, cliffs, fast chutes gullies and big natural banks allowing for some big air. The Mt Ruapehu lift pass covers both Whakapapa and Turoa.

FREERIDERS who know what's what, will be aware of the awesome area known as the Pinnacles. Simply put, if you're not a damn good advanced rider, then stay away. The Pinnacles are a series of cliff runs that will wipe the lights out for good if any rider mucks up!

FREESTYLERS will be pleased to learn that management have, in the last few years, splashed out thousands of big bucks on a new Pipemaster. Having now learned how to turn it on, the halfpipe can boast perfectly groomed walls with a nice big vert and good transitions allowing for great smooth take offs.

CARVERS can carve away for days on well groomed trails and take a week to do them all a few times over, with a number to test the best of the edge merchants.

THE TOWN
Heaps of good local facilities exist in varying villages all in easy reach of the slopes. Prices vary, but on the whole well affordable and worth the effort of a weeks stay.

Capital City: Oslo
Population: 4.5 Million
Highest Peak: Galdhopiggen 2472m
Language: Norwegian
Legal Drink Age: 18/20 spirits
Drug Laws: Cannabis is illegal and frowned upon
Age of consent: 16
Electricity: 240 Volts AC 2-pin
International Dialing Code: +47

Currency: Krone
Exchange Rate:
UK£1 = 12.7
US$1 = 7
EURO = 8.4

Driving Guide
All vehicles drive on the right hand side of the road
Speed limits:
Motorways-80kph (50mph)
Highways-90kph (56mph)
Towns-50kph (31mph)
Emergency
Fire - 110
Police - 112
Ambulance - 113
Tolls
Payable when entering a few cities.
Documentation
Driving licence and motor insurance must be carried.
Speeding
On the spot fines are payable if caught speeding.

Time Zone
UTC/GMT +1 hour
Daylight saving time: +1 hour

Norwegian Snowboard Federation
Bentsebrugata 13 B
Oslo, Norway
Tel: +47 22 09 88 40
web: www.nsbf.no

Norway is famous for it's cross country skiing which is reflected in the fact that although there are over 160 resorts dotted around the country, 80% are simply not ridable. The terrain in the suitable areas is best for novices and intermediates, with little long term interest for advanced riders due to the lack of steep terrain.

Travelling around Norway is made easy by the country's excellent road and rail network, connecting well with international airports. The main gateway airport with regular international flights is Oslo, but onward travel usually means an extra 2 to 3 hours of travel.

If you're visiting Norway by car, you can take ferry crossings via ports in the UK, or short crossings from northern ports in Germany and Denmark. Driving in Norway is easy, but snow chains are a must in remote resorts.

The one common factor is Norway is its costs (super expensive in fact). Accommodation is pretty good with the most affordable type being cabins, which cater for groups. Hotels will burn a massive hole in your pocket. Beer prices are so high that evenings in the average bar are out of the question. The best advice is to bring heaps of duty free, or buy your drinks at the off licenses, but note, you have to be 18 to drink beer and 20 to buy or drink spirits.

Overall, Norway is really good but it does have some major drawbacks, like its total lack of music talent, stupidly expensive booze and the world's worst knitwear. On the other hand, the women in this part of the world are to die for.

GEILO

5 OUT OF 10

Basic but okay

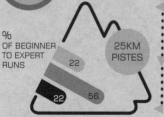

% OF BEGINNER TO EXPERT RUNS

22
22   56

25KM PISTES

1173M TOP LIFT

275M VERTICAL

800M FIRST LIFT

NUMBER OF RUNS: 39.
LONGEST RUN: 2.0km (1.2 mile)
TOTAL LIFTS: 19
4 chairs, 14 drags, 5 Children's lifts
CAPACITY (people per hour): 22,000
LIFT TIMES: 9:30 – 16:30
MOUNTAIN CAFES: 7

AVERAGE SNOWFALL:
1.25m
SNOWMAKING:
50%

WINTER PERIODS: June to Nov
Lift Passes
Afternoon pass - 235, 1 Day 275
2 Day 500, 6 Day 1150
Hire
Board & boots 310 per day
Board School
Private lesson 390 for 55 mins
Night Boarding
5 evenings a week until 20:00 from 2
January - 11 April.

FREERIDE 30%
A few trees but no backcountry
FREESTYLE 30%
Terrain park & 2 halfpipes
CARVING 40%

Tourist office Geilo
Postboks 68, N-3580
Geilo
Tel: 32 09 59 00
Web:www.geilo.no
Email:turistinfo@geilo.no

Fly
Fly to Oslo airport, which is 4 hours away.
Train
Train services are possible direct to Geilo
from Oslo and take around 2 hours.
Car
Via Oslo , head north on highway 7 via
Honefos, Gol and Hol to reach Geilo.
The distance is aound 150 miles (240 km)
and will take 2 hours .

New for 04 Season
new 150m Super Pipe (5.7m walls)at
Fugleleiken More than NOK 1.2 million
has been invested in special maintenance
equipment for the snowboard parks,

(c) Geilo tourism

Located roughly 4 hours from **Oslo** and situated in the **Hallingdal Valley**, the largest mountain area in Europe, Geilo is the oldest resort in Norway. The well laid out town is easy to get around and lies close to the slopes, making for an easy attack of the runs first thing in the morning. The slopes rise up on two sides of the valley, with terrain that is well maintained, leaving lots of corduroy tracks to mess up in the early hours. Geilo's slopes will suit intermediate and novice riders mostly, with little to set the heart racing for advanced or even competent riders, although there are a few black graded runs. The two separate areas (which aren't connected) rise up to give a maximum lift height of 1173 metres. If you want to ride both places, you'll have to take a snow taxi, which is not included in your lift pass. The Vestila area, which is actually the smaller of the two, has the longer runs, with a mixture of blues, reds and a couple of blacks.

FREERIDERS who pick a resort for powder and fast long adventurous trails, will not be satisfied here. There is no great adrenaline rush if you're a competent rider, just a couple of challenging runs to tackle and only a small amount of good powder terrain to seek out, but there are some trees to shred off the Heissen lift.
FREESTYLERS wanting air will find the 100 metre halfpipe, or the selection of hits in one of the two fun parks, the place to be. Theres a new 150m Super Pipe at **Fugleleiken**, supposedly Northern Europe's largest. Night riding in the pipe is possible, so don't fret if you miss the morning because you slept in after scoring with a local the night before.
CARVERS in shiny hard boots and race boards, give this place a miss, you'll stand out like a sore thumb and be loudly laughed at. Norwegians don't care too much for posing euro carvers. However, the number 14 trail has some nice carving spots.
BEGINNERS are presented with an excellent choice of easy slopes to tackle, starting out at the base area with good flats higher up and easy runs back into the village.

THE TOWN
Geilo also offers loads of things to do, you can try ice climbing, snow rafting or if you fancy reducing your balls to the size of two peas, you can sign up for a night in a snow hole. Geilo is a sprawling affair with good **accommodation**, but nothing comes cheap. Eating here is simple but even a basic pizza will set you back 70Kr. **Night life** will sting you if you plan to drink heavily or chat up a good looking Norwegian lass. *Hos John's, Laverb* and the *Bardola* are the places to try your luck.

wsg

HEMSEDAL

7
OUT OF 10

Norways best. Good variety of runs, a great park, cool but expensive nightlife.

pie - (c) Hemsedal tourist

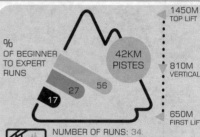

%
OF BEGINNER
TO EXPERT
RUNS

1450M
TOP LIFT

42KM
PISTES

810M
VERTICAL

650M
FIRST LIFT

17
27
56

NUMBER OF RUNS: 34.
LONGEST RUN: 6.0km (3.7 mile)
TOTAL LIFTS: 17
6 chairs, 11 drags
CAPACITY (people per hour): 22,600
LIFT TIMES: 9.30am to 9.30pm
MOUNTAIN CAFES: 6

AVERAGE SNOWFALL:
3m
SNOWMAKING:
15%

WINTER PERIODS:
Nov to May
Lift Passes
1 Day 305, 2 Days 610, 6 Days 1245
Season 4090
Hire
Several companies in town. Hemsedal
Sport Skiservice charge 310 per day for
board and boots
Board School
90 min lesson 420 (weekend)
5x90mins lesson 595 (week)
Private lesson 430 for 50mins
Night Boarding
5 evenings a week until 20:00 from 2
January - 11 April.

FREERIDE 60%
Trees and some good backcountry
FREESTYLE 30%
2 Terrain park & 2 halfpipes
CARVING 10%

Hemsedal Tourist Office
Post box 3, N-3561 Hemsedal
Tel: ++47 32 05 50 30
Fax: ++47 32 05 50 31
Web:www.hemsedal.com
Email:info@hemsedal.com

NEW

New for 04/05 Season
new 8-seater express chairlift replaces
the present 3-seater Holvinheisen
making it the biggest lift in Scandinavia.
Improved beginners area including new
terrain park.

Hemsedal has the claim of being the most photographed resort by the snowboarding press, and is no stranger to snowboarding having hosted major events for years including the Artic Challenge in 2001, and as a result has been attracting riders of all ages for years, especially freestylers. Its height, location and use of snow cannons all help to ensure a good snow record and a long season. The slopes lie about 3 kilometres from the main town and are reached by a free shuttle bus. The terrain will appeal to all standards, with 40 kilometres of well prepared piste for freeriders to carve up as well as being ideal for beginners. Freestylers will get to enjoy one of the best parks in Europe, and there's a load of good accessible back country routes. The runs are serviced by a good lift system which, unlike some neighbouring resorts, is not all drag lifts. Theres also night riding for most of the season during the week until 9pm, useful if you're trying to avoid the expensive bars.

FREERIDERS. Theres a healthy attitude towards going off piste; it's your responsibility plain and simple. So with that in mind, grab a guide or a local and head off to the **Totten** or **Røgjin** Summits. From the back of the Totten Summit, you're treated to some excellent cliffs and powder, which will test even the advanced rider. Make a bee-line for the run known locally as the Annus, a long, steep couloir that should be treated with respect. From the top of Røgjin take the sign for 13 but head for the back of the mountain and follow round, for a run known as the rubber forest. You'll start off in a powder field, but quickly heading into the trees, and they're thick and deep. These runs should lead you straight to main roads, where those canny Norwegian taxi drivers are ready to take you back to the base.

Staying within the boundary line, if you like trees you'll have no complaints here. Theres some concealed tree rails in the woods off run 7.

FREESTYLERS. There's 2 terrain parks and they're building a beginners park for the 2004/5 season.

THE TOWN & GETTING THERE

Pic - Hemsedal tourism

The intermediate park on run 33 consists of series of jumps, and a good variety of rails once you turn the corner. The main park's built well and high with a great selection of jumps, quarter pipes, rails and boxes catering for good intermediates to experts. Theres 2 half pipes including a well cut super pipe. Freestylers looking for some natural hits, should take the **Holdeskarheisen** and **Roniheisen** chairs to reach some cool terrain, including a tight gully to pull air in.

CARVERS in hard boots who dare grace the slopes will find the runs known as the **Hemsedalsloypa** and **Kuleloyas** the place to lay out turns. These may not be the longest runs in the world, but they're not for wimps. The **Sahaugloypa** is also a decent run on which to get some speed together. In many of Norway's resorts the runs are usually very short, so it comes as a big relief to find a trail that lasts more than two seconds. The **Turistloypa** is the longest descent and although

it's easy (even for novices still in nappies), it's worth a blast if only to avoid being on a lift again.

BEGINNERS seem to fare well wherever they go in Norway. Hemsedal is no exception; the only difference is that at least there is something worth progressing onto after mastering the easy flats at the base and those higher up. Instructors tend to avoid the intimidating drags at the bottom, and head up lift F, where theres a nice green all the way back down, it can get a bit busy though. Instructors do speak good english, group and 50 minute private lessons are available. The 2004/5 season sees the expansion of the beginners/family area. The area will have waves, mini quarter pipe, jumps, rails, self timer slope, and a path in the forest with animals made of wood all serviced by 2 new platter lifts.

THE TOWN

If you plan to put Hemsedal on your calling card, only do so if you have a bank balance akin to that of Richard Branson. Put simply, Hemsedal is very expensive; however it is possible to do it on a budget, just watch the alcohol and taxis and the rest is surprisingly affordable. If you need to check your email then head for the Hemsedal Cafe in town, or the restaurant at the base near the Holvinheisen lift, and its free!

Accommodation can be had near the slopes, either at *Veslestølen* or *Skarsnuten* thats serviced by its own lift. The only trouble being that you're left with an expensive taxi if you want to get to/from the main town as buses to the resort finish early, but you can easily get quality apartment for a week for about £150 based on 8 sharing. Alternativley theres plenty of accomodation in town, or if the budgets really tight then opt for a cabin or the campsite. Hemsedal Cafe does some good food at lunch, enormous portions.

Night life. Things kick off at the outside bar at the base where they'll often have live music from 4pm, then its after ski in the village. A beer will set you back at least UK£5, so hold on to it tightly. The main snowboard hang out for evening madness is the *Hemsedal Cafe*, which is expensive, cool, and full of gorgeous Norwegians. The *skogstad* hotel has a nightclub open late.

CAR
Via Oslo, head north on highway 7 via Honefos and Gol and on to Hemsedal. Oslo to resort is 137 miles (220km).
FLY
to Oslo airport, about 2 1/4 hours away. Direct sunday service from/to hemsedal NOK 375 return contact resort
TRAIN
Train services are possible to Gol from Oslo and Bergen take around 2 1/4 hours. Local bus services from Gol to Hemsedal
BUS
Direct from Oslo & Bergen, www.nor-way.no and www.bergenekspressen.no

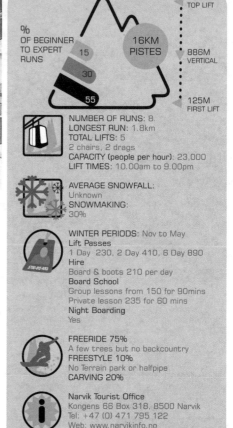

Pic - Narvik Tourism

1002M
TOP LIFT

%
OF BEGINNER
TO EXPERT   15
RUNS

16KM
PISTES

886M
VERTICAL

30

55

125M
FIRST LIFT

NUMBER OF RUNS: 8.
LONGEST RUN: 1.8km
TOTAL LIFTS: 5
2 chairs, 2 drags
CAPACITY (people per hour): 23,000
LIFT TIMES: 10.00am to 9.00pm

AVERAGE SNOWFALL:
Unknown
SNOWMAKING:
30%

WINTER PERIODS: Nov to May
Lift Passes
1 Day 230, 2 Day 410, 6 Day 890
Hire
Board & boots 210 per day
Board School
Group lessons from 150 for 90mins
Private lesson 235 for 60 mins
Night Boarding
Yes

FREERIDE 75%
A few trees but no backcountry
FREESTYLE 10%
No Terrain park or halfpipe
CARVING 20%

Narvik Tourist Office
Kongens 66 Box 318, 8500 Narvik
Tel: +47 (0) 471 795 122
Web: www.narvikinfo.no
Email: ski@narvikinfo.no

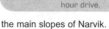

Fly
to Oslo airport and then to Evenes which
is 50 miles on.
Train
to Narvik from Oslo will take 20 hrs.
Car
Drive via Oslo , head north on E6 all the
way up to Narvik, which is at least a 20
hour drive.

About 1 hour west of the Swedish resort of **Riksgransen** lies Narvik, a hidden treasure in snowboard circles. With only 5 lifts and a summit that only just gets over 1000 metres, Narvik isn't your typical holiday resort: it's a small-town situated at the foot of a superb mountain, with lifts only opening in the afternoons on weekdays and all day on weekends and holidays. The busiest times are in February and Easter, but other than that, lift lines are practically non-existent and being located so far north, tour groups have never heard of this place. This helps to keep the slopes free of sad two plank numpties.

FREERIDERS should get the most out of this area. Much of the riding terrain is above the tree-line, but the lack of tree runs is fully compensated by plenty of natural pipes, bowls, cornices and cliffs to fly off. For fat lazy riders or those who prefer not to exhaust themselves with hiking, you'll be able to have a good blast within the lift covered area. The area known as **Fagernesfjellet** is a paradise for relatively advanced freeriders. The lifts only cover a small percentage of actual terrain available and as heli-boarding is forbidden in Norway, heaven is waiting if you're prepared to hike. There are no rules regarding where you can board, but before you take off, it's advisable to hook up with one of the locals who will show you the secret spots. In addition to Morkolla, with its enormous amount of snow, Narvik's backcountry offers wicked extreme terrain. FREESTYLERS don't have a fun park, although one is planned for the future. There is, however, plenty of good natural terrain for getting air and the flat stuff allows for loads of ground spinning.

CARVERS should check out the pistes of Fagernesfjellet which are steep, wavy and well suited to carvers. Mind you, hard booters are a rare thing here and to be honest, this place is far better challenged in a good pair of softs.

BEGINNERS will probably have a better time in **Ankernes**, a resort which is 3 miles away, rather than the main slopes of Narvik.

THE TOWN

Narvik is at the base of the slopes and everything is within walking distance. Expensive is the key word around here, but lodging in a cabin or a room at Breidablikk Inn is one of the easiest on the pocket. As for night life and partying, things happen at the Fossestua which has a pool table and is good for a beer and a late night session.

5 OUT OF 10

Nothing too pulse racing

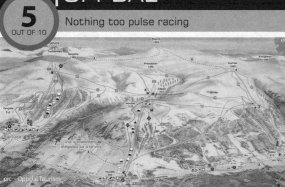

pic - Oppdal Tourism

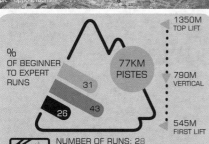

1350M
TOP LIFT

%
OF BEGINNER
TO EXPERT
RUNS

77KM
PISTES

790M
VERTICAL

31

26

43

545M
FIRST LIFT

NUMBER OF RUNS: 28
LONGEST RUN: 4km
TOTAL LIFTS: 16
2 chairs, 14 drags
CAPACITY (people per hour): 15,000
LIFT TIMES: 9.30am to 9.00pm

AVERAGE SNOWFALL:
Unknown
SNOWMAKING:
45%

WINTER PERIODS: Nov to May
Lift Passes
1 Day 280, 2 Day 495, 6 Day 1135
Night Boarding
Yes

FREERIDE 60%
A few trees and good backcountry
FREESTYLE 30%
A Terrain park & halfpipe
CARVING 10%

Tourist Office Oppdal
Po Box 50 Oppdal - N7341
Tel: ++47 (0) 72 42 17 60
Web: www.oppdal.com
Email: post@oppdal.com

Fly
to Oslo airport, about 4 hours away.
Train
to Oppdal from Oslo, and take 4hours.
Car
via Oslo, head north on E6 all the way up
to Oppdal.

Oppdal is situated 93 miles south of the town of **Trondheim**, where three valleys (originating in different parts of the country) meet. The resort is divided into four main areas, providing something for all riders with some of the best off-piste Norway has to offer. The snowboard scene is expanding in **Oppdal** (as everywhere else in the world) and most weekends the place is 'invaded' by boarders from the city of Trondheim. During the usual winter holiday period, the population doubles, so if you're not particularly fond of lines and crowds, try to stay clear. As one of Norway's biggest areas, Oppdal will appeal (as with much of this country) to easy going, piste loving freeriders. The 80 km of piste are for beginners mainly as there's nothing for advanced riders to get too excited about, and even intermediates will soon tire of the place. At the top of Vangslia there's a black run, but the mountain flattens out at the bottom making it a short and uneventful trail, unless you're a beginner joining at the top of lift A, where it becomes an excellent easy area.

FREERIDERS are kept interested with some particularly good freeride terrain to explore that includes trees, steeps and powder. The stuff found in Stolen Valley is pretty good, but due to avalanche danger, the area is often closed. However, the runs on the Vangslia mountain offer the best time, with some nice terrain features to ride, including steeps.

FREESTYLERS have a pipe (not a hot one, though) and a snowpark. The Adalen area is a natural snowpark which should keep air heads aroused for a day or two. Ground grommets will find the uneven slopes great for flatland tricks.

CARVERS can experience what it's like to fly, by cutting some lines on the Downhill World Cup arena. What's more, Oppdal's longest run reaches a respectable 2.5 miles, offering a long ride.

BEGINNERS are well catered for, with loads of novice trails stretched across the 4 connected areas all accessed with one lift pass. Snowboard instruction is also very good.

THE TOWN
In the main, local services are varied but expensive. For a convenient place to sleep, stay at the Hellaugstol camp ground, about 100 metres from the slopes, or at Landsbytorget in Stolen where a group can share an apartment. At night, check out 'The Jaeger Pub' or go skating.

N

N
O
R
W
A
Y

259

(c) Stryn tourism

Stryn is located at the base of the **Jostedalsbreen glacier** and is Norway's most famous summer resort (in fact the only one of note). The glacier gets so much snow during the winter (five metres plus), that the lifts are usually totally buried and as they couldn't run them even if they wanted to. Although this is a popular snowboarder's hangout, it should be pointed out that Stryn is also very popular with skiers, resulting in fairly long lift queues. What's more, a number of ski teams spend time on the slopes doing training sessions, swelling the numbers further. Still, leaving the two plankers aside, what you have is a small glacier mountain offering some interesting and steep riding on slopes where snow holds its condition all day. A lot of Norwegians simply come up to strip off and sunbathe (an often enjoyable sight). However, for those wanting to snowboard, the 10 kilometres of terrain are serviced by just two lifts; a double chair and a drag lift. A lot of snowboard camps are held here each year with lots of pros on the teaching staff.

FREERIDERS coming here in search of big powder bowls, dense trees and limitless off piste should forget it, Stryn has none of that. In the main, you are presented with some steep, but featureless terrain.
FREESTYLERS are the ones who are going to benefit from a trip to Stryn the most, apart from the natural hits and the famous road jumps (as seen in many a video), the man made kickers are superb. The camp's pipes are located on the higher sections, while lower down is a pipe that anyone can use.
CARVERS in hard boots get real and have the summer off, because this is not a carvers resort whatsoever. Two fat turns and you're down. This is a soft boot hangout only.
BEGINNERS that are easily intimidated may find this place a little daunting as the slopes are steep, but there are some areas to play about on if you really want to ride here.

1600M
TOP LIFT

%
OF BEGINNER
TO EXPERT
RUNS

10KM
PISTES

25

540M
VERTICAL

75

1060M
FIRST LIFT

NUMBER OF RUNS: 8
LONGEST RUN: 2.0km
TOTAL LIFTS: 2
1 chair, 1 drag
CAPACITY (people per hour): 1,000
LIFT TIMES: 9.00am to 9.30pm

AVERAGE SNOWFALL:
5m
SNOWMAKING:
none

WINTER PERIODS: Feb to March
SUMMER PERIODS: April to August
Lift Passes
1 Day 280, 3 of 4 Days 780
6 of 7 Days 1200, Season pass 3000
Hire
Board & boots 270 per day
Night Boarding
Yes till 9:30

FREERIDE 55%
No trees & no backcountry
FREESTYLE 40%
Terrain park & 2 halfpipes
CARVING 5%

Stryn Tourist Office
Telephone - +47 57 87 54 74
Tourist Info: +47 57 87 40 40
Web: www.strynefjellet.com
Email: info@strynefjellet.com

Fly
to Oslo airport & inland to Trondheim airport.
Train
to Trondheim from Oslo.
Car
via Oslo, head north on route 7 to Gol and then take the 52 to Signol onto the route 1 and route 60 via Olden to Stryn.

THE TOWN
Stryn is located along a road that is littered with campsites offering cheap places to sleep. The main hangout is the village of **Hjelle**, 15 minutes from the slopes, where you can rent a shared cabin from 420 Kr. The main **local pub** is where the only action takes place with numerous late night drinking sessions happening place on a daily basis (although it costs).

6 OUT OF 10

Not bad at all for a few days

Trysil is supposed to be Norway's largest resort and is definitely big by most Norwegian standards, and a very good place to snowboard. Situated just over two hours from **Oslo**, Trysil is a resort that caters well for its visitors, no matter what time of year. Snowboarding is possible here between the months of November and May, on slopes that cover a large percentage of the

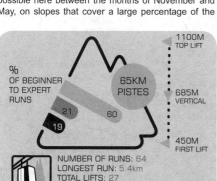

%
OF BEGINNER
TO EXPERT
RUNS

65KM
PISTES

1100M
TOP LIFT

685M
VERTICAL

450M
FIRST LIFT

21 60
19

NUMBER OF RUNS: 64
LONGEST RUN: 5.4km
TOTAL LIFTS: 27
5 chairs, 15 drags, 7 Childrens lifts
CAPACITY (people per hour): 31,400
LIFT TIMES: 9:00am to 4:30pm

AVERAGE SNOWFALL:
2m
SNOWMAKING:
30%

WINTER PERIODS: Nov to April
Lift Passes
1 Day 290, 2 Days 560
6 Day 1150, Season 3800
Hire
Board & boots 285 per day
Night Boarding
On Turistsenteret: tuesdays (8pm) and fridays (9pm)
On Høyfjellssenteret: wednesdays (8pm) and fridays (9pm)

FREERIDE 45%
Trees & some okay backcountry
FREESTYLE 35%
Terrain park & 2 halfpipes
CARVING 20%

Trysil Touristoffice
Storvegen 3, NO-2420 Trysil,
Tel: (+47) 62 45 10 00
Fax: (+47) 62 45 11 65
Web:www.trysil.com
Email:trysilfjellet@trysil.com

Fly
to Oslo which is around 140 miles away.
Train
to Zerenz, 20 minutes away.
Car
via Oslo, take E6 to Hamar then route 25

Trysilfjellet Mountain, which is predominately suited to beginners and basic intermediate riders. There are runs for advanced riders which will keep them interested for some time. Strangely the higher you go, the easier things get, notably at the top section of the slopes, where a wide open and somewhat flat snow field opens up above the tree line

FREERIDERS who venture here will find some okay tree riding and a bit of powder, but in the main the terrain is a bit dull and featureless. The runs up from **Hogegga** are the most challenging, with a series of interconnecting black runs that snake through the trees to the base.

FREESTYLERS make up a large number of the riders seen ripping up Trysil. To keep the air heads happy the management have provided them with a decent fun park and three halfpipes that are dotted around at various locations. These are all very well maintained, although on occasions a bit of 'do it your self' pipe shaping is called for though.

CARVERS if you must strap on boots that are better suited to skiers and insist on posing over your edges at speed, then Trysil allows you ample opportunity to put in some extremely wide turns (especially on the higher sections) but don't come here expecting a mass of long, super fast trails.

BEGINNERS. There are two types of orgasm, one with a good looking Norwegian chick and the other is learning to snowboard at Trysil. The place is learner heaven, with a mass of easy slopes that are well linked and well serviced by the lift system.

THE TOWN
The village of **Trysil** is 2 km from the slopes and offers good local facilities, although what is on offer is stupidly expensive and would make a weeks stay a struggle with funds, and impossible on a low budget. **Accommodation** is offered in a huge number of cabins and hotels, (all will burn deep into the pocket). Still, a few beers will help dampen the shock of prices (once pissed, you no longer care what the next things costs).

N
O
R
W
A
Y

261

AI
Super boring place, 2 1/2hrs from Oslo

FILEFJELL SKIHEISER
This is one of Norways smallest resorts and also one of the most boring. There is very little on offer, other than a few over rated intermediate and beginner runs. There is a small terrain park with an equally small halfpipe. In its defense its well looked after by local riders. The nearby village offers very basic lodging and other services all of which come at a high price.

Ride area: 8km
Top Lift: 1125m
Total Lifts:3
Contact:
Tyin-Filefjell Skisenter
N-2985 Tyinkrysset
Tel +47 (0) 613 675 75
Fax +47 (0) 613 675 76
How to get there: Fly to: Fagerness 2 hours away

GAUSDAL
A bit dull, but okay. 9 lifts, 20 runs

GAUSTABLIKK
A few okay runs, 5 lifts, 8 runs

GOL
Total waste of time, about 20mins from Hemsedal

GRONG
Forget it altogther, 6 lifts, 10 runs.

HOVEN
Okay night riding. 4 lifts & 12 runs

HAFJELL/LILLEHAMMER
Improved terrain park, snowmaking, kids areea

pic - Hafjell Tourism

expanded.
This is Norway's famous resort if for know other reason other than it once hosted the winter Olympics. However, just because they flew the '5 rings', doesn't mean that its a good measure of what's on offer. What you get here is a narrow cluster of runs with an okay mixture of all ability terrain that includes a long black run from almost the top to the bottom.
Freestylers have an okay halfpipe for catching air. Theres a good variety of jumps and rails for all levels. **Beginners** have a few easy to reach novice slopes although crowded

Ride area: 33km
Runs: 29
Easy 30%
Intermediate 41%
Advanced 18%
Expert 11%
Longest run: 7km
Top Lift: 1050m
Vertical Drop: 830m
Total Lifts:22 - 3 chairs, 18 drags, 1 Magic Carpet
Lifts Open:9.30am to 3.30pm 9.30am to 4.30pm (floodlit slopes)
Contact:
Hafjell Alpinsenter
AS 2636 Øyer Norway
Tel.: +47 61 27 47 00
www.hafjell.no
How to get there: FLY: Fly to: Oslo 2 hours away.
BUS: Free shuttle bus from Lillehammer, and good local bus service www.opplandstrafikk.no
DRIVING: 15km from Lillehammer, follow exit to Hafjell. 200 km (2.55 hrs) from Oslo, follow E6 north.

KVITFELL
2 good halfpipes, 7 lifts 20 runs, 60

minutes from Oslo

RUSTADHOGDA
Small pipe, but nothing else. 3 lifts, 3hrs from Oslo

SJUSJOEN
Only good for no hopers, 1 lifts, 80mins from Oslo

STRANDA
Okay for slow beginners, 5 lifts, 2hrs from Oslo

TROMSO

pic - Tromso Tourism

Famous for holding the finale of the 2004 TTR series, the Artic Challenge. Very basic resort, miles from anywhere, but have the capacity to build a good park & pipe.

www.tromsoalpinsenter.com

VALDRES
Valdres is a small unassuming typical Norwegian resort with a good reputation amongst Norway's snowboard population. The tree lined runs will suit intermediate freeriders and air heads.There is some extreme terrain with trees to check out that should keep the average freerider happy for a day or two.
Grommets will find enough logs to slide down. The fun park and pipe are also good and offer the best chance of pulling some good air.
Carvers looking for lots of wide open flats will be disappointed, as will advanced riders looking for major hits or deep gullies

First timers should have no problem here, the flats at the base area are full-on for collecting the first bruises with ease.

Lodging is the usual Norwegian offerings, with a number of decent chalets or apartments to choose from. **Night wise**, simply crank up the walkman and down your duty free booze.

Ride area: 10km
Longest run: 7km
Top Lift: 1050m
Total Lifts:4
Contact:
Valdres Tourist Office
P.O.Box 203
N-2901 Fagernes
Tel - (+47) 61 35 94 10
Fax - (+47) 61 35 94 15
www.valdres.com
How to get there: Fly to: Oslo 2 hours away

VASSFJELLET

pic - Vassfjellet Tourism

Vassfjellet is not a tourist resort perched way up high on a mountain and boasting millions of square miles of ridabe piste backed up with a modern base complex decked out with purpose built hotels and other tourist traps. No, this is a locals place and serves the masses from neighbouring towns and the city of Trondheim a few miles away. If you're on a road trip and fancy something different then check this place out, it's pretty cool and very snowboard friendly, with a large number of student riders

from Trondheim's University. They are given student concessions on lift passes, so if you're doing the college or Uni number, be sure to carry your student card. The terrain is fairly well matched in terms of level and styles and although the slopes here can be described as dull, most riders will find something to keep them content for an hour. By most standards this is a very small resort with only around 6 miles of piste (half of which is flood lit for night riding). This place is by no means going to hold the attention of advanced riders for too long, especially if you're looking for big powder bowls and large cliff drops. Still there is a 2 mile run to keep you occupied for a few minutes, (which offers the opportunity to ride at speed and take out a few skiers en route). If you really want to find out where the best ride areas are, contact the guys at the local snowboard club, there are no guides here but they will give you a few pointers.

Freeriders have a few wooded sections to cut through, but they won't take long to ride through.

Freestylers roaming around will find some banked walls to check out, as well as a pipe and park.

Carvers who can will have the whole area done in five minutes.

Beginners will find this place more than adequate with a good selection of easy runs.

At the end of the day, every one heads off back to Trondheim by a regular bus service. There's a good selection of places to sleep, eat and drink at almost affordable prices.

Night-life is also pretty good but booze will cost you dearly.

Ride area: 10km
Easy 25%
Intermediate 25%
Advanced 30%
Expert 20%
Longest run: 3.5km
Top Lift: 670m
Vertical Drop: 460m
Total Lifts:6
Contact:

Vassfjellet Skiheiser AS
P.b. 6079
7003 Trondheim
Tel: ++47 (0) 72830200
How to get there: Fly to: Oslo 3 hours away

VOSS

Voss is a very popular resort with over 40km of well groomed trails that will please carvers and basic freeriders.

The limited off-piste on offer is not bad and allows the chance to go steep and deep above and below the tree line in a number of spots.

Freestylers should avoid trying to catch air out of the permanent ski jump here, as you're not allowed too. Instead check out the pipe or the numerous natural hits dotted around the whole area.

Ride area: 40km
Top Lift: 945m
Total Lifts:10
Contact:
++47 (0) 56 51 12 12
How to get there: Fly to: Bergen 21/2 hours hours away

You can choose one of the five real snow areas or from the many artificial ski slopes dotted around the country. At the time of writing there was still some uncertainty over two of the resorts that went into receivership last season. Glencoe have now found new owners and should be open for the new season, however Glenshee's future is still in the balance.

Scotland's conditions are extremely variable and snow conditions can be poor, and the wind can blow so hard that it hurts as it hits you at 70 miles an hour. All the resorts are similar: low level

Capital City: Edinburgh
Population: 5 Million
Highest Peak: Ben Nevis 1347m
Language: English
Legal Drink Age: 18
Drug Laws: Cannabis is illegal and frowned upon
Age of consent: 16
Electricity: 240 Volts AC 3-pin
International Dialing Code: +44

Currency: Pounds Sterling
Exchange Rate:
US$1 = 0.6
EURO = 0.7

Driving Guide
All vehicles drive on the left hand side of the road
Speed limits:
Motorways-70mph (113kph)
Highways-60mph (97kph)
Towns-30mph (51kph)
Emergency
Fire, Police & Ambulance - 999
Tolls
Payable on some bridges
Documentation
A driving licence must be carried as well as insurance.

Time Zone
No UTC/GMT
Daylight saving time: +1 hour

British Snowboard Association
Web: www.thebsa.org
Email: info@thebsa.org

Visit Scotland
23 Ravelston Terrace
Edinburgh
EH4 3TP
Tel: 0845 22 55 121
www.visitscotland.com

hills, with uneven trails that get stupidly crowded. Halfpipes are rare due to the weather conditions and you won't find any wide motorway runs. But the most notable point about Scotland is the costs: lift tickets are a total rip off and offer very bad value for money. However getting to any of the areas should pose no problems with good air, rail and road links.

Season riders will find employment and lodging easily. If you want to teach snowboarding, you can do it legally without an instructor's certificate. However, it may help you get work.

In short, Scotland is a great country for its scenery, natural beauty and history, but not a great destination for boarding or skiing. This is a place for purists' not cheap gimmicks.

CAIRNGORM

Okay when theres snow

pic · Paul Tomkins/STB

The Cairngorms is a unique place for all sorts of reasons. For some this is a great place to visit to see some of Scotland's wild life, while others venture to these hostile hills to walk along some of the well worn paths. But this is not a proper ski/board destination and doesn't even

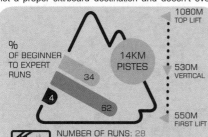

%
OF BEGINNER
TO EXPERT
RUNS

14KM PISTES

34
4
62

1080M TOP LIFT

530M VERTICAL

550M FIRST LIFT

NUMBER OF RUNS: 28
LONGEST RUN: 1.8miles (2.9km)
TOTAL LIFTS: 17
1 Funicular Train, 2 chairs, 14 drags
CAPACITY (people per hour): 12,000
LIFT TIMES: 8.30am to 4.30pm
MOUNTAIN CAFES: 3

AVERAGE SNOWFALL:
Unknown
SNOWMAKING:
none

WINTER PERIODS: Jan to April
Lift Passes
1 Day £25, 5 Days £102, Season £340
Hire
1 day £15.50,5 days £50.50
Board School
Group lessons £35/day, Private £120/day

FREERIDE 30%
No trees or backcountry
FREESTYLE 5%
Ocassionally a Terrain park & halfpipe
CARVING 65%

Tourist office Aviemore
Grampian Road,
Aviemore. Inverness-shire
Tel: +44 (0) 1479 810 363
Cairngorm info:+44 (0) 1479 861 261
Web:www.cairngormmountain.com

Fly
to Glasgow international. Transfer time to resort is 2 1/2 hours.Local airport is Inverness 45 minutes away.
Train
services are possible to the centre of Aviemore, 15 mins from the slopes.
Bus
Bus services from Glasgow airport are available on a daily basis to Aviemore.
Car
from Inverness, head south on A9 and travel to Aviemore. From London, head north via the M1, M6, A74, M8 to Perth and the A9 to Aviemore. Drive time from London is 9 hours. 535 miles (860 km).

begin to compare with resorts on main land Europe. The Cairngorms will give locals, those who live close and the casual visitor the chance to have a few hours fun on snow. If you live far away, check on conditions before leaving. This region has a poor annual snow record and suffers from very harsh winters which entail strong winds and ever changing weather patterns. The mountain layout also leaves a lot to be desired, however the introduction the new funicular train makes getting around the runs a lot easier but the cost of using the train and the other lifts is horrendous. However, its not all bad news on Cairngorm, and when it has snowed and the sun is out, you can have a great days riding. What's more, local boarders are very friendly and will be happy to show you were the best spots are to ride.

FREERIDERS won't find any trees, bowls or powder and experienced riders used to long testing steeps won't find anything to tackle apart from the West Wall, the only black run. The White Lady run can be good when it's not riddled with moguls.
FREESTYLERS who like to go big off natural hits, forget it. However, there is a good terrain park which has a series of big hits. The park also has its own boarder patrol and when snow permits there is a half pipe.
CARVERS turning up here expecting to find loads of wide open cruising slopes, will be disappointed. On the longest runs, you will be lucky to complete two big turns before you're back in a lift line. Nothing takes more than a minute.
BEGINNERS, this place is definitely not for you. There are hardly any nursery slopes, and the ones you do find are sandwiched between snow fences and choked up with ski classes. Beginners are far better off going to 'The Lecht', 40 minutes away.

THE TOWN
Spey Valley is home to a number of good local villages. For a small village Aviemore has a good choice of restaurants. The *Cairngorm Hotel* is very good, *Harkais* restaurant does a great hangover breakfast while the *Einich* restaurant has an excellent reputation. Nightlife in Aviemore is simple, there are no fancy clubs just a handful of bars, ranging from the now dated Chevvys to the Ibiza style Mambo Cafe.

265

4 OUT OF 10 — GLENCOE

Glencoe is **Scotland's** oldest resort and the best place to ride in the country. Unlike other Scottish resorts, this is not a poor alpine imitation and okay, Glencoe may have very harsh weather patterns, but who cares, they do things the right way here and don't try and make out that they are something that they're not. This may not be a big place, but it is exactly what Scottish snowboarding should be about: simple, friendly and without an attitude. It also has the best natural terrain. In general, the runs will suit all levels, although not testing. Glencoe's remoteness means it is far less crowded than other resorts. People who come here do so because they don't want the bull of the other places.

FREERIDERS will find some okay terrain in the main basin off either the top T-bar or top button lift. Off the top button lift you will find a couple of reds and an interesting black trail that bases out into an easy green run.

FREESTYLERS have a cool natural freestyle area, but the weather prevents the building or lasting of a halfpipe. However, ask the management and they'll happily do what they can to build you a decent series of hits.

BEGINNERS should have no problems learning here as there are some excellent short runs to try out which are easily reached.

Local services can be found in the small village of **Glencoe**, a 6 mile drive away. It offers limited, but good, accommodation with a number of cheap B & B'. Alternatively, the village of **Onich** is 12 miles away and has a bigger selection of services, including a bunkhouse with a bar. **Fort William** is 30 miles away and has an even bigger offering.

% OF BEGINNER TO EXPERT RUNS
20KM PISTES
10
37
53
1068M TOP LIFT
305M VERTICAL
457M FIRST LIFT

NUMBER OF RUNS: 19
LONGEST RUN: 1.6km
TOTAL LIFTS: 7
2 chairs, 4 drags, 1 learner tow
CAPACITY (people per hour): 4,300
LIFT TIMES: 8.30 to 5.00pm
MOUNTAIN CAFES: 2

WINTER PERIODS: Dec to April
Lift Passes
1 Day pass - £21
5 Day pass - £84
Season pass - £260
Hire
Board aand boots - £17
Board School
2 Hour lesson from - £12, Private £22/hr

Drive
Drive via Glasgow, head north on the A82, via Dumbarton and Tyndrun to Glencoe. From London, head north via the M1, M6, A74, to Glasgow.Blairgowrie

4 OUT OF 10 — GLENSHEE

Glenshee is Scotland's biggest resort, although not much different to the Country's smallest. This place was first to use snow cannons, but in truth, they haven't really helped to improve what largely is a disappointment. The runs are spread out over varying slopes and on a good day, you will find some off-piste powder. The majority of runs are short novice trails with only two steep sections.

Freeriders have no trees, but a bit of powder on Glas Maol area. **Freestylers** don't bother. **Carvers,** can crank a it down the **Cairnwell** but not for long. **Beginners** will hate the way the lifts are set out, however, the novice runs will provide some fun.

Local facilities don't exist. Within a large area there are places to stay in and villages to get a meal but nothing near the slopes.

The nearest airport is at **Aberdeen** which 1½ hours away.

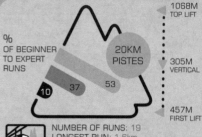

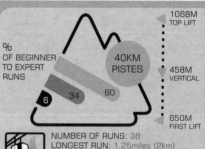

% OF BEGINNER TO EXPERT RUNS
40KM PISTES
6
34
60
1068M TOP LIFT
458M VERTICAL
650M FIRST LIFT

NUMBER OF RUNS: 38
LONGEST RUN: 1.25miles (2km)
TOTAL LIFTS: 23 - 2 chairs, 21 drags
CAPACITY (people per hour): 17,000
LIFT TIMES: 8.30 to 5.00pm
MOUNTAIN CAFES: 2

WINTER PERIODS: Dec to April
Lift Passes
1/2 Day £14.50, Day £19.50,5 Day £78
Hire
Board aand boots - £17
Board School
2 Hour lesson from - £12, Private £22/hr

Located
Glenshee is situated on the A93, 9 miles south of Braemar and 25 miles north of Blairgowrie
www.ski-glenshee.co.uk

SCOTLAND

3 OUT OF 10 — NEVIS

1220M TOP LIFT

BEGINNER
EXPERT
JNS

20KM PISTES

580M VERTICAL

25   66

10

100M FIRST LIFT

NUMBER OF RUNS: 35
LONGEST RUN: 2km
TOTAL LIFTS: 12
1 Gondola, 3 chairs, 8 drags
CAPACITY (people per hour): 9,600
LIFT TIMES: 8.30am to 4.30pm
MOUNTAIN CAFES: 4

WINTER PERIODS: Dec to April
Lift Passes
1/2 Day £15.50 ,Full day £22
5 days £84
Hire
board and boots £17.50,6 days £65
Board School
4 Hour group lesson £20, private £22/hr

Drive
From Glasgow, head north on the A82,
via Dumbarton and Glencoe.

www.nevis-range.co.uk

Nevis Range opened in 1989. The mountain has a modern lift system to rival anything in **the Alps**, but where its no match for Alps, is the weathe which is often a mixture of high winds, driving sleet and rain and havey blizzards. And Nevis gets its fair share of the lot. However, the people who run the place shrug off the problems related to the weather and do their best to look after visitors. Weekends are often very busy, while week days are generally very quite. Don't expect too many things to be laid on such as a terrain park or halfpipe, the poor snow conditions don't allow for it. What they have managed to achieve is a fairly well balanced mixture of short runs that will mainly appeal to beginners, even though most of the novice runs are serviced by drag lifts. Overall the terrain here is pretty unadventurous and an expert rider will tire of this mountain within an hour or two of being here.

FREERIDERS have a couple of good areas by **Scottish** standards to ride, namely the back bowl area which has a series of steeps.
FREESTYLERS have to make do with either building their own hits to get air, or snow permitting, the gully under the main chairlift provides a small natural halfpipe for a bit of air time.
CARVERS will find that the **Snowgoose Gully** is the area to lay some lines on. But overall Nevis is not a cruiser's resort.
BEGINNERS have a number of easy slopes located at the lower areas not far from the top gondola station.

THE TOWN.
The town of **Fort William**, 6 miles away, has a big choice of accommodation and eating spots. There is some accommodation near the slopes but it's limited and isolated. Evenings are not hot but with plenty of pubs to try out, you can have a rowdy time.

4 OUT OF 10 — LECHT

823M TOP LIFT

BEGINNER
EXPERT
JS

6KM PISTES

25   70

5

NUMBER OF RUNS: 20
TOTAL LIFTS: 14 - 1 chairs, 13 drags
CAPACITY (people per hour): 17,000

WINTER PERIODS: Dec to April
Lift Passes
1/2 Day £15,1 Day pass £20
5 Days pass £84
Hire
Board aand boots - £17
Board School
2days hire, pass and group lesson £75

Located
On the A939 Cockbridge to Tomintoul
Road. West of Aberdeen

www.lecht.co.uk

The Lecht is by far the smallest resort in Scotland, however, this is also one of the friendliest and quite simply the best beginner's resort. This value for money area, only has a handful of runs that rise up from the car park allowing for good easy access by foot to the well maintained novice runs. This is not a place for those who want long testing steeps, but it is a place with a cool attitude towards snowboarding and a genuine and welcoming feel to it.

FREERIDERS could have the whole place licked in an hour or two.
FREESTYLERS, they always try and build a park and pipe here, with locals from Aberdeen using this as a fun weekend hangout.
CARVERS of beginner to basic intermediate only.
BEGINNERS, this place is perfect for novices, the best in Scotland.

Basic but affordable local facilities can be found in Tomintoul, 15 minutes away.

S

S
C
O
T
L
A
N
D

267

If you thought Spain was only about bull fighting and tacky seaside resorts inhabited by Europe's finest villains, then think again. Spain is also about snowboarding and while it's not as intense as other parts of Europe, it's certainly worth more than a mention as well as a visit.

Spain has some thirty resorts offering every type of terrain possible and to suit all style's of riding and abilities.

Spain hasn't always had the greatest snow record and with many of the resorts not being the most up to date, there's very little artificial snowmaking to help out when the real stuff is lacking. Resort facilities are not the greatest either, with little or no snowboard facilities, poor options for places to sleep and limited snowboard hire options.

However, this is generalising because the big areas like Sierra Nevada are an easy match for the rest of Europe, indeed it will put a lot of northern places to shame.

The Spanish tend to be a bit like their Italian cousins, they love to pose and in doing so end up looking stupid in designer ski suits. Snowboarding is, however, fairly well received throughout the country.

The majority of the resorts are situated in the north of the country and can prove tricky to reach with a hit and miss public transport service. Your best bet is to hire a car at airport and drive, this way you can leave quickly if you dislike a place.

One last point, Spanish snowboarding is not as cheap as you may think. Don't think of it as just a cheap alternative to France or Austria, although Spain is certainly cheaper than Switzerland.

Capital City: Madrid
Population: 40 Million
Highest Peak: Mulhacen 3478m
Language: Spanish
Legal Drink Age: 18
Drug Laws: Cannabis is illegal
Age of consent: 16
Electricity: 240 Volts AC 2-pin
International Dialing Code: +34

Currency: Euro
Exchange Rate:
UK£1 = 1.5
US$1 = 0.8
AU$1 = 0.6
CAN$1 = 0.6

Driving Guide
All vehicles drive on the right hand side of the road
Speed limits:
Motorways 120kph (74mph)
Highways 90kph (56mph)
Towns 50kph (31mph)
Emergency
Fire - 080
Police - 091
Ambulance - 092
Tolls
Payable on a number of main roads
Documentation
Driving licence and motor insurance must be carried.

Time Zone
UTC/GMT +1 hours
Daylight saving time: +1 hour

Spanish Snowboard Association
Web: www.a-e-s.jazztel.es
Email: infoaes@telefonica.net

BAQUERIA BERET

5 OUT OF 10

An okay basic resort

Baqueria Beret is Spain's biggest and possibly most glamorous resort, but don't let that put you off because when the snow is good (which it usually is) this purpose built haunt is not too bad to ride. This hasn't been missed by the International Snowboard Federation,

pic - Edd Sayavour

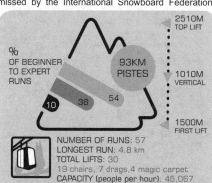

%
OF BEGINNER
TO EXPERT
RUNS

93KM PISTES

10   36   54

2510M
TOP LIFT

1010M
VERTICAL

1500M
FIRST LIFT

NUMBER OF RUNS: 57
LONGEST RUN: 4.8 km
TOTAL LIFTS: 30
19 chairs, 7 drags, 4 magic carpet
CAPACITY (people per hour): 45,067
LIFT TIMES: 9.30am to 9.00pm
MOUNTAIN CAFES: 15

AVERAGE SNOWFALL:
Unknown
SNOWMAKING:
25%

WINTER PERIODS:
Dec to April
Lift Passes
1 Day 35 Euros
6 Days 172 Euros
Hire
Board and Boots one week 75 euros

FREERIDE 40%
A few trees & a bit of backcountry
FREESTYLE 15%
a Terrain park & halfpipe
CARVING 45%

Tourist Office Baqueria Beret
SA Apartado 60, Viela, E25530
Tel: ++34 (0) 73 645 062
Web:www.baqueira.es
Email:baqueira@baqueira.es

Fly
to Barcelona airport, 4 hours away.
Train
services via a transfer by bus from the French town of Montrejea.
Car
Drive via Barcelona, head west on the N11 via Marrtorell and Lleida at which point take the N230 north to the resort.

NEW
new for 04/05 season
Ongoing work to the Bonaigua area including new chairlifts new slopes and improved village facilities.

who have held both slalom and halfpipe events here on numerous occasions, which is an indication that the place has something to offer. The terrain is spread out over four connecting areas, all of which are easy to reach and will largely appeal to intermediate piste loving carvers.

FREERIDERS looking for some cool off-piste to ride will be pleasantly surprised, with some great powder riding to be had well away from the chicken sticks in bad suits. Check out the areas on the Tuc De Dossal that are reached by chair lift, or hit the stuff up at La Bonaiqua. Advanced riders are the ones who will be most disappointed, apart from two black graded runs there's not a great deal of testing stuff.

FREESTYLERS have a rather limited amount of good natural freestyle terrain, but there is the odd good hit to get air from, plus a few drop offs to try out. The half-pipe is off the Mirador chair, but you may find it an advantage to borrow a shovel from the lift hut to do a bit of pipe shaping yourself, the resort doesn't look after itself.

CARVERS take over on the slopes here with terrain that is ideal for hard alpine riding. The resort is mainly suited to intermediates with some nice red runs but not many expert trails. For the less talented edge merchants, there are some easy blue runs.

BEGINNERS will take kindly to this place as this is a good resort to start out on and progress steadily with. Much of the terrain is easily reached by chair lifts and if you don't like Pomas or T-Bars then you'll be happy to know that you can get around the whole area without having to use them.

THE TOWN
Accommodation is close to the slopes, but eating and entertainment is not of a snowboard related nature. Still there is a supermarket for food and loads of Tapas (bar snacks). **Evenings** are OK and drinks are cheap (well compared to say drinks in France) apart from in the clubs where drinks are a flat rate of 10 euros each). Check out *Lobo* first, then *Tiffany's*, where the music is as crap and old as the name, but when you're drunk at four in the morning, who cares?

S

SPAIN

LA MOLINA

5 OUT OF 10

Okay fun resort

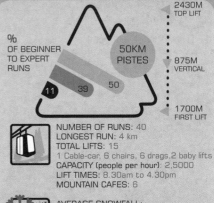

pic - La Molina Tourism

%
OF BEGINNER
TO EXPERT
RUNS

50KM PISTES

11 | 39 | 50

2430M TOP LIFT

875M VERTICAL

1700M FIRST LIFT

NUMBER OF RUNS: 40
LONGEST RUN: 4 km
TOTAL LIFTS: 15
1 Cable-car, 6 chairs, 6 drags,2 baby lifts
CAPACITY (people per hour): 2,5000
LIFT TIMES: 8.30am to 4.30pm
MOUNTAIN CAFES: 6

AVERAGE SNOWFALL:
Unknown
SNOWMAKING:
35%

WINTER PERIODS:
Dec to April
Lift Passes
1 Day pass 27/29 euros
5 Days 108 euros
Season 445 euros
Hire
Board and Boots 22 euros a day

FREERIDE 40%
Ttrees & good backcountry
FREESTYLE 20%
a Terrain park & halfpipe
CARVING 40%

La Molina Tourism
Estacion de Montana
La Molina E-17573
Tel: +34 (0) 72 892 031
Web:www.lamolina.com
Email:lamolina@lamolina.com

Fly
to Barcelona airport which is about a 2 1/2 hour transfer.
Train
services are possible direct to La Molina.
Car
Drive via Barcelona, head north on the N152 via Granollers, Ripoli and Ribes de Freser.

L a Molina is located at the end of the Moixero mountain range in the Pyrenees. Its slopes descend from the summit of the Tosa de Alp peak and connect by a short bus ride to the neighbouring and slightly larger resort of Masella. These are both welcome alternatives to big resorts scattered around the northern alps simply because mid-week, lift queues don't exist and the slopes are blissfully crowd free. The people of La Molina make you feel very welcome and coupled with neighbouring Masella, both areas have great terrain to shred, with slopes that are covered by trees up to the midway point and then clear pistes up to the summit. The terrain will capture the imagination of most intermediate riders, no matter what their style is, but advanced riders may feel a little left out.

FREERIDERS in search of extremes that require helmets should forget it, but for the rest, there's ample to search out. Off-piste opportunities present you with loads of trees, with some nice back bowls and good powder stashes on the Marsella.
FREESTYLERS get treated better here than in many other so called snowboard-friendly resorts. When snow allows, they provide a pipe and plenty of kickers on La Molina, while over on Marsella, there's a complete snowboard area called the Radical Bosc with hits galore, all of which are marked out on a rider's piste map.
CARVERS get the chance to polish up their skills on well groomed pistes and because this place isn't busy, you can go completely balls out without the worry of running over small children.
BEGINNERS in La Molina or Marsella will find that the nursery slopes are wide and spacious. Instruction services are excellent, with foreign speaking instructors available (which helps).

THE TOWN
Off the slopes, this is not a resort designed for package groups of clueless skiers without manners. No, **La Molina** is a laid back place with a simple appeal offering affordable accommodation with the chance of staying close to the slopes. Local services are very basic; however, there are enough good facilities to keep you amused with a further selection of amenities down in the village of **Puigcerda**, which is only 10 minutes away. The *El Bodegon* restaurant is the place to check out if you want to try some local dishes while night life in La Molina is what you make of it. There's no great action here but you can have a good rocking time in such places as the *Sommy Bar*.

7 OUT OF 10

Okay terrain for carvers and easy going freeriders

It seems amazing, wrong even, that you can quite easily snowboard in the morning in deep powder snow, then pop down to the beach just over an hour away for a huge seafood meal, a swim in the **Mediterranean** sea and a relax on a sun soaked coast, but that's exactly what you can do from here in this most southern resort of **Sierra Nevada,** located a short distance form the town of **Granada**. It's possible from the high point of Veleta to see the **Atlas Mountains** of Morocco across the Mediterranean. Sierra Nevada is an OK place to ride and is particularly well suited to beginners and hard boot carvers, as well as offering some cool off-piste freeriding in powder bowls. The purpose built resort is well located for the slopes. These are first accessed by the main gondola which deposits you in **Borreguilles**, directly onto fantastic beginner's piste. Go up higher

pic - Sierra Nevada Tourism

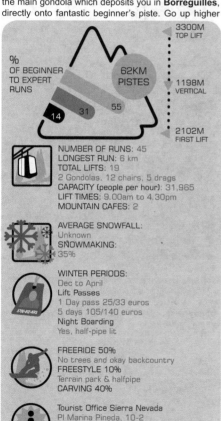

3300M
TOP LIFT

%
OF BEGINNER
TO EXPERT
RUNS

62KM
PISTES

1198M
VERTICAL

14 31 55

2102M
FIRST LIFT

NUMBER OF RUNS: 45
LONGEST RUN: 6 km
TOTAL LIFTS: 19
2 Gondolas, 12 chairs, 5 drags
CAPACITY (people per hour): 31,965
LIFT TIMES: 9.00am to 4.30pm
MOUNTAIN CAFES: 2

AVERAGE SNOWFALL:
Unknown
SNOWMAKING:
35%

WINTER PERIODS:
Dec to April
Lift Passes
1 Day pass 25/33 euros
5 days 105/140 euros
Night Boarding
Yes, half-pipe lit

FREERIDE 50%
No trees and okay backcountry
FREESTYLE 10%
Terrain park & halfpipe
CARVING 40%

Tourist Office Sierra Nevada
Pl Marina Pineda, 10-2
Granada.
General info +34 (0) 958 24 91 11
Reservations +34 (0) 958 24 91 22
Avlanche info +39 (0) 93 325 6391
Web:www.andalucia.co.uk
Email:sierran@siapi.es

and you will be on slopes whose angles are great for free carving - just that perfect angle to really lay 'em out in perfect control. Night-riding is done on the Rio slope, a 2 mile run that provides one of the best lit night trails anywhere. However, there are no set days or times for night-riding, you will need to check at the lift ticket office on a daily basis to get details.

FREERIDERS should check out the stuff just below the peak of **Veleta** at 3398m. To do this, traverse to the **Olimpica** and where this crosses the Diagonal, kick hard to your left and travel off piste on an itinerary known as **Tajos de la Virgen**. The view above you is truly stunning, (a bowl edged with dramatic cliffs). The **Dilar chair** takes you towards the Radio Telescope, where after a walk along the ridge you can see below a huge expanse of off-piste which you have just travelled over on the chair. Take any line, the slope is a good safe angle with an easy traverse back to the **Solana** piste and the Dilar chair.

FREESTYLERS have to make do most of the time, with an array of unusual natural hits. They do build a pipe when snow conditions permit it. However, if you ride over to **Tajos de la Virgen** run, you'll find rolling jumps verging into vertical kickers. Kick back again towards the **Cartujo piste** and make use of the piste edge with it's many varied banked sides to gain more air time.

CARVERS are much in evidence here as the slopes lend themselves really well to edging a board over at speed, especially on the fast black trails. Particular good blacks for this are down from the **Borreguilles**.

BEGINNERS; the Borreguilles area is full on for learning the art of hurtling down a mountain on a board, but not the only place to go. Much of this resort is excellent for novices with good snowboard instruction facilities.

S

pic - Trey Tomsik/Dutone Snowboards

THE TOWN

Off the slopes, Sierra Nevada is a cool place with a lot going on. Getting around the village, which is extremely steep, is pretty tough on foot though (especially once you have had a few beers). There is a bus service that runs until midnight, or alternatively, a chair lift that links the various levels to the centre of the village, for which you will need a valid lift pass to get on. The main set back for this place is the high cost of everything, which may have something to with the fact that the Sierra Nevada attracts a lot of the Spanish elite, and all the baggage that clings on to them. However, what is on offer is of a high standard with locals making you welcome.

Accommodation comes in all manner of styles and prices starting at super expensive. Most of the accommodation is located within easy reach of the base lifts and is pretty good, with some accommodation options at affordable prices. For budget riders, there's a hostel offering cheap beds with joint lift pass package rates.

Food. If you don't like Spanish food then don't fret, this place serves up all kinds of affordable grub from Chinese to Mexican. The main thing to watch out for, is that because this is a busy place, restaurants fill up early on in the evening and so a lot of waiting for a table is common place. Still, a meal, at a price, can be had in the likes of the Ruta del Veleta, (very posh and expensive but good). Tito Luigi is good for a cheap meal.

Night Life. If you like hard, fast and drunken action, there is plenty of it here but nothing happens until late. Bars and clubs don't get going until at least midnight, then it rocks and you'll have no trouble staying out late, drinking until you drop at 5 in the morning. The Soho Bar and La Chicle are your main late hangouts, where Senorita's are in plentiful supply all night long.

SUMMARY

Not bad for some no frills riding, with okay terrain for carvers and easy going freeriders but little for freestylers. Good value local services.

Money wise: Overall, this is a very affordable resort offering good value

CAR
Madrid to Sierra Nevada is 270 miles (435km), Drive time is about 6 1/2 hours. *From Calais, 1257 miles (2022Km), drive time is around 24 hours.
FLY
Fly to Madrid international, transfer time to resort is 3 1/2 hours. Local airport is Malaga 1 1/2 hours.
TRAIN
to Granada (20 miles).
BUS
Bus services from Madrid via a change over at Granada, on a daily basis.

S
P
A
I
N

ROUND-UP

ALTO CAMPOO

pic - Alto Campoo Tourism

Very small resort located in the Cantabrian Mountains, in the far north of Spain. The area has a series of short trails mainly of intermediate level with nothing challenging for advanced riders. Overall, this is a simple retreat that will please carvers, bore freestylers but suit novices. **Off the slopes** there is a couple of small hotels and limited basic local services near the

base area.
Ride area: 19km
Number runs: 16
Top Lift: 2175m
Bottom Lift: 1650m
Total Lifts:13
Contact:
Alto Campoo Tourist Office
Codigo de pais
Spain (34)
Tel: ++34 (0) 942/77 92 23
Fax: ++3 (0) 942/ 77 92 23
www.altocampoo.com
How to get there: Fly to: Madrid 3 hours away

ASTUN
Astun is a fairly decent resort which lies in the Astun Valley in the north of Spain. Although a rather featureless resort, Astun nevertheless has some interesting terrain that will keep freeriders of all levels happy for a few days and intermediates content for a week. **Carvers** have a number of long sweeping trails to do their thing on. **Beginners** have a good series of easy slopes. **Local services** at the base area are basic and affordable.

Number runs: 28
Top Lift: 2324m
Total Lifts:14
Contact:
Astun Tourist Office
22889 Valle de Astun
Huesca
Tel: ++34   (0)
34974373088
Fax: ++   (0)
34974373295
www.astun.com
How to get there: Fly to: Pamplona 1-1/2 hours away

BOI TAULL
A resort in the far north that will bore the tits off you if you know how to ride and spend more than two days here. There is also the odd natural hit for freestylers to gain some air off. There is still a couple of fast blacks for carvers to try out. Not to say this place is no good, its just that its a bit limited unless you're a total beginner. However, there are no convenient local services

Ride area: 1359 acres
Number runs: 41
Top Lift: 2750m
Bottom Lift: 2020m
Total Lifts:15 - 6 chairs, 9 drags
Contact:

Amigs, 14-16
08021 Barcelona
Spain
Tel: 902 40 66 40
Fax: 93 209 46 10
www.boitaullresort.e
How to get there: Fly to: Madrid 3 hours away

CERLER
Although not a very big resort, with only 30km of marked piste, Cerler is one of Spain's best natural freeride/freestyle resorts. it is laid out above the ancient village of Benasque up in the Pinneos Mountains in the north of Spain. On the slopes, **freeriders** will find an abundance of fast trails both on and off the piste with numerous areas where its possible to shred through some tight trees and down some deep powder. Most of the runs are graded red and will appeal to intermediate riders, however advanced riders wanting an easy time with a bit of a challenge, will also like it here especially on the runs that descend from the Cogulla peak. **Freestylers** will find some nice hits. **Beginners** will find this place is perfect. Good local facilities are provided a short distance from the main base area, with hotels and shops

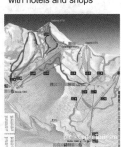

Number runs: 21
Top Lift: 2364m
Total Lifts:13
Contact:
Cerler Tourist Office
Estacion de Esqui de Cerler
telesilla B-1
22449 CERLER
Tel: ++34 (0) 974 55 10 12
Fax: ++34 (0) 974 55 16 17
www.cerler.com
How to get there: Fly to: Barcelona 2 hours away

EL FORMIGAL
Located way up in the north of the country on the French border, El Formigal is a modern purpose built affair. It offers some very good snowboarding on its wide open crowd frees slope that will appeal to piste loving carvers and beginners mostly. Fast riding freeriders and hard core freestylers are not going to be tested too much. There is no pipe or park but there is a lot of good natural freestyle terrain to get air from.
Off the slopes you will find a good selection of affordable slopeside services

Number runs: 48
Easy 29%
Intermediate 46%
Advanced 25%
Top Lift: 2200m
Vertical Drop: 377m
Total Lifts:21
1 Gondola, 5 chairs, 15 drags
Contact:
Tel - ++34 (0) 974 490 000
Fax - ++34 (0) 974 490 231
www.formigal.com
How to get there: Fly to: Barcelona 3 hours away

Sweden emulates Norway in almost every aspect; cold climate, short winter days and expensive beer. Like Norway, Sweden has a lot of listed resorts - approximately 150. However, 80% cater just for cross country skiing, so most Swedes head down to France and Austria to ride, leaving their own resorts generally crowd free, which helps when you see the size of them.

In general, 99.9% of all resorts are small and at a low level. Terrain will suit mainly intermediate freeriders and freestylers with treeriding and excellent off piste opportunities. Fast carvers won't be too impressed and advanced boarders may find things a bit limiting, but novices will have a good time on loads of easy slopes.

Capital City: Stockholm
Population: 8.9 million
Highest Peak: Kebnekaise 2111m
Language: Swedish & Lapp
Legal Drink Age: 18/20 spirits
Drug Laws: Cannabis is illegal
Age of consent: 16
Electricity: 240 Volts AC 2-pin
International Dialing Code: +46

Currency: Krona
Exchange Rate:
UK£1 = 13.6
EURO - 9
US$1 = 7.5

Driving Guide
All vehicles drive on the right hand side of the road
Speed limits:
Motorways-80kph (50mph)
Highways-90kph (56mph)
Towns-110kph (68mph)
Emergency
Fire/Police/Ambulance - 112
Documentation
Driving licence, insurance certificate and vehicle registration, passport

Time Zone
UTC/GMT +1 hours
Daylight saving time: +1 hour

Swedish Snowboard Association
www.svensksnowboard.net

Sweden Tourist Board
Swedish Travel & Tourism Council
P O Box 3030
Kungsgatan 36
SE-103 61 Stockholm
www.swetourism.se

Getting around the country is easy, although you may have to do some travelling to reach some of the far flung resorts. Air, bus and rail services are damn good, but all are very expensive.
Sweden has the reputation of being very expensive, especially booze. Resort facilities and services are of a high standard. Accommodation is in the form of hotels, little wooden cabins or hostels. A basic Bed and Breakfast home costs from 350kr per night while a bunk in a hostel is around 150kr or a cabin from 170Kr a night.

Over all, Sweden may not be the most adventurous country in which to ride, but it's worth a road trip in June when you can still ride in T-shirts: What's more, Swedes are cool people and the girls are gorgeous and absolutely stunning.

ARE

7 OUT OF 10 — Very good resort

Åre is the biggest and most developed resort in the whole of Scandinavia and unlike many Swedish resorts, this isn't a poxy little hill ! This is a good sized mountain that will give all rider levels a good time. It is situated in the middle of Sweden, near the town of **Ostershund**.

1420M TOP LIFT	
% OF BEGINNER TO EXPERT RUNS	90KM PISTES
880M VERTICAL	
10 40 50	
400M FIRST LIFT	

NUMBER OF RUNS: 102
LONGEST RUN: 4miles (6.6km)
TOTAL LIFTS: 40 - 1 Gondola, 1 cable-car, 6 chairs, 31 drags
CAPACITY (people per hour): 47,390
LIFT TIMES: 9.00am to 4.30pm

AVERAGE SNOWFALL:
Unknown
SNOWMAKING:
50%

WINTER PERIODS:
Nov to May
Lift Passes
1 Day 305, 3 Days 875
6 Days 1,515, Season pass - 3750
Hire
Complete snowboard rental;
1 day 310SEK, 3 days 780, 6 Days 1070
Board School
They offer a range of snowboard instruction including freestyle instruction, private lessons and off piste.
Night Boarding
There is a floodlight system covering 5 pistes including Gästrappet and Lundsrappet

FREERIDE 50%
Lots of trees & good backcountry
FREESTYLE 35%
a Terrain park & halfpipe
CARVING 15%

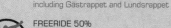

Tourist office Are
Arefjall AB, Box 53. S-830
ARE
Tel: ++46 (0) 46 647177 50
Web:www. areresort.se

Fly
to Stockholm and then inland to Ostersund airport.
Train
services are possible direct to Are from Stockholm which takes around 10 hours.
Car
Drive via Stockholm, take the E4 north to Gavle and then to Bergby at which point you head north west along the E14 via Ostersund to Are

The runs here cover three main mountains all accessed by one lift pass, although the lifts themselves don't link up. Åre is the largest area with the most challenging terrain while runs on

pic - Mats Olofsson/Are Tourism

Duved and **Bjornange** are a lot shorter and will appeal mostly to novices and intermediates.

FREERIDERS will find a lot of varied terrain, from cornices and wind lips to steeps, as well as some cool tree runs. If you can afford it, you can also explore the off-piste by helicopter (but it's not cheap). However, if you can't afford a heli-trip, you can catch a lift on a piste basher up to the top of Åre's Areskuten 1400m summit. This allows you to descend some excellent terrain that goes off in different directions but still allows you to get back to the base (study a lift map first).

FREESTYLERS have a great funpark known as The Snowboard Land Park, which is on the Brackemyren run and comes loaded with a number of big hits to gain maximum air from. There are also two pipes, one in the park and the other at the base of lift 10. The pipe has 3 metre plus walls and is regularly used to host international competitions that attract the worlds top pros.

CARVERS who like laying out big arcs will find the well groomed pistes ideal for leaving a signature in the snow. The long red run from the top of the Kabinbanan cable car that eventually takes you home via some wood, is perfect for this.

BEGINNERS should not feel left out here, there are plenty of easy slopes which run from the top lift to the base area. The of runs on the Duvedsomradet area are cool with varying terrain features.

THE TOWN

Off the slopes, what you get here is similar to what you would find in any top resort in the Alps. However, this will hurt the wallet and you shouldn't bother trying to do a week here on a tight budget, you won't last. Still, you won't be disappointed with the level of services and convenience of the accommodation. For **food**, check out *Broken Dreams* for a burger and local grub or *Bykrogens* for a pizza. **Night-life** is very pricey, but don't hold back, spend and be merry as you can have a great night out here in places like the *Sundial* or *the Diplomats*.

RIKSGRANSEN

5 OUT OF 10 — Okay for a few days

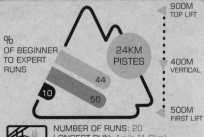

pic - Riksgransen Tourism

%
OF BEGINNER
TO EXPERT
RUNS

24KM PISTES

900M TOP LIFT

400M VERTICAL

500M FIRST LIFT

44
10
50

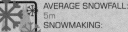

NUMBER OF RUNS: 20
LONGEST RUN: 1mile (1.6km)
TOTAL LIFTS: 6 - 2 chairs, 4 drags
CAPACITY (people per hour): 7,500
LIFT TIMES: 9.30am to 11.59pm!

AVERAGE SNOWFALL:
5m
SNOWMAKING:
none

WINTER PERIODS:
Feb to June
Lift Passes
1 Day pass - 200
3 Day pass - 450
6 Day pass - 1,000
Night Boarding
In perfect daylight until midnight

FREERIDE 60%
No trees & good backcountry
FREESTYLE 35%
a Terrain park & 3 halfpipes
CARVING 5%

Riksgransen Tourist Office
S-980 28 Riksgransen
Tel: ++46 (0) 980 400 80
Web:www.riksgransen.nu
Email:reservation@riksgransen.nu

Fly
to Stockholm and then inland to Riksgransen airport.
Train
services are possible direct to Riksgransen which is a 20 hour journey from Stockholm.
Car
Riksgransen is located close to the Swedish/Norweigan border east of the Norweigan town of Narvik off the E6 and E10 routes.

In the far north of Sweden and close to the Norwegian border lies the remote resort of Riksgansen; a place with one of the most unusual seasons in Europe, and one that has become a snowboarder's favourite for summer road trips and snowboard camps. Riksgransen is located just 125 miles from the Arctic Circle which would suggest that this is a cold place, but because of its proximity to the Gulf Stream and the Atlantic Ocean, riding in a T-shirt is quite normal in the latter months of the season. Un-like most resorts in Europe, Riksgransen doesn't open until mid February and stays open until late June, or as long as the snow allows the lifts to be used. You can ride all day in a T-shirt, and strangely enough you can still snowboard right up until midnight when there is still bright natural day light. Although no one tends to hang out here for more than a week to ten days, you won't be too disappointed if you're a no-nonsense freerider, or a full on freestyler.

FREERIDERS will find some good off piste with steeps, windlips, and cool hits for getting air born. If you sign up for heli-boarding, you get the chance to see the best of Lapland's backcountry terrain, but is not cheap whatsoever.

FREESTYLERS are attracted to Riksgransen in big numbers. They hold the Swedish Snowboard Cup here and Swedes like their hits big and laid on. So apart from loads of really good natural freestyle terrain to check out, they also build and maintain a damn good halfpipe and fun park (mainly for the camps), with loads of hits for pulling air off, this includes an awesome quarter pipe for those who know what it's about.

CARVERS will feel out of place here and to be honest, the terrain is not really that good for laying out big turns on. However, via the Ovre lift you do get access to a decent red that joins up to a black.

BEGINNERS do make it up here, but in truth, it's a long way to come just for a couple of small easy flats.

THE TOWN

Riksgransen Hotel is where it all happens off the slopes. Beds and food are offered at reasonable prices. Summer up here is for riders in a van, equipped with a tent, loads of duty free booze and a copy of Penthouse. You can also pig out at *Lappis cafe*. There's no **night-life** as such here, in fact there is none at all, however, you can have a very good drinking session in the *Riksgransen Hotel* which often last all night.

SWEDEN

ROIUND-UP

BJORKLIDEN
By any stretch of the imagination, Bjorkliden is a small resort with a mixture of basic beginner terrain to simple intermediate carving slopes. Still, overall it?s not a bad resort and offers a lot of interesting opportunities, just not of a very advanced level.

Freeriders who find the marked out runs a bit of a bore could sign up for a heli-board trip and enjoy some cool backcountry riding. Freestylers can make do with a decent sized terrain park with a good halfpipe and hits. Nothing local near the slopes but what is available a few miles away is okay but pricey.

BJORNRIKE
Small resort that offers the average rider an afternoons okay carving on a number of trails which include a couple of fast blacks. But in the main, this is a resort we if it's justified with a please beginners with a low IQ. Slope side lodging and accommodation and other resort facilities are expensive but okay.

YDALEN
overall, this is not a bad place to spend a few days if you are beginner wanting ice and easy runs or a eerider looking for easy to egotiate tree runs. Riders no rate themselves can e if it's justified with a ood selection of black runs try out. Freestylers don't ave too much to test them, t as with most Swedish sorts, locals build their n hits and session them day long.
ere is also some fast rving runs to suit the rvers.
e area: 50km
Lift: 1010m

Total Lifts:11
Contact:
Tel: +46 (0) 643 32011
How to get there: Fly to:
Stockholm 51/4 hours away

FUNASDALEN
Fundasdalen is rated by many as one of Sweden's best resorts, offering a good level of varied terrain and with plenty to keep expert and beginner riders happy for a good few days. Riders who like to go fast can do so here on a series of black runs and a great selection of red intermediate trails.t If back country riding without the hiking is your thing, heli-boarding is available to those with sufficient means. Freestylers don't need to go heli-boarding as they are provided with 2 halfpipes and a number of terrain parks that all house some mighty big hits with spines, gaps and quarter pipes. Beginners have an equally good number of basic trails. About town theres okay slope side lodging and services
Ride area: 90km
Top Lift: 1200m
Total Lifts:34
Contact:
S-840 95 Fundsdalen
Tel: +46-(0)684-164 10
Fax: +46-(0)684-290 26
How to get there: Reach Funasdalen via Roros airport in Norway 1 hour away

HEMAVAN
Hemavan is a rather unusual resort that has a reasonable marked out ride area and an even bigger unmarked backcountry terrain accessible by helicopter. For those freeriders who can't fly off to secret powder bowls, there are some nice areas close to the lifts including lots of trees at the lower section of the slopes. This is not a resort noted for its advanced terrain, indeed

there is only a couple of advanced graded runs, but for intermediates and first timers, this is a fine place to check out and spend a few days. If you do decide to visit this place then be prepared to put yourself out as there are no local facilities on the slopes and although accommodation and other amenities are not too far away, it's very spread out and will require a car.
Ride area: 30km
Top Lift: 1135m
Total Lifts:7
Contact:
Hemavan-Vaxholm AB
Hemavans Hvgfjdllshotell
Box 162
S- 920 66 Hemavan
Tel: +46 (0)954-301 50
Fax: +46 (0)954-303 08
How to get there: Fly to:
Stockholm 12 hours away

HOVFJALLETT
Hovfjallett is basically a waste of time unless you are aged 80, wearing a hearing aid and excel at speeds of one mile an hour. Although the area has a few black runs and half a dozen red trails, all can be licked by an average rider in the time it takes to have a curry induced crap. However, the place is friendly and provides a good halfpipe for air heads.

IDRE FJALL
In the top ten ranking of Sweden's resorts Idre Fjall is a place that will suit all levels and rider styles. The area has a combination of easy runs and a number of testing black runs. Nothing here is all that long, indeed the longest trail measures just under 3km, however, this is a place that can take a good few days to explore, especially if you sign up for a heli-board trip.

Freestylers have a terrain park and a halfpipe which the locals take great pride in and keep in good condition. Off the slopes you will find a good choice of slope side lodging and places to eat and drink in.

SALEN
Salen is about as big as they get in Sweden, with over 155 km of marked rideable terrain spread out over four areas offering every thing you could want both on the slopes and off. The terrain is split evenly between all levels and with a host of advanced runs that will have the hardest of riders tested to the limits and needing a week to conquer what is on offer. Freeriders will be pleased to find lots of cool areas to get a fix with deep powder stashes and fast steeps off-piste. For those wanting to go high off man made hits, then there is a host of terrain parks and halfpipes to satisfy your needs. Resort services are extreme with literally dozens of hotels, restaurants and night time hangouts much of which is either on the slopes or very close to them.

STORLIEN
Storlien is a small affair with nothing great to shout about unless you are a novice or intermediate rider who looks for simple slopes. There is nothing much here to please advanced riders, with only a couple of black runs. Freeriders will find that this place has some nice off-piste areas although very limited. Freestylers have numerous natural hits to get air from and a pipe. Basic lodging is available but none of it is that cheap

S

SWEDEN

277

PIC - SWITZERLAND TOURISM

The Swiss have gained their riches by shrewdness and getting in on the act early. So it's no wonder their resorts have been welcoming snowboarders for some time and providing them with a huge variety of services. It's never been a big deal for Swiss areas to build halfpipes and fun parks.

What you find in Switzerland is a decent mixture of the old and new. Many resorts are made up of old chalets that look the part, while others are sprawling modern affairs. Verbier is a huge and very impressive place, spoilt only by the fact that it's damn expensive and that it attracts Royalty and idiots on Big Foot skis.

Travelling around the country is made easy with a good road network that links up well with the rest of Europe. To drive on Swiss motorways you need to buy a road tax called the Vignette, which costs around Sfr 30 and can be purchased from

Capital City: Bern
Population: 7.3 Million
Highest Peak: Mont Rosa 4634m
Language: German/French/Italian
Legal Drink Age: 18
Drug Laws: Cannabis is illegal but laws are slack
Age of consent: 16
Electricity: 240 Volts AC 2-pin
International Dialing Code: +41

Currency: Swiss Franc (CHF)
Exchange Rate:
UK£1 = 2.3
EURO = 1.5
US$1 = 1.3

Driving Guide
All vehicles drive on the right hand side of the road
Speed limits:
Motorways-120kph (74mph)
Highways-80kph (50mph)
Towns-50kph (31mph)
Emergency
Fire - 118
Police - 117
Ambulance - 117
Tolls
Drivers on motorways must have permit which costs CHF40 available from most garages.
Documentation
Driving licence, vehicle registration document and motor insurance must be carried. Passport will be needed for photo ID

Time Zone
UTC/GMT +1 hours
Daylight saving time: +1 hour

Swiss Snowboard Association
Webereistrasse 47,
Postfach 8134
Adliswil 1
Switzerland
Tel: +41 1 711 82 82
Web: www.swisssnowboard.ch
Email: info@swisssnowboard.ch

PIC - SWITZERLAND TOURISM

FRANCE

GERMANY

✈ Friedrichshafen

Zurich ✈

LIECH.

E41

E25　E41　E60

✈ Bern

E35

E27

E25

Grindelwald

Wengen

Engelberg

Andermatt

Flims
Laax

Davos

Arosa

Savognin

St.Moritz

Gstaad

Leysin
Villars

eneva

Adelboden

Crans Montana
Anzere
Nendaz

Verbier

Saas Fee

Zermatt

E25

ITALY

E35

▲Mont
Blanc

Milano

Automobile Associations or at border crossings. The tax disc must be shown in the window and fines are payable if you are caught without it.

Flying options are excellent in Switzerland, with most resorts reachable within a 3 hour transfer from the main gateway airports. For such a small country with so many high mountainous areas, it's amazing how good and how many direct train routes there are to resorts. Trains wind their way up to some of the smallest places, travelling up such steep inclines that you're left wondering just how good the brakes are! Few resorts don't have their own train station, or one more than 15 km from away. Bus services are also good, especially from airports, but although they're cheaper than the trains, the buses are slower and less frequent.

Switzerland is not a member of the EU, so all foreign nationals need a passport. However, visas are not required for many nationals, but you must obtain proper permits if you want to work, even as a kitchen porter. You can get cash in hand work with no questions asked, so long as you don't draw attention to yourself.

When it comes to money, Switzerland is costly - budget riders be warned nothing is cheap, and this is not a country where you can scam your way around easily, although thankfully a lot of resorts have bunk houses and youth hostels that help to keep costs down.

ST.MORITZ TOURISM - PETER DONATSCH

wsg

ADELBODEN

6 OUT OF 10 Okay but basic resort

S
W
I
T
Z
E
R
L
A
N
D

% OF BEGINNER TO EXPERT RUNS

2350M TOP LIFT

170KM PISTES

994M VERTICAL

1356M FIRST LIFT

8   44   48

NUMBER OF RUNS: 85
LONGEST RUN: 7km
TOTAL LIFTS: 56
8 Gondolas, 3 cable-cars, 8 chairs, 12 drags, 14 Children's lifts
CAPACITY (people per hour): 33,000
LIFT TIMES: 8.30am to 4.30pm

AVERAGE SNOWFALL:
Unknown
SNOWMAKING:
5%

WINTER PERIODS:
Nov to May
Lift Passes
1 Day 51, 6 Days 228, Season 745
Hire
Many shops in the town around 50CHF for board & Boots per day
Board School
Halfday 2 hr lesson 40 or 88 CHF inc equipment. Private 70 CHF per hour

FREERIDE 30%
A few trees & a bit of off-piste
FREESTYLE 30%
2 Terrain parks & 3 halfpipes
CARVING 40%

Adelboden Tourismus
Dorfstrasse 23
CH-3715 Adelboden
Tel. +41 (0) 33 673 80 80
Fax +41 (0) 33 673 80 92
Web: www.adelboden.ch
Email:info@adelboden.ch

Fly
to Geneva airport, 3 hours away.
Train
to Frutigen station (15 minutes).
Car
via Geneva, take the N1 to Lausanne, the N9 to Aiglg and then the B11 before taking the B73 to the resort.

Adelboden, which links with **Lenk**, is a decent sized picture postcard swiss resort, located a short distance from the resort of **Gstaad** and close to the glitzy resorts of **Wengen Grindelwald** and **Murren**. However, unlike its neighbours, this is a less popular place making it that bit quieter with crowd free slopes. This is also not a resort favoured by tour operators, although a few do bus in the two plankers to mess things up. What you get to ride here is split into 6 areas all linked by lifts. Collectively, all the areas provide terrain that will keep novices and intermediates happy for a week, while expert riders will have things sorted in a few days after tackling the blacks on the **Geils** area. The mountain has some nice diverse terrain that will bring a smile to most freeriders. It also has some okay backcountry riding offering a few powder stashes and some fun pisted areas.

FREERIDERS will find plenty to keep themselves occupied with here. The Geils area offers some good off-piste riding coupled with a series of black runs that will test the best and draw tears if you fail to respect the terrain.

FREESTYLERS are spoilt for choice here, with the option to ride two funparks, one at **Sillerenbuhl** and the other on the **Hahnenmoos** area. Both parks come equipped with a good selection of gaps and some nice kickers. There's also a cool man made half-pipe and as various naturally formed pipes with big walls for getting maximum air. Locals here like to ride the natural hits and have a number of secret spring boards that are tucked away, so hitch up with a local and go big.

CARVERS will find that Adelboden will suit their needs perfectly; especially competent intermediate hard-booters who like to leave a signature in the snow on wide open trails.

BEGINNERS have a mountain that caters for them in every aspect, good novice areas with easy access from the village, excellent snowboard tuition at the local snowboard school and runs serviced by easy to use lifts, although many are drag lifts.

THE TOWN

Off the slopes, Adelboden offers plenty of slope side accommodation with various hotels and a number of chalets to choose from, all in a relaxed setting. **Eating out** here is mixed with affordable options coming from traditional swiss style restaurants. **Night life** is also okay, but on the whole, not rocking. Check out such bars as the *Alpenrosli* and *Lohner*.

280

7 OUT OF 10 — Very good resort

pic - Andermatt Tourism

Andermatt is a very small resort, located close to the **St.Gotthard Pass tunnel** with a reputation for excellent powder snow that other resorts can only dream about. This may not be a massive resort, but what it does have is a respectable 1500 metres of vertical with some damn fine steeps, lots of off-piste and crowd-free slopes that are generally also skier free (apart from major holiday times) making **Andermatt** a great place to snowboard There is excellent terrain for advanced riders in soft

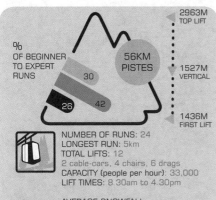

%
OF BEGINNER
TO EXPERT
RUNS

30

56KM PISTES

26 42

2963M
TOP LIFT

1527M
VERTICAL

1436M
FIRST LIFT

NUMBER OF RUNS: 24
LONGEST RUN: 5km
TOTAL LIFTS: 12
2 cable-cars, 4 chairs, 6 drags
CAPACITY (people per hour): 33,000
LIFT TIMES: 8.30am to 4.30pm

AVERAGE SNOWFALL:
8.5m
SNOWMAKING:
none

WINTER PERIODS:
Dec to April
Lift Passes
1 Day 53, 2 Days 89, 5 Days 189
Night Boarding
None

FREERIDE 70%
A few trees & some off-piste
FREESTYLE 10%
Terrain park & halfpipe
CARVING 20%

Verkehrsbüro Andermatt
Gotthardstrasse 2
6490 Andermatt
Tel: +41 (0) 41 887 14 54
Fax +41 (0) 41 887 01 85
Web:www.andermatt.ch
Email:info@andermatt.ch

Fly
to Zurich airport 2 hours away.
Train
possible direct in to Andermatt.
Car
via Zurich, head south on N3 & turn of at
signs for Schwyz onto the A8 and N2 to
Andermatt. Zurich to resort = 72 miles

boots and is noted for its testing runs that also appeal to intermediates who are beginning to sort out their riding. The area is split into four areas with the most testing terrain to be found on the **Gemsstock** slopes, easily reached from Andermatt by a two stage cable ride. From the top, you get to ride down some serious open steep bowls that eventually make their way to the base. However, to guarantee that you do get back to the base, you are well advised to use the services of a local guide.

FREERIDERS have an excellent resort to explore, with great off-piste riding in big powder areas. If your thing is fast steeps and banked walls, Andermatt is a resort that will serve your needs well and will easily keep you interested for a week or so.

FREESTYLERS are provided with a fun park and half-pipe on the Gemsstock area, but they're not particularly hot. However, there is plenty of good natural terrain to get from with big naturally formed banks and some cool drop offs.

CARVERS who like to perform will be pleased to find that there's plenty of fast sections to really crank some big turns on. The **Sonnenpiste** is a decent run to try out before hitting some of the blacks on the **Gemsstock** area.

BEGINNERS usually head for the **Natschen** area, but if you're a slow learner this may not be your resort The slope graduation goes quickly from easy to very hard.

THE TOWN

Good **accommodation** can be found in chalets or in one of the hotels, with access to the slopes very easy by foot. The old village is as Swiss as they come: somewhat boring and somewhat basic. However, it's not as expensive as some other Swiss resorts and as you can ride hard all day, who needs major night-life? A few beers in a **bar** free of moaning package tour apres numpties should do the trick. Nights can rock and the locals help to make the action take off, but don't expect lots of it.

S

SWITZERLAND

6 OUT OF 10 Good basic resort

pic - Anzere Tourism

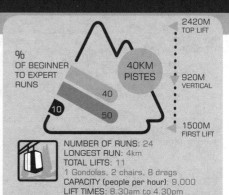

%
OF BEGINNER
TO EXPERT
RUNS

40KM PISTES

40

10

50

2420M
TOP LIFT

920M
VERTICAL

1500M
FIRST LIFT

NUMBER OF RUNS: 24
LONGEST RUN: 4km
TOTAL LIFTS: 11
1 Gondolas, 2 chairs, 8 drags
CAPACITY (people per hour): 9,000
LIFT TIMES: 8.30am to 4.30pm

AVERAGE SNOWFALL:
8m
SNOWMAKING:
5%

WINTER PERIODS:
Nov to April
Lift Passes
1 Day 42, 6 Days 199
Board School
from 60 chf 1 day with meal.
30 chf 1/2 day
Hire
Central Sports is the place to rent
snowboard gear and have your board
serviced.

FREERIDE 40%
A few trees & a bit of off-piste
FREESTYLE 15%
A Terrain park & halfpipe
CARVING 45%

Office du Tourisme de Anzere
Maison du Tourisme 1874 Anzere
Tel: +027/395 50 55
Fax: +027/395 28 46
web:www.anzere.ch
email: infos@anzere.ch

Fly
to Geneva airport, 3 hours away.
Zurich also close
Train
to Sion station (15min). TGV from paris.
Car
via Geneva, east on the N1 and N9 to
Sion and turn left and then drive up the
steep road to Anzere.

NEW

New for 04/05 season
Boardercross

Anzere is one of **Switzerland's** custom built resorts that dates back to the sixties. This small resort with a modest 25 miles of piste, sits at an altitude of 1500m. This has helped to ensure a good annual snow record of over 800 centimetres a season on slopes that get a lot of sun. This allows for plenty of tanning as you ride the slopes or sip a beer at a mountain bar. Overall, Anzere is a fun, happy-go-lucky place that will appeal to the laid back snowboarder. A lot of families and older skiers hang out here, but snowboarders can mingle with ease with both and riders are not ignored or snubbed. The 25 miles of runs are simple and all styles will find something to keep them happy, but it appeals mostly to novices and riders just getting things dialled. **Anzere** would be worth a visit for a few days if you're on a road trip, but a two week trip will prove to be a bit of a bore for those riders who rate themselves at an advanced level.

FREERIDERS in soft boots will fair well on the areas found off the **Les Rousses** and **Le Bate** chair lifts. The trees at the lower parts although not extensive, do offer some pine shredding. The Swiss don't particularly like the woods being cut up, so beware, you may encounter a few sharp tongues from the locals.
FREESTYLERS can spin off a number of natural hits and there are ample areas for practising your switch stance, especially on the runs frequented by the oldies who are leisurely sliding around on their two wooden planks. There's now a fun park with pipe and boardercross.
CARVERS are much in evidence here, with the terrain lending itself well to some good edge-to-edge riding. Competent riders will find the black under the Pas-de-**Maimbre** gondola worth a visit. It should be said that this run could be a red, but it's OK and allows for a few quick turns.
BEGINNERS should achieve the most on the well matched and easy slopes which can be tackled by taking the **Pralan-Tsalan** chair lift and then by using the drags (hold on tight, wimps).

THE TOWN
Anzere is a well laid out village, with a good choice of accommodation (mostly expensive) but budget snowboarders will find affordable beds in a selection of apartments and chalets. *Village Camp* offers decent priced lodgings while the *Avenir* does the best pizza. For evenings, it's best to check out *La Grange* or the *Rendezvous*.

6 OUT OF 10 — Good freeriding

PIC AROSA TOURISM

Arosa is all Swiss, and a place that fits in perfectly in with how the Swiss marketing chiefs would have you see it. This is one of those cosy Swiss hamlets perched high above the tree drenched valley floor. This is a high altitude resort which sits above 1800 metres and is located in the eastern sector of the country not far from the town of **Chur** and the better known resort of **Davos**. However, unlike Davos, this is not a massive sprawling mountain town, Arosa is a quiet traditional swiss village loaded with all the charm you could hope for, although spoilt slightly by its glitzy stuck up image. Still, the area offers some good snowboarding opportunities and will make a week's trip a good one if you're a novice or intermediate rider. Advanced riders have very little to keep them interested beyond a day or so. The 40 plus miles of open wide trails are serviced by a modern and well appointed lift system that can shift over 22,000 people an hour uphill with just 16 lifts Although Arosa is not on the calling card of every tour operator, the few that do use this place help to cause a few lift lines and the odd bottle neck on certain slopes. The runs are spread out over two areas, that of **Hornli** and **Weisshorn** where the most challenging terrain is located.

% OF BEGINNER TO EXPERT RUNS

2653M TOP LIFT

64KM PISTES

914M VERTICAL

38

6 56

1740M FIRST LIFT

NUMBER OF RUNS: 55
LONGEST RUN: 5.5km
TOTAL LIFTS: 16
3 cable-cars, 7 chairs, 6 drags
CAPACITY (people per hour): 22,000
LIFT TIMES: 8.30am to 4.30pm

AVERAGE SNOWFALL:
unknown
SNOWMAKING:
10%

WINTER PERIODS:
Dec to April
Lift Passes
1 Day 54, 6 Days 182
Night Boarding
None

FREERIDE 50%
Trees & good off-piste
FREESTYLE 20%
Terrain park & halfpipe
CARVING 30%

Arosa Tourist Office Arosa. Ch-7050
Tel: +41 81 378 70 20
Fax: +41 81 378 70 21
Web:www.arosa.ch
Email:arosa@arosa.ch

Fly
to Zurich airport about 3 hours away.
Train
direct into Arosa via Chur
Car
via Zurich, head south on the N3 to Chur and then take the winding road up to Arosa ,around 100miles (160km).

PIC AROSA TOURISM

FREERIDERS who want to sample some tracks at speed, should check out the black on the **Weisshorn**. If you want to get into some freshies then take the off-piste track to the resort **Lenzerheide** via the Hornli slopes, but do so only with a guide.

FREESTYLERS have a good half-pipe located at **Carmennahue**. This is also the location for the fun park which is equipped with a standard series of hits including one or two nice kickers. However, this is also a place that offers some good natural freestyling, but you have to look for it.

CARVERS who like to slide around on gentle well prepared slopes and without any surprises, will find Arosa ideal for their needs.

BEGINNERS in Arosa could do a lot worse. The slopes here provide novices an easy time and allow for some quick progression.

THE TOWN

Off the slopes you will find a limited selection of facilities, but enough to get by with. **Accommodation** is well stationed for the lifts and comes in the standard grade Swiss hotel format. Warm, cosy, charming and costly. **Eating out** and night time action is not hot at all, but if you're only out for a quiet time away from the crowds, this place will do nicely.

283

CRANS MONTANA

8 OUT OF 10

Big snowboarders resort offering something for everyone

PIC -CRANS MONTANA TOURISME

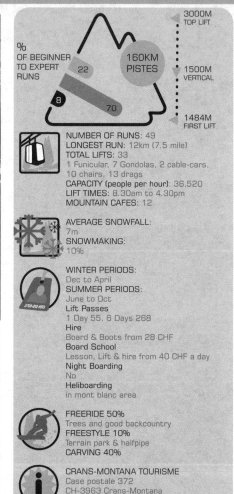

%
OF BEGINNER
TO EXPERT
RUNS

22

160KM
PISTES

8

70

3000M
TOP LIFT

1500M
VERTICAL

1484M
FIRST LIFT

NUMBER OF RUNS: 49
LONGEST RUN: 12km (7.5 mile)
TOTAL LIFTS: 33
1 Funicular, 7 Gondolas, 2 cable-cars,
10 chairs, 13 drags
CAPACITY (people per hour): 36,520
LIFT TIMES: 8.30am to 4.30pm
MOUNTAIN CAFES: 12

AVERAGE SNOWFALL:
7m
SNOWMAKING:
10%

WINTER PERIODS:
Dec to April
SUMMER PERIODS:
June to Oct
Lift Passes
1 Day 55, 6 Days 268
Hire
Board & Boots from 28 CHF
Board School
Lesson, Lift & hire from 40 CHF a day
Night Boarding
No
Heliboarding
in mont blanc area

FREERIDE 50%
Trees and good backcountry
FREESTYLE 10%
Terrain park & halfpipe
CARVING 40%

CRANS-MONTANA TOURISME
Case postale 372
CH-3963 Crans-Montana
Tel.: +41(0)27 485 04 04
Fax: +41(0)27 485 04 60
Web:www.crans-montana.ch
Email:information@crans-montana.ch

One of Switzerland's top snowboard areas is made up of two linking towns, that of **Crans** and **Montana**. Both of which are pretty outstanding and make a totally full-on place with plenty of interest for all. Both areas fuse together to provide over 100 miles (160km) of all-level and all-rider style terrain. Snowboarders have been cutting up these slopes for years, which has lead to a resort with some of the best snowboard instruction and facilities anywhere in Europe. Unfortunately the popularity of this area does mean some stupidly long lift queues with skier cluttered slopes. A lot of tour operators throughout Europe come here with package groups (especially from the UK) and so there's a lot of idiots messing up early morning runs. Still, for all the area has to offer, advanced riders are not always tested, with the terrain largely covering intermediate or novice levels. The hardest listed run is the black that runs down from the **Toula chair**, which is best tackled in softs as the unevenness in parts is better ridden in something where you can easily absorb the bumps at speed.

FREERIDERS in search of off-piste and fresh powder need to hook up with a guide and set off to areas around the **Plaine Morte Glacier**, where you can make your way to nearby **Anzere**. The route goes through some tunnels, which makes it well worth the effort. The area known as the **Faverges** is cool and for

riders with some idea of what they're doing, there are some decent steeps to tackle - but watch out for the thigh burning traverse on the way back. For those who can afford it, you can do some cool heli-boarding on some major terrain.

FREESTYLERS are well catered for, with a good pipe on Pas du Loup, which can be reached by the

THE TOWN & GETTING THERE

Montana-Arnouvaz gondola. The fun park at Aminona is loaded with rails spines and gaps, so new schoolers will love it and for those who want to find out how to ride a pipe correctly or to get big air, there is a number of schools that will help out, all of which offer some of the highest levels of snowboard tuition in Europe (they practically invented snowboard instruction here).

CARVERS have plenty of long reds to check out. In particular the red run that drops away from the **Plaine Morte** down to the village of **Les Barzettes**, is perfect to lay out some big lines and with a length of 7.5 miles, you have plenty of time to get it right.

BEGINNERS are treated to a variety of no nonsense blues which may require some navigation to avoid drag lifts. That said, this is a good novices resort, apart from the sometimes busy slopes. What really stands out is the superb level of snowboard tuition available, with a 3 hour group lesson costing from 40 Cfr.

THE TOWN
As well as supposedly having the largest linked resort in Switzerland, Crans-Montana also said to have the largest number of hotels and accommodation options of any mountain resort in the country. However, you could actually be forgiven for not classing this place as resort at all, but rather a large bustling town which in effect is what it is. The whole area is serviced by a regular bus service which is the best way to get around if you don't have a car (taxi prices are criminal). There are loads of sporting outlets, dozens of shops, (check out *The Avalanche* ++41 (0) 402 2424 for snowboard hire) a cinema and if you are feeling really lucky, a casino.

ACCOMMODATION. The 40,000 plus tourist beds are spread throughout a large area with the option to stay in either Crans or Montana Lodging options are fairly extensive with a good choice of slope side hotels or a large selection of self catering apartment blocks for groups, but on the whole nothing comes cheap wherever you stay.

FOOD. Around town you are spoilt for choice when it comes to restaurants with a selection of over 80 eateries no one need starve here. This place is blessed with simply loads of places to get a meal and even though this is an expensive resort, there are affordable joints such *San Nick's*, which offers some good pub grub or *Mamamias* for a slice of pizza or a bowl of pasta at just about affordable prices. If you wish to splash out, try *Le Sporting's*

NIGHT LIFE is pretty damn good here and well in tune with snowboard lifestyle, although it is carried out along side some very sad Swiss style après ski nonsense (simply to please holiday crowds who don't know how to have a good time). Cool hangouts to have a beer in include The *Amadeus Bar* and *Constellation*, both with a party mood and loud music. The *Memphis Bar* is a good bar.
SUMMARY
A big snowboarders resort offering something for everyone. Great carving and excellent freeriding areas. Lots of local services but a very busy place.
On the slopes: Excellent
Off the slopes: Very good
Money wise: Overall, a very expensive resort but well worth the money.

S W I T Z E R L A N D

PIC -CRANS MONTANA TOURISME

CAR: A9 to Sierre then 15 km to resort
FLY: 2.5 hours from Geneva, Zurich 4hrs. Sion nearest airport, 40 mins away.
TRAIN : To Sierre then Funicular 12 mins or 30min drive
BUS: Buses between Sierre-Montana-Crans via Chermignon or Mollens

10 OUT OF 10

Great carving and excellent freeriding areas, but comes at a price

pic -San Tang

2844M
TOP LIFT

%
OF BEGINNER
TO EXPERT
RUNS   30

310KM
PISTES

2034M
VERTICAL

30   40

810M
FIRST LIFT

NUMBER OF RUNS: 110
LONGEST RUN: 12km (7.5 mile)
TOTAL LIFTS: 57
4 Gondolas, 11 cable-cars, 10 chairs,
29 drags
CAPACITY (people per hour): 64,400
LIFT TIMES: 8.30am to 4.30pm
MOUNTAIN CAFES: 15

AVERAGE SNOWFALL:
5.5m
SNOWMAKING:
8%

WINTER PERIODS:
Nov to April
Lift Passes
1 Day 61, 6 Days 280
Hire
Loads of hire shops in town
Board School
3 x 2.5hrs 260Chf
Top Secret & Schweizer Schneesport-
schule run sbowboarding lessons inc
backcountry & freestyle
Night Boarding
Yes, Halfpipe illuminated
Heliboarding
Yes

FREERIDE 60%
Trees and good backcountry
FREESTYLE 30%
3 Terrain parks & 2 halfpipes
CARVING 10%

Davos Tourismus
Promenade 67 CH-7270 Davos
Tel: +41 (0)81/ 415 21 21
Fax: +41 (0)81/ 415 21 00
Web: www.davos.ch
Email:davos@davos.ch

Davos is not just a major snowboard resort, it's also a massive town that offers just about all you need to have a cool time. This very happening place offers the lot; tons of deep powder, loads of trees, big natural hits, half-pipes, fun parks, a boardercross circuit and night riding. All this on 200 miles (320km) of fantastic snowboard terrain, on slopes that hold the snow well. Davos is located in an area that makes it ideal to check out many other resorts, including the famous retreat of **Klosters** (the place where Prince Charles and Prince Harry first tried snowboarding Points for Harry, he has the makings of a rider, but dad, stick to skis Sir). However, back to Davos which is a resort that needs to be visited a number of times if one is to ride the whole area. Davos itself, has a bit of an attitude when it comes to money, but it's a working town and so far less snobby than other similar places. More importantly, Davos offers access to some major snowboarding terrain - there's enough stuff here to keep any rider busy for a long time. There are two main areas and most snowboarders head for the runs on the Jakobshorn, which can be reached with ease.

FREERIDERS will wet themselves when they see the off-piste opportunities, which are mega and best checked out with the services of a guide. The run down to **Teufi** from **Jakobshorn** is pretty cool, but you will have to bus back to Davos. From the top station (which is well above the tree lines), advanced or intermediate freeriders will find a number of testing

blacks which mellow out into reds as they lead straight back down to the **Ischalp** mid-section. From here you could carry on down through the trees to the base or if you want an easy final descent, there's an easy blue that snakes it's way home, ideal for novice freeriders.

FREESTYLERS have long been provided with a good pipe and park area, however, they weren't always well maintained, apart from at competition times. Now that

THE TOWN & GETTING THERE

pic - Davos Tourism

has changed and the new park, with its two pipes on the Parsenn slopes, is excellent as is the abundance of natural freestyle terrain.

CARVERS won't be disappointed here, the 6 mile red run into the village of **Serneus** is full-on and you should be carving big style at the end of this one.

pic - Davos Tourism

BEGINNERS wanting to get to grips with things should go see the guys at the '*Top Secret snowboard school*', the instructors really know how to turn you from a side standing fool into a powder hound. At the top station of **Jackobshorn**, novices are treated to wide open easy flats which are serviced by drag lifts or a short cable car ride. Alternatively, there are plenty of very easy runs lower down on the **Parsenn** slopes.

THE TOWN

If you're the sort of individual that wants to be housed, fed and watered in a charming sweet little village with cow bells hanging from rickety old sheds, don't bother with this place. Despite its some- what glitzy image, off the slopes, Davos doesn't muck around, lacks style, doesn't come cheap nor is this a visually pleasing joint. What you have here is a massive drab mountain town offering a huge choice of everything. Although this is a super expensive place that attracts international conferences and all that goes with them, you still get a large slice of snowboard lifestyle. Local facilities include sports centres, lots of shops, and even a Casino

Accommodation in Davos is second to none. On top of there being loads of expensive hotels, Davos also has an affordable snowboarders hostel come hotel called the The *Bolgenschanze* which offers a number of ride and stay packages at reasonable prices (++41 81 43 70 01). The town also boast a host of bed and breakfast joints.

Food. Two words that don't go together in Davos, cheap and eating out, but if you have the cash then the options for dining high on the hog are excellent. There is a good choice of restaurants offering every type of cuisine, ranging from local dishes to Chinese. You will also find a few fast food joints serving cardboard burgers and horrid euro style fries (chips should be fat and greasy UK style).

Night life in Davos rocks despite being so damn expensive. There is a good choice of bars and late night clubs, with live bands and artists playing seven nights a week. Most places pump out modern music but a few play sickening euro pop to please the après skiing nerds. The *Bolgenschanze* Hotel is one of the best hangouts, providing the full snowboard lifestyle package and gets packed out with loads of chicks.

S

SWITZERLAND

CAR
Drive from Zurich to Klosters/Davos = 95 miles (159km). Drive time is about 2 1/2 hours.
*From Calais = 620 miles (997 Km). Drive time is around 13 hours.
FLY
Fly to Zurich international Transfer time to resort = 2 1/2 hours
TRAIN
Trains to Davos centre.
BUS
Bus services from Zurich take around 2 1/2 hours direct to the centre of the Davos.

6 OUT OF 10

Good for a week

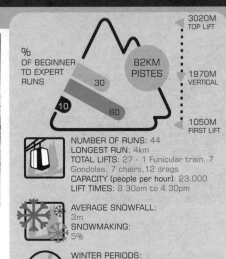

pic - Engelberg Tourism

%
OF BEGINNER
TO EXPERT
RUNS

82KM PISTES

30

10

60

3020M TOP LIFT

1970M VERTICAL

1050M FIRST LIFT

NUMBER OF RUNS: 44
LONGEST RUN: 4km
TOTAL LIFTS: 27 - 1 Funicular train, 7 Gondolas, 7 chairs,12 drags
CAPACITY (people per hour): 23,000
LIFT TIMES: 8.30am to 4.30pm

AVERAGE SNOWFALL:
3m
SNOWMAKING:
5%

WINTER PERIODS:
Nov to April
Lift Passes
1 Day 58, 6 Days 250
Board School
Swiss Snowboard School (www.skischule-engelberg.ch)& boardlocal (lucerne@boardlocal.ch) run lessons
Hire
board and boots from 45 Chf/day

FREERIDE 45%
A few trees & a bit of off-piste
FREESTYLE 15%
A Terrain park & halfpipe
CARVING 40%

Engelberg-Titlis Tourismus AG
Tourist Center, Klosterstrasse 3
6390 Engelberg
Tel: +41 (0)41 639 77 77
Fax: +41 (0)41 639 77 66
Web:www.engelberg.ch
Email:welcome@engelberg.ch

Fly
to Zurich airport, about 2hrs train away.
Train
possible to Lucerne station (45 mins)
Car
Via Zurich, head south on the routes A123/N4a/N14/N2 to Stans and turn off at signs for Engelberg.

Engelberg is a cool resort located slap bang in the middle of the country, not far from the town of **Lucerne** or the resort of **Andermatt**. By any standards, Engelberg has a very impressive rideable vertical drop which is said to be the longest in Switzerland. The beauty of this place is that it's left alone by mass ski crowds so the place has a cool laid back feel about it, without the hype. The ride area is a bit unusual and spread out from the village area. This is a resort noted for its avalanches so lots of attention is called for before trying out any of the slopes. The main happenings are offered on the Titlis area noted for its intermediate terrain but somewhat lacking for those who like to shine. The **Gerschnialp** area is for those sucking on a dummy (beginners).

FREERIDERS have a very good mountain here with some great off-piste to check out, but be warned, avalanches are common here. Some of the best off-piste terrain can be found having taken the **Jochstock** drag lift to reach the slopes on the **Alpstublii**, where you will find some amazing runs. Another easy to reach gem is the **Laub area**, which bases out conveniently to allow you to do it again. But this pleaser should not be tried out unless you know the score and can handle fast steeps, because this one will wipe your lights out for good if you balls up. Guide services are available here so use them, and stay alive.
FREESTYLERS who like it done for them will find the pipe and park on the **Jochpass area** the place to head for, but it has to be said that this is not a resort that's hot on pipe shaping. Still, who cares, the area has plenty of good natural hits to check out.
CARVERS have a fair selection of well looked after pisted runs or some fine unpisted slopes. Check out the Jachpass trails for a burner, but the best advice is leave your hard boots at home and do some soft boot carving, this place is good for it.
BEGINNERS, 30% of the slopes are said to be easy terrain, but in truth if you're a fast learner, then you soon get to ride a further 60% of slopes which are rated intermediate.

THE TOWN
Local services at the base area are of a high standard located in a traditional Swiss setting. The village offers some affordable **accommodation** but don't expect cheap digs near the slopes. There is a number of restaurants here which are all similar in style and price, but as for **night life**, it's a bit dull.

9 OUT OF 10

Excellent riding area

Flims is often over shadowed by its bigger brother, **Laax**. However, this gem of a place deserves to be given a platform of its own and although Laax is far bigger with more rideable terrain, **Flims** can hold its own. What's more, being the junior partner, Flims tends to be a little less crowded even though the two resorts link up on the slopes by lifts and share a joint lift pass. Flims sits at a slightly higher altitude than Laax but on the whole,

pic - Flims Tourism

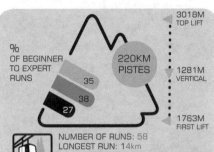

3018M TOP LIFT

%
OF BEGINNER
TO EXPERT
RUNS

220KM PISTES

35

38

27

1281M VERTICAL

1763M FIRST LIFT

NUMBER OF RUNS: 58
LONGEST RUN: 14km
TOTAL LIFTS: 29 - 7 Gondolas, 4 cable-cars, 7 chairs,8 drags, 3 kids lifts
CAPACITY (people per hour): 42,000
LIFT TIMES: 8.30am to 4.30pm

AVERAGE SNOWFALL:
7.2m
SNOWMAKING:
20%

WINTER PERIODS:
Nov to April
Lift Passes
1 Day 61, 6 Days 300

FREERIDE 45%
Trees & good off-piste
FREESTYLE 25%
2 Terrain parks & 3 halfpipes
CARVING 30%

Tourist Office Flims
CH-7017 Flims Dorf
Tel: +41 (081) 920 92 00
Fax: +41 (081) 920 92 01
Web: www.flims.ch
Email:tourismus@alpenarena.ch

Fly
to Zurich, airport, about 3 hours away.
Train
to Chur with a 40min transfer to Flims.
Car
Via Zurich, head south on the E3 to Chur and then head west on the route 19 to Flims via Laax. Zurich to resorts = 88 miles.
Drive time from Calais is 10 hours. 585 miles (941 km).

the slopes are the same in both areas. Indeed on the mountain you would be forgiven for thinking that this was two resorts although in many ways it's not. Both places share a lift pass and the series of pisted runs connect well with each other. The trails above Flims are well prepared and offer a mixture ranging from gentle blues, to a fast black trail running down the **Cassons slopes** which falls away sharply.

FREERIDERS, have for a number of years been aware of what is on offer here, whether up on Flims or over on the Laax slopes. For a nice long freeride trail that's not over testing, try out the **Segnes trail** which is a red run that shoots down from the Cassons and arrives to connect up with the **Grauberg trail**.
FREESTYLERS wanting a fix from a well shaped half-pipe wall, will need to make their way up to the Crap Sogn area above Laax. Here you find an extremely well maintained pipe and park shaped by a pipe dragon. There is another pipe open during the summer months further up on the Vorab Glacier.
CARVERS sticking to Flims will not have themselves overtaxed, but there is a nice series of good red runs below Narus that will make for a few good lines at a controlled speed. The **Heini** is a long red that starts out as a black down from the Cassons and will sort out the boys from the men (or birds from the skirt).
BEGINNERS have a well set out series of novice trails from the base area of **Flims Dorf**. The easy blues start out from the Narus and allow first timers a good choice of easy to negotiate descents back down to the base area.

THE TOWN
Flims offers a good choice of slope side **accommodation** and places to eat. Riders on a budget, book in at *Gliders* which is a cool backpackers place where a bed will cost around 45 CHF a night with breakfast available for an extra fee. **Night life** in Flims is not too hot, but what's on offer is okay in the likes of the *Albana bar* which has a good vibe about it.

S

SWITZERLAND

6 OUT OF 10

Good carvers resort

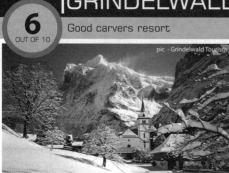

pic - Grindelwald Tourism

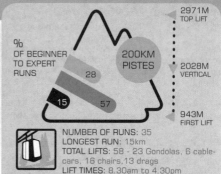

% OF BEGINNER TO EXPERT RUNS

28

15 57

200KM PISTES

2971M TOP LIFT

2028M VERTICAL

943M FIRST LIFT

NUMBER OF RUNS: 35
LONGEST RUN: 15km
TOTAL LIFTS: 58 - 23 Gondolas, 6 cable-cars, 16 chairs,13 drags
LIFT TIMES: 8.30am to 4.30pm

AVERAGE SNOWFALL:
5.3m
SNOWMAKING:
10%

WINTER PERIODS:
Dec to April
Lift Passes
1 Day 55, 6 Days 254
Jungfrau region:
2 day 118 CHF, 6 days 282
Board School
Private lesson CHF 320 for full day
Group 3 day 185 CHF, 1 week 255
Hire
6 days Snowboard & boots CHF 219

FREERIDE 50%
A few trees & good off-piste
FREESTYLE 25%
2 Terrain parks & 3 halfpipes
CARVING 25%

Grindelwald Tourism
P. O. Box 124
CH-3818 Grindelwald
Phone +41 33 854 12 12
Fax +41 33 854 12 10
Web:www.grindelwald.ch
Email: touristcenter@grindelwald.ch

Fly
Zürich Kloten and Geneva Cointrin have rail services to Interlaken. Bern Belp have airport taxis available to take you to the train station.
Train
to Interlaken Ostthere, then train to Grindelwald (approx 35min)
Car
Motorway to Bâle, Geneva or Zürich to Spiez, then to Grindelwald via interlaken

NEW

New for 04/05 season
new quad-chairlift from Innerwengen to Allmend-Wengen. Improved train service from Grindelwald to the Kleine Scheidegg

Grindelwald is one of the resorts that helps form the area more commonly known as the **Jungfrau Region**. The other resorts that make up this sector are Wengen (very posh and super up its arse attitude), and **Murren** the most laid back and snowboard friendly of the three. **Grindelwald** sits up at an altitude of some 1034 metres and scenically, is an impressive place. However, the same can't be said of the rideable terrain that is immediately on offer from the base village, for this is not an adventurous mountain resort and freeriders will soon get bored of the place, although it is a very good carvers resort. The 200 plus kilometres of marked piste stretch out across two large wide open plateaus that stretch up from both sides of the village, with the slopes on the **Mannlichen** and **Kl.Scheidegg** side linking up with the runs that descend back down into Wengen. You can also reach Murren via the slopes but in truth, it can be a bit of a pain the arse. Grindelwald is a large sprawling resort that attracts a lot of visitors, there is no such thing as a good time to visit to avoid crowds, the place is always packed. The main access lifts are not only slow but the queues for them can be hellish and can often mean a 50 minute wait in line. Still, once you do get up on the slopes and the conditions prove to be favourable, provided you do not want to be tested, you will be able to have a good time.

FREERIDERS who stick to Grindelwald are not going to find a great deal to keep them entertained, not because it's crap, there's just not that much to appeal. The best freeriding terrain is in Murren
FREESTYLERS don't tend to head here on mass, as this is didn't use to be a freestylers' resort,. Theres now 2 parks and sometimes 3 pipes on the **Oberjoch area**.
CARVERS should fair well here. The slopes may be busy, but there is still plenty of piste to lay out lots of wide linked turns on.
BEGINNERS have a host of nice gentle open slopes to learn on, the only draw back being that the access to them is not convenient.

THE TOWN
The village at the base of the slopes has a number of hotels and chalets to choose from, but nothing comes cheap as this place is stupidly expensive. Not all the **accommodation** is close to the slopes so expect to do some hiking to and from the base lifts. The resort has a host of sporting attractions, a lot of hotel restaurants but little or no cheap fast food, the night-life also sucks.

GSTAAD

6 OUT OF 10

Okay but a bit snobish

Gstaad is part of a massive slope linked area void of the mass holiday groups. What you get here is crowd free snowboarding with miles of backcountry adventures and over 150 well prepared pistes covered by a single lift pass. Welcome to Gstaad, a place where snowboarding comes as second nature and a place that despite its appeal for attracting far too many poncy image junkies with designer eye-wear, is a

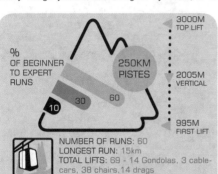

%
OF BEGINNER
TO EXPERT
RUNS

250KM PISTES

3000M
TOP LIFT

2005M
VERTICAL

995M
FIRST LIFT

10 30 60

NUMBER OF RUNS: 60
LONGEST RUN: 15km
TOTAL LIFTS: 69 - 14 Gondolas, 3 cable-cars, 38 chairs,14 drags
LIFT TIMES: 8.30am to 4.30pm

AVERAGE SNOWFALL:
Unknown
SNOWMAKING:
5%

WINTER PERIODS:
Nov to April
SUMMER PERIODS:
May to Sept (Les Diablerets)
Lift Passes
1 Day 52, 6 Days 257

FREERIDE 50%
Trees & good off-piste
FREESTYLE 20%
Terrain park & halfpipe
CARVING 30%

SKI GSTAAD
Promenade CH-3780 Gstaad
Tel: ++41 (0)33 748 81 81
Fax: ++41 (0)33 748 81 83
Web:www.gstaad.ch
Email:gst@gstaad.ch

Fly
to Geneva airport 2 1/2 hours away. Berne-Belp Airport 91 km away.
Train
Train services are possible to Gstaad/Vevey station.
Car
From Geneva, take the N1/N9 via Lusanne to Aigle at which point turn of on to the A11 to Gstaad just after the village of Saanen.

pic - Gstaad Tourism

place that has a good snowboard feel to it and one where you can ride hard. Despite the sad gits that flock here, the area has long allowed snowboarders freedom to roam its slopes, which are split between a number of areas with Gstaad sitting mid-way between them. The areas most favoured by snowboarders are **Saanenmoser** and **Schonried** which can be reached without any hassle from Gstaad. Further a field is **Les Diablerets** which is a glacier that's open in the summer months.

FREERIDERS are somewhat spoilt for choice here with some notable freeriding terrain over on the Saanen area where with aid of a guide, you can ride out some great powder fields. Alternatively, for something a little more testing you should head up to the **Les Diablerets** glacier.

FREESTYLERS have a number of half-pipes to choose from, with the best offering of park and pipe on the **Sanserloch** area. However, constructed half-pipes are not always necessary here as there is a lot of diverse natural terrain with some notable cliffs and big wind lips. Check out the cliffs up at **Huhnerspiel**.

CARVERS who like to lay a board over at speed on super steeps, have few options on where to do it. Much of what is levelled out here can be tackled by a competent intermediate rider. However, don't be put off as overall this is a good carver's area with some nice red trails to blast on the Lauenen slopes.

BEGINNERS have the biggest percentage of easy slopes around here much of which is not linked and spread out between the areas with some of the best runs on the **Saanenmoser** slopes.

THE TOWN

Gstaad is not for those with a weak stomach as on the snobbish, fur clad scale, this joint rates high and therefore is very expensive. Good affordable **lodging** can be had in places like the *Snoeb Hotel*, a specialist riders hangout. **Night life** here can also be good with an okay selection of bars that allow for some hard core drinking sessions.

S

SWITZERLAND

291

9 OUT OF 10

Excellent resort that can be ridden all year round

Laax and its smaller brother **Flims** (due to the access to the slopes on the **Vorab glacier**) are all year round Swiss treasures and pure snowboard heaven. This place is highly regarded by those snowboarders who know about it and what you have here is a full on snowboarder's resort that links up with Flims/Dorf (a more sedate skier's hangout). Together they form an area regarded as one of the most snowboard friendly places in Switzerland. The resort bosses go out of their way to help snowboarders and it's no wonder that when there's a boarder event, the world pro's all seem to make it here. The resort now plays host to a Boardercross competition that is growing in stature season by season. When events are held here, it's not just the top riders that come to perform, some big name pop stars and DJ's also put in an appearance. It is also notable that not many tour operators (the dreaded Brits in particular) plague these slopes. If ever there was a mountain meant for snowboarders free of two plankers, this is it. Every level of snowboarder will be able to enjoy it here. The initial access to the slopes is at **Murschetg**, where a cable car whisks you up to the slopes on the area known as **Crap Sogn Gion**. Its here you'll find one of the halfpipes, but if it's freeriding terrain you're after, check out the offerings on the Vorab area.

FREERIDERS are tempted by some amazing off-piste opportunities with some cool tree riding and full-on powder. The ride down from **La Siala** summit, off lift 15, is a real pleasure and can be tackled by most intermediates. Alternatively, for some easy to reach, classic off-piste riding, check out the **Cassons area**, which is on the slopes above Flims and forms the top area, but it's not for the faint-hearted.

FREESTYLERS are coaxed here with the choice of two halfpipes, which incidentally are shaped with the first Pipe Dragon in Europe. To tempt you further there's also an absolutely awesome fun park which is packed with an array of hits to test all level of air heads. The main pipe is the one located on the **Crap Sogn Gion** off lift number 10 or 2, while the other pipe is up at the **Vorab Glacier** and is open in the summer months.

CARVERS can cut most of the slopes here in style as they piste the runs regularly (and to perfection), making it a great place for laying big turns. It's not the most testing carvers resort, but those with balls should try out the long black race run, Crap Sogn, back down to the base station of **Murschetg**.

BEGINNERS have a great mountain where learning the basics is a joy on simple, hassle free slopes, which are easy to reach from all parts of the resort.

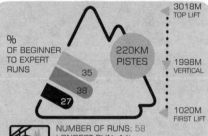

%
OF BEGINNER TO EXPERT RUNS

220KM PISTES

35
38
27

3018M
TOP LIFT

1998M
VERTICAL

1020M
FIRST LIFT

NUMBER OF RUNS: 58
LONGEST RUN: 14km
TOTAL LIFTS: 29 - 7 Gondolas, 4 cable-cars, 7 chairs,8 drags, 3 kids lifts
CAPACITY (people per hour): 42,000
LIFT TIMES: 8.30am to 4.30pm

AVERAGE SNOWFALL:
7.2m
SNOWMAKING:
20%

WINTER PERIODS:
Nov to April
Lift Passes
1 Day 61, 6 Days 300
Board Schools
Snowboard Fahrschule offer freestyle and freestyle lessons email fahrschule@weissearena.ch
Hire
Plenty of hire shops, some allowing a try before you buy.

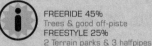

FREERIDE 45%
Trees & good off-piste
FREESTYLE 25%
2 Terrain parks & 3 halfpipes
CARVING 30%

Tourist Office Flims
CH-7017 Flims Dorf
Tel: +41 (081) 920 92 00
Fax: +41 (081) 920 92 01
Web: www.laax.ch
Email:tourismus@alpenarena.ch

LAAX

pic - Laax Tourism

THE TOWN
Both the villages of **Laax** and **Flims** (which are 10 minutes apart by road) sit at different levels and offer a host of good local facilities that will make a two weeks stay well worth the effort. Mind you, neither come cheaply and two weeks will burn a big hole in your wallet. Laax is the smaller of the two villages and has more of a ski outlook and attitude, but nevertheless, Laax has a good choice of apartments or hotels, if you shop around you will find budget options. The village has a host of attractions from squash courts to an outdoor ice rink.

ACCOMODOATION. Some 6000 visitors are offered somewhere to sleep here, and although the choice of lodging and the prices are good, most places are a little spread out and for most, may entail a walk to the slopes. For those on a tight budget, the *bunk house*, *Gliders Paradise*, is the place to check into.

FOOD is much the same as in any other high mountain retreat, that is lots of hotel restaurants all serving up generally bland, traditional Swiss meals at very high prices. Still, there is a number of notable places to get a good meal including the odd pizza joint such as *Pomodoro* in Flims. If you fancy a fish meal then look no further than *Crap Ner* restaurant in Laax, which is noted for its food (and its prices).

NIGHT-LIFE in either Laax or Flims is very good and fairly well suited to snowboard lifestyle (apart form the cost of a beer). Nothing here is of mega status but the bars on offer are good for getting messy in while listening to some good tunes. But do remember, this is Switzerland, so tank up on supermarket or your duty free supplies beer before going out, all the bars are expensive.

SUMMARY
Excellent resort that can be ridden all year round. The slopes are great for freeriders and freestylers as well as suiting beginners. Good local services.
On the slopes: Fantastic
Off the slopes: Very good
Money wise: Top value resort but also a very expensive place all year round

CAR
Zurich via Chur to Laax = 90 miles (145 km). Drive time is about 21/2 hours. From Calais 585 (941 Km). Drive time is around 10 hours
FLY
to Zurich international. Transfer 2 1/2 hrs
TRAIN
to Chur, 40 mins away.
BUS
from Zurich take around 2 1/2 hours direct to Laax via Chur.

293

wsg

LEYSIN

10 OUT OF 10

First class ultra friendly snowboard resort with terrain to suit all levels and styles

pic - Leysin Tourism

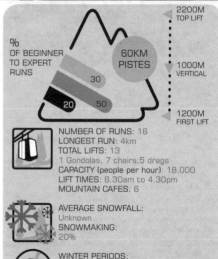

Leysin is located in the French speaking part of Switzerland and has become one of the best and most happening snowboard haunts in the country. Unlike many more popular ski resorts, this place isn't really known for its skiing which has allowed it to be adopted by snowboarders. This has helped to ensure that the place has a low key friendly appeal about it with- out any bull or hype. Leysin connects with the two alpine villages of Villars and Les Diablerets to create a very acceptable 60 km of piste. This resort goes out of its way to be snowboard friendly and since 1992 played host to the International Snowboard Federation World Pro Tour event.; an event attended by the world's top riders where the whole place turned into a festival occasion lasting for at least a week. Leysin is in fact an old and rather large sprawling mountain town and not a modern purpose built resort like some found nearby. What you get here is a high up mountain that in a good winter, offers everything to keep adventure seeking advanced riders happy, while also appealing to first timers who don't want to use a drag lift straight away. A notable point about Leysin is that it's not a popular resort with holiday companies, which is a good thing as the slopes don't get clogged up although weekends can still be a bit busy with locals and punters from Geneva. However, once you do get up on the slopes, you can roam freely over acres of great terrain without seeing another soul for hours

FREERIDERS have plenty of great terrain to explore, with tree runs down to the village, or extreme terrain with bowls and cliffs which you can reach by dropping in to your right on the Berneuse. You should also check out the official off-piste runs that give you the feeling of backcountry riding, for example try the route behind Tour D' Ai, starting at the top of Chaux de Mont.

FREESTYLERS will be able to spin huge airs in the ISF pro tour pipe, which is normally maintained, but don't be shy to ask for a shovel at the nearby lift hut. As well as the pipe, the fun park (located between Berneuse and Mayen) has quarter pipes and gaps to ride. Mind you, it's not usually built until the end of February.

S

S
W
I
T
Z
E
R
L
A
N
D

%
OF BEGINNER
TO EXPERT
RUNS

60KM
PISTES

30

20   50

2200M
TOP LIFT

1000M
VERTICAL

1200M
FIRST LIFT

NUMBER OF RUNS: 16
LONGEST RUN: 4km
TOTAL LIFTS: 13
1 Gondolas, 7 chairs,5 drags
CAPACITY (people per hour): 18,000
LIFT TIMES: 8.30am to 4.30pm
MOUNTAIN CAFES: 6

AVERAGE SNOWFALL:
Unknown
SNOWMAKING:
20%

WINTER PERIODS:
Dec to April
SUMMER PERIODS:
At Les Diablets
Lift Passes
1 Day 42, 6 Days 255
Board Schools
Snow sports Leysin charge 45CHF for half-day lessons, 205 for 6 half days. Private lessons 60 CHF per 60 CHF
Heliboarding
on one of the four Glaciers

FREERIDE 50%
Trees & good off-piste
FREESTYLE 30%
Terrain park & halfpipe
CARVING 20%

Tourist Office Leysin
Place Large
CH-1854 Leysin
Tel: +41 (0) 24 494 2244
Fax: +41 (0) 24 494 1616
Web: www.leysin.ch
Email: tourism@leysin.ch

THE TOWN & GETTING THERE

CARVERS with only hard boots and alpine boards are the ones who are going to be disappointed. There is some good carving to be had, but overall, this is a soft boot resort. The Berneuse is a good place to lay out some big turns.

BEGINNERS can get going at the nursery slopes which have easy to use rope tows, before venturing up to slopes on the Berneuse. The drag lift at the Chaux de Mont will be difficult for first timer and beginners should not use this lift, even for the lower section, as the exit point is on a very steep piece of terrain. The local ski schools handle all the snowboard tuition here.

pic - Leysin Tourism

THE TOWN
Being such a spread out place means that depending on where you're booked into, you could end up doing a lot of hard walking, unless you have a car. Around the town, life is very easy going with a lot of Americans hanging around due to the American colleges based here. Local services are basic but acceptable, offering a well located sports centre equipped with a swimming pool and indoor tennis and squash courts. If you happen to speak the language (French and German) you could even while away your evening at the cinema. Anyone who fancies a skate can check out the ramps down in Aigle, about 40 minutes away, however there's plenty of street in Leysin which the locals will happily share with you.

pic - Leysin Tourism

Accomodation. The options for a bed range from a classy hotel to the normal array of pensions along the main high street. One of the best options is the really cool bunk house called The Vagabond, which offers cheap nightly rates and has a cool bar. Alternatively, Chalet Ermina is a really good bed and breakfast place and great value.

Food. Plenty of restaurants to choose from, but a few of them are tucked away so you will need to study your tourist guide to search them all out. Generally, prices are in the middle to high bracket but affordable food is available, especially if you check out the offerings at the cool bunk house called Club Vagabound which is located away up on the back road. The town also has a couple of cheap pizza restaurants.

Night-life in Leysin is just as it should be nothing major but plenty going down with a lively crowd that's always ready to party. The partying is aided by a lot of young American students (none of whom can drink anything like the amounts the Europeans sup). The main spots are Club Vagabound, although on Saturday nights it gets way too busy, and Top Pub which is much quieter.

SUMMARY
First class ultra friendly snowboard resort with terrain to suit all levels and styles. Great freestyle terrain and ok for novices. Great local services.
On the slopes: Fantastic - Great
Off the slopes: Very good
Money Wise: Generally an expensive resort, however, lots of budget options.

CAR
Geneva via Aigle to Leysin = 151 miles (241 km). Drive time is about 2 3/4 hours.
From Calais 518 (833 Km). Drive time is around 9 1/4 hours.
FLY
Fly to Geneva international. Transfer time to resort = 2 3/4 hours.
TRAIN
Trains to Leysin central.
BUS
Bus services from Geneva take around 2 hours direct to Leysin via Aigle.

S
W
I
T
Z
E
R
L
A
N
D

7 OUT OF 10

Great ride area

pic - Nendaz Tourism

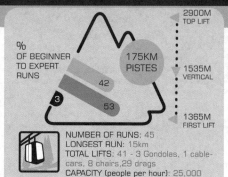

2900M
TOP LIFT

%
OF BEGINNER
TO EXPERT
RUNS

175KM
PISTES

1535M
VERTICAL

42

3

53

1365M
FIRST LIFT

NUMBER OF RUNS: 45
LONGEST RUN: 15km
TOTAL LIFTS: 41 - 3 Gondolas, 1 cable-cars, 8 chairs,29 drags
CAPACITY (people per hour): 25,000
LIFT TIMES: 8.30am to 4.30pm

AVERAGE SNOWFALL:
Unknown
SNOWMAKING:
15%

Being in the shadow of a big brother can often have its draw-backs, and the little guy may get left out and dismissed as not worth the effort. Not in this case. Nendaz is the lesser known relation of **Verbier** and along with a number of other resorts, forms the collective '**Les 4 Vallees**', located 2 1/2 hours east of Geneva just up from the town of Sion. Although linked by lift with Verbier, Nendaz offers an entirely different experience and is a lot less formal and populated. What you have here is a resort with a selection of runs starting right from it's base. It then connects up with the neighbouring hamlets and slopes of **Veysonnaz, Thyon and Siviez**. What's more, with the **Mont Fort** area offering some great summer snowboarding, this place becomes a bit of an all year round treasure. Apart from Nendaz's unique piste markings and the fact that they have installed snowmaking facilities all the way to the top, this place is one of only a few locations in Europe to offer Heli-boarding with passenger collection and mountain guides. You can fly to the heart of the **Rosablanche glacier** to ride major backcountry powder spots.

FREERIDERS will be pleasantly surprised when they arrive and see what this area has to offer both on and off-piste. Both advanced and timed riders will find a weeks stay a pleasure while thrill seekers can test themselves to the limits.
FREESTYLERS are provided with loads of possibilities for gaining air (and not just in a helicopter).There are numerous fun parks and half-pipes around here, the closest to Nendaz being the park up on the **Veysonnaz** slopes. If it's natural hits that you favour, you will find loads of banks, gullies and cool areas with logs to grind.
CARVERS have as much here as any other style of rider, particularly on the series of red trails above **Siviez** and on **Veysonnaz** slopes where you can shine on your edges at speed.
BEGINNERS should leave after a week's visit at a new level. The gentle slopes directly above Nendaz will suit you're every need.

THE TOWN

Off the slopes, Nendaz offers a quality selection of places to sleep, eat and drink in at prices to suit everyone, not just the elite, as is often the case in many resorts. Furthermore, basic local services are well appointed and you can sleep close to the slopes. Locals make you very welcome which helps to give this place a good snowboard vibe and these are some good night posts to check out.

WINTER PERIODS:
Nov to April
SUMMER PERIODS:
Possible in the general area
Lift Passes
1 Day 46, 6 Days 235
Board School
3 schools offering the usual group & private lessons.
Ski Nendez offers half day lessons (3hrs) for 39 CHF. 5 full days 340 CHF. 90min privcate lesson 85 CHF.
Freeride & Freestyle lessons available
Heliboarding
Available through Ski Nendez

FREERIDE 45%
Trees & good off-piste
FREESTYLE 20%
2 Terrain parks & 2 halfpipes
CARVING 35%

Nendaz Tourisme
1997 Nendaz
Tél. +41 (0)27 289 55 89
Fax +41 (0)27 289 55 83
Web:www.nendaz.ch
Email:info@nendaz.ch

Fly
to Geneva airport, about 1 1/2 hours away 165km. Zürich, 2 1/2 hrs, Bâle 2 1/2 hrs. Nearest airport is Sion, 15km from resort
Train
possible to Sion station (15 minutes).
Car
Motorway A9 to Sion, exit Sion-Ouest in the direction of Nendaz. Then 15 minutes drive (15km) up to the center of the resort.
*Drive time from Calais is 9 1/2 hours. 544 miles
Bus
from Sion Airport to Nendaz. Taxis , Taxi Praz tel: +41 (0)79 409 32 15

S
SWITZERLAND

Saas-Fee has been a resort well known to snowboarders for many years. They have been building half-pipes, parks and other obstacles since way back and before many others areas had even heard of snowboarding. With its high altitude glacier, Saas-Fee also provides a mountain where you can ride fast and hard in the summer months, indeed for some, this is the only time worth visiting. Winter or summer, this is still a

pic - Saas-fee Tourism

3600M TOP LIFT

% OF BEGINNER TO EXPERT RUNS

100KM PISTES

1800M VERTICAL

25   50

25

1800M FIRST LIFT

NUMBER OF RUNS: 40
LONGEST RUN: 9km
TOTAL LIFTS: 22 - 1 Cable Railway, 7 cable-cars, 1 chairs,13 drags
CAPACITY (people per hour): 22,400
LIFT TIMES: 8.30am to 4.30pm
MOUNTAIN CAFES: 10

AVERAGE SNOWFALL:
Unknown
SNOWMAKING:
5%

WINTER PERIODS:
Nov to April
Lift Passes
1/2 day 49 CHF
1 Day pass 60 Chf
6 Day pass 299 Chf
Board School
Several options. www.skischule-saas-fee.ch runs group lessons for 44 CHF per day and private for 59 CHF per hour
Heliboarding
Yes
Night Boarding
Thursdays 8 to 10pm in Saas-Balen
Tuesdays 7 to 9:45pm in Furggstalden

FREERIDE 25%
Trees & good off-piste
FREESTYLE 25%
A Terrain park & a halfpipe
CARVING 50%

Saas-Fee Tourismus
Postfach
3906 Saas-Fee
Tel. +41 27 958 18 58
Fax +41 27 958 18 60
Web:www.saas-fee.ch
Email:to@saas-fee.ch

cool place that stages numerous competitions in both seasons and snowboard manufactures do a lot of product testing. Saas Fee is a resort with two faces. In summer the small glacier area has a snowboard park which boasts three half pipes, a boardercross course, and various hits. However, in winter the snowboard park shuts down and the resort focuses itself on family skiers. They do maintain a half-pipe, but that's the nearest you'll get to specialist snowboard terrain. Most of the mountain is geared to skiers and possibly hard-booters. There's a variety of red and black runs, as well as nursery slopes and top to bottom blue runs, but nothing to really test you (although the runs off the Hinterallalin - when open - are supposed to be more challenging). Pisting is somewhat haphazard away from the main stations at the mid point and top glacier, so expect moguls on red and black runs

FREERIDERS will be disappointed to find that the off-piste is limited by crevasse danger around the glacier - but there are some nice tree runs off **Platjen**. Alternatively, the runs off the **Hinterallalin** drag lift will sort out the wimps, with some cool freeriding to be had and some fast steep sections to try out.

S

SWITZERLAND

THE TOWN & GETTING THERE

FREESTYLERS could be excused for thinking something is amiss as the natural hits are few and far between - locals tend to build their own hits and session them. Still, you may find some hits off the **Mittaghorn** and **Langfluh** lifts. There's also a few drop offs to be enjoyed near the Langfluh and Platjen areas.

CARVERS will favour Saas Fee the most, with a host of pisted runs on which to lay out some wide tracks. No matter what your level, you'll soon be carving in and out of the two plankers in style on graded runs from steep blacks to tame blues. The runs under the **Mittelallalin** restaurant are a great area for carvers.

BEGINNERS are not left out, Saas Fee has plenty of novice runs, but some of the blue pistes have long flat sections to catch you out, resulting in a fair bit of skating along. You'll also get really used to T-bars by the time you leave this place. The lower runs have a reputation for rocks and worn patches, so take care when you first head out. However, the best way to find out what's what, is to call in on the boys at the Paradise Snowboard School, they'll show you how to get around any obstructions

pic Saas-Fee Tourism

THE TOWN
Saas Fee is a car-free place where you get around by either electric vehicles or on foot. However, everything is located close to each other and the slopes. The town is a cool place, with options to sleep close to the slopes in hotels or chalets. Money wise, Saas-Fee can be very expensive if you're staying in a hotel and eating out in restaurants, but on the other hand, you can do things cheaply by staying in an apartment and feasting on supermarket produce. The resort crams in loads of amenities, from swimming pools, a cinema, a museum, an ice rink to heaps of shops, including a couple of cool snowboard shops centrally located; *Popcorn* +41 (0) 958 19 14 and *Powder Tools* +41 (0) 89 220 7792.

Accommodation: 7500 visitors can be housed here. Hotels come as one would expect, standard Swiss and expensive. However, with this place comes a good number of affordable bed and breakfast places apartment and chalets for those wanting to go self catering. Whereever you stay, nothing is too far from the slopes.
Food. Being a modern and popular resort, Saas Fee is well equipped to feed all its visitors no matter what

their chosen diet is. There are well over 50 restaurants here many based in hotels but also a good number of independent ones. Notable places to pig out in are the Boccalino for pizza or the Lavern for traditional Swiss food. Hotel Allalin is a good restaurant with affordable meals set in a rustic style.

Night life is very good here despite there being a few places offering the ski après crap. Snowboard life-style centres around the *Popcorn bar* and snowboard shop, but the *Happy bar* is cheaper (especially at happy hour 7:30 - 8:30 daily). There are a few other bars worth checking out. If you decide to stay in and party, watch out for the 'hush police' - too much noise after 10pm and you'll get fined around 120 Sfr.

SUMMARY
Sass-Fee is a great summer snowboard destination, but it's not as hot in winter, but still worth a visit. Local services are great with a good vibe.
On the slopes: Okay **Off the slopes:** Good
Money Wise: Very expensive resort but budget riders can get good deals

CAR
Geneva via Aigle, Saas Fee is 145 miles (235 km, drive time is about 3 hours. Resort is car free
From Calais 582 (936 Km). Drive time is around 10 1/2 hours.
FLY
Fly to Geneva international, Transfer time to resort 2 hours.
TRAIN
Trains to Brigg (20 minutes).
BUS
Bus services from Geneva take around 3 hours direct to Saas-Fee via Brigg.

S
W
I
T
Z
E
R
L
A
N
D

SAVOGNIN

6
OUT OF 10

Okay for a few days

Two wo hours south of **Zurich** lies the relatively unknown resort of **Savognin** that is fast becoming a magnet for snowboarders out for a good time and for riders who want to steer clear of the big resorts because they don't want to get caught up in the hustle and bustle of large ski crowds. Fortunately the ski press don't mention Savognin, which helps to keep this gem a small secret for snowboarders to do as they please with. The natives are super friendly and happy to have

pic Savognin Tourism

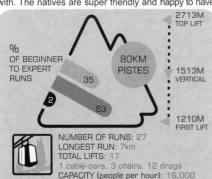

		2713M TOP LIFT
% OF BEGINNER TO EXPERT RUNS	80KM PISTES	
35		1513M VERTICAL
2		
63		1210M FIRST LIFT

NUMBER OF RUNS: 27
LONGEST RUN: 7km
TOTAL LIFTS: 17
1 cable-cars, 3 chairs, 12 drags
CAPACITY (people per hour): 16,000
LIFT TIMES: 8.30am to 4.30pm

AVERAGE SNOWFALL:
4m
SNOWMAKING:
10%

WINTER PERIODS:
Nov to April
Lift Passes
1 Day 45, 6 Days 230 CHF
Night Boarding
Yes

FREERIDE 20%
Some tree runs & good off-piste
FREESTYLE 15%
A Terrain park & halfpipe
CARVING 65%

Tourist Office Savognin
Stradung, 7460 Savognin
Tel: +41 81 659 16 16
Fax: +41 81 659 16 17
Web:www.savognin.ch
Email:ferien@savognin.ch

Fly
to Zurich airport, 2 hours away.
Train
to Tiefencastelt 5 mins away.
Car
Via Zurich, head south on the N3 to Chur and take the A3 via Tiefencastelt to Savognin.
*Drive time from Calais is 10 1/2 hours, 603 miles (970 km).

snowboarders on their slopes. The local snowboard scene is cool with its own riders club where you can find out all there is to know about this place, such as the best hits or runs and where to get messy in the evenings when the lifts are closed. The 50 miles of piste will make a weeks stay well worth it, appealing to novice carvers

FREERIDERS of an advanced level are going to be disappointed if its testing stuff you crave for, there is none really. You can have a bit of excitement on the black run known as the **Pro Spinatsch**, running down from the **Tiggignas** chair lift, it is also the location of Savognin's fun park. It doesn't take too long to conquer if you know what you're doing on your edges.

FREESTYLERS will find the best air to be had is either off the nicely shaped walls in the half-pipe or in the fun park which is tooled up with fun boxes, gaps, spines, rails and a quarter pipe. For some natural hits there are a few cliff drops and some air to be had on the area called Tiem.

CARVERS have some particularly well groomed runs for arcing over on in full view of the lifts, allowing those clad in Oxbow gear to show off their latest designer jumpers and sad flower patterned yellow pants. A good piste to suit all levels whether you're in soft or hard boots, is the **Cresta Ota**, which runs down from the **Piz Cartas** summit and makes for a good time.

BEGINNERS are looked after with a number of easy blues and the option of being able to slide back to base at the end of the day on easy to handle runs. However, uplift is mainly via drag lifts.

THE TOWN
Savognin is a small village with nothing major going on, although it's affordable and doesn't come infested with apres ski crowds. **Accommodation** is a mixture of Swiss pensions and hotels, all of which are well located for the slopes. There are one or two good evening haunts, with the best place to get a **beer** being the *Zerbratent Paulin*.

S
W
I
T
Z
E
R
L
A
N
D

DIAVOLEZZA / LAGALB

% OF BEGINNER TO EXPERT RUNS

354KM PISTES

35
25
40

3303M TOP LIFT

1503M VERTICAL

1850M FIRST LIFT

NUMBER OF RUNS: 88
LONGEST RUN: 8km
TOTAL LIFTS: 56
3 Funiculars, 1 cable railway, 6 Gondolas, 7 cable-cars, 18 chairs,27 drags
CAPACITY (people per hour): 65,000
LIFT TIMES: 8.30am to 4.30pm
MOUNTAIN CAFES: 37

AVERAGE SNOWFALL:
3.5m
SNOWMAKING:
15%

WINTER PERIODS:
Nov to April
SUMMER PERIODS:
May to Nov at Diavolezza (sometimes)
Lift Passes
Half-day 43CHF
1 Day Pass - 58Chf
6 Day Pass - 320Chf
Board School
group 1/2 day lesson from 45CHF
6 half-day lessons from 230CHF
Private lesson half-day 180CHF
Heliboarding
No
Night Boarding
No

FREERIDE 45%
A few trees & lots of good off-piste
FREESTYLE 25%
3 Terrain parks & a halfpipe
CARVING 30%

Tourist Office of St. Moritz
Via Maistra 12
7500 St. Moritz
Guest consulting
Tel. +41 (0)81 837 33 33
Fax +41 (0)81 837 33 77
Web:www.stmoritz.ch
Email:information@stmoritz.ch

S
SWITZERLAND

St Moritz has two classic distinctions, on the one hand this has to be one of the finest natural backcountry freeride places to ride in **Switzerland**, but on the other hand, St Moritz happens to be top of the league when it comes to snobbery. With out doubt this is one of the most expensive resorts on the planet, and not with-standing the outrageous costs here, the place attracts so many stuck-up rich idiots, that you can smell the fur clad sods a mile away. St Moritz is a high altitude resort that along with the areas of **Pontresina** and **Diavolezza**, form the Upper Engadine region. Diavolezza is a glacier mountain that host summer snowboarding allowing for all year round riding. St Moritz, which gives access to the slopes on the **Corviglia** and **Marguns**, is an area that is largely made up of intermediate pisted runs which get stupidly busy on most days and unfortunately there are not too many expert pisted trails to escape the hordes of learning skiers. However, there is heaps of adventurous off piste terrain to check out, but only do so with the advice and services of a local guide

FREERIDERS have a huge amount of great backcountry terrain will blow you're mind beyond, with lots of steeps, gullies, cliffs and virgin powder to seek out. Some of the best freeriding can be found up on the **Diavolezza glacier**, which is for serious riders only. St Moritz's number steep is the slope that drops down from the **Piz Nair summit** of the top cable car.

FREESTYLERS have a park and pipe but neither are that well looked after. The mega heaps of natural is far better of getting big air.

CARVERS will find lots of fairly easy and ordinary well pisted runs to cruise down. But really you should

freeride only at this place.

BEGINNERS may not have the best selection of novice trails to start out with, but what is on offer is superb if only too busy.

pics - St.Moritz Tourism

THE TOWN

Off the slopes St Moritz can easily be summed up as an over priced, over hyped ugly sham that rips you off big style for everything and attracts some very sad gits in designer wear and fur hats.

Accommodation, which is provided by an array of hotels and chalets, is available in a spread out area.

Food. There are plenty of places to get a meal, but you have to look hard to find an inexpensive burger bar.

Night-life. As for having a good night out and a few beers, unless you're a brain dead mutant who owns a gold credit card, forget it, it's sucks big style.

S

SWITZERLAND

CAR
From Zurich, head south on the N3. Turn off at Landquart on to the route 28 to Zernez and then take the R-28 down to St mortiz (200km)
From Calais the journey is 9 1/2 hours. 516 miles (830 km)
FLY
Fly to Zurich/Milan airport, 3 hours drive away. Munic h/Basel, 4 hrs away. Local airport is Samedan - St. Moritz, most airports offer connecting flights
TRAIN
Take a train to Chur, then take Rhätische Bahn direct to resort. www.rhb.ch for more info

pic - Verbier Tourism

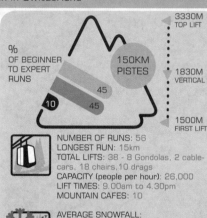

%
OF BEGINNER
TO EXPERT
RUNS

150KM
PISTES

45
10 45

3330M
TOP LIFT

1830M
VERTICAL

1500M
FIRST LIFT

NUMBER OF RUNS: 56
LONGEST RUN: 15km
TOTAL LIFTS: 38 - 8 Gondolas, 2 cable-cars, 18 chairs, 10 drags
CAPACITY (people per hour): 26,000
LIFT TIMES: 9.00am to 4.30pm
MOUNTAIN CAFES: 10

AVERAGE SNOWFALL:
3.5m
SNOWMAKING:
5%

WINTER PERIODS:
Nov to April
SUMMER PERIODS:
No longer
Lift Passes
1 Day pass - 52Chf
6 Day pass - 266Chf
Board School
La Fantastique have Mountain Guides available 440 CHF per day, Full day private lesson 370 CHF per day
Hire
Board & Boots froom 43CHF per day (verbier.com)
Heliboarding
www.lafantastique.com offer heliboarding from 360 CHF each based on 4 people
Night Boarding
Yes

FREERIDE 60%
Trees & good off-piste
FREESTYLE 20%
2 Terrain parks & 2 halfpipes
CARVING 20%

Téléverbier SA
Case Postale 419
CH - 1936 Verbier
Tél. : +41 27 775 25 11 -
Fax : +41 27 775 25 99
Web : www.verbier.ch
Email : verbiertourism@verbier.ch

Verbier is a big resort in more ways than one: Big slope area, big mountain and big on extreme terrain. However, Verbier is also big on the stuck and poncy scale being a resort that goes out of its way to attract the rich, the stuck up elite, disposed European royals and their side kicks. Despite its great terrain and summer snowboarding opportunities, this is also a resort where snowboarding is still fairly small (less than 5% of slope users) but don't fret, the attitude is pretty cool and snowboarders are welcome everywhere, although you have to share the slopes with a lot of scum bags in fur hats poncing around the mountain on their stupid Big Foot skis. Still, on the plus side of things Verbier offers all year round snowboarding up on the **Mont Fort Glacier,** although you won't be riding down to the village in June. The snow record here is good and even in a poor season it's still possible to ride to the resort in April. Generally, the terrain gives over to all levels, offering every rider something to get their teeth into. However, Verbier is essentially a freerider's resort, with easily accessible powder, trees, hard-pack, cliffs, hits and extremes, some of which necessitate a hike first. Verbier joins with **Nendas**, **Veysonnaz, La Tzoumaz** and **Val de Bagnas** to crate the 4 Vallees with 94 lifts and over 400km of piste, which can be serviced by one lift pass.

FREERIDERS who know just what snowboarding is all about will be very impressed with Verbier. The Verbier Extreme competition is now regularly held here which should give you an idea of what awesome terrain is on offer. The **Mont Gele** cable car serves no piste, just a series of off-piste runs and couloirs of varying extremity; tuck your balls (or equivalent) away before you get up here. The less squeamish should check out the areas round the back of **Lac des Vaux!** The **Col des Mines**, and **Vallon d' Arbi** routes steer you towards wide open powder fields with the words 'session me' written all over them. If trees are your thing, Verbier has loads of them, especially in the **Bruson** area, but remember, Switzerland is the one country that protects its forests, so shredding the spruce is not always appreciated.

VERBIER

pic - Verbier Tourism

FREESTYLERS have a park and pipe to ride all year round, located up on **Mont-Fort,** although pipe bashing is not Verbier's strong point. Anyway, the natural stuff around **La Chaux** and **Lac des Vaux** lifts, are the places to get air. Check out this years **O'Neil Xtreme** Snowboard Contest 18/20-03.05.

CARVERS in hard boots will enjoy several different runs, but the best is undoubtedly the long, wide red piste that goes from the top of Attelas all the way back to the **Medran** lifts. There's also some cool stuff at **Savoleyres and Ruinettes**.

BEGINNERS will find that the main areas are actually closed to snowboarders, which means that first timers are faced with steeper slopes. The best option is the runs at **Savoleyres**, where you are certain to be end up doing a few 180 butt spins. Some lifts can be tricky, so

keep to the slower chair lifts. Lift pass checking is slack, so think on, but don't get caught as they jail you here.

THE TOWN
Off the slopes, Verbier is a Royals, city slickers & lottery winner's only place, with prices that exclude everyone else. There's no such thing as a cool scene unless you can pay for it. The place is over populated with farts and their spoilt off spring (rich kids with attitude but no brains). Bedding down is costly and if you get caught scamming on someone's floor, you could face a 200 Swiss Franc fine. However, the resort is well set out and can sleep over 15,000 rich skiers. Overall, Verbier simply is not a place to visit on a tight budget, unless you have a degree in scamming. To get the information on Verbier, check with the guys at 'No Bounds' or 'Extreme' snowboard shops.

Accomodation.There are 15,000 beds on offer in Verbier but as with everything else its at a high price, but thats not to say you won't be able to get a bed somewhere. The best two options open to you are **1)** take a package tour, or **2)** hook up with a local bird, no matter how ugly, and promise her the earth in order to get in her bed.
Food. Bring stacks of tins of baked beans with you and a cooker, as unless your name is Princess Lucky, you simply won't be able to afford any of the restaurants or even the supermarkets. Food in a town that attracts the super rich, is not easy to come by cheaply, although there are loads of restaurants to choose from with a cross the board range of menus from Chinese to bland Swiss fondues.
Night life, take a fork lift truck and ram in through the doors of the main bank, then take you're spoils to any one of the bars and if your lucky, you may just have enough francs to get a fruit juice. Night-time costs the earth here unless you can scam your way into a club pretending that you're Sara Ferguson's lap dog. The clubs are not only costly but play crap music to please the lame heads who don't know any better.

SUMMARY. Extremely good resort with some of the best extreme terrain in Switzerland, but this place is hellish in terms of being stuck up.,
On the slopes: Excellent riding
Off the slopes: Criminally expensive
Money wise: Criminally expensive to help make the place attractive to the rich

S

**S
W
I
T
Z
E
R
L
A
N
D**

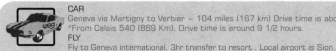

CAR
Geneva via Martigny to Verbier = 104 miles (167 km) Drive time is about 2 hours.
°From Calais 540 (869 Km). Drive time is around 9 1/2 hours.
FLY
Fly to Geneva international, 3hr transfer to resort . Local airport is Sion
TRAIN
Trains to Le Chable (10 minutes). More info www.rail.ch
BUS
Bus services from Geneva take around 3 hours direct to Verbier via Martigny, and cost 55CHF, its 95CHF and 4 1/2 hours from Zurich

6 OUT OF 10   Basic but okay

pic: Villars Tourism

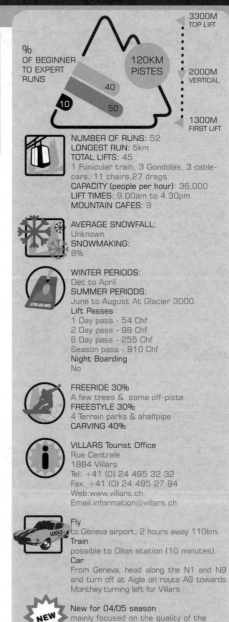

%
OF BEGINNER
TO EXPERT
RUNS

120KM
PISTES

10

40

50

3300M
TOP LIFT

2000M
VERTICAL

1300M
FIRST LIFT

NUMBER OF RUNS: 52
LONGEST RUN: 5km
TOTAL LIFTS: 45
1 Funicular train, 3 Gondolas, 3 cable-cars, 11 chairs,27 drags
CAPACITY (people per hour): 36,000
LIFT TIMES: 9.00am to 4.30pm
MOUNTAIN CAFES: 9

AVERAGE SNOWFALL:
Unknown
SNOWMAKING:
8%

WINTER PERIODS:
Dec to April
SUMMER PERIODS:
June to August At Glacier 3000
Lift Passes
1 Day pass - 54 Chf
2 Day pass - 98 Chf
6 Day pass - 255 Chf
Season pass - 910 Chf
Night Boarding
No

FREERIDE 30%
A few trees & some off-piste
FREESTYLE 30%
4 Terrain parks & ahalfpipe
CARVING 40%

VILLARS Tourist Office
Rue Centrale
1884 Villars
Tel: +41 (0) 24 495 32 32
Fax: +41 (0) 24 495 27 94
Web:www.villars.ch
Email:information@villars.ch

Fly
to Geneva airport, 2 hours away 110km.
Train
possible to Ollon station (10 minutes).
Car
From Geneva, head along the N1 and N9 and turn off at Aigle on route A9 towards Monthey turning left for Villars

NEW
New for 04/05 season
mainly focused on the quality of the resort's services and the development of children and family activities

Villars, in the French speaking part of Switzerland, is a simple place that sits in view of the high peaks of the **Les Diablerets Glacier**, where you can snowboard winter and summer. Villars is a popular place that gets its fair share of visitors throughout the season. The slopes are well spread out covering the **Les Chaux** and **Bretaye** areas and linked after some careful navigation, with the base area at Les Diablerets. Overall the place is not noted for being a hardcore destination; in fact, it's true to say that this is a resort that favours piste loving hard boot carvers and family ski groups. However, the resort has a good attitude towards snowboarding and regularly allows its slopes to be used for various competitions. If you get a bit tired of it here and fancy something a more challenging, you can easily head up to Les Diablerets and ride harder and faster.

FREERIDERS are not known for flocking to this place because although there is some okay freeriding terrain, it's not that extensive in terms of steep blacks on or off-piste. That said, the black trail running down from **Les Chaux** is a real pleaser which if you stick to the left, can also be tackled by intermediates as it mellows out the further it spreads across the slope. The place for some great freeriding is up on the Les Diablerets slopes.
FREESTYLERS can either decide to ride the pipe and park areas that are split between the Bretaye slopes and Les Chaux slopes. However, this is not one of those resorts where one can get too excited about the man made frills, and coupled with the fact that this place is not as snow sure as the slopes up on Les Diablerets, sculptured hits are not always guaranteed.
CARVERS have the best of the slopes here from the long gentle blues and a couple of steep blacks on the Les Chaux area, to the excellent pisted reds on the Bretaye area.
BEGINNER'S slopes are out numbered by intermediate ones, but don't be put off, this is a good first time resort although the place has a lot of drag lifts.

THE TOWN
Local services and **accommodation** options are comfortably provided in the setting of a traditional Swiss village located close to the slopes. The amenities on offer are some what basic but perfectly adequate for a weeks family fun holiday; In general an affordable week can be had. **Night-life** is on the dull side with only a few okay bars and the odd disco.

SWITZERLAND

WENGEN

6
OUT OF 10

Spoilt by the stuck-up attitude

Wengen, which is part of the **Jungfrau Region**, is one of Switzerlands more famous resorts, but why it should be is a mystery really, it can't just be for the terrain on offer, which although not bad, is not major, nor can it be for the welcome you get here. No Wengen

Wengen Tourism

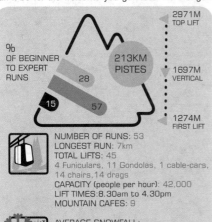

%
OF BEGINNER
TO EXPERT
RUNS

213KM PISTES

28

15   57

2971M
TOP LIFT

1697M
VERTICAL

1274M
FIRST LIFT

NUMBER OF RUNS: 53
LONGEST RUN: 7km
TOTAL LIFTS: 45
4 Funiculars, 11 Gondolas, 1 cable-cars,
14 chairs,14 drags
CAPACITY (people per hour): 42,000
LIFT TIMES:8.30am to 4.30pm
MOUNTAIN CAFES: 9

AVERAGE SNOWFALL:
5.3m
SNOWMAKING:
15%

WINTER PERIODS:
Nov to April
Lift Passes
1 Day Pass 55Chf
6 Day Pass 254Chf
Night Boarding
No
Board School
private lesson 65 CHF per hour

FREERIDE 50%
Trees & good off-piste
FREESTYLE 25%
Terrain parks & halfpipe
CARVING 25%

Tourist Information Wengen
CH-3823 Wengen
Tel +41 (0)33 855 14 14
Fax +41 (0)33 855 30 60
Web:www.wengen-muerren.ch
Email:info@wengen.ch

Fly
to Zurich airport, about 2 hours away.
Train
possible to Interlaken (10 minutes).
Car
From Zurich, head south on the E41, N4a/
N14 via Hergiswil and then the N8 to Interlaken. From here follow the Lauterbrunnen
and then signs for Wengen.

has simply become well known because the idle rich deposed European royals and a certain class of scum bag skiers from Britain who frequent this resort en-mass. The place reeks of snobbery, which is a bit of a shame because this is not a crap resort, far from it, with the slopes on offer here and at **Grindelwald** and at neighbouring Murren, a rider can have a good weeks riding on terrain that have something for all, although not a great deal for expert riders. Wengen, which shares direct slope access with Grindewald, lies at an altitude of 1274 metres and is reached via the village of **Lauterbrunnen**, which is also the main access point for **Murren**. Wengen and Grindelwald are much the same, with Wengen having a few more interesting spots to try out. You can also decent from a height of 2971 metres, which is higher than Grindewald, but in truth there is not much to separate the two places. However, Murren, the least crowded of the three resorts, offers the most challenging terrain and out of the three areas, it is also the most snowboard friendly. Wengen hasn't got a clue what its policy is towards snowboarding. A couple of seasons ago, the management set up a really good terrain park with loads of features, then the following year they decided not to build a thing for freestylers preferring to make a euro carvers (David Seaman look-alikes in hard boots and head bands) area.

FREERIDERS are best off on the runs at Murren, off the **Schilthon**. Great powder stashes are can be found in a number of spots.
FREESTYLERS have pipe and park up on the **Oberjoch area** via Grindewald. Wengen also has some natural hits.
CARVERS will blend in well here as there's a lot of Euro's with head bands and one piece suits posing on Wengen's slopes.
BEGINNERS will only be put off by the crowds of skiers falling around on the gentle slopes. Wengen has the best novice terrain, while Murren has the worst.

THE TOWN
Wengen offers a lot of local facilities with lodging close to the slopes. However, if you decide to stay here, it's going to cost you dearly with night-life totally geared around après-ski rich gits.

S

SWITZERLAND

8 OUT OF 10 — extremely good resort with terrain for all styles and levels

pic - Zermatt Tourism

%
OF BEGINNER
TO EXPERT
RUNS

23

245KM
PISTES

44

33

3820M
TOP LIFT

2200M
VERTICAL

1620M
FIRST LIFT

NUMBER OF RUNS: 132
LONGEST RUN: 13km
TOTAL LIFTS: 73
2 Funicular trains, 6 Gondolas, 17 cable-cars, 14 chairs, 34 drags
CAPACITY (people per hour): 64,500
LIFT TIMES: 8.30am to 4.30pm
MOUNTAIN CAFES: 38

AVERAGE SNOWFALL:
3m
SNOWMAKING:
25%

WINTER PERIODS:
Nov to April
SUMMER PERIODS:
May to Sept
Lift Passes
1 Day pass - 72Chf
6 Day pass - 362Chf
Board School
Group lessons from - 40CHF
Hire
Board & Boots daily rates from - 28CHF
(Kids from 22CHF)
Heliboarding
Flights to Monte Rosa
Night Boarding
No

FREERIDE 50%
Some tree runs & good off-piste
FREESTYLE 20%
2 Terrain parks & 2 halfpipes
CARVING 30%

Tourist Office of Zermatt
3920 Zermatt
Switzerland
Tel +41 27 966 81 00
Fax +41 27 966 81 01
Web:www.zermatt.ch
Email:zermatt@wallis.ch

Take the Autobahn N1 and N9 and travel along the E62 and then head up the mountain pass via **Stadlen** and **St Niklaus** and you will eventually arrive at Zermatt which is an impressive resort and sits in the direct shadow of the mighty **Matterhorn**. Zermatt is money mountain and not on the calling card of many snowboarders because its so damn expensive, although to be fair things seem to have got easier and more and more riders on a budget are managing to get by here, this is despite the fact that it is one of the most famous resorts in Europe, although it could be questioned why. Maybe its to do with it's very elitist status, but what the heck, this is a place that can be ridden in the summer up on **Theodul Glacier** when all the fur clad poser's have gone home, so it's not all bad news. Zermatt, with it's 230 kilometres of marked piste and countless acres of backcountry terrain is a very impressive place with a great mountain to ride that can also be covered with the opportunities of extensive heli-boarding on offer with trips up to the **Monte Rosa** at 4250 metres, the **Alphubeljoch** at 3782 metres and up to the **Plateau Rosa** at 3479 metres. The heli-boarding is not cheap at Zermatt with trips costing from 450 Chf. Still you don't need to take a helicopter in order to explore Zermatts fantastic terrain, because once you have made the hike to the first lifts form the main town, or in some cases taken the bus, and hit the slopes the array of lifts will whisk you up the mountain to numerous start of points. The mountain layout is a bit confusing and will take some piste map navigating before you can ride all the areas with ease, but stick in there because its worth getting it right in order to not got lost or not miss out on the best trails. On the slopes you will notice a lot of Italian poser's and your lift pass also covers the neighbouring Italian resort of **Cervina**.

THE TOWN & GETTING THERE

FREERIDERS on the lookout for open powder bowls and couloirs to ride will be kept busy in a number of areas. Zermatt offers a lot of advanced off-piste riding, with some excellent runs on the **Stockhorn** or over at the **Schwarzsee** areas. If riding trees is your thing, note that Zermatt totally restricts riding through the forest areas. If you have the money, you can also take a day's heli-boarding. Air Zermatt, but it is very expensive: two flights over the **Monte Rosa** will cost you around 440 Chf.

FREESTYLERS are provided with 2 ever improving half-pipes, but as there is so much good natural terrain, it's not that important. Two fun parks have been built in recent years.

CARVERS are much in evidence here, preferring to cut up the number of good and long testing runs that descend en-route to the village via some extremely crowded lower novice trails.

BEGINNERS may find Zermatt a bit tricky but not a big problem, just a bit tainted with too many first timers on skis clogging up the easy trails. However, you can ride easily higher up the mountain, making for some long, easy runs to progress on.

THE TOWN

ff the slopes, Zermatt is a large, car free town that is also stupidly pricey which may call for some major scamming to get by. A useful tip when travelling here from abroad is, if you fly in to **Geneva** and plan to take the train down to Zermatt, buy your train ticket at a Swiss Tourist office in you're home country before you enter **Switzerland**, as it can work out a lot cheaper. Around the town you are presented with loads of shops, various sporting centres and other visitor attractions, however, the town also comes with an over kill in snooty ski punters many on over priced ski tours. Not that getting around the main part of town is not much of a problem, but in parts you will find that a lot of walking is required. Cars are banned here and only local taxis and buses are available to shuttle you around at a price.

Accommodation can super expensive, and beyond the budget of most snowboarders. However, there is a youth hostel located about 400 metres from the main lifts in the centre of town, which is cheap and offers

pic - Zermatt Tourism

half board accommodation.

Food. Any snotty resort that over charges for lifts and accommodation, also means getting a reasonable meal is beyond the pale of most. There is however, a *McDonalds* for a cheap Mac attack (you have to forget McDonalds disgusting ethics when you're starving!). The supermarket located near the train station offers cheap eateries and for many a diet of crisps, biscuits, mars bar and cheap beer is enough.

Night life is spoilt by the rich après ski scene and the costs of everything, but that's not so say you can't have a good time here, you can. There is a cool snowboarder's bar located on the bridge en-route to the Matterhorn lift in the Swartzee area. Around town there is a large selection of bars offering different themes and some being quite lively. There are also a number of late night discos such as the *Pink Elephant* or *Le Broken*, but all have shockingly expensive booze.

SUMMARY

Zermatt is an extremely good resort with terrain for all styles and levels. The resort has a lot of good facilities, but do not this is a very very snobbish place. **Money wise**: Prices at this resort are simply criminal and not justified.

CAR
From Geneva, take the N1/N9 via Sion to Sierre. Then take the E62 to Visp at which point turn right and travel via Stalden to Zermatt. Savognin.
Drive time from Calais is 10 hours. 665 miles (1070 km).
FLY
Fly to Geneva airport, 4 hours away.
TRAIN
Train services direct to Zermatt from Geneva 4 hrs. 5hrs from Zurich. More info www.rail.ch
BUS
Bus services from Geneva take around 4 1/2 to 5 hours direct to Zermatt.

S

SWITZERLAND

BEATENBERG

Beatenberg is a blip of a place not far from Interlarken and above Lake Thun. The 10 miles of beginner friendly, intermediate dull and advanced crap terrain is spread out over a slope area unspoilt by mass crowds. In truth this is not a snowboarders destination unless you're recovering from piles and need somewhere out of the way to convalesce in peace.

Local services are very basic but at the same time offer more than what is on the slopes.

Ride area: 16km
Top Lift: 1905m
Total Lifts:5
Contact:
+41 (0) 33 841 1818
How to get there: Fly to: Zurich 2 hours away.

BETTMERALP

On its own, Bettmeralp offers a mere 20 miles of basic carving terrain, but by linking with the Aletsch area, you suddenly have a more respectable 60 plus miles of okay freeride terrain in an area that also has a number half-pipes and a couple of fun parks for big air possibilities. Generally, the slopes here will suit beginners and mid way merchants as well as giving advanced riders something to look forward too. Okay local services but costly

Ride area: 32km
Top Lift: 2710m
Total Lifts:12
Contact:
Tel: +41 (0)27 928 60 60
Fax: +41 (0)27 928 60 61
How to get there: Fly to: Zurich 2 1/2 hours away

BRAUNWALD

Braunwald is located two hours from Zurich. This small place has gained a reputation as a friendly freestyle outpost where locals and those in the know spend the weekend getting air.t The terrain itself is nothing to shout about but is still cool and rarely attracts more than a 5 minute lift queue. They regularly build decent half-pipes and parks here for which they stage various events in. **Off the slopes** things are laid back, good but basic.

Ride area: 24km
Top Lift: 1900m
Total Lifts:8
Contact:
Tel: +41 (0)55 643 30 30
Fax: +41 (0)55 643 10 00
How to get there: Fly to: Zurich 1 hour away

CHAMPERY

Champrey is a resort that forms part of the massive Portes du Soleil area, which boast a lift linked area of over 400 miles. Champery itself has 62 miles of terrain, with something for all but nothing that outstanding. An intermediate freerider will like this place although the slopes do get busy. They have a park and half-pipe here, but are not known for their up-keep. Local services are very good in a village full of character.

Ride area: 99km
Top Lift: 2277m
Total Lifts:35
Contact:
Tel: +41 (0) 24 479 20 20
Fax: +41 (0) 24 479 20 21
How to get there: Fly to: Geneva 1 1/2 hours away

CHAMPOUSSIN

Champoussin is yet another resort that helps to make up the Portes du Soleil area. This is a major plus because you would by no means want to get stuck with what's on offer here. A rider who knows what?s will have this place done and dusted in an hour, even a quick learning novice could lick the place in a day or two. This a resort that old timers wanting to find their youth will like, but any- one else will find it dull. Local services near the slopes

Ride area: 24km
Top Lift: 2150m
Total Lifts:8
Contact:
Tel - +41 24 477 20 77
Fax - +41 24 477 37 73
How to get there: Fly to: Geneva 1 1/2 hours away

CHATEAU D'OEX

Chateau d'Oex is a place that is relatively unknown by the masses. When you see what's on offer its soon clear to see why. Famed more for balloon races, the slopes here are very ordinary and won't take a good rider that long to conquer. However with a further 150 miles of terrain in the area to check out, a week's visit here will be worth the effort. Freestylers get to ride a pipe and beginners have some good slopes. Good slope side services

Ride area: 48km
Top Lift: 1800m
Total Lifts:10
Contact:
Chateau-d'Oex Tourist Office
Tel: +41 (0) 26 924 25 25
Fax: +41 (0) 26 924 25 26

How to get there: Fly to: Geneva 2 hours away

KLOSTERS

Forget the reason for Klosters fame, this resort offers any rider a challenging time with good off-piste that will please freeriders. Carvers have some excellent runs to try out and freestylers have a fun park (not hot mind, better to use the one at nearby Davos). Great also for beginners. The biggest let down here is the brown nosed ski snobs from the UK, hoping to be seen with a royal. Okay local services but pricey

Ride area: 160km
Top Lift: 2844m
Total Lifts:12
Contact:
Tourist Office Klosters
Alte Bahnhofstrasse 6
CH-7250 Klosters
Tel: +41 (0) 81 410 20 20
Fax: +41 (0) 81 410 20 10
How to get there: Fly to: Zurich 2 hours away

pic.- Klosters/ Swiss Tourism

LENZERHEIDE

Lenzerheide is a big place that covers two mountain slopes, offering some really nice open riding with tree line trails to the base area. Intermediate freeriders and carvers are in for a treat here, with the biggest cluster of runs to be found on the Statzerhorn slopes. **Freestylers** have an okay half-pipe and park on the Rothorn slopes. **Beginners** should love this place with easy trails all over the place high and low. Good laid back local services slope side.

Ride area: 152km
Easy 46%
Intermediate 41%
Advanced 13%
Top Lift: 2865m
Total Lifts:35
Contact:
Lenzerheid Tourist Office
CH-7078 Lenzerheide
Tel: +41 (0)81 385 11 20
Fax: +41 (0)81 385 11 21
How to get there: Fly to: Zurich 2 hours away

LES DIABLERETS
Les Diablerets is a cool snowboarders hangout that offers summer riding on the glacier. This is not a place for piste loving carvers, no, this is a freeriders retreat offering some great backcountry riding in deep powder, but not for the fainthearted, some of this stuff will take you out quick style if you balls up. Although not a big place, this is a good unspoilt haunt that caters well for freestylers and novices. Good slope side services.

Les Diablerets Tourism

Ride area: 125km
Runs: 77
Easy 50%
Intermediate 42%
Advanced 8%
Top Lift: 3000m
Bottom Lift: 1200m
Vertical: 1800m

Total Lifts:46 - 3 Cable Cars, 3 Gondolas,11 Chair Lifts & 28 Drags
Lift Pass: 1 day 39 euros for Isenau 1 day 46 euros Diablerets 1 day 54 euros Glacier 920 euros season
Board School: 1 morning (adult) 35 CHF 4 mornings 120 CHF private lesson 60/250 per hour/day
Contact:
Les Diablerets Tourist Office
1865 Les Diablerets
Tel: +41(0)24-492.33.58
Fax: +41(0)24-492.23.48
How to get there: FLY: Geneva : 120 km Zürich : 250 km Bâle : 200 km BUS: Shuttle bus runs everyday during winter when Glacier 3000 is open. The stops are situated at the hotel Le Chamois, at the train station, at the bottom of the Meilleret area, at the Sport Center, at the bottom of Isenau, at the hotel Les Diablotins, at the Belvédère and at the Col du Pillon.
TRAIN: direct trains to Aigle and then a mountain train to Les Diablerets. Lausanne - Aigle : 30 min Aigle – Les Diablerets : 50 min
DRIVING: Motorway A9, direction Grand St Bernard, exit Aigle. Then, road Aigle - Les Diablerets (20 km).

MEIRINGEN-HASLIBERG
Meiringen-Hasliberg has a history related to Sherlock Holmes, but today what you have is great snowboarders out back close to the Jungfrau Region. There?s no hype here, no mass holiday crowds, just a cool mountain with something for everyone. There are wide powder fields, gullies and big cliffs on a mountain that is majorly snowboard friendly providing a decent pipe and park and good beginner areas. Good lodging and local services close by.

Ride area: 64km
Top Lift: 3000m
Total Lifts:28

Contact:
Meiringen Haslital Tourism
CH-3860
Meiringen
Tel: +41 (0)33 972 50 50
Fax: +41 (0)33 972 50 55
How to get there: Fly to: Zurich 1 1/2 hours away

MORGINS
Morgins, on the Swiss side, is yet another resort that forms part of the massive Portes du Soleil area which crosses into France. On the Swiss side, Morgins is the highest resort and not a modern imitation of some of its cousins. What this place has to offer is easy access to over 40 miles of direct terrain and a further 360 miles of linked terrain. Collectively, there is something for everyone. Good slope side local services

Ride area: 67km
Top Lift: 2000m
Total Lifts:16
Contact:
Morgins Tourist Office
Tel - +41 24 477 23 61
Fax - +41 24 477 37 08
How to get there: Fly to: Geneva 11/2 hours away

ROUGEMONT
Rougemont is a tiny place that links indirectly with its bigger and more famous cousin Gstaad. This helps boost the 12 miles of terrain on offer here to a respectable 150 miles plus. Rougemont on its own is not a place that you would book a week's holiday at, indeed only a rider so stoned that an inch seems like a mile will enjoy this place. However, there is a small half-pipe and an 80 year old beginner will fair well. There are slope side facilities, but over all, this place is very dull.

Ride area: 19km
Top Lift: 2156m
Total Lifts:3
Contact:
Rougemont Tourist Office
Batiment Communal
CH - 1838 Rougemont
Tel: +41 (0)26 925-83-33
Fax: +41 (0)26 925-89-67
How to get there: Fly to: Geneva 21/2 hours away

S

SWITZERLAND

309

pic - Diamond Peak Resort , Lake Tahoe, California

There are hundreds of resorts in the US spread out over the northern eastern states, the central Rockie states and the north western states, however, many are no more than a backyard affair operated by a dollar-hungry hillbilly.

The usual season lasts from November until mid-April, with a few northern areas staying open until mid-May. US resorts are generally much smaller than ones in Europe. However, the Rockies do have peaks that rise up to 3,000 metres.

Flights to US cities are frequent, with many having transfer flights to resorts. From various airports you can reach the resorts by bus (sometimes a free shuttle service), or by hire car. If you're touring around the US, you can fly very cheaply using an Air Pass costing from $375.

Travel to a resort by **train** is limited in terms of direct routes. In most cases you will need to take a train to the nearest city and then transfer by bus. East coast resorts are the easiest to reach by train from international airports. A 30 day rail pass for unlimited travel costs from $400.

Greyhound **Buses** operate the largest cross-country network of routes, with dozens of options. Like trains, it may be necessary to take a Greyhound bus to a city and then transfer by a local bus. A 30-day adult Ameripass costs from $450.

Visa requirements vary, but generally, Europeans can enter without a visa and stay for 90 days. All foreigners need a valid passport. If you want to work in the US, you will need to obtain a work visa, which is difficult. If you are caught working without a visa, you will be deported.

Capital City: Washington D.C.
Population: 293 million
Highest Peak: Mt. Mckinley 6194m
Language: English
Legal Drink Age: 21 (most states)
Drug Laws: Cannabis is illegal and frowned upon
Age of consent: 16
Electricity: 110 Volts AC 2-pin
International Dialing Code: +1

Currency: US Dollar (US$)
Exchange Rate:
UK£1 = 1.8
EURO = 1.2
AU$1 = 0.7
CD$ = 0.7
NZ$ = 0.6

Driving Guide
All vehicles drive on the right hand side of the road
Speed limits:
Varies per state
Emergency
Police/Fire/Ambulance - 911
General police enquiries 625-5011
Tolls
Called Turnpikes and payable on many highways
Documentation
Driving licence and motor insurance must be carried.

Time Zone
5 time zones (see states)
UTC/GMT -5 to -10 hours

USA Snowboard Association
PO Box 3927
Truckee, CA 96160
Tel: (800)404-9213
email: karen@usasa.org
web: www.usasa.org

pic - Larry Pierce / Steamboat, Colorado

Accommodation comes in the form of hotels, motels, guest houses and condominiums (apartments), which are reasonably priced and usually of a very high standards. A low cost option would be to stay in a youth hostel or a ski dorm.

Restaurants vary considerably in price from cheap to ridiculous, and remember that you are expected to tip in restaurants.

Proof of age is constantly required when buying alcohol, so keep some form of ID on you wherever you go. Baby-faced snowboarders forget it.

True backcountry boarding

If you mention the name Alaska to most people, they will shiver with the thought of huge icebergs, wild snow cape mountain ranges and ridiculously cold temperatures.

In terms of terrain for snowboarding, most believe that the only people who can snowboard in **Alaska** are expert riders who know how to ride high altitude, steep, extreme back- country areas. While much of this is true with some 90% of the ridable terrain only accessible via a helicopter or by long hikes form barren and remote out-posts, Alaska is infact not just for a select few of big headed sponsored riders doing a video shoot, its a place that welcomes all riders no matter what you're ability, and although this is a very cold state with recorded low temperatures of -70°C, don't be put of. Alaska has all the modern resort facilities found in any other US snowboard/ski resort. The only difference is that what Alaska offering are a lot more limited with infact only one major developed resort, **Alyeska** which is a fully developed resort with some 62 runs and many purpose built facilities at the base of the slopes (see next page). As well as Alyeska, there are a number of smaller ridable areas, but the remainder are very basic and are not resorts as we know them. They are more or less for locals and run by clubs and private companies. One thing to put a big smile on your face is the 20 metres of snow most of the resorts get on average.

Where you won't get any of the standard resort set up style of services is in **Valdez**, which lies some 300 miles east of **Anchorage**. Valdez, which is actually a busy oil port, is the snowboarders heaven and for the place for purist only. This is where backcountry, means 'Backcountry'. There are no lifts with lines of skiers in sad clothing and headbands moaning about snowboarders, no groups of ski classes getting in the way all over the place, no ski patrols, no marked runs, no pisted runs. Nothing other than pure virgin terrain that should only be ridden if one, you can ride, and two, you only ride in a group and with a local guide and are properly equipped with backcountry clothing and safety equipment.

A number of established and professional companies are based here and operate proper backcountry tours with local guides who know the mountains and are fully trained in mountain safety and rescue. Organised trips in areas such as the **Chugach Mountains** and the **Thompson Pass** can be arranged with travel

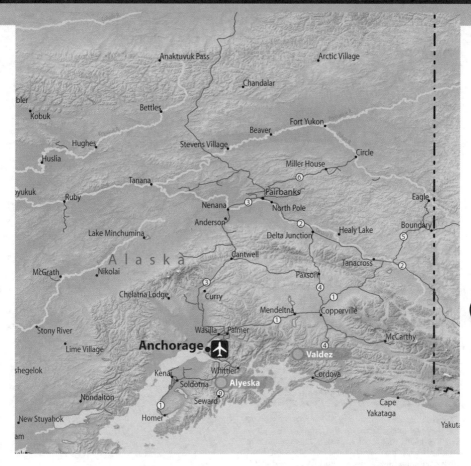

options that range from flying in by helicopter, snow-plane, snow-cat or on foot by hiking. Its even said that if you can show that you are the first to ride a particular slope, you get the honour of naming the slope or face, after your self or what ever name you choose.

Fully inclusive trips that include travel, accommodation, food and guiding are available all year round and although a weeks all in tour will cost you dearly, it will be a trip of a life time. Valdez Heli-Camps, www.valdezhelicamps.com offer numerous heli and snowcat packages.

As for local amenities, accommodation and restaurants, Valdez is a hard town that is home to oil workers who can drink stupid amounts of alcohol and who don't give a shit what snowboard you ride. The town has a number of lodges and bed and breakfast homes with affordable rates. The *Totem Inn* is one of the main places to hang out in the evenings, where you can get a decent meal, shoot some pool or drink yourself stupid well into the night trying to keep up with the locals.

8
OUT OF 10

Excellent resort with great freeriding that will please freeriders of all levels

pic - Alyeska Resort

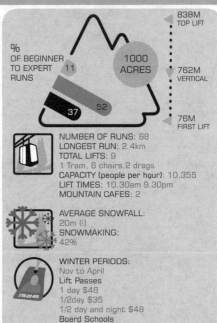

838M
TOP LIFT

%
OF BEGINNER
TO EXPERT   11
RUNS

1000
ACRES

762M
VERTICAL

37   52

76M
FIRST LIFT

NUMBER OF RUNS: 68
LONGEST RUN: 2.4km
TOTAL LIFTS: 9
1 Tram, 6 chairs,2 drags
CAPACITY (people per hour): 10,355
LIFT TIMES: 10.30am 9.30pm
MOUNTAIN CAFES: 2

AVERAGE SNOWFALL:
20m (!)
SNOWMAKING:
42%

WINTER PERIODS:
Nov to April
Lift Passes
1 day $48
1/2day $35
1/2 day and night $48
Board Schools
2 hour group $35
1 hour private $60
Hire
board and boots $30 to 38 a day
Snowmobiles
1/2 day to all day trip starts at $150
Night Boarding
Friday & Saturday 27 trails lit from 4:30
to 9:30 (night only $21)
Heliboarding
6/7 drops a day from Feb 14 to April 12
$650pp

FREERIDE 60%
Good tree runs & superb backcountry
FREESTYLE 20%
Terrain park & a halfpipe
CARVING 20%

Alyeska Resort
P. O. Box 249
Girdwood, AK 99587
Tel: 907.754.1111
Web:www.alyeskaresort.com
Email:guestservices@alyeskaresort.com

U
S
A

A
L
A
S
K
A

Travel 40 miles south west of **Anchorage** and you will eventually arrive at the somewhat unusual, but interesting resort of **Alyeska**. It happens to be **Alaska's** only traditional purpose-built resort which, now celebrating its 40th year and has a lot going for it. Forget the impression of severe weather conditions and ice slabs that one normally associates with Alaska. What you find here is a great mountain, with excellent terrain serviced by a modern lift system and is spread out over a series of slopes that begin at almost sea-level. Over the years, places like Alyeska have been largely left alone by the mass holiday crowds. Hardly any ski guides or magazines feature this resort, which is a shame because despite its location in the far northern reaches of the US and Canada, Alyeska has as much to offer, if not more, than many Rocky Mountain-based resorts. A huge plus for this resort is not only its excellent snow record, with average yearly dumps of 20m, but also the fact that you can ride deep powder in early and late spring. The 1000 acres are excellent and offer something for every style and ability, especially advanced riders. The double black diamond runs on the **North Face** are a match for anything found anywhere else in the US. There's plenty of diverse terrain with a number of damn good bowls and gullies. Across the lower slopes are glades, while higher up you will find nice open slopes and well groomed trails.

ALYESKA

FREERIDERS who know the score, have a damn fine mountain to check out with some very challenging terrain on offer. The double blacks on **North Face** will give you the chance to go wild at speed, as will the double black listed as **Max's**. There is also plenty of intermediate freeride terrain with lots of okay red and blue trails both on and off-piste. If you hike to the summit, you can gain access to the **Glacier Bowl** which has a superb descent down a wide, open expanse of deep snow. For those not content with the easy access slopes there is heli-boarding and snowcats tours in the **Chugach** mountain range, where you will get to see Alaska as it should be, wild, un-tamed, spectacular, orgasmic.

FREESTYLERS are well catered for here with an abundance of natural hits to get air, such as the nice banks on the **Mambo**. The resort also has a good terrain park which is furnished with a good set of obstacles. Alyeska 300 foot halfpipe is located on the **Don's Gully** area off lift 4, and is groomed to perfection with Alaska's only pipe grooming machine providing 10 foot high walls.

CARVERS would be the ones to feel a little left out here, as this place couldn't really be described as a good carvers resort.

BEGINNERS don't have a vast area of novice slopes but what is on offer is not bad especially on the lower areas off Lift 3. Avoid this area at the end of the day as it becomes the busy homebound route for everyone coming down off the mountain.

THE TOWN

Off the slopes you will find all the creature comforts required to make your stay a pleasant one and although not extensive, local services are very good. There is a good choice of lodging and eating joints conveniently located either at the base of the slopes or in the small town of **Gridwood**, a few minutes away by shuttle bus. The area also boasts an array of local activities ranging from river rafting, to para -gliding on skis or a board. You can even do a cruise around some of the glaciers or try your hand at salmon fishing.

Accomodation. You can lodge at the base of the slopes, most notably in the *Westin Alyeska Prince* Hotel which is located just yards from the cable car's base station. Around **Gridwood** there's a good selection of condos and B&B's, but it's not the cheapest place to stay. The cheaper option is to lodge in **Anchorage**, which has a far bigger selection.

Food. Alaska my not be world renowned for its culinary skills, however, the choice and quality of restaurants along with fast-food outlets is particularly good in and around the resort. You can pig out on fine Cajun food at *Double Dusky's* Inn, or sample some well-prepared sea food at *Simon's Saloon*. The *Bake Shop* is a local's favourite for quick snacks, whilst the *Teppanyaki Katsura* offers traditional Japanese nosh, but at a price.

Night-life around Gridwood is somewhat tame, but nevertheless not bad. There is a decent selection of laid back hangouts. The *Sitzmark* and *Aurora* bars are well visited and lively spots. But if you want some real late night action, check out what's going down 40 miles away in **Anchorage**, where you are able to party hard.

Alyeska Trail Map

CAR
from Anchorage take New Seward Highway , take left to Alyeska Highway at mile 90 (after approx 40miles).Total distance 45 miles (72km), drive time is about 50 minutes.
FLY
to Anchorage International (64km), transfer time to resort is 50 mins.
TRAIN
Train Direct to Girdwood (Alyeska)
BUS
There is a daily bus service between Alyeska and Anchorage run by Gray Line Buses. A return ticket cost from $12 or $8 single.

ALPINE MEADOWS

9 OUT OF 10

Great freeriding and natural freestyle resort with a good annual snow record

Alpine Meadows only opened its doors to snowboarders in 1996, but within that short space of time, Alpine has now become one of the most popular boarding mountains in the Tahoe region. For years, Alpine was the number

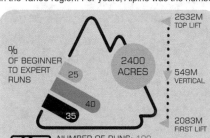

% OF BEGINNER TO EXPERT RUNS

2632M TOP LIFT

2400 ACRES

549M VERTICAL

2083M FIRST LIFT

25
40
35

NUMBER OF RUNS: 100
LONGEST RUN: 4km (2.5 miles)
TOTAL LIFTS: 14
11 chairs,2 drags, 1 magic carpet
CAPACITY (people per hour): 16,000
LIFT TIMES: 9.00am to 4.00pm
MOUNTAIN CAFES:3

AVERAGE SNOWFALL:
18m
SNOWMAKING:
80%

WINTER PERIODS:
Nov to May
Lift Passes
1 Day pass $39
1 Day High season $59
Season $1240
Board Schools
Group inc hire day@$79
Private 1hr $85
2/4 people 3hrs@$135
Hire
Standard package 1day $35 additional day $30. Premium $50 addit day @$45
Snowmobiles
Yes
Night Boarding
Friday & Saturday 27 trails lit from 4:30 to 9:30 (night only $21)

FREERIDE 60%
Good tree runs & superb backcountry
FREESTYLE 20%
Terrain park & a halfpipe
CARVING 20%

Alpine Meadows Ski Resort
PO Box 5279
2600 Alpine Meadows Road
Tahoe City, CA 96145
Tel: 530.583.4232
Fax:530-583-0963
Snow phone: 530.581.8374
Web:www.skialpine.com
Email:info@skialpine.com

pic - Palmer Snowboards

one ski resort in the US for skiers - and now we know why they kept it to themselves for so long! **Alpine Meadows** has all sorts of natural terrain that lends itself to the specific needs of snowboarders. There is a wide variety of trails from beginner to expert, lots of tree runs, great off-piste with amazing views of **Lake Tahoe**, if you care to stand and stare. On a week-day, you will hardly ever stand in line for the lifts, giving maximum riding time and ample reason to rest and chill at one of the mountain restaurants. Combine all this with a very snowboard-friendly and generally mellow attitude; Alpine Meadows is simply magic place for all snowboarders.

FREERIDERS of an advanced level should take the high speed, 6-person **Summit Six** chair for access to endless off-piste, via short traverses and hikes. On powder days check out some awesome off-piste available from **Scott chair** and **Lake View**. Unlike other nearby resorts, Alpine has an 'open boundary' policy, meaning that providing the area boundary is marked 'OPEN', you can ride wherever you desire. However, you **must observe all 'CLOSED' signs**, or risk riding in dangerous areas and losing both your lift pass and your life. If you are prepared to explore at Alpine you will find some excellent powder, long

U
USA
CALIFORNIA

pic - Martin Robinson

after a storm - it's worth hiring a guide for the day. Intermediates can enjoy long cruises from the **Roundhouse** detachable quad, and also over the back of **Alpine** on **Sherwood**, where the best early sun can be found.

FREESTYLERS have a great half-pipe known as the **Gravity Cavity** which is now shaped by a new device called the Scorpion. The pipe is located on **Sympathy Face** off the **Roundhouse** chair, while the Roos Ride terrain park, which is open to skiers and snowboarders, can be found off the **Kangaroo** chair. For those who like their hits spread naturally across the mountain, you may need to ask a local where the best ones are located as they are not always obvious but are in abundance. Be sure to use a spotter for reasons of safety.

CARVERS are presented with great corduroy slopes, with the best advanced and intermediate stuff off the **Summit** chair lift, where you will find some nice blacks that mellow out into blue trails.

BEGINNERS may only have a few marked green runs, but they are more than adequate. First timers should ride the chair lifts at the bunny slopes on the base of the mountain, before graduating to the Weasel chair for smooth, wide, open runs. The local ski-school offers a high level of tuition, with a full day's package costing from $59. Novice's can even have freestyle lessons

THE TOWN

Alpine Meadows, doesn't have any real slope side services. However, just about anything you need can be found in nearby **Tahoe City**. Tahoe City has a surplus of accommodation, eating out and sporting facilities. There are loads of shops, including loads of souvenir outlets so beloved by tourists and skiers. With the Tahoe area being so popular, it is quite possible that you could be hanging out, on or off the slopes, with some of the biggest names in snowboarding as a number of pros live in the area.

Accomodation. Alpine doesn't offer any convenient slope side lodgings, but with over 10,000 visitor beds spread throughout the **Tahoe** area, you can't fail to find suitable and affordable accommodation. The nearest lodging for Alpine is at **Tahoe City** which is 6 miles away. Here you can find a good selection of hotels, condos, apartments or cabins.

Food. If you can't find anywhere in this area to suit your taste buds, then you have a serious medical problem. There are loads of eating outlets in every price range - the choice and range are excellent. For a decent breakfast before hitting the slopes, check out The *Alpine Riverside Cafe*. For good food at reasonable prices, check out *Bridgetender* or the *Mandrian Villa* in Tahoe City. *Jasons Saloon* also serves up some decent nosh.

Night-life here is pretty cool with lots of night spots in the area. Partying options are great, with excessive drinking and chatting up of local birds made easy. Some of the best talent can be found in places such as *Naughty Dog, Pierce St Annex*, or *Humpty's*. The *River Ranch*, which is en-route to Alpine, is also noted for being a lively place.

SUMMARY
Great freeriding and natural freestyle resort with a good annual snow record. No slope side facilities, but excellent services within easy reach.
On the slopes: Super excellent
Off the slopes: Extensive
Money wise: Very expensive, on and off the slopes, but budget lodging available

CAR
From Reno take Interstate 80-West to Truckee (45 miles) then State Route 89-South exit (10miles), then right onto Alpine Meadows Road (3 miles). Drive time is about 1 1/2 hours.
FLY
Fly to Reno International, transfer time to resort 1 1/2 hours. 4 hrs from San Francisco
TRAIN
Trains: to Truckee, 6 miles away
BUS
A bus from Reno takes around 1 hour. A Grey Hound bus from San Francisco takes 5 hours via Tahoe City, 6 miles away. Free Ski shuttle buses run from most Tahoe towns (tel 530.581.8341.)

U
S
A

C
A
L
I
F
O
R
N
I
A

7 OUT OF 10

Okay slopes but dull off

pic - Bear Mtn Resort

Bear Mountain Valley is home to two mountain resorts, **Big Bear** and **Snow Summit.** Both play host to numerous top snowboarding events including the Annual Board Aid Festival at Snow Summit. As a rule, resorts' marketing slogans are trite and meaningless, but Bear Mountain's billing as a 'Good Time' place is quite accurate. Anyone who has ridden the parks or pipes,

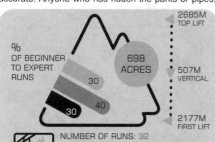

% OF BEGINNER TO EXPERT RUNS

698 ACRES

2685M TOP LIFT

507M VERTICAL

2177M FIRST LIFT

30 / 40 / 30

NUMBER OF RUNS: 32
LONGEST RUN: 3km (1.9 miles)
TOTAL LIFTS: 12
9 chairs, 3 drags
LIFT TIMES: 8.30am to 4.00pm

AVERAGE SNOWFALL:
2.54m
SNOWMAKING:
100%

WINTER PERIODS:
Dec to April
Lift Passes
1/2 Day Pass$38/40
full day $48/55
Night Boarding
Yes

FREERIDE 40%
Trees & good backcountry
FREESTYLE 40%
4 Terrain parks & 2 halfpipes
CARVING 20%

Bear Mountain Resort
P.O. Box 6812,
Big Bear Lake, CA 92315
Tel: 909.585.2519
Fax: 909.585.6805
Web:www.bearmtn.com
Email:info@bearmtn.com

Fly
Fly to Los Angeles, with a transfer time of around 2 hours.
Bus
Bus services from Los Angeles can be taken to the resort.
Car
From Los Angeles, use Interstate 10 east to Redlands. Then Hwy 15 north to San Bernardino and west on route 18. Los Angles to resort, 99 miles. 2 hrs drive.

and afterwards sat in the sun on the outdoor deck for lunch, would be hard-pressed to dispute this claim. Part of the deck's inherent allure is the fact that riders need a place to kick back after spending time on Bear's slopes, where vertical is the name of the game. The high speed quad, Big Bear Express, reaches the top of **Goldmine Mountain** in about seven minutes, where you can ride the Claim Jumper trail to notch up over 500 vertical metres. Bear Mountain offers riding for all abilities, from carving to freestyle and all species in-between. Big Bear is a black diamond bliss but also okay for intermediates.

FREERIDERS have a good choice of areas to ride. The double black diamond **Geronimo run** is a real tester, however **Gambler**, a nugget most riders never find off the top of **Showdown Mountain**, is also super cool. FREESTYLERS now have four big terrain parks and halfpipes. **The Zone** is located immediately above the deck. There is a snack shack at the top of the pipes called **The Yurt** with a judging stand and a DJ station. The **Outlaw Snowboard Park** features enormous table tops, and the famous Serpentine. There's 117 jumps, 57 jibs and 2 pipes set in 195 acres. CARVERS have a number of good trails to cruise, although in fairness this is not a Euro-carver's place. For a quick burst plus a show-off, check out **Grizzly**, a short but steep trail. BEGINNERS, Bear is an excellent place to learn. The local snowboard school offers an introduction to Snowboarding scheme, and a Vertical Improvement Program for riders who want to enhance their carving and jumping skills. Kids under 9 can also sign up for the **magic Minors** Snowboard Camp.

THE TOWN. There is a huge range of accommodation available at Big Bear Lake with apartments to rent at the base of the slopes. Local services are varied, with hundreds of places to eat and drink. The Grizzly Manor Cafe is the place for breakfast or lunch, whilst Village Pizza is the place for a take-away. As for night-life, with a choice of over 50 bars, no-one should miss out.

U

USA

CALIFORNIA

DIAMOND PEAK

5 OUT OF 10

Great views of the lake but you'll be bored after a day

pic - WSG

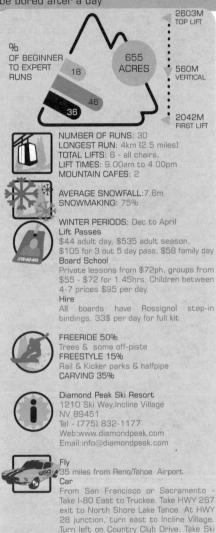

2603M
TOP LIFT

%
OF BEGINNER
TO EXPERT
RUNS

18

655 ACRES

560M
VERTICAL

46

36

2042M
FIRST LIFT

NUMBER OF RUNS: 30
LONGEST RUN: 4km (2.5 miles)
TOTAL LIFTS: 6 - all chairs,
LIFT TIMES: 9.00am to 4.00pm
MOUNTAIN CAFES: 2

AVERAGE SNOWFALL: 7.6m
SNOWMAKING: 75%

WINTER PERIODS: Dec to April
Lift Passes
$44 adult day, $535 adult season,
$105 for 3 out 5 day pass, $58 family day
Board School
Private lessons from $72ph, groups from
$55 - $72 for 1.45hrs. Children between
4-7 prices $95 per day.
Hire
All boards have Rossignol step-in
bindings. 33$ per day for full kit

FREERIDE 50%
Trees & some off-piste
FREESTYLE 15%
Rail & Kicker parks & halfpipe
CARVING 35%

Diamond Peak Ski Resort
1210 Ski Way, Incline Village
NV 89451
Tel - (775) 832-1177
Web: www.diamondpeak.com
Email: info@diamondpeak.com

Fly
35 miles from Reno/Tahoe Airport
Car
From San Francisco or Sacramento -
Take I-80 East to Truckee. Take HWY 267
exit to North Shore Lake Tahoe. At HWY
28 junction, turn east to Incline Village.
Turn left on Country Club Drive. Take Ski
Way to the top.

NEW New for 03/04 season
High speed quad (crystal express) added
for 2004 season

Of all the resorts in **Tahoe**, Diamond Peak doesn't quite mix it with the likes of Squaw and Heavenly but that's not necessarily a bad thing; as the weekends swell the other resorts, Diamond Peak promise amazing views, no crowds and good value. Built after Squaw hosted the Winter Olympics in 1960, and extended to its current size in the 80's. Diamond Peak is a resort that places a strong emphasis on fun, families and snow, and they succeed in many ways as this is a cool hang-out that attracts all ages with the slopes getting a good annual snow covering. The slopes are set out in a simple manner with a good mixture of runs spread out over the whole mountain. Being a quiet resort, the trails don't get busy and there aren't long lift lines. The 2003/4 season saw the replacement of its longest chair with a high speed quad, and boy did it need it. The rest of the lifts are still painfully slow, but does give you plenty of opportunity to sample the amazing views of Tahoe. If you're up there on a Sunday and missed your regular church service then they hold a special service up and Snowflake lodge.

FREERIDERS who can cut the mustard, will find the longest and most challenging terrain up in the area known as the **Solitude Canyon**, which is reached off the **Crystal Express** chair. But note you are not allowed to go past the marked boundary and if you do you will be prosecuted, so study your lift map.

FREESTYLERS head for the new terrain park located half way along **Spillway**. It has a badly maintained pipe and 4 kickers. Its not fenced off so you get a lot of idiot skiers ruining your approach. Up at **Lakeview** theres a rail park, again nothing too taxing.

BEGINNERS, the **school yard** run the obvious place to start. There is a special lift pass available that only covers the 2 beginner lifts and will save you a lot of money. Some of the other lifts have such as **Ridge** have a nice steep exit as you leave the lift, so its worth spending a while watching the beginners clatter into each other while you do up your bindings.

THE TOWN. There's no accommodation at the resort but **incline village** has the closest hotels. There's plenty of accommodation to choose from around Tahoe though, plenty of parking and there is a free shuttle bus available.

6 OUT OF 10

Small and pefectly formed

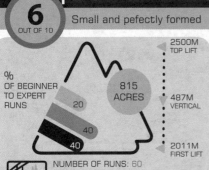

%
OF BEGINNER
TO EXPERT
RUNS

815
ACRES

2500M
TOP LIFT

487M
VERTICAL

2011M
FIRST LIFT

20
40
40

NUMBER OF RUNS: 60
LONGEST RUN: 3.2km (2 miles)
TOTAL LIFTS: 11
9 chairs, 2 drags
CAPACITY (people per hour): 15,700
LIFT TIMES: 9.00am to 4.00pm
MOUNTAIN CAFES: 3

AVERAGE SNOWFALL:
7.5m-12m
SNOWMAKING:
Unknown

WINTER PERIODS: Dec to April
Lift Passes
Day Pass $44
1/2 day $35
Hire
board and boots from $35/day
helmet $10/day

FREERIDE 40%
Trees & some off-piste
FREESTYLE 30%
3 Parks & a halfpipe
CARVING 35%

Dodge Ridge
P.O. Box 1188
#1 Dodge Ridge Road
Pinecrest, CA. 95364
Tel: 209.965.3474
Fax: 209.965.4437
Web:www.dodgeridge.com
Email:info@dodgeridge.com

Fly
to San Francisco, transfer is 2 1/2 hours.
Bus
services from San Francisco are available.
Car
30 minutes from Sonora; 90 minutes
from the Central Valley; 3 hours from
the Bay Area. Directions: 580 East
to the 205 East past I-5 and 99. At
Manteca take 120 East toward Sonora.
Stay on the 120/108 through Escalon
to Oakdale. At Oakdale turn left on
108 East to Sonora. Stay on 108 East
through Sonora to Pinecrest (30 miles).
Turn right on Dodge Ridge Road.

Dodge Ridge Resort

Dodge Ridge is not one of those resorts that springs to mind when one is thinking about where to go for a few days riding. Come to think about it, Dodge Ridge is almost unknown outside of those who live in the area or by a few hardcore riders who travel around in a van searching out the small haunts. Anyway, why would this relatively new resort be of much interest? After all, it's only been going for 15 years. Well Dodge Ridge has some 60 trails with 12 lifts which take you over a mountain that has a lot to offer, especially advanced riders, with a good series of double black diamond runs such as the trails that can be found off of lift 3. The slopes are well maintained and well set out offering something for all levels with a good mixture of trails.

FREERIDERS who like to experience rough, hard core and fast terrain will like what they find here. There is a good selection of expert runs to take on with the most interesting being the **Six Shooter** and the **Sonora Glades**, which is a tricky steep section with heaps of trees. Little more sedate trails to try out are the **Sunrise** or the **Exhibition** while the **Gentle Ben** is even easier.
FREESTYLERS have had a halfpipe and terrain park here for years. The **Santa Cruz** Snowpark and **DC Rythm Zone** are loaded with hits and a 300foot long pipe both are located off the number 5 lift, but note, this is a steep trail and not for novices. A new Santa Cruz sponsored pipe is located on a more gentle area at the top of lift 1 while lower down there is an area called the **Mountain Dew Fun Zone** designed for younger riders just learning to get air.
CARVERS have a couple of cracking trails to let loose on, namely the **Sunrise** if you have the balls or the **Quicksilver** which is a nice long blue trail off lift 8. **Fools Gold** is another cool fast trail.
BEGINNERS will find the best areas to take on are located at the lower sections of lifts 2 and 1. Please note that these are novice areas and although tame, should not be at speed.

THE TOWN
Off the slopes things suddenly change and become a little different as well as very basic indeed. Local services, provided in nearby town of **Pinecrest** are very good with good rates for accommodation and other services. There are a number of good eating joints but don't expect a lot of night life. There is none of note really, which is not to say that you can't have a good time out.

U
S
A

C
A
L
I
F
O
R
N
I
A

3060M TOP LIFT

%
OF BEGINNER
TO EXPERT
RUNS

20

4800 ACRES

1067M VERTICAL

45

35

1993M FIRST LIFT

pic - Steve Barker

NUMBER OF RUNS: 86
LONGEST RUN: 8.8km (5.5 miles)
TOTAL LIFTS: 29 - 1 Aerial Tram
1 gondola, 18 chairs, 8 drags
LIFT TIMES: 8.30am to 4.00pm
MOUNTAIN CAFES: 7

AVERAGE SNOWFALL:
8.64m
SNOWMAKING:
69%

WINTER PERIODS:
Nov to April
Lift Passes
1 Day $44
3 Days $120
6 Days $192
Board Schools
2 hour group $35
1 hour private $60
Hire
from $32/day
Snowmobiles
Yes
Night Boarding
No

FREERIDE 45%
Good tree runs & good backcountry
FREESTYLE 25%
3 Terrain parks & a halfpipe
CARVING 30%

Heavenly Mountain Resort
P.O. Box 2180
Stateline, NV 89449
Tel: (775) 586-7000
Web:www.skiheavenly.com
Email:info@skiheavenly.com

new for 04/05 season
NEW
$10 million being spent. Powder Bowl
and Waterfall lifts replaced with 6-
seater. 5 new grooming machine, more
snowmaking and East Peak Lodge is
getting a makeover

This is an over hyped resort. The new gondola that runs from downtown **South Lake Tahoe** makes access to the mountain easier but you can't make use of this facility if you are still a beginner as it does not access any beginner slopes. This is something that the resort is looking into. You can, however, ride up to look at the beautiful views of the Lake for a steep price. **Heavenly** is a large resort that stretches across the two states of **California** and **Nevada**. Heavenly has over 40 years of operation under its belt, as well as some of the largest snowboard/ski acreage in the US, and by far the biggest vertical out of the **Lake Tahoe** resorts. Snowboarders are drawn from afar, especially at weekends and during holidays. In the past, the International Snowboard Federation has held world cup events that have attracted riders from around the world, who came for the challenge of a big mountain with hardcore terrain. However, Heavenly is not just for the pro's - there is something here for everyone - but the slopes do favour riders of intermediate and advanced levels, with steeps and big air possibilities on double black diamond runs, like those of Mott & Killebrew Canyons and the Gunbarrel.

FREERIDERS will find the most challenging terrain is located on the **Nevada** side of the resort in the **Milky**

Way bowl. However, it does become tracked out very quickly and would be best left until just after a fresh dump. Still, the Milky Way Bowl is major and offers some great powder. Advanced riders who like their slopes steep and covered with trees should check out the **North Bowl**. But for those who really want to fill

HEAVENLY

THE TOWN & GETTING THERE

pic - Heavenly Resort

their pants should make for the white-knuckle rides on the **Mott & Killebrew Canyon** area. Here you will find a series of expert double black diamond runs through a series of chutes. For something a little less intimidating try the blues off **Tamarack** and **Sky chairs**.

FREESTYLERS are provided with four terrain parks and a boarder cross trail that may alter depending on the snow depths. They are spread out across both sides of the mountain. One of the terrain parks, which is designed by top riders, is built to accommodate all riders whatever your ability. However, for those who prefer natural hits, Heavenly has an abundance of them all over the place.

CARVERS are not to be outdone since Heavenly is a highly rated carvers' resort. There are plenty of well prepared pistes for laying out big tracks on, such as **Liz's** and **Big Dipper**.

BEGINNERS may at first feel a little left out with the lack of green runs. However, there are plenty of excellent blue trails to check out. Be aware that in various areas there are a number of blacks that turn off and drop away from some of the easier trails, so check your piste map. The cluster of greens off the **Waterfall lift**, on runs like **Mombo Meadows**, are good for whetting the appetite before trying the blues off **Ridge** and **Canyon lifts.**

THE TOWN
Off the mountain, local action is lively and plentiful. The choice of accommodation, eating and booze joints is massive and many within easy reach of the slopes. However, local services are a bit spread out and having a car here is a must. Locals make you feel at home and services are of a very high standard. However, the popularity of the area does mean that the place can be excessively busy, especially at weekends. South Lake Tahoe has heaps of shops and loads of sporting facilities

Accommodation: Although there is lodging within walking distance of the slopes, it is very expensive. South Lake Tahoe is heaving with hotels and motels from very cheap to very expensive. If you are on a budget try 'Doug's Mellow Mountain Retreat' (916) 544 8065 at $13-$15 per night for a small dormitory. The Blu Zu Hostel 4140 Pine Park (916) 541 9502 $15 per night for a bed in the dormitory.

Restaurants are plentiful and at prices to please everyone, there are also various fast-food joints. Every type of food is available here from Chinese, Italian, Mexican to standard American fair. It's all on offer. The list of good eating places is too long to mention in this short journal, but loacls will point you in the right direction if you ask for some recommendations. In the meantime Red Hutt or Chris's are both good.

Nightlife in Heavenly is dull. However in South Lake Tahoe there is plenty of gambling if that is your thing and many of the casinos have nightclubs. Some of the better ones are Club Z and Nero's. Hoss Hogs host some great band nights and Mulligans Irish bar is always a favourite for late night drinking.

SUMMARY
Great all-round freeriding and carving with some excellent steeps. Very busy most of the time especially holidays. Good local services.
Money wise; Overall this is a very expensive resort, but good value.

CAR
From Reno take highway 395 to Carson City, then highway 50 & folllow the signs (58 miles)
From San Francisco take highway 80 through Sacramento, then highway 50 to tahoe
FLY
Reno via Carson City, Heavenly = 58 miles (93). Drive time is about 1 hour.
TRAIN
Nearest station at Reno
BUS
A bus from Reno takes 1 1/2 hours. A Grey Hound bus from San Francisco takes 6 hours via South Lake Tahoe, 6 miles away.

JUNE MOUNTAIN

pic - June Mountain Resort

9 OUT OF 10 — Superb

June Mountain is located in the **Eastern High Sierra**, 17 miles north of its sister resort **Mammoth**. For an area of such modest size, June offers a richness of riding terrain that is often not found in even in many larger resorts. It's as though some of the best mountain features have been selectively picked and welded together to form a neat package that is user-friendly to a multitude of disciplines. This place has something to offer carvers, freestylers or freeriders of any level. There is a welcome blend of energy-sapping steeps and mellower stuff perfect for cruising. Because of the small size of June it doesn't have package tour status and it has a minimal number of ski schools, making the place a bit of a secret for those in the know and leaving you without lift queues even in peak periods. This all makes the place sound a bit like something resembling heaven, and in many respects is, especially if there's been a dump and if the park and pipe have been recently re-shaped. Having said that, June can't offer the variety of the decent larger resorts. Nevertheless, if you don't mind riding the odd run more than once and having to take one foot out along some of the flat green runs, you will get a lot out of the relaxed attitude here, away from the big resort experience.

FREERIDERS can feel free to use any of the perfectly good pistes if they wish, but when there's trees-a-plenty to circumnavigate like there is here, you'd be mad to limit yourself. At June **Mountain Summit** are some steep natural chutes and bowls. From the June Meadows Chalet those who can should be sure to drop off blind in to **Gull Ridge** for a tasty black run or two back down to June Lake.
FREESTYLERS fortunate enough to find themselves at June have at their disposal the world class super pipe in front of June Meadows Chalet and the Boarder Town Snowboard Park located on **Gunsmoke** off of lift J4. The fantastic board park is out of bounds to bi-plankers, a testament to June's snowboard policy, and consists of about 20 hits, tabletops and banks of all sizes plus another half pipe upon which those skills can be honed. A beginners park is located under **chair J2**, then step up to the **Sunrise park** which has some bigger kickers.
CARVERS have a choice of well-groomed slopes to take advantage of. The selection of black rated slopes from June Mountain Summit are great for the speed freaks to let loose, while the green and blue runs down from **Rainbow Summit** offer something far less daunting.
BEGINNER freeriders can take their time on a few gentle, un-crowded slopes. This can be attempted alone or under the laid back tuition of the instructors available. For those novice freestylers who wish to learn the art of the pipe there are also instructors around to teach you what you need to know. In fact, not just the novices need benefit from their guidance as upper level tuition is offered too.

THE TOWN. June Lake is the residential area of the June Mountain resort; the population is a mere 600. It's a very relaxed community and there are a number of cabins and motels at which to stay, as well as plenty of fine eateries.

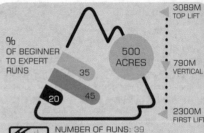

**%
OF BEGINNER
TO EXPERT
RUNS**
35
20
45

500 ACRES

3089M TOP LIFT
790M VERTICAL
2300M FIRST LIFT

NUMBER OF RUNS: 39
LONGEST RUN: 4km (2.5 miles)
TOTAL LIFTS: 7 - 6 chairs,1 drag
CAPACITY (people per hour): 10,000
LIFT TIMES: 8.30am to 4.00pm
MOUNTAIN CAFES: 2

AVERAGE SNOWFALL:6.3m
SNOWMAKING: 10%

WINTER PERIODS: Dec to April
Lift Passes
1/2 Day $50,Day Pass - $38
5 Days - $179,Season $500 (early bird
Board School
Beginner package lesson, pass & rent $140 a day. Lesson only $80. Private lessons £75 per hour
Hire
Board & Boots $30 per day

FREERIDE 40%
Trees & some off-piste
FREESTYLE 40%
3 parks & a halfpipe
CARVING 20%

June Mountain,P.O. Box 146,
June Lake,California 93529
Tel - 760.648.7733
Web:www.junemountain.com
Email:junemtn@qnet.com

Fly
to Reno, a short trip south. Mammoth has a small airport
Car
From Los Angeles: Hwy 14 to Hwy 395 north to Hwy 158; 327 miles.
From San Francisco & Sacramento: Interstate 80 to Hwy 50 to the Kingsbury Grade cutoff to Hwy 395 south to Hwy 158; 300 miles.

KIRKWOOD

Okay on the slopes, dull of it

pic - Kirkwood Resort

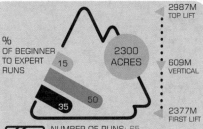

2987M TOP LIFT

% OF BEGINNER TO EXPERT RUNS

15

2300 ACRES

609M VERTICAL

35   50

2377M FIRST LIFT

NUMBER OF RUNS: 65
LONGEST RUN: 4km (2.5 miles)
TOTAL LIFTS: 12 - 10 chairs, 2 drags
CAPACITY (people per hour): 17,905
LIFT TIMES: 9.00am to 3.30pm

AVERAGE SNOWFALL: 12m
SNOWMAKING: 10%

WINTER PERIODS: Dec to April
Lift Passes
1/2 Day $23, 1 Day $46, Season $419
Board School
Beginners day package (pass, lesson, hire)
$80. 2hr group lesson $40. Private lesson
$90 per hour. Pipe & park lesson $25
Hire
board and boots $35/41 per day

FREERIDE 50%
Trees & good off-piste
FREESTYLE 25%
3 parks & a halfpipe
CARVING 25%

Kirkwood Mountain Resort
P.O. Box 1, Kirkwood, CA 95646
Tel: (209)258-6000
Web: www.skikirkwood.com
Email: info@kirkwood.com

Fly
to Reno, 70 miles from the resort
Bus
Bus journeys from Reno, take 90 minutes
Car
From Reno take the US route 395
south and then state route 88 west to
Kirkwod. Reno to resort = 70 miles. 90
minutes drive time.

Kirkwood has the reputation of being an advanced rider's mountain, and in many ways it is, as proved by their hosting of a leg of the US Extremes Pro-snowboard Tour. With a number of steep, double black diamond trails and the highest base elevation in the area, Kirkwood has great freeriding, on and off-piste, excellent carving and full-on freestyle terrain. The resort is located south of **South Lake Tahoe**, along Highways 88 and 89. Although it's not far from the resort of **Heavenly**, it is far less crowded, leaving the slopes free for riders who know what they are doing.

FREERIDERS in particular will like the natural terrain here, like open tree-riding in areas like **Larry's Lip**, and fast steeps on the double black diamond trails below an area known as **The Sisters**, which is reachable off Wagon Wheel chair lift. Don't venture into these trails if you're not up to the mark as they are steep runs which mellow out only at the lower sections. If it's powder you're after, look no further as Kirkwood receives lots of it annually.
FREESTYLERS get an excellent mountain to discover lots of natural hits. **Snowsnake Gully** offers all sorts of excitement, but the super-park, located under **chair 2**, is loaded with so many toys that freestylers hardly need go in search of anything else. Beginner air-heads should take a look under chair 7 at the **terrain garden**.
CARVERS are presented with some first class carving terrain that is a match for anywhere else in the Tahoe region. For a long, fast descent, you should give **Thunder Saddle** or **Larry's Lip** a try, but be warned - this is not for knuckle heads. For something a little less daunting, **Buckboard** is fun.
BEGINNERS need to get their act together fast if they want to appreciate Kirkwood's offerings to the full, and with the fact that this resort has some great novice trails, it shouldn't be too long. Although the piste map shows a low percentage of easy trails, there are plenty of rideable areas to be found at the lower section, like **Graduation**, which has its own easy-to-use lift. Make it to **Timber Creek** and you can practice with ease, before having a killer hot-dog at the cafe.

THE TOWN. If your name is Mr/Mrs Dull then you will love what is on offer at the base of **Kirkwood**. What you get is not up to much with expensive accommodation, dull eateries and dull night-life. For the best local happenings and night-action, head to **South Lake Tahoe**, which is only 15 miles away.

U
S
A

C
A
L
I
F
O
R
N
I
A

3 OUT OF 10

Come on, you're in Vegas man

Pic - Lee Canyon Resort

%
OF BEGINNER
TO EXPERT
RUNS

20

40 ACRES

20

60

2899M
TOP LIFT

305M
VERTICAL

2594M
FIRST LIFT

NUMBER OF RUNS: 10
LONGEST RUN: 914m
TOTAL LIFTS: 3 - all chairs
CAPACITY (people per hour): 2,500
LIFT TIMES: 9am - 4pm

AVERAGE SNOWFALL:
3m
SNOWMAKING:
50%

WINTER PERIODS:
Dec to April
Lift Passes
1/2 day $25, Day $33, Season $499
Board Schools
Group lessons $25 for 1 1/2 hours
Private lessons $70 ph
Hire
Boards & Boots $25 per day

FREERIDE 40%
A few tree & limited backcountry
FREESTYLE 20%
A Terrain park & halfpipe
CARVING 40%

Lee Canyon
State Route 156, Nevada
tel :001 (709) 593 9500
Web:www.skilasvegas.com
Email:ridenski@lvssr.com

Bus
from Las Vegas take around 1 hour.
Fly
to Reno or Las Vegas International
Drive
Route 95 out of Las Vegas towards Reno.
After 30 miles turn left onto Route 156,
then 15 miles or so to Lee Canyon.

NEW new for 04/05 season
A 150m Magic Carpet, More Snowmaking
with New tower guns, fan guns & 25%
increase in on-slope coverage.

Not many people will know this or indeed will believe it, but yes it's true, it's a fact, it exists: a snow-capped mountain to ski and ride on just outside the world's gambling heaven **Las Vegas**. Lee Canyon is a small resort only 45 miles from the Las Vegas Strip. It is weird to drive up from the heat of the desert to arrive in just 20 minutes at altitude with snowdrifts all around. The mountains get regular snow throughout the winter with an average of 3m a year. The resort can also cover 50% of the slopes with artificial snow should the real stuff be lacking. Set at 8500ft in the **Spring Mountains** to the north west of Las Vegas, what you actually get is a slope area offering a respectable 1000ft of vertical drop. There are three slow chairlifts, one on the nursery slopes accessing a total of 11 trails, one of them dotted with ramps and kickers (plus a sign that says "No aerial flips allowed" (most people seemed to ignore it!). All standards from beginner to snowgod would find something here to keep them amused for a while - if only an afternoon or two. What's more, this place never gets too crowded. The car park often seems full yet the slopes never seem to number more than 50 people at a time. At the slopes you can get full snowboard hire but like most hire kit the quality varies - getting there early gets you better equipment. There is also a shop, bar and cafe for your standard burger hit.

FREERIDERS should find the 4 black runs, which are not groomed and are basically mogul fields, a cool place to ride offering a fun challenge. Two of the blacks descend through some trees which only adds to the fun. There are a few bits where you can get off piste but the powder soon gets shredded out so don't expect any hardcore backcountry terrain.
FREESTYLERS are best looking out for natural hits as the man made offerings are a bit lame. The snowboard park, which is designed as a long trail, has a pretty mundane halfpipe which looked more like a long depression in the snow although this year a new pipe grinder will help maintain the 500 foot pipe and moneys been spent on new rails a 1/4 pipe and snow making.
CARVERS may find that this is not a place for them due to the lack of pisted trails. The terrain is often to bumpy to hold a good edge.
BEGINNERS only have a few rather dull areas to slide around on. A new 150' Magic Carpet will help increase uphill capacity and make learning easier.
THE TOWN. To find out what's going on off the slopes, get your self a guide book on **Las Vegas** as there is no way that we can even begin to tell you all that is on offer in this massive gambling city.

California has given us Hollywood, Daffy Duck and thankfully, **Mammoth Mountain**. Located in the **Eastern Sierra** region, Mammoth has welcomed snowboarders onto its slopes for many years, and with a good snow record (11m in 2003/4 season), riding is often possible into June. The past few years have seen huge

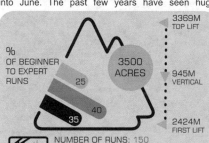

% OF BEGINNER TO EXPERT RUNS

3500 ACRES

3369M TOP LIFT

945M VERTICAL

2424M FIRST LIFT

25
40
35

NUMBER OF RUNS: 150
LONGEST RUN: 4.8km (3 miles)
TOTAL LIFTS: 27 - 3 gondolas, 24 chairs
LIFT TIMES: 8.30am to 4.00pm
MOUNTAIN CAFES: 9

AVERAGE SNOWFALL:
11m
SNOWMAKING:
33%

WINTER PERIODS:
Nov to June
Lift Passes
1 Day $62, 4 Days - $248
Season Pass - $1200
Board Schools
Group lessons $60 for 3hrs
Private lesson $450 per day
Hire
Board & boots $30 per day
Snowmobiles
Yes
Night Boarding
No

FREERIDE 45%
Good tree runs & good backcountry
FREESTYLE 35%
3 Terrain parks & 3 halfpipes
CARVING 30%

Mammoth Mountain
P.O. Box 24,#1 Minaret Road,
Mammoth Lake,California 93546
Tel: 001 760.934.0745
Web:www.mammothmountain.com
Email:info@mammoth-mtn.com

new for 04/05 season
Chair 17 replaced with a high-speed quad. Mammoth Mountain inn has final refit. New sound system in Unbound Park (hopefully some new music!). Increase in snowmaking

NEW

pic - WSG

investment by Intrawest (owners of Whistler & Squaw), much of this evident in the huge terrain parks and fast lift system, but also the construction of the new village resort that opened last season. The new village sits on the edge of town with a Gondola taking you to **Canyon Lodge**, this season should see a trail back to the village completed. Mammoth's slopes can often get busy at weekends when the place fills up with California's city dwellers. Don't let that put you off though as by normal American standards, Mammoth is a pretty big place. In fact, it's one of the biggest resorts in America, with over 150 trails set out on a long-since dead volcano; no matter what your style or ability, there's plenty to do. Mammoth's terrain parks have achieved legendary status, for the third year running picking up **Transworlds best pipe award**, and runner up to Whistler for best terrain park. Its not just for the pro's either, there's parks and pipes designed for every ability. Overall Mammoth is a great resort for boarders, there's good variety in terrain from trees to open bowls, an efficient lift system; the last drag lift was removed last season. One gripe is the piste markings which are a bit of a nightmare as they seem to just disappear.

FREERIDERS have a great mountain to ride with trees, big bowls and loads of natural hits to catch air, especially in areas such as **Huevos Grande** and **Hangman's Hollow**. Experienced riders normally head up to the ridge reached by **Gondola 2** Here there is a host of chutes that lead into a wide bowl, perfect for freeriders to show what they're made of. The **Cornice** run is the one to go for - it's awesome and will give you a major buzz. If you really have the balls, check out **Wipe Out**, a double black run off Chair 23. If you emulate the name of this run, not only will it make your eyes water, but everyone on the chair lift above will be able to watch and

USA
CALIFORNIA

laugh as you wipe out in style (give them two fingers and then get on your way).

FREESTYLERS have a resort that is well in tune with their needs, whether you're after natural hits or purpose built jumps. A good spot to check out is the area known as **Lower Dry Creek** which is a natural halfpipe. Alternatively, the **Dragon's Back** gives the advanced freestyler plenty of air time. Theres 3 terrain parks suitable for all levels. The family park near **Canyon Lodge** has a beginner's half-pipe (10ft walls) and a few boxes, but the real fun starts on the unbound parks. The unbound team keep the parks & pipes maintained perfectly all season. Depending on the snow conditions there's a huge number and variety of rails and the awesome 16'x36' wall ride.

pic - WSG

Unbound south is a great long park full of intermediate to advanced jumps, rails and boxes with lifts to take you straight back up. The **main unbound** park is across by the main lodge with great views of the park as you ascend on the lifts crossing it. Here you'll find the super pipe with its 15ft walls and next to it the massive super duper pipe. They try and

pic - WSG

open the pipes as soon as the resort opens, and when things start getting slushy in April, they build a spring pipe in the saddle bowl off the face lift express. You'll also find some huge table tops, and jumps up to 80 foot in length. To the side of the main unbound is a good run through the trees full of easy jumps on the right and tables to the left. Jump straight back on the lift and you can easily get up and down in 10 minutes. For complete beginners check out the area under the lift between the **sesame street** runs. There

are some bumps to get some credit card air on, and some boxes. If you're still not happy then **June Mountain** is only a 30 drive away.

CARVERS who like to sign the snow with their tracks will love Mammoth. The runs are super-well pisted and make for good carving terrain, both for those wanting to go at speed or for the more sedate carver. Check out the trail known as the **Saddle Bowl,** where you will find a nice, tame, long blue run.

BEGINNERS, if you can't learn or improve at Mammoth, then you're into the wrong sport. The area is perfect for novices, with plenty of green and easy progression blue runs at the lower sections and excellent snowboard tuition available. **Sesame Street** run off chair 11 near the main lodge is perfect for beginners, theres no pistes joining it so you won't get flustered by other riders, and under the chairlift are a series of bumps and boxes to try if you're not bruised enough already. Special beginner packages including lesson, lift and gear start from $87 and are well worth the money and the local snowboard school has a good reputation.

pic - WSG

THE TOWN

At the base area you will find some accommodation and basic facilities. However, the best value is to stay down in the town of **Mammoth Lakes** which is 4 miles from the mountain. Mammoth Lakes has a huge selection of good local services and although the area is not noted for being affordable, riders on a budget will still be able to swing it with a number of cheap supermarkets and low priced dorms to lodge at. For all your snowboard needs, Mammoth has a number of snowboard shops, such as *Stormriders* tel (760) 934 2471 and *Mountain Riders,* tel (760) 934 0679.

Accommodation. There's plenty of accommodation to be found in the town of Mammoth Lakes which is about 4 miles from the main lodge, but note on the whole most are very expensive. You will find condo-overload plus a few B&B joints and a hostel. The *Ullr Lodge* on Minaret Rd is a reasonable priced hostel with beds from $20 a night. The new village on the edge of town has various apartments available and means you can practically ski-in/out every day, but at a cost. The *Mammoth Mountain Inn* is situated near the main lodge and offers some good room and lift deals, but the development work going on nearer town however leaves it feeling increasingly isolated. The rooms have been refurbished and a free night bus now runs into town, so it's not a bad choice if you want to be one of the first on the slopes.

Food. You can get almost any type of food here, ranging from expensive to mega bucks. There are a number of cheaper food-stops such as Berger's, where you can dine on chicken or burgers. The Breakfast Club is the place for early starters, while *Roberto's* serves hot Mexican nosh. If pizzas are your thing, then try a slice at *Nik-N-Willie's* which is noted for its food. *Grumpy's* is noted for chicken served up in a sporting setting. *Hennessey's* in the new village is ok, but if you fancy something that's not in breadcrumbs then take a look along the old Mammoth road, the *Alpenrose* comes highly recommended. For a great coffee and to check your email go to *Looney Beans*, 3280 Main Street.

Night-life hits off in **Mammoth Lakes** and while not fantastic; it is still pretty good with bars playing up-to-date sounds. Amongst the more popular hangouts are *Whiskey Creek* and the *Stonehouse Brewery*. *Grumpy's* is a cool place that serves booze and burgers, set to a back drop of TV screens showing the latest slope action. In the new village *Dublins* does the beer/TV thing well, and has a nightclub called *Fever* next door, but pick of the bunch is *Lakanuki's*. The *Innsbruck* near the main lodge is good for a beer after a long day.

SUMMARY

Great freeriding on open slopes, impeccable terrain parks, but very busy at weekends and over holiday periods. Good local facilities but limited, affordable slope side beds

U
U
S
A

C
A
L
I
F
O
R
N
I
A

CAR
From LA follow US 395 north to Hwy. 203 (at Mammoth Lakes Junction) - 307 miles.
Reno - US 395 south, to Hwy. 203 - 168 miles.
San Francisco Area - Interstate 80 or Interstate 50 to US 395 south, to Hwy. 203 - 320 miles.
FLY
Fly to Reno International, transfer time to resort is 4 hours, Local airport is Mammoth Lakes, 20 miles away. There are plans to upgrade airport to handle larger planes.
BUS
A bus from Reno takes 3 1/2 hours. CREST bus service from Reno/Tahoe 3 days a week, call (800) 922-1930 for info.

pic - Mountain High Resort

%
OF BEGINNER
TO EXPERT
RUNS

25

35

40

220 ACRES

2500M
TOP LIFT

671M
VERTICAL

1829M
FIRST LIFT

NUMBER OF RUNS: 46
LONGEST RUN: 2.6km (1.6 miles)
TOTAL LIFTS:13
10 chairs,1 drag, 2 magic carpets
LIFT TIMES: 8.30 am- 10.00 pm
MOUNTAIN CAFES: 7

AVERAGE SNOWFALL:
4.5m
SNOWMAKING:
95%

WINTER PERIODS:
Nov to April
Lift Passes
1/2 day $44.
Day $44.
Season $499 ($249 early bird).
Free day pass if its your birthday!
Board School
Beginner lesson includes pass, lesson &
hire $55.
Standard lesson & day pass $75.
Private $75 an hour
Hire
Board & Boots $30 per day
Night boarding
Till 10pm every day

FREERIDE 55%
Trees & some off-piste
FREESTYLE 25%
2 parks & a halfpipe
CARVING 35%

Mountain High Resort
PO Box 3010,24510 Highway 2
Wrightwood, CA 92397
Telephone: (760) 249-5808
Fax: (760) 316-7893
Web:www.mthigh.com
Email:jmcolly@mthigh.com

U

**S
A**

**C
A
L
I
F
O
R
N
I
A**

Have you heard about the resort that although located in the southern reaches of **California** and only ninety minutes from **Los Angeles**, boasts at having five terrain parks, two half pipes, forty-seven named trails, twelve lifts and night riding seven days a week over seventeen flood lit slopes? No? Well let me introduce to you **Mountain High**, a no nonsense resort with riding over two mountain areas with a summit of over 2499 metres. By no means is this a big resort, indeed Mountain High is relatively small when compared to the likes of its more northern neighbour **Mammoth Mountain**. However, unlike Mammoth Mountain this place is far less over-hyped, far less crowded and a lot more affordable. There may only be just over 200 acres of ridable terrain, but as the saying goes, 'size doesn't always matter, it's what you do with the size that counts. And to be fair, Mountain High does very nicely with what it has with tow mountain areas covered in tight trees and offering a good selection of well laid out trails. The **East Resort** mountain has the highest summit elevation of 2499 metres but the smallest selection of trails, while the **West Resort** has the largest selection of trails. Both mountain areas have terrain parks and halfpipes however, the two areas are not connected by mountain lifts and you can't ride between the two, instead you will need to take the resort shuttle bus to reach either. They have been doing things here on the mountains since 1937 so in that time the management have learnt a thing or two. Along with standard tickets they operate lift ticket schemes such as the Flexi ticket system where you buy a pass for a certain number of hours or the Point system which is a system where you buy points that let you ride whenever you want throughout the season. You can even transfer the points to a friend.

FREERIDERS will no doubt find the slopes on the East Resort to there liking, especially the **Olympic Bowl** which is a double black diamond stretch. On the West Resort there are a number of nice trails to check out with lots of trees and some fine steeps. The runs off the **Inferno Ridge** are particularly good as is the **Vertigo**. For those who like to take it easy then the

Upper and Lower **Chisolm trails** are first class trails.

FREESTYLERS are extremely well looked after here with choice of five terrain parks and two halfpipes as well as loads of natural hits from which to get air from. The terrain parks, which are sponsored by Vans are spread across both mountains and known as the **Faultline**. Two of the parks are for beginners while both half pipes have their own drags lifts.

MOUNTAIN HIGH

THE TOWN & GETTING THERE

pic - Mountain High Resort

CARVERS will find that the **East Resort** offers some of the best cruising with a good selection of runs from the top.

BEGINNERS should like Mountain High with a nice selection of gentle slopes laid out at the base areas with the best runs on the **West Mountain** off the **Coyote** and **Roadrunner** lifts.

THE TOWN
Off the slopes things are somewhat different and not what you would totally expect. The resort itself, doesn't own or provide any slope linking accommodation or provide a multi complex resort with all the normal holiday attractions. Around the base areas are a few sport shops and snowboard hire outlets and cafeterias, but that's about it. However, Mountain High is located next to the town of Wrightwood which provides a host of local facilities from lodges to bed and breakfast joints. Los Angeles is only 90 minutes away so you could even base yourself there or at any one of the many towns en route. Where you eat depends basically on where you decided to stay. Most

lodges and hotels in the area have restaurants or are close to one. There are also loads of fast food joints to seek out all the way back to Los Angeles.

Nightlife and other evening entertainments vary from place to place, but basically things in Wrightwood are laid back and not very exciting while Los Angeles rocks big style and offers millions of things to do.

CAR
Ontario to Mountain High via Wrightwood. Drive time is about 45
FLY
to Ontario airport with a transfer time to the resort of 45 minutes.
BUS
from Ontario airport takes around 45 mins to Mountain High. Buses from Los Angeles take around 90 hours and from Orange County the time is 75 minutes.

6 OUT OF 10 Okay freestylers place

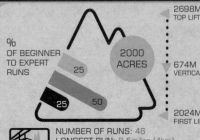

pic - Sierra at Tahoe Reesort

% OF BEGINNER TO EXPERT RUNS

2698M TOP LIFT

2000 ACRES

674M VERTICAL

25

25 50

2024M FIRST LIFT

NUMBER OF RUNS: 46
LONGEST RUN: 2.5miles (4km)
TOTAL LIFTS: 10
9 Chairs, 1 magic carpet
CAPACITY (people per hour): 14,920
LIFT TIMES: 8.30am to 4.00pm

AVERAGE SNOWFALL:
12.2m
SNOWMAKING:
20%

WINTER PERIODS:
Nov to April
Lift Passes
1 Day pass - $49
3 of 5 Day pass - $162
Season pass - $649 (unlimited Northstar & Sierra)
Board Schools
group from $35/39 hire and lesson $73/78
private $80/90 hour
Hire
board and boots $37 per day

FREERIDE 40%
Trees & good backcountry
FREESTYLE 50%
4 Terrain park & a halfpipe
CARVING 10%

Sierra-at-Tahoe Resort
1111 Sierra-atTahoe Road,
Twin Bridges, CA 95735
Tel: 001 (530) 659 7453
Web:www.sierratahoe.com
Email:sierra@boothcreek.com

Bus
from Reno to South Lake Tahoe.
Fly
to Reno, transfer time of 35 mins.
Drive
From Reno, use Interstate 395 south via Carson City and Hwy 50 to Echo Summit and then left to Sierra-at-Tahoe.Reno to resort is 31 miles. 35 mins drive-time.

Sierra-at-Tahoe is located south-west of **Lake Tahoe** and is one of the lesser known or visited resorts in the Lake Tahoe Region. This means that the 2,000 acres of freeriding and freestyle terrain is left relatively crowd-free. 46 trails cut through thick trees that spread out over three areas, offering excellent snowboarding for all abilities, but mainly favouring intermediates. Advanced riders are provided with some very challenging riding on a number of good black trails, especially those found under the **Grand View Express**.

FREERIDERS who get their fix by shredding trees will love this resort. Sierra is covered with tight trees that will rip you apart if you drop down the wrong line. However, much of the area is rated as intermediate standard.
FREESTYLERS will find this mountain a bit of a gem, apart from the shameful fact that fun-parks are open to skiers. However, **Pipeline** is a long, well looked after pipe, that is snowboard-only. There are four parks here called Fun Zones which are dotted around the slopes and marked out on the piste map in pink. For those who like their hits to come naturally, you will find plenty of banks and big walls to ride, especially where snow banks up alongside the trees.
CARVERS who look only for perfectly flat, bump less slopes may not be too impressed. This is not a resort that can lay claim to having lots of great piste on which to lay some fast turns. In general the terrain is a little unforgiving. However, there is some quite good riding to be had on the **West Bowl** Slopes where carvers can show off in style and at speed.
BEGINNERS will find plenty of easy slopes, with the chance of riding from the summit down the green **Sugar 'n' Spice** trail. Other cool novice trails are off **Rock Garden** and **Nob Hill** lifts. **Broadway**, located at the base area, is good for the total beginner and it even has its own beginner chair so you won't have to suffer the embarrassment of continually falling off a drag lift.

THE TOWN. There is some basic slopeside accommodation, but for the best local happenings and night-life, head back down to the **South Lake Tahoe** area, only 12 miles away. Get the free shuttle bus if you don't have car. Around town you will find every thing you could possibly want to make your stay a worth while one.

SQUAW VALLEY

Great all-round resort, excellent halfpipe and good novice slopes

Squaw Valley is full-on and has been snowboard-friendly for many years. Squaw is a total snowboarder's resort in every sense and is one of the best known in the **Tahoe** area. With its European-alpine feel, and its history in hosting the 1960 Winter Olympics,

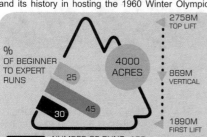

% OF BEGINNER TO EXPERT RUNS

2758M TOP LIFT
4000 ACRES
869M VERTICAL
1890M FIRST LIFT

25 — 30 — 45

NUMBER OF RUNS: 100
LONGEST RUN: 3.2miles (4.8km)
TOTAL LIFTS: 33 - 2 Gondolas, 1 cable-car, 35 chairs, 4 drags, 1 Magic carpet
CAPACITY (people per hour): 49,500
LIFT TIMES: 8.30am to 9.00pm
MOUNTAIN CAFES: 3

AVERAGE SNOWFALL:
11m
SNOWMAKING:
50%

WINTER PERIODS:
Nov to May
Lift Passes
1 Day pass - $54 Night pass - $20 2 Day pass - $98 5 Day pass - $230 Season pass - $1,495. with 1 day and afternoon pass you get free night boarding
Board Schools
group $43/2hr, private $90/hr
Hire
board & boots $37/day, 5 days/$148
Night Boarding
4pm-9pm, costs $20. Pipe & lit

FREERIDE 50%
A few tree & good backcountry
FREESTYLE 25%
3 Terrain parks & 2 halfpipe
CARVING 25%

Squaw Valley Ski Corporation
P.O. Box 2007
Olympic Valley CA 96146
Tel: 001 (530) 583-6985
Fax: 001 (530) 581-7106
Snowphone: 001 (530)583-6955
Web:www.squaw.com
Email:squaw@squaw.com

NEW new for 04/05 season
Beginner double chairlift at the Papoose Learning Area, a second magic carpet transport lift for the Squaw Kids Children's Center

Squaw is well used to looking after its visitors, with a substantial mountain on which to do so. 4000 acres of open bowl riding, 6 peaks, 30 lifts, a total capacity of 49,500 people per hour, 3 fun-parks and 2 halfpipes, combined with an average of 450 inches of snow a year (with massive amounts of snowmaking too), makes Squaw a great riders' hangout. Countless snowboard action videos feature the slopes of Squaw and it's easy to see why. Located a stone's throw from its neighbour **Alpine Meadows**, Squaw has heaps of terrain for all styles of rider to conquer - steeps, trees, long chutes, as well as easy flats for novices. Like many of the resorts in the Tahoe region, Squaw serves the weekend city dweller. Don't despair though as the slopes can still be fairly quiet during the week-days leaving plenty of powder and open runs to shred.

FREESTYLERS have been able to ride Squaw's excellent halfpipes and parks for a good number of years. The **Belmont park's** a good place for first timers to head, and you won't get too much stick if you mess up an approach. The **Central Park** fun-park geared towards the intermediate and features many obstacles to catch air and is one the best kept terrain parks in the US. There's a 250ft halfpipe, 4 or so rails, and and a couple of table-tops. **Mainline parks**, where you'll find the 500ft superpipe; shaped with a Pipe Dragon and has perfectly cut walls that most resorts only dream about. There's a variety of rails and jumps, and the staff keep things regularly changed, so you're not sure what you'll get, but you can be sure it'll be loaded. You can also ride the park and pipe at night until 9 pm

U S A   C A L I F O R N I A

333

THE TOWN & GETTING THERE

FREERIDERS wanting an adrenalin rush will be able to get it in an area known as the **KT22**. This particular area is rated double expert, and it's for no mean reason. Lose it up here and its all over - your own dear mother wouldn't even recognise your body, so be warned. Powder-seekers will find some nice offerings around **Headwall**, or over at **Granite Chief** which is a black graded area (not for wimps) with well spread out trees.

pic - Squaw Resort

pic - WSG

CARVERS in hard boots and piste-loving freeriders in softs, will not want to leave the amazingly well groomed slopes at Squaw. The runs off Squaw and **Siberia Express** are superb for laying big carves and can be tackled by all levels. **Gold Coast** is a long trail that will leave you breathless if do it in one.

BEGINNERS have a great resort to start mastering the art of staying upright. Much of the novice terrain is to be found at the base area, while the bulk of easy trails are located further up the slopes and reached off Super Gondola or the cable car. Once up, the smattering of greens and blues are serviced by a number of chair lifts, so you can avoid the T-bars during the early stages of snowboarding.

THE TOWN

Away from the slopes, Squaw has gained a reputation of being both expensive and a bit snobbish, and in both cases, it's true. But don't be put off as the place has a good buzz about it, and the locals are really friendly. Lodging, feeding, partying and all other local services are convenient for the slopes. The village packs in a raft of activities with ice skating, climbing walls and a games hall. Getting around is easy, although having a car would allow you to travel around at your own leisure.

Accommodation is offered with a number of places close to the slopes. But it will cost you. Condo's are plentiful and well equipped, but not all affordable. For a cheap and comfortable place to stay, check out the *Youth Hostel* - it has bunks at happy prices but bring your own sleeping bag. Check Squaws web site for the latest deals.

Food. Like any dollar-hungry mountain resort, expect to notch up some mileage on the credit card. Even a burger can set you back a small fortune. But as there are so many eating options, even the tightest of tight riders will be able to grab some affordable scram.

Night-life is aimed at the rich, so if you find that Squaw's local offerings are not your style, then try out the far more extensive facilities on offer in nearby **Truckee** or **Tahoe City** where you'll find the best night spots and local talent. You can either drive down, or catch a bus or taxi. Check out *Red Dog* or *Naughty bar*.

SUMMARY. Great all-round resort with snowboarding to suit all levels and styles. Excellent halfpipe and good novice slopes. Very good local services.

CAR
42 miles from Reno, NV, 96 miles from Sacramento, and 196 miles from San Francisco via Interstate 80. Resort is 8 miles from Truckee and 6 miles from Tahoe City and the North Shore of Lake Tahoe, on Hwy 89
FLY
to Reno International (42miles), transfer time to resort is 1 hour
TRAIN
Amtrak to Truckee, 6 miles away
BUS
from Reno takes around 1 hour. A Grey Hound bus from San Francisco takes 5 hours via Tahoe City, 6 miles away. Local service runs between Truckee/Tahoe to Squaw. Call (530) 550-1212

U
S
A

C
A
L
I
F
O
R
N
I
A

Sugar Bowl has numerous points that it likes to draw to people's attention, such as the fact that it is one of the oldest resorts in **California** and was fathered by no less than **Walt Disney** many years ago. However, don't

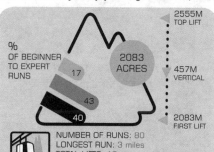

%
OF BEGINNER
TO EXPERT
RUNS

2555M
TOP LIFT

2083
ACRES

457M
VERTICAL

17

43

40

2083M
FIRST LIFT

NUMBER OF RUNS: 80
LONGEST RUN: 3 miles
TOTAL LIFTS: 13
1 gondola, 10 chairs, 2 drags
LIFT TIMES: 9am - 4pm

AVERAGE SNOWFALL:
12.7m
SNOWMAKING:
13%

WINTER PERIODS:
Nov to April
Lift Passes
1/2 Day Pass - $35, Day Pass - $50
Season Pass - $900
Board Schools
private $90/hr
Hire
Boards & Boots from $39/day

FREERIDE 50%
Lots of tree & good backcountry
FREESTYLE 25%
A Terrain park & halfpipe
CARVING 25%

Sugar Bowl
P.O. Box 5 (Mailing)
629 Sugar Bowl Road (Physical)
Norden, CA 95724
Phone: (530) 426-9000
Snow Phone: (530) 426-1111
Fax: (530) 426-3723
Web:www.skisugarbowl.com
Email:info@sugarbowl.com

Bus
from Reno to the resort.
Fly
to Reno, transfer time is 40 minutes.
Drive
From San Francisco - Take Bay Bridge
to Interstate 80, head east toward
Sacramento/Reno. exit at the Norden/
Soda Springs off ramp. Turn right on
Highway 40 eastbound, continue 3 miles

be alarmed; Donald Duck and Mickey Mouse are nowhere to be seen, although many of the skiers here do resemble a bunch of Plutos. Sugar Bowl is a nice little gem of a place that should keep you amused for a few days, but it should be pointed out that this place can become a little crowded over holiday periods etc. The terrain is evenly split over three main areas that are connected, **Lincoln, Mt Judah**, and **Mt Disney**. Lincoln and Mt Disney offer some of the most testing runs with a cool selection of black trails and a couple of double black diamonds. Mt Judah has the most sedate terrain and best for beginners and intermediates. The resort offers base facilities where you can get snowboard hire.

FREERIDERS will be pleased with Sugar's nice offering of trees, back bowls and morning powder trails. The black runs on **Mt Disney** will sort out the wimps from the men, with some very challenging trails especially the area off the **Silver Belt** chair lift where you will find a steep cliff section.

FREESTYLERS are more than welcome here and have full access to all three areas. On **Mt Judah** there is an extremely well constructed terrain park which was originaly designed by the one time pro-rider **Noah Salasnek.** The park is easily accessed via the Mt Judah lift and is loaded with a cool series of hits. The resort also boasts a well carved out halfpipe known as **Scorpion Halfpipe**, where air heads can get some big air. CARVERS are not noted for loving this place as either the trails are a little uneven or not particularly long, but that said Sugar Bowl is still okay with a few good cruising trails.

BEGINNERS will find that the best laid out easy terrain is available on **Mt Judah**, which has a particularly good easy section for novices to shine on. The section of the **Christmas tree** chair is also noted for being a good easy area.

THE TOWN

Off the slopes there is some very limited accommodation in the base lodge, which houses a hotel and can be reached via the gondola. However, the best option and biggest choice of local services can be found in the nearby town of **Truckee** which is only 10 miles away.

U
S
A

C
A
L
I
F
O
R
N
I
A

335

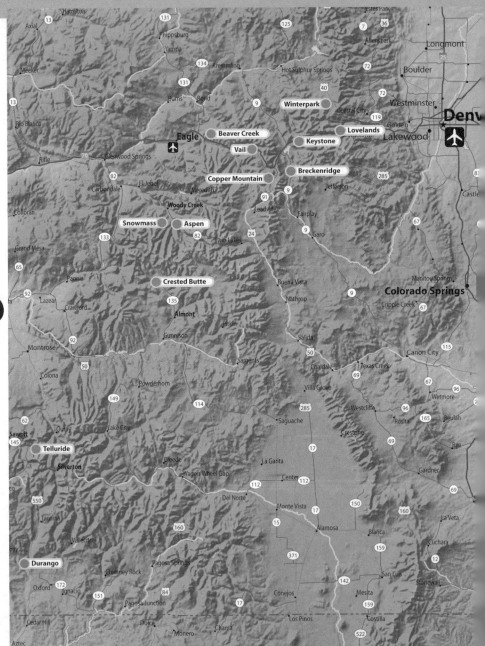

pic - Bob Winsett

8 OUT OF 10

Good riders resort with good carving and freestyling

pic - bdk Affect Beaver Creek Resort

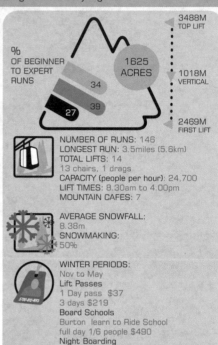

%
OF BEGINNER
TO EXPERT
RUNS

1625 ACRES

34
39
27

3488M TOP LIFT

1018M VERTICAL

2469M FIRST LIFT

NUMBER OF RUNS: 146
LONGEST RUN: 3.5miles (5.6km)
TOTAL LIFTS: 14
13 chairs, 1 drags
CAPACITY (people per hour): 24,700
LIFT TIMES: 8.30am to 4.00pm
MOUNTAIN CAFES: 7

AVERAGE SNOWFALL:
8.38m
SNOWMAKING:
50%

WINTER PERIODS:
Nov to May
Lift Passes
1 Day pass $37
3 days $219
Board Schools
Burton learn to Ride School
full day 1/6 people $490
Night Boarding
No

FREERIDE 55%
Good tree runs & good backcountry
FREESTYLE 25%
4 Terrain parks & 2 halfpipes
CARVING 20%

Beaver Creek Resort
P.O. Box 915 Avon
CO 81620
General info: 001 (970) 949 5750
Reservations: 001 (800) 404 3535
Snowphone: 001 (970) 476 4888
Web:www.beavercreek.com
Email:bcinfo@vailresorts.com

U

U
S
A

C
O
L
O
R
A
D
O

Beaver Creek, a short distance from its more famous cousin **Vail**, has a classy and expensive reputation - an ex-US President even has a house here. But don't let that put you off as this is a resort that has come of age with a really healthy attitude towards snowboarding, as seen by the provision of so many snowboard services. Even some of the local riders give up their time to board what they call the Snowboard Courtesy Patrol, which is a group of snowboarders that patrol the area's slopes to offer assistance and keep everyone in check. **Beaver Creek** is a relatively new resort, but unlike some old timers, it has managed to get things right. The well set out lift system is located on four areas, with runs that favour intermediate riders for the most part. The trails, which are cut through thick wooded areas, are shaped in a way that allows you to get around with ease, making riding here an ideal experience

FREERIDERS are presented with a series of slopes, covered in trees from top to bottom. If you like to ride hard and fast, then the double black diamonds on **Grouse Mountain** off the Grouse chair will satisfy you. Here you can drop down a line of four steep trails, where the longest, **Royal Elk,** sweeps in an arc through trees, whilst **Osprey** is the shorter of the four. Alternatively, the **Half Hitch** and single black trails found off the **Centennial** chair are less daunting, but just as much fun. If you prefer tree runs, make sure to check out the areas in the **Bachelor Gulch & Arrowhead Villages.** Enjoy established runs such as **Coyote Glade** and **Renegade**, or carve your own runs through the powder-filled trees in both Villages. To ride the best spots, hook up with a local snowboard guide.

FREESTYLERS will find plenty of big natural hits to float air. If you're a park rider, then head for any of the three parks Beaver Creek has to offer depending on your ability. For the 03/04 season, Beaver Creek introduced a new park system with it's "**Park-ology.**" The new system features three parks, beginning with **Park 101** for those new to the park that features rollers, dots and other terrain features that will allow lower level riders of all ages to learn. For intermediate park riders, **Zoom Room** features small rollers, tables and rails, and moves to progressively larger features and rails throughout. The most advanced park, **Moonshine**, is designed to be user friendly for

THE TOWN & GETTING THERE

pic - Jack Affleck/Beaver Creek Resort

THE TOWN

Beaver Creek is a major in terms of dullness. However, the village is a laid back place and locals are very friendly. Beaver is a much quieter hangout than nearby Vail, which may be why the place attracts nice family groups that walk around holding hands and smiling as they go. The resort offers all the normal **Colorado** tourist attractions from hot air baloon rides to sleigh rides and an attraction called the Adventure Ridge. You can hire full snowboard equipment at Beaver or in Vail with prices much the same wherever you go, from around $35 a day. Check out the Otherside Snowboard Shop at 001 (970) 845- 8969

intermediate to expert riders looking to improve their skills on a wide variety of features, including tables, hips, spines, rails, logslides and half-pipe.

CARVERS are much in evidence here, and with so many good carving trails, it's no wonder. Edge-to-edge stylers are attracted by the extremely well groomed trails that descend from all areas of the resort, which twist and wind their way through the tree-lined trails. The **Centennial** trail is an extremely popular run that starts off at the top of the Centennial lift. Starting as a black run and descending into a more sedate blue down to the base area, it can be done in a short space of time if you can hang on at the start.

BEGINNERS will find the best easy trails are to be found at the top of the **Cinch Express** Lift. To get down from the beginner area, take the Cinch green run back to the village. A nice touch at Beaver Creek is the kid's fun-park, **Chaos Canyon** Adventure Zone, which has a series of small hits. Riders who have never been on a snowboard will learn quickly if they visit the local snowboard school, which has a high reputation. Burton runs a learn to ride Method Center here.

Accomodation. There are no real cheap options for lodging in Beaver - in short, prices start at silly and go up to downright criminal. There are plenty of beds with many close to the slopes, but for budget riders, you are better looking for somewhere to kip in the small, nearby hamlet of Avon.

Food. If your sole reason for visiting Beaver is the food, you will find a variety of mostly costly, but good restaurants to choose from. Vegetarians, vegans, or monster meat lovers will find their every desire well catered for from one end of the village to the other. The Coyote Cafe, which is near the lift ticket office, is noted for good food at okay prices. Other good eateries to try, are The Saddleridge, the Mirabelle or On The Fly for great sandwiches.

Night-life: put simply, is dull and basically non-existent. The bars cater in the main for rich ski-types in expensive cowboy boots, who prefer to sit around log fires talking bull. However, the *Coyote Cafe* is good and worth a visit for a few beers. The best thing to do is head for **Vail** - but remember to have plenty of dollars on you.

U

U S A

C O L O R A D O

CAR
Denver via Interstate 70. Beaver Creek = 120 miles. Drive time is about 2 1/4 hours. Exit Avon
FLY
Fly to Denver International, Transfer time to resort is 2 1/4 hours. Local airport is Eagle County, 10 miles away.
BUS
There are daily bus services from both Denver and Vail/Eagle County airports direct to Beaver Creek

Despite the price, a good resort with some great terrain

Jack Affleck/Brekenridge Resort

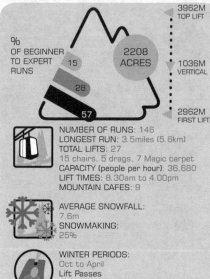

%
OF BEGINNER
TO EXPERT 15
RUNS

2208
ACRES

28

57

3962M
TOP LIFT

1036M
VERTICAL

2962M
FIRST LIFT

NUMBER OF RUNS: 146
LONGEST RUN: 3.5miles (5.6km)
TOTAL LIFTS: 27
15 chairs, 5 drags, 7 Magic carpet
CAPACITY (people per hour): 36,680
LIFT TIMES: 8.30am to 4.00pm
MOUNTAIN CAFES: 9

AVERAGE SNOWFALL:
7.6m
SNOWMAKING:
25%

WINTER PERIODS:
Oct to April
Lift Passes
1 Day pass - $57
3 Day pass - $105
Board Schools
3 days of lessons from $165 with
beginers lift pass for $11/day
park and pipe lasson $60/75
Night Boarding
No

FREERIDE 60%
Trees & good backcountry
FREESTYLE 30%
4 Terrain parks & 4 halfpipes
CARVING 10%

Breckenridge Resort
PO Box 1058
Breckenridge, CO 80424
General: (970) 453-5000
Snow Report: (970) 453-6118
Toll-Free: (800) 789-SNOW
Web:www.breckenridge.com
Email:breckguest@vailresorts.com

new for 04/05 season
Breckenridge 20th anniversary of
Snowboarding is marked with 4 parks and
4 pipes, a new small Zaugg Monster pipe
cutter, a whole series of new rails and an
x-box café for the kids.

NEW

Breckenridge is a true snowboard classic, and has been for many years, having played a leading role in the development of snowboarding in the US. The resort is constantly improving by adding new features to the mountain and around town. Located off Interstate 70, to the west of **Denver** and part of the **Ten Mile Range**, Breckenridge is a big and impressive area with terrain that spreads over four excellent snowboarding peaks, all offering something different for everyone. Some say that the 'new school' style of snowboarding started here, but whether you're from the new or the old, you should have no problems cutting big turns on the mainly wide, open flats

FREERIDERS with their powder-searching heads on will not have to hunt for long when they see what's available in the Back Bowls off **Peak 8** and off **Peak 9**'s North Face. Here you'll find plenty of terrain for riders who know how to snowboard. At the top of Chair 6, you'll find loads of good hits and drop offs, while lower down there are some wicked tree runs. You'll find good powder here, even after everywhere else has been tracked out. The **Imperial Bowl** on Peak 8 has over 1,000 metres of vert to tackle, but there's no lift, so you will need to hike up.

FREESTYLERS should have no reason to complain as apart from having some fantastic natural freestyle terrain, there are also four terrain parks and four pipes of competition standard. The latest addition to Breckenridge is what they call a 'Super Pipe Dragon', the only one in the US which can cut perfectly smooth deep walls. The **Lechman** trail is known for being one of the best natural freestyle runs on the mountain, with loads of hits formed from big wind-lips running down the sides of certain sections. Head for Peak 9 and you'll find the **Gold King** fun-park which is pretty awesome and well-maintained: there are some big, big jumps to go for and thankfully it's groomed at least twice a week, although it does gets icy. There is also a halfpipe, located just above the park, which is shaped with the Pipe Dragon every Thursday and is therefore closed on that day. However, when it's re-opened on Friday mornings, it's perfect - but get up early, because everyone wants to get there first. Peak 8 is home to another park and pipe on the **Fairway** area.

CARVERS have a mountain here that will allow for some very fast and challenging riding on well groomed alpine trails. Speed-freaks should try out the **Centennial** trail, which is a long flat and perfect for cranking big turns on. Intermediates will find the runs off Peak 10 the place to be, in particular the **Crystal**.

BEGINNERS have plenty of easy runs, many of which can be found on Peaks 8 and 9. The fact that novice trails like **Silverthorne** are wide enough for all newcomers helps to make this a great beginners' resort, especially around the **Quicksilver** lift.

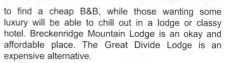

pic - Jack Affleck/Brekenridge Resort

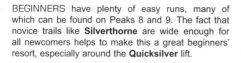

THE TOWN
As with many of Colorado's resorts, **Breckenridge** can be uncomfortably expensive. However, for riders on a tight budget, providing you shop around for accommodation and other local services, you will be able to stay here. The town is spread out, and has a rustic wild west feel about it. You can spend until you drop here with a staggering 225 plus shops, including a number of good outlets for snowboard hire with the option to rent demo boards and step-in set. Other attractions include a new 5 million dollar ice ring and a cool area for skateboarders to do their thing.

Accommodation
options are vast with some 23,000 visitor beds up for grabs. Those on a tight budget will manage to find a cheap B&B, while those wanting some luxury will be able to chill out in a lodge or classy hotel. Breckenridge Mountain Lodge is an okay and affordable place. The Great Divide Lodge is an expensive alternative.

Food, Around town you will find a massive selection of good restaurants and fast food joints ranging from cheap to steep with over 100 places to choose from. Breakfast is dished up in numerous places. The *Prospect* does a nice sunny side up as does the *Mountain Lodge Cafe* . Veggies should head to *Noodle & Bean* for the very same, while meat lovers may want to try a grill at '*Breckenridge Cattle Co*' which is also noted for its fish food.

Night-life is pretty good and rocks until late. There's plenty of beer, dancing and fine local talent to check out, including four main nightclubs and some 80 ood bars. Head to the *Underworld Club*, or *Jake T Pounders* which is young, trendy, fun and one of the main hangouts that has darts, football and pool tables. *Eric's* is another cool hangout.

SUMMARY
Despite being an expensive location, this is a super good resort with great snowboard terrain, and excellent local services.

U

S
S
A

C
O
L
O
R
A
D
O

CAR
Denver via Interstate 70 & Hwy 9. Breckenridge is 81 miles,Drive time is about 1 1/2 hours.
FLY
Fly to Denver International, Transfer time to resort is 1 1/2 hours. Local airport = Eagle Airport (Vail). 63 Miles
BUS
There are daily bus services from both Denver and Vail/Eagle County airports direct to Breckenridge

wsg

COPPER MOUNTAIN

9 OUT OF 10

One of Colorado's best resorts, with some great natural freestyle terrain.

pic - Copper Mountain Resort

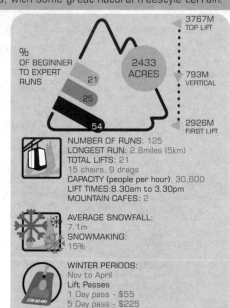

%
OF BEGINNER
TO EXPERT
RUNS

2433
ACRES

21
25
54

3767M
TOP LIFT

793M
VERTICAL

2926M
FIRST LIFT

NUMBER OF RUNS: 125
LONGEST RUN: 2.8miles (5km)
TOTAL LIFTS: 21
15 chairs, 9 drags
CAPACITY (people per hour): 30,600
LIFT TIMES:8.30am to 3.30pm
MOUNTAIN CAFES: 2

AVERAGE SNOWFALL:
7.1m
SNOWMAKING:
15%

WINTER PERIODS:
Nov to April
Lift Passes
1 Day pass - $55
5 Day pass - $225
Season pass - $1000
Board Schools
Various beginner, progression, park &
freeride lesson packages available
Night Hire
Board & Boots package $37/day
Heliboarding
Yes

FREERIDE 45%
Trees & good backcountry
FREESTYLE 25%
2 Terrain parks & 2 halfpipes
CARVING 30%

Copper Mountain Resort
PO Box 3001 (USPS)
209 Ten Mile Circle (FedEx, UPS)
Copper Mountain, CO 80443
Tel: 866-841-2481
Web:www.ride-copper.com

Copper Mountain is considered by many to be one of the best mountains in the USA and since being bought by Intrawest Resorts, the whole place has seen heavy investment to greatly improve a place that was good before. Copper's crowd free slopes with long trails and few traverses appeal to tree-riding fans, and those looking for something interesting to tackle. Powder is in abundance here with four big bowls holding massive amounts of it. Most of the main chairs take around ten minutes to reach their drop off points, although it seems double that time when you're dangling hundreds of feet in the air, with wind driving snow up your nose and down your neck. Still, the lifts are modern and connect well with the runs. Once you get to the top of each run, you will not regret the chair ride as you are presented with a mountain that is lovingly pisted, and well marked out and will make for a great time.

FREERIDERS, welcome to sex on snow! Copper has it all for you. Powder, deep bowls and trees all on offer from expert double blacks to tame piste trails. Take the Flyer chair to reach the Flyer area where you will find a series of blue runs that cut through trees. Alternatively ride the **Sierra lift** to get a powder fix. More advanced riders should take **Lift E** to take on a cluster of short blacks. These are perfect for freeriders, especially the **Union Bowl**. If you keep right off the E-lift, you hit some decent trees. Intermediate freeriders will find plenty to interest them on the run known as **Andy's Encore,** reached off the B-1 chair.

FREESTYLERS have a great mountain to explore with great natural terrain and numerous man made hits in the shape of two halfpipes and a cool terrain park. The Tsunami halfpipe is a massive pipe that's is regularly used for competitions. To get to it, simply take the **American Flyer lift** via the Carefree trail. Coppers

Terrain Park is noted for having a great series of hits furthermore all the hits are colour-graded for different rider standards, just like the runs. Natural terrain seekers should find **Union** and **Spaulding Bowls** the areas to check out for wind-lips, rock jumps and hits galore. Copper has a programme called the Team. If you volunteer to help look after the park and pipe, you will get a free season pass. tel 001 970 968 2318 for details.

CARVERS will find that this is definitely a place for them, with plenty of advanced and intermediate wide

U
S
A

C
O
L
O
R
A
D
O

open trails to choose from. Trails are groomed to perfection and runs like **Bittersweet** are a carvers dream.

BEGINNERS who come here won't be disappointed. Copper has more than sufficient areas for learning the basics and progressing onwards. There are plenty of easy green trails. The tree-lined runs of the American Flyer Quad are a real joy. The flats of K and L lifts are also perfect for first timers.

THE TOWN

Copper Mountain is very much a snowboard-friendly place and the locals will make your stay a good one. However, **Copper** has the usual pitfalls of many Colorado resorts - it can be painfully expensive. But if you're a good scammer, you can stay here on a low budget if you put yourself about and get to know the locals. The resort facilities are very good and un-like many resorts, Copper isn't overloaded with dozens of soppy tourist shops, but rather a need to have selection. There is also a sports centre a swimming pool and gym.

Accommodation in Copper offers slopeside beds, but prices range enormously from $20 up to $800 a night. Staying in nearby Dillon or Frisco would be a good alternative if you're on a tight budget , both have a good selection of cheaper accommodation. For all your lodging needs, contact Copper Mountain Lodging Services.

Food. The menus on offer here are perfect for the holiday crowds, but nothing comes cheap - a burger and a coke at Copper Commons is about $6. Still, Farley's does do an affordable steak, while O'Shea's serves up killer breakfasts at very reasonable prices. Pesce Fresco's is another noted eatery with a big menu to choose from. However, for a burger and other light snacks, check out the B-Lift Pub, a favourite with locals and visitors alike.

Night-life around Copper is somewhat tame. The main hang outs being B-Lift Pub, O'Shea's and Farleys. However, the better option for a night out drinking or pulling a local bit of skirt, is in nearby Breckenridge or Vail. The choice of bars is much better, but unless you're 21+, and have ID to prove it, you're going to be seriously bored.

SUMMARY

One of Colorado's best resorts, with some great natural freestyle terrain. Excellent for beginners. Limited but very good local services.

Money wise: High prices for most things but damn good value for you money

pic - Copper Mtn Resort

CAR
Denver via Interstate 70, Copper Mountain is 78 miles, drive time is about 1 1/2 hours.
FLY
Fly to Denver. International Transfer time to resort 1 1/2 hours. Local airport is Eagle County, 20 miles away.
BUS
Colorado Mountain Express run transfers from Denver airport to resort every 90 minutes. Price is $108 return and takes 2 hours. Call 970-241-1822 for details

343

Pic - Joseph Rehana

U
S
A

C
O
L
O
R
A
D
O

Crested Butte is one of Colorado's ex-mining haunts and well worth a visit. It has gained a good reputation as a snowboard-friendly resort, but is best known for is its extreme and hard core terrain. Indeed, you could call this place the extreme freerider's heaven in the USA, as it has successfully staged several US Extreme Snowboarding Championships. The resort was bought in 2004 by the Muellers who also own **Okemo Mountain Resort** in Vermont. They are planning some huge investments in the resort, with the long term aim to expand terrain to nearby **Snodgrass Mountain**. Crested Butte easily offers some of the most challenging snowboarding in America. What you get is a serious mountain for serious riders, and not your typical dollar-hungry **Colorado** destination. If you like your mountain high with steeps, couloirs, trees, major off-piste in big bowls, then Crested Butte is for you. With 85 runs, spread over 1,160 acres, no-one needs to feel left out, on crowd-free slopes, with a good average snow record. What's more, if you fancy riding during November, pre-Christmas, as well as the latter part of April, you can ride for nothing, or put another way, free of charge!

FREERIDERS are in command here, with much of the terrain best suited to riders who know how to handle a board and prefer off-piste. Extreme Limits is a gnarly, un-pisted heaven for extreme lovers wanting big hits and steeps. Check out **Headwall** and **North Face** for some serious double black diamond trails, offering cliffs, couloirs and trees. In order to stay safe and appreciate Crested Butte's extreme terrain, you are strongly advised to get a copy of the **Extreme Limits Guide**, which is a separate lift and trail guide, pinpointing how and where to ride. Ignore its advice, and you may not live to regret it. However, don't simply read the guide and head off, you **MUST** also seek

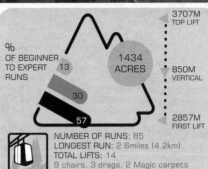

% OF BEGINNER TO EXPERT RUNS

1434 ACRES

13

30

57

3707M
TOP LIFT

850M
VERTICAL

2857M
FIRST LIFT

NUMBER OF RUNS: 85
LONGEST RUN: 2.6miles (4.2km)
TOTAL LIFTS: 14
9 chairs, 3 drags, 2 Magic carpets
LIFT TIMES: 8.30am to 4.00pm
MOUNTAIN CAFES: 8

AVERAGE SNOWFALL:
6.1m
SNOWMAKING:
25%

WINTER PERIODS:
Nov to April ,
Lift Passes
1 day $63
5 days $280
Board Schools
Private lesson $195 for 2hrs. Varrious 2hr group workshops around $80 for beginners to advanced
Hire
Board & boots $21.25 per day. Top demo kit available for $32.40 per day

FREERIDE 60%
Trees & good backcountry
FREESTYLE 25%
1 Terrain park & 1 halfpipe
CARVING 15%

Crested Butte Mountain Resort
12 Snowmass Road
P.O. Box 5700
Mt. Crested Butte, CO 81225
Web:www.skicb.com
Email:info@cbmr.com

NEW

new for 04/05 season
Under new ownership (they also own Okemo resort). Prospect lift with 3 new trails with 15 acres of intermediate terrain. Magic carpet lengthened for beginers, much improved beginners park.

Pic - Joseph Rehana

CRESTED BUTTE

THE TOWN & GETTING THERE

the services of a local snowboard or ski guide as well.

FREESTYLERS will find that a two week stay would still not be enough time to check out all the natural options for going airborn. Check out Crested Butte's gnarly fun-park, which has rails, logs, table-tops, quarter-pipes and is also skier-free. To get to the park, take the Silver Queen or Keystone lift.

CARVERS who choose a resort because of its motorway-wide, perfectly groomed slopes without

Pic - Joseph Rehana

a bump in sight, may feel a bit left out, but not too disappointed. You can still carve hard on a number of selected trails. For a fast trail, give **Ruby** a try, or check out the flats on the **Paradise Bowl.**

BEGINNERS cutting their first runs would do best to ride on the lower slopes near the village, before trying out **Poverty** or **Mineral Point** off the Keystone lift. There are a number of green runs to tackle before trying some of the easy connecting blues. The runs off **Gold Link** lift are pretty cool and worth a go. A beginners learn to snowboard programme with lift, lessons and hire, costs from around $80.

THE TOWN
Visitors coming here expecting to find the all too often horrible Colorado-style, glitzy ski-tourist trap, will be pleased to note that **Crested Butte** is none of that. This is a friendly and welcoming place with services located at the base area or in the old town, a short bus journey away. Wherever you stay, there is plenty to keep you entertained at prices that don't always hurt. Local facilities include basic sporting outlets, a

swimming pool, a gym, and an ice rink. There is also a cinema with the latest movies on show. But note, this is not a place loaded with attractions, but more of a place where you can sit back and relax without being over pampered. Colorado Boarders Shop is the place for hire and snowboard sales.

Accommodation is available at the slopes or in the old town, and together they can sleep 5,000 visitors in a choice of condos, hotels and B&B's. Prices vary, with rates as low as $25 a night in a B&B, or as high as $300 in a fancy hotel. The nearer you stay to the slopes, the more costly things are, making the old town the cheapest option.

Food. Fatties on a mission to eat fast, hard and cheaply, welcome - you have arrived in heaven. This place is littered with eateries in every price range. For a hearty breakfast, there are a number of good places to visit such as *Forest Queen*, The *Woodstone Grill* or the *Timberline Cafe*, all three open early. Later on in the day, check out *Idle Spur* where they serve damn fine steaks cooked exactly to the way you like it.

Night-life comes with a cowboy theme without the flashiness or bright lights. You can drink in a relaxed atmosphere at a number of joints that go on until the early hours. *Talk of the Town* has a punkish reputation and worth a visit. The *Idle Spur* is another cool hang which offers a good selection of beers and often has live music.

SUMMARY
The dog's balls for backcountry riding, but also a piste-loving carver's destination and good for beginners. Good and friendly local services.

Pic - Joseph Rehana

CAR
From Denver take Highway 285 south to Poncha Springs ,Highway 50 west to Gunnison , then Highway 135 north into Crested Butte, total 233 miles, drive time is about 6 1/2 hours.
FLY
Fly to Denver International, transfer time to resort is 6 1/2 hours. Local airport = Gunnison, 30 miles south.
BUS
There are daily bus services from both Denver and Gunnison airports direct to Crested Butte.

7 OUT OF 10

Good resort for all

U
S
A

C
O
L
O
R
A
D
O

%
OF BEGINNER
TO EXPERT
RUNS

3299M
TOP LIFT

1200
ACRES

618M
VERTICAL

23

26   51

2680M
FIRST LIFT

NUMBER OF RUNS: 85
LONGEST RUN: 2miles (3.2km)
TOTAL LIFTS: 11 - 9 Chairs, 2 drags
CAPACITY (people per hour): 15,600
LIFT TIMES: 8.30am to 4.00pm

AVERAGE SNOWFALL:
6.6m
SNOWMAKING:
20%

WINTER PERIODS:
Nov to April
Lift Passes
Day Pass $55/59, 4 Days $200/216
Board Schools
Group $40 2.5 hours
Private lessons $140 for 2hrs, $300 all day
Snowmobiles
$50 one hour, $170 four hours
Hire
board and boots $28/32 per day

FREERIDE 40%
Lots of trees & good backcountry
FREESTYLE 30%
2 Terrain parks & a halfpipe
CARVING 30%

Durango Mountain Resort
#1 Skier Place
Durango
Co 81301
Tel - 970.247.9000
Web:www.durangomountainresort.com

Bus
Bus services from Denver are available
but not direct.
Fly
American Airlines offers daily nonstop
jet service from Dallas to Durango whic
means a one-stop connection from mos
anywhere in the country. Additionally,
connecting flights into Durango are
offered from Denver on United Express,
from Phoenix on America West Express
and from Albuquerque on Rio Grande Ai
Drive
30-minute drive from downtown Durango
Roads to the resort are multi-lane, and
there are no mountain passes to cross.
Albuquerque is a 3 1/2 hour drive to the
south. Denver is 6 hours northeast, and
even Phoenix is an easy day's drive.

Durango Mountain Resort was formerly known has **Purgatory** and changed its name when it was taken over in 2000. Its a fantastic place and one that doesn't come with all the razzamatazz and ponciness that many of **Colorado's** other resorts have. What's more, this place is not an over priced hunt designed for Dot.Com millionaires, this is a place where riders who like to ride hard and then relax with ease, can do so at resort that is friendly and extremely well set out. This can be said for both on and off the mountain and down town in Durango, which is 25 miles away. Although Durango is under new management, there has been a ski centre here for the past 36 years, and the future looks good for this place with a number of major developments taking place up on the slopes and down in the base village of Purgatory. On the slopes you have a surprisingly well laid out selection of runs that provide something for everyone with a good choice of advanced and excellent intermediate slopes.

FREERIDERS have a wonderful mountain to play on. A weeks visit won't be wasted here with a good selection of runs to choose from with some very fast descents through trees and some fine powder stashes to seek out. The runs located under and around the **Grizzly chair** lift are cool and will offer the advanced rider a good time. The **Bull Run** is especially good but be warned, the lower section is not for the faint hearted. For some less daunting descents try the runs off the **Hermosa** Quad. Snowcat boarding is a good option to find some great untracked lines.
FREESTYLERS have plenty to do here with a choice of terrain parks and halfpipes. **Paradise Terrain Park** has a 450ft half-pipe, hits, rails & drops. **Pitchfork Terrain Park** features hips, rails, table tops, gaps, big air hit.
CARVERS have a series of cool cruising trails but in truth this place is more of a freerider's resort. Still, runs like the **Path** of Peace is a good intermediate cruising trail.
BEGINNERS can almost ride from the top to the bottom on a nice cluster of easy green trails reached off the Hermosda lift.

THE TOWN
If you wish to lodge close to the slopes, then theres 3,120 beds near the resort , but a cheaper bet is to head 25 miles over to **Durango**. Theres 7,000 beds there, as well as okay restaurants and bars.

KEYSTONE

Not really up to much

Keystone has been a ski resort since 1970, but it was only in 1997 that the management finally broke down and allowed snowboarders to use their mountain. The new found

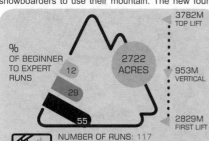

%
OF BEGINNER
TO EXPERT
RUNS

12
29
55

2722 ACRES

3782M
TOP LIFT

953M
VERTICAL

2829M
FIRST LIFT

NUMBER OF RUNS: 117
LONGEST RUN: 3miles (5km)
TOTAL LIFTS: 20 - 2 Gondolas, 12 Chairs, 2 drags,4 magic carpet
CAPACITY (people per hour): 35,175
LIFT TIMES: 8.30am to 8.00pm

AVERAGE SNOWFALL:
5.84m
SNOWMAKING:
35%

WINTER PERIODS:
Nov to April
Lift Passes
1 Day pass - $55
2 Day pass - $110
Night ride - $39
Board Schools
Full-day lesson, lift and equipment - $103
Hire
board and boots $28 per day
Night Boarding
closes 8.00pm 15 trails, half pipe & park

FREERIDE 60%
Lots of trees & good backcountry
FREESTYLE 20%
A Terrain park & halfpipe (floodlit)
CARVING 20%

Keystone Resort
PO Box 38
Keystone, CO 80435
Tel: 001-970-496-2316
Web:www.keystoneresort.com
Email;keystoneinfo@vailresorts.com

Bus
from Denver take 1 1/4 hours and from Vail 1 hour.
Fly
to Denver Int a 1,3/4hr transfer time.
Drive
From Denver, head west on I-70 via the Eisenhower tunnel to Dillion. Exit at the junction 205 to Hwy 6 onto Keystone, a further 6 miles.

pic - Tim Axe/Keystone Resort

tolerance of 'knuckle draggers' has not impressed all parties, (ie skiers) especially since Keystone seems to have embraced snowboarding whole-heartedly. A snowboard-specific section combines a halfpipe with a snowboard park. There's also a snowboard school and the largest board rental shop in North America. Keystone is owned by **Vail** Associates, who also own Vail, Beaver Creek, Breckenridge and Arapahoe Basin - all these resorts offer a multi-area pass. Boarders were excited at the opening of Keystone for many reasons: they have the only gondola in Summit County and it also offers the county's only night-boarding area, where you can ride 15 lit trails until 8pm.

FREERIDERS can roam freely over Keystone's three connected mountains: **Keystone** Mountain, **North Peak** and The **Outback**. Keystone is the front mountain and is laden with jib runs like Paymaster and Spring Dipper. It's a good idea to have someone to spot your blind landings off the big rollers as it gets real busy. North Peak and Outback offer steeps and open tree runs.
FREESTYLERS now have a 20 acre fun-park and two halfpipes located in the Packside Bowl. The main pipe is widely hailed as excellent, with walls reaching 3m in high season. The park's hits and layout have received less praise, but it's hoped that the new season will see changes. One major problem with the park is that it is next to the slalom course and the main ski-school area: more than one day-glow, spandex-clad racer has nearly been decapitated as they stupidly take a short cut across the park.
CARVERS will be delighted to know that Keystone grooms some of their runs twice a day, leaving lots of terrain to lay out big turns.
BEGINNERS may find that overall the area is not a great novice resort as there are too many flats and too much traversing.

THE TOWN
Over the past few years Keystone has been engaged in a multi-dollar redevelopment plan. This has lead to the building of the River Run area which is a collection of condos within walking distance of the slopes. Keystone overall offers a lot of condos and a handfull of hotels with nothing coming in that cheaply. However, eating and drinking options are plentiful, although night time action is lame to say the least.

U
S
A

C
O
L
O
R
A
D
O

347

6 OUT OF 10

Good compact resort

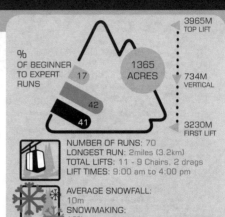

%
OF BEGINNER
TO EXPERT
RUNS

17

1365 ACRES

42

41

3965M
TOP LIFT

734M
VERTICAL

3230M
FIRST LIFT

NUMBER OF RUNS: 70
LONGEST RUN: 2miles (3.2km)
TOTAL LIFTS: 11 - 9 Chairs, 2 drags
LIFT TIMES: 9:00 am to 4:00 pm

AVERAGE SNOWFALL:
10m
SNOWMAKING:
12%

WINTER PERIODS:
Nov to April
Board Schools
Group lessons $40 for 2 1/2 hrs,
packages available that include hire & lift
pass from $63. Private lessons from $70
per hour
Hire
Board & Boots $28 per day

FREERIDE 60%
Lots of trees & good backcountry
FREESTYLE 20%
A Terrain park & a halfpipe
CARVING 30%

Loveland Mountain Resort
Po Box 899
Georgetown CO 80444
Phone: 303-571-5580
Web:www.skiloveland.com
Email:loveland@skiloveland.com

Bus
from Denver available by arrangement.
Fly
to Denver, transfer time 1 hour.
Drive
From Denver, head west on I-70 via Idaho
Springs and turning left onto the route 6
past Georgetown, to reach Loveland. The
distance from Denver is 56 miles.

Lovelands is a resort that has a reputation for good snow, a long season, and a claim to have the world's highest quad chair lift which lets you off at an elevation of 3871 metres. Located close to **Denver**, is definitely a place that is worth a visit and a great one for day trippers, especially for the city slickers from Denver. Despite being close to Denver, however, overcrowding is not a problem and both the lift lines and pistes are often deserted. The resort has recently been investing a lot of dollars in expanding the terrain with the addition of another 400 acres of extreme slopes at the area known as **the Ridge**. A lot of money has also been spent on upgrading the snowmaking facilities to help boost the snow cover. Loveland is not the biggest hill in **Colorado**, but what you get is more than adequate and there are certainly smaller places than this one. What you have is a ridable area that stretches up from two points, Loveland Valley and Loveland Basin that are linked by chairlift and road. Loveland Valley is the smaller of the two areas with a cluster of runs that rise up through some thick wooded glade's that eventually thin out the further up you go. **Loveland Basin**, who's slopes stretched out around a high bowl above the entrance to the **Eisenhower Tunnel**, is the main area to ride with a good choice of runs from basic intermediate trails to some hardcore extreme runs with a few double black diamond extreme slopes.

FREERIDERS should grab the number 2 lift and head up to the Ptarmigan area where you will find lots of cool freeriding terrain. However, some of the best freeride terrain can be found off lift 8 in the **Zip Basin**. Here you will find some nice backcountry type terrain with a few gullies and bowls.

FREESTYLERS have a decent terrain park along with an okay pipe, but in truth some of the natural features are better for air.
CARVERS have a good resort with well maintained trails that are nicely laid out. Some of the best carving is off the number 6 lift.

BEGINNERS can take a lesson here to help then tackle what is largely not a beginner's resort. That's not to say novices should stay away, it's just that the resort is more of an intermediate level.

THE TOWN
While there area boasts a few shops and places to eat, this is not a resort as such. One okay option would be to stay down in Denver where you can't fail to find good local facilities.

SNOWMASS

6
OUT OF 10

Okay, but expensive

Snowmass is the biggest of the resorts that make up the Aspen area, and the second largest resort in **Colorado**. With its four separate peaks, Snowmass is an impressive resort with a lot going for it and warmly

pic - Aspen/Snowmass Resort

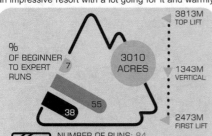

3813M
TOP LIFT

%
OF BEGINNER
TO EXPERT
RUNS

7

3010
ACRES

1343M
VERTICAL

38

55

2473M
FIRST LIFT

NUMBER OF RUNS: 84
LONGEST RUN: 5.05miles (8.2km)
TOTAL LIFTS: 21
17 Chairs, 2 drags,2 magic carpets
CAPACITY (people per hour): 27,978
LIFT TIMES: 8.30am to 4.00pm

AVERAGE SNOWFALL:
7.62m
SNOWMAKING:
5%

WINTER PERIODS:
Nov to April
Board Schools
Full day private $479
Full Day Group $109
Hire
Number of hire shops on mountain

FREERIDE 50%
Trees & good backcountry
FREESTYLE 25%
3 Terrain parks & 2 halfpipes
CARVING 25%

Aspen Skiing Company
Post Office Box 1248
Aspen,
CO 81612
Tel - 800-308-6935
Web:www.aspensnowmass.com

Bus
Bus journeys from Denver, take around
2 1/4 hours.
Buses run between aspen and
snowmass until 2am
Fly
to Denver, with a 3 1/2 hour transfer,
local airport is Aspen, 3miles
Train
Nearest station is Glenwood Springs about
(64 km) from Aspen. www.amtrak.com
Drive
Snowmass Village is located 5 miles off
Colorado 82 via Brush Creek Road. Aspen
is located 5 miles past Brush Creek road
via Colorado 82

welcomes snowboarders. This has not always been the case within the Aspen group, where snobbish areas such as **Aspen Mountain**, still ban snowboarders. However, the 1,246 metres of vertical available here, means you don't have to go anywhere else. Snowmass is mainly an advanced/intermediate rider's retreat, with a good choice of double black diamond runs and trails through trees, steeps and awesome powder making this a place where everyone can get a fix.

FREERIDERS will go crazy here. Snowmass is a real pleasure and offers fantastic riding. Those wanting to cut some serious terrain should check out **Hanging Valley** and **Cirque** for some double black steeps and powder bowls. The run known as **Baby Ruth** is also where advanced riders will get a real buzz. Snowmass offers plenty of backcountry riding with organised tours: Aspen Powder Tours runs trips for riders wanting the ultimate thrill, from around $230 a day.

FREESTYLERS have two halfpipes and a three terrain park, as well as a mountain riddled with natural hits. The main pipe is some 500ft long, with big walls and perfect transitions for getting massive amounts of air. The pipe was originally designed by pro Jimi Scott, and is easily reached off the Funnel lift. There is also a very good fun-park reached off the **Coney Glade** chair lift.

CARVERS have a good selection of wide, open motorway flats for putting in some big carves, with an array of all-level, well groomed trails set out across the area. Big Burn reached off Lift Number 4 is a good intermediate trail.

BEGINNERS cutting their first snow should start at the base area from the Fanny Hill chair lift, before trying out the steeper stuff on the Big Burn. The local ski-school has a 3 day beginner's programme that guarantees you will learn to ride: if you don't, you get an extra day's tuition free.

THE TOWN
The base village has dozens of lodging options, with beds within easy reach of the bottom runs. Evenings are not up to much, but there is a lot more going on in nearby Aspen. For a drink, check out the *Copper Street Pier*, or *Eric's* for a game of pool. Be aware that **Aspen** is super $$$ dollar-hungry.

U
S
A

C
O
L
O
R
A
D
O

349

8 OUT OF 10

Some excellent treeriding, but off the slopes the place is way too stuck up

PIC- Steamboat /Larry Pierce

%
OF BEGINNER
TO EXPERT 13
RUNS

2939 ACRES

56
31

3224M TOP LIFT

1118M VERTICAL

2103M FIRST LIFT

NUMBER OF RUNS: 142
LONGEST RUN: 3miles (4.8km)
TOTAL LIFTS: 20
1 Gondola, 17 chairs, 2 drags
CAPACITY (people per hour): 36,195
LIFT TIMES: 8.30am to 3.30pm

AVERAGE SNOWFALL:
8.19m
SNOWMAKING:
15%

WINTER PERIODS:
Nov to April
Lift Passes
Day Pass - $69
5 out of 6 Day Pass - $335
Season Pass - $1450 (early bird $885)
Board Schools
group clinic all day $27
private 2 hours $235 all day $475
Hire
board and boots $33/day
Snowmobiles
2hr $80, 4hrs $135, all day $175

FREERIDE 60%
Trees & good backcountry
FREESTYLE 20%
4 Terrain parks & 2 halfpipes
CARVING 20%

Steamboat Ski & Resort Corporation
2305 Mt. Werner Circle
Steamboat, CO 80487
Tel: 970-879-6111
Web:www.steamboat.com
Email:info@steamboat.com

NEW new for 04/05 season
$1.3 million spent on new wind powered
chair lift which replaces the old Burgess
Creek Double lift. $2 million spent in
03/04 on various resort infrastructure
improvements.

Steamboat is a curious place in more ways than one. What you get is an old mining town with a seemingly laid back approach coupled with a mountain that offers some great riding with over 2939 acres of terrain that is spread out over four tree-lined mountain peaks. Unfortunately, many will find Steamboat is certainly not the best place to spend a weeks vacation. Although this is not a bad place to visit in terms of the riding opportunities and the good annual snow record, its tacky dollar hungry, fur-clad ski-cowboy image will make most normal snowboarders want to throw up. However, Steamboat has a growing snowboard population and has made a real effort to drag itself into the 21st century (although having live bands playing on the lower slopes on a Friday afternoon is hardly ground breaking stuff). Still, the resort has several things in its favour. The resort offers some fantastic tree-riding, there's ample deep powder and some great carving slopes. There is also a couple of double black diamond trails offering extreme slopes for advanced riders to tackle along with some over-rated blacks for intermediate riders to try out. What is most notable here, are the trees and the options for backcountry snowboarding, which can be explored by taking a snowcat trip organised locally.

FREERIDERS can have a good time at Steamboat. If you're up to the grade, try riding the steeps on the Meadows of Storm Peak, where **Christmas Tree Bowl** and the neighbouring chutes will give you a good challenge. Alternatively, try cutting some deep powder tracks in areas like **Toutes**.

U
USA
COLORADO

STEAMBOAT

FREESTYLERS can catch some decent natural air or sample the man-made hits in the Maverick terrain park on **Big Meadow**. There is also a good pipe called **Dude Ranch** ('Dude' - what a seriously lame name) which is located on the Bashor area and is of competition standard cut by a Pipe Dragon. Less poorly named is the **Beehive**, a small fun-park with a series of mini-hits for kids only, located on the Spike trail reachable off the South Peak lift.

CARVERS have a number of very good descents on which to perfect their technique. Steamboat is also noted for its Olympic race runs, which can be used by snowboarders. Further more, this is also a place where speed skiers, and indeed extreme down hill mountain bikers, often come to practice their thing. Which means the mountain certainly has a number of very gnarly slopes where you can cut it at great speed, but don't go racing down fast runs in an out of control or dangerous manner, because not only will someone get seriously hurt, but the ski patrol will take a very dim view of your actions and throw you off the mountain.

BEGINNERS and total novices will feel most left out here, for apart from some green runs snaking in and out of the higher grade trails, the easy stuff at the base area is often very tiresome. Steamboat has an excellent ski and snowboard school.

THE TOWN
Steamboat is a welcoming town even if it has a poncy feel about it. The town is loaded with all manner of attractions and is well equipped for making your stay

PIC- Steamboat /Larry Pierce

a good one. You can choose to stay on or close to the slopes and the main resort facilities are well located to each other and for the slopes. However, being a dollar-hungry place, those of you on a tight budget may not be able to survive beyond a couple of days here. The cost of most things is unjustifiably high. Which is a shame (perhaps its a deliberate resort policy so they can attract dot.com millionaire's and keep low-lifes away). Around town you will find a host of things to do, from a climbing gym to an indoor ice rink. The town also has a number of shops, with most now catering for snowboarders, some even offer good deals on board sales.

Accomodation. Steamboat has a very good selection of accommodation with loads of lodges, chalets and condo's to choose from.

Food. Steamboat has a good selection of restaurants from fancy dining out joints to a number of fast food places, whether you have a steak or a burger, one thing is for sure, you can guarantee it will be top notch (mind you so will the price). You can eat out in style on the mountain at places like the *Bear River Bar & Grill* or the *Rendezvous Saddle* cafeteria.

Night-life in this over hyped town leaves a lot to be desired and can be best described as crap and aimed at middle-aged skiers with sad dress sense. They have way too much après-ski nonsense here. However, the *Cellar bar* has a good deal going. For $12 you get to drink as much as you can for two hours.

SUMMARY
On the mountain this a great place to ride with some excellent treeriding to try out and some cool carving runs. But off the slopes the place is way too stuck up

PIC- Steamboat /Larry Pierce

U

U
S
A

C
O
L
O
R
A
D
O

CAR
From Denver, head west on I-70 via the Eisenhower tunnel, leave the Silverthrone exit. Then head north along Hwy 9 and Hwy 40. Denver to resort is 167 miles.
FLY
Fly to Denver, with a 4 hour transfer Yampa Valley airport is 22miles from the resort, theres 5 flights daily from Denver & Houston
BUS
Buses from Denver take around 3 hours 20 mins from Yampa.

8 OUT OF 10

Great no nonsense freeriders resort

pic - Telluride Resort

3735M
TOP LIFT

%
OF BEGINNER
TO EXPERT
RUNS

1700
ACRES

24

38

38

1075M
VERTICAL

2660M
FIRST LIFT

NUMBER OF RUNS: 84
LONGEST RUN: 4.6miles (7.36km)
TOTAL LIFTS: 16 - 2 Gondolas, 11
Chairs, 2 drags,1 Magic Carpet
CAPACITY (people per hour): 21,186
LIFT TIMES: 9:00 am to 4:00 pm

AVERAGE SNOWFALL:
7.9m
SNOWMAKING:
15%

WINTER PERIODS:
Nov to April
Board Schools
Beginners and various clinics available
800-801-4832
Hire
Board & Boots $33 per day

FREERIDE 60%
Trees & good backcountry
FREESTYLE 20%
A Terrain park & a halfpipe
CARVING 20%

Telluride Ski and Golf Company
565 Mountain Village Boulevard
Telluride CO 81435
Tel - 970-728-6900
Snow Phone 970.728.7425
Web:www.telski.com
Email: info@tellurideskiresort.com

Fly
Montrose Airport is 65 miles from the
Resort flights from Chicago, Dallas
Houston & Newark. Telluride Airport i
6 miles from the resort & connectin
flights from Denver and Phoenix
Drive
From Denver by way of Grand Junction
- Take Interstate 70 West to Gran
Junction, go South on Route 50 t
Montrose. Continue South on Route 55
to Ridgway then turn right onto Rout
62. Follow this to Route 145 and tur
left. Follow the signs into Telluride.Trave
time - 7 hours
From Colorado Springs - Take Rout
24 West. Turn south on 258/24 an
proceed to Route 50. Turn right on Rout
50. Proceed over Monarch Pass ont
Gunnison and finally Montrose. Turn le
and go South on Route 550 to Ridgwa
then turn right onto Route 62. Follo
this to Route 145 and turn left. Follo
the signs into Telluride. Travel time -
hours.

Telluride sticks two fingers up to convention when it comes to the norm in **Colorado**! Why? Well it's simple, no tackiness, no bull, no hype, no snotty nose yuppies; none of it, what you have here is easily summed up as 'superb'. Telluride, which is said to have been robbed over a hundred years ago by Butch Cassady, is full on, but unlike other resorts in Colorado, this Wild West town won't rob you blind. Telluride, which is an old mining town, is set in the **San Juan Mountains** and is a skiers and snowboarders' heaven that offers every style and ability of rider something to saviour, especially beginners as this place has to be one of the best novices resort in the whole state. Now in it's third year and $14mill later the **Prospect Bowl** area is great, accessed by three high speed quad lifts which lead you to varied runs and the **Ute Park**; It's really opened up this hill.

FREERIDERS who like fast hard steeps will love it here as Telluride offers some fantastic riding. The **Kant-Mak-M**, the **Spiral** and the **Plunge** runs are a series of really challenging steeps that will either leave you seriously bruised if you bail, or make you feel like a god if you complete them in style. These are serious double black diamond trails and not for wimps.

FREESTYLERS who are happy to roam around riding off natural hits are in for a pleasant surprise. The mountain has a number of natural pipes and banks. The **West Drain** slope offers some cool riding due in part to it being a natural half pipe. The **Air Garden Terrain Park** covers 10 acres and features a number of boxes, rails, kickers, table tops and a halfpipe designed for a variety of abilities. You'll find it on **Lower See Forever** area.

CARVERS have a mountain that lends itself perfectly well to cruising at speed, although it should be said that many of the trails are a bit short. Note also that some runs are only pisted on oneside, which means one side being smooth and the other bumpy.

BEGINNERS are probably the one group who will feel most pleased here and most at ease because Telluride not only has a good percentage of easy trails, they are also well set out and very easy to negotiate.

OFF THE SLOPES things are just as good as on them. There are two options to choose from for lodging and local facilities in either **Telluride's** main town or up in the **Mountain Village.** Which every you choose you wont be disappointed as both offer good accommodation, great places to dine and a number of cool bars.

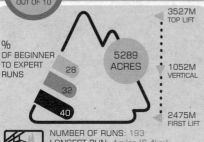

10 OUT OF 10

Fantastic mountain offering great riding for ever style and level of rider

%
OF BEGINNER
TO EXPERT
RUNS

28
32
40

5289 ACRES

3527M
TOP LIFT

1052M
VERTICAL

2475M
FIRST LIFT

NUMBER OF RUNS: 193
LONGEST RUN: 4miles (6.4km)
TOTAL LIFTS: 34
1 Gondola, 23 chairs, 10 drags
CAPACITY (people per hour): 53,281
LIFT TIMES: 8.30am to 4.00pm
MOUNTAIN CAFES: 20

AVERAGE SNOWFALL:
8.5m
SNOWMAKING:
5%

WINTER PERIODS:
Nov to April
Lift Passes
Discounts available by buying in advance
from website. 2004/5 pricing not
released at time of press.
Board Schools
one day group $90/100
1 Hour Private Lesson - $110
3 hours park lesson $80
Hire
board and boots $27/day
Snowmobiles
1 hour from $62
Night Boarding
Yes

FREERIDE 60%
Trees & good backcountry
FREESTYLE 20%
3 Terrain parks & a halfpipe
CARVING 20%

Vail Resorts
PO Box 7
Vail, CO 81658
(970)476-5601
Web:www.vail.com
Email:vailinfo@vailresorts.com

new for 04/05 season
Snowmaking line is being installed at
Golden Peak this summer with new
hydrants and fan guns which will enable
the resort to make more snow faster
on the eastern side of the mountain,
including the eastern off-mountain
routes. A snowmaking project also in
underway on Simba.
- Grooming: 10 new cats to Vail's
snowcat fleet will add 33 percent more
grooming this season,

NEW

PIC- Jack Affleck / Vail Resorts

U
USA
COLORADO

Vail has the reputation of being one of America's most prestigious (ie snobbish) ski resorts, and in some respects it's true. The town of Vail, a bizarre imitation of a 'typical' Swiss alpine village, is centred around the base of the resort and is hellishly expensive. However, there are loads of good reasons to visit Vail, which include the large amount of terrain on offer (over 4,000 acres) and Vail's extremely healthy and positive attitude towards snowboarding. The terrain park has 3 halfpipes and 12 runs, and is also open to skiers although thankfully, it's frequented almost exclusively by snowboarders. One major point regarding Vail is that it is a very popular resort resulting in some long lift queues throughout the season. But in terms of climate and cost, a good time to visit is late season when the snow is soft and the price of lift tickets drop dramatically.

FREESTYLERS are extremely well catered for on Vail's slopes. Vail also provides a major half pipe and terrain park known as the **Golden Peak**. Both park and pipe are groomed to perfection. The pipe has huge walls offering great transitions while the park is loaded with not only a major series of gaps, spines etc, but also a chill out area that has video screens, pumping music and drink vending services.

CARVERS have some excellent blue trails and some challenging fast blacks. Many of the runs start out as one grade and then suddenly become another, so study a lift map in order to negotiate the best spots with ease. The **Avanti** lift gives access to some really nice carving trails. The **Mountain Top** lift also allows you to ride in style on a number of extremely good trails.

PIC- Jack Affleck / Vail Resorts

FREERIDERS will find this place heaven. Vail's Back Bowls will stoke you beyond belief when you see what is on offer. In order to find out where the best places are, you should pick up a copy of the free pocket-sized snowboard mountain map which will point you in the direction of the best boarding trails and hits. The most popular backcountry includes **Ptarmigan Ridge**, a 25ft cornice jump and **Kengis Khan**, another cornice not suitable for sufferers of vertigo. The cliffs under Chair 4 are easier to access, as long as you don't mind your slams being applauded by everyone on the lift. The tree run **Cheeta Gully** is marked as one of the special snowboard trails and will test the most proficient rider.

BEGINNERS have a mountain with so many easy trails and excellent progression possibilities, that if you fail here, you must be a complete loser. The areas of **Golden Peak** are perfect for learning the basics, although it can become a little clustered around midday, especially at weekends and holidays. Vail's snowboard school is excellent and has a number of instruction programmes.

THE TOWN
If you reckon that **Vail** is just about the slopes, think again as there are heaps of things going on with an amazing amount of great local services. The area is huge, so use of the free shuttle bus may be necessary depending on where you base yourself. Recently, merchants & restaurant owners have taken a much-needed approach to offering lower priced options for visitors, including apres, dinner & drink specials. Do your homework before making a choice and you will save much more $$ than you thought. Locals know exactly what to do to make your stay a good one. They offer a high level of service whether you're buying a burger or checking in to a hotel.

Accommodation consists of a selection of some 30,000 visitor beds and providing you don't mind not being slopeside, you will find affordable lodging. Many opt to stay out in one of the nearby villages with cheaper housing and on average, only a 20 minute 'commute' to the slope. Check Vails web site for a full listing of accommodation.

Food. Eating in the resort or around the main area may destroy your bank balance or father's credit card if you don't choose carefully. Some prices are silly, but there are plenty of semi-affordable, fast-food joints to check out. To tickle your taste buds, why not check out *Pazzo's*, which serves a good helping of cheap pasta or where you can have a 'do it yourself pizza'. The *Red Lion* also features good, cheap burgers, sandwiches & fries in one of the most convenient, frequently visited village locations (On Bridge Street, in the heart of all the action).

Night-life, as you'd hope, is extremely good. The offerings are excellent, with good bars and okay places to boogie well into the early hours. Contrary to popular belief, you CAN find cheap drink specials in the heart of the village. Two frequented stops this season included *Fubar* and *8150*, which both featured a $10(US $) all-you-can-drink special on Sunday & Monday nights (we hope to see the return of this unbelievable deal in the 04/05 season). You can also checkout the many après specials, which include $3 beers and discounted appetizers.

SUMMARY
Absolutely fantastic mountain offering great riding for ever style and level of rider. Great local services in and around the resort with lots going on.

CAR
Denver via Interstate 70, take Main Vail Exit (176), 97 miles (156km). Drive time is about 1 3/4 hours.
FLY
Fly to Denver International (110 miles), transfer time to resort is 2 hours. Local airport is Eagle County, 30 miles away, 13 airports offer connection
BUS
There are daily bus services from both Denver and Vail/Eagle County airports direct to Vail.

U
S
A

C
O
L
O
R
A
D
O

6 OUT OF 10

Slopes ideal for pensioners, luckily saved by the terrain parks

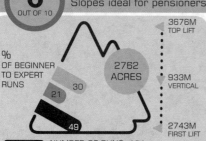

3676M
TOP LIFT

% OF BEGINNER TO EXPERT RUNS

2762 ACRES

30
21
49

933M
VERTICAL

2743M
FIRST LIFT

NUMBER OF RUNS: 134
LONGEST RUN: 5.1 miles (8.2km)
TOTAL LIFTS: 21- 18 chairs, 2 Magic Carpets, 1 Rope tow
CAPACITY (people per hour): 35,030
LIFT TIMES: 8.30am to 4.00pm

AVERAGE SNOWFALL:
9.1m
SNOWMAKING:
20%

WINTER PERIODS:
Nov to April
Lift Passes
1 Day $59,5 of 6 Day pass - $295
Board Schools
Beginners package lift, hire & 2 1/2hr lesson $89/99 per day.
Various group lessons 2 1/2hrs $49/59
Hire
Beginners Board & Boots $28/32
Demo Board & Boots $40/44

FREERIDE 50%
Trees & good backcountry
FREESTYLE 30%
3 Terrain park & 2 halfpipes
CARVING 20%

Winter Park Resort
150 Alpenglow Way,P.O. Box 36
Winter Park, Colorado 80482
tel: (970) 726-5514
Web:www.skiwinterpark.com
Email: wpinfo@skiwinterpark.com

Bus
Bus journeys from Denver take 1 hour.
Fly
to Denver Int, transfer 1 1/2 hours
Drive
From Denver, head west on I-70 via the Eisenhower tunnel to exit 232 on Hwy 40 direction Granby. 67 miles. 1 1/2 hours drive time.
Train
Amtrak's California Zephyr goes to Winter Park daily from Chicago & LA. Ski train weekends from Denver

NEW

New for 04/05
Nothing this season, but Intrawest invested heavily in the terrain parks in 03/04 season

pic - Winterpark Resort

U
S
A

C
O
L
O
R
A
D
O

Winter Park - a mere 67 miles from **Denver,** nestling at the base of Berthoud Pass at an altitude of 2,743 feet, is said to be the fifth largest resort in the USA, with over 2886 acres of terrain. The old saying that 'size always matters' doesn't ring true at winter, since although this place is vast, it is not as great as the hype dictates. However, Colorado is famous for its powder snow and in fairness; Winter Park snags more than its fair share, with an average annual snowfall of 350 inches and plenty of blue sky days. The high tree line of Winter Park means that even when there is low cloud, visibility is still good. Winter Park is actually two mountains, **Winter Park** and **Mary Jane.** Winter Park has trails for all standards of rider and is well groomed. What makes this place somewhat dull is that it is really tame, with hardly any fast, challenging terrain. The best runs (if such exist) are on the Mary Jane slopes and are mostly black trails. There have been some big improvements in the terrain parks in the last couple of years.

FREERIDERS will find plenty of okay tree runs around both mountains with near perfect spaced trees. However, don't expect to ride all the ferns at any great speed. There is some good riding to be had in **Parsenn Bowl** on June Mountain, and on the runs of the **Challenger**.

FREESTYLERS are presented with two fun-parks. The **Rail yard** is the big one designed for the advanced rider. Conditions depending, it has 25 rails, 16 jumps and a superpipe organised into various lines. The **Jack Kendrick** park is set-up for more intermediate riders it has a number of rails and kickers and a less intimidating halfpipe.

CARVERS content with wide pistes where they can pose doing big arcs, will find Winter Park right up their street. Much of what you find on Winter Park Mountain will suit carvers.

BEGINNERS also fair well here. The easy trails, and indeed some of those classed as intermediate, can be ridden within a few days if you put your mind to it.

THE TOWN
Winter Park's lodging is 6 miles down the valley, where you can find a good selection of places to stay at affordable prices. The evenings are not too hectic, but you can party. Check out *Lord Gore Arms* which shows videos every night with DJ's and bands, or The Pub for Sunday night disco mayhem.

355

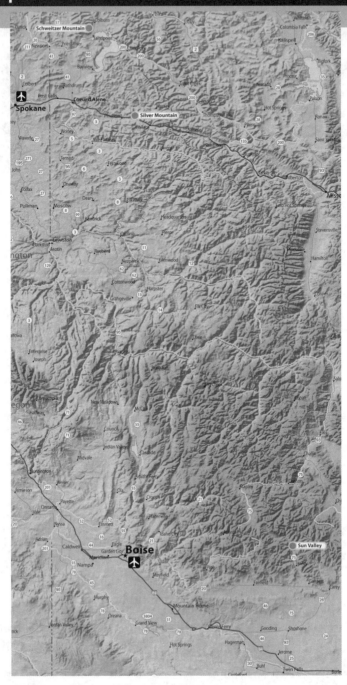

7 OUT OF 10

Really cool resort

1951M TOP LIFT

% OF BEGINNER TO EXPERT RUNS

20
40
40

2500 ACRES

732M VERTICAL

1217M FIRST LIFT

NUMBER OF RUNS: 59
LONGEST RUN: 2.7miles (4.3km)
TOTAL LIFTS: 9
6 chairs, 2 drags, 1 Rope tow
CAPACITY (people per hour):8,092
LIFT TIMES: 9.00am to 4.00pm

AVERAGE SNOWFALL:
7.6m
SNOWMAKING:
10%

WINTER PERIODS:
Nov to April
Lift Passes
1 Day pass - $44/48 .Night pass - $25
Season pass - $709 (early bird discounts available)
Board Schools
One day with pass and board/boots $59
Three days with pass and board/boots $99
Hire
Board and Boots $30/40 day
Helmets $7 day
Night Boarding
Friday/Sat 3pm till 8pm 19 Dec-13Mar

FREERIDE 50%
Trees & good backcountry
FREESTYLE 25%
A Terrain park & halfpipe
CARVING 25%

Schweitzer Mountain Resort
10,000 Schweitzer Mountain Road
Sandpoint, ID 83864
Tel: 001 208-263-9555
Fax: 001 208-263-0775
Web:www.schweitzer.com
Email:ski@schweitzer.com

Bus
from Spokane to resort takes 90 mins
Fly
to Spokane Int. 86 miles south west is served by most carriers. Sandpoint airports handles the seriously minted
Drive
From Spokane, take I-90 east and then Hwy 95 north via the town of Sandpoint. Schweitzer is another 2 miles on.
Train
Sandpoint is nearest station. Amtrak has trains from Chicago & Seattle, 2 miles from resort

pic -Schweitzer Resort

L ying about an hour's drive north of **Couer D'Alene, Idaho**, (and about an hour and a half south of the **Canadian border**) is the town of **Sandpoint**. Sandpoint is in the lucky position of having one of the coolest snowboarding spots in the North-western United States. A mere 10 minutes drive up a beautiful wooded ascent takes you to the Schweitzer basin. Probably unheard of by anyone that hasn't spent time in the area. On top of the amazingly laid back atmosphere of the Northwest in general, Schweitzer enjoys a very low "I snowboard so I'm great" bullshit factor, a problem that needs addressing both in the UK and central states like Utah and Colorado. The resort has a good lift system with reasonably priced lift tickets at $35 a day for the whole mountain - this may also include some excellent night riding on one of the many well lit runs. If you haggle, you might get some bargains for multi-day tickets, or if you are with a group.

FREERIDERS are assured plenty of powder days and an enormously varied selection of terrain from the super steep chutes on the west side of the front half of the mountain, to an amazingly long (and tiring) blue run that starts from one of several high speed, no-queue lifts about 100 feet from the day-lodge. The ridge that links the runs together along the top of the mountain also provides a breathtaking view of **Lake Pend O'Reille**.

FREESTYLERS have a magical mountain do to their tricks on. A favourite with local students, this overlooked mountain provides some great natural kicks, a fantastic half pipe, a boardercross course and an altogether impressive fun park called **Stomping Grounds** where competitions are held throughout the season period.

CARVERS have plenty of groomed stuff on offer and speed perverts can make good on runs such as **Cathedral** and **Zip**

BEGINNERS have no need to worry here as all the novice runs are well away from the main runs so helping to prevent mass collisions, and serviced by a separate chair lift.

THE TOWN
All your local needs are mainly provided down in **Sandpoint** 2 miles away. There is some accommodation available at the base area close to the slopes such as The *Green Gables Lodge* or in one of the condos. Far cheaper lodging can be found in Sandpoint where you will find a basic but okay selection of shops, restaurants and bars. For a burger try the *Powder House* and for a beer give *Roxy's* a try.

U

USA

IDAHO

357

SILVER MOUNTAIN

5 OUT OF 10

Okay but basic

pic -Silver Mountain Resort

% OF BEGINNER TO EXPERT RUNS
20
40
40
1500 ACRES

1920M TOP LIFT
671M VERTICAL
1250M FIRST LIFT

NUMBER OF RUNS: 67
LONGEST RUN: 2.5miles (4km)
TOTAL LIFTS: 7
1 Gondola, 5 chairs, 1 drag
CAPACITY (people per hour):8,200
LIFT TIMES: 9.00am to 3.30pm

AVERAGE SNOWFALL:
6.35m
SNOWMAKING:
15%

WINTER PERIODS:
Nov to April
Lift Passes
Weekday - $23 ,Weekend - $30
Night pass - $12, Season pass - $329
Board Schools
Group lesson from $20, Private 1 hr $49
Night Boarding
Yes

FREERIDE 30%
Trees & some backcountry
FREESTYLE 20%
A Terrain park & halfpipe
CARVING 50%

Silver Mountain Ski Area
610 Bunker Avenue, Kellogg ID 83837
Tel: 001 (208) 783 1111
Web:www.silvermt.com
Email:infosm@silvermt.com

Bus
from Spokane takes 80 mins to Kellogg.
Fly
to Spokane Int, which is 70 miles west
of the resort. Missoula 130miles,
Seattle 350 miles
Drive
From Spokane, take I-90 west past
Coeur d'Alene and then a further 40
miles on to Kellogg. Silver Mountain is
only 1/4 of a mile from Kellogg.

A smaller resort than **Schweitzer**, and much closer to civilisation, is **Kellogg, Idaho**. A small mining town in north central Idaho, about 40 minutes from Couer **D'Alene**, Kellogg has the honour of running the longest gondola ride in the world, which culminates at the day lodge of Silver Mountain. Essentially composed of two resorts, the new Silver Mountain lift system and the incorporated **Jackass Ski Bowl** provide a superb set of runs, although the intermediate rider is better catered for than freestylers or super euro-carvers. In fact, the only real downside to this hidden gem of a mountain is the fact that it is infested with cat tracks linking one run to the next. Easy on skis, a real drag on a board. However, to be fair to the resort management, they are dealing with the problem by getting rid of a lot of the cat tracks. Overall, the mountain offers a fair selection of long steeps with generally great snow and weather conditions. The seven lifts are quick and easy to negotiate and mercifully lift lines are tiny. Slope facilities are a bit suspect, the day lodge is far less impressive than that at Schweitzer, and the food is both mediocre and extortionate. But a major plus is the very low lift prices, with a day pass from only $24 bucks during the week.)

FREERIDERS will find that the backcountry stuff is thin on the ground - unlike tree stumps, grit, and large rocks, which seem to litter a good deal of the area outside the fences. However, some very nice, but challenging, freeriding can be had on areas like the **Rendezvous** or down the **Warner Peak**.

FREESTYLERS note that this is not a place loaded with natural freestyle terrain. However, to counter this there is a good terrain park and halfpipe called the **Trench** which is built and shaped to conform with competition standards located up on Noah's.

CARVERS can ride with some degree of style here, with a number of long cruising trails that are groomed to perfection. The Tamarack is a fantastic two and a half mile long trail to try out.

BEGINNERS have a mountain that is well suited to their needs, with a host of novice trails offering easy sedate descents.

THE TOWN
You can lodge close to the slopes, but in general the main thing to do is base yourself down **Kellogg**, which is 2 minutes away. The town offers a good choice of local facilities with very reasonable prices for lodging and general living. The *Silver Ridge Mountain Lodge* offers some good packages.

SUN VALLEY

A resort that will suit all riders

Sun Valley dates back decades and comes with a fair share of its own history. Said to be the USA's oldest ski resorts, Sun Valley has managed stay up with the times and today is a resort that is a match for any other destination in

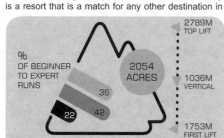

% OF BEGINNER TO EXPERT RUNS

2054 ACRES

36
22
42

2789M
TOP LIFT

1036M
VERTICAL

1753M
FIRST LIFT

NUMBER OF RUNS: 75
LONGEST RUN: 3 miles(5km)
TOTAL LIFTS: 19 - 16 chairs, 3 drags
CAPACITY (people per hour):26,780
LIFT TIMES: 9.00am to 4.00pm

AVERAGE SNOWFALL:
6m
SNOWMAKING:
Unknown

WINTER PERIODS:
Dec to April
Lift Passes
1 Day Pass $48, 6 days $235
Board Schools
2 hours group $453
3 days 6 hours $115
Private 1 hour $95
Night Boarding
No

FREERIDE 50%
Lots of trees & good backcountry
FREESTYLE 20%
A Terrain park & halfpipe
CARVING 30%

Sun Valley Company
Post Office Box 10
Sun Valley, Idaho 83353
Tel: 208-622-2001
Web:www.sunvalley.com
Email:ski@sunvalley.com

Bus
Shuttle bus from Boise, Twin Falls, Pocatello and Idaho falls
Fly
into Sun Valley/Friedman Memorial Airport in Hailey, connections from Salt Lake City,Boise & Utah
Drive
From Boise, head south on I-84 and then via hwy 20 at Mountain Home to hwy 75 heading north following signs for Ketchum and then onto Sun Valley.

pic - Sun Valley Resort

the country. Located in the southern part of Idaho and east of the capital **Bosie**, what you have here is a resort for every one from advanced air heads to total first timers, although it's fair to say that the beginner terrain is a bit limited. On and off the slopes the whole area has a rather strange feel to it with a mixture of the Old Wild West and a hint of Europe thrown in. Its set to a back drop of a large rideable area which covers over 2000 acres and split over two main areas known as **Dollar/Elkhorn** and **Bald Mountain**. Dollar/Elkhorn area the smaller and best for beginners while Bald Mountain is the place to head for to ride some advanced steeps. Whichever area you try out, you will be met with excellent slope facilities which incorporates a high tech snowmaking system that covers over 78% of the slopes.

FREERIDERS who know what life is about and can handle a board at speed will be able to prove it on the slopes up on Bald Mountain which has a good selection of advanced and intermediate trails. The bowls below the Seattle Ridge are superb and will keep you amused for days with some nice powder stashes.
FREESTYLERS are well catered for here with a halfpipe that measures 350 foot long by 80 foot wide and is located on the Dollar area. Riders can also purchase a budget priced lift ticket that covers Dollar and the pipe area. Around the whole area freestylers will find loads of awesome natural hits to get air off.
CARVERS who consider themselves to be of the advanced grade, should look no further than the slopes off Bald Mountain where you'll find a first class selection of long, well pitched cruising runs.
BEGINNERS should be aware of the difference between the main areas. If you are a total first timer to snowboarding then stay away from Bald Mountain and check out the offerings on Dollar. The local ski school offers clinics from $40 a session for all grades.

THE TOWN
Off the slopes, **Sun Valley** is a resort that is fully geared up to handle visitors needs. There is a good selection of slope-side accommodation and excellent resort services with some nice restaurants and good bars, but note this is not a cheap resort.

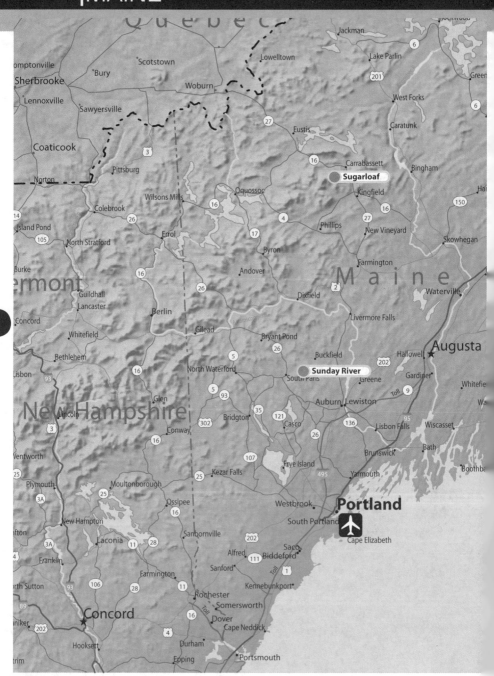

MAINE

SUGAR LOAF

7 OUT OF 10

Some good challenging terrain

By east coast standards, Sugarloaf/USA is a big resort and a highly rated one that is well worth taking the time to visit. Located around two and a half hours drive time from **Portland**, this is a relatively easy place to get to and one could quite easily spend a week riding here on a mountain that has the only treeless summit with lift access in the east. Another notable point is that unlike many other east coast resorts, Sugarloaf/USA

pic - Sugarloaf Resort

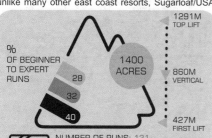

%
OF BEGINNER
TO EXPERT
RUNS

1291M
TOP LIFT

1400 ACRES

860M
VERTICAL

28

32

40

427M
FIRST LIFT

NUMBER OF RUNS: 131
LONGEST RUN: 3.5miles (5.6km)
TOTAL LIFTS: 15 - 13 chairs, 2 drags
CAPACITY (people per hour): 21,810
LIFT TIMES: 8.30am to 3.50pm

AVERAGE SNOWFALL:
5.23m
SNOWMAKING:
92%

WINTER PERIODS:
Nov to May
Lift Passes
Day $57, 2 Days $106 ,6 Days $294
Season Pass - $1295
Board Schools
board clinics $70 inc board and pass
Hire
$32/day, 6Days $153

FREERIDE 35%
Trees & some off-piste
FREESTYLE 20%
A Terrain park & halfpipe
CARVING 45%

Sugarloaf/USA
5092 Access Road
Carrabassett Valley, ME 04947
Snow Phone: 1-207-237-6808
Web:www.sugarloaf.com
Email:info@sugarloaf.com

Bus
from Portland can take a good 3 hours.
Fly
to Portland which is 110 miles away.
Drive
From Portland travel north on the I-95 to Augusta, then take the 27 via Farmington to reach the resort. The journey by car will take about 2 1/2 hours.

manages a longer season than many other east coast destinations as the resort is able to keep hold of its snow very well. What's more, they back up their real snow with snowmaking facilities that cover almost 92% of the mountain. In truth this is a mountain that will mainly appeal to freeriders and carvers. The 131 well groomed and well set out runs offer some very challenging runs with the option to ride down some extreme steeps and fast double diamond black trails.

FREERIDERS are going to feel very much at home here, with a good choice of descents that include acres of **summit bowl** riding and over 500 acres of treeriding terrain. Some of the most challenging terrain to check out can be found off the **Spillway chair** lift, while for a less stressing descent, the **Gauge** is okay. FREESTYLERS can be seen kicking off natural hits all over this mountain as the place lends itself very nicely to natural freestyling. If you can't find a decent hit to please your desires, than Sugarloaf/USA has a massive terrain park and large halfpipe with huge walls and nice transitions. The terrain park comes loaded with hits galore with rails, spines and big gaps, there is also a boarder cross circuit with a number of hits and banks.
CARVERS of all levels will find an abundance of runs to choose from which are laid out all over the mountain starting out at the summit and allowing for long cruising runs all the way back home.
BEGINNERS are presented with numerous trails that are mainly laid out across the lower section of the mountain and although the resort has a lot of good novice areas, the main section is often clogged up with skiers and others using the routes as access to the base, and base lifts.

THE TOWN
Local facilities are well placed for the slopes with lots of condo's available for letting at reasonable rates. Around the resort you will find a good selection of restaurants and a number of nightspots.

U
S
A

M
A
I
N
E

361

pic - Sunday River Resort

975M
TOP LIFT

%
OF BEGINNER
TO EXPERT
RUNS

25

640
ACRES

713M
VERTICAL

35

40

244M
FIRST LIFT

NUMBER OF RUNS: 128
LONGEST RUN: 3miles (5km)
TOTAL LIFTS: 18
15 chairs, 3 drags
CAPACITY (people per hour): 32,000
LIFT TIMES: 8.00am to 4.00pm

AVERAGE SNOWFALL:
6.35m
SNOWMAKING:
92%

WINTER PERIODS:
Oct to May
Lift Passes
1 Day pass - $57
3 Day pass - $150
6 Day pass - $294
Board Schools
Beginner packages inc lift ticket, lesson
& rentail 1 day $75 . 2 days $120.
Private lessons $70 1hr, $110 2hrs
Hire
Board & Boots $30 per day
Night Boarding
No

FREERIDE 40%
Trees but poor backcountry
FREESTYLE 40%
5 Terrain parks & 2 halfpipes
CARVING 20%

Sunday River Ski Resort
P.O. Box 450
Bethel, ME 04217
phone: (207) 824-3000
fax: (207) 824-5110
Web:www.sundayriver.com
Email:info@sundayriver.com

Sunday River, which happens to be one of the major resorts in the American Skiing Co's portfolio, has rapidly grown from a local snowboarder's haunt to a fairly happening place in a very short space of time. Located a stone's throw away from the state border with **New Hampshire**, Sunday River attracts a lot of city dwellers from **Portland** and other nearby towns, to its simple but extremely well laid out slopes that cover eight linked mountains with three resort base areas. Once you arrive, it's not long before you appreciate just why this place is a popular destination with many of Maine's snowboarders and skiers alike as this is an excellent east coast resort which is thick with trees from the top to bottom on all the mountains. All the runs are hacked out from the dense pine to form a cluster of trails suitable for all styles and level of rider, in particular freeriders who know how to go for it. The eight mountain peaks are all open to snowboarders, with over 120 well looked after runs that get a good annual covering of real snow and are backed up by major snowmaking facilities that covers nearly all of the trails. The one off putting point is the crowds, particularly at weekends when the whole mountain can become a bit busy.

FREERIDERS will find that a week's stay here will not be wasted provided you get out and explore all eight mountains. Each one offers something a little different to the last, although in the main they don't vary too much. Still, the resort management have planned the runs and offer different slope pitches and terrain features that will catch you out if you are not concentrating on what you are doing. For those riders who can handle fast steeps, the double blacks on **Oz Peak** and **Jordan Bowl** (especially the double black **Caramba**) are the places to head for. However, beware of **Kansas**, a long, flat muscle-pumping traverse used to get you back to the main area, the trick here is to keep you speed up. Some good tree-riding can be found on the **Baker Mountain**.

FREESTYLERS will find lots of natural hits to catch air, and plenty of places for jibbing off logs and other obstacles. However, for those who like things laid on, Sunday offers a lot more than many other resorts by providing five terrain parks loaded with all sorts of hits, a boardercross circuit and three halfpipes.

CARVERS who like speed and steeps mixed in together can crank some fast turns on the White Heat trails, which is one of the steepest runs on the east coast. The trails on the **North Peak** are ideal

pic - John Quigley

for intermediate riders who like to take it easy.

BEGINNERS here have a resort that is superb for learning at with a large choice of easy runs to try out. The local ski-school offers a great teaching programme called the 'Perfect Turn Snowboard 'Clinic', where they guarantee to teach you to ride in a day, with a maximum of six people in a class.

THE TOWN
Off the slopes, local services are initially provided in the base areas where you will find a good selection of slope side lodging with condo's being the main choice. However, you may find it better to take the four mile drive back down to **Bethel** which plays host to all your needs. This is an easy-going and laid back kind of place that offers far more options for lodging, eating out or going for a beer. Bethel also offers cheaper facilities because as with most resorts, if you stay on or near the slopes, prices go up, and this place is no exception.

Good **accommodation** exists at the base of Sunday's slopes with a big choice of condo's. For riders on a budget then The *Snow Cap Lodge* Dorm is a good place to stay. On the other hand, if you have the cash then the *Jordan Grand Hotel*, which is on the slopes, is the place. Here they have all the facilities of a hotel which include a swimming and health club, bar lounge and dining room.

Food. Sunday River hasn't always had a good reputation for it's eating out. But things are changing with a good selection of restaurants on the slopes, or close by. In many of the lodges or hotel-condo's one is able to fine something that will please. You can get a decent steak in places like the *Hill Trading restaurant*, or a good Italian meal at *Rosett's*.

Nightlife is probably Sunday River's main let down. This is basically a place for lame heads into apres and all the horrible stuff that comes with it. There are a number of okay bars such as *Bumps*, the *Foggy Goggle* or *Suds Pub* and the *Sunday River Brewery*, but they all seem to think that sad music and silly games are cool.

SUMMARY
This is a place that offers some great all round freeriding to suit all levels. There is some excellent treeriding to be had and good beginner areas.

U
S
A

M
A
I
N
E

CAR
From Portland, head north on I-95 to exit 11 and then take Hwy 26 to Bethel which is 6 miles from Sunday. Portland to resort = 65 miles. 3 1/4 hours drive time.
FLY
Fly to Portland Int, with a transfer time of 1 3/4 hours.
BUS
Bus services from Portland can take 1 3/4 hours.

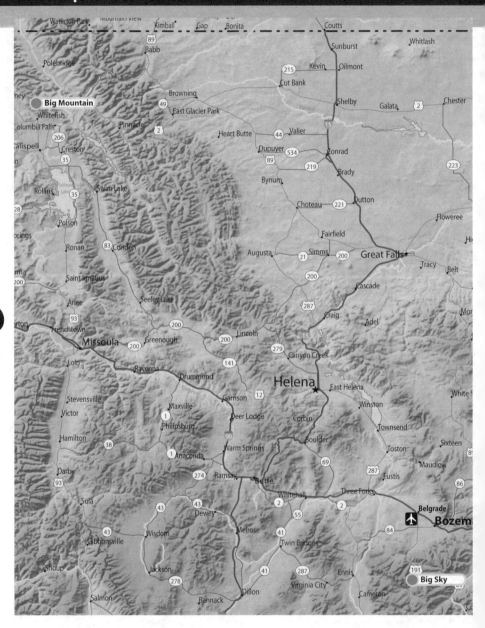

9
OUT OF 10

Top resort that is a riders dream and very welcoming

Question, Big Mountain, have you heard of it? Answer no? Well other than those in the area and those from surrounding states, not many people have, and those in the know who have discovered this gem, may want to keep this place a secret. But it could be said that to not tell others about this rider's heaven could be criminal. Located in the far north of **Montana**, Big Mountain has attracted a lot of attention recently and is steadily growing in popularity due to it not only having great riding available, but also because of the resort's super laid back attitude and no nonsense approach. This place isn't one of those horrible glitzy haunts

pic - Big Mountain Resort

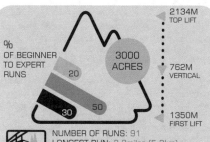

2134M
TOP LIFT

%
OF BEGINNER
TO EXPERT
RUNS

20

3000
ACRES

762M
VERTICAL

30

50

1350M
FIRST LIFT

NUMBER OF RUNS: 91
LONGEST RUN: 3.3miles (5.3km)
TOTAL LIFTS: 11 - 9 chairs, 2 drags
CAPACITY (people per hour): 13,800
LIFT TIMES:9.00am to 9.00pm

AVERAGE SNOWFALL:
7.62m
SNOWMAKING:
Unknown

WINTER PERIODS:
Nov to April
Lift Passes
1/2 Day $41 ,Day Pass - $49
Season Pass - $990
Board Schools
Full day group $50 Half Day $35
Full Day Private $310 Half Day $160
Hire
Board and boots $20/30, Helmet $5
Snowmobiles
1/2 day $130, Full day $230
Night Boarding
4pm to 9pm Fri and Sat. Pass $14

FREERIDE 55%
Trees & good off-piste
FREESTYLE 25%
A Terrain park but no pipe
CARVING 20%

Big Mountain
PO Box 1400, Whitefish MT 59937
Tel - 1-(800) 858-3930
Web:www.bigmtn.com
Email:bigmtn@bigmtn.com

visited by fur clad skiers out to pose as is so often the case in many of **Colorado's** resorts. No, this is a purist's resort, a place where you come to ride and take it easy without gimmicks. Big Mountain, which is closely linked to the nearby town of **Whitefish**, attracts visitors from places such as Seattle and up in neighbouring Canada. However, it doesn't attract too many of them so it never becomes overpopulated here. Excellent transport links exist making this an easy place to get to either by plane or by train. Amtrax runs a daily service to Whitefish, called the Empire Builder Passenger service to and from major cities like **Seattle** and even **Chicago**. Overall this is a place that keeps things simple and affordable, both on the mountain and around town. The slopes operate a good lift system and provide heaps of annual snow. They don't bother with snowmaking here as they simply don't need it. The real stuff covers a mountain that offers a mixture of wide open bowls, wooded glades and great cruising runs.

FREERIDERS are in for a major treat at this place with a fantastic offering of deep powder, big bowls, lots of trees and great natural terrain features. Basically, the mountain splits into three marked out areas. There's the **Main Mountain**, which has the most trails and something for every level, the **North Side**, which has a splattering of tree line black and blue runs and the **Hellroaring Basin**, which is an area mainly suited to advanced freeriders with riding on black and double black trails.

U
S
A

M
O
N
T
A
N
A

365

THE TOWN & GETTING THERE

FREESTYLERS can have lots of fun here and any rider that doesn't appreciate this mountain should give up boarding and become a girl guide. This place is ideal for freestylers. Apart from lots of natural features, there is a massive terrain park off the **Tenderfoot** chair 3.

CARVERS will appreciate the long and wide corduroy trails that can be found all over the mountain.

BEGINNERS have a great mountain with lots of easy trails especially at the lower sections. A number of the blues are also suitable for quick learners and allow novices to ride from the top to bottom.

pics - Big Mountain Resort

THE TOWN

Big Mountain offers a good choice of local services with a wide range of options for lodging, eating and having a good night out. The facilities at the base of the slopes are very good and will provide you with most of your basic needs with condo's that have restaurants and bars. Around the base village you will also find a few shops, but in truth the biggest choice of shops and all other local services can be found back down in the sprawling and old fashioned town of **Whitefish**. Here you will find a place where locals treat you with respect.

Accommodation is provided at the slopes or in Whitefish. If you stay near the slopes you will be able to find a condo or a bed in one of the lodges at reasonable prices. Rates start from $60 per person a night, but if you base yourself down in **Whitefish**, you will be able to get better deals. There is a hostel called the *Non Hostile Hostel* that offers cheap bunks 001 (406) 862 7383.

Food. Big Mountain and Whitefish provide good and simple choices for going out and filling your stomach at a price to please everyone. You can pig out at The *Stube & Chuckwagon Grill* which serves excellent food

all day long. The *Moguls Bar and Grill* is an ideal place to get breakfast before hitting the slopes and is located near the base of Swift Creek chair lift. In Whitefish the *Buffalo Cafe* is a good place to eat.

Nightlife here is very laid back, but that's not to say that you can't have a stomping time. Highly rated by the visiting ski groups is the *Stube & Chuckwagon Grill* which goes in for too much apre ski stuff, is still a cool bar. The *Great Northern* in Whitefish is not a bad joint which has a good selection of beers.

CAR
In the US, take Interstate 90 until you're eight miles west of Missoula. Take US Highway 93 north 110 miles to Kalispell. From US-93 toward Whitefish, turn RIGHT (North) onto Baker Ave, City Hall will be on your right. Head (North) over the Viaduct, go straight onto Wisconsin Ave through the lights. 3 miles ahead, turn RIGHT (North) onto Big Mountain Rd. 8 miles up the road you'll find Big Mountain Village.
FLY
Glacier Park International Airport (FCA) has non-stop flights from Salt Lake (Delta), Minneapolis (Northwest), Spokane and Seattle (Horizon) arriving daily.
BUS
services from Calgary, but not direct. Local bus services are available from Glacier and nearby towns of Browning and Whitefish.
TRAIN
take Amtrak from Seattle, Portland and points east, including Minneapolis and Chicago. Multi-night package deals, including lodgings and ski tickets, are available by calling (800) 858-3930. Shuttle services ferry skiers from the Whitefish station to Big Mountain.

U S A M O N T A N A

6 OUT OF 10

Good freeriding area

3398M
TOP LIFT

%
OF BEGINNER
TO EXPERT
RUNS

3600
ACRES/
136KM

1325M
VERTICAL

42

37

21

2072M
FIRST LIFT

NUMBER OF RUNS: 100
LONGEST RUN: 6miles (9km)
TOTAL LIFTS: 17 - 1 Gondola, 1 cable-
car, 12 chairs, 3 drags
CAPACITY (people per hour): 20,000
LIFT TIMES: 8.30am to 4.00pm

AVERAGE SNOWFALL:
10m
SNOWMAKING:
75%

WINTER PERIODS:
Nov to April
Lift Passes
1 Day pass - $61
4 of 5 day pass £232
Season (unlimited) pass $1060
Board Schools
2 hours group $42
Private 2hours $195
Hire
Board and boots $34/day

FREERIDE 45%
Trees & backcountry
FREESTYLE 35%
2 Terrain parks & a halfpipe
CARVING 20%

Big Sky Resort
P.O. Box 160001
1 Lone Mountain Trail
Big Sky, MT 59716
Tel: 001 800-548-4486
Fax: 001 406-995-5001
Snow phone - 001 406-995-5900
Web: www.bigskyresort.com
Email: info@bigskyresort.com

Bus
from Bozeman take about 1 1/2hrs
Fly
to Bozeman Int, with a transfer time of
1 1/2 hours.
Drive
From Bozeman, head south on Hwy 191
direct to Big Sky. Bozeman to resort =
45 miles. 1 hour drive time.

NEW

New for 04/05
new high-speed quad to replace fixed
grip lift on Southern Comfort terrain.
Three more gladed ski runs and building
12 more cabins.

pic - Big Sky Resort

Big Sky is a typical corporate style resort which only goes back to around 1973, when the place was first built aided by millions of corporate dollars. Located just south of **Bozeman** in the **northern Rockies**, Big Sky is an impressive place, where you can do some serious riding on crowd-free slopes that rise above the tree lines. The rideable area is reached by Big Sky's tram and is spread over **Andesite Mountain** and **Lone Mountain**, which rise up to 3,400 meters. This has led to the claim that Big Sky has the largest vertical in the US. The two mountains, with a total of 100 trails, are connected by just seventeen lifts, consisting of some very fast chair lifts that can move 20,000 people uphill per hour.

FREERIDERS will find this is a great place to get a fix. A good trail is the **Big Horn** which begins as an unchallenging trail that passes through woods, before dropping sharply into a bowl with banks and some good hits. Some of the most challenging terrain can be found if you first take the **Lone Peak** chair, and then hike up to reach the ridge off the south-facing summit. For those who know what they're doing, you get the option to go for it down loads of chutes. FREESTYLERS looking for some natural hits would do well to check out the gully formed down the side of Lower Morning Star, which is pretty cool. And if this is not enough, then Big Sky has a wheel-carved halfpipe and a good series of hits in the terrain park, which will keep grommets happy for days on end.

CARVERS should get a good buzz out of these slopes, with plenty of wide open flats that allow for some serious carving. Check out the stuff off the **Ram Charger** quad, where you can lay out with style. Carvers will also prefer the wide terrain on **Elk Park Ridge**, where you can crank some wide turns.

BEGINNERS will find plenty of easy terrain to practice their first moves, with the best novice stuff on the south side of **Andesite**, off **Southern Comfort chair** lift. The local ski-school handles all levels of tuition with full beginner programmes.

THE TOWN
Big Sky is not a place for the budget conscious. The modern town is a friendly place which looks after its visitors well and offers all the things you would expect of a tourist trap. Lodging is a mixture of condos and hotels along with a number of expensive restaurants and a few okay bars.

U

USA

MONTANA

4 OUT OF 10

Simple and unadventurous resort, suits beginners

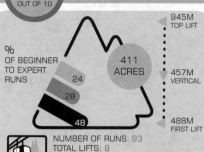

%
OF BEGINNER TO EXPERT RUNS

411 ACRES

24
28
48

945M
TOP LIFT

457M
VERTICAL

488M
FIRST LIFT

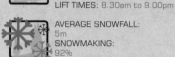

NUMBER OF RUNS: 93
TOTAL LIFTS: 9
6 chairs, 3 drags
CAPACITY (people per hour): 14,000
LIFT TIMES: 8.30am to 9.00pm

AVERAGE SNOWFALL:
5m
SNOWMAKING:
92%

WINTER PERIODS:
Nov to April
Lift Passes
1 Day $52/59
5 Days $176/219
Night 4/9pm $19
Season $1180
Board Schools
1 1/2 Hour Group lesson - $27
Hire
Board and boots $33/day
Night Boarding
Yes

FREERIDE 40%
Trees & some backcountry
FREESTYLE 15%
A Terrain park & a halfpipe
CARVING 45%

Bretton Woods Mountain Resort
Route 302, Bretton Woods,NH 03575
Tel - 603-278-3320
Web:www.brettonwoods.com

Bus
Services from Boston will take 3 hours.
Fly
to Boston, in Maine, transfer time of 2 1/2 hour.
Drive
From Boston, head north on I-93 via Manchester and Concord turning left at signs for Twin mountain along route 302. Boston to the resort is 165 miles

NEW

New for 04/05
new Rosebrook Summit Express high-speed detachable quad. 3 new black-diamond trails (Bode's Run, McIntire's Ride and Fire Tower) from new lift

pic - Bretton Woods Resort

Bretton Woods lies 165 miles north of **Boston** and 100 miles north of **Manchester** and claims to be the largest resort in **New Hampshire**. However, claiming to be the biggest at something is not always an indicator of how good you are. What you have here is a respectable mountain that by east coast standards is fairly decent. Some 93 runs are hacked out of dense trees that cover the whole mountain from the summit to base. The slopes, which are in view of **Mt Washington**, are currently spread out over two peaks, **Mt Rosebrook** and **West Mountain** with the trails all working their way back down into one main base area. Soon to open will be another ridable area, that of **Mt Stickney**. What Bretton seems to be about to the casual observer, is a place that likes to keep things simple and one that attracts a lot of family ski groups. Constantly expanding, this is a resort that is best suited to beginners and intermediate carvers although freeriders who like easy slopes with trees will also fair well here. In recent years major expansion plans have lead to the area almost doubling in size with the opening of the West Mountain which is a nice area for advanced riders who like to shred tight trees. All the trails and lifts connect up well and getting around the three slope faces can be done with ease. But that said, riders who prefer steep trails that last more than a few turns, may find that anything more than a couple of days on these slopes may become a bit tedious. On the other hand, a 10 year old kid taking their first snowboard trip with their parents will enjoy a weeks stay.

FREERIDERS do have a mountain that allows for easy going riding which also means taking in some treeriding. But this place is by no means a good freerider's resort, there's nothing that adventurous to take on and the few advanced runs that there are, don't take long to conquer.
FREESTYLERS are presented a mountain that is basically dull when it comes to finding good natural hits. They do exist but not many. However, there is a halfpipe to check out.
CARVERS who like to take it easy will enjoy Brettons Woods. In the main, this is a good simple cruising resort, with a number of decent trails especially those on Mt Rosebrook.

THE TOWN. Local attractions and services are provided at the base of the slopes. What you are offered is of a very high standard, the only problem being that the place is very boring and not much fun.

U
S
A
.
N
E
W
H
A
M
P
S
H
I
R
E

369

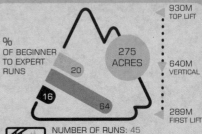

LOON MOUNTAIN

6 OUT OF 10

A bit dull but okay

pic · Loon Mountain Resort

%
OF BEGINNER
TO EXPERT
RUNS

20

275 ACRES

16

64

930M
TOP LIFT

640M
VERTICAL

289M
FIRST LIFT

NUMBER OF RUNS: 45
LONGEST RUN: 2.5miles (4km)
TOTAL LIFTS: 9
1 Gondola, 6 chairs, 2 drags
CAPACITY (people per hour): 10,550
LIFT TIMES: 8.30am to 4.00pm

AVERAGE SNOWFALL:
3m
SNOWMAKING:
96%

WINTER PERIODS:
Oct to May
Lift Passes
1 Day pass $49/54
5 Days $220/270
Board Schools
Half day Group $35/39
Full Day Group $74/79
Hire
Board and boots $38/day, 5 days $180
Night Boarding
No

FREERIDE 50%
Trees but poor backcountry
FREESTYLE 20%
A Terrain park & a halfpipe
CARVING 30%

Loon Mountain Resort
RR1, Box 41 , Kancamagus Hwy
Lincoln, NH 03251
Tel: 603-745-8111
Fax: 603-745-8214
Web:www.loonmtn.com
Email:info@loonmtn.com

Bus
Bus services from Boston can take 21
hours to Loon.
Fly
to Boston, with a transfer time of 2
1/4 hours.
Drive
From Boston, head north on I-93 to ex
32 at Lincoln. Then go east along R-12
to Loon Mountain. Boston to resort is
132 miles. 2 hours drive time.

NEW

New for 04/05
new Doppelmayr CTEC high-spe
detachable quad chairlift on its North Pe
widening of the Flume trail and clearing
glades, plus the addition of a deck arou
the Camp III mid-mountain lodge

New Hampshire breeds a lot of resorts, most of which are frankly crap. However, Loon Mountain is one of the state's better offerings with a good friendly snowboard attitude. Located in **White Mountain National Forest**, Loon is the highest mountain in New Hampshire and a very popular resort that attracts a lot of punters. The resort has been going through a multi-million dollar expansion programme and has recently expanded the ride area with new lifts and services. The 275 acres of terrain is nearly all covered by snow cannons, so when the real stuff is lacking, they can still ensure good coverage. Despite Loon's small size and the odd lift line, it's a good place to ride, with a mixture of varied terrain to appeal to most recreational boarders of intermediate standard

FREERIDERS have a tree-covered mountain that allows for some good riding experiences. The **Kissin' Cousin** is a popular warm-up area, before trying out the likes of **Speakeasy**, reached by the **Kancamagus** chair. The **East Basin** is also a popular freeride area, where you'll find some decent wind-lips to track up.
FREESTYLERS have a full-on fun-park called **Loon Mountain Park** (how do they come up with these names eh?), which snowboarders travel a long way to ride. Located on **Lower Picked Rock** and approximately 1,500m long, the park has plenty of very big hits & rails including a 400-foot superpipe. Theres a few other mini-parks dotted around the mountain, and new for the 04 season was a beginners park on **Lower Northstar**.
CARVERS will soon realise that Loon is the mountain for them. It offers a great chance to perform to watching onlookers, as you carve big turns on long, well prepared trails. Some of the best runs are the **Flume** and the Upper and Lower **Walking Boss**, an area that offers some cool carving on either blue or black trails. There is also plenty for novice and intermediate alpine riders.
BEGINNERS will find plenty here. The best and easiest stuff is found on the **West Basin**, while the mid-section of the **Seven Brothers** chair offers something a little more testing. Loon Ski School offers a very good learning snowboard clinic

THE TOWN. Local services are plentiful in either **Loon**, **Lincoln** or **down** in the famous hippy hangout of **Woodstock**. All three towns are friendly and look after their visitors well. **Food** around the area caters well for all tastes and pockets. The *Old Mill* is good for seafood, while *Elvios* is the pizza place, and The *Woodstock Inn* is good for bar food. There are also a few good late-night hangouts in either Loon, Lincoln or Woodstock.

6 OUT OF 10

Not hot, but not bad

Waterville is an easy-going, laid back place that is part of a programme called the Peaks of Excitement, a group of resorts working together. This means that your lift pass can be used at over 20 other places, giving a combined area of around 2,000 acres. The resort

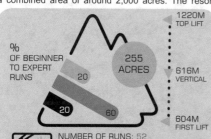

1220M
TOP LIFT

% OF BEGINNER TO EXPERT RUNS

255 ACRES

20

616M
VERTICAL

20   60

604M
FIRST LIFT

NUMBER OF RUNS: 52
LONGEST RUN: 3.1miles (5km)
TOTAL LIFTS: 12 - 8 chairs, 4 drags
CAPACITY (people per hour): 14,867
LIFT TIMES: 9.00am to 3:45pm

AVERAGE SNOWFALL:
3.55m
SNOWMAKING:
100%

WINTER PERIODS:
Nov to April
Lift Passes
Standard Day $39, Peak $53
Board Schools
Beginners package of lift pass, rental & lesson $56/60 per day. 2hr lesson $31.
Private lessons $67/75 per hour
Hire
Burton Board & Boots $31/33 per day.
Helmets $10/12 per day

FREERIDE 40%
Trees but poor backcountry
FREESTYLE 40%
3 Terrain parks & 2 halfpipes
CARVING 30%

Waterville Valley Resort
1 Ski Area Road,PO Box 540
Waterville Valley, NH 03215
Tel: 1-800-GO-VALLEY (468-2553)
Fax: (603)-236-4344
Web:www.waterville.com
Email:info@waterville.com

Bus
from Boston take 2 hours to Waterville.
Fly
to Boston, with a 2 hour transfer time.
Drive
From Boston, 130 miles, 2hrs. Take I-93 N to Exit 28, 11 miles via Rt. 49 to resort.
From New York, 325 miles, 6hrs. Take I-95 to I-91 to I-84 to Mass. Turnpike to I-290 to I-495 to Rt. 3 N to I-93 N to Exit 28, then 11 miles via Rt. 49 to resort.

Pic - Waterville Valley

is only two hours from **Boston** and can be easily reached by bus or car. The slopes are a two minute drive from the village and serviced by a regular shuttle bus to the lifts. Waterville really tries hard to please snowboarders, with four fun-parks. However, the resort is a busy place at weekends, and being quite small, it can feel a bit cluttered at times. Advanced riders don't have a host of challenging trails, in the main this is an intermediate's and fast learning novice's resort.

FREERIDERS may not have the biggest or most happening playground at **Waterville**, but you still have areas to cut, with plenty of trees to shred like **Lower Bobby's.**
FREESTYLERS and trick merchants have three fun-parks and a massive halfpipe to play in. The parks (shamefully open to skiers), are spread out around the slopes and offer something for all levels. The **Exhibition Terrain Park** (located near the base) is a pro-level park and features quarter-pipes, rail slides, table-tops and gaps and the superpipe. The **Boneyard** (located on Periphery) is a step down for more intermediate riders. The **little Slammer** is for junior grommets, and has some 8-10ft jumps of various guises and a few wide rails.
CARVERS who can handle a board on its side have just one steep double black to go for - True Grit. Alternatively, the cluster of blues that descend from the summit make for nice easy carving on pleasant and well groomed trails.
BEGINNERS only have a couple of dull green trails at the base, with a number of over-rated blues higher up that can be tackled quite easily by those with a few days under their belt.

THE TOWN. Local facilities, a few minutes from the slopes, are without frills. **Accommodation** covers condos, hotels and an array of B&B's. Prices are affordable and a number of weekly packages are available at reduced rates. **Dining out** offers no great surprises, with a simple choice of restaurants providing local dishes, fast-food and deli stuff. For some decent food check out Chile Peppers or Alpine Pizza. **Night action** is dull, but the Zoo Station and Legends 1291 are okay for a beer.

U
S
A

N
E
W

H
A
M
P
S
H
I
R
E

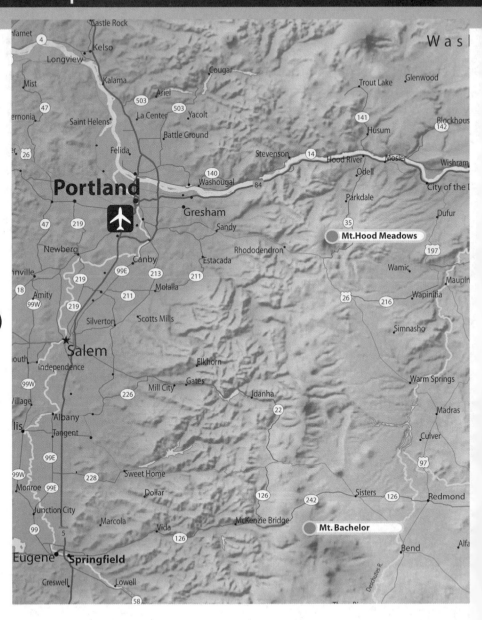

Rider KellyClark Photo JeffCurtes, Burton Snowboards

MT BACHELOR

10 OUT OF 10

Full-on freeriders resort offering great open and tree-lined riding

Pic - Peter Butsch/Mt.Bachelor

Mt Bachelor is located in the **Cascade Mountains** of **Central Oregon**, 20 miles from the booming resort town of **Bend**. The snow-capped, dormant volcano is unique in that it is conical-shaped with seven high-speed quads, offering 360 access to the whole area. Chutes and gullies created long ago by lava flows, gives the terrain a shape and contour found in few other places. Combine 370 inches of annual snowfall, howling winds, that create fairy-tale wind-lips, and you're left with acres of terrain that rival the best of any man-made park. Weekly storms rock the mountains, forcing you to frequently use force to steer through the dense weather systems. But even before the clouds clear and the sky is blue again, Mt Bachelor is damn fun!

FREERIDERS-if the summit is open, be sure to make the 10 minute hike to the top of the **Cirque Bowl**. You will find here an extra large cornice (that grows to 45 feet) and the infamous **Jamo Jump**, where you can fling yourself silly. Also accessible from the summit chair is Mt Bachelor's Backside, where you are sure to find fresh snow and solitude. You can use the new 2 mile long **Northwest Express** chair to access a vast amount of steep bowls and perfect tree runs. There are minimal man-made runs here, and the ones that are cut are narrow and winding.

FREESTYLERS-the **Outback** has many BMX and skate park-like runs that are easy to find by following the tracks. On crowded days, head over to **Rainbow chair**, which unfortunately is as slow as shit, but there are many natural quarter-pipes and rollers untouched by the weekend crowd. If you're man enough, ask some local jackass about the **Compression jump**, which on good days allows you to travel an unlimited distance before shooting up the side of the **Cindercone**. If natural terrain is not for you, Mt Bachelor maintains Mt Bachelor maintains four terrain parks, and a Superpipe built for the Olympic Qualifiers in 2000.

CARVERS will find that Bachelor has them in mind and grooms its trails to perfection. The runs off **Skyliner** and **Pine Marten** chairs are great intermediate and

2763M TOP LIFT

% OF BEGINNER TO EXPERT RUNS

15
25
60

3683 ACRES

946M VERTICAL

1818M FIRST LIFT

NUMBER OF RUNS: 71
LONGEST RUN: 1.5miles (3.5km)
TOTAL LIFTS: 12
10 chairs, 2 drags
CAPACITY (people per hour): 21,000
LIFT TIMES: 9.00am to 4.00pm
MOUNTAIN CAFES: 20

AVERAGE SNOWFALL:
8.89m
SNOWMAKING:
none

WINTER PERIODS:
Nov to june
Lift Passes
1 Day pass $37/47
5 Day pass $202/235
Season pass -$910
Board Schools
3 hours group inc board and pass $50
private $60/hr
Hire
board and boots $26/day
Snowmobiles
Yes
Nightboarding
Yes

FREERIDE 70%
Trees & good backcountry
FREESTYLE 20%
4 Terrain parks & 2 halfpipes
CARVING 10%

Mt. Bachelor, Inc.
P.O. Box 1031
Bend, OR 97709
Tel: (800) 829-2442
Snowfone: (541) 382-7888
Web:www.mtbachelor.com
Email:info@mtbachelor.com

novice trails, but if you have the bottle then head to the summit and ride the unpisted open steeps of the **Cirque** - but don't bail!

BEGINNERS-this is a mountain that you'll appreciate, with its selection of good, easy green runs that can be ridden from the mid-section of the **Pine Marten** chair. The runs descend in a manner that allow you to steer onto a more interesting and challenging blue

MT BACHELOR

THE TOWN & GETTING THERE

Pic - BB/Mt.Bachelor

Good snowboard hire services are at Bachelor Ski & Sport and Side Effects Snowboard Shop.

Accomodation. The area can accommodate over 7,500 visitors, but nothing directly on the slopes. The nearest lodging is only a few miles from the slopes at the Inn of The *Seventh Mountain*, but the best choice of condos, B&B's and lodges can be found in the town of Bend, 20 miles away from Bachelor.

Food. There are no big surprises when it comes to restaurants. What you are offered is a good, but somewhat basic selection of eatries where you can wine and dine down in Bend, or have a snack attack up on Bachelor. The *Taco Stand* is the place to fill yourself with a burrito bomber: this beauty will clog up any 15 gallon pressure-locked toilet. *Stuft Pizza* is the place for pasta dishes.On the Mountain locals call *Scapolo's* in the Pine Marten Lodge from the chairlift and have pizza waiting when they arrive.

as you gain confidence. The local snowboard school is really good, and the staff know how to turn you into a fast freeriding god within a day or two. A day's all-in programme will set you back just $40, and for those who want to make it big, sign up for one of High Cascade's winter camps.

Night-life at Bachelor is not exactly the most happening. However, things liven up in **Bend** where there are enough joints to drink and dance in until you drop. Try *Evil Sister Saloon* if you're inclined to the 'alternative' end of the spectrum. *Legends* is also a cool hangout with large screens and a decent beer.

THE TOWN

Mt Bachelor doesn't offer any substantial slopeside facilities. However, excellent laid back local services with a warm welcome are available 20 miles away in **Bend** or **Sunriver**. A free, daily and regular shuttle bus service runs to and from the slopes. Hitching to the mountain is also a good bet and cars do stop to pick you up. Bend and the surrounding area has everything you need for your stay, shops, banks, postal services and a huge array of in and out-door sporting attractions.

SUMMARY

Full-on freeriders resort offering great open and tree-lined riding on crowd free slopes ideal for all levels. Excellent local facitities of a high quality.

Moeny Wise: Prices vary for lodgings, but overall this is a very affordable resort

CAR
Portland via Madras & Bend. Mt Bachelor is 203 miles. Drive time is about 3 1/2 hours.
FLY
Fly to Portland International, transfer time to resort is 3 1/2 hours. Local airport is Redmond, 15 miles from Bend
BUS
There are daily bus services from both Portland airport and Redmond domestic airport.
TRAIN
to Chemult 60 miles away

MT HOOD MEADOWS

10 OUT OF 10

Full-on freerider's resort offering great, open and tree-lined terrain

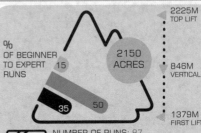
pic s - Mt.Hood Meadows Resort

There are three main resorts on Mt Hood, a dormant (not extinct!) volcano: **Mt Hood Meadows**, **Ski Bowl** and **Timberline**. Although small, Meadows is the most popular and has a huge range of interesting riding crammed into its space and, joy of joys, virtually no traversing anywhere. It maybe tempting fate, but it is hard to get lost on Hood. You can spend a whole day taking different lines, but know that you are not too far from where you started. This is a very mixed ability mountain, with some nice basic novice terrain to pockets of testing trails for the more advanced rider, but in truth this not the most testing place, Steep descents will only be found in very short doses, like on **Waterfall** or around the back of **Nightmare Knoll** (a 40+ft cliff). The locals have their own names for most of the stuff they ride and are more than happy to show you their favourite little stash(!). The lifties are cool too, and a large proportion ride. If you can't afford the daily rates, the mountain is open for night-riding until March, although not extensively: take advantage of the special offers at Safeway's Supermarkets ($8.50 for Sunday 4pm-10pm) and you can't complain. Meadows is a popular destination for **summer riding**, with *Tim Windell's High Cascade* and *Mt Hood Snowboard Camp,* but you have to be enrolled on a camp to use their facilities.

FREERIDERS-this mountain is very much for you: the terrain, which may not offer a super amount of challenging stuff or be the most extensive in the world, is still perfect wherever you go. The **Super Bowl** is a black graded area, with a series of descents on open terrain. The notable thing about the Super Bowl, is that

% OF BEGINNER TO EXPERT RUNS

2225M TOP LIFT
2150 ACRES
15
846M VERTICAL
35   50
1379M FIRST LIFT

NUMBER OF RUNS: 87
LONGEST RUN: 3 miles (5km)
TOTAL LIFTS: 10 - all chairs
CAPACITY (people per hour): 16,145
LIFT TIMES: 8.00am to 10.00pm
MOUNTAIN CAFES: 2

AVERAGE SNOWFALL:
9.15m
SNOWMAKING:
none

WINTER PERIODS:
Nov to June
SUMMER PERIODS:
July to August
Lift Passes
1 Day pass $44/48
Night only $20
4 of 6 Days $150
Super Bowl Snow Cat provides 1,700ft vertical dropping into Heather Canyon. Head to top of Cascade Express $10 a trip.
Board Schools
Group lessons $35 for 90mins
Beginner package $99 for 3 days lift, lesson & hire
Private lessons $65 per hour
Hire
Board & boots $28 per day, demo kit $40 per day
Night Boarding
240 acres including park & pipe. Wednesday, Thursday and Sunday nights until 9:00 PM. Friday and Saturday nights until 10:00 PM.

FREERIDE 60%
A few trees & good backcountry
FREESTYLE 30%
3 Terrain parks & a halfpipe
CARVING 10%

MT. HOOD MEADOWS SKI RESORT
P.O. Box 470
Mt. Hood, OR 97041-0470
Tel: 503.337.2222
Fax:503.337.2217
Web:www.skihood.com
Email:info@skihood.com

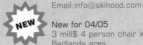

NEW

New for 04/05
3 mill$ 4 person chair will open up the Badlands area

THE TOWN & GETTING THERE

it's not serviced by a lift line; instead you get up on a snowcat for around $10 a go

FREESTYLERS-there are natural hits everywhere and also a good fun-park off the **Hood River chair**. However, the fact that skiers are allowed in the park with so much good natural terrain on offer, make it hardly worth using. You can have a great time riding the hits around **Chunky Swirl** and the **Texas run**. If you're a pipe hound, then you'll usually find it well maintained but often very busy with local air heads.

CARVERS-the runs from **Cascade** are the best in terms of wide, open carving trails, with a couple of decent blue trails down to choose from. There isn't an abundance of steeps for long fast carving, but what is there is is excellent.

BEGINNERS are treated to a good number of trails that are easy to reach and easy to negotiate. **Mt Hood Express** gives access to some interesting green runs and some tame blues. The local snowboard school has a host of teaching programmes for all levels, including a Mountain Master Programme

THE TOWN

If you're the sort of person that doesn't want the normal, tacky, overpriced tourist facilities found in many resorts, then this place will please you. What you have is a laid back and very basic place where the locals are cool. *Timberline Lodge* (the location for the film 'The Shining') has recently had an overhaul and is the only real slopeside accommodation which is open all year, but prices can be a bit steep. A good option would be to stay down in **Government Camp** opposite **Ski Bowl** which is only a few miles away. Alternatively you could base yourself in the town of **Hood River**, 36 miles away, which has loads of facilities.

Accommodation is provided in various locations, with the more expensive near the slopes at Mt Hood. Mt Hood Hamlet B&B has rates from $95 tel (800) 407 0570. While down on **Hood River** you can get a bed at *Prather's Motel* for around $40 a night. The *Bingen School Hostel* has nightly rates from $15 and is a good budget hangout.

Food. If you're the sort of person that wants to dine out night after night eating fine haute cuisine dressed in a tuxedo, then firstly see a shrink, and secondly visit another resort. This place is for those who like their food served man style, big portions no frills and cheap. Wherever you stay, there are plenty of budget food-stops. *Huckleberry's* does a damn fine breakfast and is open 24 hours. While down in Hood River, *Big City Chicks* is good.

Night Life. Hood may seem to be quiet and tame from the outside, but in fact things can get very lively and in a snowboard way, kick off nightly with a lot of hardcore boozing, especially in the no frills Government Camp or in Mt Hood at the likes of the *Alpenstube*. The biggest selection of night action takes place in **Hood River**.

U S A

O R E G O N

CAR
From Portland take Hwy 26 east to Government Camp; then north on Hwy 35 - 10 miles to Meadows. 75 miles total, drive time is about 1 1/2 hours.
FLY
Fly to Portland International. Transfer time to resort is 1 1/2 hours. Vancouver 74 miles
BUS
There are daily bus services from Portland airport as well as good car hire services. Weekend day trip specials from Portland, return $20 leaves 6:40am returns 4:00pm tel: 503. BUS. LIFT /287.5438/
TRAIN to Portland 69 miles on

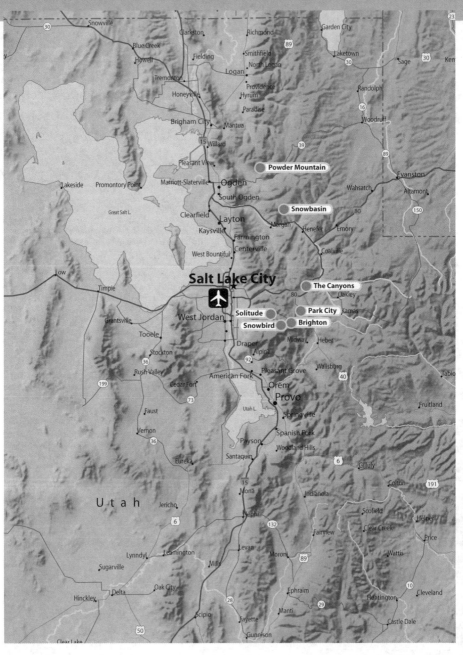

5 OUT OF 10 — Over-rated resort, but some good freeriding if you're prepared to hike

Brighton is generally talked of as the snowboarding capital of **Utah**, but that is over-rated. **Brighton** is located at the top of **Big Cottonwood Canyon** and most of the mountain

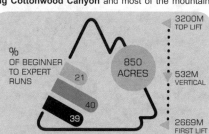

% OF BEGINNER TO EXPERT RUNS

21
40
39

850 ACRES

3200M TOP LIFT

532M VERTICAL

2669M FIRST LIFT

NUMBER OF RUNS: 66
LONGEST RUN: 3 miles
TOTAL LIFTS: 8 - 7 chairs, 1 drags
CAPACITY (people per hour): 10,100
LIFT TIMES: 9.00am to 9.00pm

AVERAGE SNOWFALL:
12.7m
SNOWMAKING:
24%

WINTER PERIODS:
Nov to April
Lift Passes
1/2 Day Pass $35
Full Day $41
Season $895
Night pass $30
Board Schools
2 Hour lesson, lift and equipment - $61
private $145 Half day $295 Full Day
Hire
Board and boots - $26/32 per day
Night Boarding
200 acres, 20 runs are floodlit & oper
Monday-Saturday from 4:00pm-9:00pm

FREERIDE 60%
Trees & some cool backcountry
FREESTYLE 20%
A Terrain park & 2 halfpipes
CARVING 20%

Brighton Resort 12601 E. Big
Cottonwood Cyn Brighton, Utah 84121
Tel: 801.532.4731
Web:www.skibrighton.com
Email:info@skibrighton.com

Bus
from Salt Lake City takes 45 mins
Fly
to Salt Lake City, with transfer time of
35 minutes.
Drive
From Salt Lake City head east along
highway 190 Canyon Road all the way
up to Brighton. Salt Lake City to the
resort is 35 miles.

is lacking in vertical and challenging terrain. The pipe sucks and the regulars here are not a friendly crowd. There are some really good riders but they don't appreciate visitors crowding the snowboard parks and they will always be the first to let you know it. However, Brighton has been welcoming pleasure seekers to its slopes since 1936 and is fully open to snowboarders. Brighton is also close to the snowboard friendly resort of Solitude.

FREERIDERS will want to head straight for the **Millicent** lift. The **Wolverine Cirque backcountry** is out of this world. This area may require a hike out, but it is well worth the effort. Scree-Slope rocks too. It accesses a sweet cliff/shoot area, which goes all the way over to **Camera Land** and **Mary Chutes** backcountry. An easy hike to the top of Preston Peak from the **Snake Creek Express** leads to some super tree runs in Snake Bowl. **Hidden Country** backcountry also has a limitless possibility of tree runs and powder shoots after a good storm, but it tends to get tracked out pretty fast.

FREESTYLERS will be disappointed with the pipe but the park is very well maintained. It has a bunch of decent table tops and spine jumps and is not usually crowded during the week.

CARVERS will find that Brighton doesn't have a lot to offer. There are only a few fast groomers off of Millicent and Evergreen. The rest of the mountain just does not maintain enough vertical.

BEGINNERS would really enjoy learning on this mountain. A large portion of the terrain is not too steep or technical. The **Explorer lift** is a great place to start and there are numerous runs off of the **Majestic lift** that beginners would be comfortable with. **Sunshine** off the Snake Creek Express is a long run, but mellow.

THE TOWN
Off the slopes things are remarkably different to on the slopes because in truth there is nothing here other than a couple of basic lodges and a few bed and breakfasts haunts. You should stay in a neighbouring resort or down in **Salt Lake City**.

U
USA
UTAH

379

7 OUT OF 10

Good freeriders resort

Pic - Eric Schramm/Park City

% OF BEGINNER TO EXPERT RUNS

3050M TOP LIFT

3300 ACRES

18

945M VERTICAL

44

38

2100M FIRST LIFT

NUMBER OF RUNS: 100
LONGEST RUN: 3.5miles (5.6km)
TOTAL LIFTS: 14 - all chairs
CAPACITY (people per hour): 27,200
LIFT TIMES: 9.00am to 9.00pm
MOUNTAIN CAFES: 5

AVERAGE SNOWFALL: 8.89m
SNOWMAKING: 47%

WINTER PERIODS: Nov to April
Lift Passes
Day Pass - $61
Board Schools
Group 3 hours from $70
Hire
Board & Boots $31 per day
Snowmobiles:90 mins $50
Night Boarding:Yes

FREERIDE 50%
Lots of trees but poor backcountry
FREESTYLE 20%
2 Terrain parks & 2 halfpipes
CARVING 30%

Park City Mountain Resort
P.O. Box 39
Park City, UT 84060
Tel: 435.658.5560
Web:www.parkcitymountain.com
Email:info@pcski.com

Fly
to Salt Lake City, 45 mins transfer
Drive
Interstate highway 80 exit Kimball Park
City #145 southbound ut-224 to resort

New for 04/05 season
Additional rails, funboxes, jumps and
music will be added to the Resort's
terrain parks. New 4 person begginers
chair lift.

Park City, which played host to the 2002 Olympic Winter Games, is by far the most famous resort in Utah and also one of the most expensive. However, don't let the fact that this is a costly place with a bit of an attitude put you off. In terms of what there is to ride and the way the place is laid out, **Park City** is cool. With some 100 named trails and over 3300 acres of linked terrain, no-one is going to feel left out here. For the 2002 Olympic Winter Games, Park City was home to skiing's giant slalom and as well as the snowboard races and when you see this place, it's easy to see why. This is a place that knows how to put on a show, (even if the snow can often be a bit dodgy).

FREERIDERS will be wetting themselves once they see what awaits them on these slopes, which stretch out over a number of peaks. If you like backcountry riding then check out **McConkey's bowl** where there are some great double diamond runs that weave through the trees. If riding deep powder in bowls is your thing then this place has some fantastic bowls that involve some hiking and then dropping in, notably the trails on **Jupiter**. Here you will find some black diamond rated trails that can be ridden down to a chair lift, but be warned, this area is for experts.

FREESTYLERS who want to catch big air off natural hits are going to love this place. The mountain is littered with hits galore whether it be up in the bowls or down on the lower pisted areas. The resort also builds numerous terrain parks with man-made hits of every shape, and to cap it all, there is a serious halfpipe located at the top of the **Payday trail.** The pipe is also flood lit for night riding.

CARVERS are also in for a good time here. There is a fine choice of good cruising trails such as the runs off the **King Con** chair lift.

BEGINNERS who have never ridden will soon be able to get to grips with things here, as this is a very good first timers resort.

THE TOWN. Around town there are lots of things to do as well has offering fantastic nightlife. No other resort in Utah packs in as many facilities as this one. There is every imaginable type of accommodation available although not many are aimed at budget riders. However, a good cheap option is the *Park City Youth Hostel* (www.parkcity.com tel 435 655 7255). Don't listen to the stories about the Mormon **drinking** laws, they do exist but they just make things more amusing. Ask a local bartender what the score is on this.

7 OUT OF 10

Great freeriders resort with some cool cat boarding

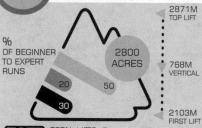

2871M
TOP LIFT

% OF BEGINNER TO EXPERT RUNS

2800 ACRES

768M
VERTICAL

20

50

30

2103M
FIRST LIFT

TOTAL LIFTS: 7
4 chairs, 2 Drags, 1 Platter
LIFT TIMES: 9:30 AM - 4:00 PM
MOUNTAIN CAFES: 4

AVERAGE SNOWFALL
8.89m
SNOWMAKING
Unknown

WINTER PERIODS
Dec to April
Lift Passes
1 day lift pass $43
6 day lift pass $219
$7 snowcat (for lightning ridge backcountry)
season from $470
Board Schools
Private lesson $59 per hour
Group lessons $30 for 2.5 hours
Hire
Board & Boots $27 per day
Heliboarding
For heli-boarding around the Ogden area call Diamond Peaks Heli-Ski Adventures (801) 745-4631.
Night Boarding
Off Sundown Lift & Tiger t-bar till 10pm

FREERIDE 60%
Trees & huge backcountry
FREESTYLE 20%
A Terrain park & halfpipe
CARVING 20%

Powder Mountain Inc
PO Box 450
Eden, UT 84310
Tel: (801) 745-3772
Web:www.powdermountain.com
Email:powdermountain@powdermount
ain.com

Fly
to Salt Lake City, transfer time of 1 hour.
Drive
From Salt Lake City head north on the I-15 north to Ogden 12th Street exit. Salt Lake City to the resort is 55 miles.

Powder Mountain

Powder Mountain can be considered as Utah's best kept secret. It is just outside of the small mountain town of **Eden**, north of **Salt Lake City**, and does not attract the crowds like many of the larger resorts near Salt Lake City and Park City.

FREERIDERS will be stoked to find that Powder Mountain is one giant playground. Most of the terrain is a variety of tree shots, rock drops, and open powder fields. There are great lines off either side of **Straight Shot** and from the top of **Cobabe Canyon**. Powder has super **cat skiing** to the top of **Lightning Ridge**. Riders will also fall in love with the backcountry area known as **Powder Country** which is well known throughout the region, in total theres another 2800 acres of accesible backcountry. These impressive steeps are easily accessible from the **Sundown lift** and drop to the highway where a shuttle service runs for another ride up.

FREESTYLERS will find a decent well maintained halfpipe off the **Hidden Lake Run** and a smaller pipe off Sundown lift near Confidence. Unfortunately, there is not a designated park area. If you search a little, you can find plenty of natural hits to play on. The boulder field on lower Straight Shot and the trees off of East 40 have some nice kickers.

BEGINNERS should all learn to ride at this resort with ease. **Sunrise, Sundown**, or **Hidden Lake** lift would be good places to start while the **Picnic** and **Mushroom** runs are nice mellow runs to follow up on.

THE TOWN
Resort lodge restaurants are the only places to eat nearby and the only accommodation at the mountain is the *Columbine Inn,* where rooms and condos are available. The best bet for inexpensive food and accommodations is 19 miles away in the city of **Ogden**. Here you will find a large selection of everything, birds, booze and music, to mention but a few.

U
U S A
U T A H

5 OUT OF 10

Decent terrain, but too commercial

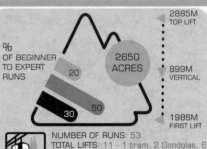

% OF BEGINNER TO EXPERT RUNS: 20 · 50 · 30

2650 ACRES

2885M TOP LIFT

899M VERTICAL

1986M FIRST LIFT

NUMBER OF RUNS: 53
TOTAL LIFTS: 11 - 1 tram, 2 Gondolas, 6 chairs, 2 magic carpets
CAPACITY (people per hour): 14,650
LIFT TIMES: 9:00 a.m. to 4:00 p.m

AVERAGE SNOWFALL
10m
SNOWMAKING
22%

WINTER PERIODS
Dec to April
Lift Passes
Day $55
Season $875
Board Schools
Group lessons $35 for 2 hours
Private lessons $129 for 2 hours
Night Boarding
No

FREERIDE 40%
A few trees but good backcountry
FREESTYLE 20%
2 Terrain parks
CARVING 40%

Snowbasin: A Sun Valley Resort
3925 E. Snowbasin Rd.
Huntsville, UT 84317
tel: (801) 620-1000
Web:www.Snowbasin.com
Email:info@snowbasin.com

Fly
to Salt Lake City, transfer time of 50 mins
Drive
From Salt Lake city take US-89 northbound, take exit 326, onto I-84 eastbound, exit 92. Take Old Highway and turn left on State Road 167 , then turn left on State Road 226 heading west for 3 miles. 33 miles in total.
Bus
services from Salt Lake City take 50 mins

U
S
A

U
T
A
H

Snowbasin is located north of the city of **Ogden**. Unfortunately, they hold so many races here that the **John Paul Express**, which takes you to the men and women's downhill courses and which accesses a large kick ass part of the mountain, is usually closed of for competitions. Still, there are a lot of other runs to check out with a good supply of black ones at the upper area and a number of intermediate trails leading from the top to the bottom, taking in a few trees en-route. The whole mountain is open to boarders, but only if you have a safety strap on your board. If you arrive without one, you won't be allowed up.

FREERIDERS will like this mountain more than anyone else. In general the mountain is not extensive and a week's stay would be overdoing it. However, there is a good selection of black marked slopes to keep most riders interested for a day or two. The **Strawberry Express** is good for access to backcountry gates.

FREESTYLERS will find 2 terrain parks, one at the base and another on Porky Face. The **little park** at the base has some boxes, a couple of rails and a table top, while the **big park** at the top of Porcupine lift has some bigger jumps and a 1/4 pipe.

CARVERS have some nice options like the men's and women's downhill courses when races are not going on. Most of the mountain is intermediate groomers with some nice long trails.

BEGINNERS have a good resort for learning the basics at and although there are not loads of green easy trails, what is on offer is okay, especially the beginner terrain off of **Becker Chair.**

THE TOWN
Forget about any slope side facilities, however, **Ogden** has everything you could possibly want. The *Alaskan Inn* 001 (801)-621-8600 is pricey and the rooms fill up fast, but it is fun and is right in *Ogden Canyon*, closer to the resorts.

SNOWBIRD

Epic mountain for good riders

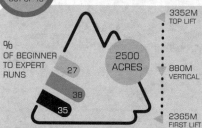

3352M
TOP LIFT

%
OF BEGINNER
TO EXPERT
RUNS

27

2500
ACRES

880M
VERTICAL

38

35

2365M
FIRST LIFT

NUMBER OF RUNS: 85
LONGEST RUN: 2.5miles
TOTAL LIFTS: 12
1 tram, 10 chairs, 2 drags
CAPACITY (people per hour): 16,800
LIFT TIMES: 9am to 4:30 pm

AVERAGE SNOWFALL
12.7m
SNOWMAKING
1%

WINTER PERIODS Nov to May
Lift Passes
Lift pass $57,5 day pass $220
Board Schools
Half-day improvers workshops $56.
Beginners package inc lift, lesson, hire
$99 for 1 day, $149 3 days. Private 3hr
$275. Secret spots day for advanced
freeriders $90 per day
Hire
Board & Boots $31 per day, $45 for
demo equip
Heliboarding
7 runs/day $525/770
Night Boarding
Chickadee lift open until 8:30 p.m for night
boarding on wednesdays and fridays

FREERIDE 60%
A few trees & good backcountry
FREESTYLE 20%
2 Terrain parks & 2 halfpipes
CARVING 20%

Snowbird Ski and Summer Resort
P.O. Box 929000
Snowbird, UT 84092-9000
Tel: 1-801-742-2222
Web: www.snowbird.com
Email: info@snowbird.com

Fly
to Salt Lake City, transfer time 45 mins
Drive
From Salt Lake City head east along I-80
and I-215 south and leave at exit 6 following
the route for little Cottonwood Canyon.
Salt Lake City to the resort 25 miles.
Bus
services from Salt Lake City takes 45 mins

NEW

New for 04/05 season
new superpipe

pic - Snowbird Resort

Snowbird is unquestionably the choice mountain for intermediate and expert snowboarders. It has the most vertical terrain of any **Utah** resort and a pretty decent halfpipe, and a superpipe being built for the 04/05 season. Skiers tend to out-number riders on this mountain, but the attitude is not competitive. Over the years, this is a resort that has become well known for its steep terrain and fantastic powder, trees, bowls and gullies along with some okay novice terrain. In all honesty, this place is for riders who can ride, because nearly half of the mountain is rated as advanced. If you like going balls out down serious steeps then Snowbird is your heaven, but be warned, if you fail to respect any of the slopes, you may go home in a body bag.

FREERIDERS should take the **Mineral Basin** lift off the backside of **Hidden Peak** which accesses some of the most epic snow and terrain imaginable. It is easy to spend an entire day there after a good storm and never get bored. On the other hand, once you take the tram to the top of Hidden Mountain, you can't really go wrong no matter what face you drop in off. There are plenty of cool runs like **Silver Fox, Great Scott,** and **Upper Cirque,** and **Gad Valley**. It is also not a bad idea to save some quality time for **Thunder Bowl,** accessible by the Gad 2 lift.

FREESTYLERS have a decent pipe accessed by the Mid-Gad lift, and 2 parks designed for all abilities. Besides that, you will have to use some creativity to find hits.

BEGINNERS will quickly find that Snowbird is really an intermediate to expert mountain and might get bored on the limited availability of easy runs. However, the easy area known as the Baby Thunder, is good.

THE TOWN
Local services are sparse to say the least. There are a couple of lodges close to the base lifts along with a few restaurants and a couple of bars. But don't expect much, or anything cheap.

U

7 OUT OF 10

Super terrain but limited air possibilities

pic - Solitude Resort

%
OF BEGINNER
TO EXPERT
RUNS
20

1200
ACRES

30   50

3058M
TOP LIFT

624M
VERTICAL

2434M
FIRST LIFT

NUMBER OF RUNS: 64
LONGEST RUN: 3.5 miles (5.6km)
TOTAL LIFTS: 8 - all chairs
CAPACITY (people per hour): 12,550
LIFT TIMES: 9:00 a.m. to 4:00 p.m
MOUNTAIN CAFES: 3

Solitude is a nice change of pace because it does not seem to attract hoards of people like the other **Salt Lake** resorts, plus the mountain kicks ass! There is also a great variety of terrain and a way of spreading out the crowds so that the lines in any one area do not get too long. The attitude is low key and the regulars are super friendly. They used to have a weird no air policy at this resort., but they now boats a family terrain park with a couple of lumps and a few boxes. Another major complaint is the electronic pass card and gate system used at every lift which is a real pain in the ass.

FREERIDERS will have no problem having the time of their lives at this resort. The summit lift is sure access to some of the sweetest powder country in Utah. **Honeycomb Canyon** is long and extreme and offers freeriding at its best. The **Evergreen** area is a must and the Headwall Forest rarely gets tracked out. The best freeriding on this mountain is the **Solitude backcountry** area, only accessible by hiking. These impressive steeps and powder fields drop down onto **Brighton Ski Resort**, but by staying far left, you will find trails that wrap back around to Solitude.

FREESTYLERS will probably hate it here. Unless you're first timers the new **family terrain park**s' not going to get your pulse racing
CARVERS will want to concentrate on the area accessed by the **Eagle Express** where there are plenty of fast cruiser runs like the **Challenger**, **Gary's Glade** and Inspiration. Carvers will also be happy with a handful of smooth runs off of the Summit chair such as **Dynamite** and **Liberty**. The Apex chair will get you to a few short groomers as well.

BEGINNERS will find that this mountain is a great place to first try snowboarding at. There is a good area for learning right off of the **Moonbeam II** chair, where you will find plenty of good easy runs to keep you happy for a while. **North Star** and **South Star,** off the Sunrise lift, are also great beginner runs. First timers can also warm up on Easy Street off the Link chair.

AVERAGE SNOWFALL
12.5m
SNOWMAKING
30%

WINTER PERIODS
Nov to April
Lift Passes
Lift pass $45 for 1 day
Board Schools
Beginners package $85 for day hire, lift pass & 2hr lesson
Hire
Board & Boots $30/day $20/half day

FREERIDE 65%
Trees & backcountry
FREESTYLE 5%
A family terrain park (ie shite)
CARVING 30%

Solitude Mountain Resort
12000 Big Cottonwood Canyon
Solitude, UT 84121
Phone: 801.534.1400
Web:www.skisolitude.com
Email:info@skisolitude.com

Fly
to Salt Lake City, transfer time of 50 mins
Drive
From Salt Lake City head east along I-80 and south on I-215 and exit at junction 6 to Wasatch. You'll find the resort 14 miles up Big Cottonwood Canyon
Bus
services from Salt Lake City take 50 mins

THE TOWN
You can stay close to the slopes in one of the lodges or condo units offering a choice rooms at generally high rates. The _Powderhorn_ is Solitude's newest place for lodging offering visitors somewhere to stay that is both good and convenient, but it's not cheap. Eating out options are basic, however, the _Creekside_ makes fantastic pizza's.

THE CANYONS

great boarders resort, perhaps not for absolute beginners though

The Canyons is **Utah's** newest resort and one of the largest with over 3625 acres of fantastic terrain to check out that makes this part of the **Rockies** a pure dream. Newest Canyons may be, but in fact this place has been around for quite some time but under another name, that of **Park West**. However, that's neither here nor there, what this place is about is the future. This massive mountain, which is covered in trees from top to bottom, is constantly expanding by opening new areas all the time and upgrading base facilities year on

year off. Indeed Canyons has big ambitions and plans to one day be the biggest resort in the US. And when you see what they have achieved so far, perhaps it could happen. But for now this is a mountain that has everything to turn the aspiring freestyle junkie into a pro air head, or a freeride grommet into a mountain guru. You have deep gullies, massive powder bowls and natural hits galore wherever you go.

FREERIDERS have landed in paradise when they get here. You simply won't believe not only the amount of terrain, but also the diversity of it all. The **Tombstone Express** will take you to some super terrain, but make sure you study your lift map, it would be easy to head off down a steep trail above your ability. However, one of the best areas to visit is the **South Side Chutes** off the Condor chair lift, where you will find a series of steep chutes.

FREESTYLERS who have been wondering which place to check out in Utah, should look no further than this resort. The Canyons is a mega freestylers hangout having loads of natural halfpipes with excellent banked walls. And as if having perfectly formed natural pipes wasn't enough, the resort also has a first class superpipe called the **Sobe**, take the Saddleback chair to Snow Canyon where you'll find the extensive **CIA terrain park**.

CARVERS of any level will find that this is a fine resort to practice carving at. There are loads of carefully prepared pistes that will keep you happy for days on end.

BEGINNERS must study a lift map or seek advice from a local in order to get to the best of the easy terrain, which in truth, is rather limited. However, if you're a quick learner then it's fine.

THE TOWN
The Canyons has some base area accommodation and other local services. However, the best option in terms of choice and prices is either down in **Park City** or back along in **Salt Lake City**.

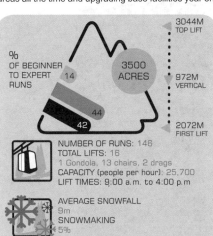

%
OF BEGINNER
TO EXPERT
RUNS

3044M TOP LIFT

3500 ACRES

14

44

42

972M VERTICAL

2072M FIRST LIFT

NUMBER OF RUNS: 146
TOTAL LIFTS: 16
1 Gondola, 13 chairs, 2 drags
CAPACITY (people per hour): 25,700
LIFT TIMES: 9:00 a.m. to 4:00 p.m

AVERAGE SNOWFALL
9m
SNOWMAKING
5%

WINTER PERIODS
Nov to April
Board Schools
$64 2hr group lesson
$110 private lesson
Hire
Board & Boots $34 per day, demo stuff
$45

FREERIDE 40%
Lots of trees & backcountry
FREESTYLE 20%
A terrain park & pipe
CARVING 40%

The Canyons
4000 The Canyons Resort Drive
Park City, UT 84098
Phone: 435-649-5400
Web:www.thecanyons.com
Email:info@thecanyons.com

Fly
to Salt Lake City, with transfer time of 45 minutes (32 miles).
Drive
Salt Lake City head east along I-80.
Salt Lake City to the resort is 32 miles.

U
S
A

U
T
A
H

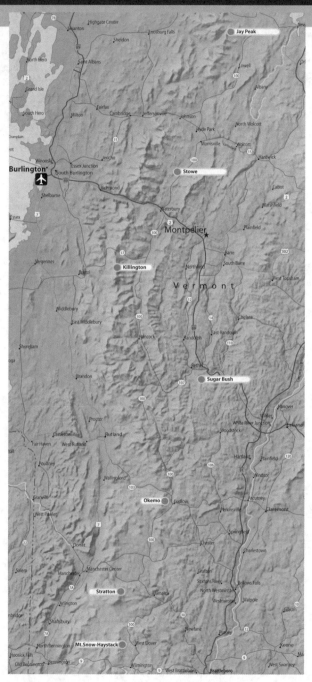

JAY PEAK

5
OUT OF 10

Okay East coast freeriding

Jay Peak, located in the far northern part of **Vermont** and close to the **Canadian border,** is not a bad place and one that attracts a fair few riders from within the state and

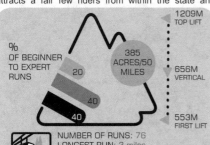

% OF BEGINNER TO EXPERT RUNS

20
40
40

385 ACRES/50 MILES

1209M TOP LIFT
656M VERTICAL
553M FIRST LIFT

NUMBER OF RUNS: 76
LONGEST RUN: 3 miles
TOTAL LIFTS: 8 - 1 Gondola, 5 chairs, 1 drags, 1 magic carpet
CAPACITY (people per hour): 12,175
LIFT TIMES: 8.30am to 4.00pm

AVERAGE SNOWFALL
9m
SNOWMAKING
85%

WINTER PERIODS:
Nov to April
Lift Passes
1 Day $40 , 5 Days $200
Hire
Day $30, 5 Days $115

FREERIDE 50%
A few trees & good backcountry
FREESTYLE 30%
4 Terrain parks & a halfpipe
CARVING 20%

Jay Peak Resort
Route 242, Jay Peak. VT 05859.
Tel: 001 (802) 988 2611
Web:www.jaypeakresort.com
Email:info@jaypeakresort.com

Fly
Fly to Monteal in Canada, transfer time of 1 1/2 hours.
Drive
From Montreal head south on I-10, 35 & 91 & Hwy 100 via Newport. Montreal to the resort = 70 miles. Boston is 3 1/2 hours New York City is 6 1/2 hours.
Bus
services from Montreal takes 1 1/2 hours.
Train
AMTRAK Vermonter to St. Albans, 45 minutes away. Ground transfers available to Jay Peak.

NEW

New for 04/05 season
Will have 4 distinct parks this season, built on the idea of "progressive accessibility".

Pic - Henry Georgi/Jay Peak

across the border in Canada. Indeed the resort is actually owned by a Canadian resort company and you can even use Canadian dollars to pay for your lift ticket. For an east coast resort, Jay has a fairly good annual snow record, and although the amount of snow that falls here is no match for the resorts in the Rocky Mountains, is still good for the east and you can usually be guaranteed some fine powder each year. It is also notable that although it may not be a very big place, the amount of good hardcore and tree riding stands out's. Much of the mountain is fully open to snowboarders and is rated for advanced and intermediate riders, novice terrain is very limited. The resort has a modern lift system which includes a 60 person tramway and a series of chair lifts and T-bars. The location of Jay Peak may be the chief reason for this place for not becoming overcrowded while lift lines are either nonexistent or very small, except over holiday periods and weekends.

FREERIDERS will find that the offerings on Jay Peak are pretty good and will allow advanced and intermediate riders the chance to ride hard and fast with some excellent powder spots, some very fast chutes and lots of tight trees. Note, the resort has a strict policy when it comes to riding in the woods. Basically you must take responsibility for your own actions if you ride out of bounds, you must be a competent rider and you must not go alone. Areas such as **Buckaroo**, the **Everglade** or the **Beaver Ponds Glades** are pure nectar and will excite all riders.

FREESTYLERS have 4 terrain parks and a boardercross trail. But with so much natural freestyle terrain on offer, the man made hits are almost not needed but great to learn on. The **Canyonland** is home to an amazing natural halfpipe that should keep you amused for hours.

CARVERS have a nice number of cruising trails set out everywhere.

BEGINNERS are the one group who may find this place not for them. There are novice areas but they are very limited.

THE TOWN

Jay Peak is a small town and has a limited amount of accommodation on offer. However, prices are not too bad and around town you will be able to go out and get a good meal with a reasonable choice of restaurants. Night life, however, is tame.

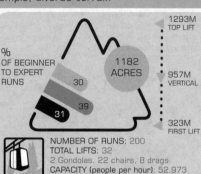

1293M
TOP LIFT

%
OF BEGINNER
TO EXPERT
RUNS

30

1182
ACRES

957M
VERTICAL

31

39

323M
FIRST LIFT

NUMBER OF RUNS: 200
TOTAL LIFTS: 32
2 Gondolas, 22 chairs, 8 drags
CAPACITY (people per hour): 52,973
LIFT TIMES: 8.30am to 4.00pm
MOUNTAIN CAFES: 9

AVERAGE SNOWFALL:
6.4m
SNOWMAKING:
72%

WINTER PERIODS:
Oct to May
Lift Passes
1 Day pass $67/72
5 Days $248
Board Schools
Group lessons $35 for 90mins
Beginner package $99 for 3 days lift,
lesson & hire
Private lessons $65 per hour
Hire
2 Days Lift Pass and Hire $181
Board & Boots $31 per day
Night Boarding
No

FREERIDE 45%
Trees & good backcountry
FREESTYLE 30%
4 Terrain parks & a halfpipe
CARVING 25%

Killington Resort
4763 Killington Road
Killington, VT 05751
Tel: 001 (802) 422 - 6200
Snowphone: 001 (802) 422 - 3261
Web:www.killington.com
Email:info@killington.com

Killington is a big resort - the Beast of the East as the locals like to call it. If you thought the east coast of America was lame and no match for the central or western resorts then think again. Killington has seven mountains of steeps, bumps, mega carving terrain, loads of fun-parks and halfpipes, all serviced by a modern and well equipped lift system that includes an artistically painted and heated gondola. Visitors arriving here thinking that they will have the place licked in a day or two will be surely tested. You will need at least a couple weeks to ride all the runs and then a further month just to get to know what you have just been down. Killington reportedly has the largest snow-making facilities in the east, and like a number of other US resorts, it's a particularly snowboard-friendly place having hosted many snowboard events. The United States Amateur Snowboard Association once chose Killington as its training ground, and it's easy to see why: the terrain is perfect for all levels and all styles. One thing that boarders should be aware of is traversing, as it's very easy to end up spending a lot of time travelling across the mountain, trying to get around. An excellent tool here is the **free Ride Guide** which tells you everything worth knowing, from a snowboarder's perspective, about the mountain and surrounding town - you can pick up a copy at the ticket office.

FREERIDERS have a mountain that often seems to vary at every turn: you get to ride lots of bumps - Superstar on **Skye Peak** and **Outer Limits** on **Bear Mountain** for instance; plus there are lots of trees to ride in, with numerous 'secret' trails to search out. If you're after a heart tester, check out the steeps at **Killington Peak** off the Cascade chair, where you have a choice of tree-lined steep blacks.

FREESTYLERS have two terrain parks and two halfpipes. The main pipe with its 12ft walls is superb

and located close to the base lodge. And as well as the pipe having great transitions and sounds blasting out, you can also get a burrito pipe side. As well as featuring two terrain parks, one of which is now on the **Timberline**, there is now a boardercross course on the **Dream Maker** area. Killington offers a pipe-only pass for $20.

CARVERS will love Killington's steep terrain, which ranges from ultra-wide, straight down trails like **Double**

THE TOWN & GETTING THERE

Dipper (which is good for big carves), to narrower, more traditional runs such as **East Fall** or **Royal Flush**. Other notable carving spots are on **Ram's Head, Snowdon** or **Skye Peak**.

BEGINNER'S areas are excellent. However, like a lot of New England resorts, they can get busy at weekends. Stick to mid-week if possible as there are no crowds and empty runs. The *Killington Snowboard School* is excellent and offers every level of tuition, at prices worth paying. A day's ride package costs $65.

THE TOWN

Local facilities are extensive and varied, with a purpose-built village at the base of the slopes. However, by far the bulk of local hospitality is stretched along the access road. If you're prepared to pay for the convenience, then try to stay at the base; the cheaper thing to do is move away from **Killington** and hang out in one of the smaller hamlets. This way you get a better feel of the place and the locals are easier to get to know. Wherever you stay, it's always good to have a car, although there are shuttle bus services. For snowboard services check the *Ride On* or *Darkside* shops.

Accommodation here is a bit hit and miss in the sense that there is no real town to speak of. There are

Pic -Killgton Resort

some slopeside condos, but they don't come cheap. A full range of lodging options can be found stretched along the five mile access road, and offers dozens of cheap B&B joints to motels.

Food is standard grade, east coast, with big portions, lots of variety with over 60 restaurants throughout the area and in every price bracket. *Churchills* is noted for its steaks but isn't cheap and may entail a drive to get to it along route 4. Also highly rated is *Hemingways*, a super dollar hungry restaurant. For a decent and filling breakfast, why not check out the *Kodiak Cafe*. Or for a reasonably priced burger visit *Peppers bar*.

Pic -Killgton Resort

Night-life in and around Killington is noted for being well suited to snowboarders. There is a host of evening spots where beer and local birds are available to all ,and which can be very lively most evenings while rocking 'til late. The *Pickle Barrel* is known for having a good vibe as is the *Wobbly Barn* with live bands and rowdy crowds.

SUMMARY

Very good snowboarder's resort with ample, diverse terrain to suit all styles and levels. Lots of good local services but not a convenient layout.

Money wise: In the main very pricey but with options for budget riders to make it.

U
S
A

V
E
R
M
O
N
T

CAR
2 3/4 hours from Boston I93 to south of Concord,NH. I89 north to us 4 Rutland, Exit 1 in Vermont. Follow US4 west to Resort
FLY
to Boston, but theres no direct transfers.

6 OUT OF 10

Basic but good riding

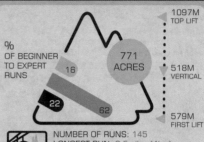
Pic MtSnow Resort

%
OF BEGINNER
TO EXPERT
RUNS

16

771 **ACRES**

22

62

1097M
TOP LIFT

518M
VERTICAL

579M
FIRST LIFT

NUMBER OF RUNS: 145
LONGEST RUN: 2.5miles (4km)
TOTAL LIFTS: 23
18 chairs, 2 drags, 3 magic carpet
CAPACITY (people per hour): 36,944
LIFT TIMES: 8.30am to 4.00pm

AVERAGE SNOWFALL
4.21m
SNOWMAKING
50%

WINTER PERIODS:
Nov to April
Lift Passes
Day pass $55/65 (hi/low season)
Board Schools
private $87/hr 6 hours $360
Hire
Board and Boots $36/day 5 Days $121

FREERIDE 40%
Trees but poor backcountry
FREESTYLE 25%
4 Terrain parks & a halfpipe
CARVING 35%

Mt Snow
105 Mountain Road
VT 05356
Tel: 001 (802) 464 3333
Web:www.mountsnow.com
Email:info@mountsnow.com

Fly
to Boston Int. or Bradley Int. both with
a transfer time of around 23/4 hours .
Drive
From Boston, head west along Hwy 2,
then north on I-91,west along Rte 9 and
then finally north on Rts 100 to Mt Snow..
Boston to resort is 134 miles, 2 3/4
hours drive time.
Bus
services from Boston and Bradley.

Mount Snow and Haystack are located in the **Green Mountain National Forest**, and like many of the east coast resorts within easy reach of major towns and cities, the area sees plenty of weekend ski-dwellers. Mount Snow and Haystack are, in fact, two separate resorts that are not, unfortunately, linked by lifts or snow trails. However, they are only a few minutes apart via the regular shuttle bus operating between the two areas. Collectively, the two areas have some 145 trails that are sold as one when you buy a lift pass. In the main, the whole place forms a cruisy mountain, best suited to intermediates and novices, with some decent-sized runs and interesting terrain features with hits, rollers, flats and trees. Be warned that at weekends and holiday periods, long lift queues do appear.

FREERIDERS coming here for the first time will find that the slopes on Mount Snow will offer challenging and difficult terrain. Advanced freeriders should head up to North Face with its series of blacks and double blacks which will test you with a mixture of bumps and groomed terrain. On Haystack, The **Witches** double blacks offer some interesting riding, but they're quite short.

FREESTYLERS are best checking out the slopes on Mount Snow, where you'll find a good series of well constructed man-made hits in **Inferno terrain park** fun-park, which is over 1,000 metres long. Close by, is the **Gut** 120 metre professional superpipe, which has flood lights and is shaped to competition level.

CARVERS wanting to lay down arcs can do so with ease on Snowdance, one of the blues from the Summit Cafe. The **North Face** area on Mount Snow is good for fast carving on steeps.

BEGINNERS tend to stay on Mount Snow, where there is a good layout of easy trails. Haystack has a complete beginner-only area. Ride On Snowboard School offers a Guaranteed Learn to Ride session, at $50 all-in.

THE TOWN
There is accommodation at the base of the slopes. *Mount Snow Condominiums* offer very good facilities which include a pool, but it's not a cheap option. A far greater selection of services can be found at **West Dover** or **Wilmington**, both inside a 10 mile radius. The lifestyle here is nothing amazing: a few bars and a number of places to eat give a laid back feel to the place, without any ego.

U S A

V E R M O N T

OKEMO

Stacks of diverse terrain to ride

Jay Peak, located in the far northern part of **Vermont** and close to the **Canadian border,** is not a bad place and one that attracts a fair few riders from within the state and across the border in Canada. Indeed the resort is actually owned by a Canadian resort company and

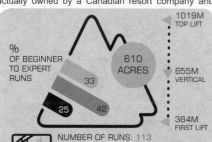

%
OF BEGINNER
TO EXPERT
RUNS

610 ACRES

33
25 42

1019M
TOP LIFT

655M
VERTICAL

364M
FIRST LIFT

Pic - Okemo Resort

NUMBER OF RUNS: 113
LONGEST RUN: 4.5miles (7.2km)
TOTAL LIFTS: 18
12 chairs, 5 drags, 1 magic carpet
CAPACITY (people per hour): 32,050
LIFT TIMES: 8.00am to 4.00pm

AVERAGE SNOWFALL:5.08m
SNOWMAKING:95%

WINTER PERIODS:Nov to April
Lift Passes
2 days $96/112, 5 Days $210/245
Hire
Group $33hr, Private $80/hr
Board School
Board and Boots $33/day, 5 Days $135

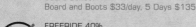

FREERIDE 40%
Trees but poor backcountry
FREESTYLE 30%
3 Terrain parks & 3 halfpipes
CARVING 30%

Okemo Mountain Resort
77 Okemo Ridge Road
Ludlow VT 05149
Tel - (802) 228-4041
Fax - (802) 228-2079
Snow Phone - (802) 228-5222
Web:www.okemo.com
Email:info@okemo.com

Fly
to Boston, with a transfer time 3 hours. Albany 2Hrs
Drive
From Boston, head north on I-93 to Hwy 89, turning off at junction 9 for route 103 via Ascutney and Ludlow.,Boston to resort is 150 miles. 3 hours drive time.
Bus
services from Boston can take 3 hours.

NEW

New for 04/05 season
Two new gladed trails have been added at Jackson Gore.

you can even use Canadian dollars to pay for your lift ticket. For an east coast resort, Jay has a fairly good annual snow record, and although the amount of snow that falls here is no match for the resorts in the Rocky Mountains, is still good for the east and you can usually be guaranteed some fine powder each year. It is also notable that although it may not be a very big place, the amount of good hardcore and tree riding stands out's. The location of Jay Peak may be the chief reason for this place for not becoming overcrowded while lift lines are either nonexistent or very small, except over holiday periods and weekends.

FREERIDERS will find that the offerings on Jay Peak are pretty good and will allow advanced and intermediate riders the chance to ride hard and fast with some excellent powder spots, some very fast chutes and lots of tight trees. Note, the resort has a strict policy when it comes to riding in the woods. Basically you must take responsibility for your own actions if you ride out of bounds, you must be a competent rider and you must not go alone. Areas such as **Buckaroo**, the **Everglade** or the **Beaver Ponds Glades** are pure nectar and will excite all riders.

FREESTYLERS have 4 terrain parks and a boardercross trail. But with so much natural freestyle terrain on offer, the man made hits are almost not needed but great to learn on. The **Canyonland** is home to an amazing natural halfpipe that should keep you amused for hours.

CARVERS have a nice number of cruising trails set out everywhere.

BEGINNERS are the one group who may find this place not for them. There are novice areas but they are very limited.

THE TOWN

Jay Peak is a small town and has a limited amount of accommodation on offer. However, prices are not too bad and around town you will be able to go out and get a good meal with a reasonable choice of restaurants. Night life, however, is tame.

Pic Stratton Resort

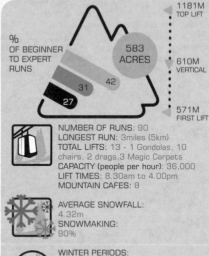

%
OF BEGINNER
TO EXPERT
RUNS

583 ACRES

1181M TOP LIFT

610M VERTICAL

571M FIRST LIFT

42
31
27

NUMBER OF RUNS: 90
LONGEST RUN: 3miles (5km)
TOTAL LIFTS: 13 - 1 Gondolas, 10 chairs, 2 drags,3 Magic Carpets
CAPACITY (people per hour): 36,000
LIFT TIMES: 8.30am to 4.00pm
MOUNTAIN CAFES: 8

AVERAGE SNOWFALL:
4.32m
SNOWMAKING:
90%

WINTER PERIODS:
Nov to May
Lift Passes
1 day $59/72
5 days $198/215
Board Schools
1 3/4hr group from $35
1 3/4hr private from$85
Hire
burton boards $39/45 day
kids $35/39 day
Night Boarding
No

FREERIDE 40%
Trees but poor backcountry
FREESTYLE 35%
5 Terrain parks (3 beginners) & a halfpipe
CARVING 25%

Stratton Mountain Resort
RR 1 Box 145
Stratton Mountain, Vermont 05155-9406
Tel: 802-297-4000
Snowfone: 802-297-4211
Web:www.stratton.com
Email:infostratton@intrawest.com

Stratton is generally recognised as the home of snowboarding, well at least on the east coast. A decent-sized resort, **Stratton** was one of the first areas in the US to give snowboarders access to its mountain. It is also noted for not only being the original home and test area for **Jake Burton** and his Burton Snowboards, but also as the place where America's first pro-snowboard school was set up and the home to the world's longest running snowboard competition, The US Open, which uses what is reputed to be the best halfpipe on the planet. The Green Mountain Race Series also comes to Stratton for a couple of events. Midweek you are up and down the mountain in a flash, but at the weekend, lift queues appear as everybody from **New York** and **Boston** arrive en-mass. However, with 40 years history as a ski resort, the management know how to keep things moving along to everyone's satisfaction. Riding here will suite everyone although riders who look for extreme or big cliff jumps may be a little disappointed. Still this is a resort that has a good annual snow record and one which offers snowmaking facilities covering over 82% of the terrain on offer.

FREERIDERS who like their terrain carved out of tight trees, won't be disappointed as all the trails are hacked out of thick wood from top to bottom. For a good ride fix, the rollers and banks on the intermediate/novice terrain of **Black Bear** and the **Meadows** should do the trick. Riders with some know-how should check out the

Upper Tamarack and if you are looking for some open trees, Freefall is the place.

FREESTYLERS hanging around the lower mountain can use the high-speed, six-person chair to access one of five fun-parks and the superpipe. All the parks have a series of table-tops, gaps and ramps and to keep you interested they regularly build new hits. The pipe also has a loud sound-system, and floodlights for hitting the walls at night. On the lower mountain

THE TOWN & GETTING THERE

Pic Stratton Resort

is the **Upper & Lower East Meadow terrain parks**, the upper is a novice park set out with a series of small hits for catching your first air without too much landing pain, the lower park takes things up a level. **The Power park** is strictly for pros or those with balls as big as the huge table-tops, this is also where you'll find the superpipe.

CARVERS will notice that **North American, Upper Standard** and **Lifeline** will grab the alpine rider for big turns. The runs are well pisted and wide enough to allow you to put in some long, continuous turns, without too much fear of a collision.

BEGINNERS and novice riders will have the whole of the lower mountain to explore, plus easy routes from the summit. The runs are particularly well suited for first timers, but at weekends the flat pitches become crowded, so expect a few collisions. Snowboard tuition is first class at Stratton with loads of lesson programmes.

THE TOWN

Whether you're planning a week's trip or a two week stay, you won't be disappointed with what you find both on the slopes and off them. At the base of the mountain is a compact alpine style village with more or less everything you need. The scene can't be described as wild and in your face, but it is out there and with plenty going on. The place has a warm and welcoming atmosphere, and although you pay for it, services are very good. Shopaholics will love it here as there are dozens of stores and malls to help while away your time. There's also a very good sports centre in Stratton, where you can tone up, have a massage, or simply perve at the women doing their exercises.

Accomodation. With nigh on 20,000 visitor beds around the area, lodging options are really good, with the usual offerings of condos, lodges, fancy, over-priced hotels or basic B&B haunts. The Lift Line Lodge has rates from $70, while the Stratton Mountain Inn has rates from $90 and offers good services in the centre of the village.

Food. Eating out options are a little disappointing, with the choice of expensive, bland food in a pompous restaurant, or cheap, bland nosh at a fast-food outlet.

However, if you search around, you will find something to please your pallet. The *Sirloin Saloon* fries up some damn fine steaks and the Base Lodge Cafeteria dishes up a decent breakfast. Pizza lovers should check out the offerings from *La Pizzeria* while *Red Fox* is the Italian place.

Night-life in Stratton is okay but not spectacular. The *Base Lodge* is the first port of call in the early evening hours, where you can play pool, pinball and a juke box pumping out up-to-date sounds. Later on, check out the *Green Door Pub* for a few lively beers, or *North Grill* to sample some blues in a laid back atmosphere.

SUMMARY

Good snowboarder's resort with ample, diverse terrain to suit all styles and levels. Lots of good local services, but a bit hit and miss!

CAR
Take Route 2 west to I-91. Go north to exit 2 and follow signs to Route 30 north, then drive 38 miles north to Bondville, VT. Total distance 146 miles, drive time is about 3 1/4 hours.
FLY
Fly to Boston International. Transfer time to resort is 3 1/4 hours. Local airport is Albany 90 miles.
TRAIN
to Brattleboro, 40 miles away
BUS
There are daily bus services from Boston airport and from Albany airport.

5 OUT OF 10 — Okay fun resort

Pic -Stowe Resort

1109M TOP LIFT

% OF BEGINNER TO EXPERT RUNS

16

480 ACRES

720M VERTICAL

25

59

290M FIRST LIFT

NUMBER OF RUNS: 46
LONGEST RUN: 3.7miles (6km)
TOTAL LIFTS: 11
1 Gondola, 8 chairs, 2 drags
CAPACITY (people per hour): 16,600
LIFT TIMES: 8.30am to 9.00pm

AVERAGE SNOWFALL
6.35m
SNOWMAKING
75%

WINTER PERIODS:Nov to April
Lift Passes
1 Day $56 , 5 Day $282
Night pass $20,Season pass $1,435
Board Schools
privte 1hr/$93 half day $216
group from $37
Hire
board & boots $31 additional days $25
Night Boarding
thursday-saturday 4/9pm on 2 trails

FREERIDE 40%
Trees but poor backcountry
FREESTYLE 25%
3 Terrain parks & a halfpipe
CARVING 35%

Stowe Mountain Resort
5781 Mountain Road
Stowe, VT 05672
Tel: 1-800-253-4754
Web:www.stowe.com

Fly
to Boston Int, transfer time 2 1/2 hrs.
Drive
From Boston, head north on 89 and turn
off at junction 10 on to route 100 to
Stowe. Boston to resort is 198 miles. 2
1/2 hours drive time.
Bus
services from Boston take 3 3/4 hours

If you're after some serious east coast riding, then the popular resort of **Stowe** is your place. It's a proper mountain spread over three distinct areas, each one lending itself to a different level of ability: **Spruce Peaks** is the beginner/intermediate area (a little isolated from the main ride area); **Mt Mansfield** is accessed by the fastest 8-person gondola in the world, and is an intermediate's paradise with great cruising terrain, perfect for those who like to carve. The final area is the largest, and a perfect mix for each style in the advanced stages. Because Stowe is a popular hangout with city slickers and weekend tourists, the lifts can get clogged on weekend mornings, but don't be put off - a short wait will be awarded with a good long run.

FREERIDERS may find the area under the gondola fun with heaps of tracks through trees, and plenty of places within the main area to disappear into. Liftline and National are rather tame trails having been widened over the years, and are only cool if you are into bumps. **Nosedive** is good for freeride and carving, with the rest of the **Mansfield** area consisting of intermediate terrain, including a few good natural hits and jumps on the trail's edge.

FREESTYLERS are going to kick arse on any mountain after a session in one of four fun-parks at Stowe. The top choice park is the specially designed **Jungle**, located on the Lower Lord area which is easily reached from Lift 4. Stowe also has a pipe, and the resort even provides a park for beginners and novices, alongside 20 minute lessons called Quick Trick at $15.

CARVERS are much in evidence at Stowe, with the runs on **Mt Mansfield** having some nice, tame carving trails.

BEGINNERS will surprise themselves when they see how quickly they can progress on the abundance of easy slopes, especially if they are aided by the teaching staff at the local snowboard school who have more teaching programmes available than you could poke a stick at, ranging from novice to freestyle camps.

THE TOWN

The village is about six miles from the main slopes and is reached by a free shuttle bus. There are plenty of places to lay your head along the road to the lifts, with the usual choice of condos and B&B's. Stowe doesn't have the most radical **night-life**, although you can eat and drink well in a number of restaurants and bars, with the cool, friendly locals. The *Rusty Nail* is a hot spot for beer and music.

SUGAR BUSH

6 OUT OF 10

Not a bad series of mountains

Pic-Sugarbush Resort

1260M
TOP LIFT

%
OF BEGINNER
TO EXPERT
RUNS

18

54
MILES

807M
VERTICAL

39

43

452M
FIRST LIFT

NUMBER OF RUNS: 115
TOTAL LIFTS: 17 - 14 chairs, 3 drags
CAPACITY (people per hour): 25,463
LIFT TIMES: 8.30am to 4.00pm
MOUNTAIN CAFES: 5

AVERAGE SNOWFALL: 6.6m
SNOWMAKING: 68%

WINTER PERIODS:Nov to April
Lift Passes
1 day $48/59, 6 days $296
Board Schools
group 2 hours $37
private 1 hour $82 all day $297
Hire
board and boots $30/day

FREERIDE 40%
Trees but limited backcountry
FREESTYLE 20%
2 Terrain parks & a halfpipe
CARVING 40%

Sugarbush Resort
1840 Sugarbush Access Rd.
Warren, VT 05674
Phone: (802) 583-6300
Web:www.sugarbush.com

Fly
to Burlington Airport which is a 45min
taxi away from resort. Boston airport
approximately 3 hours drive/bus away.
Drive
Southbound: take I-89 south to Exit
10 Waterbury,Route 2 south to Route
100, through Waitsfield then right onto
Sugarbush Access Road. Northbound:
take I-89 Exit 9 on to Route 100b onto
to 100 through Waitsfield, then right
onto Sugarbush Access Road.
Bus
services available from Boston
Train
Waterbury and Rutland nearest stations.
Amtrak runs trains from Washington
DC,Baltimore,Philadelphia and New York

NEW
New for 04/05 season
On Mt Ellen 40 acres of terrain,
Progression Park with plans for 9 parks
of varying difficulty. Burton LTR centre.
Mt Ellen only lift pass.

Located along the **Mad River Valley** is the very snowboard friendly resort of Sugarbush, a mountain resort that is not bad and well worth a visit if you are in the area. Sugarbush is split over six connected mountain areas, all of which offer different features for different abilities. A short distance from Sugarbush is a resort called **Mad River Glen**, however, don't bother with this arse of a place because seven years ago they banned snowboarders due to a dispute with the management. Still, today there's no such problem here at Sugarbush, which has been operating as a resort since 1958. Today Sugarbush is a modern and well equipped resort with state of the art snowmaking facilities that reach almost 70% of the slopes. Mind you the resort has a respectable real annual snow fall of some 716 cm per season, making artificial snow not always so important. The six rideable areas are split up as, **Castlerock Peak,** which is home to some major expert terrain, **Cadd Peak,** which is the location for the Mountain Range Snow Park and good intermediate runs, **Lincoln Peak**, which has a splattering of good carving trails and some trees, **Mount Ellen**, which is the highest in the resort, **North Lynx Peak** home to a lot of novice terrain and finally **Slide Brook Basin**. You can ride all the areas on one lift pass and all are connected by the array of chair and drag lifts.

FREERIDERS should first make for the **Lincoln Peak** where you will be able to sample some major runs via the **Castlerock chair.** This area is mainly for riders who know the score, if you are easily frightened, forget it. However, if you are up to it then you won't be disappointed.
FREESTYLERS have a new **Progression Park** on Mount Ellen for beginners. The pro park has moved to the Sunny D area and has it's own lift. Around the resort there is also an abundance of natural hits for catching air off.
CARVERS can pick and choose really. The area has a cool choice of groomers. Some of the runs on **Lincoln** are ideal for carving.
BEGINNERS can take a lesson at the local ski school before trying out the easy slopes on **Lincoln Peak** or the **North Lynx Peak**

THE TOWN
Off the slopes Sugarbush offers a large number of accommodation options, from quality hotels to basic bed and breakfast homes. Dining out is also rather good around here, however, the same can't be said for the nightlife, it's very lame indeed.

U

U
S
A

V
E
R
M
O
N
T

Rider Terje Haakonsen pic- JeffCurtes, - burton snowboards

CRYSTAL MOUNTAIN

6
OUT OF 10

Pretty good resort

Located mid-way into **Washington State**, an hour and twenty minutes from **Seattle**, Crystal is yet another yankee freeride classic, unspoilt by skiers, for riders in the know. The terrain is spread out over four peaks, with an awesome amount of backcountry riding. Over the next few years,

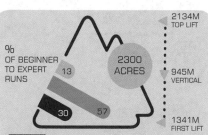

%
OF BEGINNER TO EXPERT RUNS

13

2300 ACRES

30   57

2134M
TOP LIFT

945M
VERTICAL

1341M
FIRST LIFT

NUMBER OF RUNS: 50
LONGEST RUN: 2.5miles
TOTAL LIFTS: 9 - 1all chairs
CAPACITY (people per hour): 19,110
LIFT TIMES: 8.30am to 4.00pm

AVERAGE SNOWFALL
9.65m
SNOWMAKING
none

WINTER PERIODS
Nov to April
Lift Passes
Half Day $40, Full Day $45
Night $20
Board Schools
2Hr Group $35
Private 1 Hr $65
Hire
board and boots $30/day
Night Boarding
4pm-Close Fri/Sat night

FREERIDE 50%
Trees & backcountry
FREESTYLE 25%
A Terrain parks & a halfpipe
CARVING 25%

Crystal Mountain Resort
1 Crystal Mtn Blvd. Crystal Mt
WA 98022
Tel: 001 (630) 663 2265
Web:www.skicrystal.com
Email:comments@skicrystal.com

Fly
to Seattle, 76 miles north of Crystal.
Drive
From Seattle head south on I-5 and exit onto Hwy 164 and then Hwy 410 east to Crystal Mountain. Seattle to resort 76 miles. 1 1/2 hours drive time.
Bus
services from Seattle take 1 3/4 hours.

Pic-Cyrtal Mountain Resort

the planned investment programme will deliver new lift facilities and improve existing services. It will also raise Crystal's profile which may have the adverse effect of bringing in more skiers - presently there is a balanced mix, leaving the slopes crowd-free and lift queues short.

FREERIDERS, miss this place and you're missing out on life; the terrain is pure freeriding and South Back is the place to check out if you're willing to do some hiking. From the summit of **Throne**, you get to ride what can best be described as heaven - unfortunately it is not for wimps being a steep with a double black diamond rating. Less daunting but still a big buzz are the runs off **Summit House**, while the trails in the North Back area on the likes of **Paradise Bowl** are total joy.

FREESTYLERS won't need man-made facilities at Crystal Mountain, as there is plenty of natural freeride terrain to catch big air. However, there is a pipe off the **Rendezvous chair**, but it's not up to much. The Boarder Zone fun-park, located off the **Quicksilver** chair, has a number of hits, but like the halfpipe, it doesn't live up to what nature can offer.

CARVERS can have as good a time as freeriders, with a choice of excellent slopes that will please advanced and intermediate riders, even if some of the trails are not too long.

BEGINNERS can't do much worse than at Crystal. Only 13 of its trails are fine for novices, but what is on offer is excellent and easily reached from the base. And like many US resorts, a number of the higher rated runs are not that tricky, so many of the red trails can be licked by a competent, fast-learning novice.

THE TOWN
No big surprise here, the village at the base of the slopes is simple, basic, but good enough, with affordable places to sleep and eat in to suit all tastes and pockets. For a **bed** check out The *Alpine Inn*, which is close to the slopes and good value. For a feed try the *Cascade Grill* which serves a good breakfast. The main hangout for booze is the *Snorting Elk Cellar*, but unfortunately it's not a place for babes.

U

USA   WASHINGTON

wsg

MT BAKER

10 OUT OF 10

Fantastic snowboarder's resort

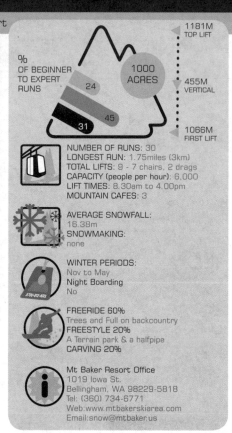

% OF BEGINNER TO EXPERT RUNS

24

1000 ACRES

31

45

1181M TOP LIFT

455M VERTICAL

1066M FIRST LIFT

NUMBER OF RUNS: 30
LONGEST RUN: 1.75miles (3km)
TOTAL LIFTS: 9 - 7 chairs, 2 drags
CAPACITY (people per hour): 6,000
LIFT TIMES: 8.30am to 4.00pm
MOUNTAIN CAFES: 3

AVERAGE SNOWFALL:
16.38m
SNOWMAKING:
none

WINTER PERIODS:
Nov to May
Night Boarding
No

FREERIDE 60%
Trees and Full on backcountry
FREESTYLE 20%
A Terrain park & a halfpipe
CARVING 20%

Mt Baker Resort Office
1019 Iowa St.
Bellingham, WA 98229-5818
Tel: (360) 734-6771
Web:www.mtbakerskiarea.com
Email:snow@mtbaker.us

If sex was a mountain, Mt Baker would be the orgasm, because this treasure is pure snowboarding heaven, with a snowboard history that is written in big letters. In the early days when other ski resorts had their heads up their arses and were banning snowboarders, this amazing place took a far different view. That foresight has crowned Baker as one of the best unspoilt snowboard resorts in the world, with a snow record to be envious of. It also holds the world record for most snowfall for a resort in a season, set back in 98/99 with a staggering 29m. On average they get 16m which explains why theres never been any plans, nor will there be of adding snowmaking to their facilities. Mt Baker is also the home to the legendary Banked Slalom race, which is held every year. Located in the far north of Washington state, Mt Baker was home to the late legend Craig Kelly, who liked riding Baker's terrain so much, he moved there. Due to Baker's isolation it has the added advantage that it doesn't attract hoards of day-tripping skiers, leaving the slopes bare and the lift queues at a big fat 'zero'. The slopes span two mountains - **Mount Shuskan** rising to 2,963m (9,720ft), and **Panorama Dome** with its more modest summit of 1,524m (5,000ft). Both mountains offer the opportunity to ride steeps and deep powder, with the majority of advanced piste set

out on the Panorama side. Runs like the **Chute** are set to test anyone, but be warned, parts of it are really steep and carry avalanche warnings. Overall, Baker is a mountain where you need to be fully aware of your surroundings and not take any chances. One wrong turn could easily see you returning home to mum in a black body bag!.

FREERIDERS wanting to explore the amazing off-piste should seek the advice of a local rider; it's the only way to locate the best stuff, of which there are heaps. The amazing amount of unrestricted freeriding terrain is truly awesome and will keep you riding happily forever and a day. For the less adventurous, the blue off Number 8 chair in the **Shuskan** area is well worth a ride, offering piste-loving freeriders the opportunity to shine at speed.

FREESTYLERS will love the whole area, particularly the natural halfpipe that runs from the top of the two **Shuskan** chair lifts. This is where the Banked Slalom

Pics -Mt Baker Resort

may be a bit thin on the ground, but don't let that put you off. What is offered is cheap and damn good value, making a week or even two, well worth the trip up. The town of Bellingham, just over an hour away has an even greater selection of lodgings, sporting facilities and other visitor attractions.

Accommodation is only possible down in **Glacier** which has a number of options at very reasonable prices. Cool places to contact for a bed, are *Glacier Creek Lodge, Mt Baker B&B, Diamond Ridge B&B* or a condo at the Mt Baker Chalets & Condos.

is held and, apart from beginners, is a must for all freestylers and freeriders. The run drops down a long winding gully and is totally magic.

CARVERS who only want to pose whilst laying fast tracks on perfectly prepared piste should stay away. Mt Baker is not a hard-booter's resort, although there are some runs to blast down. Instead, buckle in with soft boots and go freeriding which this places is meant for, (lame heads who want to pose in hard boots stay away).

BEGINNERS won't be disappointed with Mt Baker, with the option of learning on plenty of easy runs that are spread out around the area, the best being located on Shuskan. The local snowboard school is well established and offers a number of teaching programmes for all levels, with an emphasis on general freeriding.

THE TOWN
Riders who like everything on their doorstep will not be happy as the only facility at the base is a car park. Baker is not a gimmick, so you do have to put yourself out which is another reason why it's so good. The slopes of Mt Baker are located 17 miles from the main local services which can be found in the low-key town of **Glacier**, a simple and unspoilt place. Local services

Food. The options for getting a meal on the slopes or down in Glacier may be a bit limited in terms of choices of restaurants, but what is available will do nicely. During the day you can pig out on the slopes at the White Salmon Day Lodge which has very reasonable rates. The new Raven Hot cafe has fast become a major day time hangout whilst also serving up some wicked food. Down in Glacier, Milano's Cafe is the place to check out, where they do great pasta dishes.

Night-life. One of the beauty's of this place is it's laid back atmosphere, which applies equally to the night life in Glacier, the perfect snowboard scene-laid back and cool. There is no hype, no après-ski crap and no gits in silly hats playing party games. What you get is basic, offering a good laugh and messy late night drinking sessions, resulting in some killer hangovers.

SUMMARY
Fantastic snowboarder's resort with ample diverse terrain to suit all styles and levels. Lots of good local services but not convenient for the slopes.

U
S
A

W
A
S
H
I
N
G
T
O
N

CAR
Seattle via Bellingham. Mt Baker is 107 miles (172km). Drive time is about 2 hours.
FLY
Fly to Seattle International. Transfer time to resort is 2 hours. Local airport is Bellingham 56 miles away.
TRAIN
to Bellingham (56 miles)
BUS
Buses from Seattle take 3 hours and 1 1/4 hours from Bellingham airport.

399

Pic Ride Snowbo

GRAND TARGHEE

8 OUT OF 10

A resort for powder hounds

3110M
TOP LIFT

BEGINNER
EXPERT
INS

10

2500
ACRES

729M
VERTICAL

35

55

2438M
FIRST LIFT

NUMBER OF RUNS: 62
LONGEST RUN: 2.5miles (4km)
TOTAL LIFTS: 5
4 chairs, 1 Magic Carpet
LIFT TIMES: 9.30am to 4.00pm

AVERAGE SNOWFALL
12.8m
SNOWMAKING
5%

WINTER PERIODS
Nov to April
Lift Passes
1 Day $53, 5 Days - $250
Board Schools
2hr group $45, 1 hr private $70
Mountain guide 3 hrs $175
Hire
Board & Boots $29 per day pro kit $40
Snowmobiles
Targhee Snowmobile Tours offer day trips
through Yellowstone National Park, www.
tetonvalleyadventures.com
Cat Boarding
Full day: $299,Half Day: $225
Reservations and deposit are required,
call ext. 1355

FREERIDE 70%
Trees & backcountry
FREESTYLE 20%
A natural halfpipe
CARVING 10%

Grand Targhee Ski & Summer Resort
Box Ski, Wyoming 83422
Tel: 001 (307)-353-2300
Web:www.grandtarghee.com
Email:info@grandtarghee.com

Fly
to Salt Lake City International.Transfer
time to resort = 5 3/4 hours. Local
airport = Teton Peaks 13 miles away.
Drive
Idaho Falls via Driggs.Grand Targhee is
87 miles. Drive time is about 1 3/4
hours. *Salt Lake City is 289 miles,
which will take about 5 3/4 hours.
Bus
from Idaho Falls take 1 1/2 hours and
5 3/4 hours from Salt Lake City airport
(289 miles).

Freeriders in search of powder and lots of it, will find that Grand Targhee is the perfect place to find it. This fantastic resort is a US powder heaven, with an average snowfall of over 1,280cm a year making riding powder a buy word here, even the piste map shows the powder terrain levels so novices can even try out powder stashes. What you have here in this low key resort are two mountains - **Fred's Mountain** which can be reached via three chair lifts and a drag lift, and **Peaked Mountain** accessible only by snowcats. Both mountains offer the chance to do some full-on freeriding on crowd free slopes that will suit advanced and intermediate riders in the main. The trails on Fred's Mountain are a collection of short blacks that snake through a smattering of trees with a couple of nice, wide open blue runs. If you're the adventurous sort, then Peaked Mountain should be the place to get your fix. This is where you get to ride perfect freeride territory with the help of snowcats - a local company offers snowcat tours for around $299 a day. Tours are accompanied by guides and limited to 10 people per cat; prices include a lunch. Peaked Mountain is not exclusively for advanced riders; in fact most of what is on offer is graded green and blue, with a couple of black descents that take in some thick trees.

FREERIDERS will soon work out that this is a resort for them. The terrain on both mountains lends itself perfectly for both piste and backcountry riding. You'll find a number of steep black trails on **Fred's Mountain**, but most of them are quite short.
FREESTYLERS have a naturally formed halfpipe that provides air heads with some interesting walls to ride up. There is also a killer boardercross circuit that needs to be treated with full respect. However, man-made obstacles aren't really necessary in Targhee; the place is riddled with natural hits, many of which are known only to the locals. However, the riders here are cool and will happily take you to the best launch pads and show you how much diverse, natural freestyle terrain there actually is.
CARVERS forget it, especially Euro-faggots who only own a pair of hard boots. The terrain here is not really suited to big arcs and posey turns for lift-line riders. What's more, as there's not too much smooth grooming here, the generally uneven slopes will take you out if you edge over without good speed control.
BEGINNERS are the one group who may feel left out here. Although there is some novice areas around the base, there's not much of it. Still, if you're a fast learner then don't be put off.

Off the slopes what you get is both basic and very limited. There is only a handful of buildings at the base area offering a number of high quality lodges, hotels and a few local shops all close to the slopes. The village has a very relaxed and laid back appeal to it, but if you're the sort that wants a resort loaded with the usual tourist gizmo's, forget it.

U

U
S
A

W
Y
O
M
I
N
G

JACKSON HOLE

Lots of challenging terrain offering some excellent backcountry freeriding

pics - Jackson Hole Resort

3185M
TOP LIFT

%
OF BEGINNER
TO EXPERT
RUNS

10

2500
ACRES

40

50

1216M
VERTICAL

1924M
FIRST LIFT

NUMBER OF RUNS: 62
LONGEST RUN: 4.5miles (7.2km)
TOTAL LIFTS: 11 - 1 Aerial tram, 1 Gondola, 8 chairs,1 Magic Carpet
CAPACITY (people per hour): 8,600
LIFT TIMES: 8.30am to 4.00pm
MOUNTAIN CAFES: 3

AVERAGE SNOWFALL:
11.6m
SNOWMAKING:
10%

WINTER PERIODS:
Dec to April
Lift Passes
1 Day pass $49/67
6 Day pass $294/$372
Board Schools
Private lessons half/all day $265/$445
3 Day beginner package lesson, lift pass, hire $210
Group lessons 3hr $80
Hire
Burton Board & Boots $26.5 per day

FREERIDE 55%
Trees & full on backcountry
FREESTYLE 25%
A Terrain park & a halfpipe
CARVING 20%

Hole Mountain Resort
Box 290, 3395 West Village Drive
Teton Village, WY 83025
Tel: 1-307-733-2292
Web:www.jacksonhole.com
Email:info@jacksonhole.com

NEW

New for 04/05
Opening of Crags Terrain 200 new acres
of once closed Bowls Chutes and Trees
a must do, accessible via the Headwall
"Stairway to Heaven" or via a more
gradual hike from the top of Apres Vous

Jackson Hole is a truly all American resort and comes with cowboys, saloon bars and high peaks. Not the typical tree-lined rolling mountains found in a lot of US resorts, Jackson is a high peaked mountain resort that is located in a large valley some 10-40 miles wide and 50 miles long. At the base of the slopes is a small village called **Teton**, 10miles away from the main town of Jackson Hole, which has the much smaller resort of **Snow King** rising out of it. Jackson Hole is a resort that will appeal to snowboarders that like a challenge. Much of the terrain is rated black, offering some steep sections with trees and long chutes. Back country riding is also a major option as there are vast amounts of terrain to check out. To get the best of it, there are a number of specialist backcountry tour operators, offering daily tours with prices starting at around $300.

FREERIDERS should love it on Jackson's slopes, with a host of marked out trails and acres of backcountry terrain to explore in areas such as the **Green River Bowl** or **Cody Bowl**. Backcountry guides are on hand to help you, and you can sign up for half day, full, or two day guiding sessions for around $325. But note that you are strongly advised to always check with the areas **Bridger-Teton** Backcountry avalanche hazard and weather forecast before going anywhere. Some of the

best riding can be found on **Rendezvous mountain** which was once noted for having the biggest vertical descent in the US, some 1261 metres. Once you get off Rendezvous' old tram, you drop down into a cool playground, offering a great selection of chutes, jumps and big drop-ins, Jackson also features **Corbett's Couloir**, a famous vertical drop into a marked run that will leave you breathless.

THE TOWN & GETTING THERE

FREESTYLERS will certainly appreciate Jackson. From the Thunder Chair you will be able to reach a natural pipe. The **Paintbrush** and **Toilet Bowl** also offer loads of hits, where you can ride for hours off and over loads of good natural stuff. If this isn't enough, then check out the man-made pipe of the **Teewinot** chair lift.

CARVERS who can and like to do so at speed, should check out **Gros Venture** as this is the place for experienced speed merchants. The run is over 3 km long and drops away, forming an excellent testing trail Intermediates (and those not so sure of themselves) should try out **Casper Bowl** or **Moran Face** on **Apres Vous Mountain**.

BEGINNERS will find Jackson's mostly steep and testing terrain a bit daunting, but don't fret; most novices should manage to get around after a few days, although they should probably avoid the **Rendezvous** area. First timers have the chance to progress quickly, especially on the runs found at the bottom of Apres Vous mountain, reached off the Teewinot chair. A high level of instruction is available including halfpipe training run camps for women.

THE TOWN
Immediately at the base area of the slopes lies the resort of **Teton Village** which is more or less your typical horrid ski resort all in set up. That's not to say it's not welcoming, it is, and locals will make your stay a good one. However, the town of **Jackson** which is a 20 minute bus ride away operating on an-all day basis, offers a more sedate time with a heavy dose of pure outback Americana. Around town there is a lot of activities and not all costing the earth, which makes the place cool and worth it. There is a number of good snowboard shops to check out: such as the *Hole in the Wall*, or the *Bomb Shelter*.

Accomodation. The area has a vast array of lodging. There is plenty near the slopes in **Teton Village** where you can kip close to the slopes at the Hostel for around $5 a night. For a bigger selection and cheaper prices check out the offerings in Jackson, 10 miles from the slopes.

Food. If you don't leave here over weight, then see a shrink. The place has dozens of places to get food from, whether it is a supermarket, fast food joint or an up-market restaurant frequented by fur clad clueless city slickers. Prices to suite all are possible but on the whole, dining out is not a cheap experience here. However, *Bubba's* is comes highly recommended and serves some great chicken dishes. The *Snake River* and *Otto Brothers brew pub* are also noted for their good food.

Night life here is just how it should be, with something for all with a snowboard flavour. Options for some night action exist in either **Teton Village** or **Jackson** itself. Tretton is a lot quieter than Jackson, with *Mangy Moose, the Stagecoach* or the *Rancher* all being popular hangouts. As for local talent, the place seems a bit of a guy place but there is some skirt to be had.

SUMMARY
Great resort with lots of challenging terrain offering some excellent backcountry freeriding. Good and friendly local services, although a bit spread out..
Money Wise: This is an expensive resort but it can be done on the cheap

CAR
Idaho Falls via Victor. Jackson Hole is 111 miles. Drive time is about 1 3/4 hours.*Salt Lake City is 299 miles, which will take about 5 3/4 hours.
FLY
Fly to Salt Lake City International.Transfer time to resort is 5 3/4 hours. Local airport is Jackson, 10 miles away.
BUS
Buses from Idaho Falls take 1 1/2 hours and 5 3/4 hours from Salt Lake City airport (299 miles).

U
S
A

W
Y
O
M
I
N
G

BASIC WORDS

Yes - Oui	How - Comment	When - Quand	Sixteen - Seize
No - Non	Lift - Soulever	Why - Pourquoi	Seventeen - Dix-sept
Please - Sil vous plait	Look - Regarder		Eighteen - Dix-huit
Thank you - Merci	Meet - Rencontrer	NUMBER - NOMBRE	Nineteen - Dix-neuf
Hello - Bonjour	None - Aucun	Zero - Zero	Twenty - Vingt
	Open - Ouvrir	One - Un	
Call - Appeler	Pull - Tier	Two - Deux	Day: - Jour:
Carry - Porter	Push - Pousser	Three - Trois	
Change - Changer	Rain - Pluie	Four - Quatre	Sunday - Dimanche
Close - fermer	Release - Lacher	Five - Cinq	Monday - Lundi
Come - Venir	Slide - Deraper	Six - Six	Tuesday - Mardi
Drink - Boire	Snow - Neiger	Seven - Sept	Wednesday - Mercredi
Eat - Manger	Speak - Parler	Eight - Huit	Thursday - Jeudi
Exhausted - Epuise	Take - Prendre	Nine - Neuf	Friday - Vendredi
Fall - Tomber	There- La	Ten - Dix	Saturday - Samedi
Get - Recevoir	To - A	Eleven - Onze	
Give - Donner	Turn - Tourner	Twelve - Douze	Time - Temps
Help - Aider	Wait - Attendre	Thirteen - Treize	
Here - Ici	Wear - Porter	Fourteen - Quatorze	
Hold - Tenir	Week - La semaine	Fifteen - Quinze	

COMMON PHRASES

Do you speak English? - Vous parlez anglais?
I don't speak French - Je ne parle pas francais
I don't understand - Je ne comprends pas
Please speak slowly - Veuillez parler lentement
I hope you understand my English - J'espere que vos comprenez mon anglais
Where do you come from? - D'ou venez-vos?
I come from..... - Je viens de.......
I live in London - J'habite a London
My name is - Je m'appelle
I am _ _ years old - J'ai-__ans
I am marred and I have children - Je suis marie et j'ai enfant
What's your name? - Comment vous appelez-vous?
What time is it? - Quelle heure est-il?
It is eight o'clock -Il est huit heures
Good Morning - Bonjour

Good Afternoon - Bonjour
Good Evening - Bonsoir
Good Night - Bonne nuit
I would like to make a telephone call/reverse the charges to....- Je voudrais telephoneren/telephoner en PCV a....
The number is - Le numero est
I would like to change these travellers cheques/this currancy/this Eurocheque - J'aimerais changer ces cheques de voyage/ces devises/cet Eurocheque
Can I obtain money with my? creditcard? - Puis-je avoir de L'argent avec ma carte de credit
How much is this? - C'est combien
Money - Argent
Credit card - Carte de credit
Bank - Bank
Change - Changement

TRAVEL TERMS

Flying - Volant
Passport - Passeport
Airport - Aeroport
Customs - Douane
Passports please - Les passeports, s'il vous plait
I have nothing to declare - Ja n'ai rien a declarer
Excuse me, where is the check-in for? - Excusez-moi, ou est le comptoir d'enregistrement de....?
What is the boarding gate? - Quelle est la porte d'embarquement?
Which way is the baggage reclaim? - Ou se trouve l'aire de reception das bagages?
How long is the delay likely to be? - Le retard est de combien?
Driving - Conduite
No parking - Stationnement interdit
Car - Voiture
Stop - Stop
One way - Sens unique
Give way - Cedez la
No Entry - Sens interdit

How much dose it cost to hire a car for one day? - Quel est le prix de location d'une voiture pour un jour?
I have ordered a car in the name of - J'ai reserve une voiture au nom de
Is insurance and tax included? - Est-ce que l'assurance et les taxes sont comprises?
By what time must I return the car? - A quelle heure dois-je ramener la voiture?
I've had a breakdown at......... - Je suis tombe en panne a.........
I am on the road from.......... - Ju suis sur la route de........
Please call the police - Vous pouvez appeler la police
There has been an accident - Il y a eu un accident
Train - Train
Railway Station - Gare
Where is the ticket office - Ou se trouvre le guichet?
May I have a single/return ticket? - Puis-je avoir un aller/un aller retour ticket?
Does this train go to? - Est-ce que cet autobus va a....?

FRENCH LANGUAGE GUIDE

FOOD AND DRINK

Bread - Pain
Cheese - Fromage
Chips - Pommes frites
Coffee - cafe
Dessert - Dessert
Egg - Oeuf
Fish dishes - Poissons
Food - Nourriture
Fruit - Fruits
Lemon - Citron
Main Courses - Plats principaux
Meat dishes - Viandes
Milk - Lait
Mushroom - Champignon
Poulet - Chicken
Red wine - Rouge vin
White wine - Blanc vin
Potatoes - Pommes de terre
Rice - Riz

Salt - Sel
Seafood - Fruits de mer
Sausage - Saucissee
Vegetables - Legumes
Vinegar - Vinaigre
Vegetarian dishes - Plats vegetariens
Waiter - Monsieur

Enjoy your meal - Bon appetit
Can you recommend a restaurant?
- Pouvez-vos recommander un bon restaurant?
I would like a table for - Je voudrais une table pour
May I have the menu - Puis-je avoir la carte?
Do you have any vegetarinan dishes?
- Avez-vous des plats vegetariens?
Could I have a wellcooked/medium/

rare - Je le voudrais bien cuit/a point/ saignant
The food is cold - C'est froid
I would like a cup of tea - Je voudrais une tasse the
I would like a beer please - Je voudrais une biere s'il vous plait
Trappistes - a beer brewed from malt

AROUND THE RESORT

Bakers - Boulangerie
Bed & Breakfast - Chambre
Bath - Baigner
Chalet - Chalet
Gifts - Kahdow
Hairdresser's - Coiffeur
Hotel - Hotel
Shower - Douche
Shop - Boutique
Shoes - Chaussures
Stationery - Pahpaytehree
Tourist Office - l'office de tourisme
Travel Agent - Bureau de voyages

Do you have a map of the area? - Avez-vous une carte de la region?
I would like to go to..... - Je voudrais aller a.....
I would like to order a taxi - J voudrais eserver un taxi
How much will it cost? - Ca coutera

combien?
Can I reserve accommodation here? - Puis-je reserver un longement ici?
Do you have a list of accommodation?
- Vous avez une liste d'Hotels?
I have a reservation in the name of... - J'ai fait une reservation au nom de
Do you have any rooms free? - Vous avez des chambres?
How much is it per night? - Quel est le prix pour une nuit?
At what time is breakfast? - A quelle heure petit-dejeuner?
What time do I have to check out? - A quelle heure dois-je laisser la chambre?
Can I have the key to the room?.. - Je voudrais la cle de la chambre?..
My room number is - Le numero de ma chambre
May I have the bill please?- L'addition si vous plais

I think there is a mistake on my bill
- Mais je crois qu'il ya a une erreur dans la note
What time do the shops open/close?
- A quelle heure ouvrent/ferment les magasins?
Can I try this on? - Puis-je essayer ceci??
I'll take this one - Je prends celui-ci
I would like a film for my camera - Ja voudrais une pellicule pour cet appareil photo
I would like some batteries - Je voudrais des piles

ON THE SLOPES

Snow - Neiger
Course - la course
Winter - Hiver
Steep Slope - la pente difficile
Avalanche - L'avalanche
Gentle Slope - la pente facile
Danger - Le danger
Bumpy Slope - la piste bosselee
Rescue - Sauver
Mogul - la bosse
First Aid Kit - La pharmache de secours
Ski Area - le domaine skiable
Ski Patrol - Le patrouilleur
T-Bar - Le teleski a archets
Beginner - le debutant
Chairlift - le telesiege
Intermediate - le moyen

Cable Car - le telepherique
Advanced - le avance
Gondola - la cabine
Lift Station - la station
Narrow Pass- la trace etroite
Powder Snow - la neige poudreuse
Fall Line - la ligne de pente
Fresh Snow - la neige fraiche
Traverse - la traversee
Sticky Snow - la neige collante
Summit - le sommet
Wet Snow - la neige mouillee
Off Piste - le ski hors-piste
Icy - la neige glacee
Valley- la vallee
Crevasse - la crevasse
Rock - le caillou / le roc

Glacier - le glacier
Slope - la pente
Lift Ticket - le billet
Piste - la piste
Ski Instructor- Le professeur de ski
Run - la descente
Lesson- le lecon
Track - la trace
Meeting place - le rassemblement
One lession costs........ - Une lecon coute........

GERMAN LANGUAGE GUIDE

COMMON PHRASES

Do you speak English? - Sprechen Sie Englisch?
I don't speak German - Ich spreche kein Deutsch
I don't understand - Ich verstehe Sie nicht
Please speak slowly - Sprechen Sie bitte langsam
I hope you understand my English - Ich hoffe, mein Englisch is verstandlich
Where do you come from? - Woher komme Sie
I come from - Ich komme von
I live in London - Ich wohne in London
My name is - Ich heisse

I am _ _ years old - Ich bin _ _ jahre alt
I am marred and I have children - Ich bin verheiratet und habe kinder
What's your name? - Wie heisst Du?
What time is it? - Wie spat ist es?
It is eight o'clock - Es ist acht Uhr
Good Morning - Guten Morgen
Good Afternoon - Guten Morgen
Good Evening - Guten Abend
Good Night - Gute Nacht

AROUND THE RESORT

Tourist Office - TouristenInformationsburo
Do you have a map of the area? - Haben sie eine Stadtkarte?
I would like to go to..... - Ich mochte nach.....
I would like to order a taxi - Ich mochte gerne ein Taxi
How much will it cost? - Wieviel lostet das?
Can I reserve accommodation here? - Kann ich hier eine Unterkunft reservieren?
Do you have a list of accommodation? - Haben Sie ein Unterkunftsverzeichnis?

Hotel - Hotel Bath - Bad
Chalet - Chalet Shower - Dusche
Bed & Breakfast - Pension

I have a reservation in the name of... - Ich habe eine Reservierung foor..
Do you have any rooms free? - Haben Sie Zimmer frei?
How much is it per night? - Wieviel kostet das pro Nacht?
At what time is breakfast? - Um wieviel Uhr Fruhstuck?
What time do I have to check out? - Um wieviel Uhr mussen wir das zimmer verlassen?
Can I have the key to the room? - Konnen Sie mir bitte den Schlussel fur Zimmer?
My room number is - Meine Zimmernummer ist
May I have the bill please? - Die Rechnung, bitte?

I think there is a mistake on my bill - Ich glaube auf dieser Rechnung ist ein Fehler.

Shop - Geschaft
Shoes - Schule
Stationery - Schreibwaren
Hairdresser's - Friseur
Gifts - Geschenke
Bakers - Backerei
Travel Agent - Reiseburo

What time do the shops open/close? - Um wieviel Uhr offnen/schliessen die Geschafte?
Can I try this on? - Kann ich das anprobieren?
I'll take this one - Ich nehme das
I would like a film for my camera - Ich mochte einen Film fur meinen Fotoapparat
I would like some batteries - Ich mochte einige Batterien

ON THE SLOPES

Snow-Schneien
Powder Snow - Pulverschnee
Fresh Snow - Neuschnee
Sticky Snow - Klebriger Schnee
Wet Snow - Nassschnee
Winter-Winter

Steep Slope - Steiler Hang
Gentle Slope - Leichter Hang
Bumpy Slope - Buckelpiste
Mogul - Buckel

Danger - Gefahr
Avalanche - Lawine
Rescue - Retten
Ski Area - Skigebiet
First Aid Kit - Notapotheke
Ski Patrol - Pistendienst

T-Bar - Bugellift
Chairlift - Sessellift
Cable Car - Luftseilbahn
Gondola - Gondel

Beginner - Anfanger
Intermediate - Mittlerer

Advanced - Fortgeschrittener

Narrow Pass - Enger Durchgang
Lift Station - Liftstation
Fall Line - Fallinie
Traverse - Traverse
Summit - Gipfel
Off Piste - Abseits der Piste
Valley - Tal
Icy - Eisig
Rock - Felsen
Crevasse - Spalte
Glacier - Gletscher
Lift Ticket - Lift Billett
Slope - Hang
Piste - Piste
Ski Instructor - Skilehrer
Run - Abfahrt
Lesson - Lektion
Track - Spur
Meeting place - Sammelplatz
Course - Kurs
One lession costs........ - Eine lektion kostet.........

NORWEIGEN LANGUAGE GUIDE

PRONOUNCIATION

æ – as in the vowel sound in "man"
å – as in the vowel sound in "thought"
ø – as in the vowel sound in "first"

sj and skj – as sh in "shoe"
j , hj and gj – as in y in "yes"

BASIC WORDS

s – Ja
– Nei

Please – Vær så snill
Thank you – Takk

How? – Hvordan
Hello – Hallo/Hei

NUMBERS & DAYS

o - null
e - en
o - to
ee - tre
r - fire

Five - fem
Six - seks
Seven – sju
Eight - åtte
Nine - ni

Ten - ti
Day:
Sunday - søndag
Monday - mandag
Tuesday - tirsdag

Wednesday - onsdag
Thursday - torsdag
Friday - fredag
Saturday - lørdag

COMMON PHRASES

you speak English? – Snakker du engelsk?
n't speak Norwegian. – Jeg snakker ikke norsk.
n't understand. – Jeg skjønner ikke.
name is – Jeg heter
at time is it? – Hva er klokka?
s eight o'clock – Klokka er åtte
od Morning – God morgen
od Afternoon – God ettermiddag
od Evening – God kveld
od Night – God natt
uld like to change these travellers cheques/this currancy/this

Eurocheque – Jeg vil gjerne veksle disse reisesjekkene/pengene/
denne eurosjekken
How much is this? – Hvor mye koster denne/dette
Can you please write it down – Kan du være så snill å skrive det
ned?
I come from....- Jeg er/kommer fra....
Control your speed – Kontroller farten din
How are you today? – Hvordan har du det i dag? (Not a common
phrase in Norwegian)
Where are you from? – Hvor er/kommer du fra?

FOOD & DRINK

it - frukt
iter - kelner
tchup - ketchup
mon - sitron
k - melk
tatoes - poteter
e - ris
in Courses - hovedretter
t - salt
h dishes - fiskeretter
afood - sjømat
at dishes - kjøttretter
getables - grønnsaker
getarian dishes - vegetarretter
egar - eddik
icken - kylling

Sausage - pølse
Mushroom - sopp
Bread - brød
Cheese - ost
Chips – pommes frites (pronounced as in
French)
Coffee - kaffe
Red wine - rødvin
Dessert - dessert
White wine - hvitvin

I'd like a table for...... – Jeg vil gjerne ha
et bord til…
Do you have a set menu? – Har dere en
fast meny?
Do you have any vegetarinan dishes? – Har

dere noen vegetarretter?
Can you recommend a restaurant? – Kan
du anbefale en restaurant?
May I please have the menu? – Kan jeg få
menyen, takk?
I would like a cup of tea – Kan jeg få en
kopp te, takk?
I would like a beer please – Kan jeg få en
øl, takk?
The food is cold – Maten er kald
Cheers – Skål!

TRAVEL TERMS

ssport please – Passet takk
ve nothing to declare – Jeg har ingenting å fortolle
at is the boarding gate? – Hvilken gate er det?
e way - Enveis
had a breakdown at....... – Jeg har fått motorstopp ved….
n on the road from.......... – Jeg er på veien fra
ase call the police – Vennligst ring politiet

There has been an accident – Det har skjedd en ulykke
How much does it cost to hire a car for one day? – Hvor mye koster
det å leie en bil for en dag?
Is insurance and tax included? – Er forsikring og skatt inkludert?
Does this train go to? – Går dette toget til?
Where is the ticket office?- Hvor er billettkontoret?
When is the next train to? – Når er neste tog til?

ON THE SLOPES

anche – snøskred
ger - fare
cue - redning
t Aid Kit - førstehjelpsskrin
irlift - stolheis
le Car -
dola - gondolbane
der Snow - puddersnø

Old Snow – gammel snø
Sticky Snow – kram snø
Wet Snow – våt snø
Glacier - isbre
Slope - bakke
Piste - løype
Run - nedfart
Mogul - kuleløype

Beginner - nybegynner
Intermediate- viderekommende
Advanced - avansert
Traverse - krysse
Off Piste – frikjøring/off piste
Lift Ticket - heiskort
Ski Instructor – ski instruktør
Lesson - time

ITALIAN LANGUAGE GUIDE

NUMBERS & DAYS

Zero - Zero
One - Uno
Two - Due
Three - Tre
Four- Quattro
Five - Cinque
Six - Sey

Seven - Sette
Eight - Otto
Nine - Nove
Ten - Dieci
Eleven - Undici
Twelve - Dodici
Thirteen - Tredici

Fourteen - Quattordici
Time- Tempo
Fifteen - Quindici
Sixteen - Sedici
Seventeen - Diciassette
Eighteen - Dicitto
Nineteen - Diciannove

Twenty - Venti

Day: - Giorno:
Sunday - Domenica
Monday - Lunedi
Tuesday - Martedi
Wednesday - Mercoledi

Thursday - Giovedi
Friday - Venerdi
Saturday – Sabato

COMMON PHRASES

Do you speak English? - Parla inglese?
I don't speak Italian - Non parlo italiano
I don't understand - Non capisco
Please speak slowly - La prego di parlare lentamente
I hope you understand my English - Spero che tu capisca il mio inglese
Where do you come from? - Da dove viene?
I come from... - Vengo da....
I live in London - Vivo a Londra
My name is - Mi chiamo

I am _ _ years old - Ho...anni
I am marred and I have children - Sono sposato e ho bambini
What's your name? - Come ti chiami?
What time is it? - Che ore sono?
It is eight o'clock - Sono le otto
Good Morning - Buon giorno
Good Afternoon - Buon pomeriggo
Good Evening - Buona sera
Good Night - Buona notte

The number is - Il numero e......

I would like to change these travellers cheques/this currancy/this Eurocheque - Vorrei cambiare questi assegni turistici/ questa valuta/questo euroassegno
Can I obtain money with my creditcard? - Posso incassare contanti con il carta di Credito
How much is this? - Quant'e?
 Money - Denaro
Credit card - Carta di Credito
Bank - Banca
Change – Cambiare

FOOD & DRINK

Food - Cibo
Waiter - Cameriere
Enjoy your meal - Buon Appetito
Can you recommend a restaurant? - Puo raccomandarmi un ristorante?
I'd like a table for...... - Vorrei un tavolo per...
May I have the menu? - Per favore, mi puo dare il menu?

I would like a cup of tea - Vorrei una tazza di te
I would like a beer please - Per cortesia vorrei una birra
Scura - is a dark beer
Main Courses - Piatti principali

Fish dishes - Piatti di pesce

Meat dishes - Piatti di carne

Vegetarian dishes - Piatti vegetariani
Bread - Pane
Cheese - Formaggio
Chips - Patatine fritte
Coffee - Caffe
Dessert - Dolce
Fruit - Frutta
Lemon - Limone
Milk - Latte

Potatoes - Patate
Rice - Riso
Salt - Sale
Seafood - Frutti di mare
Vegetables - Verdure
Vinegar - Dell'aceto
Pollo - Chicken
Salsiccia - Sausage
Fungo - Mushroom
Red wine - Rosso vino
White wine - Bianco vino

AROUND THE RESORT

Tourist Office - L'ufficio informazioni
Do you have a map of the area? - Ha una mappa della zona?
I would like to go to..... - Vorrei andare a......
I would like to order a taxi - Vorrei prenotare un tassi
How much will it cost - Quant'e?
Can I reserve accommodation here - Posso prenotare qui l'alloggio?
Do you have a list of accommodation - Ha un elenco di alloggi?

Hotel - Albergo Chalet
Bed & Breakfast - Pensione
Bath- Bagno Shower - Doccia
Do you have any rooms free? - Avete camere libere?
How much is it per night? - Quante'e per notte?
At what time is breakfast? - A che ora viene servita la colazione?
What time do I have to check out? - A che ora devo lasciare libera la camera?
Can I have the key to the room? - Posso avere la chiave della camera?

My room number is? - La mia camera ha il numero?
May I have the bill please? - Mi da il conto per favore?
I think there is a mistake on my bill - Credo ci sia un errore nel conto.

Shop - Negozio
Stationery - Cartoleria
Gifts - Articoli da regalo

Shoes - Scarpe
Hairdresser's - Parrucchiere
Bakers - Panificio

Travel Agent - Agenzia di viaggi
What time do the shops open/ close - A che ora aprono/chiudono i negozi?
Can I try this on? - Posso provarlo?
I'll take this one - Prendero questo
I would like a film for my camera - Vorrei una pellicola per questa macchina fotografica
I would like some batteries the same size as this old one. - Vorrei delle pile della stessa grandezza di quella vecchia.

ON THE SLOPES

Snow - Nevicare
Winter - l'inverno
Avalanche - Valanga
Danger - Pericolo
Rescue - Salvare
First Aid Kit - Farmacia di primo soccorso
Ski Patrol - Pattugliatore
T-Bar - Ancora
Chairlift - Seggiovia
Cable Car - Funivia
Gondola - Gondola
Lift Station - Partenza dello sci-lift

Powder Snow - Neve polverosa
Fresh Snow - Neve fresca
Sticky Snow - Neve che attacca
Wet Snow - Neve bagnata
Icy - Ghiacciato
Crevasse - Crepaccio
Glacier - Ghiacciaio
Slope - Il pendio
Piste - La pista
Run - La discesa
Track - Traccia

Course - Percorso
Steep Slope - La pista ripida
Gentle Slope - La pista facile
Bumpy Slope - I dossi
Mogul - I motti
Ski Area - Regione Sciistica

Beginner - Il principiante
Intermediate - Il medio sciatore
Advanced - L'esperto

Narrow Pass - Passaggio stretto
Traverse - La diagonale

Hill - La collina
Off Piste - Il fuori pista
Valley - La valle
Rock - La roccia

Lift Ticket - Il biglietto

Ski Instructor - Il maestro di sc
Lesson - La lezione
Meeting place - Il punto d'incontro
One lession costs - Un........ lezione costa.......

JAPANESE LANGUAGE GUIDE

BASIC WORDS

Good morning - ohayo gozaimasu
Good afternoon - konnichiwa
Good evening - konbanwa
 Excuse me - sumimasen ga
Goodbye - sayonara
Goodnight - oyasumi nasai
Thank you - arigatou
Yes - Hai
No - lie

USEFUL PHRASES

Do you speak English? - Eigoga hanasemasu ka
 I don't speak Japanese - Watashi wanihon-go ga hanasemasen
Where Is_station? - eki wa doko desu ka
A return ticket please - ofuku onegaishlmasu
One way kala mlchi onega is hi masu
Does this train stop at ..... - kono densha wa ..... ni tomarimasu ka
How much Is it? - Ikura desu ka
Can you tell me the name of a good hotel?- ii hoteru wo shoukai shite kudasai
What is the (hotel's) telephone number?- (hoteru no) denwa bango wa nan ban desu ka

A half-day lift pass, please - han nichi ken one gaishimasu
A one-day lift pass, please - ichi nichi ken onegaishimasu
A two-day lift pass, please - futsuka ken onegaishimasu
Where Is the lift/pipe/gondola/ski area? - lift/pipe/gondola/ski job wa doko ni ari masu ka
Is all the area open to boarders? - snowboard wa dokodemo dekimasu ka

TYPICAL MENU

Menrui (noodles):
Ramen - Chinese noodles
which are served in steaming hot soy sauce soup with pork Japanese spring onion, fish paste and seaweed Many varieties of this exist - find your favourite.

Soba - Noodles - buck- wheat noodles often served in a hot soup with vegetables and seaweed, fried tofu or tempura (green peppers/pumpkin/shrimp squid deep-fried In batter)
Udon - Noodles a thicker variety of noodles served in a hot soup as above.
Donburi (rice dishes)

Katsu don - pork cutlet with egg and onions in sweet soy sauce on ricE

Gyudon - Thin strips of beef on rice

Oden - Eggs/giant radish/fish paste/thick sea- weed stewed in fish stock and served hot.

Man - Soft Chinese filled rolls with meat, curry, pizza or sweet red bean.

Onigiri - Rice balls wrapped in seaweed paper often with different fillings.
The tuna-mayonnaise rice- ball is well adapted to western palettes.
Umeboshi (pickled plum) is a little more difficult to stomach.

SPANISH LANGUAGE GUIDE

NUMBERS & DAYS

Zero Cero	Four Cuatro	Eight Ocho	Day:	Wednesday Miercoles
One Uno	Five Cinco	Nine Nueve	Sunday Domingo	Thursday Jueves
Two Dos	Six Seis	Ten Diez	Monday Manana	Friday Viernes
Three Tres	Seven Siete		Tuesday Martes	Saturday Sabado

BASIC WORDS

Yes - Si
No - No
Please - Por favor

Thank you - Gracias
How? - Como?
Hello – Hola

COMMON PHRASES

Do you speak English? - Habla usted ingles?

I don't speak Italian. - No hablo espanol

I don't understand. - No entiendo

My name is - Me llamo
What time is it? - Que hora es?

It is eight o'clock - Son las ocho
Good Morning - Buenos dias
Good Afternoon - Buenas tardes
Good Evening - Buenas noches
Good Night - Buona notte
I would like to change these travellers cheques/this currancy/this Eurocheque - Quisiera cambiar estos cheques de viaje/dinero/este Eurocheque

How much is this? - Cuanto es?
Can you please write it down - Lo puede escribir, por favor
I come from....- Soy de.....
Control your speed - Controla la velocidad
How are you today? - Que tal estas hoy?
Where are you from? - De donde eres?

FOOD & DRINK

Cheers - Salud
Waiter - Camarero
Can you recommend a restaurant? - Puede recomendarme un buen restaurante?
I'd like a table for...... - Quisiera una mesa para.....
May I please have the menu? - Puedo ver la carta, por favor?
Do you have a set menu? - Tienen menu del Dia
Main Courses - Platos principales
Fish dishes - Pescados
Meat dishes - Carnes
Vegetarian dishes - Platos vegetarianos
Do you have any vegetarinan dishes? -

Dan comidas vegetarians, por favor?
The food is cold - L comida esta fria
I would like a cup of tea - Quisiera una taza de te
I would like a beer please - Quisiera una cerveza, por favor

Red wine - Tinto vino
White wine - Blanco vino

Bread - Pan
Cheese - Queso
Chips - Patatas fritas
Coffee - Cafe
Dessert - Postre

Fruit - Frutas
Ketchup - Salsa de tomate
Lemon - Limon
Milk - Leche
Potatoes - Patatas
Rice - Arroz
Salt - Ensalada
Seafood - Mariscos
Vegetables - Legumbres
Vinegar - Vinagre
Gallina - Chicken
Salchicha - Sausage
Seta - Mushroom

TRAVEL TERMS

Passport please - Los oassaportes por favor
I have nothing to declare - No tengo nada que declarar
What is the boarding gate? - Por que puerta?
One way Sentido unico - No Entry Prohibido el paso

I've had a breakdown at....... - El coche se ha averiado en.
I am on the road from.......... - Estoy en la carretera de......
Please call the police - Llame a la policia
There has been an accident - Ha habido un accidente

How much does it cost to hire a car for one day? - Cuanto cuesta alquilar un coche por un dia?
Is insurance and tax included? - Esta incluido en el precio los impuestos y el seguro?
Does this train go to? - Quest'

treno va a....?
Where is the ticket office?- Donde esta la taquilla de billetes?
When is the next train to? - A que hora sale el proximo tren para....?

ON THE SLOPES

Avalanche - El alud
Danger - El peligro
Rescue - Salvar
First Aid Kit - El botiquin

Chairlift - El telesillas
Cable Car - El teleferico
Gondola - La cabina

Powder Snow - Nieve polvo
Old Snow - Nieve asentada

Sticky Snow - Nieve primavera
Wet Snow - Nieve pesada
Glacier - El glaciar
Slope - La pendiente
Piste - La pista
Run - La bajada
Mogul - La banera

Beginner - El principiante
Intermediate- El esquiador de nivel intermedio

Advanced - Avanzado

Traverse - La Traversa
Off Piste - Fuera de la pista

Lift Ticket - El billete
Ski Instructor - El monitor de esqui
Lesson - La leccion

INDEX

wsg

INDEX

INDEX

INDEX

INDEX

NOTES

CLASSIFIEDS

TRAVEL/BREAKS & CHALETS

RECRUITMENT

VERBIER & ELSEWHERE

For the most suitable accomodation and no-hassle holidays call Mountain Beds for expert advice

Ski Resorts

Tel: 07000 780 333
Fax: 07000 780 334
www.mountainbeds.com

46 Resorts Worldwide
Chalets, Hotels & Apts
8 UK Regional Airports
Group Discounts & Special Offers

Tel: 01738 840 888
www.skiactivity.com

NATIVES.CO.UK

Fancy working a season in the Alps? 100's of vacancies, including Bar, Rep, Hotel and Chalet work.

web: www.natives.co.uk
tel: 08700 463377
email: jobs@natives.co.uk

natives.co.uk
the uk's no.1 ski job website

SHOPS

Stores at:
Lichfield - City Precinct
Stafford - Guildhall Centre

Telephone:
01543 411422

- Skiing & Snowboarding
- Clothing & Accessories
- Ski/Board Clothing To Hire
- Expert Advice

or buy online...

INSURANCE

THE experts in
SNOWBOARD & SKI
Insurance

www.fogginsure.co.uk

simple online steps to purchase your winter sports insurance securely.

Premiums from
£18.25 single trip - £49.95 annual

Fogg Travel Insurance Services Limited

SPORTSCOVER DIRECT
SPORTS LEISURE AND TRAVEL INSURANCE

VENTUREGUARD

Competitive Travel
Insurance - Annual cover or Single trips

Tel: 0845 120 6400 Fax: 0845 120 6401
Online @ www.sportscover.co.uk
email: info@sportscover.co.uk
33 Corn Street, Bristol BS1 1HT
"Get covered before you hit the slopes!"